Texts in Computing

Volume 9

Logic for

Artificial Intelligence

&

Information Technology

Texts in Computing Series Editor
Ian Mackie   mackie@lix.polytechnique.fr

Logic for
Artificial Intelligence
&
Information
Technology

Dov M. Gabbay

ISBN 978-1-904987-39-0
College Publications
Scientific Director: Dov Gabbay
Managing Director: Jane Spurr
Department of Computer Science
King's College London
Strand, London WC2R 2LS, UK

Original cover design by Richard Fraser

Cover produced by orchid creative   www.orchidcreative.co.uk

CONTENTS

Preface

Logic is now widely recognized to be one of the foundation disciplines for information technology. It has been said that logic may come to play a role in information technology similar to that played by calculus in physics. Like calculus, logic has found applications in virtually all aspects of the subject, from software engineering and hardware design to programming and artificial intelligence. Moreover, it has served to stimulate the search for clear conceptual foundations, a quest which has recently acquired a certain urgency. While progress in the past has been enhanced by theoretical development, it has to a significant degree proceeded independently of theory. In the future this is unlikely to be the case. Many of the current aspirations are seen to require major theoretical advances, and many lie in areas where logic is one of the basic disciplines. If these aspirations are to be fulfilled, logic and information technology must enter a more intimate and enduring relationship. Logic must be adapted and changed to suit its new applications.

The paradigm of logic as an executable language is currently based on the Horn clause fragment of classical logic, and yet there is no existing formulation of classical logic which leads naturally to and supports this paradigm, from the point of view of either teaching or research. Furthermore, existing theorem provers are based on various resolution methods which reformulate and rewrite well-formed formulae in normal forms which are quite alien to the way we perceive the meaning of the classical connectives.

In recent years many extensions of classical logic such as temporal, modal, relevance and fuzzy logics have been used extensively in computer science. Resolution becomes even less intuitive when extended, where possible, to handle these logics. A new formulation of classical logic is needed which can naturally be modified to yield the effect of non-classical logics.

In this book we present classical and non-classical logic and develop a theorem prover for classical logic, in a way which tries to maintain a procedural point of view and has the following main characteristics:

1. The intuitive meaning of the connectives will be retained and no unintuitive

translation of well-formed formulae will be used unless it has a natural and intuitive meaning beyond mere logical equivalence.

2. The reasoning rules and the theorem prover will follow as closely as possible the intuitive reasoning procedures employed by humans.

3. The principles involved in the reasoning of the logic and the theorem prover are layered and structured. We show a range of stronger and stronger fragments from intuitionistic logic to full classical logic.

4. Variations on the principles involved in the proof procedures and the theorem prover allow for variations of classical logic in a natural way. The methods can be extended to handle modal and temporal logics.

5. The above set-up and presentation of classical logic has theoretical value for pure logic itself. The trade-off between logical principles and restrictions on the proof procedures and theorem prover yields (owing to points 3 and 4) a better understanding of classical logic and its variations.

This will show that the role of logic in computing is not only that of an essential tool but that of a true partnership.

This book is taken from lecture notes for an introductory logic course which has been taught by the author in the Department of Computing at Imperial College, London, since autumn 1984.

The course was given to a class of 120 first-year computer science students. There were 18–20 hours of lectures over nine weeks and 9 hours of tutorials in parallel sessions of four groups of 30 students each, involving four tutors. Weekly meetings between the tutors and the author assessed the delivery of the material. The material covered was more or less as follows:

Chapter 1   3 hours
Chapter 3   3 hours
Chapter 4   3 hours
Chapter 8   3 hours
Chapter 9   4 hours

Another 2–4 hours were spent on a selection of topics from Chapters 2, 4 and 10. Chapter 7 was never taught but was of course available in the notes.

We also had the backward rules theorem prover implemented by Mr Frank Kriwaczek, and the students could play with it.

Another, more advanced 16 hour course was taught by the author, based on Chapters 2, 4, 10, 11. This course was given to MSc students.

Chapter 7 was not taught, even to the MSc students. Computer science students do not seem to like completeness theorems or indeed mathematics, although they do seem to feel more secure to have full mathematical backup to the material they are taught.

In 1998 we all moved from Imperial COllege to King's College London. The course was taught in the years 1999–2000 and 2001 and then again in 2006 and 2007. The students at King's are as enthusiastic and well-motivated as those at Imperial but generally there was less support for teaching at Kings', especially in 2006–2007, due to a general period of hardship which computer science departments are enduring across the country.

Chapter 12 is based on a survey written for the layperson and circulated in the department. Chapters 11 and 12 were not taught to the first-year students. The first-year student reader of this book will probably find it a bit overwhelming but will recognize the ideas. These chapters give a glimpse into the real challenges to logic!

Acknowledgements

Thanks are due to Jane Spurr for producing the camera-ready version and for her general super-efficient support over the years.

I am also grateful to Valentin Shehtman for going over the text and supplying most of the worked examples. Some of the worked examples are extracted from [Lavrov and Maksimova, 1995; Mendelson, 1964; Bizam and Herczeg, 1978; Spivak, 1995].

The author is a Leverhulme major Research Fellow.

Dov Gabbay

London
July 2007

Introduction

There are many logics in existence, and more seem to be devised each year. They range from the rules of argumentation experimented with by Ancient Greek philosophers to arcane and highly abstract formalisms used by computer scientists to give meaning to the more complex operations that computers carry out. At first, logics from these extremes seem to have little in common, yet we claim that they are all logics. What common properties do they have that allow such a claim?

Essentially logics are systems for reasoning that some statement is true, given that some statements are true. (We put aside the question of what it means for a statement to be true, for now.) Logics differ in the kinds of statements which can be described, and the truth of statements relative to other statements. In other words, in one logic we might be able to show that John is sometimes at home, given that John is always at home. In a second logic, this may not be the case, and in a third logic we may not be able even to state that John is sometimes at home, let alone decide whether it is true or not! As for most tools, there are various logics, some of which are useful for some problems, and not for others. Therein lies the reason for this book's existence.

This book is devised to introduce classical logic in such a way that we can easily deviate into discussing non-classical logics as well. Rather than be bemused by the variety of logics displayed, we would have you concentrate on their similarities. Seemingly large differences between two logics often arise from a small difference in their definition. Understanding these small differences and their magnified effects is necessary for you to comprehend the concepts common to all logics.

Overview of the book

Chapter 1 introduces the most common logic, *classical propositional logic*, and with it the basic notions which we shall transfer to each of the logics we examine. We immediately start to interfere with the definition of classical propositional logic to reach a number of *non-classical* logics in Chapter 2, before returning to the classical world in Chapter 3 to present a natural deduction method for determining the

truth of statements from other statements. While this method is historically important, and useful in certain circumstances, it is difficult to automate. Therefore, in
Chapter 4 we tinker with the method to produce a goal-directed automated version.
Chapter 5 further modifies the automated reasoning method to handle certain non-
classical logics. Chapter 6 deals with probabilistic logics. In Chapter 7 we take
a step back from reasoning within logic, to consider methodological properties of
the logic itself, and of the reasoning methods we use. We show that our reasoning
method is both sound and complete.

   We then move on to predicate logics, which are introduced in Chapter 8, with
the concepts being presented informally before a mathematical definition is given.
Chapter 9 continues with classical predicate logic, showing how reasoning can be
carried out with the additional features that predicate logic offers. Chapter 10 looks
at some features of predicate forms of modal and related non-classical logics. We
conclude with Chapters 11 and 12, which introduce non-monotonic logic and give
the reader a glimpse into the real challenges facing applied logic.

   The book contains many exercises, the answers to which are to be found at the
back of the book. We urge the reader to attempt all the exercises, as they have
been included to support the main body of the text by illustrating and sometimes
expanding upon points raised in the preceding material. There are also worked
examples which should be attempted without looking at the answers.

   The following diagram gives the schematic dependence of the chapters:

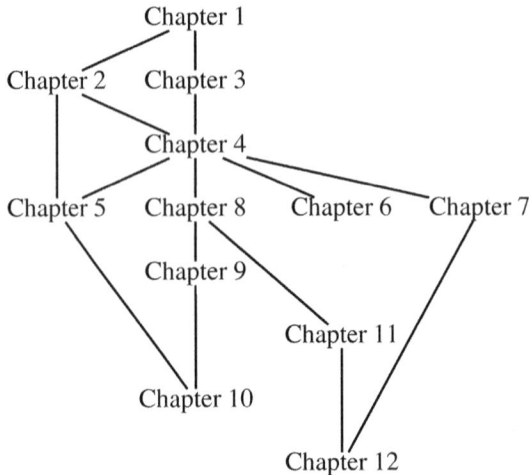

CHAPTER 1

Propositional logic and truth tables

This book is about logical systems. Our view of such systems is that they consist of three major components:

1. a formal language,

2. an intended semantic interpretation,

3. a family of reasoning rules.

The formal language is used to represent knowledge, i.e. collections of assumptions. The intended interpretation, which could be either purely mathematical or just intuitive, represents our perception of the connection between the formal language and the knowledge. The reasoning rules allow us to draw logical conclusions from the representation of the knowledge. The most common and most widely used logical system is known as *classical first-order predicate calculus*. The power of the predicate calculus means that it (or its extensions) can be used for most application areas.

The general field of logic has many applications. It started in *philosophy* for the analysis of human arguments and of various concepts we use, such as causality, necessity, time, concepts in the philosophy of religion, ethics, etc. Logic is used to analyze the foundations of *mathematics*. Some parts of logic such as set theory, model theory, recursion theory, constructive mathematics and topoi are now considered as mathematics subjects in their own right. In *linguistics* suitable logics and logical grammars are constructed to analyze our use of language; for example, how we use pronouns, quantifiers, tenses and so on. The use of logic in linguistics is important for natural language processing in computer science. The logical analysis of the language must, in many cases, be done first, in order to enable us to apply computer science to language. In addition, logic is used to study cognition in *psychology*, and special quantum logics have been constructed for the study of the foundations of quantum mechanics in *physics*. However, our formulation of logic in this book is motivated by its use in computing. Logic is used directly in computer science, especially in the areas of:

- *specification and verification of programs*
  Logic sentences are used to describe the desired behaviour of a program, and the program itself; manipulating the sentences can show whether the program implements the specification.

- *distributed computing, concurrency and process control*
  Certain forms of logic are devised specifically to reason about physical phenomena, such as time and space, and these are used to reason about interacting processes.

- *database management*
  Querying databases is essentially a matter of testing to see if one sentence is a logical consequence of some other sentences; similarly, updating and consistency maintenance can also be viewed as logical operations.

- *circuit design and VLSI*
  Logic has been applied to the problem of describing and verifying the behaviour of electronic circuits.

- *expert systems, planning and artificial intelligence*
  These areas are substantially based on the application of rules to data, which is the *raison d'être* for logic.

- *natural language processing*
  The semantics of sentences such as 'Alun ate the cake that Bethan had bought that morning' can be represented by logic formulae. These formulae can then be used to reason about the consequences of the sentences.

- *logic programming*
  This is the most obvious connection between computing and logic, where a special formulation of logic (called Horn clause logic) is used as a basis for the programming language Prolog.

1   Introducing classical propositional logic

We begin with the simplest of logics: the *classical propositional logic*. The rest of this chapter will describe the language of classical propositional logic, which essentially can contain all the characteristic elements of many major logical systems. Many different logics, formulations and styles can all be recognized through their propositional parts.[1]

---

[1]This footnote can be appreciated after reading Chapters 8 and 9: different propositional logics can be presented through their own characterisitic propositional axioms and rules. They can be turned into

The first assumption of classical logic is that we are dealing with atomic propositions (statements), which can receive a truth value of true ($\top$) or false ($\perp$), in any given situation. By situation we mean a local snapshot, a description of what is happening at a certain place at a certain time from a fixed and agreed point of observation. The classical logic is two valued, i.e. propositions can only have a truth value of true or false. Here we are already making a very serious assumption with far-reaching logical consequences. Statements like

> John loves Mary.

may not in reality have a clear-cut truth value. In situations where it may not be possible for propositions to have a precise truth value, a *non-classical* logic may be required. We present a logic for such situations in Chapter 2.

The second assumption of classical logic is that we are dealing with a single situation, or snapshot. A notable different assumption could be that we are dealing with a sequence of snapshots, a changing situation over time. This gives rise to the so-called *temporal logics*.

The third assumption for classical logic, as for most other logics, is that the truth value of a complex structured sentence depends only on the truth value of its parts. Thus the value of the complex sentence

> John and June got married and John and June had a child.

depends on whether the two sentences

> John and June got married.
> John and June had a child.

are true or false.

There are many intensional sentences whose truth value does not depend on the truth values of the components. For example,

> Tom believes that John and June had a child.

may be true or false independently of whether John and June did indeed have a child or not.

1.1 Formal language

The formal language of propositional logic consists of a set of symbols (typically $\{p, q, r, \ldots\}$) which are the atomic propositions, and the symbols $\wedge$ for conjunction (pronounced 'and'), $\vee$ for disjunction ('or'), $\Rightarrow$ for implication ('implies') and

---

predicate logics by enriching the language and adding more axioms for the quantifiers. Up to very recently the quantificational component of a logic was more or less a standard addition (with some variation) to its propositional part. (See Remark 9.3.8 below.) It is only recently that general theories of quantifiers are being developed.

¬ for negation ('not'), to build up more complex sentences. If A and B are the components, we can build up the formulae $(A)\wedge(B), (A)\vee(B), (A)\Rightarrow(B)$ and $\neg(A)$ from them. The truth values of the more complex sentences are determined by the truth values of the atomic propositions and the logical symbols in the complex sentences. Take the sentence $\neg(p)$, and suppose that the proposition p is given the value $\perp$ (false). We find the value of $\neg(p)$ by looking up the value given by $\neg$ when applied to $\perp$, in the table

A	$\neg A$
$\top$	$\perp$
$\perp$	$\top$

For an argument which is $\perp$, $\neg$ produces $\top$ (true), so $\neg(p)$ is true when p is false. Now consider the sentence $(p)\wedge(q)$. The table for $\wedge$ is

A	B	$A\wedge B$
$\top$	$\top$	$\top$
$\perp$	$\top$	$\perp$
$\top$	$\perp$	$\perp$
$\perp$	$\perp$	$\perp$

Suppose that p is given the value $\top$ and q is given the value $\perp$; then we can see that $(p)\wedge(q)$ has the value $\perp$. Similarly if both p and q are given the value $\top$, then $(p)\wedge(q)$ has the value $\top$ as well, which is why $\wedge$ is pronounced 'and'.

The $\vee$ operator has the table

A	B	$A\vee B$
$\top$	$\top$	$\top$
$\perp$	$\top$	$\top$
$\top$	$\perp$	$\top$
$\perp$	$\perp$	$\perp$

and thus $(p)\vee(q)$ has the value $\top$ whenever either p or q is given the value $\top$; hence $\vee$ is called 'or'. Finally, the table for $\Rightarrow$ is

A	B	$A\Rightarrow B$
$\top$	$\top$	$\top$
$\top$	$\perp$	$\perp$
$\perp$	$\top$	$\top$
$\perp$	$\perp$	$\top$

so that when p is $\top$ and q is $\perp$, $(q)\Rightarrow(p)$ is $\top$.

The table for $\Rightarrow$ is less straightforward than the previous ones, so let us check the rationale behind it. Suppose we see an advertisement for a shop which claims: 'For payment in cash we give a 25% reduction on the price of all television sets.' We decide to check the truth of this advertisement and go into the shop to buy a TV set. There are four possible outcomes:

1. We pay cash and get a 25% reduction.

2. We pay cash, but do not get a 25% reduction. (The shop clerk tells us 'this is our last set, take it or leave it!')

3. We do not pay cash (i.e. we get credit), but nevertheless we get the 25% reduction. (The shop clerk is very nice and says 'Well, if you can't pay now, pay when your next salary cheque comes in'.)

4. We do not pay cash and we do not get the 25% reduction.

We summarize these outcomes in the following table:

	Pay Cash	Get 25%	Advert
1	True	True	
2	True	False	
3	False	True	
4	False	False	

What do we put in the right-hand column of this table? When is the advertisement misleading? We cannot complain about outcomes 1 and 3 since in both cases the 25% reduction was given. Outcome 2 would, if true, clearly make the advertisement false, so the only case which may leave us in doubt about what to put in the table is outcome 4. We cannot say with conviction that the advertisement is misleading, because we did not pay cash. On the other hand, neither can we confirm that the advertisement is true, since we did not test the condition of paying by cash. We need to place some value there, if we are to continue to use truth tables, so we must decide on some convention. Classical logic is content with assuming truth for outcome 4, (see however, Section 1.6).

	Pay Cash	Get 25%	Advert
1	True	True	True
2	True	False	False
3	False	True	True
4	False	False	???

Later in the book we will introduce other views of $\Rightarrow$.

If we have nested complex sentences, such as $\neg((p)\lor(q))$, we work out the value of the innermost sentences first, working outwards, so that we evaluate $(p)\lor(q)$ and use the result of that to evaluate the $\neg$. If p and q are both $\bot$, then $(p)\lor(q)$ is also $\bot$, and thus $\neg((p)\lor(q))$ is $\top$.

EXERCISE 1.1. Work out the truth values of the following formulae when p has the value $\top$, and q has the value $\bot$:

1. $\neg((p)\land(q))$

2. $(p){\Rightarrow}(p)$

3. $(p){\Rightarrow}({\neg}(p))$

4. $((q){\vee}({\neg}(q))){\wedge}(p)$

We now formally define the notion of a well-formed formula (wff) of classical propositional logic and the truth values given to the various operators.

DEFINITION 1.2 (Classical propositional logic).

1. The language of classical propositional logic contains a set $\mathcal{L}_p$ of atomic propositions with typical members $\{p, q, r, s, q_1, q_2, q_3, \ldots\}$ and a set of connectives $\{\wedge, \vee, \neg, \Rightarrow\}$.

2. The notion of a well-formed formula (wff) is defined inductively by the following conditions:

   (a) Any atom $p \in \mathcal{L}_p$ is a wff. We say it is built up from $\{p\}$.

   (b) If A and B are wffs then so are: $\neg(A), (A){\wedge}(B), (A){\vee}(B), (A){\Rightarrow}(B)$. If A is built up from the atoms $\{p_1, \ldots, p_n\}$ and B is built up from the atoms $\{q_1, \ldots, q_k\}$, then $\neg(A)$ is built up from the same atoms as A and $(A) \wedge (B), (A) \vee (B)$ and $(A) \Rightarrow (B)$ are built up from $\{p_1, \ldots, p_n, q_1, \ldots, q_k\}$.

   (c) Let A be a formula built up from $q_1, \ldots, q_k$. We indicate this fact by writing $A(q_1, \ldots, q_k)$. Let $B_1, \ldots, B_k$ be wffs. We define by structural induction the result of substituting in A the formulae B_i for the atom q_i, for $i = 1, \ldots, k$. We denote this substitution by $A(q_1/B_1, \ldots, q_k/B_k)$ and refer to it as a substitution instance of A.

   - For atomic $A(q) = q$, we let $A(q/B) = B$.
   - $(\neg(A))(q_1/B_1, \ldots, q_k/B_k) = \neg(A)(q_1/B_1, \ldots, q_k/B_k)$
   - $((A) \Rightarrow (B))(q_1/B_1, \ldots, q_k/B_k) = A(q_1/B_1, \ldots, q_k/B_k) \Rightarrow B(q_1/B_1, \ldots, q_k/B_k)$ and similarly for $(A) \wedge (B)$ and $(A) \vee (B)$.

3. An *interpretation* (or *assignment*) is any function h assigning truth values to the atomic propositions. h is a function from $\mathcal{L}_p$ into $\{\top, \bot\}$, i.e. $h : \mathcal{L}_p \mapsto \{\top, \bot\}$.

4. We can extend the definition of h from atomic propositions to any wff A by induction, as follows:

   (a) $h(\neg(A)) = \top$ if $h(A) = \bot$, otherwise the value is $\bot$.

   (b) $h((A){\wedge}(B)) = \top$ if $h(A) = \top$ and $h(B) = \top$, otherwise the value is $\bot$.

   (c) $h((A){\vee}(B)) = \top$ if $h(A) = \top$ or $h(B) = \top$ or both, otherwise the value is $\bot$.

(d) $h((A) \Rightarrow (B)) = \top$ if $h(A) = \bot$ or $h(B) = \top$ or both, otherwise the value is $\bot$.

The above definition of $h(A)$ agrees with our understanding of the meaning of the connectives as presented in the truth tables.

5. We find it convenient to assume that our language contains as atomic propositions the constant atoms $\top$ and $\bot$. $\top$ is always true and $\bot$ is always false.

By defining a precedence hierarchy for each of our connectives, we can omit many of the brackets which clutter our formulae. Let us agree that the precedence of the connectives is as follows: $\neg$ is stronger than $\wedge$ which is stronger than $\vee$ which is stronger than $\Rightarrow$. This is similar to the situation we have in algebra, where $-$ (unary minus) is stronger than $\times$, which is stronger than $+$. Thus $-2 + 5 \times 3$ is equivalent to $(-2) + (5 \times 3) = 13$. Similarly $\neg q \vee r \wedge s \Rightarrow q$ is $((\neg q) \vee (r \wedge s)) \Rightarrow q$. To clarify the structure of written formulae further, we will sometimes use [and] instead of (and), e.g. as in $[(\neg q) \vee (r \wedge s)] \Rightarrow q$.

In general $A \wedge B \wedge C$ means $(((A) \wedge (B)) \wedge (C))$ and similarly for $A \vee B \vee C$.

1.2 Computing truth tables

To calculate the truth values of complex wffs for arbitrary truth values of propositions, we build a truth table for the sentence. This is how to compute a truth table for the wff $A = (\neg p \Rightarrow q) \vee r$.

Step 1 Count the number of atoms in A. In this case it is 3 (p, q and r).

Step 2 Form a table with $2^3 = 8$ rows and with as many columns as there are subformulae (i.e. nested sentences) of A. In our case the table is shown below, where r is the first atom, q is the second atom and p is the third atom (from the right).

p	q	r	$\neg p$	$(\neg p \Rightarrow q)$	$(\neg p \Rightarrow q) \vee r$
1					
2					
3					
4					
5					
6					
7					
8					

Step 3 Fill in the columns of the atoms with $\top$ and $\bot$ by alternating *downwards* $\top\bot\top\bot$... for the first atoms, $\top\top\bot\bot$... for the second atoms and so on in powers of 2:

	p	q	r	$\neg p$	$(\neg p \Rightarrow q)$	$(\neg p \Rightarrow q) \vee r$
1	T	T	T			
2	T	T	⊥			
3	T	⊥	T			
4	T	⊥	⊥			
5	⊥	T	T			
6	⊥	T	⊥			
7	⊥	⊥	T			
8	⊥	⊥	⊥			

Step 4 Compute the values in the other columns row by row using the basic truth tables for the connectives:

	p	q	r	$\neg p$	$(\neg p \Rightarrow q)$	$(\neg p \Rightarrow q) \vee r$
1	T	T	T	⊥	T	T
2	T	T	⊥	⊥	T	T
3	T	⊥	T	⊥	T	T
4	T	⊥	⊥	⊥	T	T
5	⊥	T	T	T	T	T
6	⊥	T	⊥	T	T	T
7	⊥	⊥	T	T	⊥	T
8	⊥	⊥	⊥	T	⊥	⊥

EXERCISE 1.3. Compute the truth tables of the following sentences:

1. $\neg A \vee B$

2. $\neg(\neg A \wedge \neg B)$

3. $A \vee \neg A$

4. $((A \wedge B) \Rightarrow C) \Rightarrow (A \Rightarrow (B \Rightarrow C))$

5. $(A \Rightarrow B) \wedge (B \Rightarrow A)$; this formula is abbreviated $(A \Leftrightarrow B)$

6. $(A \Rightarrow (B \wedge C)) \Rightarrow ((A \Rightarrow B) \wedge (A \Rightarrow C))$

Most wffs have contingent truth tables, meaning that they become true or false depending on the truth values of their atoms. For example, the following can be made either true or false depending on the values of p and q:

$$[(p \Rightarrow q) \wedge q] \Rightarrow p$$

If p is intended to mean 'you are a heavy smoker' and q 'you cough', then the above might be read (more or less) as [if you are a heavy smoker then you cough, and you cough, then you are a heavy smoker].

Now if you cough, and yet are not a heavy smoker, then the above formula is false. On the other hand, if you are a heavy smoker, the formula is true regardless of whether you cough or not.

We saw that every wff has a truth table, but is the converse true? For a given truth table for, say, p, q and r, is there a corresponding formula $A(p,q,r)$ with the given truth table? The answer is yes. We demonstrate this by means of an example. Can we find a formula $A(p,q,r)$ with the following truth table?

	p	q	r	A
1	T	T	T	T
2	⊥	T	T	T
3	T	⊥	T	T
4	⊥	⊥	T	⊥
5	T	T	⊥	⊥
6	⊥	T	⊥	⊥
7	T	⊥	⊥	⊥
8	⊥	⊥	⊥	⊥

The wff with the above table is

$$A = [p \wedge q \wedge r] \vee [\neg p \wedge q \wedge r] \vee [p \wedge \neg q \wedge r]$$

How do we find A? We go over the table and take out the rows for which the table for A gives a value of T to A. In this example there are three such rows:

	p	q	r	A
1	T	T	T	T
2	⊥	T	T	T
3	T	⊥	T	T

For each such row we describe what the values of p, q and r are as indicated:

- For T T T write $[p \wedge q \wedge r]$

- For ⊥ T T write $[\neg p \wedge q \wedge r]$

- For T ⊥ T write $[p \wedge \neg q \wedge r]$.

A is the disjunction (a combination using $\vee$) of all the wffs for the rows, i.e.

$$A = [p \wedge q \wedge r] \vee [\neg p \wedge q \wedge r] \vee [p \wedge \neg q \wedge r]$$

What we said in symbols means the following in English: A is T *exactly when* p, q and r are all true, or when p is false and q and r are true, or when p is true, *q* is false and *r* is true. We should show that *A* has exactly the required table. In other words, that it is impossible for our formula *A* to be true under an assignment of truth values to *p*, *q* and *r* for which the truth table records a value of ⊥ for *A*. No such situation can arise, since for the wff *A* to be true, one of its disjuncts must be true. Each of its disjuncts uniquely describes one row in the truth table, in particular a row which gives a value of ⊤ to *A*.

EXERCISE 1.4.

1. Find a wff *A* for each of the following tables:

p	*q*	*A* =?
⊤	⊤	⊤
⊤	⊥	⊥
⊥	⊤	⊥
⊥	⊥	⊤

p	*q*	*r*	*A* =?
⊤	⊤	⊤	⊤
⊤	⊤	⊥	⊥
⊤	⊥	⊤	⊥
⊤	⊥	⊥	⊤
⊥	⊤	⊤	⊥
⊥	⊤	⊥	⊤
⊥	⊥	⊤	⊤
⊥	⊥	⊥	⊥

2. Can the following be all true?

> The television is switched on. If the television is switched on and has power then there is a picture. There is no picture.

(Hint: translate into symbols and check the truth table for a row in which the conjunction of the sentences is true.)

2   Notions of truth and validity

We have seen in the exercises that some wffs have truth tables with the value ⊤ throughout in the right-hand column. Such wffs are called *tautologies*. They are always true no matter what truth values their atoms have. We can also define a tautology in terms of the truth assignment *h*.

DEFINITION 1.5. A wff *A* is a *tautology* iff for every assignment *h*, $h(A) = \top$. The symmetric concept is that *A* is a *contradiction* iff for every *h*, $h(A) = \bot$. If *A* is a tautology we denote it by ⊨*A*.[2]

Some commonly encountered tautologies include

---

[2]Tautologies are also called *theorems* of logic, especially in the context of some other ways of generating them. See next chapter.

$$p \lor \neg p$$
$$[p \land (p \Rightarrow q)] \Rightarrow q$$
$$p \land q \Rightarrow q$$
$$p \Rightarrow \neg \neg p$$
$$q \Rightarrow p \lor q$$

$$p \Rightarrow p$$
$$p \land q \Rightarrow p$$
$$\neg \neg p \Rightarrow p$$
$$p \Rightarrow p \lor q$$
$$[(p \Rightarrow q) \land \neg q] \Rightarrow \neg p$$

Tautologies are logical truths. Contradictions, on the other hand, are logical falsities, and can never be true. Here are some example contradictions:

$$p \land \neg p$$
$$\neg (p \Rightarrow p)$$
$$p \land (p \Rightarrow q) \land \neg q$$

Notice that if A is a tautology, $\neg A$ is a contradiction. If a formula A is not a contradiction, then there is at least one assignment h to its atoms which gives $h(A) = \top$. When this is the case, the formula A is said to be *consistent* or *satisfiable*. Some examples of consistent (but not tautological) sentences are

$$p$$
$$\neg q \lor (q \Rightarrow p)$$
$$q \land (p \Rightarrow p)$$

2.1 Equivalences

Two formulae A, B which have the same truth table (i.e. $h(A) = h(B)$ for all h) are said to be *equivalent*. Logically they 'say' the same thing. We indicate equivalence by writing $\equiv$ (pronounced 'if and only if', or 'iff'). Thus $A \equiv B$ means that A and B have the same truth table. For example,

$$\neg \neg p \;\equiv\; p$$
$$\neg (p \lor q) \;\equiv\; \neg p \land \neg q$$
$$\neg (p \land q) \;\equiv\; \neg p \lor \neg q$$

These first three are called the De Morgan laws. Others include

$$\neg (p \Rightarrow q) \;\equiv\; p \land \neg q$$
$$p \land (q \lor r) \;\equiv\; (p \land q) \lor (p \land r)$$
$$p \Rightarrow q \;\equiv\; \neg q \Rightarrow \neg p$$
$$p \lor (q \land r) \;\equiv\; (p \lor q) \land (p \lor r)$$
$$p \land p \;\equiv\; p$$
$$p \land q \;\equiv\; q \land p$$
$$(p \land q) \land r \;\equiv\; p \land (q \land r)$$

$$p \vee p \ \equiv \ p$$
$$p \vee q \ \equiv \ q \vee p$$
$$(p \vee q) \vee r \ \equiv \ p \vee (q \vee r)$$
$$p \wedge \neg p \ \equiv \ \bot$$
$$p \vee \neg p \ \equiv \ \top$$

Using equivalences, we can define some of the truth connectives in terms of each other:

$$p \Rightarrow q \ \equiv \ \neg p \vee q$$
$$p \wedge q \ \equiv \ \neg(\neg p \vee \neg q)$$
$$p \Rightarrow q \ \equiv \ \neg(p \wedge \neg q)$$
$$p \vee q \ \equiv \ \neg(\neg p \wedge \neg q)$$
$$p \wedge q \ \equiv \ \neg(p \Rightarrow \neg q)$$
$$p \vee q \ \equiv \ \neg p \Rightarrow q$$

We can also use the equivalences to transform formulae to other equivalent formulae like we do in school algebra. See Exercise 1.2.5 and its solution.

EXERCISE 1.6.

1. Let $p|q$ be defined as the wff with p, q having the table below:

p	q	$p|q$
$\top$	$\top$	$\bot$
$\bot$	$\top$	$\top$
$\top$	$\bot$	$\top$
$\bot$	$\bot$	$\top$

Define $\wedge, \vee, \neg$ and $\Rightarrow$ using $|$. (Hint: let $\neg p$ be $p|p$.) The '$|$' operator is known as the Sheffer stroke.

2. Which of the following are tautologies?

   (a) $(p \vee q) \wedge \neg p \Rightarrow q$

   (b) $(\neg q \Rightarrow \neg p) \Rightarrow (p \Rightarrow q)$

   (c) $(p \wedge q \vee r) \Rightarrow (p \wedge q \wedge r)$

   (d) $((p \Rightarrow q) \Rightarrow p) \Rightarrow p$

DEFINITION 1.7 (Normal forms). There are two basic normal forms in which sentences can be written, based on disjunctions (combinations using $\vee$) and conjunctions (combinations using $\wedge$). Such normal forms are sometimes used for automatic methods of checking whether a sentence is a tautology.

1. *Disjunctive normal form* — a formula of the form

$$A_1 \vee A_2 \vee \cdots \vee A_k$$

where each A_i is a conjunction of either atoms or their negations, is called a wff in a disjunctive normal form. These are formulae we get out of tables in the manner we described in the previous section.

The formula $\perp$ is considered to be in a disjunctive normal form in which the number of disjuncts is $k = 0$.

2. *Conjunctive normal form* — a formula of the form

$$A_1 \wedge A_2 \wedge \cdots \wedge A_k$$

where each A_i is a disjunction of atoms or their negations, is called a wff in a conjunctive normal form. This is the dual to disjunctive normal form where $\wedge$ and $\vee$ are interchanged.

The formula $\top$ is considered to be in a conjunctive normal form in which the number of conjuncts is 0.

3. One can give a more strict definition of normal forms. First we do not allow repetition; thus $p \wedge p$ is not allowed. Second we want each atom p appearing in the formula to appear either as p or $\neg p$ in each basic component of the normal form. Thus for example $p \vee q$ is not acceptable. It should be $(p \wedge q) \vee (p \wedge \neg q) \vee (\neg p \wedge q)$ which is equivalent. Such a normal form we shall call a strict normal form.

We can prove that all wff can be rewritten into either of the normal forms by using the equivalences we have presented above. In fact every formula can be put into an equivalent strict normal form if we first build the full truth table for it and then construct the corresponding formula for this truth table as done in Section 1.1.2.

THEOREM 1.8. *For any wff A, there are equivalent formulae A^c and A^d where A^c is in conjunctive normal form and A^d is in disjunctive normal form.*

Proof. We prove the theorem by induction over the structure of the formula A.

1. The base case is when A is an atomic proposition, so that $A = A^c = A^d$.

2. When A is $\neg B$, by induction we can rewrite B into the normal form formulae B^c and B^d. By applying the De Morgan laws, negating B^c gives a formula in disjunctive normal form, and negating B^d gives a formula in conjunctive normal form. Hence if $B^c = B^c_1 \wedge \cdots \wedge B^c_n$ where the B^c_i are conjunctions of propositions or their negations, then each B^c_i can be negated to become a disjunction $(\neg B^c_j)^d$ so that $A^d = (\neg B^c_1)^d \vee \cdots \vee (\neg B^c_n)^d$. Similarly $A^c = (\neg B^d_1)^c \vee \cdots \vee (\neg B^d_n)^c$.

3. When A is $B \vee C$, by induction we can rewrite both B and C into the normal form formulae B^c, B^d, C^c and C^d. Clearly $B^d \vee C^d$ is in disjunctive normal form. Now $B^c \vee C^c$ can be transformed into conjunctive normal form by repeated use of the equivalence

$$p \vee (q \wedge r) \equiv (p \vee q) \wedge (p \vee r)$$

Assume that $B^c = B^c_1 \wedge \cdots \wedge B^c_m$ and $C^c = C^c_1 \wedge \cdots \wedge C^c_n$. Now

$$(B^c_1 \wedge \cdots \wedge B^c_m) \vee (C^c_1 \wedge \cdots \wedge C^c_n)$$
$$\equiv ((B^c_1 \wedge \cdots \wedge B^c_m) \vee C^c_1) \wedge \cdots \wedge ((B^c_1 \wedge \cdots \wedge B^c_m) \vee C^c_n)$$
$$\equiv ((B^c_1 \vee C^c_1) \wedge \cdots \wedge (B^c_m \vee C^c_1)) \wedge \cdots \wedge ((B^c_1 \vee C^c_n) \wedge \cdots \wedge (B^c_m \vee C^c_n))$$

The B^c_i and C^c_j are all disjunctions of propositions or their negations; hence the entire formula is in conjunctive normal form.

4. A similar argument holds for when A is $B \wedge C$.

5. When A is $B \Rightarrow C$, we can rewrite A to be $\neg B \vee C$, and then the proof continues as for disjunction above.

∎

EXERCISE 1.9. Transform the following to both disjunctive normal form and conjunctive normal form:

$$[(p \Rightarrow q) \vee r] \wedge \neg q \Rightarrow p$$
$$(p \vee q) \wedge r$$
$$p \wedge q \wedge \neg r$$

2.2　Arguments and consequence relations

An *argument* is a claim that one formula B (called the *goal* or the *conclusion*) follows logically from a set of formulae $A_1, \ldots, A_n$ (called the *data* or the *assumptions*). The set of assumptions may be empty (i.e. no assumption). In such a case $A_1, \ldots, A_n$ do not appear. We can formally use the trick of saying this is the case of $n = 0$. Representing the assumptions by $A_1, \ldots, A_n$ and the goal by B, we represent the argument by

$$\frac{A_1,\dots,A_n}{B}$$

or alternatively $A_1,\dots,A_n \vdash B$, which has the virtue of being a more compact notation. Here is an example of an argument:

$$\frac{\text{Either John is at home or John is in his office.}}{\text{Therefore John is at home.}}$$
John is not in the office.

Writing this formally with propositional symbols h for John being at home, and and o for John being at the office, we have

$$\frac{h\lor o}{\frac{\neg o}{h}}$$

or $h\lor o, \neg o \vdash h$. Perhaps the most well-known argument is

$$\frac{A, A\Rightarrow B}{B}$$

or $A, A\Rightarrow B \vdash B$. This is known as *modus ponens* and will be used extensively in future chapters.

DEFINITION 1.10 (Validity of arguments).   An argument with assumptions $A_1,\dots,A_n$ and conclusion B is logically *valid* when the formula $[(A_1)\land\dots\land(A_n)] \Rightarrow B$ is a tautology, otherwise the argument is *invalid*. Hence an argument is valid if, whenever the assumptions of the argument are true, the conclusion is true.

Given the following information,

Assumptions	Conclusion
$(p\Rightarrow q)$	$\neg q$
$\neg p$	

does the conclusion follow? To answer, we check if $[(p\Rightarrow q)\land\neg p]\Rightarrow\neg q$ is a tautology. We can write $A_1,\dots,A_n \vdash ?B$ when we are not sure whether the argument is valid. Otherwise the question mark is omitted. We leave the reader to check whether the argument is valid or not.

A valid argument from a set of assumptions to a conclusion can be considered to form a relationship between the assumptions and the conclusion, namely that the conclusion is true as a consequence of the assumptions being true. Thus the $\vdash$ symbol is often referred to as the *consequence relation*. Consequence relations satisfy the following properties:

- *Reflexivity*
  If the conclusion is also one of the assumptions then the argument is valid, i.e. $A_1,\dots,A_n, B \vdash B$.

- *Monotonicity*
  If a conclusion from a set of assumptions is valid, then the same conclusion is valid from the set of assumptions with some additional formulae added, i.e. if $A_1, \ldots, A_n \vdash B$ then $A_1, \ldots, A_n, C \vdash B$ for any C.

- *Cut*[3]
  If a conclusion from a set of assumptions is added to that set of assumptions, and this larger set is used to make a second conclusion, then the second conclusion can be made from the original assumptions, i.e. if $A_1, \ldots, A_n \vdash B$ and $A_1, \ldots, A_n, B \vdash C$ then $A_1, \ldots, A_n \vdash C$.

In fact one can define the notion of a logical system on the set of wffs to be any relation satisfying the above three properties. Different logical systems satisfy different *additional properties*. For example, the above $\vdash$ for classical logic (defined using truth tables) also satisfies

$$A_1, \ldots, A_n, A \vdash B \vee C \quad \text{iff} \quad A_1, \ldots, A_n \vdash (A \Rightarrow B) \vee C$$

Note that the presence of C is important. In some other logics (such as intuitionistic logic which we will discuss in Chapter 2), C is not allowed. Further discussion is postponed to Chapter 7.

Here is a list of valid arguments. They are so basic that they are called *rules*.

List of valid rules

1. $\dfrac{A \wedge B}{A}$ and $\dfrac{A \wedge B}{B}$ ($\wedge$ *elimination*)

2. $\dfrac{A, B}{A \wedge B}$ ($\wedge$ *introduction*)

3. $\dfrac{A}{A \vee B}$ and $\dfrac{B}{A \vee B}$ ($\vee$ *introduction*)

4. $\dfrac{A \Rightarrow C, \ B \Rightarrow C, \ A \vee B}{C}$ ($\vee$ *elimination*)

5. $\dfrac{A, \ A \Rightarrow B}{B}$ This *modus ponens* rule has a related form:

   $\dfrac{\neg A, \ A \vee B}{B}$ ($\Rightarrow$ *elimination*)

6. $\dfrac{B, \neg B}{C}$ ($\neg$ *elimination*)

---

[3]The notion of cut is central in logic. A full discussion is given in Chapter 3. Monotonicity or non-monotonicity is also very central. This will be discussed in Chapter 11.

7. $\dfrac{B\Rightarrow C,\; B\Rightarrow\neg C}{\neg B}$ ($\neg$ *introduction*)

8. If we want to show that $\dfrac{B_1,\ldots,B_k}{A\Rightarrow C}$ is a valid argument we can show instead that $\dfrac{B_1,\ldots,B_k,\,A}{C}$ is valid.

EXERCISE 1.11.

1. Show that A logically implies B, i.e. $A \vdash B$, is a valid argument if and only if $A\wedge\neg B$ is not consistent.

2. Is $A\Rightarrow B$, $B\Rightarrow C\vdash A\Rightarrow C$ valid?

DEFINITION 1.12 (Consistency of a set of formulae). A set of wffs

$$\{A_1,\ldots,A_n,C\}$$

is consistent if there is a row in the truth table of their conjunction which makes the conjunction true. In other words, if values can be given to all the atomic sentences in $\{A_1,\ldots,A_n,C\}$ which make all of $A_1,\ldots,A_n,C$ true.

For example, consider the set $\{p\Rightarrow q,\ \neg p,\ \neg q\}$, which is consistent if we can find values for p and q which will make all members of the set true. Assigning falsity to both p and q achieves this. Now consider the set $\{r\Rightarrow s,\ r,\ \neg s\}$. In this case we cannot find any such values for r and s (try drawing a truth table for the formula $r\Rightarrow s\wedge r\wedge\neg s$).

EXERCISE 1.13.

1. There are n people standing in a queue. The first person says

    'The last person in the line is lying.'

    The other people in the line say

    'The person in front of me is lying.'

    We can write one sentence of the form 'person 1 is telling the truth iff person n is not telling the truth' for the first person in the queue, and $n-1$ sentences of the form 'person i is telling the truth iff person $i-1$ is not telling the truth', for the other people in the queue. We use p_i to represent the sentence 'person i is telling the truth'

$$
\begin{array}{lll}
A_1 & \text{is} & p_1 \Leftrightarrow \neg p_n\\
A_2 & \text{is} & p_2 \Leftrightarrow \neg p_1\\
& \vdots &\\
A_n & \text{is} & p_n \Leftrightarrow \neg p_{n-1}
\end{array}
$$

Is the set $\{A_1, \ldots, A_n\}$ consistent, i.e. can you give values to $p_1, \ldots, p_n$ so that all of $A_1, \ldots, A_n$ are satisfied? Does it matter whether n is odd or even?

We have learnt the notion of contradiction. A is a contradiction if $\neg A$ is a tautology, i.e. if the truth table for A is all the $\bot$ in the right-hand column. A is not consistent if and only if A is a contradiction. This gives us the connection of consistency with arguments. If $\{A_1, \ldots, A_n, C\}$ is not consistent, and if $\{A_1, \ldots, A_n\}$ is true (in some interpretation) then $\neg C$ is true (in that interpretation). Thus $A_1 \wedge \cdots \wedge A_n \Rightarrow \neg C$ is a tautology. The other direction is also true. If $A_1 \wedge \cdots \wedge A_n \Rightarrow \neg C$ is a tautology, then any row in the truth table which makes $A_1, \ldots, A_n$ true must also make $\neg C$ true, i.e. make C false. Thus we cannot make all of $\{A_1, \ldots, A_n, C\}$ all true.

The practical conclusion from the above is that checking whether $A_1, \ldots, A_n \vdash B$ is a logically valid argument is the same as checking whether $\{A_1, \ldots, A_n, \neg B\}$ is inconsistent. Another view of the argument

$$\frac{A_1, \ldots, A_n}{B}$$

is to consider $A_1, \ldots, A_n$ as *data* and to consider B as a *query* to be asked of the data. B follows logically from $A_1, \ldots, A_n$ if the answer to the query B should be yes.

Thus we have the following three ways to look at the formula (i.e. 1, 2 and 3 below are equivalent).

$$A_1 \wedge \cdots \wedge A_n \Rightarrow B$$

1. as a tautology,

2. as a valid logical argument

$$\frac{A_1, \ldots, A_n}{B}$$

with assumptions $A_1, \ldots, A_n$ and conclusion B,

3. as a statement that if we query a database with goal B and the database contains $A_1, \ldots, A_n$ among its data, then the answer is yes.

$$\frac{\text{Data}}{A_1, \ldots, A_n} \quad ? \quad \frac{\text{Query}}{B}$$

In Chapters 3 and 4 we shall look at some rule-based methods for answering the question 'does the query logically follow from the data?' In the next chapter, we broaden our horizons by beginning to look at so-called *non-classical* logics where components of the classical logical system have been changed, offering in some cases more expressive logics, and in others more restrictive logics.

EXERCISE 1.14.

1. Let *p* stand for 'John loves Mary', *q* stand for 'Mary loves John', *r* stand for 'John is tall', and *s* stand for 'Mary is tall'. Translate the following into symbols (you may need to introduce other atoms):

    (a) John loves Mary only if she loves him and she is not tall.

    (b) If John is tall and Mary loves him then Mary is not tall.

    (c) If John and Mary love each other then Mary loves herself.

2. Use the equivalence rules (see Section 2.1) to push all occurrences of the negation symbol '¬' next to the atoms in the following expressions:

$$\neg((a{\Rightarrow}b)\vee(a{\Rightarrow}c)\wedge\neg a)$$
$$\neg(a\wedge\neg b){\Rightarrow}a$$

3. Show the equivalences below:

$(A{\Rightarrow}\top)$	≡	$\top$	$(A{\Rightarrow}\bot)$	≡	$\neg A$
$(\bot{\Rightarrow}A)$	≡	$\top$	$(\top{\Rightarrow}A)$	≡	A
$(A\vee\top)$	≡	$\top$	$(A\vee\bot)$	≡	A
$(A\wedge\top)$	≡	A	$(A\wedge\bot)$	≡	$\bot$

4. Below are several arguments in English. For each argument:

   - define a dictionary using the atoms *p*, *q*, *r*, *s*, . . ., i.e. assign one of these symbols to stand for each relevant proposition in the argument,

   - translate the argument into logic using the dictionary,

   - check whether the argument is logically valid.

    (a) Either it is warm or it is raining. Unless it is not warm, we go outside. *Therefore* we go outside.

    (b) If the king is in the room, then the courtiers laugh only if he laughs. The courtiers always laugh when the jester is in the room. The king never laughs when the jester is in the room. *Therefore* either the king or the jester is not in the room.

    (c) If we are not hungry, and the food is very hot, we eat slowly. If we are not hungry, either we eat slowly or the food is very hot. The food is not very hot. *Therefore* we are hungry.

(d) If Jones did not meet Smith last night, then either Smith was a murderer, or Jones is telling a lie. If Smith was not a murderer, then Jones did not meet Smith last night, and the murder happened after midnight. If the murder happened after midnight, then either Smith was a murderer, or Jones is telling a lie, but not both. *Therefore*, Smith was a murderer.

3 Worked examples

EXAMPLE 1.15 (Worked examples for Section 1.1.1).
Exercises

1. Following the definition, show that in every formula the numbers of left and right brackets are equal.

2. Explain why the following expression is not a formula:

$$\neg((p) \wedge (q)) \vee (p)$$

3. According to the definitions, show that if A is a formula, then $(A)(q/B)$ is a formula.

4. Let $l(A)$ be the length of a formula A (i.e. the total number of characters in the expression (A)). Prove that $l((A)(q/B)) \geq l(A)$.

5. Show that for any formula A, 3 divides $(l(A) - 1)$.

6. Show that if A, B are formulae and q is an atom occurring n times in A, then
$l((A)$
$(q/B)) = l(A) + n \cdot (l(B) - 1)$.

7. Find an example showing that formulae $(A)(p, q/B, C)$ and $((A)(p/B))$ (q/C) may be distinct.

Solutions

1. For atomic propositions there is nothing to prove. If the claim is true for A, then it is true for $\neg(A)$, where the numbers of left and right brackets increase by one. If it is true for A and B, then it is true for $(A) \wedge (B), (A) \vee (B), (A) \Rightarrow (B)$, because the total numbers of left and right brackets increase by two.

2. Suppose it is. This expression does not begin with '(' and is not an atomic proposition. So it is $\neg(B)$ for some formula B. But the expression $B = (p) \wedge (q)) \vee (p$ is not a formula, because every non-atomic formula ends with ')'.

3. By induction. If A is atomic then $(A)(q/B)$ is either A or B. If $A = \neg(C)$ then $(A)(q/B) = \neg((C)(q/B))$. $(C)(q/B)$ is a formula by the induction hypothesis. Hence $(A)(q/B)$ is a formula by 1.1.2(b). The cases when A is an implication, disjunction or conjunction are similar.

4. By induction. If A is atomic then $l(A) = 1$, and the claim is trivial.

   If $A = (C) \vee (D)$ then $l(A) = l(C) + l(D) + 5$.

   $(A)(q/B) = ((C)(q/B)) \vee ((D)(q/B))$, and so $l((A)(q/B)) = l((C)(q/B)) + l((D)(q/B)) + 5$. By the induction hypothesis, $l((C)(q/B)) \geq l(C)$, and $l((D)(q/B)) \geq l(D)$. Therefore $l((A)(q/B)) \geq l(A)$.
   Other cases are similar.

5. By induction. The case when A is atomic is clear.

   If $A = \neg(B)$, and $l(B) = 3n + 1$, then $l(A) = l(B) + 3 = 3(n + 1) + 1$. If $A = (B) \triangledown (C)$, $\triangledown$ being $\Rightarrow, \vee$ or $\wedge$, and $l(B) = 3m + 1, l(C) = 3n + 1$ then $l(A) = l(B) + l(C) + 5 = 3m + 3n + 7 = 3(m + n + 2) + 1$.

6. Again by induction. We use the notation $A' = (A)(q/B)$.

   If A is atomic, $A \neq q$, then $A' = A$, $n = 0$, and thus $l(A') = l(A) + n(l(B) - 1)$.

   If $A = q$, then $A' = B, n = 1$, and so $l(A') = l(B) = 1 + (l(B) - 1) = l(A) + n(l(B) - 1)$.

   If $A = \neg(C)$ then $A' = \neg(C')$ by 1.1.2(c), and $l(A) = l(C)+3, l(A') = l(C')+3$. If q occurs n times in A, then it occurs n times in C, and so by the induction hypothesis, $l(C') = l(C) + n(l(B) - 1)$. Hence $l(A') = l(C') + 3 = l(C) + n(l(B) - 1) + 3 = l(A) + n(l(B) - 1)$.

   If $A = (C) \triangledown (D)$ then $A' = (C') \triangledown (D')$, and $l(A) = l(C) + l(D) + 5, l(A') = l(C') + l(D') + 5$. If q occurs n times in A, x times in C, y times in D, then $n = x + y$. By the induction hypothesis, $l(C') = l(C) + x(l(B) - 1), l(D') = l(D) + y(l(B) - 1)$. Thus

$$
\begin{aligned}
l(A') &= l(C') + l(D') + 5 \\
&= l(C) + x(l(B) - 1) + l(D) + y(l(B) - 1) + 5 \\
&= l(A) + n(l(B) - 1)
\end{aligned}
$$

7. This may happen when q occurs in B. For instance, take $A = (p) \vee (q)$, $B = q, C = p$. Then $(A)(p, q/B, C) = (q) \vee (p)$, but $((A)(p/B))(q/C) = ((q) \vee (q))(q/C) = (p) \vee (p)$.

EXAMPLE 1.16 (Worked examples for Section 1.1.2).

Exercises

1. Find all values of the atoms p, q, r, s, t, u for which the following formula is false:

   (a) $((p \Rightarrow q \wedge r) \Rightarrow (\neg q \Rightarrow \neg p)) \Rightarrow \neg p$

(b) $(p \wedge q) \vee (p \wedge r) \vee (q \wedge r) \vee (s \wedge t) \vee (s \wedge u) \vee (t \wedge u) \vee (\neg p \wedge \neg s)$

(c) $p \vee q \vee r \Rightarrow (p \vee q) \wedge (p \vee r)$

(d) $(p \vee q) \wedge (q \vee r) \wedge (r \vee p) \Rightarrow p \wedge q \wedge r$

(e) $p \vee q \Rightarrow (\neg p \wedge q) \vee (p \wedge \neg q)$

2. Consider the following propositions about a natural number n:

$$n < 100$$
$$n > 35$$
$$n > 9$$
$$n > 10$$
$$n > 5$$

Find n, for which two of these propositions are false, and three others are true. Is such n unique?

3. m, n are natural numbers. Of the following four propositions

(a) n divides $(m + 1)$

(b) $m = 2n + 5$

(c) 3 divides $(m + n)$

(d) $(m + 7n)$ is prime

three are true, and one is false. Find all possible pairs a, b.

4. Three runners A, B, C had a race and finished almost at the same time. Three sports commentators gave the following immediate reports:

(a) A has won.

(b) B has not won.

(c) C was not the last.

It turned out that exactly one of the commentators was right. What was the result of the race?

5. After racing, four jockeys (A, B, C, D) made the following statements about their results:

(a) 'I was neither the first, nor the last.'

(b) 'I was not the last.'

(c) 'I was the first.'

(d) 'I was the last.'

Three of these statements are true, and one is false. Find, who was telling a lie and who came first.

6. A professor of logic meets 10 of his former students, Albert, Alice, Bob, Bertha, Clifford, Connie, David, Dora, Edgar and Edith, who have become five married couples. When asked about their husbands, the ladies gave the following answers:
Alice: My husband is Clifford, and Bob has married Dora.
Bertha: My husband is Albert, and Bob has married Connie.
Connie: Clifford is my husband, Bertha's husband is Edgar.
Dora: My husband is Bob, and David has married Edith.
Edith: Yes, David is my husband. And Albert's wife is Alice.
Additional true information coming from the men was that every lady gave one correct and one wrong answer. This was sufficient to find out the truth. Reproduce the professor's argument.

7. Each of four dwarfs, Ben, Ken, Len and Vin, is either always telling the truth or always lying. Here is their chat:
Ben (to Ken). You are a liar.
Len (to Ben). You yourself are a liar!
Vin (to Len). They are both liars. And you too.
Who is telling the truth?

Solutions

1. (a) The implication $((p \Rightarrow q \wedge r) \Rightarrow (\neg q \Rightarrow p)) \Rightarrow \neg p$ is false iff $(p \Rightarrow q \wedge r) \Rightarrow (\neg q \Rightarrow \neg p)$ is $\top$, and $\neg p$ is $\bot$. Then p is $\top$ and it remains to consider only q, r:

q	r	$q \wedge r$	$p \Rightarrow q \wedge r$	$\neg q \Rightarrow \neg p$	$(p \Rightarrow q \wedge r) \Rightarrow (\neg q \Rightarrow \neg p)$
$\top$	$\top$	$\top$	$\top$	$\top$	$\top$
$\top$	$\bot$	$\bot$	$\bot$	$\top$	$\top$
$\bot$	$\top$	$\bot$	$\bot$	$\bot$	$\top$
$\bot$	$\bot$	$\bot$	$\bot$	$\bot$	$\top$

So the answer is: p is $\top$; q, r are arbitrary.

(b) All possible combinations of truth values are listed in the table:

p	q	r	s	t	u
T	⊥	⊥	T	⊥	⊥
T	⊥	⊥	⊥	T	⊥
T	⊥	⊥	⊥	⊥	T
T	⊥	⊥	⊥	⊥	⊥
⊥	T	⊥	T	⊥	⊥
⊥	⊥	T	T	⊥	⊥
⊥	⊥	⊥	T	⊥	⊥

Comment. The formulae $p \wedge q, p \wedge r, q \wedge r, s \wedge t, s \wedge u, t \wedge u, \neg p \wedge \neg s$ must be false, and thus $(p \vee s)$ must be true. So we notice that at least one of the following combinations appears:

- p is T, and q, r are ⊥
- s is T, and t, u are ⊥.

Having three values fixed, we compute the truth table for the other three.

(c)

p	q	r
⊥	⊥	T
⊥	T	⊥

Comment. $p \vee q \vee r$ is T and ($p \vee q$ is ⊥ or $p \vee r$ is ⊥).

(d)

p	q	r
⊥	T	T
T	⊥	T
T	T	⊥

Comment. $p \vee q, q \vee r, p \vee r$ must be true, and $p \wedge q \wedge r$ false (i.e. at least one of the atoms is ⊥). If p is ⊥ then q, r are T. Two other cases are analogous.

(e) p, q must both be true.

2. Denote these propositions by $p_1, \ldots, p_5$. Then the following formulae are true:

$$\neg p_1 \Rightarrow p_2, p_2 \Rightarrow p_4, p_4 \Rightarrow p_3, p_3 \Rightarrow p_5$$

We notice that if p_2 is T then the three other propositions (p_3, p_4, p_5) are T. Hence p_2 is ⊥.

Since $\neg p_1 \Rightarrow p_2$ is $\top$ we get that p_1 is $\top$. But then p_4 is false (otherwise, four propositions are true).

Therefore p_1, p_3, p_5 are true; p_2, p_4 are false.

That is, we have: $n < 100, n \leq 35, n > 9, n \leq 10, n > 5$. Thus $n = 10$ is the unique possibility.

3. The argument is similar to the previous exercise. Let $p_1, \ldots, p_4$ be the propositions in question. Then one can check that the following formulae are true:

$$p_3 \Rightarrow \neg p_2, p_3 \Rightarrow \neg p_4$$

Since exactly one of the atoms is false, it follows easily that p_1, p_2, p_4 are $\top$ and p_3 is $\bot$. Then the following is true:

   (a) n divides $(m + 1)$.

   (b) $m = 2n + 5$.

   (c) $(m + 7n)$ is prime.

By (a), (b), n divides $2n + 6$, and thus n divides 6, i.e. $n = 1, 2, 3$ or 6. Taking (c) into account, we get the two possibilities:

   (i) $n = 2, m = 9$.

   (ii) $n = 6, m = 17$.

4. Consider the statements a, b, c as atoms. Clearly, $a \Rightarrow b$ is true. So there are the following two possibilities:

   (i) a, b are $\top$, c is $\bot$.

Then the positions of A, B, C are 1,2,3.

   (ii) c, b are $\top$, a is $\bot$.

Then A has not won, B has not won either, and C was the last. This is impossible. Therefore only the first possibility remains.

5. Consider the statements of A, B, C, D respectively as atoms a, b, c, d. The following two propositions are obviously true:

$$d \Rightarrow b, c \wedge d \Rightarrow a$$

Since exactly one of a, b, c must be false, there are two possibilities for their truth values:

   (i) a, b, d are $\top$, c is $\bot$.

(ii) a, b, c are $\top$, d is $\bot$.

In the case (i) only B might be the first. (Note that D was the last, and the positions of A, C cannot be found exactly.) In the case (ii) we obtain a contradiction, because nobody can be the last. Therefore, B has won, and C was lying.

6. There are 25 atomic propositions of the form 'a man whose name begins with X and a woman whose name begins with Y are married', which we denote by $p_{AA}, p_{AB}, \ldots, p_{EE}$. The information at the professor's disposal is expressed by a rather long conjunction including clauses $(p_{XY} \Rightarrow \neg p_{XZ})$ and $(p_{YX} \Rightarrow \neg p_{ZX})$ for any triple X, Y, Z where $Y \neq Z$, and also the following ones:

(a) $p_{CA} \Leftrightarrow \neg p_{BD}$

(b) $p_{AB} \Leftrightarrow \neg p_{BC}$

(c) $p_{CC} \Leftrightarrow \neg p_{EB}$

(d) $p_{BD} \Leftrightarrow \neg p_{DE}$

(e) $p_{DE} \Leftrightarrow \neg p_{AA}$

It will be convenient to show truth values of the atoms in a 5×5 table. The first part of our conjunction means that $\top$ occurs exactly once at each row and each column of the table.

Now assume that p_{CA} is $\top$ and start filling in the table:

	A	B	C	D	E
A	$\bot$				
B	$\bot$				
C	$\top$	$\bot$	$\bot$	$\bot$	$\bot$
D	$\bot$				
E	$\bot$				

Since (a) and (c) are true, we have that p_{BD} is $\bot$, p_{DE} is $\top$, and

	A	B	C	D	E
A	$\bot$				$\bot$
B	$\bot$			$\bot$	$\bot$
C	$\top$	$\bot$	$\bot$	$\bot$	$\bot$
D	$\bot$	$\bot$	$\bot$	$\bot$	$\top$
E	$\bot$				$\bot$

Using (c) we get

	A	B	C	D	E
A	⊥	⊥			⊥
B	⊥	⊥		⊥	⊥
C	⊤	⊥	⊥	⊥	⊥
D	⊥	⊥	⊥	⊥	⊤
E	⊥	⊤	⊥	⊥	⊥

and eventually

	A	B	C	D	E
A	⊥	⊥	⊥	⊤	⊥
B	⊥	⊥	⊤	⊥	⊥
C	⊤	⊥	⊥	⊥	⊥
D	⊥	⊥	⊥	⊥	⊤
E	⊥	⊤	⊥	⊥	⊥

We have to check also another assumption: p_{CA} is ⊥. Then if we fill in the table according to (a), (d), (e), we have

	A	B	C	D	E
A	⊤	⊥	⊥	⊥	⊥
B	⊥	⊥	⊥	⊤	⊥
C	⊥			⊥	
D	⊥			⊥	⊥
E	⊥			⊥	

and we observe that (b) becomes false.

Therefore the solution is unique.

7. Let B, K, L, V be the atoms stating that corresponding dwarfs are truthful. The following formulae are known to be true:

(a) $B \Leftrightarrow \neg K$

(b) $L \Leftrightarrow \neg B$

(c) $V \Rightarrow \neg B \wedge \neg K \wedge \neg L$

(d) $\neg V \Rightarrow \neg(\neg B \wedge \neg K) \wedge L$

Now assume that V is true. Then B, K must be ⊥ by (c), and so (a) becomes false.

Hence V is ⊥. By (d) L is ⊤, and by (b), (a) we get that B is ⊥, K is ⊤. (a)–(d) are true for these values of atoms. Therefore only Len is telling the truth.

EXAMPLE 1.17 (Worked examples for Section 1.2.1).

Exercises

1. Show that $A \equiv B$ iff $(A \Leftrightarrow B)$ is a tautology.

2. Show that if $A_1 \equiv B_1$ and $A_2 \equiv B_2$ then $(A_1 \Rightarrow A_2) \equiv (B_1 \Rightarrow B_2)$.

3. Prove that if $A \equiv B$ then $(C)(p/A) \equiv (C)(p/B)$.

4. Show that every substitution instance of a tautology is also a tautology.

5. Prove that if $A \equiv B$ then$(A)(p/C) \equiv (B)(p/C)$.

6. Check the following equivalences:

   (a) $A \vee (A \wedge B) \equiv A$

   (b) $A \wedge (A \Rightarrow B) \equiv A \wedge B$

   (c) $A \vee (B \wedge \neg A) \equiv A \vee B$

   (d) $A \Rightarrow (B \Rightarrow C) \equiv A \wedge B \Rightarrow C$

   (e) $A \Rightarrow (B \Rightarrow C) \equiv B \Rightarrow (A \Rightarrow C)$

   (f) $(A \Rightarrow B) \Rightarrow A \equiv A$

   (g) $(A \Rightarrow B) \Rightarrow B \equiv A \vee B$

   (h) $(A \Leftrightarrow B) \Leftrightarrow C \equiv A \Leftrightarrow (B \Leftrightarrow C)$.

7. Find disjunctive normal forms for the formulae

   (a) $p \Leftrightarrow q$

   (b) $\neg(p \Leftrightarrow q)$

   (c) $(p \Leftrightarrow q) \Leftrightarrow r$

8. Explain how to find $(\neg A)^d$ provided A^d is given as a strict normal form.

9. Find a formula A built of three atomic propositions, such that the strict normal forms A^d and $(\neg A)^d$ have an equal number of disjuncts.

10. Let X be the set of all formulae built of three atomic propositions. Find a consistent formula $A \in X$ with the following property:

    for any $B \in X$, if $B \Rightarrow A$ is a tautology, then either $A \equiv B$ or B is a contradiction.

11. Find a formula A, such that the formula

$$(A \wedge q \Rightarrow \neg p) \Rightarrow ((p \Rightarrow \neg q) \Rightarrow A)$$

   is a tautology.

Solutions

1. Exercise 1.1.3.5 shows that for any assignment h, $h(A \Leftrightarrow B) = \top$ iff $h(A) = h(B)$. Hence the claim follows.

2. Immediately by definitions: given that $h(A_1) = h(B_1)$ and $h(A_2) = h(B_2)$ we obtain that $h(A_1 \Rightarrow A_2) = h(B_1 \Rightarrow B_2)$.

3. By induction. For example, if $C = D \wedge E$ then

$$(C)(p/A) = (D)(p/A) \wedge (E)(p/A),$$
$$(C)(p/B) = (D)(p/B) \wedge (E)(p/B).$$

   If the claim holds for D, E we obtain that $(C)(p/A) \equiv (C)(p/B)$ as in the previous exercise.

4. Let A be a tautology. To show that $A' = (A)(q_1/B_1, \ldots, q_k/B_k)$ is a tautology take any assignment h and prove that $h(A') = \top$. Let h_1 be an assignment such that $h_1(q_1) = h(B_1), \ldots, h_1(q_k) = h(B_k), h_1(r) = h(r)$ for any other atom r. It suffices to prove that $h(C') = h_1(C)$ for any formula C (because then we have: $h(A') = h_1(A) = \top$). This is easily done by induction on C. For example, if $C = D \wedge E$ and $h(D') = h_1(D), h(E') = h_1(E)$ then $C' = D' \wedge E'$, and so $h(C') = \top$ iff $h(D') = h(E') = \top$ iff $h_1(D) = h_1(E) = \top$ iff $h_1(C) = \top$.

5. If $A \equiv B$ then $(A \Leftrightarrow B)$ is a tautology (Exercise 1 above). Then $(A \Leftrightarrow B)(p/C)$ is also a tautology (Exercise 4 above). But this is the same as $(A)(p/C) \Leftrightarrow (B)(p/C)$. Now apply Exercise 1 above again.

6. Sometimes it is easier to compute truth tables, and sometimes straightforward arguments work better.

   (a) For any assignment h, $h(A \vee (A \wedge B)) = \top$
      iff $h(A) = \top$ or $h(A \wedge B) = \top$
      iff $h(A) = \top$ or $h(A) = h(B) = \top$
      iff $h(A) = \top$. Hence $h(A \vee (A \wedge B)) = h(A)$.
      Another method: compute the truth table of $A \vee (A \wedge B)$:

A	B	$A \wedge B$	$A \vee (A \wedge B)$
$\top$	$\top$	$\top$	$\top$
$\top$	$\bot$	$\bot$	$\top$
$\bot$	$\top$	$\bot$	$\bot$
$\bot$	$\bot$	$\bot$	$\bot$

(b) $h(A \wedge (A \Rightarrow B)) = \top$ iff $h(A) = \top$ and $h(A \Rightarrow B) = \top$
iff $h(A) = \top$ and $(h(A) = \bot$ or $h(B) = \top)$
iff $h(A) = h(B) = \top$
iff $h(A \wedge B) = \top$.

(c) $h(A \vee (B \wedge \neg A)) = \top$ iff $h(A) = \top$ or $h(B \wedge \neg A) = \top$
iff $h(A) = \top$ or $h(B) = h(\neg A) = \top$
iff $h(A) = \top$ or $(h(B) = \top$ and $h(A) = \bot)$
iff $h(A) = \top$ or $h(B) = \top$.

(d) The easiest way is to use equivalences mentioned in the text:

$$
\begin{aligned}
A \Rightarrow (B \Rightarrow C) &\equiv \neg A \vee (B \Rightarrow C) \\
&\equiv \neg A \vee (\neg B \vee C) \\
&\equiv (\neg A \vee \neg B) \vee C \\
&\equiv \neg(A \wedge B) \vee C \\
&\equiv A \wedge B \Rightarrow C
\end{aligned}
$$

(e) Use the previous equivalence:

$$
\begin{aligned}
A \Rightarrow (B \Rightarrow C) &\equiv A \wedge B \Rightarrow C \\
B \Rightarrow (A \Rightarrow C) &\equiv B \wedge A \Rightarrow C
\end{aligned}
$$

(f) Compute the truth table:

A	B	$A \Rightarrow B$	$(A \Rightarrow B) \Rightarrow A$
$\top$	$\top$	$\top$	$\top$
$\top$	$\bot$	$\bot$	$\top$
$\bot$	$\top$	$\top$	$\bot$
$\bot$	$\bot$	$\top$	$\bot$

(g) Compute the truth table:

A	B	$A \Rightarrow B$	$(A \Rightarrow B) \Rightarrow B$	$A \vee B$
$\top$	$\top$	$\top$	$\top$	$\top$
$\top$	$\bot$	$\bot$	$\top$	$\top$
$\bot$	$\top$	$\top$	$\top$	$\top$
$\bot$	$\bot$	$\top$	$\bot$	$\bot$

(h) One way is to compute truth tables. Another way is to observe that $(p \Leftrightarrow q)$ has the same table as addition in the two-element Abelian group in which $\top$ is the null element. Group addition is always associative.

7. (a) $(p \wedge q) \vee (\neg p \wedge \neg q)$

(b) $(p \land \neg q) \lor (\neg p \land q)$

(c) $(p \land q \land r) \lor (\neg p \land \neg q \land r) \lor (p \land \neg q \land \neg r) \lor (\neg p \land q \land \neg r)$

8. $(\neg A)^d$ consists exactly of those disjuncts built of atoms and their negations which are missing in A^d. This follows immediately if we remember correspondence between truth tables and normal forms.

9. Use the previous exercise. A^d should have four disjuncts. For example,

$$(p \land q \land r) \lor (p \land \neg q \land r) \lor (p \land \neg q \land \neg r) \lor (\neg p \land q \land r)$$

10. Take an A such that in its truth table only one line gives the value $\top$. If $B \Rightarrow A$ is a tautology, B can be true only at the same line.

   So, for example, we can take $A = p \land q \land r$ or $A = \neg p \land q \land \neg r$, etc.

11. It is sufficient to make $(p \Rightarrow \neg q) \Rightarrow A$ a tautology. And this happens if $A = (p \Rightarrow \neg q)$.

EXAMPLE 1.18 (Worked examples for Section 1.2.2).

Exercises

1. (a) Find formulae A, B, C such that $\{A, B\}, \{A, C\}, \{B, C\}$ are consistent, while $\{A, B, C\}$ is not.

   (b) For any n find an inconsistent set of n formulae, of which every $(n-1)$ formulae are consistent.

2. Find four pairwise inconsistent non-contradictory formulae.

3. What is the maximal number of pairwise inconsistent non-contradictory formulae with two atomic propositions p, q?

4. Check validity of the rules 1–8 of page 16.

5. Given that $A_1, \ldots, A_n, B \vdash C$ and $A_1, \ldots, A_n, C \vdash B$ show that $A_1, \ldots, A_n \vdash B \Leftrightarrow C$.

Solutions

1. (a) For example, if $A = p, B = q, C = \neg(p \land q)$.

   (b) For example, $A_1 = p_1, \ldots, A_{n-1} = p_{n-1}, A_n = \neg(p_1 \land \cdots \land p_{n-1})$. The set $\{A_1, \ldots, A_{i-1}, A_{i+1}, \ldots, A_n\}$ is consistent because all these formulae are true when every atom but p_i is $\top$.

2. $p \wedge q, p \wedge \neg q, \neg p \wedge q, \neg p \wedge \neg q$.

3. Four, because for every formula there is at least one line in the truth table when it is true, and no line fits for two distinct formulae.

4. Rules 1, 2, 3 are straightforward.

   Rule 4. We have to show that $(A \Rightarrow C) \wedge (B \Rightarrow C) \wedge (A \vee B) \Rightarrow C$ is a tautology. Instead of drawing the truth table we can do it as follows.

   Assume that $A \Rightarrow C, B \Rightarrow C, A \vee B$ are true. Then A is true or B is true (or both). If A is $\top$ and $A \Rightarrow C$ is $\top$ then C is $\top$. If B is $\top$ and $B \Rightarrow C$ is $\top$ then C is $\top$. Therefore C is true under our assumption.

   Rules 5, 6 are checked easily.

   Rule 7. Assume that $B \Rightarrow C, B \Rightarrow \neg C$ are both true. If B were true then $C, \neg C$ would be both true. Thus B is false, i.e. $\neg B$ is true.

   Rule 8. Suppose $\dfrac{B_1, \ldots, B_k, A}{C}$ is valid. Then $\dfrac{B_1, \ldots, B_k}{A \Rightarrow C}$ is valid, because if $B_1, \ldots, B_k$ are true then the truth of A implies the truth of C.

5. By rule 8 we obtain $A_1, \ldots, A_n \vdash B \Rightarrow C$ and $A_1, \ldots, A_n \vdash C \Rightarrow B$. Hence $A_1, \ldots,$
   $A_n \vdash B \Leftrightarrow C$, because if $A_1, \ldots, A_n$ are true then both $B \Rightarrow C, C \Rightarrow B$ are true.

Intermediate Summary

In this chapter so far we learnt the following main ideas:

- A logical system consists of a formal language, a semantic interpretation and a set of reasoning rules.

- The language of classical propositional logic uses letters such as p, q, r, etc. to represent atomic sentences, and connectives $\wedge$, $\vee$, $\neg$ and $\Rightarrow$ to combine sentences into more complex sentences.

- Truth tables can be used to interpret the sentences of classical propositional logic.

- Sentences which are always true are called tautologies; those which are always false are contradictions. If a sentence is not a contradiction then it is said to be consistent.

- Sentences can be put in a convenient normal form.

- A valid argument is a relationship (known as the consequence) between a set of assumptions and a conclusion, and holds provided the conclusion is true whenever the assumptions are all true.

- The consequence relation for any logical system possesses three properties: reflexivity, monotonicity and transitivity. Differing additional properties distinguish differing logical systems.

- If a set of assumptions and a negated formula are not consistent, then the formula is a conclusion in a valid argument from the assumptions.

4 Model theory

We take the view that a formula A is saying something about the truth values of the atoms appearing in A. It says that the atoms can get only truth values that make A true (i.e. h such that $h(A) = \top$) are accepted. We can thus view the semantic meaning of A as the set M_A of all assignments to h which make A true, i.e.

$$M_A = \{h \mid h(A) = \top\}.$$

We call such assignments models of A.

The elementary model theory we have in this section studies such sets of models.

We need some basic concepts

DEFINITION 1.19.

1. An assignment h of $\top, \bot$ to all the atoms of the langauge is also called a *model*. See Definition 1.2.

2. Let A be a formula. Let $M_A = \{h \mid h(A) = \top\}$.

   In words: M_A is the family of all models which make A true.

   Let Θ be a set of formulas, then let $M_\Theta = \{h \mid h(A) = \top \text{ for all } A \in \Theta\}$.

3. Let M be a class of models. Then we say that M is a *EC*-class iff for some formula A we have that $M = M_A$. We say that M is an EC_Δ class iff for some Θ we have $M = M_\Theta$.

4. Clearly a theory Θ is consistent if and only if $M_\Theta \neq \varnothing$.

DEFINITION 1.20. A theory Θ is said to be *compact* iff for every finite subset $\Delta \subseteq \Theta$ we have that $M_\Delta \neq \varnothing$.

THEOREM 1.21 (Compactness theorem). *Let Θ be a set of wffs such that for any finite subset $\Delta \subseteq \Theta$, there exists a model h such that $h \in M_\Delta$. Then there exists a model g such that $g \in M_\Theta$.*

Proof. Let $A_1, A_2, A_3, \ldots$ be a complete enumeration of all wffs of the language. Define sets $\Theta_n, n = 0, 1, \ldots$, as follows:

step 0: Let $\Theta_0 = \Theta$.

step *n+1*: Assume Θ_n has been defined and that it is compact, i.e. every finite subset $\Delta \subseteq \Theta_n$ has a model $h \in M_\Delta$. We show that either $\Theta_n \cup \{A_{n+1}\}$ or $\Theta_n \cup \{\neg A_{n+1}\}$ is compact. If not, then for some finite $\Delta_1 \subseteq \Theta_n$ and $\Delta_2 \subseteq \Theta_n$, we have that $\Delta_1 \cup \{A_{n+1}\}$ and $\Delta_2 \cup \{\neg A_{n+1}\}$ have no models. Consider $\Delta_1 \cup \Delta_2$. This is a finite subset of Θ_n and hence has a model h. Therefore in this model either A_{n+1} or $\neg A_{n+1}$ holds. Thus either $\Delta_1 \cup \{A_{n+1}\}$ or $\Delta_2 \cup \{\neg A_{n+1}\}$ does have a model, contrary to what we assumed. Thus either $\Theta_n \cup \{A_{n+1}\}$ of $\Theta_n \cup \{\neg A_{n+1}\}$ is compact. We can thus let $\Theta_{n+1} = \Theta_n \cup \{A_{n+1}\}$ if it is compact or otherwise we let $\Theta_{n+1} = \Theta_n \cup \{\neg A_{n+1}\}$.

Let $\Theta_\infty = \bigcup_n \Theta_n$. We claim Θ_∞ is compact. For let $\Delta \subseteq \Theta_\infty$, Δ finite, then being finite $\Delta \subseteq \Theta_m$ for some large m and so it has a model.

We now construct a model g of Θ_∞. Let $g(q) = \top$ iff $q \in \Theta_\infty$.

We now claim that for any formula $A : g(A) = \top$ iff $A \in \Theta_\infty$.

The proof is by induction on the strucure of the formula A.

case 1: $A = q, q$ atomic. We cannot have that both q and $\neg q$ in Θ_∞ because the set $\{q, \neg q\}$ will not have a model and Θ_∞ is compact. So at most one of $q, \neg q$ is in Θ_∞. One of them must be there because for some $m, q = A_m$ in the enumeration and so one of them was put into $\Theta_m \subseteq \Theta_\infty$. We thus indeed have $g(q) = \top$ iff $q \in \Theta_\infty$.

case 2: $A = \neg B$. We have $g(A) = \top$ iff $g(B) = \bot$ iff $B \notin \Theta_\infty$ iff $\neg B \in \Theta_\infty$.

case 3: $A = A_1 \wedge A_2$.

$g(A_1 \wedge A_2) = \top$ iff $g(A_1) = g(A_2) = \top$ iff $A_1 \in \Theta_\infty$ and $A_2 \in \Theta_\infty$ iff $A_1 \wedge A_2 \in \Theta_\infty$ (otherwsie $A_1, A_2, \neg(A_1 \wedge A_2) \in \Theta_\infty$ and this is impossible as this finite subtheory of Θ_∞ has no models).

Similar considerations apply to the clases of $A_1 \vee A_2$ and $A_1 \Rightarrow A_2$.

We thus conclude that Θ_∞ has a model and hence $\Theta \subseteq \Theta_\infty$ has the same model. ∎

THEOREM 1.22. *Let M be a class of models such that both M and its complement $\bar{M}$ are EC_Δ. Then M is an EC class.*

Proof. Assume $M = M_\Theta$ for some theory (set of wffs) Θ and $\bar{M} = M_\Delta$ for some theory Δ. Consdier the theory $\Delta \cup \Theta = \Gamma$. This theory has no models.

By the compactness theorem for some finite $A_1, \ldots, A_n \in \Theta$ and $B_1, \ldots, B_m \in \Delta$ we have that $\Gamma_0 = \{A_1, \ldots, A_n, B_1, \ldots, B_m\}$ has no models. We have $n, m \geq 1$. Since both Θ and Δ have models.

The above implies that

$$(*)\qquad A_1 \wedge \ldots \wedge A_n \Rightarrow \neg B_1 \vee \ldots \vee B_m \text{ is true in every model}$$

because to be false in a model h we must have $h(A_i) = \top$ and $h(B_j) = \top$ contradicting our assumption that Γ_0 has no models.

We now show that

$$M = M_{A_1 \wedge \ldots \wedge A_n}.$$

We need to show that for any model h:

$$h \in M \text{ iff } h \in M_{A_1 \wedge \ldots \wedge A_n}.$$

First note that since $\{A_1, \ldots, A_n\} \subseteq \Theta$ we have that $h \in M$ implies $h(A_i) = \top$ for $i = 1, \ldots, n$ and hence $h \in M_{A_1 \wedge \ldots \wedge A_n}$.

Assume that $h(A_i) = \top$ for $i = 1, \ldots, n$. Then, by (*), for some $B_j, 1 \leq j \leq m$ we have $h(B_j) = \bot$. Thus h cannot be in $\bar{M}$ and so $h \in M$. ∎

THEOREM 1.23. *There are EC_Δ classes which are not EC.*

Proof. Let M be the class of all models giving all atoms value $\top$. This is an EC_Δ class. We can let Θ be the set of all atoms and $M = M_\Theta$. M cannot be *EC* class. For any wff A, M cannot be M_A. For A is built up from a finite number of atoms. If h is such that $h(A) = \top$ then h can be changed to give $\bot$ on all atoms not in A. Call the result h'. Then we still have $h'(A) = \top$ but $h' \notin M$. ∎

THEOREM 1.24. *There are classes of models which are not EC_Δ.*

Proof. Consider M and its complement as defined in the previous theorem. We cannot have that both are EC_Δ becasue M is not *EC*. ∎

We now give some applications of the compactness theorem.

DEFINITION 1.25.

1. A graph is a set G of nodes together with a set $\mathbb{C}$ of pairs of nodes $\{x, y\}$, where x, y are from G, indicating which nodes are connected (i.e. (x, y) in $\mathbb{C}$ means that x and y are connected).

2. Let $P_1, \ldots, P_m$ be m distinct colours. The graph is said to be m-colourable iff each point of the graph can be assigned a unique colour such that for any two different nodes x, y, if they are connected then their colours are different.

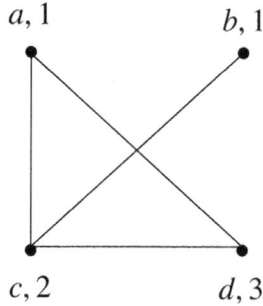

Figure 1.1.

EXAMPLE 1.26. Consider the graph with nodes $\{a, b, c, d\}$ and connections as in Figure 1.1

This graph can be coloured by 3 colours but not by two colours. The colouring is indicated in Figure 1.1 by the nubmers 1, 2, 3 next to the nodes.

DEFINITION 1.27.

1. Given a graph G, we can express its colouring and connections in propositional logic as follows:

   - Let p_x^i be an atom for each $x \in G$ and colour P_i saying that the colour of x is P_i.

   - Let $c_{\{x,y\}}$ be an atom for each $x \neq y$ in G saying that x and y are connected.

2. Consider the following theory $\Delta(G)$:

   $\Delta(G)$ contains:

   (a) $\bigvee_{i=1}^n q_x^i \wedge \bigwedge_{j \neq i} \neg q_x^j$, x in G.
       This formula says that x is coloured by exactly one colour for each $x \in G$.

   (b) $c_{\{x,y\}} \Rightarrow \bigwedge_{i=1}^n \neg(q_x^i \wedge q_y^i)$ for all x, y in G, such that $x \neq y$.
       This formula says that connected nodes have different colours.

   (c) $c_{\{x,y\}}$ for $\{x, y\}$ connected in G, $x \neq y$.
       This formula says that x, y are connected as in G.

THEOREM 1.28. *Let G be a graph. If every finite subgraph of G can be coloured with n-colours, then G itself an be coloured with n colours.*

Figure 1.2.

Proof. Consider the theory $\Delta(G)$ of the previous definition. A finite subgraph of G generates a finite subset of $\Delta(G)$. If it can be n-coloured then it means it has a model. In fact, every finite subset of $\Delta(G)$ involves only a finite number of nodes from G (as indices in atoms of the form $c_{\{x,y\}}$ or p_x^i) and hence can be extended a little further to be the theory of a finite subgraph of G based on the same atoms. We can also add for each x in the subgraph that x is coloured by exactly one colour. Since this subgraph can indeed be coloured with n colours, we get that the finite subtheory of $\Delta(G)$ has a model.

By the compactness theorem $\Delta(G)$ has a model h. h would be an n colouring of G.   ∎

EXAMPLE 1.29 (Sudoku). The Japanese game of Sudoku is a propositional logic game that has become very popular in the UK in recent months. The game involves a grid with 9×9 boxes which can contain single numbers from 1 to 9. Some of the boxes already contain numbers, as in Figure 1.2.

See www.sudoku.org, the figure is copied from this website.

The purpose of the puzzle is to fill in the remaining boxes in such a way that every row, every column and every 3×3 box (as indicated in the grid) contains the numbers 1 through 9.

Let us express this in propositional logic. Let $q_{i,j}^m$ be an atomic propositon saying that at box i, j $(1 \leq i \leq 9, 1 \leq j \leq 9)$ the number m is entered $(1 \leq m \leq 9)$.

For example, in the figure at box $(2,1)$ we have the number 4 and at box $(2,9)$ we have the number 6.

So according to the figure $q_{2,1}^4 = \top$ and $q_{2,9}^6 = \top$ but $q_{2,1}^1 = \bot, q_{2,1}^2 = \bot$, etc.

Let us now write the conditions of the game.

1. (a) $q_{i,j}^m \to \bigwedge\limits_{\substack{x \neq m \\ 1 \leq x \leq 9}} \neg q_{i,j}^x.$

   (b) $\bigvee\limits_{x=1,\ldots,9} q_{i,j}^x$

   every box has a unique number.

2. Let σ denote an arbitrary permutation of the numbers 1 to 9. So $\sigma = (\sigma(1),\ldots,\sigma(9))$. The restrictions are

   (a) $\bigwedge_i \bigvee_\sigma \bigwedge_{j=1,\ldots,9} q_{i,j}^{\sigma(j)}$. Every column has numbers 1 to 9

   (b) $\bigwedge_j \bigvee_\sigma \bigwedge_i q_{i,j}^{\sigma(i)}$. Every row has the number 1 to 9.

   (c) Let η be any one to one fucntion of the numbers $(1,1)$, $(1,2)$, $(1,3)$, $(2,1)$, $(2,2)$, $(2,3)$, $(3,1)$, $(3,2)$, $(3,3)$ onto the numbers 1 to 9.

   - $\bigwedge\limits_{\substack{i = 0,3,6 \\ j = 0,3,6}} \bigvee_\eta \bigwedge\limits_{\substack{k = 1,2,3 \\ r = 1,2,3}} q_{i+k,j+r}^{\eta(k,r)}.$

     The rule says that every 3×3 box must have all numbers 1 to 9 in it.

3. The data of any particular box is entered as is. In our diagram we take:

$$q_{1,3}^5 \wedge q_{1,4}^7 \wedge q_{1,6}^8 \wedge q_{1,7}^2$$

$$\wedge q_{2,1}^4 \wedge q_{2,9}^6$$

$$\wedge q_{)}^7 3,2 \wedge q_{3,5}^6 \wedge 1_{3,8}^8$$

$$\wedge q_{4,1}^5 \wedge q_{4,2}^2 \wedge q_{4,4}^9 \wedge q_{4,6}^4 \wedge q_{4,8}^3 \wedge q_{4,9}^1$$

$$\wedge q_{6,1}^8 \wedge q_{6,2}^6 \wedge q_{6,4}^1 \wedge q_{6,6}^7 \wedge q_{6,8}^5 \wedge q_{6,9}^4$$

$$\wedge q_{7,2}^9 \wedge q_{7,5}^3 \wedge q_{7,8}^6$$

$$\wedge q_{8,1}^7 \wedge q_{8,9}^5$$

$$\wedge q_{9,3}^2 \wedge q_{9,4}^4 \wedge q_{9,6}^6 \wedge q_{9,7}^1$$

Let Θ be the conjunction of all the above formulas. Then any assignment h making Θ true ($h \in M_\Theta$) is a solution to the Sudoku problem.

For example there will be exactly one number $1 \leq m \leq 9$ such that $h(q_{9,9}^m) = \top$. Then m is what goes at the top right and box.

Figure 1.3 gives you a solution (the figure is from the same website).

9	6	3	1	7	4	2	5	8
1	7	8	3	2	5	6	4	9
2	5	4	6	8	9	7	3	1
8	2	1	4	3	7	5	9	6
4	9	6	8	5	2	3	1	7
7	3	5	9	6	1	8	2	4
5	8	9	7	1	3	4	6	2
3	1	7	2	4	6	9	8	5
6	4	2	5	9	8	1	7	3

Figure 1.3.

EXAMPLE 1.30 (Simplified Sudoku problem). We give here a simplified version of Sudoku,which is easier to write in logic.

Consider 4×4 squares:

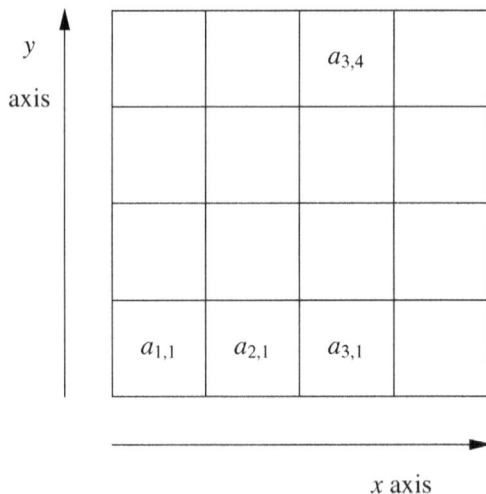

A Sudoku problem for 4×4 matrix would require that every row, every column and every 2×2 square as indicated in the grid would contain all the numbers 1

to 4. The simplified Sudoku problem wants to make life easier by replacing the requirement on the 2×2 squares by a requirement on the two major diagonals.

In the simplified case, we logically want to put the numbers $1, \ldots, 4$ in such a way that every row, every column and every major diagonal has all numbers from 1 to 4.

Note that in the simplified case, we have the condition on the diagonals instead of the condition on internal boxes that we had in the case of the real Sudoku on 9×9 square.

Let us write $q_{i,j}^x = \top$ to means that the number $a_{i,j}$ in the box (i, j) is x, with $1 \le x \le 4$.

That is $q_{i,j}^x \equiv (a_{i,j} = x)$

Here is an example

2	1	4	3
4	3	2	1
3	4	1	2
1	2	3	4

Note that this example also satisfies the condition on the four internal boxes as well.

We then say

- $\bigwedge_{i,j=1}^{4} \bigvee_{x=1}^{4} q_{i,j}^x$

- $\bigwedge_{i,j=1}^{4} \bigwedge_{\substack{x \neq y \\ 1 \le x \le 4 \\ 1 \le y \le 4}} \neg(q_{i,j}^x \wedge q_{i,j}^y)$

Let σ be any permutation of the numbers $\{1, 2, 3, 4\}$. Then

- $\bigwedge_{i=1}^{4} \bigvee_{\sigma} \bigwedge_{j=1}^{4} a_{ij} = \sigma(j)$

- $\bigwedge_{j=1}^{4} \bigvee_{\sigma} \bigwedge_{i=1}^{4} a_{ij} = \sigma(i)$

- $\bigvee_{\sigma} \bigwedge_{i} a_{ii} = \sigma(i)$

1	7	4	2	3	8	9	5	6
5	2	9	1	6	4	8	7	3
6	8	3	7	9	5	2	4	1
2	9	5	4	7	1	3	6	8
8	1	6	3	5	2	4	9	7
3	4	7	9	8	6	1	2	5
9	5	8	6	4	3	7	1	2
7	3	1	5	2	9	6	8	4
4	6	2	8	1	7	5	3	9

Figure 1.4.

- $\bigvee_{\sigma} \bigwedge_{i=1}^{4} a_{i,5-i} = \sigma(i)$.

A machine oriented way of implementing this is to take

$$
\begin{aligned}
p_1 &= 2 \quad \text{prime} \\
p_2 &= 3 \quad '' \\
p_3 &= 5 \quad '' \\
p_4 &= 7 \quad ''
\end{aligned}
$$

So $x_1, \ldots, x_4 \in \{1, 2, 3, 4\}$ are all different iff $p_{x_1} \cdot p_{x_2} \cdot p_{x_3} \cdot p_{x_4} = 210$,

So we write

$$
\begin{aligned}
\bigwedge_{i=1}^{4} \Pi_j p_{a_{i,j}} &= 210 \\
\bigwedge_{j=1}^{4} \Pi_i p_{a_{i,j}} &= 210 \\
\bigwedge_{i=1}^{4} \Pi_i p_{a_{i,j}} &= 210 \\
\bigwedge_{i=1}^{4} \Pi_i p_{i,5-i} &= 210
\end{aligned}
$$

The above is more efficient but is machine oriented.

The real Sudoku game is a 9×9 square. We can use the same idea. We may be able to optimise the calculations using good prime numbers and running up and down the matrix in a certain way. At the end we may get a program that is really machine oriented and only the end result (of whether the conditions hold) is logically huamn oriented and meaningful.

It is possible to add the condition requiring that the major diagonals also have no repetition of any number from 1 to 9. Figure 1.4 is a sample solution.

5 Semantic Tableaux

Given a wff A, we want to know whether there exists an assignment h to its atoms such that $h(A) = \bot$. There is an algorithm for answering this question. We compute the full truth table for A, as suggested in Section 1.1, and if one of the rows gives value $\bot$, then the answer is yes.

This procedure is of exponential complexity in the number n of atoms appearing in A. We need a truth table with 2^n rows.

The question to ask now is whether there are some quicker methods which might give an answer, in many particular cases, in a polynomial number of steps? It is not known whether there exists a polynomial algorithm which can check in *all* cases in polynomial time for any wff of the classical propositional logic whehter it is a tautology or not.

To motivate some possibly quicker methods which work on many examples, let us check some examples. We aim to present the tableaux method through these examples. So we first go through the examples with some explanation and then we present the tableaux rules in detail.

EXAMPLE 1.31.

1. Let us check whether $((a \Rightarrow b) \Rightarrow a) \Rightarrow a$ is a tautology. To check this let us see if we can give it the value $\bot$.

   To get $\bot$, we must give $(a \Rightarrow b) \Rightarrow a$ the value $\top$ and give a the value $\bot$. (Let us write $A = \top$ or $A = \bot$ to indicate we want to give A the value indicated.) Let us create a box, a tableau, and in the left-hand side of the box, let us write what we want to get $\top$ and in the right-hand side let us write what we want to get $\bot$. We use the notation

   $$(A_1, \ldots, A_n) \| (B_1, \ldots, B_n)$$

   or when it is clear we omit the parenthesis and write $A_1, \ldots, A_n \| B_1, \ldots, B_m$, where $(A_1, \ldots, A_n)$ are the formulas we want to be $\top$, written as a sequence and $(B_1, \ldots, B_m)$ are the formula we want to get $\bot$, also written as a sequence. The vertical double line is the dividing line.

   Note that $A_1, \ldots, A_n$ and $B_1, \ldots, B_m$ are sequences, and so order does matter (especially when we insert and/or delete formulas into or from the seqeunce).

   So in our example we have

   $$(a \Rightarrow b) \Rightarrow a \| a$$

   Since we already want $(a \Rightarrow b) \Rightarrow a$ to be $\top$, we have two options. Either a is $\top$ or $a \Rightarrow b$ is $\bot$.

Since we want a to be $\perp$, the only option remaining to us is $a \Rightarrow b = \perp$. So we need to put $a \Rightarrow b$ on the right.

Let us append it to the right-hand side. We get

$$(a \Rightarrow b) \Rightarrow a \| (a, a \Rightarrow b).$$

Note that if we were a computer program executing this algorithm, it would be simpler for the program to execute both options. In this case the option which does not work will have the atom a present both on the right and on the left of the tableau. A clear contradiction.

In other words, we get that

$$(a \Rightarrow b) \Rightarrow a \| a$$

splits into two tableaux

$$(a \Rightarrow b) \Rightarrow a, a \| a \quad \text{and} \quad (a \Rightarrow b) \Rightarrow a \| a, a \Rightarrow b$$

Clearly the first one is not possible because it has the same atom in both sides.

Note that in fact, it is sufficient to write

$$\varnothing \| (a, a \Rightarrow b)$$

since $a \Rightarrow b = \perp$ or $a = \top$ will automatically make $(a \Rightarrow b) \Rightarrow a$ to be $\top$ so we can throw $(a \Rightarrow b) \Rightarrow a$ out.

This policy of replacing formulas will make the process more efficient.

Now to make $a \Rightarrow b$ to be $\perp$, we need to make $a = \top$ and $b = \perp$ and so we append them from the right-hand side of each sequence. We get

$$((a \Rightarrow b) \Rightarrow a, a) \| (a, a \Rightarrow b, b).$$

Again, we do not need to record $a \Rightarrow b$ on the right any more. So really the end tableau is:

$$a \| (a, b).$$

So it is clear that it is not possible to make the formula $((a \Rightarrow b) \Rightarrow a) \Rightarrow a$ false.

Figure 1.5 records the computation steps.

Obviously we cannot satisfy the requirement of the bottom tableau because we cannot make a both $\top$ and $\perp$. The technical term used is that the tableau is *close*. Otherwise it is *open*.

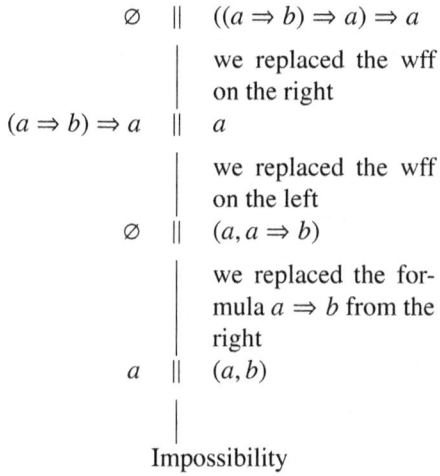

$$\varnothing \quad \| \quad ((a \Rightarrow b) \Rightarrow a) \Rightarrow a$$

we replaced the wff
on the right

$$(a \Rightarrow b) \Rightarrow a \quad \| \quad a$$

we replaced the wff
on the left

$$\varnothing \quad \| \quad (a, a \Rightarrow b)$$

we replaced the for-
mula $a \Rightarrow b$ from the
right

$$a \quad \| \quad (a, b)$$

Impossibility

Figure 1.5.

2. Let us do another example.

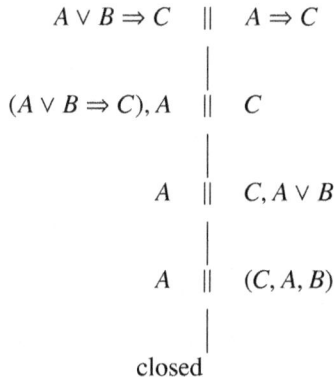

$$A \vee B \Rightarrow C \quad \| \quad A \Rightarrow C$$

$$(A \vee B \Rightarrow C), A \quad \| \quad C$$

$$A \quad \| \quad C, A \vee B$$

$$A \quad \| \quad (C, A, B)$$

closed

3. Another example

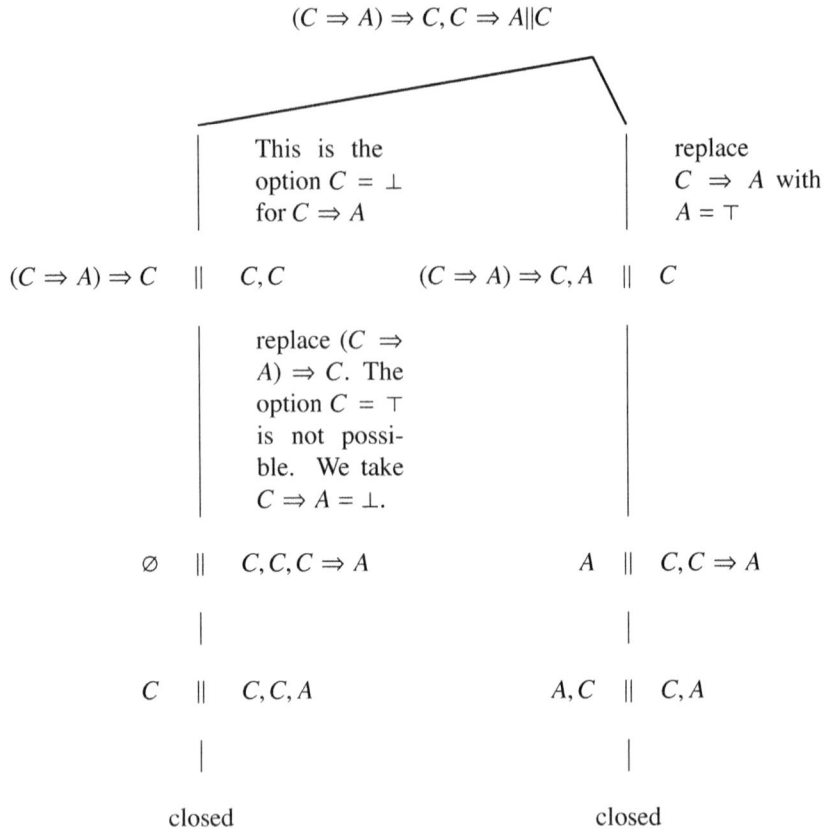

$$(C \Rightarrow A) \Rightarrow C, C \Rightarrow A \| C$$

	This is the option $C = \bot$ for $C \Rightarrow A$		replace $C \Rightarrow A$ with $A = \top$

$(C \Rightarrow A) \Rightarrow C \quad \| \quad C, C$ $(C \Rightarrow A) \Rightarrow C, A \quad \| \quad C$

	replace $(C \Rightarrow A) \Rightarrow C$. The option $C = \top$ is not possible. We take $C \Rightarrow A = \bot$.		

$\varnothing \quad \| \quad C, C, C \Rightarrow A$ $A \quad \| \quad C, C \Rightarrow A$

$C \quad \| \quad C, C, A$ $A, C \quad \| \quad C, A$

closed   closed

4. and another example

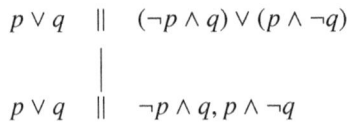

$$p \vee q \quad \| \quad (\neg p \wedge q) \vee (p \wedge \neg q)$$

$$p \vee q \quad \| \quad \neg p \wedge q, p \wedge \neg q$$

Now we use the wff $p \vee q$ on the left. We have two options for $p \vee q = \top$. These are $p = \top$ or $q = \top$. So we split:

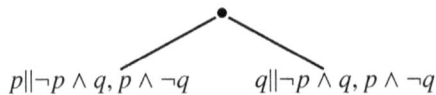

$$p \| \neg p \wedge q, p \wedge \neg q \qquad q \| \neg p \wedge q, p \wedge \neg q$$

Let us continue with the left one and work on $p \wedge \neg q$. For $p \wedge \neg q = \bot$ we have either $p = \bot$ or $\neg q = \bot$. So we split

$$p\|\neg p \wedge q, p \wedge \neg q$$

$$p\|\neg p \wedge q, p \qquad\qquad p\|\neg p \wedge q, \neg q$$

closed

Since $\neg q = \bot$ iff $q = \top$

$$p, q\|\neg p \wedge q$$

$$p, q\|\neg p \qquad\qquad p, q\|q$$

$$p, q, p\|\varnothing \qquad\qquad \text{closed}$$

open

Let us now work on the right. This would be the same development as the left except that we have q on the left hand side of the tableaux. Thus we get:

$$q\|\neg p \wedge q, p \wedge \neg q$$

$$q\|\neg p \wedge q, p \qquad\qquad q\|\neg p \wedge q, \neg q$$

$$q\|\neg p, p \qquad\qquad q\|q, p \qquad\qquad q, q\|\neg p \wedge q$$

$$q, p\|p \qquad\qquad \text{closed} \qquad q, q\|\neg p \qquad\qquad q, q\|q$$

closed

$$q, q, p\|\varnothing \qquad\qquad \text{closed}$$

open

We thus conclude from the two open tableaux that the assignment h such that $h(p) = h(q) = \top$ will accomplish the task of making the left hand sequence of the original tableau all $\top$ and the right-hand sequence all $\bot$.

We use the terminology that h *satisfies* the tableau.

REMARK 1.32 (Discussion of tableaux structures). We now discuss the main points involved in the tableaux algorithm. This is prior to giving a formal definition.

Point 1: **Structure**. We have to decide what structures to use in the tableaux. In classical logic, the basic intuition is to want some formulas to be $\top$ and some formulas to be $\perp$. So we can take as tableau structure two sets

$$\Delta\|\Gamma$$

Δ is the set of wffs to be true and Γ the set of wffs to be false.

This intuition can be generalised in two ways, in anticipation of the next chapter, where other non-classical logics are introduced. One directionis to let Δ and Γ have a more complex structure, like sequences, or trees or sequences of sequences, etc. Another direction is to anticipate many truth values, say $\top, \perp$ and $\frac{1}{2}$, and thus have for example tableaux of the form $\Delta\|\Theta\|\Gamma$ where Δ is the set of formulas we want to have value $\top$ each Θ is the set we want to have value $\frac{1}{2}$ each and Γ is the set we want to ahve value $\perp$ each.

It is best in this chapter not to complicate matters too much; we can always return to tableaux in the next chapter, so we choose Δ, Γ to be sequences of formulas of the form:

$$A_1, \ldots, A_n \| B_1, \ldots, B_m$$

Point 2: **Insertion and Deletion**. Once we decided we are dealing with sequences, we have to specify how to insert or delete from them.

Consider the sequence

$$(A_1, \ldots, A_i, X, A_{i+1}, \ldots, A_n)$$

1. If we want to replace X by $(Y_1, \ldots, Y_k)$ do we insert the replacement in the same position (of X) or do we put the insertion somewhere else?

   We choose for this chapter to replace X in the same position, to get:

   $$(A_1, \ldots, A_i, Y_1, \ldots, Y_k, A_{i+1}, \ldots, A_n)$$

2. If we want to insert B, do we put it at the beginning or the end of the sequence? We choose to insert at the end to get

   $$(A_1, \ldots, A_n, B)$$

   Similarly for the right hand side we get $(B_1, \ldots, B_m, B)$. Note that we could, in principle, have different insertions for the left and the right sides of the tableaux

Point 3: **Closure**. We saw that a tableau is considered closed if the same atomic wff appears in the sequences both on the left and on the right. For example

$$A_1, \ldots, A_i, q \ldots \| B_1, \ldots, B_j, q, \ldots$$

The idea is that the left side wants $q = \top$, while the right side wants $q = \bot$ and it is impossible to get both.

In classical logic, where really all we need is sets on the right and left sides, we can declare the tableau closed if the same q appears anywhere in each sequence.

In other logics, where the fact that we have sequences and structure does make a difference, we may declare a tableau closed only if q appears both on the right and left in certain positions but not in other postions. For example, we may declare a tableau closed only if for some q we have

$$A_1, \ldots, q, , \ldots, A_n \| B_1, \ldots, B_m, q$$

(i.e. q must appear on the left but must be the last one on the right hand side). These detailed variations and their logical meanings will be discussed in the next chapter.

Point 4: **Repetition**. We also encounter repetition, say

$$p, q, p \| r, r, r$$

What do we make of this?

For classical logic, we treat the sequence as a set and so repetition is ignored.

For other logics, we may decide that adjacent repetition can be collapsed e.g. $(\ldots r, r \ldots)$ can be collapsed to $(\ldots, r, \ldots)$, but non adjacent repetitions remain. We shall leave the details to the next chapter in the appropriate context. For this chatper, all repetitions are ignored.

Point 5: **Size**. We can also decide on the length of the sequence on the right-hand side. Do we allow for only one formula at most on the right-hand side or do we allow for more? There does not seem to be any meaningful restrictions for the length of the left-hand sequence. For the right-hand side the meaningful option sito allow for at most one element.

For this chapter we allow the right-hand sequence to be of any length.

REMARK 1.33 (Discussion of tableaux rules). We now discuss the option for tableaux rules for the various connectives, given that we have already chosen the structure of a single taleau to be a pair of sequences of formulas:

$$t : A_1, \ldots, A_n \| B_1, \ldots, B_m$$

where t is the name of the tableau.

The idea is to assume that one of the formulas on the right or on the left is non atomic: say the formula is one of the following

$$E = \neg D_1$$

or

$$E = D_1 \Rightarrow D_2$$

or

$$E = D_1 \vee D_2$$

or

$$E = D_1 \wedge D_2$$

E may appear either on the right or the left. We would like to simplify the tableau by replacing E either by D_1 or D_2 in the right or left, and reduce the question posed by the original tabeau (of finding an assignment which satisfies the tableaux) to the two questions posed by the new tableaux. We call the new tableaux say s_0 and s_1 and say that s_0 and s_1 are *obtained from t* by replacing the key formula E. E is the formula 'used' or 'replaced' in the transaction. The rules, which we will discuss below, will be the rules 'applied' (to E in t) in the transaction and replace t by s_0 and s_1. We examine for each connective the problem of reduction for each case; when E is on the right and when E is on the left. We use the following notation to refer to the cases **left** $\neg$, **right** $\neg$, **left** $\Rightarrow$, **right** $\Rightarrow$, **left** $\wedge$, **right** $\wedge$, **left** $\vee$, **right** $\vee$.

To discuss the fine points of our options we look at several cases:

1. **case of negation** $\neg$: Consder the case of **left** $\neg$

$$t_1 : A_1, \ldots, \neg D_1, \ldots, A_n \| B_1, \ldots, B_m$$

and similarly the case of **right** $\neg$:

$$t_1 : A_1, \ldots, A_n \| B_1, \ldots, \neg D_2, \ldots, B_m.$$

First of all in classical logic we have $X = \top$ iff $\neg X = \bot$ and $X = \bot$ iff $\neg X = \top$. So obviously, we need to move D_1 or D_2 to the other side. The question is where do we insert the formula? At the beginning of the seqeunce? Or at the end? Or maybe at the mirror place of where the original negation was on the other side? For classical logic it does not matter. We shift it to the right-hand side of the sequence and insert from the right end of the sequence as already agreed for insertion.

2. **Case of $E = D_1 \Rightarrow D_2$**: Consider the case of **left** $\Rightarrow$:

$$t : A_1, \ldots, A_n \| B_1, \ldots, B_i, D_1 \Rightarrow D_2, \ldots, B_m$$

$D_1 \Rightarrow D_2$ is supposed to be false. There is only one way to do that in classical logic. Make $D_1 = \top$ and $D_2 = \bot$. So clearly we append (insert) D_1 at the end of the sequence on the left, i.e. the new left becomes $A_1, \ldots, A_n, D_1$. How about the insertion of D_2 into the right-ahnd side of the tableau? We have three options:

(a) Form

$$B_1, \ldots, B_i, \ldots, B_m, D_2$$

(with $D_1 \Rightarrow D_2$ deleted from its position)

(b) Form

$$B_1, \ldots, B_i, D_2, \ldots, B_m$$

(with D_2 replacing $D_1 \Rightarrow D_2$)

(c) Form

$$B_1, \ldots, B_i, D_2$$

i.e. we replace $D_1 \Rightarrow D_2$ by D_2 and abandon the rest of the sequence.

In classical logic we choose option (a). The other options are meaningful in other logics.

Thus the tableau t is replaced by the tableau

$$s : A_1, \ldots, A_n, D_1 \| B_1, \ldots, B_m, D_2$$

we now check $D_1 \Rightarrow D_2$ on the left, i.e. the case of **left** $\Rightarrow$.

We have

$$A_1, \ldots, A_i, D_1 \Rightarrow D_2, \ldots, A_n$$

Obviously either $D_1 = \bot$ or $D_2 = \top$.

For the option $D_1 = \bot$ we just append it to the right-hand side. We delete $D_1 \Rightarrow D_2$ from the left.

For $D_2 = \top$ we delete $D_1 \Rightarrow D_2$ from the left and add D_2 to the left. We have similar options here, analogous to (a), (b), (c) of the **right** $\Rightarrow$ case. Again for classical logic we choose (a), i.e. append at the end.

Thus the tableau t is replaced by the two tableaux s_1 and s_2.

$$s_1 : A_1, \ldots, A_n, D_2 \| B_1, \ldots, B_m$$
and
$$s_2 : A_1, \ldots, A_n \| B_1, \ldots, B_m, D_1$$

3. **Case of** $E = D_1 \vee D_2$. If E is on the right-hand side of the tableaux, then we have

$$t : A_1, \ldots, A_n \| B_1, \ldots, D_1 \vee D_2, \ldots, B_m$$

We simply replace $D_1 \vee D_2$ by D_1, D_2 in the same position, to obtain

$$s : A_1, \ldots, A_n \| B_1, \ldots, D_1, D_2, \ldots, B_m.$$

The reader may ask why not append D_1, D_2 to the right-hand side of B_m to obtain

$$A_1, \ldots, A_n \| B_1, \ldots, B_m, D_1, D_2$$

The answer is that in the majority of logics $\wedge$ and $\vee$ are 'local' connectives, while $\Rightarrow$ and $\neg$ have a variety of meanings. So we retain the positon for the cases of $\wedge$ and $\vee$.

When E is on the left we have

$$t : A_1, \ldots, D_1 \vee D_2, \ldots, A_n \| B_1, \ldots, B_m$$

we split t an replace it by the two tableaux

$$s_1 : A_1, \ldots, D_1, \ldots, A_n \| B_1, \ldots, B_m$$

and

$$s_2 : A_1, \ldots, D_2, \ldots, A_n \| B_1, \ldots, B_m$$

and expect at least one of them to be closed.

4. **Case of** $E = D_1 \wedge D_2$. This is very similar to the $\vee$ case when $D_1 \wedge D_2$ is on the left. We replace it by D_1, D_2 namely

$$t : A_1, \ldots, D_1 \wedge D_2, \ldots, A_n \| B_1, \ldots, B_m$$

becomes

$$s : A_1, \ldots, D_1, D_2, \ldots, A_n \| B_1, \ldots, B_m.$$

When $D_1 \wedge D_2$ is on the right, we split into two tableaux, namely:

$$t : A_1, \ldots, A_n \| B_1, \ldots, D_1 \wedge D_2, \ldots, B_m$$

splits into two options

$$s_1 : A_1, \ldots, A_n \| B_1, \ldots, D_1, \ldots, B_m$$

and

$$s_2 : A_1, \ldots, A_n \| B_1, \ldots, D_2, \ldots, B_m$$

We retain the position of E.

5. **Case of closure**. Note that the replacements involved in the cases (1)–(4) above always reduces the number of more complex formulas in the tableaux. Evenutally we may be dealing with a tableaux with atomic formulas onlu. Assume the form is

$$p_1, \ldots, p_n \| q_1, \ldots, q_m$$

The idea is that all atoms on the left must get true and all atoms on the right must get false.

Certainly if $p_1 = q_1$, then this is not possible to do and so we declare the tableau as *closed*. Certainly if $p_i \neq q_j$ for all i, j then this is possible to do and so we declare the tableau as *open*.

What do we do when say $p_1 = q_2$? Is the tableaux open or closed? This depends on the logic. For classical logic the tableau is closed whenever for some $i, j, p_i = q_j$. For other logics it may be different. If the meaning of the sequence is temporal, then p_1 and $q_2 = p_1$ may refer to different times and so it may be possible to make p_1 true at time 1 and false at time 2.

So to summarise, the notion of closure has to be defined separtely for each lgoic. So we refer to the notion as Closure Rule whcih can decide when a tableau t is 'closed'.

6. **Summary and notation**. We would like to introduce a convenient notation and use of words for the rules introduced in (1)–(5) above. We started witha tableau

$$t_1 : A_1, \ldots, E, \ldots, A_n \| B_1, \ldots, B_m$$

with E on the left or

$$t_2 : A_1, \ldots, A_n \| B_1, \ldots, E, \ldots, B_m$$

with E on the right.

We considered E as the key formula to be dealt with and depending on the form of E ($E = D_1 \wedge D_2$ or $E = D_1 \vee D_2$ or $E = \neg D_1$ or $E = D_1 \Rightarrow D_2$) and whether it is on the right or the left we split (or replaced) the original tableau into one or two tableaux s_1 and s_2 using one of the rules for $\Rightarrow, \vee, \wedge$ or $\neg$.

We present this situation as

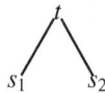

and say that t was replaced by reducing formula E using rule so and so.

Let $t : A_1, \ldots, A_n \| B_1, \ldots, B_m$ be a tableau and let h be an assignment to the atoms appearing in the tableau. We say that h *satisfies* t iff h makes all of a_i true and all of B_j false.

LEMMA 1.34. *Let t be a tableau and assume that s_1, s_2 (or just s_1) are tableaux obtained from t by applying a rule to a key formula E. Let h be an assignment to the atoms. Then (1) is equivlent to (2).*

1. *In either s_1 or s_2 we have that all formulas on the left get balue $\top$ under h and all formulas on the right get value $\perp$ under h.*

2. *In the tableau t, all formulas on the left get value $\top$ and all falulas on the right get value $\perp$*

Proof. We examine each case (1)–(4) in Remark 1.33 and verify case by case that the lemma holds. we leave the details as an exercise for the reader. ∎

DEFINITION 1.35 (Tableaux algorithm).

1. Consider the propositional language with connectives $\wedge, \vee, \Rightarrow$ and $\neg$. By a tableau t in this language we mean two sequences of formulas written in the form

$$t : A_1, \ldots, A_n \| B_1, \ldots, B_m.$$

   t is the name of the tableaux, $A_1, \ldots, A_n$ is the left side and $B_1, \ldots, B_m$ is the right side of the tableau.

2. Let $V = \{v_1, \ldots, v_k\}$ be a set of distinct elements.

   We denote by $t, s, \ldots$ sequences of elements from V, including the empty sequence $\varnothing$. Let $*$ denote concatenation of sequences. So if $\mathbf{t} = (x_1, \ldots, x_n)$ and $\mathbf{s} = (y_1, \ldots, y_m)$ are two sequences of any kind, we let $\mathbf{t} * \mathbf{s}$ be $(x_1, \ldots, x_n, y_1, \ldots, y_m)$.

   We define the relation $t R_i s, i = 1, \ldots, k$ between sequences as follows:

   $t R_i s$ iff $s = t * (v_i)$. We define $t R s$ to mean that for some sequence t' we have $s = t * t'$, (i.e. t is an initial segment of s).

3. By a finite V-tree, we mean a finite set T of sequences of elements from V satisfying the following conditions

   (a) $\varnothing \in T$

   (b) If $s \in T$ and $t R s$ then $t \in T$.

4. Let $(T, R, \varnothing)$ be a finite tree. An endpoint $t \in T$ is a point such that for any point $s \in T$ if tRs then $t = s$. A path π in T is a maximal sequence of points of the form $(\varnothing, t_1, \ldots, t_k)$ such that t_k is an endpoint and ofr every $1 \leq j \leq k$ $t_j R_i t_{j+1}$ for some $1 \leq i \leq k$.

A path can also be defined as a maximal linearly ordered (by R) subset of T containing $\varnothing$.

5. A tableax tree has the form $(T, R_0, R_1, R, \varnothing, \tau)$ satisfying the following conditions.

   (a) $(T, R_i, R, \varnothing)$ is a binary tree based on $V = \{0, 1\}$

   (b) τ is a function giving for each $t \in T$ a tableau $\tau(t)$.

   (c) Whenever $\tau(t)$ is $A_1, \ldots, A_n \| B_1, \ldots, B_m$ and $tR_0 s$ and $tR_1 s_1$ then for some formula $E = D_1 \vee D_2$ on the left of $\tau(t)$ or $E = D_1 \wedge D_2$ on the right of $\tau(t)$ or $E = D_1 \rightarrow D_2$ on the left of $\tau(t)$, we have that $\tau(s_0)$ and $\tau(s_1)$ are the two replacement tableaux introduced in Remark 1.33

   (d) Whenever $\tau(t)$ is as before and $tR_0 s$ holds and t has s as the only successor, then for some formula $E = \neg D_1$ on either the righ tor the eft or $E = D_1 \wedge D_2$ on the left or $E = D_1 \vee D_2$ on the right or $E = D_1 \Rightarrow D_2$ on the right the tableau $\tau(s)$ is the result of replacing E according to the rules of Remark 1.33.

   (e) All tableaux $\tau(t)$ for endpoints t contain atomic formulas only.

THEOREM 1.36 (Completeness for classical logic). *Consider the closure rule for tableaux of classical logic stating that a tableau is closed whenever the same atom appears both on the right-hand side and on the left-hand side. Let $\varnothing$: $A_1, \ldots, A_n \| B_1, \ldots, B_m$ be a tableau. Then the following are equivalent.*

1. *There exists an assignment h to the atomic propositions in the tableau such that*

$$h(A_i) = \top, i = 1, \ldots, n$$

and

$$h(B_i) = \bot, i = 1, \ldots, m.$$

2. *There exists a tableaux tree in the sense of Definition 1.35 with $\tau(\varnothing) = A_1, \ldots, A_n \| B_1, \ldots, B_m$ such that at least one endpoint at the tree is not closed.*

Proof.

1. Assume first that we have a tree with an endpoint s with a tableau which is not closed. Let π be the direct path in the tree starting with $\varnothing$ and ending with s.

   Let h be the assignment with $h(q) = \top$ if q is in the left-hand side of the tableau of s and $h(q) = \bot$ if q is in the right-hand side.

   h can be defined properly because the atoms on the left an on the right are different sets. By Lemma 1.34 applied repeated through the path π h should also make all formulas of the left of the tableau at $\varnothing$ true and all formulas on the right false.

2. Assume we have a tableau

$$\varnothing : A_1, \ldots, A_n \| B_1, \ldots, B_m.$$

   We can construct a tree tableau $(\top, \varnothing, \tau)$ for it as follows:

   Step 0. Put $\varnothing$ in the tree with the above tableaux. Thus $T_0 = \{\varnothing\}$, $\tau_0(\varnothing) = A_1, \ldots, A_n \| B_1, \ldots, B_m$.

   Step $n + 1$. Assume we already constructed a tree in step n with endpoints $t_1, \ldots, t_k$ Call this tree $(T_n, \varnothing, \tau_n)$. If all tableaux at $t_1, \ldots, t_k$ have only atoms in them we stop. Otherwise there is a t and a complex formula E either in the right or in the left-hand side which is not atomic. Apply the appropriate rule to E from the rules in (1)–(4) of Remark 1.33 to obtain one or two tableaux to replace it. Say these tableaux are s_0 and s_1. Add two (or one) new points to the existing tree T_n, namely $t * (0)$ and $t * (1)$ and extend τ_n and let $\tau(t * (0)) = s_0$ and $\tau(t * (1)) = s_1$. Let the new tree be named $(T_{n+1}, \varnothing, \tau_{n+1})$, where τ_{n+1} is the extended τ_n to the new nodes. Note that the endpoints of T_{n+1} have now a less complex formula in its endpoints. Overall because we replaced E by simpler formulas.

   After a while all the endpoints constructed will have atomic formulas only in their tableaux. r Now assume that there exists an assignment h whcih makes all formulas on the left-hand side of $\varnothing : A_1, \ldots, A_n \| B_1, \ldots, B_n$ true and all formulas on the right hand side false. We now find an endpoint in the tree whcih is not closed. We construct the path in steps

   Step 0 Take $\varnothing$ as the first element in the path.

   Step $n + 1$ Assume we construct a path $\varnothing, t_1, \ldots, t_n$. Also assume that h makes all formulas in the left hand side of the tableau at t_n true and all formulas at the right-hand side false. If t_n is an endpoint we stop. The tableau of t_n is not closed.

Otherwise t_n splits into $t_n * (0)$ and $t_n * (1)$. By Lemma 1.34 at least on of the tableau at $t * (0)$ and $t * (1)$ is such that h makes the left all true and the right all false. Let t_{n+1} be $t * (0)$ if this is the one and $t * (1)$ otherwise

Eventaully we shall reach an endpoint ∎

6 Non-deterministc truth tables

In section 1.1, page 5, we discussed the following table:

	Pay Cash	Get 25%	Advert
1	True	True	True
2	True	False	False
3	False	True	True
4	False	False	???

We dedided in classical logic that the truth value in case 4 be true. This is a conservative appraoch. A more realistic approach would be to say that it can be either True or False depending on the situation at hand. If we adopt this point of view we get a new type of implication, whcih we can denote by $\Rightarrow$ with the following non-deterministic truth table

A	B	$A \Rightarrow B$
$\top$	$\top$	$\top$
$\top$	$\bot$	$\bot$
$\bot$	$\top$	$\top$
$\bot$	$\bot$	$\top$ or $\bot$

The question is how do we compute the truth tablke of a more complex formula? Let us try a few examples so that you can see how it is done.

EXAMPLE 1.37. Consider items 2 and 3 of Exercise 1.26

p	$\neg p$	$p \Rightarrow p$	$p \Rightarrow \neg p$	$(p \Rightarrow p) \Rightarrow p$	$\neg(p \Rightarrow p)$
$\top$	$\bot$	$\top$	$\bot$	$\top$	$\bot$
$\bot$	$\top$	Two possibilities 1.$\top$ 2.$\bot$	$\top$	For possibility 1 we get $\bot$ For possibility 2 we get 2 further possibilities 2.1.$\top$ 2.2.$\bot$	For possibility 1 we get $\bot$ For possibility 2 we get $\top$

EXAMPLE 1.38. As a further example let us redo the table on page 8 for the formula $(\neg p \Rightarrow q) \vee r$. This time we do it for $(\neg p \Rrightarrow q) \vee r$.

Here it is.

	p	q	r	$\neg p$	$(\neg p \Rrightarrow q)$	$(\neg p \Rrightarrow q) \vee r$
1	$\top$	$\top$	$\top$	$\bot$	$\top$	$\top$
2	$\top$	$\top$	$\bot$	$\bot$	$\top$	$\top$
3	$\top$	$\bot$	$\top$	$\bot$	$\top$ or $\bot$	$\top$
4	$\top$	$\bot$	$\bot$	$\bot$	$\top$ or $\bot$	$\top$ or $\bot$
5	$\bot$	$\top$	$\top$	$\top$	$\top$	$\top$
6	$\bot$	$\top$	$\bot$	$\top$	$\top$	$\top$
7	$\bot$	$\bot$	$\top$	$\top$	$\bot$	$\top$
8	$\bot$	$\bot$	$\bot$	$\top$	$\bot$	$\bot$

REMARK 1.39 (Beziau negation). Example 1.38 shows that we can define a new connective:

$$\sim A = \text{ definition } \neg(A \Rrightarrow A)$$

whose table is
Table for $\sim$:

A	$\sim A$
$\top$	$\bot$
$\bot$	$\top$ or $\bot$

The connective $\sim$ is known as the Beziau connective. Note that using the connectives and $\Rrightarrow$ we can get $\neg$ back as

$$\neg A = \text{ definition } A \Rrightarrow \sim A$$

We can also define $A \Rrightarrow B$ using $\sim$ and $\Rrightarrow$ by writing:
$A \Rrightarrow B = \text{ definition } B \vee (\neg A \wedge \neg B \wedge \sim (A \vee B))$ or by
$(A \Rrightarrow B) \wedge (\neg B \Rrightarrow \sim (A \vee B))$.

Here is the table for $(A \Rrightarrow B) \wedge (B \Rrightarrow \sim (A \vee B))$. Obviously it is the same as the table for $A \Rrightarrow B$.

A	B	$\neg B$	$A \Rrightarrow B$	$A \vee B$	$\sim (A \vee B)$	$\neg B \Rrightarrow \sim (A \vee B)$	$(A \Rrightarrow B) \wedge$ $(\neg B \Rrightarrow \sim (A \vee B))$
$\top$	$\top$	$\bot$	$\top$	$\top$	$\bot$	$\top$	$\top$
$\top$	$\bot$	$\top$	$\bot$	$\top$	$\bot$	$\bot$	$\bot$
$\bot$	$\bot$	$\bot$	$\top$	$\top$	$\bot$	$\top$	$\top$
$\bot$	$\bot$	$\top$	$\top$	$\bot$	$\top$ or $\bot$	$\top$ or $\bot$	$\top$ or $\bot$

DEFINITION 1.40. Let h be an assignment and let A be a formula built up from the atoms $q_1, \ldots, q_n$ and the connectives $\wedge, \vee, \neg \Rrightarrow$ and $\sim$. We define the set of

values $h[A]$, which A can get under the assignment h. Since the table of $\sim$ is non-deterministic, $h[A]$ is a set of values, rather than a single value. The definition is by induction on the structure of A.

1. For $A = q, q$ atomic, $h[q] = \{h(q)\}$.

2. If A is $B \wedge C$ and $h[B] = \{x_1, x_2\}$ and $h[C] = \{y_1, y_2\}$, where we allow $x_1 = x_2$ and we allow $y_1 = y_2$ and x_i, y_j are either $\top$ or $\bot$, then

$$h[A] = \{x \wedge y \mid x \in h[B], y \in h[C]\}$$

   where $\wedge$ is considered as a function on the truth values operating like its truth table.

3. Similarly, for the cases of $A = B \vee C, A = B \Rightarrow C$ and $A = \neg B$.

4. For $A = \sim B$ we let $h[A] = \{\sim x \mid x \in h[B]\}$, namely if $\top \in h[B]$ then $\bot \in h[A]$ and if $\bot \in h[B]$ then both $\bot$ and $\top$ are in $h[A]$.

Note that if A does not contain the connective $\sim$ then $h[A] = \{h(A)\}$.

DEFINITION 1.41. Let A be a formula built up from the atoms $q_1, \ldots, q_n$ and the connectives $\wedge, \vee, \Rightarrow, \neg$ and $\sim$. Then the non-deterministic truth table for A is the table associating with each different assignment h of truth values to $q_1, \ldots, q_n$ the set $h[A]$. The table can be displayed as done in Section 1.1, except that under the column for A we put sets of values obtained and not single values (obtained in the deterministic case).

The table will look as follows:

	q_1	$, \ldots,$	q_n	A
h_1	$\top$	$\top \ldots \top$	$\top$	$h_1[A]$
h_2				
$\vdots$	$\vdots$	$\vdots$	$\vdots$	$\vdots$
h_{2^n}	$\bot$	$\bot \ldots \bot$	$\bot$	$h_{2^n}[A]$

THEOREM 1.42. *Let* $\mathbf{h}$ *be a function, giving for each sequence* $\mathbf{s} = (x_1, \ldots, x_n)$ *of values from* $\{\top, \bot\}$ *a non-empty set of values* $\mathbf{h}(\mathbf{s}) \subseteq \{\top, \bot\}$. *Then there exists a formula A built up from* $q_1, \ldots, q_n$ *and the connectives* $\wedge, \vee, \Rightarrow, \neg$ *and* $\sim$ *such that for every assignment h such that* $h(q_i) = x_i$, *we have that* $h[A] = \mathbf{h}(\mathbf{s})$.

Proof. If all the values $\mathbf{h}(\mathbf{s}) = \{\top\}$ or if all the values $\mathbf{h}(\mathbf{s}) = \{\bot\}$, then we can take A to be either a tautology or a contradiction.

Assume now that for some sequences $\mathbf{s}^1, \ldots, \mathbf{s}^m \in \mathbf{H}_\top$ the value is $\{\top\}$, for some $\mathbf{y}^1, \ldots, \mathbf{y}^k \in \mathbf{H}_\bot$ the value is $\{\bot\}$ and for the remaining sequences $\mathbf{z}^1, \ldots, \mathbf{z}^r \in \mathbf{H}_{\bot,\top}$ the value is $\{\bot, \top\}$.

We have $2^n = m + k + r$. Let $\mathbf{H} = \mathbf{H_\top} \cup H_\perp \cup H_{\perp,\top}$.

For each sequence of values $\mathbf{u} = (u_1, \ldots, u_n) \in \mathbf{H}$, we construct the fomula

$$E_\mathbf{u} = q_1^{u_1} \wedge \ldots \wedge q_n^{u_n}$$

where $q^\top = q$ and $q^\perp = \neg q$.

For any assignment h, clearly $h(E_\mathbf{u})$ gets value $\top$ exactly when $h(q_i) = u_i, i = 1, \ldots, n$. Otherwise the value is $\perp$.

Now construct the wff A as follows:

$$A = \bigvee_{\mathbf{s} \in \mathbf{H_\top}} E_\mathbf{s} \vee \bigvee_{\mathbf{z} \in \mathbf{H}_{\perp,\top}} E_\mathbf{z} \wedge {\sim} \neg E_\mathbf{z}$$

Assume $\mathbf{z} = \mathbf{s} \in \mathbf{H_\top}$, then $E_\mathbf{s}$ is $\top$ and therefore A is $\top$. Let $\mathbf{u} = \mathbf{y} \in \mathbf{H}_\perp$, then $\mathbf{u}$ is not any $\mathbf{s} \in \mathbf{H_\top}$ and so all the $E_\mathbf{s}$ are $\perp$. $\mathbf{u}$ is also not any $\mathbf{z} \in \mathbf{H}_{\perp,\top}$ and so $E_\mathbf{z}$ are all false and so $A = \perp$.

Suppose not $\mathbf{u} = \mathbf{z}_0 \in \mathbf{H}_{\perp,\top}$. Then $E_{\mathbf{z}_0}$ alone is $\top$ and all of $E_\mathbf{s}$, and $E_\mathbf{z}$ are $\perp$, for $\mathbf{z} \neq \mathbf{z}_0$ and $\mathbf{s} \in H_\perp$.

In this case, A is exactly ${\sim} \neg E_{\mathbf{z}_0}$.

Since $E_{\mathbf{z}_0}$ gets $\top$ then $\neg E_{\mathbf{z}_0}$ gets $\perp$ and ${\sim} \neg E_{\mathbf{z}_0}$ gets $\{\top, \perp\}$.

We have therefore seen that A has the table $\mathbf{h}$ as we claimed.   ∎

7   Tableaux worked examples

EXAMPLE 1.43.

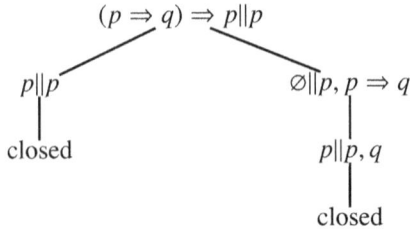

EXAMPLE 1.44.

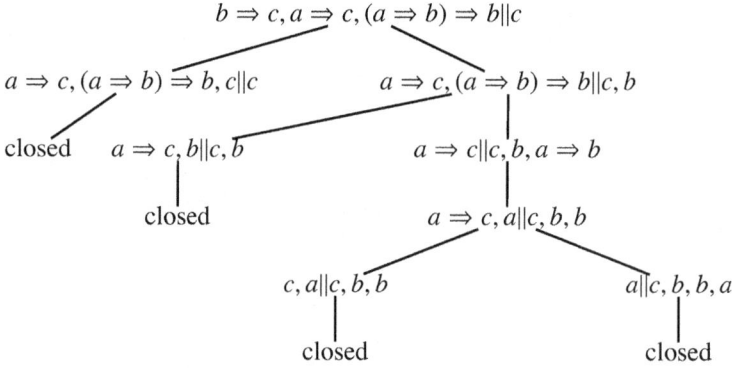

EXAMPLE 1.45.

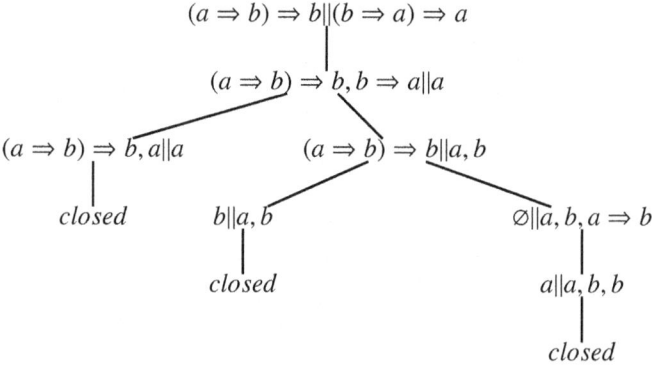

EXAMPLE 1.46.

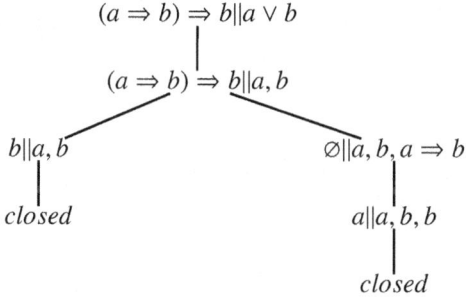

EXAMPLE 1.47.

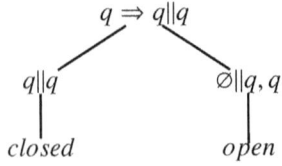

EXAMPLE 1.48.

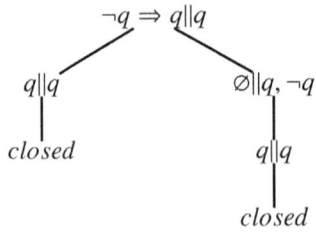

EXAMPLE 1.49.

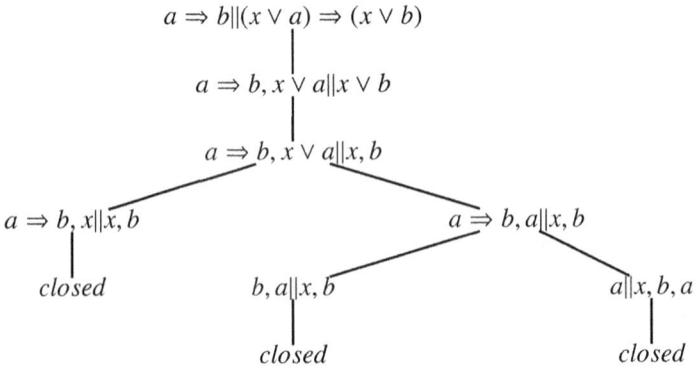

EXAMPLE 1.50.

EXAMPLE 1.51.

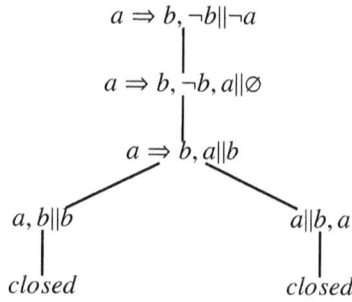

EXAMPLE 1.52.

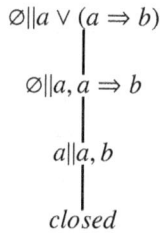

EXAMPLE 1.53.

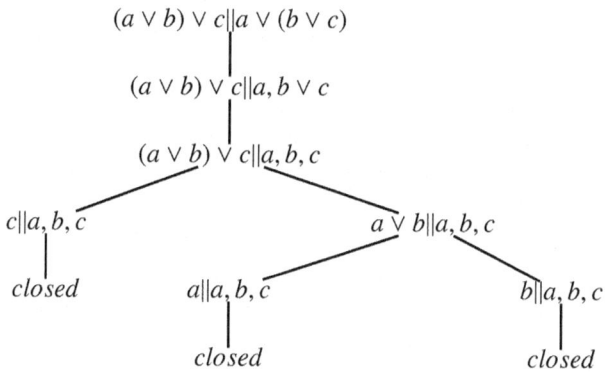

EXERCISE 1.54. Use tableaux to prove the following:

1. that ¬*p* follows from *p*⇒*q* and ¬*q*

2. that *p*∨*q* follows from ¬*p*⇒*q*

3. that ((*a*⇒*b*)⇒*a*)⇒*a* is a tautology

4. that p follows from $(p \Rightarrow q) \Rightarrow q$ and $q \Rightarrow p$

5. that $\neg(p \wedge \neg p)$ is a tautology

6. that $\neg(p \Rightarrow q) \Rightarrow p$ is a tautology

7. that $\neg(p \Rightarrow q) \Rightarrow \neg q$ is a tautology

8. that $b \vee (b \Rightarrow c)$ is a tautology

9. that $(p \Rightarrow \neg p) \Rightarrow \neg p$ is a tautology

10. that $(\neg p \Rightarrow p) \Rightarrow p$ is a tautology

11. that $(p \wedge q) \Rightarrow \neg(\neg p \vee \neg q)$ is a tautology

12. that $a \Rightarrow (\neg b \Rightarrow \neg(a \Rightarrow b))$ is a tautology

13. that $\neg p \Rightarrow ((p \vee q) \Rightarrow q)$ is a tautology

14. that b does not follow from $a \Rightarrow ((a \wedge b) \vee (\neg a \wedge \neg b))$.

8   Another version of tableaux proofs

Consider the formula $A(p, q)$ built up from the two atoms p, q. For example

$$A(p, q) = \neg p \Rightarrow ((p \vee \neg q) \Rightarrow q).$$

This formula has a truth table considering all four possibilities of truth values for the pair (p, q).

p	q	$\neg p$	$\neg q$	$p \vee \neg q$	$(p \vee \neg q) \Rightarrow q$	$\neg p \Rightarrow ((p \vee \neg q) \Rightarrow q)$
T	T	⊥	⊥	T	T	T
T	⊥	⊥	T	T	⊥	T
⊥	T	T	⊥	⊥	T	T
⊥	⊥	T	T	T	⊥	⊥

Suppose we know for sure that $p = \bot$. Then only the last two rows in the truth table become relevant. The formula $A(p, q)$ becomes $B = A(\bot, q)$, where we write $\bot$ for p. The official notation for this is $B = A(p/\bot, q)$ or $A(p, q)[p/\bot]$. Let us write it in full:

$$B = \neg\bot \Rightarrow ((\bot \vee \neg q) \Rightarrow q)$$

we have (see item 3 of Exercise 1.2.10):

$$\neg\bot \equiv \top$$
$$\bot \vee \neg q \equiv \neg q$$

and so the formula is equivalent to

$$B' = \top \Rightarrow (\neg q \Rightarrow q).$$

We also have

$$(\top \Rightarrow X) \equiv X$$

so B is equivalent to $B_\perp = (\neg q \Rightarrow q)$.

Now similarly let us put $p = \top$ in the formula A. That is we look at $A(p/\top, q)$. This gives us the first two rows in the truth tables.

We get

$$C = A(p/\top, q) = \neg\top \Rightarrow ((\top \vee \neg q) \Rightarrow q).$$

We have

$$(\top \vee X) \equiv \top$$

and we get that C is equivalent to

$$\perp \Rightarrow (\top \Rightarrow q)$$

which is equivalent to

$$\perp \Rightarrow q$$

which is equivalent to $\top$ because $(\perp \Rightarrow X) \equiv \top$.

To summarise we get that $A(p/\top, q)$ is equivalent to $\top$ and $A(p/\perp, q)$ is equivalent to $\neg q \Rightarrow q$.

Since p can be either $\top$ or $\perp$, the above two possibilities cover the entire truth table. The first two rows of the truth table give us the result for $A(p, q) \equiv \top$ and the last two rows of the truth table give us the result of $A(p, q) \equiv \neg q \Rightarrow q$. Note that $A(p/\perp, q) \wedge \neg p$ is equivalent to $(A(p, q) \wedge \neg p)$ and similarly $A(p/\top, q)$ is equivalent to $(A(p, q) \wedge p)$.

Just to make sur let us check the last two rows of the truth table

p	q	$A(p, q)$	$\neg q$	$\neg q \Rightarrow q$
$\perp$	$\top$	$\top$	$\perp$	$\top$
$\perp$	$\perp$	$\perp$	$\top$	$\perp$

We know the following

$$\begin{aligned} A(p, q) &\equiv (A(p/\top, q) \wedge p \vee A(p/\perp, q) \wedge \neg p) \\ &\equiv ((A(p, q) \wedge p) \vee (A(p, q) \wedge \neg p)) \end{aligned}$$

The above consideations give us a new way of doing tableaux. suppose we want to check whether

$$A(p, q) \| E$$

We can split the tableaux in a different way by writing

$(A(p, q) \wedge \neg p) \vee (A(p, q) \wedge p)\|E$

$A(p, q) \wedge p\|E$ $A(p, q) \wedge \neg p\|E$

$p, A(p/\top, q)\|E$ $\neg p, A(p/\bot, q)\|E$

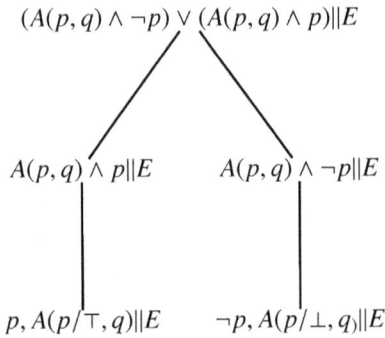

Since if $\neg p$ is true then $p = \bot$ and if p is true then $p = \top$.

The above move has simplified the left hand side considerably.

We call these kinds of rules *atomic cut rules*.

EXAMPLE 1.55. Let us check whether

$$\neg p \Rightarrow ((p \vee \neg q) \Rightarrow q)$$

can be made false, first by ordinary tableaux method and then by the new atomic cut tableaux method.

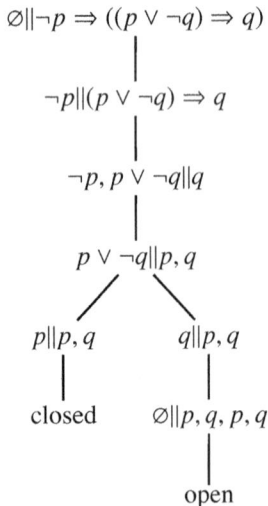

$\varnothing\|\neg p \Rightarrow ((p \vee \neg q) \Rightarrow q)$

$\neg p\|(p \vee \neg q) \Rightarrow q$

$\neg p, p \vee \neg q\|q$

$p \vee \neg q\|p, q$

$p\|p, q$ $q\|p, q$

closed $\varnothing\|p, q, p, q$

open

It an be made false by $p = q = \bot$ (as indeed seen from truth tables).

Now we use the new method for the same problem

$$\emptyset \| \neg p \Rightarrow ((p \vee \neg q) \Rightarrow q)$$

$$|$$

we use cut on p

$$|$$

$$\emptyset \| [\neg \top \Rightarrow (\top \vee \neg q) \Rightarrow q] \wedge p, [\neg \bot \Rightarrow ((\bot \vee \neg q) \Rightarrow q)] \wedge \neg p$$

$$|$$

simplify

$$|$$

$$\emptyset \| \top \wedge p, (\neg q \Rightarrow q) \wedge \neg p$$

$$\emptyset \| p, (\neg q \Rightarrow q) \wedge \neg p$$

$$\emptyset \| p, \neg p \qquad \emptyset \| p, \neg q \Rightarrow q$$

$$p \| p \qquad \neg q \| p, q$$

closed $\qquad \emptyset \| p, q, q$

$$|$$

open

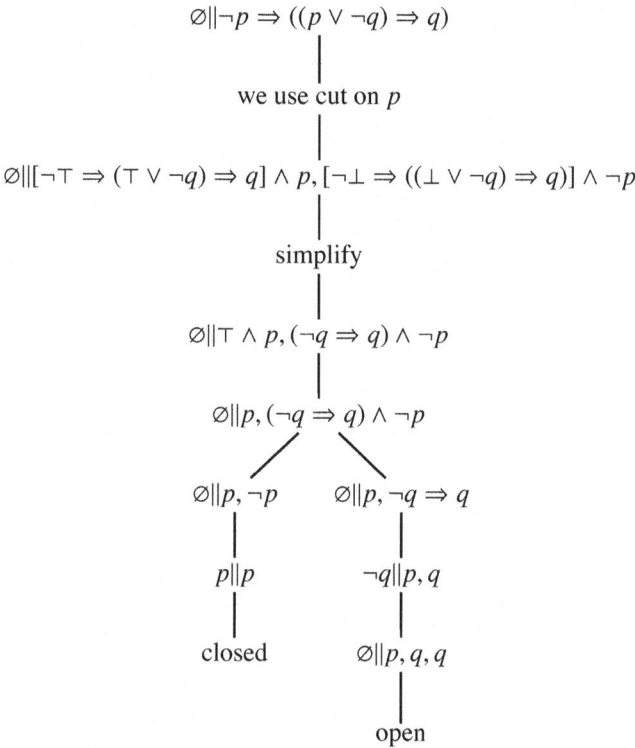

Let us now summarise the atomic cut rule:

If $\Delta \| \Gamma$ is a tableau containing $A(p, q_1, \ldots, q_k)$ either in Δ or in Γ then A can be replaced in the same position by the disjunction $(A(p/\top, q_1, \ldots, q_n) \wedge p) \vee (A(p/\bot, q_1, \ldots, q_n) \wedge \neg p)$ where $A(p, q_1, \ldots, q_k)$ is any formula built up from the atoms $p, q_1, \ldots, q_k$ and where $A(p/X)$ for a new atom X which is different from $p, q_1, \ldots, q_k$ (but could be $\top$ or $\bot$) is defined by induction as follows:

1. If A does not contain the atom p then $A(p/X)$ is A. That is there is nothing to do.

2. If $A(p)$ is the atom p, then p/X is X.

3.
$$(\neg A)(p/X) = \neg A(p/X)$$
$$(A \vee B)(p/X) = A(p/X) \vee B(p/X)$$
$$(A \wedge B)(p/X) = A(p/X) \wedge B(p/X)$$
$$(A \Rightarrow B)(p/X) = A(p/X) \Rightarrow B(p/X).$$

EXAMPLE 1.56. Let us do again Example 1.7.2. Note that replacement on the left does not necessarily simplify, because it gives a disjunction and the tableaux has to split. It may be better to replace on the right hand side. Anyway, the rule can be useful in many cases.

$$b \Rightarrow c, a \Rightarrow c, (a \Rightarrow b) \Rightarrow b \| c$$

replace $(a \Rightarrow b) \Rightarrow b$ by $a \wedge ((\top \Rightarrow b) \Rightarrow B) \vee \neg a \wedge ((\bot \Rightarrow b) \Rightarrow b)$.

We simplify $(\top \Rightarrow b) \Rightarrow b$ to the equivalent $b \Rightarrow b$ which is equivalent to $\top$, and $(\bot \Rightarrow b) \Rightarrow b$ to the equivalent b before replacing. We get

$$b \Rightarrow c, a \Rightarrow c, (a \vee (\neg a \wedge b) \| c$$

Let's do the same for $a \Rightarrow c$ and replace it with

$$((\top \Rightarrow c) \wedge a) \vee ((\bot \Rightarrow c) \wedge \neg a)$$

which is equivalent to

$$(c \wedge a) \vee \neg a$$

we get:

$$b \Rightarrow c, (c \wedge a) \vee \neg a, a \vee (\neg a \wedge b) \| c$$

We have not simplified much by using the rule.

CHAPTER 2

Some non-classical logics

Classical logic is a powerful language for certain forms of reasoning, and much can be done with it. However, it does not capture all that the natural reasoning methods of humans do. For example, we might not know for certain that an atomic sentence was true, but that there was a 75% chance that it was—this cannot be captured by classical propositional logic. As a further illustration, let the atoms p and q represent two different coins which can be exchanged for an item r. This could be easily stated by $p \wedge q \Rightarrow r$. However, to state that the amount represented by p and q is used up in the exchange cannot be done by classical reasoning. When we use an implication $A \Rightarrow B$, we assume that no change is undergone by A when it is used to conclude B. This does not carry over into the chemical example, nor for a number of problems in computer science. (Note that attempts to express the change to p and q are doomed to failure: $p \wedge q \Rightarrow r \wedge \neg p \wedge \neg q$ reduces to $\neg(p \wedge q)$.)

Many non-classical logics have been devised to handle these and other problems which exceed the capabilities of classical logic. In this chapter, we present a selection of variations of classical propositional logic to illustrate the possibilities. There are alternatives to classical logic which add more connectives to the language, and other alternatives which vary the meaning of the existing connectives. Amongst the most important of the latter are *many-valued* logics, *intuitionistic* logic, *modal* and *temporal* logics and *resource* (*relevance* and *linear*) logics.

1 Many-valued logics

The first assumption that we made in Chapter 1 was that atomic sentences were either true or false, and that no other values were permitted. In the first alternative to classical logic that we shall describe, Łukasiewicz many-valued logics, we withdraw that assumption and instead we assume that we have a range of possible values and any atom gets one of these values. Depending on the number of values in the range, different many-valued logics can be defined.

The language of propositional many-valued logic is the same as the language of the classical propositional calculus; we have a set $Q = \{q_1, q_2, \ldots\}$ of atomic sentences and a set of connectives $\{\wedge, \vee, \neg, \Rightarrow\}$. Let L_n be the set $\{0, 1/n, 2/n, \ldots, (n-1)/n, 1\}$. L_n is the set of truth values: 0 represents false (0 degree of truth), 1 represents true and the other values represent degrees of truth between the two extremes. For $n = 1$ we get $\{0, 1\}$, which is classical logic. For $n = 2$, we get $\{0, 1/2, 1\}$, a three-valued logic. The truth table for the connectives for the case $n = 2$ is defined in Table 2.1. The table also contains the general equation for computing the truth values for any value of n.

Table 2.1. The truth table for $n = 2$.

A	B	$A \wedge B$	$A \vee B$	$A \Rightarrow B$	$\neg A$
x	y	$\min(x, y)$	$\max(x, y)$	$\min(1, 1 - x + y)$	$1 - x$
1	1	1	1	1	0
1	1/2	1/2	1	1/2	0
1	0	0	1	0	0
1/2	1	1/2	1	1	1/2
1/2	1/2	1/2	1/2	1	1/2
1/2	0	0	1/2	1/2	1/2
0	1	0	1	1	1
0	1/2	0	1/2	1	1
0	0	0	0	1	1

The rationale behind the truth table is as follows. When we claim $A \Rightarrow B$, then our claim is true if B is 'at least as true as' A. This corresponds to $\bot \Rightarrow \bot$ is $\top$, $\bot \Rightarrow \top$ is $\top$ and $\top \Rightarrow \top$ is $\top$ in the classical two-valued truth tables. Our attitude towards $A \Rightarrow B$ where A is 'more true' than B might be that it is false, but this judgement is too harsh. A may be just slightly more true than B. If x is the truth value of A, and y is the truth value of B, then $x - y$ is how far $A \Rightarrow B$ is from the truth. We can thus give $A \Rightarrow B$ the value $1 - (x - y) = 1 - x + y$. Combining both cases for $x \leq y$ and $x < y$ gives the formula $\min(1, 1 - x + y)$. The functions of x and y for the other connectives, $A \wedge B$ has truth value $\min(x, y)$, $A \vee B$ has $\max(x, y)$, and $\neg A$ has $(1 - x)$, reflect the traditional way of understanding these connectives.

The value 1 is considered to be *truth*, and so any formula A is an L_n-tautology if it always gets the value 1 in the L_n truth table. For example, $A \Rightarrow A$ is an L_2-tautology, while $\neg A \vee A$ is not. When the truth value of A, i.e. x is 1/2, $\neg A \vee A$ is $\max(1 - 1/2, 1/2) = 1/2$ and hence $\neg A \vee A$ does not always get the value 1. (Contrast this with classical logic, where $A \Rightarrow A$ is equivalent to $\neg A \vee A$.) As for classical logic, A is an L_n-contradiction if it always gets the value 0 in the L_n truth table. The negation of an L_n-tautology is an L_n-contradiction, and vice versa.

Łukasiewicz also introduced the infinite-valued logic L_∞, where the truth values are all rational numbers x such that $0 \leq x \leq 1$. The same formulae given in

Table 2.1 for calculating the meaning of the connectives apply. The following formulae are all L_∞-tautologies.[1]

1. $A \Rightarrow A$

2. $A \Rightarrow (B \Rightarrow A)$

3. $(A \Rightarrow B) \Rightarrow ((B \Rightarrow C) \Rightarrow (A \Rightarrow C))$

4. $(A \Rightarrow (B \Rightarrow C)) \Rightarrow (B \Rightarrow (A \Rightarrow C))$

5. $((A \Rightarrow B) \Rightarrow B) \Rightarrow ((B \Rightarrow A) \Rightarrow A)$

6. $((A \Rightarrow B) \Rightarrow (B \Rightarrow A)) \Rightarrow (B \Rightarrow A)$

EXERCISE 2.1.

1. For the three-valued logic, can one find wffs $d_1(x), d_2(x), d_3(x)$ for atomic x, such that d_1 always gets the value 1, d_2 always gets the value $1/2$, and d_3 always gets the value 0?

2. Compute the truth table in the three-valued logic $\{0, 1/2, 1\}$ of the formulae:

   (a) $\neg A \vee B$

   (b) $\neg A \wedge \neg B$

   (c) $A \vee \neg A$

   (d) $((A \wedge B) \Rightarrow C) \Rightarrow (A \Rightarrow (B \Rightarrow C))$

   (e) $(A \Rightarrow B) \wedge (B \Rightarrow A)$

   (f) $(A \Rightarrow (B \wedge C)) \Rightarrow ((A \Rightarrow B) \wedge (A \Rightarrow C))$

3. Let $A^0 \Rightarrow B$ be B and $A^{n+1} \Rightarrow B$ be $A \Rightarrow (A^n \Rightarrow B)$.

   (a) Show that (for any assignment) the truth value of $(\neg A)^k \Rightarrow A$ is either 0 or 1 in L_n, provided $k \geq n - 1$.

   (b) Find a formula which always gets the value 1 in the truth table of $\{0, 1/n, 2/n, \ldots, 1\}$ but does not always get the value 1 in the table for $\{0, 1/(n + 1), 2/(n + 1), \ldots, 1\}$.

4. Show that $((A^n \Rightarrow B) \Rightarrow A) \Rightarrow A$ is a tautology of L_n but not of L_{n+1}.

5. Find a formula A_k of L_n with a single atom x such that

$$A_k(x) = 1 \text{ iff } x = 1/k, \text{ for } k \geq 2$$

6. Let us denote by L_n also the set of tautologies (theorems) of the logic L_n.

   (a) Show that $L_n \subseteq L_m$ if m is a divisor of n.[2]

---

[1] The same L_∞-tautologies are obtained also when we let the truth values be all real numbers $0 \leq x \leq 1$. This is so because of the continuity of the truth table functions.

[2] Actually it is also true that if m is not a divisor of n then $L_n \not\subseteq L_m$. The proof is not as easy.

(b) Show that for wffs without negation, $L_n \subseteq L_m$ iff $m \leq n$.

DEFINITION 2.2.

1. We can define a consequence relation for the logic L_n and L_∞ as follows:

   $A_1, \ldots, A_k \vdash_{L_n} B$ iff for any assignment h

   $$h(A_1) + \cdots + h(A_k) - h(B) \leq k - 1$$

   In particular, we have $\vdash_{L_n} B$ iff for all $h, h(B) = 1$.

2. $\vdash_{L_n}$ is the consequence relation which satisfies the equivalence

   $$A_1, \ldots, A_k, B \vdash_{L_n} C \text{ iff } A_1, \ldots, A_k \vdash_{L_n} B \Rightarrow C$$

3. There are other consequence relations definable using the many-valued truth table. For example, we can let $A_1, \ldots, A_n \vdash_n B$ iff for all h

   $$\min_i\{h(A_i)\} \leq h(B)$$

The above equivalence is also known as the *deduction theorem*.

EXERCISE 2.3. Verify the deduction theorem mentioned in item 2 of the previous definition.

2   Other logics

Classical logic and the many-valued logics are static systems, which rely on fixed sets of truth values which can be assigned to the atomic sentences, and the truth values of complex sentences are computed inductively according to a prescribed truth table. Thus if A is a formula built up from the propositions $q_1, q_2, \ldots, q_n$, we can evaluate the truth value of A provided we know the truth values of $q_1, q_2, \ldots, q_n$. The function giving these values is the assignment h, which for example is given by

$$
\begin{aligned}
h(p \Rightarrow q) &= \min(1, 1 - h(p) + h(q)) \\
h(\neg p) &= 1 - h(p)
\end{aligned}
$$

for the classical and many-valued logics. To introduce and explain other logics, such as intuitionistic and linear logics, we need to consider the above slightly differently. We make h context dependent on indices t from structured set T. We get different logics for different structures.

2.1 Temporal logic

We assume we have a flow of time of the form $(T, \leq)$, where T is the set of moments of time and $\leq$ is a reflexive, transitive and antisymmetric earlier–later relation on T, i.e. $\leq$ satisfies the following:

- $t \leq t$

- $t \leq s$ and $s \leq r$ imply $t \leq r$

- $t \leq s$ and $s \leq t$ imply $t = s$.

Note that we do not require that $(T, \leq)$ be linear. Thus we are allowing for a branching future in our time flow.

Let us regard the assignment h of truth values to the propositions as being a description of the world or situation with respect to a particular time t. Thus h_t might say that the value of q_1 at time t is $\top$ and the value of q_2 is $\bot$ and so forth. According to the truth tables, we can compute a truth value for the formula A at time t, written $h_t(A)$. A wff is considered to be a tautology if, no matter what h_t is, the value of A, namely $h_t(A)$, is true.

The difference between classical logic and other many-valued logics is in how they compute the value of $h_t(A)$ at time t, given the values for the propositions, and in what values one can give to the propositions. Suppose that at time t we want to say that, always in the future, A implies B. We cannot write '$A \Rightarrow B$ holds at t' or compute $h_t(A \Rightarrow B)$ to get the required meaning because $\Rightarrow$ behaves according to the agreed truth table — we check at time t the value of A and the value of B and return the value true provided A is not true at the same time as B is false. We need a special connective, say $\Box A$, which will say that A holds at all moments from t onwards. Thus we have $h_t(\Box A) = \top$ if for all $s \geq t$ we have $h_s(A) = \top$.

This connective still satisfies the principle that the value of $\Box A$ at time t depends on the values of A (its subformula) at all other times.

Let us now consider the combination $A \twoheadrightarrow B$ which we define to be $\Box(A \Rightarrow B)$.

This is the connective we want. $h_t(A \twoheadrightarrow B)$ has to go to any future time $s \geq t$ and check the values of A and B at s and find that $A \Rightarrow B$ holds at s. Therefore

$$h_t(A \twoheadrightarrow B) \quad = \top \quad \text{iff for all } s \geq t, h_s(A) = \top \text{ implies } h_s(B) = \top$$

Let us agree from now on that $\twoheadrightarrow$ is understood to be interpreted as above. What kind of logic do we get? We present the definition of the meaning of the logic below.

DEFINITION 2.4 (Temporal many-valued logic). Let $(T, \leq)$ be a flow of time and let L be a set of truth values (e.g. L can be L_n or L_∞). An interpretation (or a model) for the language with $\{\neg, \wedge, \vee, \Rightarrow, \Box\}$ is any set of functions $\{H_t \mid t \in T\}$ assigning truth values to the atomic propositions for each moment of time t. We can extend the definition of H_t from atomic propositions to any complex formulae by induction, as follows:

$$H_t(\neg A) = 1 - H_t(A)$$

$$H_t(A \wedge B) = \min(H_t(A), H_t(B))$$

$$H_t(A \vee B) = \max(H_t(A), H_t(B))$$

$$H_t(A \Rightarrow B) = \min(1, 1 - H_t(A) + H_t(B))$$

$$H_t(\Box A) = \min_{s \geq t} H_s(A)$$

A model is presented as $(T, \leq, H)$, where H is the family of functions H_t. We say that A is a temporal L-tautology, and write $\vDash_L A$, iff $H_t(A) = 1$ for all possible H_t over all possible models of time, where L is the set of truth values..

We can define a temporal many-valued consequence relation by letting

$$A_1, \ldots, A_k \vDash_L B$$

iff for all $(T, \leq, H)$ and all $t \in T$, we have

$$H_t(A_1) + \cdots + H_t(A_k) - H_t(B) \leq k - 1$$

We assume the model of time and H_t are such that different values are given to propositions at different times, and we understand $A \twoheadrightarrow B$ to mean that at all future times A implies B. Each $A \twoheadrightarrow B$ is evaluated as for the many-valued logics at each $s \geq t$, and takes the lowest value that any of these times assigns it.

The new temporal tautologies are those formulae A for which $H_t(A) = 1$ for all times t. For example, $p \twoheadrightarrow p$ is both a classical (when $\twoheadrightarrow$ is replaced by $\Rightarrow$) and a temporal tautology, whereas $p \vee (p \twoheadrightarrow q)$ is not a temporal tautology although it is a classical tautology. A counterexample is to have p false at time t, but to have p true and q false at some time $s > t$.

To say that A will always be true, one can write $(A \twoheadrightarrow A) \twoheadrightarrow A$, which is what we denoted $\Box A$. Furthermore, to say that A will be true at some (unknown) future moment is the same as saying that its negation will not always be true, i.e. $\neg\Box\neg A$, which is denoted $\Diamond A$. The $\Box$ and $\Diamond$ are known as *modalities*.

2.2 Intuitionistic logic

So far the future allows for truth values to change in any way we want. Thus if $t < s$, we may have $H_t(q) = 1$ and $H_s(q) = 0$. Propositions can become false as time passes. In the case of many-valued logics, atoms can fluctuate in value over time, rising and falling through a series of values. A restriction on this leads naturally to intuitionistic logic. Suppose we take the two-valued $L_1 = \{0, 1\}$ and insist that truth values or propositions can only go up (or remain the same) as time goes on. In other words, propositions cannot become 'falser' over time. Formally we might write

(2.1) $t \leq s$ implies $H_t(q) \leq H_s(q)$

What impact does this restriction have? At first sight, it does not seem to be a practical restriction because we know that in reality, truth values can change either way. Is there a plausible interpretation for this restriction? Consider the following situation. We have an event at a fixed time t_0, giving values to all wffs; for example, suppose that a murder has been committed. An investigating team is set up which gathers information as time goes on. To assert A at time t means in this case that at time t the team discovered that A happened at time t_0, i.e. at the time of the murder. Thus information accumulates over time. Each formula A has three possible values:

- We record A as true if A is definitely confirmed (by some physical evidence, say).

- We record $\neg A$ as true if $\neg A$ is definitely confirmed.

- Otherwise, we record A as false.

Thus $H_t(A) = 1$ means that at time t we have definite evidence that A was true at t_0. $H_t(\neg A) = 1$ means that at time t we have definite evidence that $\neg A$ was true at t_0, and $H_t(A) = 0$ means that at time t we are unable to confirm or deny the truth of A. Because of the 'increasing truth' condition, we know that once we have ascertained that either A or $\neg A$ was true at t_0, that information will remain.

Now if $H_t(A \twoheadrightarrow B) = 1$, we know that we have firm evidence to establish that if A was true at t_0, then B was also true at t_0. This is evidence of a *link* between evidence of the truth of A which can be used as evidence of the truth of B. For example, if we can prove that the person with a particular fingerprint was the murderer, and we can prove that Alun possesses the particular fingerprint, then we can prove that Alun was the murderer.

The above interpretation yields the intuitionistic meaning of $\twoheadrightarrow$ and $\neg$. We keep the meaning of $\wedge$ and $\vee$ as before. Thus $\vDash_{L_1} A$ gives the set of all intuitionistic tautologies. If we let $L = L_n$ or $L = L_\infty$, we get a general notion of intuitionistic many-valued logic. The following is a definition of an intuitionistic many-valued logic.

DEFINITION 2.5 (Intuitionistic many-valued logic). We define the language as in Definition 2.4 with the following changes:

1. $t \leq s$ implies $H_t(q) \leq H_s(q)$ for all propositions q

2. $H_t(\neg A) = \min_{s \geq t}(1, 1 - H_s(A))$.

Note that if we use the constant $\perp$ so that $H_t(\perp) = 0$ for all values of t, then $H_t(\neg A) = H_t(A \twoheadrightarrow \perp)$ in the intuitionistic many-valued interpretation.

DEFINITION 2.6 (Kripke models for intuitionistic logic).   We give separately
the version of the previous definition for the case of two truth values $\{0, 1\}$, and
the language $\{\land, \lor, \Rightarrow, \neg, \bot\}$. A *Kripke structure*, or a *Kripke model*, has the form
$(T, \leq, h)$ where $(T, \leq)$ is a partially ordered set and h is an assignment giving for
each $t \in T$ and atom q a value $h(t, q) \in \{0, 1\}$. We require persistence for all q,
namely

- $t \leq s$ and $h(t, q) = 1$ imply $h(s, q) = 1$.

We extend h to all wffs as follows:

- $h(t, A \land B) = 1$ iff $h(t, A) = 1$ and $h(t, B) = 1$.

- $h(t, A \lor B) = 1$ iff $h(t, A) = 1$ or $h(t, B) = 1$.

- $h(t, A \Rightarrow B) = 1$ iff for all s such that $t \leq s$ and $h(s, A) = 1$ we have
  $h(s, B) = 1$.

- $h(t, \bot) = 0$.

- $h(t, \neg A) = 1$ iff for all s such that $t \leq s$ we have $h(s, A) = 0$.

- We define a semantic consequence relation $\vDash_I$ by $A_1, \ldots, A_n \vDash_I B$ iff for all
  models $(T, \leq, h)$ and all $t \in T$ we have: if $h(t, A_i) = 1$, for $i = 1, \ldots, n$, then
  $h(t, B) = 1$.

- B is an intuitionistic tautology iff $\varnothing \vDash_I B$.

EXERCISE 2.7. Show that in the previous definition the following persistence
property holds:

- $t \leq s$ and $h(t, A) = 1$ imply $h(s, A) = 1$.

EXAMPLE 2.8 (Kripke models for Gödel's logic). If we require in Definition
2.2.3 that the partially ordered set $(T, \leq)$ is linearly ordered, we get the logic known
as Gödel's logic, also known as Dummett's LC logic. Its characteristic axiom is

$$(A \Rightarrow B) \lor (B \Rightarrow A)$$

or equivalently

$$(A \Rightarrow (B \lor C)) \Rightarrow ((A \Rightarrow B) \lor (A \Rightarrow C))$$

or equivalently, using only $\Rightarrow$

$$[((A \Rightarrow B) \Rightarrow C)] \Rightarrow [((B \Rightarrow A) \Rightarrow C)] \Rightarrow C].$$

All the above axioms require linearity of the set of worlds T, i.e.

$$\forall t, s(t \le s \vee s \le t).$$

We now prove a simple assertion for such linear Kripke models.

LEMMA 2.9. *Let t, s be two worlds in a linear Kripke model such that for all atomic q we have that $h(t, q) = h(s, q)$. Then for any formula A we have $t \vDash A$ iff $s \vDash A$.*

Proof.

- The above holds for atomic A by assumption.

- For the case of $A \vee B$, we have:
  $t \vDash A \vee B$ iff $t \vDash A$ or $t \vDash B$,
  iff by the inductive assumption,
  $s \vDash A$ or $s \vDash B$ iff $s \vDash A \vee B$.

- A similar argument proves the case of $A \wedge B$.

- We now turn to the case of $A \Rightarrow B$. We have $t \nvDash A \Rightarrow B$ iff for some $y \ge t$, we have $y \vDash A$ and $y \nvDash B$. By linearity we have that either $s \le y$ or $y \le s$. If $s \le y$, then $s \nvDash A \Rightarrow B$. If $y \le s$, then we have $t \le y \le s$ and since s and t give the same values to all atomic sentences, so does y. Therefore, by the induction hypothesis we have that $s \vDash A$ and $s \nvDash B$ and therefore $s \nvDash A \Rightarrow B$.

- The case of $\neg A$ follows from regarding $\neg A = A \Rightarrow \bot$.

This concludes the inductive proof of the lemma   ∎

We can now simplify the Gödel models considerably for the case of a finite set of atoms $Q = \{q_1, \ldots, q_n\}$ as follows.

Let $\approx_Q$ be an equivalence relation on T defined by $t \approx_Q s$ iff for all atoms q in Q, $t \vDash q$ iff $s \vDash q$.

Clearly for any formula A built up from the atoms of Q we have:

$$t \approx_Q s \text{ implies } t \vDash A \text{ iff } s \vDash A.$$

Let T_Q be the set of equivalence classes of points of T. Then T_Q is finite. We define, for two classes t_Q and s_Q in T_Q, an ordering $\le_1$ by:

- $t_Q \le_1 s_Q$ iff for some $t \in t_Q$ and $s \in s_Q$ we have $t \le s$.

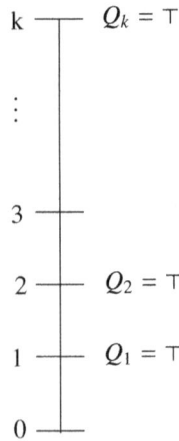

Figure 2.1.

$\leq_1$ is indeed an ordering of T_Q. It is clearly reflexive. Let us check transitivity:

Assume $t_Q \leq_1 s_Q$ and $s_Q \leq_1 r_Q$. Then for some $t \in t_Q, s \in s_Q$ we have $t \leq s$ and for some $s' \in s_Q$ and $r \in r_Q$ we have $s' \leq r$. Our aim is to show $t_Q \leq_1 r_Q$. Now by linearity, either $t \leq r$ or $r \leq t$. If $t \leq r$ then $t_Q \leq_1 r_Q$.

If $r \leq t$, then since we have also $r \leq s$ and $s \approx_Q s'$ and $s' \leq r$, we will show that we must have $t \approx_Q r$. Assume $t \vDash q$ then $s \vDash q$ because $t \leq s$, and $s' \vDash q$ because $s' \approx_Q s$ and $r \vDash q$ because $s' \leq r$. This shows that $t \approx_Q r$. But if $t \approx_Q r$ then clearly $t_Q \leq_1 r_Q$ by reflexivity.

Having proved that $(T_Q, \leq_1)$ is a linear model, we can now prove the following assertion (*)

(*) For any formula A built up from the atoms Q we have that

$$t_Q \vDash A \text{ in } (T_Q, \leq_1) \text{ iff } t \vDash A \text{ in } (T, \leq).$$

Proof of (*): Exercise

We can now count all the different finite linear models for the language of atoms of Q only. They have the form of diagram in Figure 2.1

$Q_i \subseteq Q$ are non-empty pairwise disjoint sets. At point 0 all members of Q get $\perp$. At point i all members of Q_i get $\top$ for the first time, for $i = 1, \ldots, k$.

Any element $q \in Q - \bigcup_{i=1}^{k} Q_i$ get $\perp$ all the time.

Here is how we count the models

1. fix n for $Q = \{q_1, \ldots, q_n\}$

2. choose $1 \leq k \leq n$

3. choose k disjoint non-empty subsets of Q, $Q_1 \subseteq Q, \ldots, Q_k \subseteq Q$

4. choose an ordering on $Q_1, \ldots, Q_k$ (there are $k!$ options). Say σ is a permutation, then the ordering is $Q_{\sigma(1)}, \ldots, Q_{\sigma(k)}$.

5. the model thus constructed is as in Figure 2.1, i.e. has the linear ordering $\{0, 1, \ldots, k\}$ with $h(m, q) = \top$ iff $q \in Q_{\sigma(i)}$ for some $i \leq m$.

2.3 Resource logics

We are now in a position to discuss the family of logics which are grouped under the heading of *resource* logics. The intuitionistic interpretation was not really temporal — it had to do with the accumulation of evidence, with $t \leq s$ meaning s is a time at which more evidence has been obtained than at time t. The temporal component was used as a means of ordering the increasing evidence. However, it is possible to deal directly with the additional information and do without the concept of time.

Let α_t be the information available at time t, and α_s be the information available at time s. Now $\alpha_s = \alpha_t \otimes \beta$ where β is the additional information which combined (or added) to α_t yields α_s. We can thus replace the flow of time by a flow of information. Let I be a set of pieces of information, and let $\otimes$ be a 'combining' operator for putting together members of I to obtain further members of I. $H_t(q)$ gives the truth value of q relative to the piece of information t. We can define $t \leq s$ iff for some x, $t \otimes x = s$. We also need $\emptyset$ to represent no information, so that $\emptyset \otimes t = t \otimes \emptyset = t$ for all t. We now have a new way of understanding $\twoheadrightarrow$:

$$H_t(A \twoheadrightarrow B) = 1 \text{ iff for all } s \text{ such that } H_s(A) = 1 \text{ we get } H_{t \otimes s}(B) = 1$$

This definition states that $A \twoheadrightarrow B$ is true in a situation provided that whenever a situation in which A is true is added, a situation in which B is true is reached. The definition corresponds to natural reasoning.

There are several options for understanding $\neg A$ in this context, the simplest being

$$H_t(\neg A) = 1 - H_t(A)$$

which corresponds to earlier interpretations of $\neg$. We could also use

$$H_t(\neg A) = H_t(A \twoheadrightarrow \perp)$$

as above.

Validity can be defined by $\vDash A$ iff $H_\emptyset(A) = 1$ for all information sets and definitions of the $\otimes$ operator. These different definitions of $\otimes$ yield different logics. There is a basic requirement of $\otimes$ that it be associative, i.e. $(x \otimes y) \otimes z = x \otimes (y \otimes z)$.

We can require that $\otimes$ be commutative ($t \otimes s = s \otimes t$) meaning that the order in which information is combined does not matter. A further requirement might be that information cannot be reinforced by repetition, so that $t \otimes t = t$.

We summarize the discussion in the following definition.

DEFINITION 2.10 (Many-valued resource logic).   A many-valued substructural logic has the same connectives as before, namely $\{\wedge, \vee, \Rightarrow, \neg, \perp\}$, but is interpreted with respect to $\langle I, \otimes, \emptyset \rangle$, where I is a set with an associative binary operator $\otimes$ and identity $\emptyset$ such that $\emptyset \otimes t = t$ for all t. H is an assignment associating with each $t \in I$ and proposition q, a truth value $H_t(q)$. H can be inductively extended to all wffs by

$$H_t(A \wedge B) = \min(H_t(A), H_t(B))$$

$$H_t(A \vee B) = \max(H_t(A), H_t(B))$$

$$H_t(A \twoheadrightarrow B) = \min_s \min(1, 1 - H_s(A) + H_{t \otimes s}(B))$$

$$H_t(\neg A) = H_t(A \twoheadrightarrow \perp)$$

where $\perp$ is a constant which may be interpreted by $H_t(\perp) = 0$ for all t (although logics exist which do not require this).

$\vDash A$ (A is valid) iff for all $\langle I, \otimes, \emptyset \rangle$ and H we have $H_\emptyset(A) = 1$.

EXERCISE 2.11. Check the validity of the following formulae when (a) $\otimes$ is associative and commutative, and when (b) $\otimes$ is associative and $t \otimes t = t$, and when in both cases $\emptyset \otimes t = t$.

  1. $A \twoheadrightarrow A$

  2. $A \twoheadrightarrow (A \twoheadrightarrow A)$

  3. $(A \twoheadrightarrow (B \twoheadrightarrow C)) \twoheadrightarrow (B \twoheadrightarrow (A \twoheadrightarrow C))$

  4. $(A \twoheadrightarrow (A \twoheadrightarrow B)) \twoheadrightarrow (A \twoheadrightarrow B)$

  5. $A \twoheadrightarrow ((A \twoheadrightarrow A) \twoheadrightarrow A)$

EXAMPLE 2.12 (Linear logic and relevance logic). These are very well known resource logics and this example will give a flavour of their nature. Imagine several assumptions, say

  1. A

  2. $A \Rightarrow (A \Rightarrow B)$

  3. C

We can use *modus ponens* and derive B by using A twice, i.e.

$$\frac{A, A \Rightarrow (A \Rightarrow B)}{A \Rightarrow B}$$

and again

$$\frac{A, A \Rightarrow B}{B}$$

So, in deriving B, we used assumption (1) twice, assumption (2) once and assumption (3) not at all.

In general, let $\alpha : D$ be a pair with α a list of exactly how many times each assumption was used in deriving D. We can maintain our lists by letting

$$\frac{\alpha : D; \beta : D \Rightarrow E}{\beta \otimes \alpha : E}$$

where $\beta \otimes \alpha$ is a new list giving details of what is used in the proof of E, constructed from α and β.

Relevance logic will accept a proof of E from a set of assumptions provided all assumptions were used *at least once*. Linear logic insists that each assumption is used *exactly once*.

See also Section 5.2.

3 Another look at intuitionistic logic

We saw in Chapter 1 that classical logic is content with regarding $A \Rightarrow B$ as being true when A and B are both false. Intuitionistic logic takes a more 'dynamic' view that the assertion $A \Rightarrow B$ must be properly tested. In other words, A must be made true and then we must check for B which must follow from A in all circumstances in which A is true. Thus when we are presented with a candidate for a valid argument of the form $A_1, \ldots, A_m \vdash (A \Rightarrow B)$, we do not use truth tables to confirm it, i.e. check whether $A_1 \wedge \cdots \wedge A_m \Rightarrow (A \Rightarrow B)$ is a tautology, but check instead whether by adding A to the assumptions, $A_1, \ldots, A_m, A \vdash B$ is a valid argument.

Intuitionistic logic for the language with $\wedge, \vee, \Rightarrow$ and $\neg$ can be defined as the minimal logic (by which we mean the logic with the least number of valid arguments) which allows for the equivalence

$$A_1, \ldots, A_m \vdash (A \Rightarrow B) \text{ iff } A_1, \ldots, A_m, A \vdash B$$

and satisfies reflexivity, monotonicity and cut and also rules 1, 2, 3, 4, 6 and 7 on page 16.

Classical logic allows for a stronger equivalence, namely

$$A_1, \ldots, A_n \vdash (A \Rightarrow B) \vee C \text{ iff } A_1, \ldots, A_n, A \vdash B \vee C$$

Given a set of assumptions $\{A_1, \ldots, A_n\}$ and a conclusion B, in classical logic we can look, by building truth tables, for all the possibilities (rows of the truth table) in which the assumptions are all true. For each of these possibilities we can check the truth table of B. If B is true in each of these possibilities, then classical logic will regard the argument $A_1, \ldots, A_n \vdash B$ as valid.

Intuitionistic logic would also check whether B is true in all circumstances in which the assumptions are all true. But when the conclusion is an implication, say $C \Rightarrow D$, the validity of the argument depends on just those possibilities which make the assumptions together with C true. Again, if D is true in all those possibilities then intuitionistic logic will regard the argument $A_1, \ldots, A_n \vdash B$ as valid.

We illustrate the difference with an example. Suppose that there is a single assumption $p \vee q$, and the conclusion is $\neg p \Rightarrow q$. The truth table for classical implication gives

	p	q	$p \vee q$	$\neg p \Rightarrow q$
1	$\top$	$\top$	$\top$	$\top$
2	$\top$	$\bot$	$\top$	$\top$
3	$\bot$	$\top$	$\top$	$\top$
4	$\bot$	$\bot$	$\bot$	$\bot$

Rows 1, 2 and 3 all make the assumption true, so the argument is valid in classical logic if and only if these rows make the conclusion true, which they do. Intuitionistic logic requires us to consider what happens when we demand that the antecedent of the implication $\neg p$ is true together with the assumption, which is the case in rows 2 and 3.

More formally we adopt a constructive view of $A \Rightarrow B$. To assert $A \Rightarrow B$ we must have a method which transforms any proof of A into a proof of B. For part of the language without disjunction, we are able to motivate intuitionistic logic further as a variation of classical logic. Consider the following formulation of classical logic. We know that $A_1, \ldots, A_n \vdash B$ in classical logic if, according to the truth tables, $\bigwedge A_i \Rightarrow B$ is a tautology. To check whether the above is a tautology we check each row in the truth table, and ensure that B is true in each row where all of the A_i are true. Each row in the truth table gives values to the atomic propositions. If $q_1, q_2, \ldots, q_m$ are the atoms, a row in the truth table can be taken as giving values to $q_1, q_2, \ldots, q_m$ or adding the assumptions $q_i^{\pm}$ to the data, where q_i^{+} is q_i, and q_i^{-} is $\neg q_i$. Thus we have $A_1, \ldots, A_n \vdash B$ in classical logic iff for all choices of vectors $x_1, x_2, \ldots, x_m \in \{+, -\}$, we have $A_1, \ldots, A_n, q_1^{x_1}, q_2^{x_2}, \ldots, q_m^{x_m} \vdash B$. It is enough to generate the above choices by the single rule $A_1, \ldots, A_n \vdash B$ if for all formulae C, we have both $A_1, \ldots, A_n, C \vdash B$ and $A_1, \ldots, A_n, \neg C \vdash B$. Intuitionistic logic without disjunction allows for the same equation but only for positive q_i, i.e. $A_1, \ldots, A_n \vdash B$ iff for all subsets $\{p_1, p_2, \ldots, p_k\} \subseteq \{q_1, q_2, \ldots, q_m\}$, we have $A_1, \ldots, A_n, p_1, p_2, \ldots, p_k \vdash B$.

Let us check an example to bring out the difference in the presence of ∨. Suppose there is a board meeting of Imperial Petroleum convened to vote on a motion calling for the chairman's resignation. It is expected that the vote will be very close. Information was given anonymously to the chairman that a deal was made between Mr Jones and Mr Smith, two members of the board, that for 100,000 one of them will vote in favour of the motion. It was not clear which of them sold out their vote, but one thing is clear. Either Mr Smith will vote 'yes' if Mr Jones votes 'yes', or Mr Jones will vote 'yes' if Mr Smith votes 'yes'. We can represent this in symbols as

(2.2) $(S \Rightarrow J) \vee (J \Rightarrow S)$

using J and S to stand for Mr Jones will vote 'yes' and Mr Smith will vote 'yes' respectively. The chairman was supposed to check this 'deal', but having only been taught classical logic, he did not bother. The classical truth of the allegation is logically evident, as the following truth table shows:

S	J	$S \Rightarrow J$	$J \Rightarrow S$	$(S \Rightarrow J) \vee (J \Rightarrow S)$
T	T	T	T	T
T	⊥	⊥	T	T
⊥	T	T	⊥	T
⊥	⊥	T	T	T

The formula (2.2) is true under all circumstances in classical logic. Intuitionistic logic does not follow tables. To establish the truth of $S \Rightarrow J$, we assume S is true and check J. Let us now check the first disjunct:

Database	Query
S is true	Is J true?
(Temporarily assume true)	

The answer is 'no', since we have no further evidence connecting S with J. Let us now check the other alternative:

Database	Query
J is true	Is S true?
(Temporarily assume true)	

Again the answer is 'no', since we have no further evidence connecting J with S. Therefore the allegation is not logically self-evident in intuitionistic logic and needs to be investigated.

Note that our intuitive understanding of intuitionistic implication is hypothetical. This makes intuitionistic logic and intuitionistic implication natural bases for describing database updating and time-dependent reasoning from data.

Further discussions comparing intuitionistic and classical logic can be found in Section 3.

From the point of view of intuitionistic logic, what component do we add to intuitionistic reasoning to obtain classical (logic) reasoning? We have arrived at intuitionistic logic by questioning and weakening the logic of the truth table. If we use intuitionistic logic, what is it that we can do to make the logic turn into classical logic? The answer is the following: in the course of the computation (or reasoning) in intuitionistic logic, if we fail to delete temporary assumptions when we have finished using them, we get classical logic.

If we check the validity of $(S \Rightarrow J) \vee (J \Rightarrow S)$ again and fail to delete the assumptions, we should succeed. First we check whether $(S \Rightarrow J)$ is true. To do that intuitionistically, we add (or assume) that S is true and ask for J. Since we have no further evidence, we cannot show that J is true and hence the computation (or checking) of whether $S \Rightarrow J$ is true failed. At this point of the computation, S is marked by us as true, because we temporarily assumed S is true to check whether J follows. To pass to the next stage, namely checking whether $J \Rightarrow S$, we ought to delete the S. Suppose we do not do that and continue the computation by checking whether $J \Rightarrow S$ is true. To do that we temporarily assume J is true and ask whether S must be true. But S now has to be true because it is still marked true from the previous computation. Thus $(S \Rightarrow J) \vee (J \Rightarrow S)$ comes out valid, if we leave old data around.

This happens for all formulae. Suppose we are given a proper computation procedure for asking questions A from a database $\mathcal{P}$, using intuitionistic logic. In the middle of the computation $\mathcal{P}$ may be temporarily increased to $\mathcal{P}'$ (a bigger database). If, at any time in the middle of the computation, we allow the query A to be asked again from $\mathcal{P}'$ (i.e. we *restart* with A, see Section 4.1.2), without having to return to the original $\mathcal{P}$, but continuing with $\mathcal{P}'$, then the answers we get are those of classical logic.

4 Worked examples

EXAMPLE 2.13 (Worked examples for Section 2.1).
Exercises

1. Does there exist an L_2-formula $A(p, q)$ with the following truth table?

p	q	$A(p, q)$
1	1	1
1	1/2	0
1	0	1/2
1/2	1	0
1/2	1/2	0
1/2	0	0
0	1	0
0	1/2	0
0	0	1

2. Are the formulae $A \Rightarrow B$ and $\neg A \vee B$ equivalent in the logic L_2?

3. Show that the connective $\Rightarrow$ cannot be expressed in terms of $\vee, \wedge, \neg$ in the logic L_n if $n > 1$.

4. Show that a formula without $\Rightarrow$ cannot be an L_n-tautology if $n > 1$.

5. Show that if A is an L_n-tautology for some n, then $\neg A$ is not an L_m-tautology for any m.

6. Show that $L_\infty \subseteq L_n$ for any n.

7. Show that $L_\infty \neq L_n$ for any finite n.

8. Show that $L_\infty = \bigcap \{L_n \mid n \geq 0\}$.

Solutions

1. No. Notice that every L_2-formula takes a value 0 or 1 when each of its arguments is either 0 or 1. This is easily proved by induction. But this property fails for the truth table in question.

2. No, because $1/2 \Rightarrow 1/2 = 1$, and $\neg 1/2 \vee 1/2 = 1/2 \vee 1/2 = 1/2$.

3. To show this, it is sufficient to prove that for any L_2-formula $A(p_1, \ldots, p_k)$ built up using the connectives $\neg, \vee, \wedge$ only, we have $A(1/2, \ldots, 1/2) = 1/2$. This is proved by induction.

   (a) If $A = p_i$, the claim is obvious

   (b) If $A = B \vee C$, then $A(1/2, \ldots, 1/2) = B(1/2, \ldots, 1/2) \vee$
   $C(1/2, \ldots, 1/2) = 1/2 \vee 1/2$ (by the induction hypothesis) $= 1/2$.

   (c) If $A = B \wedge C$, the proof is similar.

   (d) If $A = \neg B$, then $A(1/2, \ldots, 1/2) = \neg B(1/2, \ldots, 1/2) = \neg 1/2$ (by the induction hypothesis) $= 1/2$.

4. Similarly to the previous exercise, one can prove by induction that for every formula A of the corresponding type, $A(1/n, \ldots, \frac{1}{n}) \neq 1$.

5. To prove this, observe that $A(1, \ldots, 1) = 1$ in any logic L_m (because this is true in L_n and truth values in L_m for this specific case are computed by the same rules).

6. Note that $A(x_1, \ldots, x_k)$ in $L_n = A(x_1, \ldots, x_k)$ in L_∞ (for any $x_1, \ldots, x_k \in \{0, \frac{1}{n}, \ldots, 1\}$). This happens because truth tables in L_n and in L_∞ are computed by the same rules.

   Now if A is an L_∞-tautology, it follows that A is an L_n-tautology.

7. Otherwise $L_n \subseteq L_{n+1}$ by the previous exercise, in contradiction with Exercise 2.1.1.4.

8. $L_\infty \subseteq \bigcap\{L_n \mid n \geq 0\}$ by Exercise 7. For the converse, suppose A is not an L_∞-tautology and show that A is not an L_n-tautology for some n. By the assumption, $A(x_1, \ldots, x_k) \neq 1$ (in L_∞) for some values $x_1, \ldots, x_k$ of atoms occurring in A. Since $x_1, \ldots, x_k$ are rational numbers, there exists n, such that $x_1, \ldots, x_k \in \{0, 1/n, \ldots, (n-1)/n, 1\}$. Then $A(x_1, \ldots, x_k)$ (in L_∞) $= A(x_1, \ldots, x_k)$ (in L_n), according to the definitions. Hence A is not an L_n-tautology.

EXAMPLE 2.14 (Worked examples for Section 2.2.1).

Exercises

1. Check if the following formulae are temporal L_1-tautologies:

    (a) $B \Rightarrow (A \Rightarrow B)$

    (b) $A \wedge B \Rightarrow B$

    (c) $A \wedge B \twoheadrightarrow B$

    (d) $B \twoheadrightarrow (A \twoheadrightarrow B)$

    (e) $\Box A \twoheadrightarrow A$

    (f) $\Box A \twoheadrightarrow \Diamond A$

    (g) $\Box A \twoheadrightarrow \neg\Diamond\neg A$

    (h) $\Box A \wedge \Box B \twoheadrightarrow \Box(A \wedge B)$

    (i) $\Box(A \wedge B) \twoheadrightarrow \Box A \wedge \Box B$

    (j) $\Diamond(A \vee B) \twoheadrightarrow \Diamond A \vee \Diamond B$

    (k) $\Box\Box A \twoheadrightarrow \Box A$

2. Prove that a formula without $\twoheadrightarrow$ (and $\Box$) is a temporal L-tautology iff it is an L-tautology.

3. Show that (in L_1) the formula $\Box p$ is non-equivalent to any formula built up from the connectives $\vee, \wedge, \neg$.

4. Call formulae A, B temporally L-equivalent if $H_t(A) = H_t(B)$ in any model for any t. Show that A, B are temporally L-equivalent iff

$$\vDash (A \twoheadrightarrow B) \wedge (B \twoheadrightarrow A)$$

5. Construct infinitely many formulae with a single atom p, which are pairwise temporally L_1-non-equivalent.

Solutions

1. (a), (b). These formulae are classical tautologies. Hence they are also temporal tautologies, because truth values at every moment of time are computed according to classical rules.

    (c) We know already that $C = (A \land B \Rightarrow B)$ is a tautology. Now $\Box C$ is a temporal tautology, because $H_t(\Box C) = \top$ iff for all $s \geq t, H_s(C) = \top$, and the latter is true.

    (d) This formula is not a temporal tautology. For, let A, B be atoms, and consider a flow of time with two moments, t and s, such that $t < s$. Let $H_t(A) = H_s(A) = 1, H_t(B) = 1, H_s(B) = 0$. Then $H_t(A \twoheadrightarrow B) = 0$, but $H_t(B) = 1$; hence $H_t(B \twoheadrightarrow (A \twoheadrightarrow B)) = 0$.

    (e) This is also a temporal tautology. As in case (c), it suffices to show that $\Box A \Rightarrow A$ is a temporal tautology. For this, assume that $H_t(\Box A) = 1$, and show that $H_t(A) = 1$. By the assumption, $H_s(A) = 1$ for any $s \geq t$. Hence $H_t(A) = 1$ because $\leq$ is reflexive.

    (f) Again, it is sufficient to check that $H_t(\Box A \Rightarrow \Diamond A) = 1$ for any t.

    This follows again from the reflexivity of the time flow. For, assume that $H_t(\Box A) = 1$ then $H_t(A) = 1$, and then $H_t(\Diamond A) = 1$ (since $t \leq t$).

    (g) $\neg\Diamond\neg A = \neg\neg\Box\neg\neg A$. This formula has the same truth value (at any moment of time) as $\Box\neg\neg A$, which is equivalent to $\Box A$ (since $\neg\neg A \equiv A$ in classical logic). Therefore, $\Box A \twoheadrightarrow \neg\Diamond\neg A$ is an L_1-tautology.

    (h, i) Let us check that $H_t(\Box A \land \Box B) = H_t(\Box(A \land B))$: $H_t(\Box A \land \Box B) = 1$ iff $H_t(\Box A) = H_t(\Box B) = 1$ iff $H_s(A) = H_s(B) = 1$ for any $s \geq t$ iff $H_s(A \land B) = 1$ for any $s \geq t$ iff $H_t(\Box(A \land B)) = 1$.

    (j) Let us show that $H_t(\Diamond(A \lor B) \Rightarrow \Diamond A \lor \Diamond B) = 1$. For this assume that $H_t(\Diamond(A \lor B)) = 1$. Then $H_s(A \lor B) = 1$ for some $s \geq t$.

    Hence for this s, $H_s(A) = 1$ or $H_s(B) = 1$. Then $H_t(\Diamond A) = 1$ in the first case, $H_t(\Diamond B) = 1$ in the second.

    (k) This formula is a temporal tautology because $\Box A \twoheadrightarrow A$ is a tautology for any A (see (e) above). So we can replace A by $\Box A$.

2. Take a formula A built by $\lor, \land, \neg$. If A is an L-tautology then $H_t(A) = 1$ for any moment t, because truth values at t are found by the same rules as in L.

    For the converse, suppose $A(p_1, \ldots, p_k)$ is not an L-tautology. Then there are values $x_1, \ldots, x_k$ of atoms $p_1, \ldots, p_k$ such that $A(x_1, \ldots, x_k) \neq 1$ (in L). Take the flow of time $(T, \leq)$ with a single moment t, and the interpretation h such that

    $$H_t(p_1) = x_1, \ldots, H_t(p_k) = x_k$$

Then $H_t(A) = A(x_1, \ldots, x_k)$ in $L \neq 1$. Thus A is not a temporal L-tautology.

3. Suppose the contrary, i.e. that for some classical formula A, $\Box p \Leftrightarrow A$ is a temporal tautology. If such A exists, then we can further assume that A is built using a single variable p. Really, if $\Box p \Leftrightarrow A(p, q_1, \ldots, q_k)$ is a temporal tautology, then $\Box p \Leftrightarrow A(p, \top, \top, \ldots, \top)$ is a temporal tautology (because $\Box p$ does not depend on $q_1, \ldots, q_k$) and we can consider $A' = A(p, \top, \ldots, \top)$ instead of A.

   But in classical logic, there are only four pairwise non-equivalent formulae with one variable p, $\neg p$, $\top$, $\bot$, and none of the equivalences (1) $\Box p \Leftrightarrow p$, (2) $\Box p \Leftrightarrow \neg p$, (3) $\Box p \Leftrightarrow \top$, (4) $\Box p \Leftrightarrow \bot$ are temporal tautologies. Corresponding countermodels are:

   (1) $T = \{t, s\}, t < s, H_t(p) = 1, H_s(p) = 0$

   (2), (4) $T = \{t\}, H_t(p) = 1$

   (3) $T = \{t\}, H_t(p) = 0$.

4. Assume that A, B are temporally equivalent, and consider an arbitrary model.

   Since for any s, $H_s(A) = H_s(B)$, we have that $H_s(A \Rightarrow B) = H_s(B \Rightarrow A) = 1$. Hence $H_t(A \twoheadrightarrow B) = H_t(B \twoheadrightarrow A) = 1$ for any t, and therefore $\models_L (A \twoheadrightarrow B) \wedge (B \twoheadrightarrow A)$.

   Conversely, suppose $\models_L (A \twoheadrightarrow B) \wedge (B \twoheadrightarrow A)$, and take any model. Then for any t,

   $$H_t(A \twoheadrightarrow B) = H_t(B \twoheadrightarrow A) = 1$$

   which implies that

   $$H_t(A \Rightarrow B) = H_t(B \Rightarrow A) = 1$$

   Then by Łukasiewicz truth tables, we see that $H_t(A) \leq H_t(B)$ and $H_t(B) \leq H_t(A)$, and thus A, B are temporally L-equivalent.

5. Consider the following formulae:

   $$A_1 = \neg p$$
   $$A_2 = p \wedge \Diamond \neg p$$
   $$A_3 = \neg p \wedge \Diamond(p \wedge \Diamond \neg p)$$
   $$\vdots$$
   $$A_{2n} = p \wedge \Diamond A_{2n-1}$$
   $$A_{2n+1} = \neg p \wedge \Diamond A_{2n}, \ldots$$

Consider the following model: $(\top, \le)$ is the set $\{-1, -2, -3, \ldots\}$ ordered by the standard relation '$\le$',

$$H_t(p) = \begin{cases} 1, & \text{if } t \text{ is even} \\ 0, & \text{if } t \text{ is odd} \end{cases}$$

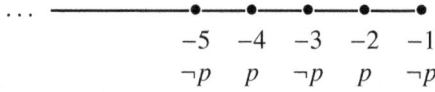

Then the following holds:

(a) $H_{-n}(A_n) = 1$;

(b) $H_{-n}(A_m) = 0$ for any $m > n$.

(a) is proved by induction. If $n = 1$ we have

$$H_{-1}(A_1) = H_{-1}(\neg p) = 1 - H_{-1}(p) = 1$$

If (a) is proved for $n = 2k - 1$, we have

$$H_{-2k}(A_{2k}) = 1 \text{ iff } H_{-2k}(p) = H_{-2k}(\Diamond A_{2k-1}) = 1$$

But $H_{-2k}(p) = 1$ by definition, and $H_{-2k}(\Diamond A_{2k-1}) = 1$ since, by the inductive hypothesis, $H_{-(2k-1)}(A_{2k-1}) = 1$. Thus $H_{-2k}(A_{2k}) = 1$.

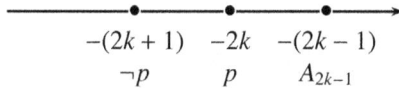

Similarly,

$$H_{-(2k+1)}(A_{2k+1}) = 1 \text{ iff } H_{-(2k+1)}(\neg p) = H_{-(2k+1)}(\Diamond A_{2k}) = 1$$
$$H_{-(2k+1)}(\neg p) = 1 \text{ since } H_{-(2k+1)}(p) = 0$$
$$\text{and } H_{-(2k+1)}(\Diamond A_{2k}) = 1 \text{ since } H_{-2k}(A_{2k}) = 1$$

This completes the proof of (a).

(b) is also proved by induction on n. Let $n = 1$. Suppose $H_{-1}(A_m) = 1$ for some $m > 1$. Then m must be odd (otherwise $H_{-1}(p) = 1$ which is not true). But if $m = 2k + 1$, we have $H_{-1}(\Diamond A_{2k}) = 1$ which implies that $H_{-1}(A_{2k}) = 1$ (because the only future of (-1) is (-1) itself).

But this cannot be true, as we have observed. Now assume that (b) is proved for any pair m', n' such that $m' > n', n' < n$, and consider a pair (m, n) such that $m > n$. Suppose $H_{-n}(A_m) = 1$. Then $H_{-n}(\Diamond A_{m-1}) = 1$ (as it follows from the definition of A_m), and thus

(i) $H_{-n}(A_{m-1}) = 1$

or

(ii) $H_{-n'}(A_{m-1}) = 1$ for some $n' < n$.

The latter contradicts our assumption because $m - 1 > n - 1 \geq n'$.

As for (i), it is incompatible with $H_{-n}(A_m) = 1$ because one of the numbers $m, (m-1)$ is even and the other is odd, and $p, \neg p$ cannot both be true at $(-n)$. Therefore $H_{-n}(A_m) = 0$.

EXAMPLE 2.15 (Worked examples for Section 2.2.2).

Exercises

1. Check, using Kripke models, if the following formulae are intuitionistic tautologies:

   (a) $\neg A \vee A$

   (b) $\neg\neg A \Rightarrow A$

   (c) $A \Rightarrow \neg\neg A$

   (d) $(A \Rightarrow B) \vee (B \Rightarrow A)$

   (e) $\neg A \wedge \neg B \Rightarrow \neg(A \vee B)$

   (f) $\neg\neg(A \vee \neg A)$

   (g) $A \Rightarrow (B \Rightarrow A \wedge B)$

2. Describe Kripke structures with the least moment of time, where the formula $p \vee \neg p$ is true at any moment.

Solutions

1.   (a) No. Take the two-element Kripke model (for A atomic):

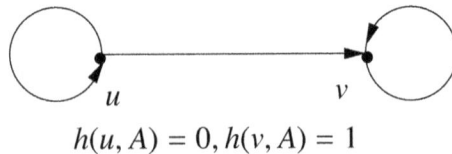

$$h(u, A) = 0, h(v, A) = 1$$

Then $h(u, \neg A) = 0$, and so $h(u, A \vee \neg A) = 0$.

(b) No. Take the same model as in the previous case. We have $h(u, \neg\neg A) = 1$ because $h(u, \neg A) = h(v, \neg A) = 0$. Also $h(u, A) = 0$, and thus $h(u, \neg\neg A \Rightarrow A) = 0$.

(c) Yes. Consider an arbitrary Kripke model, and suppose $h(t, A) = 1$. We have to show that $h(t, \neg\neg A) = 1$. Suppose the contrary. Then $h(s, \neg A) = 1$ for some $s \geq t$, which implies $h(s, A) = 0$. But this contradicts persistence of A (Exercise 2.2.4).

(d) No. Take the three-element Kripke model (for A, B atomic):

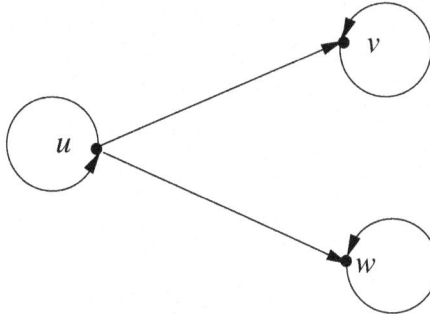

Let $h(v, A) = h(w, B) = 1$, $h(v, B) = h(u, B) = h(u, A) = h(w, A) = 0$. Then $h(u, A \Rightarrow B) = 0$ because $v \geq u, h(v, A) = 1, h(v, B) = 0$; also $h(u, B \Rightarrow A) = 0$ because $w \geq u, h(w, B) = 1, h(w, A) = 0$. Hence $h(u, (A \Rightarrow B) \vee (B \Rightarrow A)) = 0$.

(e) Yes. In any Kripke model, if $h(t, \neg A \wedge \neg B) = 1$ then $h(t, \neg A) = h(t, \neg B) = 1$, and thus $h(s, A) = h(s, B) = 0$, for any $s \geq t$.

The latter means that $h(s, A \vee B) = 0$. Therefore for every t, $h(t, \neg A \wedge \neg B) = 1$ implies $h(t, \neg(A \vee B)) = 1$.

(f) Yes. Suppose the contrary. Then in some Kripke model, for some t we have $h(t, \neg\neg(A \vee \neg A)) = 0$ and so for some $s \geq t$, $h(s, \neg(A \vee \neg A)) = 1$, and further on, $h(r, A \vee \neg A) = 0$ for any $r \geq s$, i.e. $h(r, A) = h(r, \neg A) = 0$ for any $r \geq s$. Now $h(r, \neg A) = 0$ only if $h(r', A) = 1$ for some $r' \geq r$, and on the other hand, $h(r', A) = 0$ since $r' \geq r \geq s$. This is a contradiction.

(g) Yes. It is sufficient to show that, in any Kripke model, $h(t, A) = 1$ implies $h(t, B \Rightarrow (A \wedge B)) = 1$.

So suppose $h(t, A) = 1$; take any $s \geq t$, and suppose also that $h(s, B) = 1$. Then $h(s, A \wedge B) = 1$ because $h(s, A) = 1$ due to persistence (Exercise 2.2.4).

2. These are structures where p has the same truth value at all moments of time. Really, assume that $h(t_0, p \vee \neg p) = 1$ and t_0 is the initial moment.

Then either $h(t_0, p) = 1$ or $h(t_0, \neg p) = 1$. If $h(t_0, p) = 1$ then $h(t, p) = 1$ for any t (by persistence). If $h(t_0, \neg p) = 1$ then for any t, $h(t, \neg p) = 1$ by persistence, and thus $h(t, p) = 0$.

The converse is clear, because if $h(t, p) = 0$ for any t, then $h(t_0, \neg p) = 1$. Otherwise $h(t_0, p) = 1$ (since $h(t_0, p \vee \neg p) = 1$).

EXAMPLE 2.16 (Three-valued Smetanich logic). Consider Kripke structures with two moments of time making a chain: $T_2 = \{t_0, t_1\}, t_0 < t_1$. Restrict the definition of an intuitionistic tautology to this case. That is, we define $\vDash_S A$ iff for all Kripke structures $(T_2, \leq, h), h(t, A) = 1$ for any t.

In general, the possible combinations of truth values of a formula A at the moments t_0, t_1 can be $(0, 0), (0, 1)$ or $(1, 1)$ (because of persistence). Let us consider them as corresponding to the numerical values 0 (for $(0, 0)$), 1/2 (for $(0, 1)$) and 1 (for $(1, 1)$). Then we can treat Smetanich logic as three-valued. For example, $A \wedge B$ has the following truth table:

A	B	$A \wedge B$
0	0	0
1/2	0	0
1	0	0
0	1/2	0
1/2	1/2	1/2
1	1/2	1/2
0	1	0
1/2	1	1/2
1	1	1

1. Compute truth tables for all connectives in Smetanich logic and compare them to L_2 truth tables.

2. Check if the following formulae are Smetanich tautologies:

   (a) $\neg A \vee A$

   (b) $\neg\neg A \Rightarrow A$

   (c) $(A \Rightarrow B) \vee (B \Rightarrow A)$

   (d) $\neg A \vee \neg\neg A$

   (e) $A \vee (A \Rightarrow B) \vee \neg B$

3. Let $(T, \leq)$ be a partially ordered set with the first element and at least two other elements. Show that the formula $A \vee (A \Rightarrow B) \vee \neg B$, with A, B atomic, can be refuted in some Kripke structure $(T, \leq, h)$.

4. Let S be the set of all Smetanich tautologies. Show that $L_2 \not\subseteq S$, and $S \not\subseteq L_2$.

5. Show that L_2-negation is non-expressible in Smetanich logic, but that intuitionistic negation is expressible in L_2.

Solutions

1.

A	B	¬A	A ∧ B	A ∨ B	A ⇒ B
1	1	0	1	1	1
1	1/2	0	1/2	1	1/2
1	0	0	0	1	0
1/2	1	0	1/2	1	1
1/2	1/2	0	1/2	1/2	1
1/2	0	0	0	1/2	0
0	1	1	0	1	1
0	1/2	1	0	1/2	1
0	0	1	0	0	1

If we compare this to Table 2.1, we see that $A \wedge B, A \vee B$ are the same functions, whereas $\neg A, A \Rightarrow B$ are not. In particular, $\neg A$ never gets the value $1/2$ in Smetanich logic.

2. (a) $\neg p \vee p$ is not a tautology (for p atomic). We can take the same model as in Exercise 2.4.3.1(a).

   (b) No. Use the model from Exercise 2.4.3.1(b).

   (c) Unlike the general intuitionistic case, $(A \Rightarrow B) \vee (B \Rightarrow A)$ is a Smetanich tautology.

   Indeed, consider an arbitrary Kripke model $(T_2, \leq, h)$. Owing to persistence, it is sufficient to show that the formula is true at t_0, i.e. that

   (c.1) $h(t_0, A \Rightarrow B) = 1$ or $h(t_0, B \Rightarrow A) = 1$.

   Assume that $h(t_0, A \Rightarrow B) = 0$, and show that $h(t_0, B \Rightarrow A) = 1$.
   $h(t_0, A \Rightarrow B) = 0$ implies

   (c.1.1) $h(t_0, A) = 1, h(t_0, B) = 0$, or

   (c.1.2) $h(t_1, A) = 1, h(t_1, B) = 0$.

   From (c.1.1) it follows that $h(t_0, B \Rightarrow A) = 1$ since A is persistent.
   From (c.1.2) it also follows that $h(t_0, B \Rightarrow A) = 1$ since $h(t_0, B) = h(t_1, B) = 0$, owing to the persistence of B.

   (d) Similarly to the previous one, this is a tautology. Consider a Kripke model $(T_2, \leq, h)$ and show that $h(t_0, \neg A) = 1$ or $h(t_0, \neg\neg A) = 1$.
   Assume that $h(t_0, \neg A) = 0$. Then $h(t_0, A) = 1$ or $h(t_1, A) = 1$. In both cases $h(t_1, A) = 1$, and thus $h(t_0, \neg\neg A) = 1$ (because $\neg A$ is false at t_0 and at t_1).

(e) This is a tautology. Indeed, take any model $(T_2, \leq h)$. Assume that $h(t_0, A) = h(t_0, A \Rightarrow B) = 0$, and show that $h(t_0, \neg B) = 1$.

We have $h(t_0, A) = 0$ and also $h(r, A) = 1, h(r, B) = 0$ for some $r \geq t_0$. Since $h(r, A) \neq h(t_0, A)$, it follows that $r = t_1$. Now $h(t_1, B) = 0$ implies $h(t_0, B) = 0$ by persistence. Therefore, $h(t_0, \neg B) = 1$. Thus (e) is true at t_0 and also at t_1 (by persistence).

3. Let s_0 be the first element of T and let s_1, s_2 be two other elements. We can assume further that $s_2 \not\leq s_1$ (otherwise denote them the other way round). Now take a Kripke model such that

$$h(u, A) = 1 \text{ iff } u \geq s_1$$
$$h(u, B) = 1 \text{ iff } u \geq s_2$$

Then obviously, $h(s_0, A) = 0$. Also $h(s_0, \neg B) = 0$, since $s_0 \leq s_2$ and $h(s_2, B) = 1$. Furthermore, $h(s_1, A) = 1, h(s_1, B) = 0$ (since $s_2 \not\leq s_1$) yield that $h(s_0, A \Rightarrow B) = 0$. Therefore $A \vee (A \Rightarrow B) \vee \neg B$ is false at s_0.

4. $L_2 \not\subseteq S$ for example, because $\neg\neg A \Rightarrow A \in L_2$, but $\neg\neg A \Rightarrow A \notin S$ (by 2(b)). $S \not\subseteq L_2$, because $A \vee (A \Rightarrow B) \vee \neg B \in S$ (by (2(e)), but $A \vee (A \Rightarrow B) \vee \neg B \notin L_2$. To see this, take the values $A = 1/2, B = 0$. Then $A \vee (A \Rightarrow B) \vee \neg B = 1/2 \vee (1/2 \Rightarrow 0) \vee 0 = 1/2 \vee 1/2 = 1/2$.

5. (I) To show that L_2-negation is non-expressible in S, we consider truth tables in S for the following formulae built of a single atom x:

x	$\neg x$	$x \vee \neg x$	$\neg\neg x$	$\top$	$\bot$
0	1	1	0	1	0
1/2	0	1/2	1	1	0
1	0	1	1	1	0

Let us prove that any formula A with a single atom is equivalent to one of these six; this will solve the problem, because L_2-negation has a different truth table (cf. Table 2.1).

The proof goes by induction on the length of A.

- If $A = x, \top$ or $\bot$, there is nothing to prove.
- If $A = B \wedge C$ and $B \equiv C', C \equiv C'$ and B', C' are among the six, then $A \equiv B' \wedge C'$ and there are several cases to be considered.

  (a) $C' = \top$. Then $A \equiv (B' \wedge \top) \equiv B'$ and there is nothing to prove.

  (b) $B' = \top$. Similarly to (a).

  (c) $C' = \bot$ or $B' = \bot$. Then $A \equiv \bot$.

(d) $A \equiv x \wedge \neg x$. Then $A \equiv \bot$ (this is seen from the truth tables).

(e) $A \equiv x \wedge (x \vee \neg x)$. From the truth tables one can see that $A \equiv x$.

(f) $A \equiv x \wedge \neg \neg x$. Then it follows that $A \equiv x$.

(g) $A \equiv \neg x \wedge (x \vee \neg x)$. Then $A \equiv \neg x$.

(h) $A \equiv \neg x \wedge \neg \neg x$. Then $A \equiv \bot$.

(i) $A \equiv (x \vee \neg x) \wedge \neg \neg x$. Then $A \equiv x$.

(j) $B' = C'$. Then $A \equiv B'$.

- If $A = B \vee C$, $B \equiv B'$, $C \equiv C'$ and B', C' are among the six, then $A \equiv B' \vee C'$, and again we consider cases:

  (a) $C' = \top$ or $B' = \top$. Then $A \equiv \top$.

  (b) $C' = \bot$. Then $A \equiv B' \vee \bot \equiv B'$.

  (c) $B' = \bot$. Then $A \equiv \bot \vee C' \equiv C'$.

  (d) $B' = x, C' = \neg x$. Then $A \equiv x \vee \neg x$.

  (e) $B' = \neg x, C' = x$. Then $A \equiv x \vee \neg x$.

  (f) $A \equiv x \vee (x \vee \neg x)$. Then $A \equiv x \vee \neg x$.

  (g) $A \equiv x \vee \neg \neg x$. Then $A \equiv \neg \neg x$.

  (h) $A \equiv \neg x \vee (x \vee \neg x)$. Then $A \equiv x \vee \neg x$.

  (i) $A \equiv (x \vee \neg x) \vee \neg \neg x$. Then $A \equiv \top$.

  (j) $A \equiv \neg x \vee \neg \neg x$. Then $A \equiv \top$.

  (k) $B' = C'$. Then $A \equiv B'$.

- If $A = B \Rightarrow C$, $B' \equiv B$, $C' \equiv C$ and B', C' are among the six, then again we have several cases to consider:

  (a) $C' = \top$. Then $A \equiv (B' \Rightarrow \top) \equiv \top$.

  (b) $B' = C'$. Then $A \equiv (B' \Rightarrow B') \equiv \top$.

  (c) $A = x \Rightarrow \bot$. Then $A \equiv \neg x$.

  (d) $A \equiv \neg x \Rightarrow \bot$. Then $A \equiv \neg \neg x$.

  (e) $A \equiv (x \vee \neg x) \Rightarrow \bot$. Then $A \equiv \bot$.

  (f) $A \equiv \neg \neg x \Rightarrow \bot$. Then $A \equiv \neg x$.

  (g) $A \equiv \neg x \Rightarrow x$. Then $A \equiv \neg \neg x$.

  (h) $A \equiv \neg x \Rightarrow x \vee \neg x$. Then $A \equiv \top$.

  (i) $A \equiv x \Rightarrow x \vee \neg x$. Then $A \equiv \top$.

  (j) $A \equiv x \Rightarrow \neg \neg x$. Then $A \equiv \top$.

  (k) $A \equiv x \Rightarrow \neg x$. Then $A \equiv \neg x$.

  (l) $A \equiv \neg x \Rightarrow \neg \neg x$. Then $A \equiv \neg \neg x$.

  (m) $A \equiv (x \vee \neg x) \Rightarrow x$. Then $A \equiv \neg \neg x$.

  (n) $A \equiv (x \vee \neg x) \Rightarrow \neg x$. Then $A \equiv \neg x$.

(o) $A \equiv (x \vee \neg x) \Rightarrow \neg\neg x$. Then $A \equiv \neg\neg x$.

(p) $A \equiv \neg\neg x \Rightarrow x$. Then $A \equiv x \vee \neg x$.

(q) $A \equiv \neg\neg x \Rightarrow \neg x$. Then $A \equiv \neg x$.

(r) $A \equiv \neg\neg x \Rightarrow (x \vee \neg x)$. Then $A \equiv x \vee \neg x$.

(s) $B' = \top$. Then $A \equiv (\bot \Rightarrow C') \equiv \top$.

- If $A = \neg B$, then $A \equiv B \Rightarrow \bot$, and this is reduced to the previous cases.

(II) Now let $\Rightarrow$ be the L_2-implication, $\neg$ be the L_2-negation.

Then $\neg(\neg x \Rightarrow x)$ is the intuitionistic negation. To show this, consider the truth table:

x	$\neg x$	$\neg x \Rightarrow x$	$\neg(\neg x \Rightarrow x)$
0	1	0	1
1/2	1/2	1	0
1	0	1	0

5 Numerical attack and defence

The purpose of this section is to give meaning to the concept of *one number x supporting or attacking another number y*.

We begin with a story.

Shiraz is a nice girl from a community where parents arrange their children's marriages. This community believes in the statement

$$A = \text{no sex before marriage.}$$

Recently Shiraz was going out with a nice boy called Kevin. Kevin is an American student from a decent family. Kevin followed the rules and had his parents approach Shiraz's parents with a view of negotiating for the girl. Meanwhile, the two young people were going out together and were very much in love. Kevin does not believe in A and as it was becoming more and more obvious that a deal would be struck by the parents, Kevin was trying to persuade Shiraz that perhaps under the circumstances she would concede to statement A', which is a milder version of A.

$A' = $ A little bit of 'closeness' and 'exploration' is acceptable when marriage is pending.

Shiraz stated $\neg A'$ but she was not absolutely categorical about it, and Kevin felt that a little bit of persuasion might weaken her resolve.

Here are some of the arguments Kevin used:

B_1: You don't really love me. If you did love me you would have let me 'explore' a little bit.

B_2: It is not healthy for me to be in this permanent state of internal 'pressure'.

B_3: How can we tell we are compaitble unless we try a little bit of something?

B_4: These are modern times, you should not be old fashioned and not cool! Your parents lived in different times with different values.

B_5: You also want to do it, why deny yourself?

B_6: Your 'cold' attitude is weakening your parents' negotiating position with my parents. It gives the impression that something is wrong with you.

To this Shiraz has her own arguments in favour of $\neg A'$:

C_1: My parents made me promise not to compromise myself.

C_2: You don't respect me, all you want is sex.

C_3: What if the parents do not reach agreement, what shall we do then?

Kevin has his own counter-arguments:

D_1: I'll be careful.

D_2: No-one will know.

D_3: I love you, I want to express my love to you.

Each one of these arguments has different strength.

For example B_3 and B_6 are much stronger arguments than say B_2.

Let us associate with each argument a number x between 0 and 1, where $x = 1$ indicates a 100 % strong argument and $x = 0$ indicates a very bad argument. The following diagram, Figure 2.2 describes the situation:

An arrow $\rightarrow$ means attack, a double arrow $\twoheadrightarrow$ means defence.

The question is, given this attack and defence system with concrete numbers attached, as in the diagram, what is the resulting strength of the arugment $\neg A'$? How resolved can Shiraz be now?

There is another factor we can add to the diagram. Argument D_3 (I love you) attacks argument C_2 (All you want is sex). We know D_3 is nonsense, but D_3 is an emotinal argument and so has a stronger transmission value. So really to have a more general diagram we must also add transmission numbers $0 \leq \varepsilon \leq 1$ to each arrow or double arrow.

So the general situation we need to study is the situation in Figure 2.3

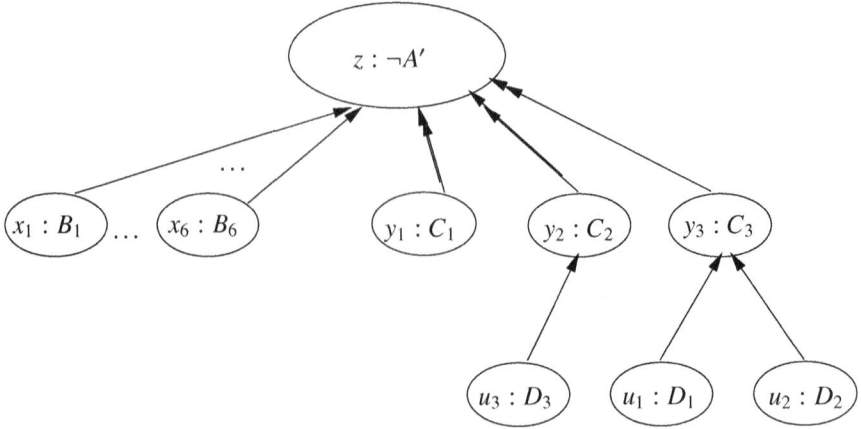

Figure 2.2.

We have a node a with a label (usually a number) x associated with it, the arrow is transmitting that label to a node b, which has a label y associated with it. ε is a transmission factor. We are interested in the new label $y' = \mathbf{f}(y, x, \varepsilon)$, which is the result of this transmission acting on node b. This situation has many interpretations. We list a few of them:[3]

1. x, y, ε are numbers in $[0, 1]$, (representing a variety of numerical evaluations), and x attacks or supports y, (i.e. x is used to decrease or increase y). For example b might be an argument and a may be another argument attacking or supporting it. The values x and y may be numerical values representing the strength of each argument.

2. ε is an action expressed in some logical system and x is the pre-condition and y is the postcondition of the action. The nodes a and b represent states. In this case ε moves the system from state a to state b. The attributes x and y have to do with describing the states.

3. Figure 2.2 is a Bayesian net with ε the conditional probability $P(b|a)$ of b given a, i.e. $y = P(b)$, $x = P(a)$ and $P(b) = P(b|a)P(a)$.

4. Figure 2.3 is part of a neural net with ε the weight and x and y the input and output respectively.

---

[3]We shall explain later in the book the meaning of items 2–5.

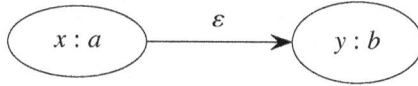

Figure 2.3.

5. a can be a theory and ε can be a revision algorithm such that when a is added to the theory b then the algorithm ε has to revise the union $a \cup b$ to maintain consistency. In this case x and y are not numbers but are contexts for the theories a and b respectively.

This example is most meaningful in the methodology of Labelled Deductive Systems. See Chapter 5.

We are interested in the case where x, y are fuzzy values (attached to a and b) in $[0, 1]$ and we want to know what our options are for x acting and changing y. Let us assume for the moment that $\varepsilon = 1$, i.e. we have full transmission. So we can ignore ε for now. Thinking in terms of fuzzy logic, we see the number 0 as representing *false* or *nil* and see 1 as representing *true*. Thus if x is attacking y, we must decrease y to y' and if x supports y then it must increase y. We expect the following properties:

1. $\mathbf{f}(y, x)$ is monotonic up for support or monotonic down for attack. Let us indicate this by writing $\mathbf{f}^+$ for support and $\mathbf{g}^-$ for attack functions.[4]

2.
   - $\mathbf{f}^+(y, 0) = y$
   - $\mathbf{f}^+(y, 1) = 1$
   - $x \leq x' \rightarrow \mathbf{f}^+(y, x) \leq \mathbf{f}^+(y, x')$
   - $y \leq \mathbf{f}^+(y, x)$

3.
   - $\mathbf{g}^-(y, 0) = y$
   - $\mathbf{g}^-(y, 1) = 0$

---

[4]A function $g(x)$ is monotonic up in x if whenever $x_1 \leq x_2$ then $f(x_1) \leq f(x_2)$. Similar definitions for monotonic down: $x_1 \leq x_2 \rightarrow f(x_1) \geq f(x_2)$.

- $x \leq x' \rightarrow \mathbf{g}^-(y, x) \geq \mathbf{g}^-(y, x')$
- $\mathbf{g}^-(y, x) \leq y$

4. Clearly if $\mathbf{f}^+$ is a support function then $\mathbf{f}^-(y, x) = 1 - \mathbf{f}(1 - y, x)$ is an attack function.

EXAMPLE 2.17 (James Bernoulli support).   The idea of Bernoulli is that the number x supports y by attacking $1 - y$. We view $1 - y$ as being the distance of y from 1. Thus by attacking $1 - y$, we are bringing y nearer to 1. The Bernoulli attack on $1 - y$ by x is executed by multiplying by $1 - x$. Thus:

$$\mathbf{f}_B^+(y, x) = 1 - (1 - y)(1 - x).$$

Indeed,

- $\mathbf{f}_B^+(y, 0) = y$

and

- $\mathbf{f}_B(y, 1) = 1$

- If $x' = x + \delta$ then

$$\begin{aligned}
\mathbf{f}_B^+(y, x') &= 1 - (1 - y)(1 - x - \delta) \\
&= 1 - (1 - y)(1 - x) + \delta(1 - y) \\
&\geq \mathbf{f}(y, x).
\end{aligned}$$

Also

$$\mathbf{f}_B^+(y, x) - y = 1 - 1 + y + x - xy - y = x(1 - y) \geq 0.$$

Let us check what the corresponding attack function $\mathbf{f}_B^-(y, x)$ is:

$$\begin{aligned}
\mathbf{f}_B^-(y, x) &= 1 - \mathbf{f}_B^+(1 - y, x) \\
&= 1 - (1 - (1 - (1 - y))(1 - x) \\
&= 1 - 1 + (1 - x)y \\
&= y(1 - x).
\end{aligned}$$

In fact this is a Bernouilli attack on y by x.

Summary of the Bernoulli case:

- x supports y yields $1 - (1 - y)(1 - x)$

- x attacks y yields $y(1 - x)$

- Note that support is symmetrical in x and y (i.e. x, y jointly cooperate with each other) while x attacks y gives $y(1 - x)$. We would have liked to take xy but attack by 0 should leave y as is. So it must be $y(1 - x)$. However the attackers do support each other, as we can see.

- x_1 and then x_2 attack y yields $y(1 - x_2)(1 - x_2)$

- x_1 and then x_2 support y yields $1 - (1 - y)(1 - x_1)(1 - x_2)$.

Analysis of the Bernoulli case:

Let us assume the case of x_1 supports and then x_2 attacks y:
  We get the value:

$$[1 - (1 - y)(1 - x_1)](1 - x_2) = (y + x_1 - x_1 y - x_2 y - x_1 x_2 + x_1 x_2 y).$$

We now examine the case of x_2 attacks and then x_1 supports y:
  We get the value of

$$
\begin{aligned}
[1 - (1 - y)(1 - x_2)](1 - x_1) &= 1 - (1 - y - x_2 + x_2 y)(1 - x_1) \\
&= 1 - 1 + y - x_2 y + x_2 - x_1 y + x_1 x_2 y - x_1 x_2 \\
&= y + x_2 - x_1 y - x_2 y + x_1 x_2 y - x_1 x_2
\end{aligned}
$$

The two values are not the same. This is not satisfactory. Furthermore, suppose we both attack and support y by x (i.e. let $x_1 = x_2$), do we get that y remains unchanged? The answer is no! For $y = 1$ and $x_1 = x_2 = x$ we get the new value $y' = 1 - x$. Obviously we need a better notion of attack and support.

Let us analyse what we get: we have a monotonic support function $\mathbf{f}^+(y, x)$, satisfying

(*1) $\mathbf{f}^+(y, 0) = y$

(*2) $\mathbf{f}^+(y, 1) = 1$

and we defined a derived attack function as:

(*3) $\mathbf{f}^-(y, x) = 1 - \mathbf{f}^+(1 - y, x)$.

Thus, given y, and attack by x_1 followed by support by x_2 gives

(*4) $y_{1,2} = \mathbf{f}^+(1 - \mathbf{f}^+(1 - y, x_1), x_2)$

Support by x_2 followed by attack by x_1 gives

(*5) $y_{2,1} = 1 - \mathbf{f}^+(1 - \mathbf{f}^+(y, x_2), x_1)$.

These two must be equal. Especially if $x_1 = x_2$, these two must cancel each other. Therefore we must have

(*6) $y = \mathbf{f}^+(1 - \mathbf{f}^+(1 - y, x), x) = 1 - \mathbf{f}^+(1 - \mathbf{f}^+(y, x), x)$

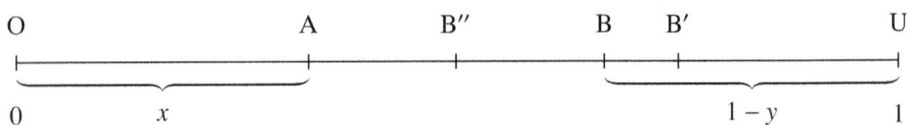

Figure 2.4.

Can such an equation hold? Let $x = 1$, we get $0 = 1$. Our problem arose from the definition of $\mathbf{f}^-(y, x)$ in (*3). Obviously we need a new point of view. Consider the situation in Figure 2.4.

The figure describes the interval $[0, 1]$. O is the origin and U is the unit 1. A is a point corresponding to the value x and B is a point corresponding to the value y. If we compare Figure 2.4 with Figure 2.3, we have that x attacks or supports y. The proposed Bernoulli support of y by x (i.e. point B by point A), we decreased the distance $(1-y) = BU$ by multiplying it by $(1-x)$, thus shifting B to B', nearer to U. Similarly, the attack of A on B was done by the distance $OB = y$, by multiplying by $1 - x$, thus shifting B to B'' to the left of B.

As we have seen, this (essentially additive) way of doing things was not satisfactory, as a combined attack and support by A on B do not cancel each other.

We now introduce our new idea. Consider the ratios

$$r_A = \frac{x}{1 - x}$$

$$r_B = \frac{y}{1 - y}$$

Let us support or attack by changing the ratios. We change the ratio r_B by multiplying by the ratio r_A. Thus

(♯1)   Attach ratio: $r_{B'} = r_B | r_A = \dfrac{y(1 - x)}{x(1 - y)}$

(♯2)   Support ratio: $r_{B''} = r_B r_A = \dfrac{xy}{(1 - x)(1 - y)}$

We find the new value z by solving the equation

$$\frac{z}{1 - z} = r$$

giving

(♯3) $z = \dfrac{r}{1 + r}$

Let us calculate the resulting z' and z'' for support and attack.

$$z' = \frac{r_{B'}}{1 + r_{B'}} = \frac{x(1 - y)}{(1 - x)y(1 + \frac{x(1-y)}{(1-x)y})}$$

$$= \frac{x(1 - y)}{(1 - x)y + x(1 - y)}$$

$$z'' = \frac{r_{B''}}{1 + r_{B''}} = \frac{xy}{(1 - x)(1 - y)(1 - \frac{xy}{(1 - x)(1 - y)})}$$

$$= \frac{xy}{xy + (1 - x)(1 - y)}$$

We now explore a connection with geometry. Consider Figure 2.3 again.

Consider the projective Cross-Ratio usually denoted by $(O, U; A, B)$ (O for origin, U for unit, A for node a in Figure 2.5, with $OA = x$ and B for node b with $OB = y$).

The Cross-Ratio is

$$\mathbb{R}(0, 1; x, y) = \frac{OA}{AU} \mid \frac{OB}{BU} = \frac{x}{1 - x} \mid \frac{y}{1 - y} = \frac{x(1 - y)}{y(1 - x)}$$

So we have

$$r_{B'} = \mathbb{R}(0, 1; x, y)$$
$$r_{B''} = \mathbb{R}(0, 1; x, 1 - y)$$

This connection is probably more than just a numerical coincidence because the Cross-Ratio is used to give the Cayley-Klein distance in Non-Euclidean geometry. Consider two points A, B inside a fixed circle (called *The Absolute*). The line AB intersects the circle at points O and U, see Figure 2.5. Then the Cayley–Klein distance $\bar{AB}$ is defined as $-k\log\mathbb{R}(O, U; A, B)$, where k is a constant. The value of k determines the nature of the resulting geometry. See [Faulkner, 1949, chapter 6] and [Adler, 1967, Sections 4.10 and 11.7].

EXAMPLE 2.18. Let us now make use of the Cross-Ratio. First we need to fix our notation.

Let $x \otimes y$ be an abbreviation for $\mathbb{R}(0, 1; x, y)$. This will help s iterate the operation. Let $x \, ®y$ be the point z such that its ratio is $x \otimes y$, that is

$$z = x \, ®u = \frac{x \otimes y}{1 + x \otimes y}$$

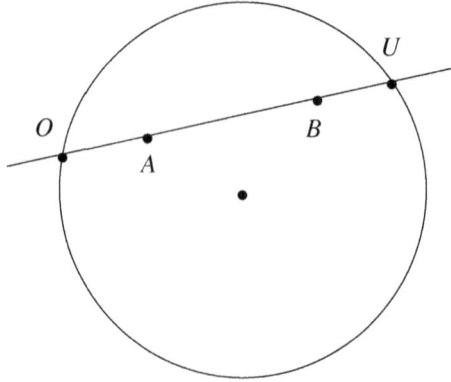

Figure 2.5.

Let

$$x \otimes y = \mathbb{R}(0, 1, x, y)$$

$$= \frac{x}{1-x} \mid \frac{y}{1-y}$$

Hence

$$-x \otimes \tfrac{1}{2} = \frac{-x}{1+x} \mid \frac{\tfrac{1}{2}}{\tfrac{1}{2}} = \frac{-x}{1+x}$$

This means in general for the one dimensional case that

$$x \circledR y = -((-x \otimes y) \otimes \tfrac{1}{2}).$$

Hence

$$-((-x) \otimes \tfrac{1}{2}) = \frac{x}{1+x}$$

Hence

$$
\begin{aligned}
r_{B'} &= x \otimes y \\
r_{B''} &= x \otimes (1-y) \\
z' &= -(-r_{B'} \otimes \tfrac{1}{2}) \\
&= -(-(x \otimes y) \otimes \tfrac{1}{2})
\end{aligned}
$$

Similarly

$$z'' = -(-(x \otimes (1-y)) \otimes \tfrac{1}{2}).$$

The above is really a geometrical construction.

Consider the line AB. Fix a coordinate system on this line so that $\bar{O}U = 1$. Thus there is a point C such that $\bar{O}C = x \otimes y$ and a point D corresponding to C to the left of O, as in Figure 2.6.

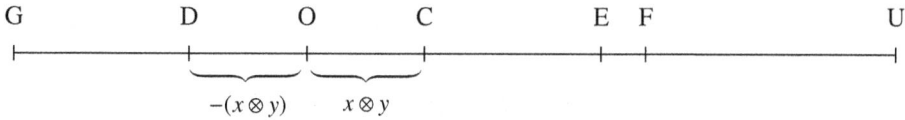

Figure 2.6.

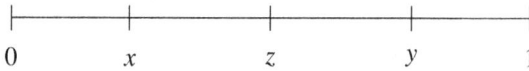

Figure 2.7.

The point E is the middle of $\bar{O}U$. Let the point F be the one corresponding to $\mathbb{R}(O, U, D, E)$ and let G be the point corresponding to F on the other side of O (i.e. $G = -F$). Then the point G corresponds to z'.

Hence we can define a geometrical construction of a new point representing the result of a point B supporting a point A. It is the third point G as constructed.

We can write

$$G = A \otimes B.$$

Note that the construction can be carried out in projective geometry (no metrics) and thus can deal with attach and support of points in higher dimensional spaces e.g. the plane. We shall investigate this idea in the next subsection 2.5.1. Furthermore, the Cross-Ratio attack and support in the one dimensional case it agrees with several forms of the Dempster–Shafer formula. This will be discussed in the next subsection.

5.1 Cross-Ratio[5]

This section further studies the connection between attack and support and the Cross-Ratio. We need to lay out the situation and notation for the one dimensional case and then generalise it to two and higher dimensions.

Let us lay out the basic situation in Figure 2.7:

The number x is supported by the number y. As a result of this support x becomes a new number z. We have

1. The support of y directed to x manifests itself by the ratio $\frac{y}{1-y}$ dividing the ratio $\frac{x}{1-x}$. Thus we get a new ratio $r = \frac{x}{1-x} \mid \frac{y}{1-y}$, which turns out to be

---

[5] Advanced material

the geometrical Cross-Ratio $\mathbb{R}(0, 1; x, y)$, which we also denoted by $x \otimes y$. The new point z which is the new result of the support of y directed to x is $z = \frac{r}{1+r}$. We denoted this point by $z = x \ \textcircled{\tiny R}\, y$.

Note that $\otimes$ is a numerical construction, while $\textcircled{\tiny R}$ is a geometrical construction, which therefore may be generalised to higher dimensions.

This is the task of this section.

Generalising to higher dimensions is of practical importance beyond mere mathematical interest. If we look at the basic attack/support situation as described in Figure 2.3, a and b may have multidimensional incomparable features that cannot be reduced to single numbers x and y and it makes more sense to regard x and y as multidimensional vectors. So we are faced with the geometrical/numerical problem as follows:

Problem

Given $\mathbf{s} = (x_1, \ldots, x_n)$ and $\mathbf{y} = (y_1, \ldots, y_n), n \geq 1, 0 \leq x_i, y_j \leq 1$. What meaning do we give to the phrase $\mathbf{s}$ attacks/supports $\mathbf{y}$, and what vector $\mathbf{y}'$ do we define as the result of this attack/support?

We offer the following solution

Solution

Given the n-dimensional vectors $\mathbf{s}$ and $\mathbf{y}$ as described, consider them elements of n-dimensional space. Let $\mathbf{S}$ be a closed surface in this space such that any two points $\mathbf{s}, \mathbf{y}, \mathbf{s} \neq \mathbf{y}$ inside the surface form a line $\mathbf{l}(\mathbf{s}, \mathbf{y})$ which intersects $\mathbf{S}$ in two points $\mathbf{A}$ and $\mathbf{B}$.

Define $\mathbf{s} \ \textcircled{\tiny R}\, \mathbf{y}$ as the point $\mathbf{z}$ on the line $\mathbf{l}(\mathbf{s}, \mathbf{y})$ which 'corresponds'[6] to the Cross-Ratio $\mathbb{R}(\mathbf{A}, \mathbf{B}; \mathbf{s}, \mathbf{y})$. Note that this solution depends on the choice of $\mathbf{S}$. We also require that the one dimensional case be embedded in the n-dimensional case.

The best way to understand this is to do some (two dimensional) examples.

We consider the plane and take as our closed surface the square with vertices $(0,0)$, $(1,0)$, $(1,1)$ and $(0,1)$. This allows us to look at all points C with coordinates inside the interval $[0,1]$.

EXAMPLE 2.19. Let $C = (0.1, 0.6)$ and $D = (0.4, 0.9)$. We are seeking to define a point $E = (x_E, y_E)$ which we can view as

$$E = C \ \textcircled{\tiny R}\, D.$$

We use the square mentioned above, see Figure 2.8:

The line through C, D is $y = mx + 0.5$.

This line meets the square in the points $A = (0, 0.5)$ and $B = (0.5, 1)$.

We now have a one dimensional attack/support problem on the line AB. We need to calculate the Cross-Ratio $f = \mathbb{R}(A, B', C, D)$ and find the corresponding

---

[6]See examples. We can take $\mathbf{z}$ such that $\mathbb{R}(\mathbf{a}, \mathbf{B}; \mathbf{z}, \infty) = \mathbb{R}(\mathbf{A}, \mathbf{B}; \mathbf{s}, \mathbf{y})$.

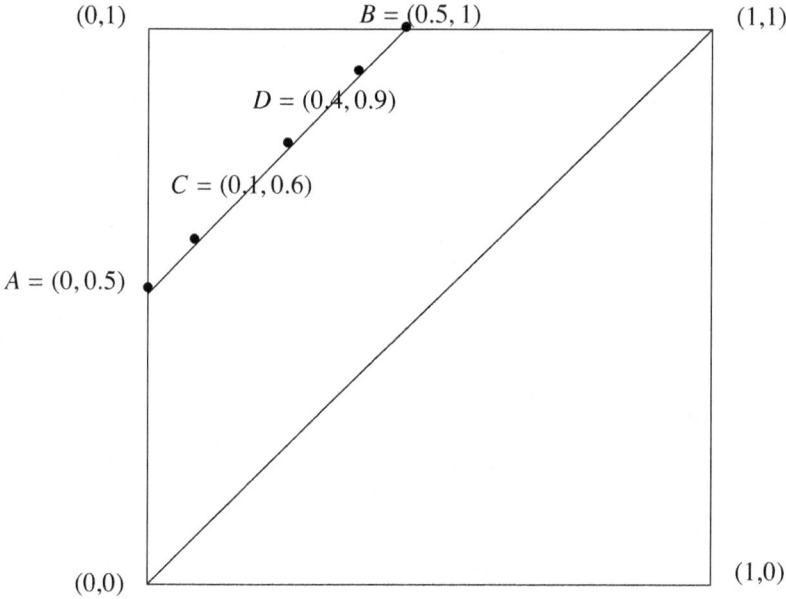

Figure 2.8.

point E. So we need to calculate the actual lengths AB, AC, CB, AD, DB and then find E and the length AE.

Let us start:

$$AB = \sqrt{\tfrac{1}{2}^2 + \tfrac{1}{2}^2} = \tfrac{\sqrt{2}}{2}$$

$$AC = \sqrt{0.1^2 + 0.1^2} = \tfrac{\sqrt{2}}{10}$$

$$CB = \sqrt{0.4^2 + 0.4^2} = \tfrac{\sqrt{2.4}}{10}$$

$$AD = \sqrt{0.4^2 + 0.4^2} = \tfrac{\sqrt{2.4}}{10}$$

$$DB = \sqrt{0.1^2 + 0.1^2} = \tfrac{\sqrt{2}}{10}$$

The cross ratio $\bar{r}$ on the line AB is

$$\bar{r} = \frac{AC}{CB} \mid \frac{AD}{DB} = \frac{\sqrt{2/10}}{\sqrt{2.4/10}} \mid \frac{\sqrt{2.4/10}}{\sqrt{2/10}} = \frac{1}{4} \mid \frac{4}{1} = \frac{1}{16}.$$

The point E must satisfy

$$\frac{AE}{EB} = \bar{r}$$

or

$$\frac{AE}{AB - AE} = \bar{r}$$

Therefore

$$AE = \frac{\bar{r}.AB}{1 + \bar{r}} = \frac{\frac{1}{16} \cdot \frac{\sqrt{2}}{2}}{1 + \frac{1}{16}} = \frac{\sqrt{2}}{34}.$$

Let (x_E, y_E) be the coordinates of E. We need to find them. We have two equations:

1. E is on the line AB. Hence

$$y_E = x_E + 0.5$$

2. We know the length AE. Hence

$$\sqrt{x_E^2 + (y_E - 0.5)^2} = \frac{\sqrt{2}}{34}.$$

Solving the equations, we get

$$\sqrt{2x_E} = \frac{\sqrt{2}}{34}$$

Hence

$$x_E = \frac{1}{34}$$

and

$$y_E = \frac{1}{34} + \tfrac{1}{2} = \frac{18}{34}$$

We therefore have the following: The result of the two dimensional support of $(0.1, 0.6)$ ©$(0.4, 0.9) = (\frac{1}{34}, \frac{18}{34})$.

EXAMPLE 2.20. We mentioned that the result of our calculations may depend on the surface chosen. We chose a square. What if we choose a circle?

Let us get on with it. First let us modify the one dimensional case a bit, to make it more convenient. Instead of [0,1] let us take [-0.5, +0.5]. This is more convenient for circles.

The Cross-Ratio is not affected. We take as our surface the circle $x^2 + y^2 = (0.5)^2$. We need to restrict our coordinates to points inside this circle. Our points C, D must be shifted to the coordinates $C' = (-0.4, 0.1)$ and $D' = (-0, 1, 0, 4)$ (by subtracting $\frac{1}{2}$ from each coordinate). C', D' do lie within the circle with radius $\frac{1}{2}$.

So we are OK. The line through C', D' is still $y = x + 0.5$. The line $y = x + 0.5$ meets the circle $x^2 + y^2 = 0.25$ at the two points, being the solutions of:

$$x^2 + (x + 0.5)^2 = 0.25$$
$$x^2 + x^2 + x + 0.25 = 0.25$$

which yields

$$2x^2 + x = 0.$$

So $x_1 = -0$. and $x_2 = 0$.

So we have $y_1 = 0$ and $y_2 = 0.5$.

The points A' and B' are

$$A' = (-0.5, 0), B' = (0, 0, 5)$$

We now calculate lengths

$$A'B' = \sqrt{2} - 0.5$$

$$A'C' = \sqrt{0.1^2 + 0.1^2} = \sqrt{2}.0.1$$

$$C'B' = \sqrt{0.4^2 + 0.4^2} = \sqrt{2}.0.4$$

$$A'D' = \sqrt{0.4^2 + 0.4^2} = \sqrt{2}.0.4$$

$$D'B' = \sqrt{0.1^2 + 0.1^2} = \sqrt{2}.0.1$$

The Cross-Ratio is

$$\bar{r}' = \frac{A'C'}{C'B'} \mid \frac{A'D'}{D'B'} = \frac{\sqrt{2}.0.1}{\sqrt{2}.0.4} \mid \frac{\sqrt{2}.0.4}{\sqrt{2}.0.1} = \frac{1/4}{4/1} = \frac{1}{16}.$$

We are looking for a point E' such that

$$\frac{A'E'}{A'B' - A'E'} = \bar{r},$$

Hence

$$A'E' = \frac{\bar{r}' \cdot A'B'}{1 + \bar{r}'} = \frac{1 \cdot \sqrt{2} \cdot 0.5}{16(1\frac{1}{16})} = \frac{\sqrt{2}}{17.2} = \frac{\sqrt{2}}{34}$$

We now need to find the coordinates of the point $E' = (x_{E'}, y_{E'})$. They satisfy

1. $y_{E'} = X_{E'} + 0.5$

Figure 2.9.

2. $\sqrt{(E_{E'} + 0.5)^2 + (X_{E'} + 0.5)^2} = \frac{\sqrt{2}}{34}$

    $\sqrt{2}(X_{E'} + 0.5) = \frac{\sqrt{2}}{34}$

    $X_E = \frac{1}{34} = \frac{17}{34} = \frac{-16}{34}$

    and therefore

    $y_E = X_{E'} + 0.5 = \frac{1}{34}$

To compare with the point E of the previous example, (where the surface was a square) let us add $\frac{1}{2}$ to each coordinate. We get $E' + (\frac{1}{2}, \frac{1}{2}) = (\frac{1}{34}, \frac{18}{34}) = E$.

    We got the same result!

We now have to check that the one dimensional case can be embedded as a two dimensional case. In other words, if we have the numbers x and y and we form the line of Figure 2.9

    and then calculate the ratio

$$ r = \frac{x}{1-x} \mid \frac{y}{1-y} $$

we get the value

$$ z = \frac{r}{1-r} $$

as the result of the support of x by y.

    We now need to embed the one dimensional case into the two dimensional case (we take the square as our surface) and get the same result. Let the embedding be $C = (x, x)$ and $D = (y, y)$.

    The line going through these points is the diagonal. Hence $A = (0,0)$ and $B = (1, 1)$ as in Figure 2.10

    We need to calculate the point E as before and show that E is the point

$$ (\frac{r}{1+r}, \frac{r}{1+r}). $$

We have

$$ AB = \sqrt{2} $$
$$ AC = \sqrt{2}x $$
$$ AD = \sqrt{2}y $$
$$ CB = \sqrt{2}(1-x) $$
$$ DB = \sqrt{2}(1-y). $$

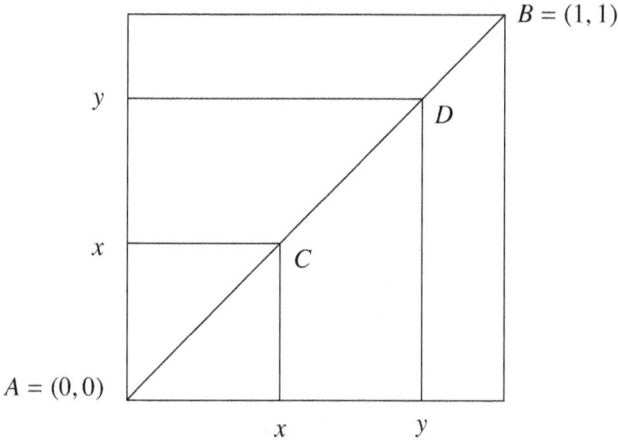

Figure 2.10.

Hence $\bar{r} = \dfrac{AB}{CB} \mid \dfrac{AD}{DB} = \dfrac{\sqrt{2}x}{\sqrt{2}(1-x)} \mid \dfrac{\sqrt{2}y}{\sqrt{2}(1-y)} = r.$

We are looking for a point E such that

$$\frac{AE}{EB} = \bar{r}$$

or

$$\frac{AE}{\sqrt{2} - AE} = \bar{r} = r$$

$$AE = \frac{\sqrt{2}r}{1+r}$$

E lies on the diagonal so its coordinates are (e, e). Hence its distance from $A = (0,0)$ s

$$AE = \sqrt{e^2 + e^2} = \sqrt{2}e = \sqrt{2}\frac{r}{1+r}$$

Hence $E = \dfrac{r}{1+r}$ as required.

Thus the one dimensional case can be embedded correctly as a two dimensional case.

5.2 The Dempster–Shafer combination

We now compare our Cross-Ratio approach with the Dempster–Shafer approach. We begin by presenting the Dempster–Shafer rule of combination.

EXAMPLE 2.21 (Dempster–Shafer rule). The range of values we are dealing with is the set of all subintervals of the unit interval [0,1]. The Dempster–Shafer addition on these intervals is defined by

$$[a,b] \oplus [c,d] = [\frac{a \cdot d + b \cdot c - a \cdot c}{1-k} , \frac{b \cdot d}{1-k}]$$

where

$$k = a \cdot (1-d) + c \cdot (1-b),$$

where '·', '+', '−' are the usual arithmetical operations. The compatibility condition φ required on a, b, c, d is

$$\varphi([a,b],[c,d]) \equiv (k \neq 1).$$

The operation $\oplus$ is commutative and associative. Let $\mathbf{e} = [0,1]$.
The following also holds:

- $[a,b] \oplus \mathbf{e} = [a,b]$

- For $[a,b] \neq [1,1]$ we have $[a,b] \oplus [0,0] = [0,0]$

- For $[a,b] \neq [0,0]$ we have $[a,b] \oplus [1,1] = [1,1]$

- $[a,b] \oplus [c,d] = \emptyset$ iff either $[a,b] = [0,0]$ and $[c,d] = [1,1]$ or
  $[a,b] = [1,1]$ and $[c,d] = [0,0]$.

In this algebra, we understand the transmission value $[a,b]$ as saying that the actual transmission value lies in the interval $[a,b]$.

Let us make three comments:

1. Let x denote $[x,x]$. We get for $0 \leq a \leq 1$ and $0 \leq c \leq 1$ the following

$$a \oplus c = \left[\frac{ac + ac - ac}{1 - a(1-c) - c(1-a)}, \frac{ac}{1 - a(1-c) - c(1-a)} \right]$$

$$= \left[\frac{ac}{1 - a - c + 2ac}, \frac{ac}{1 - a - c + 2ac} \right]$$

$$= \frac{ac}{1 - a - c + 2ac}$$

provided $(a + c - 2ac) \neq 1$.

$a \oplus c$ equals $a \, \circledR \, (1-c)$ as defined in Example 2.18. This is also the propagation method used by the MYCIN expert system. See [Hájek and Valdes, 1994].

2. Let us check for what values of a, c can we have equality, i.e. when can we have $a + c - 1 = 2ac$?

Assume $a \leq c$.

We claim the only solution to the equation $a + c - 2ac = 1$ is $a = 0, c = 1$ for $a \leq c$ and $a = 1, c = 0$ for the case $c \leq a$. There is no solution for $c = a$.

To show this, let $c = a + \varepsilon, 0 \leq \varepsilon \leq c - a$.

Then assume

$$
\begin{aligned}
a + a + \varepsilon &= 1 + 2a(a + \varepsilon) \\
2a + \varepsilon &= 1 + 2a^2 + 2\varepsilon a \\
\varepsilon - 2\varepsilon a &= 1 + 2a^2 = 2a \\
\varepsilon(\tfrac{1}{2} - a) &= a^2 - a + \tfrac{1}{2} \\
&= (a - \tfrac{1}{2})^2 - (\tfrac{1}{2})^2 + \tfrac{1}{2} \\
&= (a - \tfrac{1}{2})^2 + (\tfrac{1}{2})^2
\end{aligned}
$$

Hence

$$
\begin{aligned}
(a - \tfrac{1}{2})^2 + \varepsilon(a - \tfrac{1}{2}) + (\tfrac{1}{2})^2 &= 0 \\
[(a - \tfrac{1}{2}) + \tfrac{\varepsilon}{2}]^2 - (\tfrac{\varepsilon}{2})^2 + (\tfrac{1}{2})^2 &= 0 \\
(a - \tfrac{1}{2} + \tfrac{\varepsilon}{2})^2 = (\tfrac{\varepsilon}{2})^2 - (\tfrac{1}{2})^2 \\
&= ((\tfrac{\varepsilon}{2} - \tfrac{1}{2})(\tfrac{\varepsilon}{2} + \tfrac{1}{2})
\end{aligned}
$$

Hence $\varepsilon = 1$ and since $0 \leq c = a + \varepsilon \leq 1$ we must have $a = 0$ and $c = 1$.

In particular, we get that for $a = c = x$, $x \oplus x$ is always defined and we have

$$
x \oplus x = \frac{x^2}{1 - 2x + 2x^2}
$$

For example, we have

$$
\begin{aligned}
0 \oplus 0 &= 0 \\
1 \oplus 1 &= 1 \\
\tfrac{1}{2} \oplus \tfrac{1}{2} &= \tfrac{1}{2}
\end{aligned}
$$

3. Let us check what happens when $c = d$.

We get

$$
\begin{aligned}
[a, b] \oplus c &= \frac{bc}{1 - a(1 - c) - c(1 - b)} \\
&= \frac{bc}{1 - a + ac - c + bc} \\
&= \frac{bc}{1 - a - c + c(a + b)}
\end{aligned}
$$

5.3   Voting

Suppose we have three candidates for the presidency of a country, a, b and c. The country has a population of one million and the voters are asked to vote for one candidate. Assume that 200,000 voted for candidate a, 350,000 for candidate b and 100,000 for candidate c. 350,000 did not bother to vote. We can associate a number between 0 and 1 with each canfidate. Let $x = 0.2, y = 0.35$ and $z = 0.1$. We can write the results as

$$x : a, y : b \text{ and } z : c$$

We want to rank the relative strength of the candidates, in other words, how stronger is candidate a relative to b, a relative to c and b relative to c.

The simplest, most reasonable way is to check the relative number of votes each candidate gets relative to the other. So we have

$$S(a, b) = \frac{x}{x + y}$$

$$S(a, c) = \frac{x}{x + z}$$

$$S(b, c) = \frac{y}{y + z}$$

$$S(b, a) = \frac{y}{y + x}$$

$$S(c, a) = \frac{z}{z + x}$$

$$S(c, b) = \frac{z}{z + y}$$

We need to interpret these numbers. We can say the numbers give a measure of how much the voters prefer one candidate over another. If we look at

$$S(a, a) = \frac{x}{x + x} = \tfrac{1}{2}$$

we see that $\tfrac{1}{2}$ means equal preference. So if $S(a, b) > \tfrac{1}{2}$ then the voters prefer a to b, and if $S(a, b) < \tfrac{1}{2}$ then the voters prefer b to a. We also have

$$S(\alpha, \beta) = 1 - S(\beta, \alpha).$$

Let us now check the connections between $S(a, b), S(b, c)$ and $S(a, c)$.

$$S(a, b) = \frac{x}{x + y}$$

or equivalently

$$y = \frac{1 - S(a,b)}{S(a,b)} x$$

$$S(b,c) = \frac{y}{y+z}$$

or equivalently

$$z = \frac{1 - S(b,c)}{S(b,c)} y$$

and

$$S(a,c) = \frac{x}{x+z}$$

or equivalently

$$z = \frac{1 - S(a,c)}{S(a,c)} x.$$

Therefore we must have the following connection

$$\frac{S(a,c)}{1 - S(a,c)} = \frac{S(a,b)}{1 - S(a,b)} \cdot \frac{S(b,c)}{1 - S(b,c)}.$$

If we solve $S(a,c)$ in terms of $S(a,b)$ and $S(b,c)$ we get

$$S(a,c) = \frac{S(a,b)S(b,c)}{1 - S(a.b) - S(b,c) + 2S(a,b)S(b,c)}.$$

or recalling the Dempster–Shafer combination, we get

$$S(a,c) = S(a,b) \oplus S(b,c).$$

This means that if we know the preference numbers of a over b and of b over c then we can take the transitive preference of a over c to be the Dempster–Shafer combination.

6 Tableaux for L_2

L_2 has 3 values $\{0, \frac{1}{2}, 1\}$. The corresponding tableaux for 3 values should have 3 entries,

$$\Delta \| \Theta \| \Gamma$$

Δ is left, Θ is middle and Γ is right. To keep things simple, assume Δ, Θ, Γ are sets (not sequences).

Δ are the formulas that are supposed to get value 1, Θ are the formulas that are supposed to get $\frac{1}{2}$ and Γ is the set of formulas that are supposed to get 0. Remember that 1 corresponds to $\top$ and 0 corresponds to $\bot$.

Let us see whether $A \vee \neg A$ can get value 0.

$$\varnothing \| \varnothing \| A \vee \neg A.$$

What rule do we have for disjunction in the right position. We check the truth table for $p \vee q$ and see what values for p and q can give value 0 to $p \vee q$. We see that both p and q must be 0. Therefore:

Right $\vee$ rule:

$$\Delta \| \Theta \| \Gamma, A \vee B$$
$$|$$
$$\Delta \| \Theta \| \Gamma, A, B.$$

What happens if $A \vee B$ is in the middle? How can $A \vee B$ get alue $\frac{1}{2}$? Looking at the table there are 3 possibilities. ($A = \frac{1}{2}$ and $B = 0$) or ($A = \frac{1}{2}$ and $B = \frac{1}{2}$) or ($A = 0$ and $B = \frac{1}{2}$).

Hence the rule is

Middle $\vee$ rule

$$\Delta \| \Theta, A \vee B \| \Gamma$$

$$\Delta \| \Theta, A \| \Gamma, B \qquad \Delta \| \Theta, A, B \| \Gamma \qquad \Delta \| \Theta, B \| \Gamma, A$$

Now the last possibility, how can $A \vee B$ get value 1? For this we must have that either $A = 1$ and B does not matter or that $B = 1$ and A does not matter. So

Left $\vee$ rule

$$\Delta, A \vee B \| \Theta \| \Gamma$$

$$\Delta, A \| \Theta \| \Gamma \qquad \Delta, B \| \Theta \| \Gamma.$$

We now check negation. If $\neg A$ is X then A is $1 - X$. This means reflectin around the value $\frac{1}{2}$, i.e.

$$\neg 1 = 0, \neg 0 = 1, \neg \tfrac{1}{2} = \tfrac{1}{2}.$$

Left $\neg$ rule

$$\Delta, \neg A \| \Theta \| \Gamma$$
$$|$$
$$\Delta \| \Theta \| \Gamma, A.$$

Middle $\neg$ rule

$$\Delta \| \Theta, \neg A \| \Gamma$$
$$|$$
$$\Delta \| \Theta, A \| \Gamma.$$

Right ¬ rule

$$\Delta \| \Theta \| \Gamma, \neg A$$

$$\Delta, A \| \Theta \| \Gamma.$$

A tableaux is *closed* if the same A appears in mor than one side.

We can now do the tableaux algorithm for $\varnothing \| \varnothing \| A \vee \neg A$:

$$\varnothing \| \varnothing \| A \vee \neg A$$

$$\varnothing \| \varnothing \| A, \neg A$$

$$A \| \varnothing \| A$$

closed

How about the tableaux for giving $A \vee \neg A$ value $\frac{1}{2}$?

From the open part we see we can give A value $\frac{1}{2}$.

Let us now check another candidate for a three valued tautology, anmely

$$p \wedge q \Rightarrow p$$

Let us see if we can give it the value $\frac{1}{2}$. We want to check the tableau

$$\varnothing \| p \wedge q \Rightarrow p \| \varnothing.$$

We need rules for $\wedge$ and for $\Rightarrow$.

Right $\Rightarrow$ rule

How can $A \Rightarrow B$ get value 0? The only way is that $A = 1$ and $B = 0$. Hence

$$\Delta, \| \Theta \| \Gamma, A \Rightarrow B$$

$$\Delta, A \| \Theta \| \Gamma, B$$

Middle $\Rightarrow$ rule

How can $A \Rightarrow B$ get value $\frac{1}{2}$? There are two ways ($A = \frac{1}{2}$ and $B = 0$) or ($A = 1$ and $B = \frac{1}{2}$). Thus we have

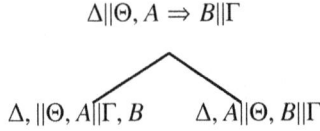

$$\Delta \| \Theta, A \Rightarrow B \| \Gamma$$

$$\Delta, \| \Theta, A \| \Gamma, B \qquad \Delta, A \| \Theta, B \| \Gamma$$

Left $\Rightarrow$ rule

For $A \Rightarrow B$ to be 1 we have six possibilities:

$$A = 0, \quad B = 0$$

$$A = 0, \quad B = \frac{1}{2}$$

$$A = 0, \quad B = 1$$

$$A = \frac{1}{2}, \quad B = 1$$

$$A = \frac{1}{2}, \quad B = \frac{1}{2}$$

$$A = \frac{1}{2}, \quad B = 1$$

$$A = 1, \quad B = 1$$

We note that if $A = 0$ we do not care what B is and if $B = 1$ we don't care what A is. So really we can simplify to three possibilities $A = 0$ or $B + 1$ or $A = B = \frac{1}{2}$. So we get

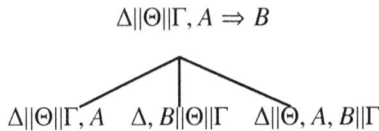

$$\Delta \| \Theta \| \Gamma, A \Rightarrow B$$

$$\Delta \| \Theta \| \Gamma, A \quad \Delta, B \| \Theta \| \Gamma \quad \Delta \| \Theta, A, B \| \Gamma$$

We now consider $\wedge$:

For $A \wedge B$ to be 0 it is enough to have $A = 0$ or $B = 0$. For $A \wedge B$ to be 1, we must have that both $A = B = 1$. For $A \wedge B$ to be $\frac{1}{2}$ we must have either ($A = \frac{1}{2}$ and $B = \frac{1}{2}$) or ($B = \frac{1}{2}$ and $A = 1$), or ($B = 1$ and $A = \frac{1}{2}$). So here are the rules.

Right $\wedge$ rule

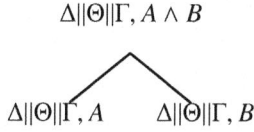

Left ∧ rule

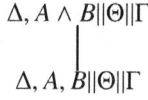

Middle ∧ rule

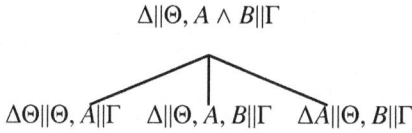

Let us now check $\varnothing \| p \wedge q \Rightarrow p \| \varnothing$.

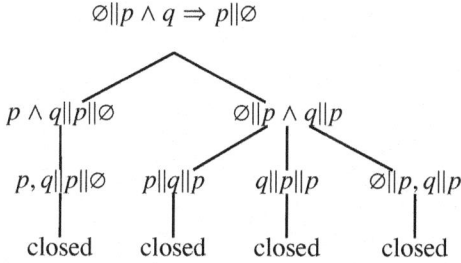

CHAPTER 3

Introducing forward rules

In Chapter 1 we presented a method for checking whether a conclusion B follows logically from a set of assumptions $A_1, \ldots, A_n$, namely that of using truth tables to check whether

$$[A_1 \wedge \cdots \wedge A_n] \Rightarrow B$$

is a tautology. This method, although always effective, is not always the most efficient and immediate. Consider the following example:

$$\frac{\begin{array}{c} p \Rightarrow q \\ \neg r \vee q \Rightarrow s \vee p \\ q \end{array}}{s \vee q}$$

If we follow our method, we have to check whether the following formula is a tautology:

$$[(p \Rightarrow q) \wedge [(\neg r \vee q) \Rightarrow (s \vee p)] \wedge q] \Rightarrow s \vee q$$

Because there are four propositions in the formula, we need a table with $2^4 = 16$ rows to do that. Yet we can immediately see that the conclusion follows from the assumption, because we have q as an assumption and $s \vee q$ as a conclusion.

This suggests a new approach. Given a set of assumptions, we would like to manipulate and combine them, step by step, until we can see that the conclusion follows. We are looking for small combinatorial steps which can lead from the assumptions to the conclusion. The approach we shall present relies on the observation that if $A_1 \wedge \cdots \wedge A_n \Rightarrow B$ is a tautology and $A_1 \wedge \cdots \wedge A_n \wedge B \Rightarrow C$ is a tautology, then $A_1 \wedge \cdots \wedge A_n \Rightarrow C$ is a tautology. We can write this in the form of an argument, so that

$$\frac{\begin{array}{c} A_1 \wedge \cdots \wedge A_n \Rightarrow B \\ A_1 \wedge \cdots \wedge A_n \wedge B \Rightarrow C \end{array}}{A_1 \wedge \cdots \wedge A_n \Rightarrow C}$$

The above rule (which is called the *cut* rule, for cutting out the intermediate formula B) allows us to find the intermediate B which help us derive the required C. We are using the B as a lemma, which is a perfectly natural way of thinking for humans. For example,

I have one orange and one apple implies I have two fruit

$$\frac{\text{I have one orange and one apple and I have two fruit implies}}{\text{I have one orange and one apple implies I have an even number of fruit}}$$

Notice that we do not need to use all of the $A_1, \ldots, A_n$ when deriving the C from the intermediate formula B. Certainly we can conclude that I have an even number of fruit from the fact that I have two fruit, without knowing what those fruit are.

EXAMPLE 3.1. From the assumptions below, we will attempt to derive D by using the *modus ponens* argument from Chapter 1, namely that from P and $P \Rightarrow Q$ we can obtain Q.

1. $A \Rightarrow B$

2. A

3. $B \Rightarrow C \lor D$

4. $\neg C$

We can argue as follows (the numbered lines give the next steps in the argument):

5. We can get B from assumptions 1 and 2:

$$\frac{A, \; A \Rightarrow B}{B}$$

6. From intermediate step 5 and assumption 3 we can get $C \lor D$:

$$\frac{B, \; B \Rightarrow C \lor D}{C \lor D}$$

7. From assumption 4 and intermediate step 6 we get D:

$$\frac{\neg C, \; C \lor D}{D}$$

Here we have only used simple elementary steps, with lines 5 and 6 being the intermediate steps for getting to the conclusion.

We want to formulate a body of rules which can be used to reach conclusions from assumptions and do the same job as the truth tables. Deriving such a method is crucial in the case of predicate logic (the topic of later chapters) because truth tables cannot be drawn up for predicate logic, and the only semi-mechanical way to generate the set of all valid formulae of predicate logic is via rules. In this book we shall present two methods of using rules. In the above two examples, we worked forwards from the assumptions to the conclusion, and thus we were using a *forward method*. In later chapters we shall change to using *backward methods* in which we start with the conclusion, and work backwards to the assumptions.

We use the notation

$$\frac{A_1,\ldots,A_n}{B}$$

to indicate a logic rule which can be used in reasoning from data. The reasoning is performed step by step; in each step we must indicate where and how the $A_1,\ldots,A_n$ are obtained and which rule is used to obtain B. The choice of rules is up to us and there are various standard systems of rules. Section 4 will give the formal definition of the reasoning process. Let us denote by

$$A_1,\ldots,A_n \vdash_R B$$

the notion of B being obtainable from $A_1,\ldots,A_n$ using the set of rules R. We must show that R does exactly what the table does, i.e. we must show that R satisfies the following *soundness and completeness* conditions:

Soundness: If $A_1\wedge\cdots\wedge A_n \vdash_R B$ then $A_1\wedge\cdots\wedge A_n\Rightarrow B$ is a tautology.

Completeness: If $A_1 \wedge \cdots \wedge A_n \Rightarrow B$ is a tautology then $A_1 \wedge \cdots \wedge A_n \vdash_R B$.

In Chapter 7, we will prove that the backward reasoning method to be introduced in Chapter 4 satisfies the soundness and completeness condition.

1   Natural deduction rules

We now discuss the rules for reasoning forwards from the assumptions to the conclusion. The rules will be divided into two categories, *introduction* rules and *elimination* rules. The introduction rules will enable us to combine formulae by introducing conjunctions, disjunctions, implications, and so forth. The elimination rules permit us to break up formulae into valid constituent subformulae. By judicious use of the introduction and elimination rules, we are able to combine subformulae of our assumptions to reach the desired conclusion (should it be a logical consequence of the assumptions). To explain further the rationale behind the rules, we will look at the individual rules, starting with those for conjunction.

1.1 Rules for conjunction

The truth table for conjunction is

A	B	$A \wedge B$
$\top$	$\top$	$\top$
$\bot$	$\top$	$\bot$
$\top$	$\bot$	$\bot$
$\bot$	$\bot$	$\bot$

We want to write rules which correspond exactly to the truth table. The rules will have two forms, corresponding to the two directions of the truth table:

1. $A = \top$ and $B = \top$ together imply $A \wedge B = \top$.

2. $A \wedge B$ is $\top$ only in the case mentioned in point 1.

The first form is dealt with in the *introduction* rules, because we introduce the conjunction $A \wedge B$ when both A and B are true. So we write

$$(\wedge I) \ \frac{A, \ B}{A \wedge B}$$

which states that $A = \top$ and $B = \top$ together imply that $A \wedge B = \top$. The $\wedge I$ stands for 'and introduction'. The *elimination* rule deals with the second rule form. Once we know $A \wedge B = \top$, what can we say about the rows in the truth table which give this result? The rule has two components, and says

$$(\wedge E) \ \frac{A \wedge B}{A} \ \text{ and } \ \frac{A \wedge B}{B}$$

which states that $A \wedge B = \top$ implies $A = \top$ and $A \wedge B = \top$ implies $B = \top$. In other words, when a conjunction is true, both its left and right conjuncts are true. The $\wedge E$ stands for 'and elimination'.

EXAMPLE 3.2. We will show that from the assumptions $p \wedge q$ and $r \wedge s$ we can derive the conclusion $p \wedge s$. Applying the first component of the $(\wedge E)$ rule to $p \wedge q$, we can derive p, and using the second component on $r \wedge s$ gives us s. Combining these via the $(\wedge I)$ rule on p and s gives us the desired $p \wedge s$.

1.2 Rules for disjunction

The truth table for disjunction is

A	B	$A \vee B$
$\top$	$\top$	$\top$
$\bot$	$\top$	$\top$
$\top$	$\bot$	$\top$
$\bot$	$\bot$	$\bot$

The first three rows in the table, those in which either $A = \top$ or $B = \top$, yield $A \lor B = \top$. Hence the 'or introduction' rule is

$$(\lor I) \; \frac{A}{A \lor B} \; \text{and} \; \frac{B}{A \lor B}$$

We could have a rule which said that $A \lor B = \top$ when $A = \top$ and $B = \top$, but this is subsumed by the two rules we have presented. No other rows give $A \lor B = \top$, and we must reflect this fact through the 'or elimination' rule. So we must say that $A \lor B$ is true only through A being true or through B being true. There are many ways of doing this; for example, we can write

$$(\lor E1) \; \frac{A \lor B, \; \neg A}{B} \qquad\qquad (\lor E2) \; \frac{A \lor B, \; \neg B}{A}$$

which will achieve the desired effect. Alternatively we can use the following rule, which is usually to be found in textbooks:

$$(\lor E) \; \frac{A \Rightarrow C, \; B \Rightarrow C, \; A \lor B}{C}$$

$(\lor E)$ is a better rule to adopt, and we take it as part of our official set of natural deduction rules. The reasons for adopting one rule and not another are mainly because of convenience, and elegance. In this book we will use all three rules for $\lor$: we use $(\lor E)$ as a basic rule, and since $(\lor E1)$ and $(\lor E2)$ can be proved from $(\lor E)$ and the rules for $\neg$, we can use them as well.

EXAMPLE 3.3. From the assumptions $p \land \neg q$ and $q \lor r$ we can derive $r \lor s$ as a conclusion. Using the second component of the $(\land E)$ rule on $p \land \neg q$, we can derive $\neg q$, and using $(\lor E1)$ on $\neg q$ and $q \lor r$ gives us r. From this, we use the $(\lor I)$ rule to introduce the new disjunct s, giving the conclusion $r \lor s$.

1.3 Rules for implication

The table for $\Rightarrow$ is

A	B	$A \Rightarrow B$
$\top$	$\top$	$\top$
$\bot$	$\top$	$\top$
$\top$	$\bot$	$\bot$
$\bot$	$\bot$	$\top$

1. If $A = \bot$ or $B = \top$ then $A \Rightarrow B = \top$.

2. There are no other cases than point 1 where $A \Rightarrow B = \top$.

We can write these as

$$(\Rightarrow I1)\ \frac{\neg A}{A \Rightarrow B} \qquad (\Rightarrow I2)\ \frac{B}{A \Rightarrow B} \qquad (\Rightarrow E1)\ \frac{A \Rightarrow B}{\neg A \vee B}$$

but these rules involve $\vee$ and $\neg$ and are thus not rules which purely deal with implication. Further on in this book, we shall show how conjunction, disjunction and negation may be expressed in terms of implication, which we shall take as a 'fundamental' connective. It is better, therefore, for us to use pure rules for $\Rightarrow$. These are

$$(\Rightarrow E)\ \frac{A,\ A \Rightarrow B}{B}$$

and

$$(\Rightarrow I)\ \text{If}\ \frac{\{\text{assumptions}\},\ A}{B}\ \text{is valid then}\ \frac{\{\text{assumptions}\}}{A \Rightarrow B}\ \text{is also valid}$$

We will use ($\Rightarrow$I) and ($\Rightarrow$E) as our rules for $\Rightarrow$.

EXAMPLE 3.4. To show s from the assumptions

1. $p \Rightarrow q$

2. p

3. $q \vee r \Rightarrow s$

we proceed as follows.

4. From assumptions 1 and 2 using ($\Rightarrow$E) we get q.

5. From intermediate result 4 using ($\vee$I) we get $q \vee r$.

6. From intermediate result 5 and assumption 3 using ($\Rightarrow$E) we get s.

We can show this as a structured argument:

$$\frac{\dfrac{\dfrac{p,\ p \Rightarrow q}{q}}{q \vee r} \qquad q \vee r \Rightarrow s}{s}$$

1.4   Rules for negation

The truth table for $\neg$ is

A	$\neg A$
$\top$	$\bot$
$\bot$	$\top$

1. If $A = \bot$ then $\neg A = \top$.

2. $\neg A = \top$ only if $A = \bot$.

If we write the rules in the usual way we get

$$\frac{\neg A}{\neg A} \text{ and } \frac{\neg A}{\neg A}$$

which are not particularly useful, so let us write other rules which are more effective:

$$(\neg E1) \frac{\neg\neg A}{A} \text{ and } (\neg I1) \frac{A}{\neg\neg A}$$

These are not enough. We must also say that any A has two possible truth values, $\top$ and $\bot$, and no more. Thus we take

$$(\neg 2) \frac{\begin{array}{c} A \Rightarrow B \\ \neg A \Rightarrow B \end{array}}{B}$$

The usual rules for $\neg$ are

$$(\neg E) \frac{\neg A \Rightarrow B, \ \neg A \Rightarrow \neg B}{A} \text{ and } (\neg I) \frac{A \Rightarrow B, \ A \Rightarrow \neg B}{\neg A}$$

We will adopt $(\neg E)$ and $(\neg I)$ as our basic rules, although we will find $(\neg E1)$, $(\neg I1)$ and $(\neg 2)$ most useful. They can be proved from the basic rules.

EXAMPLE 3.5. We must show r from these two assumptions:

1. $p \Rightarrow (q \Rightarrow r)$

2. $p \wedge q$.

We do this by the following steps:

3. From assumption 2 using $(\wedge E)$ we derive p.

4. From intermediate result 3 and assumption 1 using $(\Rightarrow E)$ we have $q \Rightarrow r$.

5. From assumption 2 using $(\wedge E)$ we derive q.

6. From intermediate results 4 and 5 using $(\Rightarrow E)$ we have r.

In argument form this is

$$\frac{\dfrac{\dfrac{p \wedge q}{p} \qquad p \Rightarrow (q \Rightarrow r)}{q \Rightarrow r} \qquad \dfrac{p \wedge q}{q}}{r}$$

EXERCISE 3.6. Reasoning with these rules is tricky, because there is very little guidance about which rule to apply in which situation. In the following exercise, the aim is to explore the possibilities that the introduction and elimination rules permit, rather than actually to prove, the conclusion from the assumptions. Using the rules is a little like playing chess—there are many ways in which the pieces may be moved, but not all moves are good ones.

Attempt to show that the following arguments are valid (they all are):

1. $\dfrac{p \wedge q}{p \vee q}$

2. $\dfrac{p \Rightarrow q,\ \neg q}{\neg p}$

3. $\dfrac{p \vee r,\ \neg p,\ r \Rightarrow q}{q}$.

2   Using subcomputations

So far we have not altered the set of assumptions during the derivation of the conclusion. The following example requires us to do just that.

EXAMPLE 3.7. This example involves showing that the implication $p \Rightarrow r$ follows from these assumptions:

1. $p \Rightarrow q$

2. $q \Rightarrow r$.

Recall that the ($\Rightarrow$I) rule is

$$\text{If } \frac{\{\text{assumptions}\},\ A}{B} \text{ is valid then } \frac{\{\text{assumptions}\}}{A \Rightarrow B} \text{ is also valid}$$

So that by ($\Rightarrow$I) it is sufficient to show that r follows from the assumptions 1, 2 and p to show $p \Rightarrow r$. Hence we make a third assumption:

3. p

before we derive r.

4. Now assumptions 1 and 3 give q by ($\Rightarrow$E).

5. Intermediate result 4 and assumption 2 give r by ($\Rightarrow$E) .

Hence we have shown that $p \Rightarrow r$ follows from the assumptions.

The preceding example was a simple illustration of a technique which we shall often employ in this book, namely reducing the problem of proving one formula to a subproblem of proving a reduced formula from an increased set of assumptions. When making use of this technique, it is important to be aware of the boundaries of the subcomputation. If we had been trying to prove that $(A \Rightarrow C) \wedge A$ followed from the assumptions in Example 3.7, it would have been no good suddenly to add a new step 6, in which we took the A that we had assumed for the subproblem and used $(\wedge I)$ to derive $(A \Rightarrow C) \wedge A$. The A must only be used within the bounds of the subproblem $(A \Rightarrow C)$. To illustrate this, we can represent the argument in Example 3.7 in the following diagram:

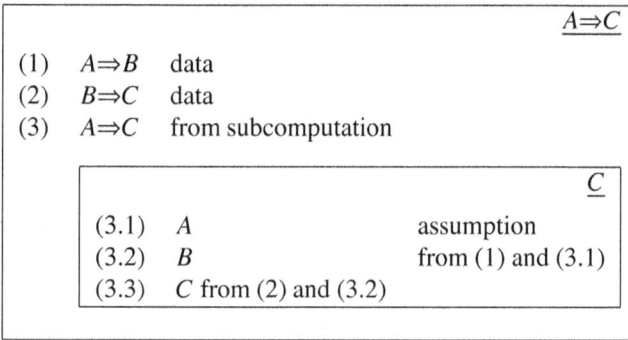

$$
\begin{array}{lll}
 & & \underline{A \Rightarrow C} \\
(1) & A \Rightarrow B & \text{data} \\
(2) & B \Rightarrow C & \text{data} \\
(3) & A \Rightarrow C & \text{from subcomputation} \\
 & & \underline{C} \\
 & (3.1) & A \text{assumption} \\
 & (3.2) & B \text{from (1) and (3.1)} \\
 & (3.3) & C \text{ from (2) and (3.2)}
\end{array}
$$

The underlined formula in the upper right-hand corner of the box is what we wish to prove. If we manage to prove it (as in this case) it will also be the last formula in the box. The first formulae in the box are the assumptions. Further formulae can be added after the assumptions by using the natural deduction rules as in the previous examples. We need to mark each line whether it is an assumption or indicate from what previous lines it is derived and by which rules. If we need to use a subcomputation to prove any of the new formulae, including the 'goal' formula, we start a new box after the formula we wish to prove. This new box has its 'subgoal' formula (in this case C) in the upper right-hand corner, and as the last formula in the box. The added assumptions are put in at the start of the box (in this case A). Again, the natural deduction rules are used to derive any intermediate formulae needed. *The added assumptions may only be used within their own box (or any box included in their box),* although subcomputations can access assumptions in their outer boxes. If we attempt to draw a diagram for the attempted derivation of $(A \Rightarrow C) \wedge A$ given above, we run into problems.

$$\begin{array}{|l|}
\hline
\qquad\qquad \underline{(A{\Rightarrow}C)\wedge A} \\
A{\Rightarrow}B \\
B{\Rightarrow}C \\
A{\Rightarrow}C \\
\qquad\boxed{\begin{array}{l} \qquad \underline{C} \\ A \\ C \end{array}} \\
\times \quad (A{\Rightarrow}C)\wedge A \\
\hline
\end{array}$$

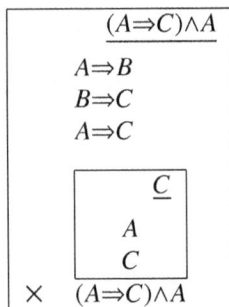

The last line in the outer box cannot be derived, because the A is not available outside the box in which it was introduced. A more formal description of the box representation of proofs will be given later.

To prove that a formula is a tautology, we must show that it can be derived from the empty set of assumptions. Recall that an argument with assumptions $A_1, \ldots, A_n$ and conclusion B is logically valid if and only if $[A_1 \wedge \cdots \wedge A_n] {\Rightarrow} B$ is a tautology. Now any formula B is equivalent to the formula $\top {\Rightarrow} B$, where $\top$ is truth. So to show that a formula B is a tautology is the same as showing that $\top {\Rightarrow} B$ is a tautology, and thus that the argument with assumption $\top$ and conclusion B is valid. Since $\top$ is always given, we should show that the argument with no assumptions and the conclusion B is valid.

EXAMPLE 3.8. $p \vee \neg p$ is a tautology provided

$$\frac{\text{nothing}}{p \vee \neg p}$$

is valid. By the ($\Rightarrow$I) rule, since

$$\frac{p}{p \vee \neg p}$$

is valid (by the ($\vee$I) rule), so is

$$\frac{\text{nothing}}{p \Rightarrow p \vee \neg p}$$

Similarly, since

$$\frac{\neg p}{p \vee \neg p}$$

is valid (again by the (∨I) rule), so is

$$\frac{\text{nothing}}{\neg p \Rightarrow p \vee \neg p}$$

By using (¬2) we have

$$\frac{\begin{array}{c} p \Rightarrow p \vee \neg p \\ \neg p \Rightarrow p \vee \neg p \end{array}}{p \vee \neg p}$$

as required.

EXERCISE 3.9. Prove the following tautologies from the earlier Exercise 1.6, this time using the forward rules instead of the truth tables used then.

1. $(p \vee q) \wedge \neg p \Rightarrow q$

2. $(\neg q \Rightarrow \neg p) \Rightarrow (p \Rightarrow q)$

Consider the tautology $((p \Rightarrow q) \Rightarrow p) \Rightarrow p$ which was also shown to be a tautology in Exercise 1.6. To show this, we must demonstrate that the argument

$$\frac{\text{nothing}}{((p \Rightarrow q) \Rightarrow p) \Rightarrow p}$$

is valid. By (⇒I) we have to show

$$\frac{(p \Rightarrow q) \Rightarrow p}{p}$$

How can we show p from the data $(p \Rightarrow q) \Rightarrow p$? The only way we have is to show $(p \Rightarrow q)$ and then use (⇒E). We thus show

$$\frac{(p \Rightarrow q) \Rightarrow p}{p \Rightarrow q}$$

which by (⇒I) is shown by proving

$$\frac{p, (p \Rightarrow q) \Rightarrow p}{q}$$

At this point we grind to a halt, as none of the rules seem to help to prove this argument. In fact this argument is invalid; we can let $p = \top$ and $q = \bot$. In Chapter 1, however, we showed our original argument to be a tautology via truth tables, so our method of reasoning with rules should be powerful enough to prove it as well.

We will leave this problem until the next chapter, since the solution lies in a different way of using rules. In the meantime remember the following: truth tables are mechanical—when you use truth tables you are assured of finding an answer. When you use natural deduction rules you need ingenuity; you may not find an answer at all. There are certain problems in the logic literature involving a few simple assumptions and a simple conclusion, which have required hundreds of reasoning steps to prove. Do not, therefore, be surprised if several intermediate steps (though hopefully not hundreds) are needed to solve Exercise 3.10 below.

EXERCISE 3.10.

1. Derive the rules ($\Rightarrow$I1), ($\Rightarrow$I2) and ($\Rightarrow$E1) from ($\Rightarrow$I) and ($\Rightarrow$E) and the negation rules.

2. Show the following using the natural deduction rules:

   (a) $\dfrac{p\Rightarrow(q\Rightarrow r)}{p\wedge q\Rightarrow r}$

   (b) $\dfrac{p\vee q\Rightarrow r}{(p\Rightarrow r)\wedge(q\Rightarrow r)}$

   (c) $\dfrac{\text{nothing}}{q\Rightarrow(p\Rightarrow q)}$

   (d) $\dfrac{\text{nothing}}{p\Rightarrow p}$

   (e) $\dfrac{\neg(p\Rightarrow q)}{p\wedge\neg q}$

   (f) $\dfrac{\neg p\vee q}{p\Rightarrow q}$

3 Example proofs

In this section, we present a series of proofs using the box notation. Together they illustrate how the natural deduction rules should be used and, in conjunction with the exercises included in the section, give proofs of some of the common equivalences of propositional logic. We begin with some proofs which use the introduction and elimination rules for $\wedge$, $\vee$ and $\Rightarrow$, before progressing to the rules for negation, which often involve more convoluted proofs.

Given a problem to prove of the form $\mathcal{P} \vdash A$ (sometimes we write $\mathcal{P} \vdash ?A$ to indicate that we want to show this) we refer to the wffs in $\mathcal{P}$ as *data* and to A as a goal.[1] In the course of the proof (computation), we may need to show $C \Rightarrow D$;

---

[1] In Section 11.1 $\mathcal{P}$ is referred to as the *database* and A as the *query*. The reasoning process in Chapter 11 is non-monotonic.

we start a new subcomputation box with C as the *assumption* (actually additional data) and D as the goal within that subcomputation.

3.1 Proofs using ∧, ∨ and ⇒ rules

We start by proving that ∧ is both commutative and associative.

1. $P{\wedge}Q \vdash Q{\wedge}P$

			$Q{\wedge}P$
(1)	$P{\wedge}Q$	data	
(2)	Q	(∧E) on (1)	
(3)	P	(∧E) on (1)	
(4)	$Q{\wedge}P$	(∧I) on (3),(2)	

2. $P{\wedge}(Q{\wedge}R) \vdash (P{\wedge}Q){\wedge}R$

			$(P{\wedge}Q){\wedge}R$
(1)	$P{\wedge}(Q{\wedge}R)$	data	
(2)	P	(∧E) on (1)	
(3)	$Q{\wedge}R$	(∧E) on (1)	
(4)	Q	(∧E) on (3)	
(5)	$P{\wedge}Q$	(∧I) on (4),(2)	
(6)	R	(∧E) on (3)	
(7)	$(P{\wedge}Q){\wedge}R$	(∧I) on (5),(6)	

Next we prove some properties of implication, showing that anything implies something which is true, that implication distributes over conjunctions on the right, and that nested implications have the effect of conjunctive conditions.

3. $Q \vdash P{\Rightarrow}Q$

			$P{\Rightarrow}Q$
(1)	Q	data	
(2)	$P{\Rightarrow}Q$	subcomputation	

			Q
(2.1)	P	assumption	
(2.2)	Q	from (1)	

4. $P{\Rightarrow}Q{\land}R \vdash (P{\Rightarrow}Q){\land}(P{\Rightarrow}R)$

		$(P{\Rightarrow}Q){\land}(P{\Rightarrow}R)$
(1)	$P{\Rightarrow}Q \land R$	data
(2)	$P{\Rightarrow}Q$	subcomputation

			Q
	(2.1)	P	assumption
	(2.2)	$Q{\land}R$	($\Rightarrow$E) on (1),(2.1)
	(2.3)	Q	($\land$E) on (2.2)

(3)	$P{\Rightarrow}R$	subcomputation

			R
	(3.1)	P	assumption
	(3.2)	$Q{\land}R$	($\Rightarrow$E) on (1),(3.1)
	(3.3)	R	($\land$E) on (3.2)

(4)	$(P{\Rightarrow}Q){\land}(P{\Rightarrow}R)$	$\land$I on (2),(3)

5. $P{\Rightarrow}(Q{\Rightarrow}R) \vdash P{\land}Q{\Rightarrow}R$

		$P{\land}Q{\Rightarrow}R$
(1)	$P{\Rightarrow}(Q{\Rightarrow}R)$	data
(2)	$P{\land}Q{\Rightarrow}R$	subcomputation

			R
	(2.1)	$P{\land}Q$	assumption
	(2.2)	P	($\land$E) on (2.1)
	(2.3)	$Q{\Rightarrow}R$	($\Rightarrow$E) on (1),(2.2)
	(2.4)	Q	($\land$E) on (2.1)
	(2.5)	R	($\Rightarrow$E) on (2.3),(2.4)

Finally in this group, we illustrate the use of ($\lor$E).

6. $B, R{\lor}S{\Rightarrow}A, R{\lor}S, A{\land}R{\Rightarrow}C, B{\land}S{\Rightarrow}C \vdash C$

```
                                                        C
   (1)   B                data
   (2)   R∨S⇒A            data
   (3)   R∨S              data
   (4)   A∧R⇒C            data
   (5)   B∧S⇒C            data
   (6)   A                (⇒E) on (2),(3)
   (7)   R⇒C              subcomputation

            ┌───────────────────────────────────┐
            │                            C        │
            │   (7.1)   R       assumption        │
            │   (7.2)   A∧R     (∧I) on (6),(7.1) │
            │   (7.3)   C       (⇒E) on (4),(7.2) │
            └───────────────────────────────────┘

   (8)   S⇒C              subcomputation

            ┌───────────────────────────────────┐
            │                            C        │
            │   (8.1)   S       assumption        │
            │   (8.2)   B∧S     (∧I) on (1),(8.1) │
            │   (8.3)   C       (⇒E) on (5),(8.2) │
            └───────────────────────────────────┘

   (9)   C                (∨E) on (3),(7),(8)
```

EXERCISE 3.11. Show that the following arguments are valid, using the rules
(∧I), (∧E), (∨I), (∨E), (⇒I) and (⇒E).

1. $P∧Q⇒R ⊢ P⇒(Q⇒R)$

2. $(P⇒Q)∧(Q⇒R) ⊢ P⇒R$

3. $P⇒R, Q⇒S ⊢ P∧Q⇒R∧S$

3.2   Proofs involving negation rules

We start with a few relatively simple proofs using the negation rules. We use the
¬I rule $A⇒B$, $A⇒¬B ⊢ ¬A$ in both proofs, in the following manner. We select a
formula to play the role of B, and use two subcomputations to show that we have
both $A⇒B$ and $A⇒¬B$ and thus we must have $¬A$.

7. $P⇒Q ⊢ ¬(P∧¬Q)$

$$\overline{\neg(P \wedge \neg Q)}$$

(1) $P \Rightarrow Q$ data
(2) $\neg(P \wedge \neg Q)$ subcomputation

$$\overline{Q}$$

(2.1.1) $P \wedge \neg Q$ assumption
(2.1.2) P ($\wedge$E) on (2.1.1)
(2.1.3) Q ($\Rightarrow$E) on (1),(2.1.2)

$$\overline{\neg Q}$$

(2.2.1) $P \wedge \neg Q$ assumption
(2.2.2) $\neg Q$ ($\wedge$E) on (2.2.1)

8. $\vdash \neg(P \wedge \neg P)$

$$\overline{\neg(P \wedge \neg P)}$$

(1) $\neg(P \wedge \neg P)$ subcomputation

$$\overline{P}$$

(1.1.1) $P \wedge \neg P$ assumption
(1.1.2) P ($\wedge$E) on (1.1.1)

$$\overline{\neg P}$$

(1.2.1) $P \wedge \neg P$ assumption
(1.2.2) $\neg P$ ($\wedge$E) on (1.2.1)

9. $P \Rightarrow Q, \ \neg Q \vdash \neg P$

$$\overline{\neg P}$$

(1)	$P \Rightarrow Q$	data
(2)	$\neg Q$	data
(3)	$\neg P$	subcomputation

$$\overline{Q}$$

(3.1.1)	P	assumption
(3.1.2)	Q	($\Rightarrow$E) on (1),(3.1.1)

$$\overline{\neg Q}$$

(3.2.1)	P	assumption
(3.2.2)	$\neg Q$	from (2)

10. $(P \Rightarrow \neg P) \Rightarrow (\neg P \Rightarrow P) \vdash P$

$$\overline{P}$$

(1)	$(P \Rightarrow \neg P) \Rightarrow (\neg P \Rightarrow P)$	data
(2)	P	subcomputations

$$\overline{P}$$

(2.1.1)	$\neg P$	assumption
(2.1.2)	$P \Rightarrow \neg P$	subcomputation

$$\overline{\neg P}$$

(2.1.2.1)	P	assumption
(2.1.2.2)	$\neg P$	from (2.1.1)

(2.1.3)	$\neg P \Rightarrow P$	($\Rightarrow$E) on (1),(2.1.2)
(2.1.4)	P	($\Rightarrow$E) on (2.1.1),(2.1.3)

$$\overline{\neg P}$$

(2.2.1)	$\neg P$	assumption
(2.2.2)	$\neg P$	from (2.2.1)

We complete this section with a convoluted example to show how involved these proofs can become, and that there may be more than one way of proving a formula.

11. $(P{\Rightarrow}Q){\Rightarrow}Q,\ Q{\Rightarrow}P \vdash P$

$$\underline{P}$$

(1)	$(P{\Rightarrow}Q){\Rightarrow}Q$	data
(2)	$Q{\Rightarrow}P$	data
(3)	P	subcomputations

$$\underline{P{\Rightarrow}Q}$$

(3.1.1)	$\neg P$	assumption
(3.1.2)	$P{\Rightarrow}Q$	subcomputation

$$\underline{Q}$$

(3.1.2.1)	P	assumption
(3.1.2.2)	Q	subcomputations

$$\underline{P}$$

(3.1.2.2.1.1)	$\neg Q$	assumption
(3.1.2.2.1.2)	P	from (3.1.2.1)

$$\underline{\neg P}$$

(3.1.2.2.2.1)	$\neg Q$	assumption
(3.1.2.2.2.2)	$\neg P$	from (3.1.1)

$$\underline{\neg(P{\Rightarrow}Q)}$$

(3.2.1)	$\neg P$	assumption
(3.2.2)	$\neg Q$	subcomputations

$$\underline{P}$$

(3.2.2.1.1)	Q	assumption
(3.2.2.1.2)	P	$({\Rightarrow}E)$ on (2),(3.2.2.1)

$$\underline{\neg P}$$

(3.2.2.2.1)	Q	assumption
(3.2.2.2.2)	$\neg P$	from (3.2.1)

(3.2.3)	$\neg(P{\Rightarrow}Q)$	subcomputations

$$\underline{Q}$$

(3.2.3.1.1)	$P{\Rightarrow}Q$	assumption
(3.2.3.1.2)	Q	$({\Rightarrow}E)$ on (1),(3.2.3.1.1)

$$\underline{\neg Q}$$

(3.2.3.2.1)	$P{\Rightarrow}Q$	assumption
(3.2.3.2.2)	$\neg Q$	from (3.2.2)

A shorter box proof is the following:

$$\underline{P}$$

(1) $(P \Rightarrow Q) \Rightarrow Q$ data
(2) $Q \Rightarrow P$ data
(3) P subcomputations

$$\underline{P}$$

(3.1.1) $\neg P$ assumption
(3.1.2) $P \Rightarrow Q$ subcomputation

$$\underline{Q}$$

(3.1.2.1) P assumption
(3.1.2.2) Q subcomputation

$$\underline{P}$$

(3.1.2.2.1.1) $\neg Q$ assumption
(3.1.2.2.1.2) P from (3.1.2.1)

$$\underline{\neg P}$$

(3.1.2.2.2.1) $\neg Q$ assumption
(3.1.2.2.2.2) $\neg P$ from (3.1.1)

(3.1.3) Q $(\Rightarrow E)$ on (1), (3.1.2)
(3.1.4) P $(\Rightarrow E)$ on (2), (3.1.3)

$$\underline{\neg P}$$

(3.2.1) $\neg P$ assumption

EXERCISE 3.12. Show, using negation rules, that the following arguments are valid.

1. $\neg(P \wedge \neg Q) \vdash P \Rightarrow Q$

2. $\vdash ((P \Rightarrow Q) \Rightarrow P) \Rightarrow P$

3. $\vdash \neg(P \Rightarrow Q) \Rightarrow P$

4   Formal descriptions of proofs

DEFINITION 3.13 (Indices).   We now give a series of precise definitions for the notion of a correct forward proof.

1. Let $\mathbb{N}$ be the set of natural numbers and let $\mathbb{N}^*$ be the set of non-empty sequences of natural numbers. For $\alpha, \beta \in \mathbb{N}^*$, let $\alpha S \beta$ mean that α is an initial segment of β.

2. Let $\alpha < \beta$ be defined as follows:[2]

$$(a_1 \ldots a_n) < (b_1 \ldots b_m) \quad \text{iff} \quad (m \geq n) \wedge \left(\bigwedge_{i=1}^{n-1} a_i = b_i \wedge a_n < b_n \right).$$

3. Let $\alpha \oplus \beta$ mean the concatenation of the sequences α and β, and let Λ be the empty sequence.

4. Let $\alpha R \beta$ mean that α comes before β in the lexicographic ordering. It can be defined as

$$\alpha R \beta \text{ iff for some } \gamma \text{ we have } [\gamma < \beta \wedge \gamma S \alpha], \gamma \text{ is possibly empty}$$

EXAMPLE 3.14. We need the above indices for the description of computations and subcomputations. Suppose we want to prove that from the data $A \Rightarrow (B \Rightarrow C)$ it follows that $B \Rightarrow (A \Rightarrow C)$. The first line of the proof would be

$$(1) \quad A \Rightarrow (B \Rightarrow C) \quad \text{data}$$

The second line of the proof is a subcomputation showing the goal $B \Rightarrow (A \Rightarrow C)$, by assuming B and showing $A \Rightarrow C$. We write

(2)	Show $B \Rightarrow (A \Rightarrow C)$	
(2.1)	B	assumption for subcomputation 2
(2.2)	Show $A \Rightarrow C$	

We show $A \Rightarrow C$ by going to another subcomputation, namely we assume A and show C. We write

(2.2.1)	A	assumption for subcomputation (2.2)
(2.2.2)	$B \Rightarrow C$	(2.2.1) and from (1) and ($\Rightarrow$E)
(2.2.3)	C	from (2.1) and (2.2.2) and ($\Rightarrow$E)

The indices tell us what is a subcomputation of what and what is a box. Given an index α then all indices (α, a) are elements of the box α. $\alpha < \beta$ means that α is an assumption or result that β can use (e.g. in the rule ($\Rightarrow$E)). $\alpha R \beta$ simply orders the lines linearly. If we were to draw the boxes we would get

---

[2] We want to say that $\alpha = (a_1, \ldots, a_{n-1}, a_n)$ and $\beta = (a_1, \ldots, a_{n-1}, b_n, \ldots, b_m)$ and $a_n < b_n$. This means that at the point $(a_1, \ldots, a_{n-1}, b_n)$ we started a new box subcomputation and β is somewhere inside the box.

$$B \Rightarrow (A \Rightarrow C)$$

(1) $A \Rightarrow (B \Rightarrow C)$
(2) $B \Rightarrow (A \Rightarrow C)$

$$A \Rightarrow C$$

(2.1) B
(2.2) $A \Rightarrow C$

$$\underline{C}$$

(2.2.1) A
(2.2.2) $B \Rightarrow C$
(2.2.3) C

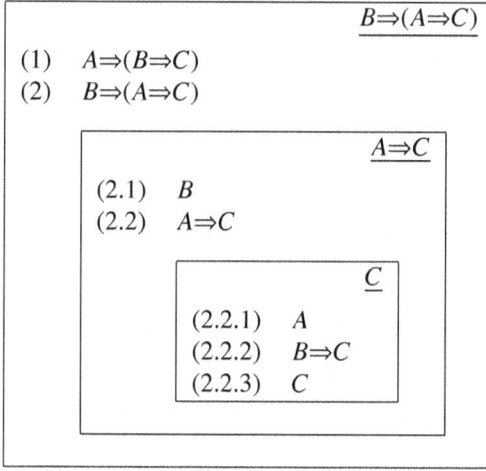

DEFINITION 3.15 (Correct annotated computation).   Let $\mathcal{P} = \{A_1, \ldots, A_n\}$ be a database and let G be a goal. Consider a set of indexed wffs $\pi = \{(\alpha_1, B_1, a_1), (\alpha_2, B_2, a_2), \ldots\}$. π is said to be a forward proof of the goal from the data iff the following conditions are satisfied:

1. π contains $((1), A_1, \text{data}), \ldots, ((n), A_n, \text{data})$ and $((m), G, a)$, for some m and a.

2. Any element $(\alpha, B, a) \in \pi$ satisfies exactly one of the following conditions.

    (a) $a = $ 'data' and $B \in \mathcal{P}$ or for some b and for some $\beta < \alpha$, $(\beta, B, b) \in \pi$ and $a = $ 'reiteration from β'.

    (b) For some a_1, a_2 and for some $\gamma_1, \gamma_2 < \alpha$, and some $B_1, B_2, (\gamma_1, B_1, a_1) \in \pi$ and $(\gamma_2, B_2, a_2) \in \pi$ and $B_2 = B_1 \Rightarrow B$ and $a = $ 'from γ_1, γ_2 using rule $(\Rightarrow E)$'.

    (c) For some b and for some $\beta < \alpha$ and some B_2, $B = B_1 \vee B_2$ and $(\beta, B_1, b) \in \pi$ and $a = $ 'from β using rule $(\vee I)$'.

    (d) For some b and for some $\beta < \alpha$, and some B_2, $B = B_2 \vee B_1$ and $(\beta, B_1, b) \in \pi$ and $a = $ 'from β using rule $(\vee I)$'.

    (e) For some b and for some $\beta < \alpha$ and some B_1, $(\beta, B \wedge B_1, b) \in \pi$ and $a = $ 'from β using rule $(\wedge E)$'.

    (f) For some b and for some $\beta < \alpha$ and some B_1, $(\beta, B_1 \wedge B, b) \in \pi$ and $a = $ 'from β using rule $(\wedge E)$'.

    (g) B is $B_1 \Rightarrow B_2$ and $(\alpha \oplus (1), B_2, \text{assumption}) \in \pi$ and for some b and for some k, $(\alpha \oplus (k), B_2, b)$ is in π, and $a = $ 'subcomputation'.

(h) B is $\neg B_1$ and for some b_1, b_2, x_1, x_2 and for some wff X, $(\alpha\oplus(1,1), B_1, b_1) \in \pi$ and $(\alpha\oplus(2,1), B_1, b_2) \in \pi$, and for some k_1 and k_2, $(\alpha\oplus(1,k_1), X, x_1) \in \pi$ and $(\alpha\oplus(2,k_2), \neg X, x_2) \in \pi$, and $a =$ 'subcomputation', and $b_1 = b_2 =$ 'assumption'.

(i) For some b_1, b_2, x_1, x_2 and for some wff X, $(\alpha \oplus (1,1), \neg B, b_1) \in \pi$, and $(\alpha \oplus (2,1), \neg B, b_2) \in \pi$, and for some k_1 and k_2, $(\alpha \oplus (1,k_1), X, x_1) \in \pi$ and $(\alpha \oplus (2,k_2), \neg X, x_2) \in \pi$, and $a =$ 'subcomputation', and $b_1 = b_2 =$ 'assumption'.

(j) For some b, b_1, b_2, x_1, x_2 and for some $\beta < \alpha$, $(\beta, C \vee D, b) \in \pi$, and $(\alpha\oplus(1,1), C, b_1) \in \pi$ and $(\alpha\oplus(2,1), D, b_2) \in \pi$, and for some k_1, k_2, $(\alpha\oplus(1,k_1), B, x_2) \in \pi$ and $(\alpha\oplus(2,k_2), B, x_2) \in \pi$, and $a =$ 'subcomputation', and $b_1 = b_2 =$ 'assumption'.

(k) $B = B_1 \wedge B_2$ and for some b_1, b_2 and for some $\beta_1, \beta_2 < \alpha$, $(\beta_1, B_1, b_1) \in \pi$ and $(\beta_2, B_2, b_2) \in \pi$, and $a =$ 'from β_1, β_2 and rule $(\wedge I)$'.

(l) α has the form $\alpha_0\oplus(1)$ or $\alpha_0\oplus(1,1)$ or $\alpha_0\oplus(2,1)$ and $a =$ 'assumption'.

DEFINITION 3.16 (Box display).   Let π be a proof. For each $(\alpha, B_1, a) \in \pi$ let $Box(\alpha) = \{(\alpha_1, C, a_1)|\alpha S \alpha_1$ and $\alpha \neq \alpha_1\}$. $Box(\alpha)$ may be empty. The following is a definition of box display. We present π linearly according to the lexicographic order of the indices. If (α, B, a) is a line we write $\alpha : \beta$; annotation.

To be a box display, each line must satisfy one of the conditions of the previous definition. The annotation of line α describes the condition which the line satisfies. If the line $\alpha : \beta$ has a box associated with it ($Box(\alpha)$ is non-empty) we indent the line inwards and put in a graphical box. At the top right-hand corner of a box we write the goal (last line of the box).

DEFINITION 3.17 (Box consequence).   Let $\mathcal{P} \vdash_{Box} G$ be defined to mean that there exists a forward proof π from $\mathcal{P}$ as data to G as goal, in the sense of Definition 3.15.

THEOREM 3.18 (Soundness of box consequence).   *If $\mathcal{P} \vdash_{Box} G$ then $\bigwedge \mathcal{P} \Rightarrow G$ is a tautology.*

Proof. Assume $\{A_1, \ldots, A_n\} \vdash_{Box} G$, with a box proof π. Then by definition, the following items are in π: $((i), A_i, \text{data}) \in \pi, i = 1, \ldots, n$, and $((m), G, a) \in \pi$ for some m. We now show that $E = \bigwedge_i A_i \Rightarrow G$ is a tautology, by induction on the size of π (complexity of the proof) and the number m.

Case 1. $m \leq n$
In this case $b =$ 'data' and $G = A_m$ and clearly E is a tautology.

Case 2. $m > n$
This case means that some proof steps were taken to get G. These steps are accord-

ing to item 2 of Definition 3.4.3, conditions (a)–(k). We examine each condition in turn.

(a) This case follows from the induction hypothesis (case (1)).

(b) By the induction hypothesis $\bigwedge A_i \Rightarrow G_1$ and $\bigwedge A_i \Rightarrow (G_1 \Rightarrow G)$ are tautologies and therefore so is E.

(c), (d) By the induction hypothesis, since $G = G_1 \vee G_2$, we get that $\bigwedge A_i \Rightarrow G$ is a tautology since $\bigwedge A_i \Rightarrow G_1$ is a tautology.

(e), (f) These cases are similar to (d) and (e).

(g) In this case G is $G_1 \Rightarrow G_2$ and we enter a subcomputation whose assumption is $((m, 1), G_1, \text{assumption})$ and conclusion (goal) is $((m, k), G_2, b)$.

Let $\pi_m = \{(\alpha^*, X, x) \mid ((m) \oplus \alpha, X, x) \in \pi\} \cup \{((i), B_i, \text{data}) \mid i = 1, \ldots m - 1$ and $((i), B_i, b_i) \in \pi\}$, where α^* is defined as follows:

$$\alpha^* = ((n + y), X, x), \text{ whenever } \alpha = (y, X, x)$$

Then π_m is a smaller proof of G_2 from $\{A_1, \ldots, A_n, B_{n+1}, B_{m-1}\}$. By the induction hypothesis $\bigwedge A_j \wedge \bigwedge B_j \wedge G_1 \Rightarrow G_2$ and $\bigwedge A_i \Rightarrow B_j, j = 1$, are all tautologies. Hence E is a tautology.

(h) In this case $G = \neg G_1$. We create $\pi_{(m,1)}$ and $\pi_{(m,2)}$ in a similar manner to the previous case, letting

$$\pi_{(m,i)} = \{(\alpha^*, X, x) \mid ((m, i) \oplus \alpha, X, x) \in \pi\} \cup$$
$$\{((i), B_i, \text{data}) \mid i = 1, \ldots, m - 1, ((i), B_i, b_i) \in \pi\}$$

We get $\bigwedge A_i \wedge \bigwedge_j B_j \wedge G_1 \Rightarrow X$ and $\bigwedge A_i \wedge \bigwedge_j B_j \wedge G_1 \Rightarrow \neg X$ are tautologies. Hence so is E.

(i) This case is similar to the previous case.

(j) This case is a combination of $C \vee D$ and $C \Rightarrow G$ and $D \Rightarrow G$. We get that $\bigwedge A_i \Rightarrow (C \Rightarrow G), \bigwedge A_i \Rightarrow (D \Rightarrow G)$ and $\bigwedge A_i \Rightarrow C \vee D$ are all tautologies and hence E is a tautology.

(k) In this case $G = G_1 \wedge G_2$ and we get by the induction hypothesis that $\bigwedge A_i \Rightarrow G_1$ and $\bigwedge A_i \Rightarrow G_2$ are tautologies and therefore so is E.

(l) This case does not arise.

This completes the proof of the theorem. ∎

Summary

Let us conclude this chapter by presenting in Figure 3.1 a summary of the natural deduction rules.

$$(\wedge I) \frac{A, B}{A \wedge B} \qquad (\wedge E) \frac{A \wedge B}{A} \text{ and } \frac{A \wedge B}{B}$$

$$(\vee I) \frac{A}{A \vee B} \text{ and } \frac{B}{A \vee B} \qquad (\vee E1) \frac{A \vee B, \neg A}{B} \qquad (\vee E2) \frac{A \vee B, \neg B}{A}$$

$$(\vee E) \frac{A \Rightarrow C, B \Rightarrow C, A \vee B}{C}$$

$$(\Rightarrow I1) \frac{\neg A}{A \Rightarrow B} \quad (\Rightarrow I2) \frac{B}{A \Rightarrow B} \quad (\Rightarrow E1) \frac{A \Rightarrow B}{\neg A \vee B} \quad (\Rightarrow E) \frac{A, A \Rightarrow B}{B}$$

$$(\Rightarrow I): \text{If } \frac{P, A}{B} \text{ is shown to be valid then } \frac{P}{A \Rightarrow B} \text{ is also valid}$$

$$(\neg E1) \frac{\neg \neg A}{A} \quad (\neg I1) \frac{A}{\neg \neg A} \quad (\neg 2) \frac{\neg A \Rightarrow B, A \Rightarrow B}{B}$$

$$(\neg E) \frac{\neg A \Rightarrow B, \neg A \Rightarrow \neg B}{A} \quad (\neg I) \frac{A \Rightarrow B, A \Rightarrow \neg B}{\neg A}$$

$$\text{Cut rule: } \frac{P}{A} \text{ and } \frac{P, A}{B} \text{ imply } \frac{P}{B}$$

The rules ($\vee$E1), ($\vee$E2), ($\neg$E1), ($\neg$2), ($\neg$I1) and ($\neg$I2) can be proved from the other rules. The cut rule can also be proved.

Figure 3.1. Summary of natural deduction rules

CHAPTER 4

From forward to backward rules

Let us summarize the knowledge we have so far. The basic problem is that we have a database (a set of assumptions) and a query (a conclusion) and we want to know whether logically the answer to the query is yes (i.e. whether the conclusion follows logically from the assumptions). We have learnt two methods for checking that this is so. The first method, introduced in Chapter 1, constructs a truth table to check whether an implication from the assumptions to conclusion is a tautology. The second method, presented in Chapter 3, uses forward rules to reason from the assumptions, searching for the conclusion. The truth table method is mechanical and always gives an answer. The forward rules method is not completely mechanical and requires some intuition and ingenuity.

Our task in this chapter is to make the method of using rules as mechanical as possible. This attempt will lead us to a third method—the method of backward-going rules and rewrites of the database. We will develop this method from the forward rules, and progress slowly through examples.

Suppose we are given the following typical situation:

$$\begin{array}{ccc} \text{Assumptions} & & \text{Conclusion} \\ \mathcal{P} & \vdash & C \end{array}$$

Our question is whether C follows from the assumptions. We would like to give advice on how to use the rules of the previous chapter so that their application becomes as automatic and mechanical as possible.

1 Introductory heuristics

Some *heuristics* might be

H1 When the argument is of the form $\mathcal{P} \vdash A \land B$ then first show $\mathcal{P} \vdash A$ and then show $\mathcal{P} \vdash B$.

H2 When the argument is of the form $\mathcal{P} \vdash A \Rightarrow B$ then add A to the assumptions and have B as the conclusion, i.e. show $\mathcal{P} \cup \{A\} \vdash B$.

H3 When the argument is of the form $\mathcal{P} \vdash \neg A$ then it is advisable to use the $\neg$I rule; that is, to show A guess a 'good' x and show $\mathcal{P} \vDash A \Rightarrow x$ and $\mathcal{P} \vDash A \Rightarrow \neg x$.

The problem is how to guess such an x. We do this by going through all the assumptions and choosing x to be a formula whose negation appears as one of the assumptions. If no negated formula can be found in the assumptions we resort to choosing x to be any formula in the assumptions. This may not always work — although if we try all the x which are subformulae of the data and the goal then it will work. However, the guessing, although systematic, is not efficient. We now give some worked examples using H1–H3 as heuristics.

EXAMPLE 4.1. We will attempt to show that $\neg A \vee B \vdash A \Rightarrow B$.

Step 1 We will apply H2. Since the conclusion has the form of an implication we ask instead whether $\neg A \vee B, A \vdash B$. Looking at the rules of Chapter 3, we see that the nearest rule to use is $(\vee E1){:}x \vee y, \neg x \vdash y$. Its form is not exactly the same as that of our problem, but if we take $x = \neg A$ and $y = B$ we get: $\neg A \vee B, \neg\neg A \vdash B$. If we could replace A by $\neg\neg A$ we could use the above rule. But we can do this because we have another rule, namely $(\neg I1)$.

Step 2 Since $(\neg I1){:}A \vdash \neg\neg A$ we can add $\neg\neg A$ and we have to show: $\neg A \vee B, \neg\neg A \vdash B$.

Step 3 We can now get B using the $(\vee E1)$ rule.

EXAMPLE 4.2. To show $A \Rightarrow (B \Rightarrow C) \vdash \neg C \wedge B \Rightarrow \neg A$ we use H2 and try to show

$$\frac{A \Rightarrow (B \Rightarrow C), \neg C \wedge B}{\neg A}$$

Since we want to show a negation $\neg A$, we follow the advice given in H3, i.e. try to guess an x with which we can show

$$\frac{A \Rightarrow (B \Rightarrow C), \neg C \wedge B}{A \Rightarrow x} \qquad \frac{A \Rightarrow (B \Rightarrow C), \neg C \wedge B}{A \Rightarrow \neg x}$$

Which x should we guess? The advice says look for negated assumptions. We have $\neg C \wedge B$ in the data which is really $\neg C, B$; thus let us try $x = C$. It may not work, in which case we shall have to try something else. We now have to show

$$\frac{A \Rightarrow (B \Rightarrow C), \neg C \wedge B}{A \Rightarrow C} \qquad \frac{A \Rightarrow (B \Rightarrow C), \neg C \wedge B}{A \Rightarrow \neg C}$$

Putting the A into the assumptions, in accordance with H2 we have to show

$$\frac{A \Rightarrow (B \Rightarrow C), \neg C \wedge B, A}{C} \qquad \frac{A \Rightarrow (B \Rightarrow C), \neg C \wedge B, A}{\neg C}$$

The right-hand argument is obvious (x was chosen especially for that purpose). We are left now with the left-hand argument. Since we have $A, A \Rightarrow (B \Rightarrow C)$ we get $B \Rightarrow C$ and since we also have B we get C. Thus we have shown what was necessary, and the exercise is solved successfully.

EXERCISE 4.3. Show $(A \Rightarrow B), \neg B \vdash \neg A$.

1.1 Adding positive and negative assumptions

We now introduce a further, very useful, heuristic rule:

H4 To show $\mathcal{P} \vdash C$ find a 'good' x and show $\mathcal{P}, x \vdash C$ and $\mathcal{P}, \neg x \vdash C$.

This rule is often useful. As for H3, the question is how to choose x? There are two criteria to help us. One is to choose x such that many conclusions can be obtained from the assumptions $\mathcal{P}, x$. For example, if $\mathcal{P}$ happens to be

$$\{A \Rightarrow B, \quad A \Rightarrow E, \quad A \Rightarrow D\}$$

then it may be worthwhile to take $x = A$. Another criterion is to choose an x which will give the conclusion C. For example, if C is $A \lor B$ we may want to take $x = B$. Let us look at an example.

EXAMPLE 4.4. To show $A \Rightarrow B \vdash \neg A \lor B$ we follow H4 and show

$$\frac{A \Rightarrow B, x}{\neg A \lor B} \quad \text{and} \quad \frac{A \Rightarrow B, \neg x}{\neg A \lor B}$$

$x = A$ will yield B for the first case, and directly give $\neg A$ for the second, and make both cases valid. We could have tried $x = B$ but that would have turned out to be fairly complicated. For the choice $x = A$ we have to show

$$\frac{A \Rightarrow B, A}{\neg A \lor B} \quad \text{and} \quad \frac{A \Rightarrow B, \neg A}{\neg A \lor B}$$

| This is valid since
we can get B
and use ($\lor$I) | valid by direct
rule ($\lor$I) |

For the choice $x = B$ we must show

$$\frac{A \Rightarrow B, B}{\neg A \lor B} \quad \text{and} \quad \frac{A \Rightarrow B, \neg B}{\neg A \lor B}$$

| valid by direct rule | valid since $A \Rightarrow B, \neg B \vdash \neg A$
by Exercise 4.3 |

Our procedures are more mechanical now than before but still they are not completely automatic. Rules H1 and H2 seem automatic enough but H3 and H4 involve choices. Consider

$$\frac{A\Rightarrow(B\wedge C),\, A}{B\wedge C} \quad \text{and} \quad \frac{A\Rightarrow(B\Rightarrow C),\, A}{B\Rightarrow C}$$

In these arguments we immediately see that the conclusion follows from the assumption because we can use *modus ponens* immediately. If we follow heuristics H1 and H2 mechanically, for the first of the examples we have to show both the following:

$$\frac{A\Rightarrow(B\wedge C),\, A}{B} \quad \text{and} \quad \frac{A\Rightarrow(B\wedge C),\, A}{C}$$

and for the second example we must show

$$\frac{A\Rightarrow(B\Rightarrow C),\, A,\, B}{C}$$

which are both more complicated. We want to make our rules very strict so that there will not be much choice left. Notice that the heuristic rules H1 and H2 reduce the complexity of the conclusion C:

H1 To check $\mathcal{P} \vdash A\wedge B$ we check $\mathcal{P} \vdash A$ and $\mathcal{P} \vdash B$.

H2 To check $\mathcal{P} \vdash A\Rightarrow B$ we check $\mathcal{P}, A \vdash B$

so the query we have to check becomes simpler and simpler. For negation, we have

H3 To check $\mathcal{P} \vdash \neg A$ we choose an x and check $\mathcal{P}, A \vdash x$ and $\mathcal{P}, A \vdash \neg x$.

Our guidelines for x were to look through the assumptions $\mathcal{P}$ for some negated formula $\neg D$ in $\mathcal{P}$ and take $x = D$. D may be, however, much more complicated than A. We encounter a similar problem in the case of $\mathcal{P} \vdash A\vee B$ where we use H4, namely:

H4 To check $\mathcal{P} \vdash A\vee B$, look for an x such that $\mathcal{P}, x \vdash A\vee B$ and $\mathcal{P}, \neg x \vdash A\vee B$ are both valid.

Again we may be making matters more complicated, unless the choice for x is a 'good' one, in which case we cannot expect a mechanical choice. We thus want to get rid of cases such as $\neg A$ and $A\vee B$, so let us agree on a new heuristic rule:

H5 To show $\mathcal{P} \vdash A\vee B$ show instead $\mathcal{P} \vdash \neg A\Rightarrow B$ which leads to showing $\mathcal{P}, \neg A \vdash B$.

Here we are using a rewrite equivalence (see Section 2.1) of $A \lor B$ in terms of $\neg$ and $\Rightarrow$. Thus we are rid of $\lor$ at the expense of gaining a negation. So using H5, instead of showing $A \Rightarrow B \vdash \neg A \lor B$ we show $A \Rightarrow B, \neg\neg A \vdash B$ which is very easy. The next example is more complicated.

EXAMPLE 4.5. To show $\neg(\neg A \land \neg B) \vdash A \lor B$, according to H5 we show $\neg(\neg A \land \neg B)$, $\neg A \vdash B$. The next step is not so obvious. It is much more convenient when all our assumptions have the form x or the form $y \Rightarrow z$, without $\neg$ in front. Now we know that

$$\neg(\neg A \land \neg B) \equiv \neg A \Rightarrow B$$

(you can check by truth tables), and so we have to show in this case that $\neg A \Rightarrow B$, $\neg A \vdash B$, which is much easier. However, we just made a lucky guess. Is there a policy we can follow?

Note that since we are dealing with an essentially mechanical procedure we have first to transform the assumptions to the 'ready for computation' form and then apply our rules. The fact that we know (or guessed) the two sides are equivalent is not relevant.

This gives us the idea that we should look into the structure of A when we are asked to show $\mathcal{P} \vdash \neg A$. Since we have the following equivalences,

$$\begin{aligned} \neg(A \land B) &\equiv& A \Rightarrow \neg B \\ \neg(A \lor B) &\equiv& \neg A \land \neg B \\ \neg(\neg A) &\equiv& A \\ \neg(A \Rightarrow B) &\equiv& A \land \neg B \end{aligned}$$

we are led to yet another heuristic:

H6 We can replace $\neg$ by these rules:

1. Replace $\mathcal{P} \vdash \neg(A \land B)$ by $\mathcal{P}, A \vdash \neg B$
2. Replace $\mathcal{P} \vdash \neg(A \lor B)$ by $\mathcal{P} \vdash \neg A$ and $\mathcal{P} \vdash \neg B$
3. Replace $\mathcal{P} \vdash \neg\neg A$ by $\mathcal{P} \vdash A$
4. Replace $\mathcal{P} \vdash \neg(A \Rightarrow B)$ by $\mathcal{P} \vdash A$ and $\mathcal{P} \vdash \neg B$.

In each case the negative conclusion to show is reduced to a simpler conclusion, or several such simpler conclusions.

Our situation now is this: given rules H1, H2, H5 and H6, we can replace any problem of the form $\mathcal{P} \vdash C$. where C is complex, by several auxiliary problems $\mathcal{P}_i \vdash x_i$ where the x_i are either atoms q_i, or negations of atoms $\neg q_i$. The reduction can be done mechanically.

EXAMPLE 4.6. To show $\neg A \vdash A{\Rightarrow}B$ using the official rules, i.e. without using rules $\Rightarrow$I1 and $\Rightarrow$I2. Using H1 we have to show $\neg A, A \vdash B$. This requires some ingenuity. Since we have the rule $\neg\neg B \vdash B$ we show $\neg A, A \vdash \neg\neg B$. (This is a non-mechanical 'guess'.) Using recommendation H3 we show for some x (which we also guess)

$$\frac{\neg A, A}{\neg B{\Rightarrow}x} \quad \text{and} \quad \frac{\neg A, A}{\neg B{\Rightarrow}\neg x}$$

i.e. we show

$$\frac{\neg A, A, \neg B}{x} \quad \text{and} \quad \frac{\neg A, A, \neg B}{\neg x}$$

The obvious 'guess' is $x = A$. The step of choosing to show $\neg A, A \vdash \neg\neg B$ instead of $\neg A, A \vdash B$ is an 'inspiration'. A machine would not have known what to do, given the rules and recommendations which we have developed so far.

EXAMPLE 4.7. Here is another example of this sort: $\neg q{\Rightarrow}q \vdash q$ is a valid argument. How can it be shown using the rules? Since $\neg q{\Rightarrow}q$ is given in the assumptions, we might attempt to show $\neg q{\Rightarrow}q \vdash \neg q$ and then use $\neg q{\Rightarrow}q, \neg q \vdash q$. However, $\neg q{\Rightarrow}q \vdash \neg q$ is not valid (take $q = \top$). We need a non-mechanical inspiration here. We take $\neg\neg q$, instead of q, and show $\neg q{\Rightarrow}q \vdash \neg\neg q$ and since $\neg\neg q \vdash q$ is a rule, we will get the desired conclusion. We show $\neg q{\Rightarrow}q \vdash \neg\neg q$. Since this is a negation we show instead (by H3)

$$\frac{\neg q{\Rightarrow}q}{\neg q{\Rightarrow}x} \quad \text{and} \quad \frac{\neg q{\Rightarrow}q}{\neg q{\Rightarrow}\neg x}$$

We have to guess a good x. The x to guess is $x = q$. We thus show

$$\frac{\neg q{\Rightarrow}q}{\neg q{\Rightarrow}q} \quad \text{and} \quad \frac{\neg q{\Rightarrow}q}{\neg q{\Rightarrow}\neg q}$$

which can be easily done.

We see that we still need to be creative. Any hope of automatic use of the rules requires better heuristics.

EXAMPLE 4.8. To show $\neg(A{\Rightarrow}B) \vdash A{\wedge}\neg B$, following H1 we show both the following:

$$\text{(a)} \quad \frac{\neg(A{\Rightarrow}B)}{A} \quad \text{and} \quad \text{(b)} \quad \frac{\neg(A{\Rightarrow}B)}{\neg B}$$

We start with (b). We choose an x and show

$$\frac{\neg(A{\Rightarrow}B)}{B{\Rightarrow}x} \quad \text{and} \quad \frac{\neg(A{\Rightarrow}B)}{B{\Rightarrow}\neg x}$$

What do we take for x? The recommendation is to look for some negative information among the assumptions. In this case we have $\neg(A\Rightarrow B)$. We thus take $x = (A\Rightarrow B)$. We thus have to show

$$\text{(b1)} \quad \frac{\neg(A\Rightarrow B)}{B\Rightarrow(A\Rightarrow B)} \quad \text{and} \quad \text{(b2)} \quad \frac{\neg(A\Rightarrow B)}{B\Rightarrow\neg(A\Rightarrow B)}$$

Using H2 we show

$$\text{(b1*)} \quad \frac{\neg(A\Rightarrow B),\, B}{A\Rightarrow B} \quad \text{and} \quad \text{(b2*)} \quad \frac{\neg(A\Rightarrow B),\, B}{\neg(A\Rightarrow B)}$$

The second case (b2*) is valid and so we are left with the first case (b1*) which can be written as

$$\frac{\neg(A\Rightarrow B),\, A,\, B}{B}$$

which is also valid. This concludes case (b) of the example. Let us return to case (a), namely $\neg(A\Rightarrow B) \vdash A$. How about our new 'inspiration' of showing $\neg\neg A$ instead of A? Let us try to show $\neg(A\Rightarrow B) \vdash \neg\neg A$. We choose an x and show

$$\frac{\neg(A\Rightarrow B)}{\neg A\Rightarrow x} \quad \text{and} \quad \frac{\neg(A\Rightarrow B)}{\neg A\Rightarrow\neg x}$$

Following our heuristics, we take $x = (A\Rightarrow B)$. We must thus show

$$\frac{\neg(A\Rightarrow B)}{\neg A\Rightarrow(A\Rightarrow B)} \quad \text{and} \quad \frac{\neg(A\Rightarrow B)}{\neg A\Rightarrow\neg(A\Rightarrow B)}$$

Applying H2, we have to show

$$\frac{\neg(A\Rightarrow B),\, \neg A,\, A}{B} \quad \text{and} \quad \frac{\neg(A\Rightarrow B),\, \neg A}{\neg(A\Rightarrow B)}$$

The first is valid because $\neg A, A \vdash B$ was shown in Example 4.6, and the second is obviously valid.

In the last two examples we had

$$\frac{\neg(A\Rightarrow B),\, \text{something}}{\neg(A\Rightarrow B)}$$

and we stopped checking and said that it was valid. What would happen if we were to use an automatic method of computation? Let us go back to Example 4.8, to the point where we have to show

$$\frac{\neg(A\Rightarrow B),\, B}{\neg(A\Rightarrow B)}$$

If we were to continue mechanically using our rules and use heuristic H6 we would continue removing the negation, and trying to show

$$\frac{\neg(A \Rightarrow B), B}{A \wedge \neg B}$$

which brings us back to showing $\neg B$ and we may enter an infinite loop.

1.2   Restart rule

Let us collect here the mechanical principles we have so far. Given a problem of the form $\mathcal{P} \vdash C$ we can mechanically use rules H1, H2, H5 and H6 to reduce the original problem to problems of the form $\mathcal{P}_i \vdash x_i$ where x_i are atoms or their negations (i.e. $x_i = q$ or $x_i = \neg q$). We also saw, through examples such as $\neg q, q \vdash p$ $\neg q \Rightarrow q \vdash q$ and $(p \Rightarrow q) \Rightarrow p \vdash p$, that we still need rules like H3 and H4 involving ingenuity, and we have just seen that we may get stuck in a loop. Can things be made more mechanical?

Let us look at H4. This rule says that when we are stuck in showing $\mathcal{P}^* \vdash C$ we choose an x and show instead $\mathcal{P}^*, x \vdash C$ and $\mathcal{P}^*, \neg x \vdash C$. Let us try to mechanize this rule and see what happens. Suppose we start our problem with $\mathcal{P} \vdash A$. We might feel that later in our mechanical attempts to get A we are going to be stuck with some $\mathcal{P}^* \vdash C$. Now $\mathcal{P}$ contains less data than $\mathcal{P}^*$ (because our computation always increases the data) so before we embark on our computation of $\mathcal{P} \vdash A$ we might use rule H4 with $x = A$ which is a good guess. We thus replace $\mathcal{P} \vdash A$ by both $\mathcal{P}, A \vdash A$ and $\mathcal{P}, \neg A \vdash A$. Of course, $\mathcal{P}, A \vdash A$ is valid, so we have to show $\mathcal{P}, \neg A \vdash A$. What have we gained? We now have $\neg A$ as an extra assumption. Imagine that we continue the computation and get stuck at the point $\mathcal{P}^* \vdash C$. Now we also have $\neg A$, so really we are stuck at $\mathcal{P}^*, \neg A \vdash C$. Here is an ingenious trick. Suppose instead of asking $\mathcal{P}^*, \neg A \vdash C$ we ask $\mathcal{P}^*, \neg A \vdash A$ and suppose we succeed in showing A. Now we are going to have

$$\frac{\mathcal{P}^*, \neg A}{A} \quad \text{and} \quad \frac{\mathcal{P}^*, \neg A}{\neg A}$$

both valid. We can certainly show C because $A \wedge \neg A \vdash C$ is a correct rule, and we have certainly shown that $\mathcal{P}^*, \neg A \vdash A \wedge \neg A$. But look what we have done. We started with $\mathcal{P} \vdash A$ and then we got to $\mathcal{P}^* \vdash C$ and were stuck; we asked $\mathcal{P}^* \vdash A$ instead and we knew that to succeed with that is the same as to succeed with $\mathcal{P}^* \vdash C$. We have thus discovered the *restart rule*:

Restart If when starting with $\mathcal{P} \vdash A$ we get stuck at $\mathcal{P}^* \vdash C$ we can *restart* A and ask $\mathcal{P}^* \vdash A$ instead.[1]

---

[1]In fact we can restart with any previous goal (to the current goal C) and not necessarily with the original goal A. Thus we can limit restart to be activated at atomic goals C only. In general, however, there are logics where restart cannot be restricted to be activated at atomic goals only. We need to prove formally that for any $\mathcal{P}$, and A we have: $\mathcal{P} \vdash A$ with restart iff $\mathcal{P}, \neg A \vdash A$ without restart. This will be done later in Lemma 7.6.6 in the context of the completeness theorem.

You may want to clarify one point about our computation: we had $\mathcal{P}^*, \neg A \vdash A$ before, while the restart rule allows for $\mathcal{P}^* \vdash A$. This is not a problem, because we saw above that we can always add $\neg A$ to the assumptions. The restart rule is mechanical. You do not have to guess an x. All you have to do is, whenever you are stuck, try to prove the original A again.

EXAMPLE 4.9. To show $(p{\Rightarrow}q){\Rightarrow}p \vdash p$ we try to get $p{\Rightarrow}q$ while remembering that the original aim was to get p. Thus we ask $(p{\Rightarrow}q){\Rightarrow}p \vdash p{\Rightarrow}q$ which by use of H1 becomes $(p{\Rightarrow}q){\Rightarrow}p, p \vdash q$. In Section 2 we saw that as an original question the above argument is invalid (because we can have, we recall, $p = \top$ and $q = \bot$ and we will get $\top \vdash \bot$). However, this is not an original question but part of the computation of the original argument $(p{\Rightarrow}q){\Rightarrow}p, p \vdash q$. We are thus allowed to use the restart rule and ask p again. So instead of $(p{\Rightarrow}q){\Rightarrow}p, p \vdash q$ we ask $(p{\Rightarrow}q){\Rightarrow}p, p \vdash p$ which succeeds.

Another way to justify the restart rule is to notice that $((q{\Rightarrow}c){\Rightarrow}q){\Rightarrow}q$ is a tautology. Thus to ask $\mathcal{P} \vdash q$ is the *same* as to ask $\mathcal{P}, ((q{\Rightarrow}c){\Rightarrow}q){\Rightarrow}q \vdash q$. By the rule ${\Rightarrow}E$ for atoms we can try and ask $\mathcal{P}, ((q{\Rightarrow}c){\Rightarrow}q){\Rightarrow}q \vdash (q{\Rightarrow}c){\Rightarrow}q$ and by the rule for $\Rightarrow$ we ask $\mathcal{P}, ((q{\Rightarrow}c){\Rightarrow}q){\Rightarrow}q, q{\Rightarrow}c \vdash q$. We are thus back to our original query q but we have $q{\Rightarrow}c$ in the data. Since c can be any proposition, we can repeat this process over and over. Therefore we can show $\mathcal{P} \vdash q$ by showing $\mathcal{P}, q{\Rightarrow}c_i \vdash q$ for $i = 1, 2, \ldots$. Thus if we have the query c_i in the middle of a computation we can always use *modus ponens* backwards on $q{\Rightarrow}c_i$ and ask for q, i.e. we can restart q.

1.3 A heuristic for negation

So far we have mechanized the computation for the cases of $\wedge$, $\Rightarrow$ and $\vee$. We have not dealt with negation—we have not replaced rule H3, which still requires intuition. H3 says that to show $\mathcal{P} \vdash \neg A$ we choose an x wisely and show both

$$\frac{\mathcal{P}}{A{\Rightarrow}x} \quad \text{and} \quad \frac{\mathcal{P}}{A{\Rightarrow}\neg x}$$

If we show $A{\Rightarrow}x$ and we show $A{\Rightarrow}\neg x$ then we have shown $A{\Rightarrow}(\neg x \wedge x)$. This is a valid intuitive rule. $\neg x \wedge x$ is always $\bot$. So $\neg A$ and $A{\Rightarrow}\bot$ have the same truth table. Thus we can always write $A{\Rightarrow}\bot$ instead of $\neg A$ and use the rules for $\Rightarrow$. Let us check.

To show $\mathcal{P} \vdash \neg A$ we choose x and show

$$\frac{\mathcal{P}}{A{\Rightarrow}x} \quad \text{and} \quad \frac{\mathcal{P}}{A{\Rightarrow}\neg x}$$

so that we must show

$$\frac{\mathcal{P}, A}{x} \quad \text{and} \quad \frac{\mathcal{P}, A}{\neg x}$$

which is the same as showing

$$\frac{P, A}{x \wedge \neg x}$$

(since $x, \neg x \vdash x \wedge \neg x$), but $x \wedge \neg x \equiv \bot$, so we therefore show $P, A \vdash \bot$. If, on the other hand, right from the start, we write $A \Rightarrow \bot$ instead of $\neg A$ and use the rule for $\Rightarrow$ then to show $\mathcal{P} \vdash \neg A$ we show $\mathcal{P} \vdash A \Rightarrow \bot$ and hence show $\mathcal{P}, A \vdash \bot$, which is the same as before.

We have seen that $A, \neg A \vdash B$ is a valid rule. In terms of $\bot$ this rule will be $\bot \vdash B$ for any B.

We are thus led to a heuristic for negation: rewrite $\neg A$ as $A \Rightarrow \bot$ and use $\Rightarrow$ rules, pretending $\bot$ is just another atom. The only additional rule needed is $\bot \vdash B$ for any B. (Check this via truth tables.)

EXAMPLE 4.10. Let us try $A, \neg A \vdash B$ which required ingenuity before we had the negation heuristic. Rewrite the argument as $A, A \Rightarrow \bot \vdash B$. Now $A, A \Rightarrow \bot \vdash \bot$ is successful since by $\Rightarrow$E we get $\bot$ and the new negation rule yields B. This was both easy and mechanical.

EXAMPLE 4.11. Showing $\neg q \Rightarrow q \vdash q$ also required ingenuity. The argument can be re- written as $(q \Rightarrow \bot) \Rightarrow q \vdash q$. To get q (our original query) we try to ask for $q \Rightarrow \bot$ because $(q \Rightarrow \bot) \Rightarrow q$ is in the data. Thus we must show $(q \Rightarrow \bot) \Rightarrow q \vdash q \Rightarrow \bot$. By using H1 we may ask $(q \Rightarrow \bot) \Rightarrow q, q \vdash \bot$. None of the normal rules now apply, so we are stuck. In this situation we are able to use restart and ask instead for the original q: $(q \Rightarrow \bot) \Rightarrow q, q \vdash q$ which succeeds. Thus the original argument is valid.

Compare with Example 4.1.9, where we can replace p by q and q by $\bot$.

Suppose we have the query $\mathcal{P} \vdash A$. We know by truth tables that $A \equiv (\neg A \Rightarrow A)$, so we can replace the above argument by $\mathcal{P} \vdash \neg A \Rightarrow A$ and hence use H1 to reduce this to $\mathcal{P}, \neg A \vdash A$, and after translation to $\mathcal{P}, A \Rightarrow \bot \vdash A$. If later in the computation of A we get stuck at $\mathcal{P}^*, A \Rightarrow \bot \vdash C$, we can always continue by using the negation rule and asking for A because if A succeeds then we get $\bot$ from $A, A \Rightarrow \bot$, and when we have $\bot$ we can get anything we want, including C.

1.4   Rewriting assumptions

We are close to having a fully mechanical reasoning method. Let us summarize where we stand now. Given $\mathcal{P} \vdash A$ to show, we can mechanize the proof as follows:

1. All negations $\neg D$ are rewritten as $D \Rightarrow \bot$, where $\bot$ is falsity.

2. $A \vee B$ is rewritten as $\neg A \Rightarrow B$ which can be further rewritten to $(A \Rightarrow \bot) \Rightarrow B$.

3. Rules H1 and H2 deal with $\wedge$ and $\Rightarrow$ and these are mechanical rules.

4. Rule H4 was replaced by the restart rule.

5. Rule H3 for $\neg$ was replaced by the rule $\bot \vdash B$.

We now have to formulate the exact mechanical use of the rules. We know that any argument $\mathcal{P} \vdash A$ can be reduced to a list of several arguments $\mathcal{P}_i \vdash x_i$ where x_i are atoms (we do not have $\neg$ any more and so x_i can be $\bot$, which is also considered to be an atom). It would be useful to have all the data in $\mathcal{P}_i$ in the form $[A \wedge B \wedge C] \Rightarrow x$, i.e.

$$['body' \text{ of formulae}] \Rightarrow [\text{atomic 'head'}]$$

so that we can, say, to show $\mathcal{P} \vdash x$ just show $\mathcal{P} \vdash A \wedge B \wedge C$.

The next step is to deal with $\mathcal{P} \vdash x$ where x is of the above form, namely an atom or $\bot$. We saw in an earlier example that sometimes we make the computation more complicated by our reduction. For example, $A \Rightarrow (B \wedge C), A \vdash B \wedge C$ becomes $A \Rightarrow (B \wedge C), A \vdash B$ and $A \Rightarrow (B \wedge C), A \vdash C$. If we reduce B and C further we get something like

$$\frac{A \Rightarrow B \wedge C}{A}$$
$$\frac{\text{extra added in the process of simplification}}{\text{atom } x}$$

where x is embedded somewhere in A, B, C. It is therefore to our advantage to make sure that the assumptions themselves have the convenient form $A \Rightarrow x$, where x is atomic or $A \Rightarrow \bot$, so that when we simplify the conclusion we get things like $A_i \Rightarrow x_i \vdash y$ and we just look whether we have y appearing among the x_i and whether we can show the relevant A_i.

We use two more equations to reduce anything of the form $A \Rightarrow B$, where B is an arbitrarily complex formula, to the form $C \Rightarrow x$, where x is atomic. These are

H7 $A \Rightarrow (x \wedge y) \equiv (A \Rightarrow x) \wedge (A \Rightarrow y)$

H8 $A \Rightarrow (x \Rightarrow y) \equiv (A \wedge x) \Rightarrow y$

Thus if $(A \Rightarrow x \wedge y)$ is an assumption we replace it by the two assumptions $A \Rightarrow x$ and $A \Rightarrow y$, and if $A \Rightarrow (x \Rightarrow y)$ is an assumption we replace it by $(A \wedge x) \Rightarrow y$. In both cases the 'head' becomes less complicated. We continue to rewrite all the assumptions until all 'heads' become atomic.

EXAMPLE 4.12. Showing $\neg(\neg A \wedge \neg B) \vdash A \vee B$ involves first rewriting wffs of the form $\neg x$ as $x \Rightarrow \bot$ and $x \vee y$ as $(x \Rightarrow \bot) \Rightarrow y$. So we show instead:

$$\frac{[(A \Rightarrow \bot) \wedge (B \Rightarrow \bot)] \Rightarrow \bot}{(A \Rightarrow \bot) \Rightarrow B}$$

Using H2 we show

$$\frac{[(A \Rightarrow \bot) \wedge (B \Rightarrow \bot)] \Rightarrow \bot, A \Rightarrow \bot}{B}$$

To continue we ask: does anything in the assumptions give B? The answer is 'no' because the heads of the assumptions are $\perp$ not B. But remember that if we can prove $\perp$ then we can prove any formula. Thus the correct question to ask is: do we have an assumption giving B or $\perp$? The answer is 'yes', two of them. We proceed by mechanically checking the first of them and, if it does not work, trying the second and so forth.

The first assumption with $\perp$ as head is $[(A\Rightarrow\perp)\wedge(B\Rightarrow\perp)]\Rightarrow\perp$. If we can show $(A\Rightarrow\perp)\wedge(B\Rightarrow\perp)$ we will get $\perp$ which will give $\neg B$. To show a conjunction we have to show each conjunct; thus we have to show

$$\frac{((A\Rightarrow\perp)\wedge(B\Rightarrow\perp)) \equiv \perp, A\Rightarrow\perp}{A\Rightarrow\perp} \text{ and } \frac{(A\Rightarrow\perp)\wedge(B\Rightarrow\perp)\Rightarrow\perp, A\Rightarrow\perp}{B\Rightarrow\perp}$$

We must remember the original query to show, which was B, as we may want to restart. Clearly the first argument is valid and can be proved mechanically. To show the second we use H2:

$$\frac{[(A\Rightarrow\perp)\wedge(B\Rightarrow\perp)]\Rightarrow\perp, A\Rightarrow\perp, B}{\perp}$$

To show $\perp$ we can use the first assumption but that will put us into a loop. Using the second assumption will lead us to try to show A which does not seem to help either. So we restart with the original B which succeeds. Thus the entire example succeeds.

EXAMPLE 4.13. To show $\neg(A\vee B) \vdash \neg A\wedge\neg B$ first we rewrite the formula $A\vee B$ as $(A\Rightarrow\perp)\Rightarrow B$, $\neg(A\vee B)$ as $((A\Rightarrow\perp)\Rightarrow B)\Rightarrow\perp$, and $\neg A$ as $A\Rightarrow\perp$ and $\neg B$ as $B\Rightarrow\perp$. We have to show

$$\frac{((A\Rightarrow\perp)\Rightarrow B)\Rightarrow\perp}{(A\Rightarrow\perp)\wedge(B\Rightarrow\perp)}$$

so by H1 we must show both $(A\Rightarrow\perp)$ and $(B\Rightarrow\perp)$. To show $A\Rightarrow\perp$ we use H2 and show

$$\frac{((A\Rightarrow\perp)\Rightarrow B)\Rightarrow\perp, A}{\perp}$$

which leads to

$$\frac{((A\Rightarrow\perp)\Rightarrow B)\Rightarrow\perp, A}{(A\Rightarrow\perp)\Rightarrow B}$$

because $((A\Rightarrow\perp)\Rightarrow B)\Rightarrow\perp$ is an assumption with head $\perp$. Now using H2 we reach

$$\frac{((A\Rightarrow\perp)\Rightarrow B)\Rightarrow\perp, A, A\Rightarrow\perp}{B}$$

To show that we match B with the $\perp$ of $A{\Rightarrow}\perp$ (if we used the first assumption we would loop) and show

$$\frac{((A{\Rightarrow}\perp){\Rightarrow}B){\Rightarrow}\perp, A, A{\Rightarrow}\perp}{A}$$

which succeeds.

To show $B{\Rightarrow}\perp$ we use H2 and show

$$\frac{((A{\Rightarrow}\perp){\Rightarrow}B){\Rightarrow}\perp, B}{\perp}$$

which leads to

$$\frac{((A{\Rightarrow}\perp){\Rightarrow}B){\Rightarrow}\perp, B}{(A{\Rightarrow}\perp){\Rightarrow}B}$$

and by H2 we must show

$$\frac{((A{\Rightarrow}\perp){\Rightarrow}B){\Rightarrow}\perp, B, A{\Rightarrow}\perp}{B}$$

which succeeds.

1.5 Summary of computation rules

H1 To show $\mathcal{P} \vdash A{\wedge}B$ show $\mathcal{P} \vdash A$ and $\mathcal{P} \vdash B$.

H2 To show $\mathcal{P} \vdash A{\Rightarrow}B$ show $\mathcal{P}, A \vdash B$.

H3 $\perp \vdash A$ for any A.

H4 If you start with $\mathcal{P} \vdash A$ then at any time later in the computation you may start showing A again.

H5 Rewrite $A{\vee}B$ as $(A{\Rightarrow}\perp){\Rightarrow}B$.

H7 Rewrite $A{\Rightarrow}(B{\wedge}C)$ as $(A{\Rightarrow}B){\wedge}(A{\Rightarrow}C)$.

H8 Rewrite $A{\Rightarrow}(B{\Rightarrow}C)$ as $A{\wedge}B{\Rightarrow}C$.

H9 Rewrite $\neg A$ as $A \Rightarrow \perp$.

Note that heuristic H6 no longer applies.

The outline computation is that to show $\mathcal{P} \vdash C$ use the rules to get to $\mathcal{P}_i \vdash x_i$ where x_i are atoms or $\perp$. Rewrite any assumption in $\mathcal{P}_i$ into the form $A{\Rightarrow}y$ where y is an atom, or $\perp$. If $x_i = y$ or $y = \perp$ then to show $\mathcal{P}_i \vdash x_i$ show $\mathcal{P}_i \vdash A$. If you need to restart with C you can show $\mathcal{P}_i \vdash x_i$ by showing $\mathcal{P}_i \vdash C$.

EXERCISE 4.14. Show

1. $(p{\Rightarrow}q){\wedge}(q{\Rightarrow}r){\wedge}\neg r \vdash \neg p$

2. $\neg\neg p \vdash p$

3. $\neg p{\Rightarrow}p \vdash p$

4. $p{\vee}q, \neg p \vdash q$

5. $q{\wedge}r{\Rightarrow}s, p{\vee}r{\Rightarrow}q, \neg p \vdash r{\Rightarrow}s$

6. $p{\vee}q, p{\Rightarrow}r, q{\Rightarrow}r \vdash r$

2 Worked examples

We now give a summary of the official backward rules for dealing with the computational problem of whether a conclusion follows from some assumptions. There are two principles to follow for representing both the assumptions and the conclusion:

use only $\wedge$, $\Rightarrow$ and $\bot$ We rewrite everything, assumptions and conclusion, with the connectives $\wedge$, $\Rightarrow$ and $\bot$. Thus we translate $\neg x$ as $x{\Rightarrow}\bot$ for any x, and we translate $A{\vee}B$ as $(A{\Rightarrow}\bot){\Rightarrow}B$. Note that $A{\vee}B$ also has the same truth table as $(A{\Rightarrow}B){\Rightarrow}B$ and the same table as $(B{\Rightarrow}A){\Rightarrow}A$, and the same table as $(B{\Rightarrow}\bot){\Rightarrow}A$, so any of the above can serve as a translation. We officially choose $A{\vee}B$ to be translated as $(A{\Rightarrow}\bot){\Rightarrow}B$. Here is a truth table showing all the equivalences:

A	B	$A{\vee}B$	$A{\Rightarrow}\bot$	$(A{\Rightarrow}\bot){\Rightarrow}B$	$(A{\Rightarrow}B)$	$(A{\Rightarrow}B){\Rightarrow}B$
T	T	T	$\bot$	T	T	T
$\bot$	T	T	T	T	T	T
T	$\bot$	T	$\bot$	T	$\bot$	T
$\bot$	$\bot$	$\bot$	T	$\bot$	T	$\bot$

$(A{\Rightarrow}B){\Rightarrow}B$ has a symmetrical table in A and B and hence equals $(B{\Rightarrow}A){\Rightarrow}A$. Notice that $(A{\Rightarrow}\bot){\Rightarrow}B$ has a symmetrical table in A and B and hence equals $(B{\Rightarrow}\bot){\Rightarrow}A$.

use only clausal form Even in the case of data (assumptions) and query (conclusion) written using $\Rightarrow$, $\wedge$ and $\bot$ only, we want to write the data in a special form, namely as a set of implications of the form $B{\Rightarrow}q$ where q is atomic, or $\bot$. Each $B{\Rightarrow}q$ is called a *clause*, with B as *body* and q as *head*.

Given a set of assumptions, can we always write the assumptions in the above form? The answer is yes. Given an assumption E, we can apply the following rules:

E has the form:	Rewrite E to:
atomic	no change
$A \Rightarrow \bot$	no change
$A \Rightarrow q$, q atomic	no change
$A \wedge B$	A and B
$A \Rightarrow (B_1 \wedge B_2)$	$A \Rightarrow B_1$ and $A \Rightarrow B_2$
$A \Rightarrow (B_1 \Rightarrow B_2)$	$A \wedge B_1 \Rightarrow B_2$

Where E is rewritten, the above rules must be applied again to the products of the rewrite of E, until there is no change. This is to ensure that assumptions such as $p \wedge q \Rightarrow (r \wedge p \Rightarrow s)$ are fully rewritten to clausal form. We thus see that any database can be rewritten and replaced by an equivalent database, whose elements have the desired form.

There are several computational steps for clausal form databases, given by the following:

For atoms q To show $\mathcal{P} \vdash q$ succeeds, we distinguish several cases:

- $q \in \mathcal{P}$, thus we succeed.

- Some $B \Rightarrow q \in \mathcal{P}$, then we must show that $\mathcal{P} \vdash B$ succeeds.

- $\bot \in \mathcal{P}$, thus we succeed.

- For some $B \Rightarrow \bot \in \mathcal{P}$, then we must show that $\mathcal{P} \vdash B$ succeeds.

For conjunction To show $\mathcal{P} \vdash A \wedge B$ we must show $\mathcal{P} \vdash A$ and $\mathcal{P} \vdash B$.

For implication To show $\mathcal{P} \vdash A \Rightarrow B$ show $\mathcal{P}, A \vdash B$. Remember that A may need to be rewritten when being added to the database. This is known as the *deduction theorem*.

Restart rule Assume our original problem is to show $\mathcal{P} \vdash A$. In the middle of the computation we have to show $\mathcal{P}^* \vdash C$. Usually C will be atomic. We can, at any time, choose to continue with $\mathcal{P}^* \vdash A$ instead (even if we do not have to).

We can now give some worked examples. After the examples we will discuss ways of automating the computation. Remember—loops are possible but if A logically follows from $\mathcal{P}$ then there is always a way to use the rules to get from $\mathcal{P}$ to A, without loops.

EXAMPLE 4.15.

$(p{\Rightarrow}q){\Rightarrow}p \ \vdash p$

$\qquad$ | rule for atoms

$(p{\Rightarrow}q){\Rightarrow}p \ \vdash p{\Rightarrow}q$

$\qquad$ | rule for $\Rightarrow$

$p,(p{\Rightarrow}q){\Rightarrow}p \ \vdash q$

$\qquad$ | restart

$p,(p{\Rightarrow}q){\Rightarrow}p \ \vdash p$

$\qquad$ |

$\qquad$ success

EXAMPLE 4.16.

$(a{\Rightarrow}b){\Rightarrow}b \ \vdash c$
$\quad a{\Rightarrow}c$
$\quad b{\Rightarrow}c$

$\qquad$ | rule for atoms used with $b{\Rightarrow}c$

$(a{\Rightarrow}b){\Rightarrow}b \ \vdash b$
$\quad a{\Rightarrow}c$
$\quad b{\Rightarrow}c$

$\qquad$ | rule for atoms used with $(a{\Rightarrow}b){\Rightarrow}b$

$(a{\Rightarrow}b){\Rightarrow}b \ \vdash a{\Rightarrow}b$
$\quad a{\Rightarrow}c$
$\quad b{\Rightarrow}c$

$\qquad$ | rule for $\Rightarrow$

$(a{\Rightarrow}b){\Rightarrow}b \ \vdash b$
$\quad a{\Rightarrow}c$
$\quad b{\Rightarrow}c$
$\quad a$

$\qquad$ | Notice here that we can use the rule for atoms for b used with $(a{\Rightarrow}b){\Rightarrow}b$ but we will loop because we will be back where we are. Let us use restart instead.

$\qquad$ | restart

$(a{\Rightarrow}b){\Rightarrow}b\ \ \vdash c$
   $a{\Rightarrow}c$
   $b{\Rightarrow}c$
    a

> Notice now that if we use the rule for atoms with $b{\Rightarrow}c$ we will ask for b and loop again. It is wise (almost mechanical though) to use $a{\Rightarrow}c$.

> rule for atoms with $a{\Rightarrow}c$

$(a{\Rightarrow}b){\Rightarrow}b\ \ \vdash a$
   $a{\Rightarrow}c$
   $b{\Rightarrow}c$
    a

   success

EXAMPLE 4.17.
$(a{\Rightarrow}b){\Rightarrow}b\ \ \vdash (b{\Rightarrow}a){\Rightarrow}a$

> rule for $\Rightarrow$

$(a{\Rightarrow}b){\Rightarrow}b\ \ \vdash a$
   $b{\Rightarrow}a$

> rule for atoms for $b{\Rightarrow}a$

$(a{\Rightarrow}b){\Rightarrow}b\ \ \vdash b$
   $b{\Rightarrow}a$

> rule for atoms using $(a{\Rightarrow}b){\Rightarrow}b$

$(a{\Rightarrow}b){\Rightarrow}b\ \ \vdash a{\Rightarrow}b$
   $b{\Rightarrow}a$

$(a{\Rightarrow}b){\Rightarrow}b\ \ \vdash b$
   $b{\Rightarrow}a$
    a

> restart

$(a{\Rightarrow}b){\Rightarrow}b\ \ \vdash (b{\Rightarrow}a){\Rightarrow}a$
   $b{\Rightarrow}a$
    a

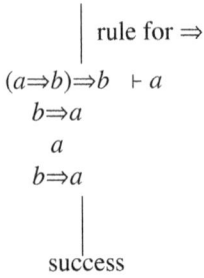

$$\Big|\quad \text{rule for} \Rightarrow$$

$(a{\Rightarrow}b){\Rightarrow}b \quad \vdash a$

　$b{\Rightarrow}a$

　　a

　$b{\Rightarrow}a$

$$\Big|$$

　success

EXAMPLE 4.18.

$(a{\Rightarrow}b){\Rightarrow}b \quad \vdash a{\vee}b$

$$\Big|\quad \text{rewrite}$$

$(a{\Rightarrow}b){\Rightarrow}b \quad \vdash (a{\Rightarrow}{\perp}){\Rightarrow}b$

$$\Big|\quad \text{rule for} \Rightarrow$$

$(a{\Rightarrow}b){\Rightarrow}b \quad \vdash b$

　$(a{\Rightarrow}{\perp})$

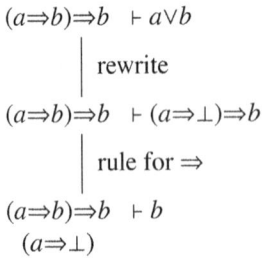

> We have two choices here. One is to use the rule for atoms with
> $a{\Rightarrow}{\perp}$ and the second to use the rule for atoms with $(a{\Rightarrow}b){\Rightarrow}b$.
> You can guess that the first case loops so we use the second case.
> A computer will use each case in the order of writing and if it
> loops (we can use loop detection techniques) will try the next.
> So we continue

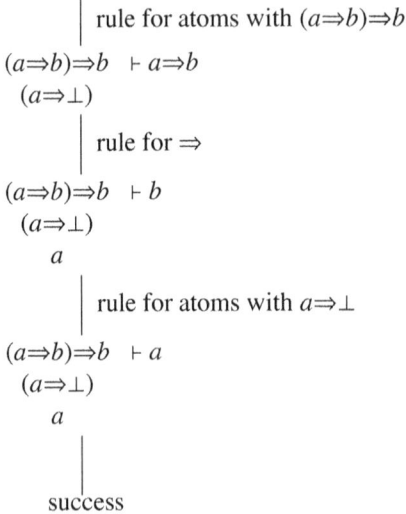

$$\Big|\quad \text{rule for atoms with } (a{\Rightarrow}b){\Rightarrow}b$$

$(a{\Rightarrow}b){\Rightarrow}b \quad \vdash a{\Rightarrow}b$

　$(a{\Rightarrow}{\perp})$

$$\Big|\quad \text{rule for} \Rightarrow$$

$(a{\Rightarrow}b){\Rightarrow}b \quad \vdash b$

　$(a{\Rightarrow}{\perp})$

　　a

$$\Big|\quad \text{rule for atoms with } a{\Rightarrow}{\perp}$$

$(a{\Rightarrow}b){\Rightarrow}b \quad \vdash a$

　$(a{\Rightarrow}{\perp})$

　　a

$$\Big|$$

　success

EXAMPLE 4.19.

$(q{\Rightarrow}q)\ \vdash q$

> (This should not succeed!)
>
> rule for atoms

$(q{\Rightarrow}q)\ \vdash q$

This loops with no way out. Even the restart rule is of no use to us.

EXAMPLE 4.20.

$\neg q{\Rightarrow}q\ \vdash q$

> This should succeed; check by truth tables.
>
> rewrite

$((q{\Rightarrow}\bot){\Rightarrow}q)\ \vdash q$

> rule for atoms

$((q{\Rightarrow}\bot){\Rightarrow}q)\ \vdash q{\Rightarrow}\bot$

> rule for $\Rightarrow$

$((q{\Rightarrow}\bot){\Rightarrow}q)\ \vdash \bot$
$\qquad q$

> Note that the rule for atoms involving $\bot$ applies only when $\bot$ is in the database, i.e. if we had $(q{\Rightarrow}\bot)\vdash a$, we could ask for q but the rule does not apply in the case above. Therefore we use the restart rule.
>
> restart

$((q{\Rightarrow}\bot){\Rightarrow}q)\ \vdash q$
$\qquad q$

success

EXAMPLE 4.21.

$(a{\Rightarrow}b)\ \vdash (x{\vee}a){\Rightarrow}(x{\vee}b)$

> rewrite

$(a{\Rightarrow}b)\ \vdash ((x{\Rightarrow}\bot){\Rightarrow}a){\Rightarrow}((x{\Rightarrow}\bot){\Rightarrow}b)$

rule for $\Rightarrow$

$(a{\Rightarrow}b)$ $\vdash ((x{\Rightarrow}\bot){\Rightarrow}b)$
$((x{\Rightarrow}\bot){\Rightarrow}a)$

rule for $\Rightarrow$

$(a{\Rightarrow}b)$ $\vdash b$
$((x{\Rightarrow}\bot){\Rightarrow}a)$
$(x{\Rightarrow}\bot)$

rule for atoms using $a{\Rightarrow}b$

$(a{\Rightarrow}b)$ $\vdash a$
$((x{\Rightarrow}\bot){\Rightarrow}a)$
$(x{\Rightarrow}\bot)$

rule for atoms using $((x{\Rightarrow}\bot){\Rightarrow}a)$

$(a{\Rightarrow}b)$ $\vdash x{\Rightarrow}\bot$
$((x{\Rightarrow}\bot){\Rightarrow}a)$
$(x{\Rightarrow}\bot)$

Note that you cannot say we have $x{\Rightarrow}\bot$ in the database and hence success, since the rules are mechanical. Success can be obtained only in the rule for atoms. $x{\Rightarrow}\bot$ is not an atom. So:

rule for $\Rightarrow$

$(a{\Rightarrow}b)$ $\vdash \bot$
$((x{\Rightarrow}\bot){\Rightarrow}a)$
$(x{\Rightarrow}\bot)$
x

rule for atoms with $x{\Rightarrow}\bot$

$(a{\Rightarrow}b)$ $\vdash x$
$((x{\Rightarrow}\bot){\Rightarrow}a)$
$(x{\Rightarrow}\bot)$
x

success

EXAMPLE 4.22.

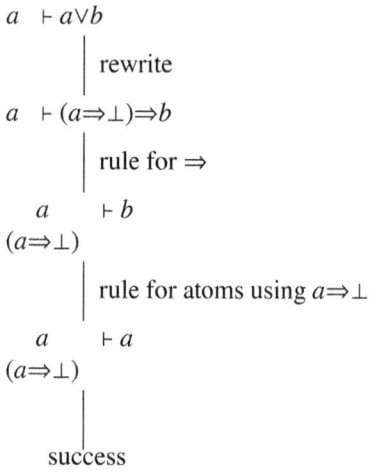

$$a \quad \vdash a \lor b$$

| rewrite

$$a \quad \vdash (a{\Rightarrow}\bot){\Rightarrow}b$$

| rule for $\Rightarrow$

$$a \qquad \vdash b$$
$$(a{\Rightarrow}\bot)$$

| rule for atoms using $a{\Rightarrow}\bot$

$$a \qquad \vdash a$$
$$(a{\Rightarrow}\bot)$$

|

success

EXAMPLE 4.23.

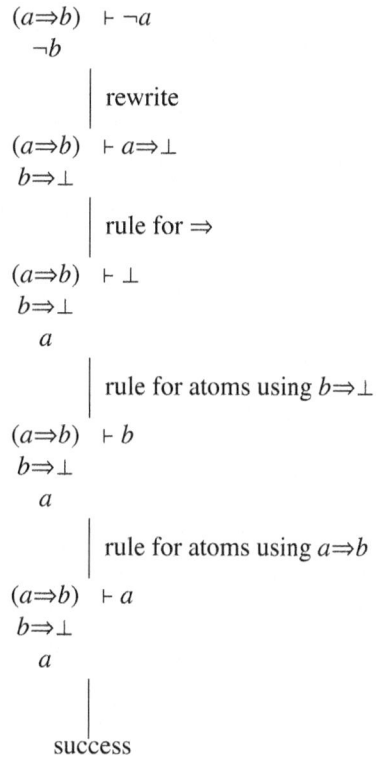

$$(a{\Rightarrow}b) \quad \vdash \neg a$$
$$\neg b$$

| rewrite

$$(a{\Rightarrow}b) \quad \vdash a{\Rightarrow}\bot$$
$$b{\Rightarrow}\bot$$

| rule for $\Rightarrow$

$$(a{\Rightarrow}b) \quad \vdash \bot$$
$$b{\Rightarrow}\bot$$
$$a$$

| rule for atoms using $b{\Rightarrow}\bot$

$$(a{\Rightarrow}b) \quad \vdash b$$
$$b{\Rightarrow}\bot$$
$$a$$

| rule for atoms using $a{\Rightarrow}b$

$$(a{\Rightarrow}b) \quad \vdash a$$
$$b{\Rightarrow}\bot$$
$$a$$

|

success

EXAMPLE 4.24.

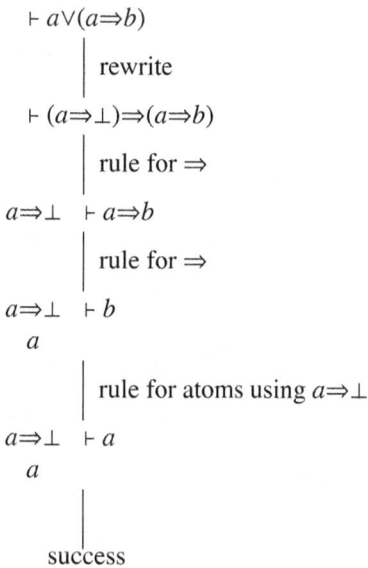

$$\vdash a \lor (a{\Rightarrow}b)$$

| rewrite

$$\vdash (a{\Rightarrow}\bot){\Rightarrow}(a{\Rightarrow}b)$$

| rule for $\Rightarrow$

$$a{\Rightarrow}\bot \quad \vdash a{\Rightarrow}b$$

| rule for $\Rightarrow$

$$a{\Rightarrow}\bot \quad \vdash b$$
$$a$$

| rule for atoms using $a{\Rightarrow}\bot$

$$a{\Rightarrow}\bot \quad \vdash a$$
$$a$$

|

success

EXAMPLE 4.25.

$(a \lor b) \lor c \vdash a \lor (b \lor c)$

| rewrite

$((a \Rightarrow \bot) \Rightarrow b) \lor c \vdash a \lor ((b \Rightarrow \bot) \Rightarrow c)$

| rewrite

$(((a \Rightarrow \bot) \Rightarrow b) \Rightarrow \bot) \Rightarrow c \vdash (a \Rightarrow \bot) \Rightarrow ((b \Rightarrow \bot) \Rightarrow c)$

| rule for $\Rightarrow$

$(((a \Rightarrow \bot) \Rightarrow b) \Rightarrow \bot) \Rightarrow c \vdash (b \Rightarrow \bot) \Rightarrow c$
$\qquad (a \Rightarrow \bot)$

| rule for $\Rightarrow$

$(((a \Rightarrow \bot) \Rightarrow b) \Rightarrow \bot) \Rightarrow c \vdash c$
$\qquad (a \Rightarrow \bot)$
$\qquad b \Rightarrow \bot$

> The rule for atoms can be used with each of the three assumptions. If you want to use the system automatically try all three. Otherwise try the first one because it will make you add to the data and thus increase the chances of success.

| rule for atoms using $(((a \Rightarrow \bot) \Rightarrow b) \Rightarrow \bot) \Rightarrow c$

$(((a \Rightarrow \bot) \Rightarrow b) \Rightarrow \bot) \Rightarrow c \vdash ((a \Rightarrow \bot) \Rightarrow b) \Rightarrow \bot$
$\qquad (a \Rightarrow \bot)$
$\qquad b \Rightarrow \bot$

| rule for $\Rightarrow$

$(((a \Rightarrow \bot) \Rightarrow b) \Rightarrow \bot) \Rightarrow c \vdash \bot$
$\qquad (a \Rightarrow \bot)$
$\qquad b \Rightarrow \bot$
$\qquad (a \Rightarrow \bot) \Rightarrow b$

| rule for atoms using $b \Rightarrow \bot$

$(((a \Rightarrow \bot) \Rightarrow b) \Rightarrow \bot) \Rightarrow c \vdash b$
$\qquad (a \Rightarrow \bot)$
$\qquad b \Rightarrow \bot$
$\qquad (a \Rightarrow \bot) \Rightarrow b$

| rule for atoms using $(a \Rightarrow \bot) \Rightarrow b$

$(((a{\Rightarrow}\bot){\Rightarrow}b){\Rightarrow}\bot){\Rightarrow}c \;\vdash a{\Rightarrow}\bot$
$\quad (a{\Rightarrow}\bot)$
$\quad\; b{\Rightarrow}\bot$
$\quad (a{\Rightarrow}\bot){\Rightarrow}b$

$\qquad\Big|\;$ rule for $\Rightarrow$

$(((a{\Rightarrow}\bot){\Rightarrow}b){\Rightarrow}\bot){\Rightarrow}c \;\;\vdash \bot$
$\quad (a{\Rightarrow}\bot)$
$\quad\; b{\Rightarrow}\bot$
$\quad (a{\Rightarrow}\bot){\Rightarrow}b$
$\qquad\; a$

$\qquad\Big|\;$ rule for atoms using $a{\Rightarrow}\bot$

$(((a{\Rightarrow}\bot){\Rightarrow}b){\Rightarrow}\bot){\Rightarrow}c \;\;\vdash a$
$\quad (a{\Rightarrow}\bot)$
$\quad\; b{\Rightarrow}\bot$
$\quad (a{\Rightarrow}\bot){\Rightarrow}b$
$\qquad\; a$

$\qquad\Big|$

success

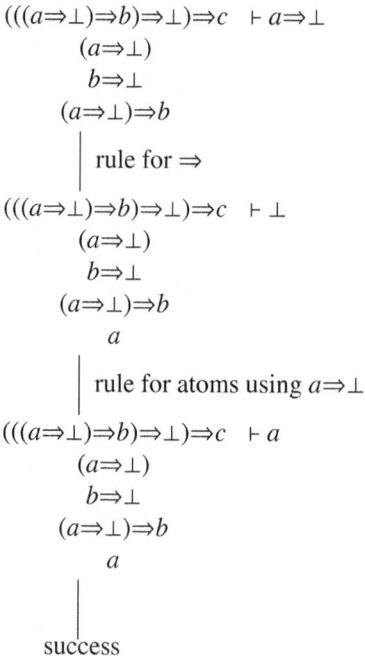

EXERCISE 4.26. Use backward rules to prove the following:

1. that $\neg p$ follows from $p{\Rightarrow}q$ and $\neg q$

2. that $p{\vee}q$ follows from $\neg p{\Rightarrow}q$

3. that $((a{\Rightarrow}b){\Rightarrow}a){\Rightarrow}a$ is a tautology

4. that p follows from $(p{\Rightarrow}q){\Rightarrow}q$ and $q{\Rightarrow}p$

5. that $\neg(p{\wedge}\neg p)$ is a tautology

6. that $\neg(p{\Rightarrow}q){\Rightarrow}p$ is a tautology

7. that $\neg(p{\Rightarrow}q){\Rightarrow}\neg q$ is a tautology

8. that $b{\vee}(b{\Rightarrow}c)$ is a tautology

9. that $(p{\Rightarrow}\neg p){\Rightarrow}\neg p$ is a tautology

10. that $(\neg p{\Rightarrow}p){\Rightarrow}p$ is a tautology

11. that $(p{\wedge}q){\Rightarrow}\neg(\neg p{\vee}\neg q)$ is a tautology

12. that $a\Rightarrow(\neg b\Rightarrow\neg(a\Rightarrow b))$ is a tautology

13. that $\neg p\Rightarrow((p\vee q)\Rightarrow q)$ is a tautology

14. that b follows from $a\Leftrightarrow((a\wedge b)\vee(\neg a\wedge\neg b))$.

3 A deterministic goal-directed algorithm

We need to write a precise algorithm of how the backward computation works. We propose the definition below. The database $\mathcal{P}$ is a sequence of assumptions of the form $B\Rightarrow q$ or $B\Rightarrow\bot$, for q atomic. When we add data to $\mathcal{P}$ we append the data to the end of the list. When we have an atomic goal q and we look for data items in $\mathcal{P}$ of the form $B\Rightarrow q$ or $B\Rightarrow\bot$, we scan the list from beginning to end and take the first such clause. If the computation fails for this first choice, then we go to the next one in the list.

Thus, for example, when we try

1. $p\Rightarrow q$

2. $q\Rightarrow q\vdash q$

3. q

we first use the $\Rightarrow$ rule with clause 1. We try $\vdash p$; this fails because we have no clause with head p. So we go back to the list and use the next clause in line with head q. This is clause 2 and so we try $\vdash q$. We now scan the list and take the first clause with head q, which is clause 1, and so we ask $\vdash p$, and we are in a loop. If we have a historical loop checker we will know that we have already tried $\vdash p$ so we stop and pass to clause 3 and succeed.

Another way of avoiding looping is to throw out clauses that have been used. This is called the policy of *diminishing resource*. If we do that then we do not need a historical loop checker. However, if we adopt the policy of diminishing resource we need to prove that there are no cases where some clauses need to be used twice, or if there are such cases, we need to compensate by additional rules.

As we shall see later, the restart rule can compensate for the policy of diminishing resource and we can manage with using clauses at most once.

DEFINITION 4.27 (Translation into ready for computation form).

1. A ready for computation clause can be defined inductively as follows:

   - An atom q or $\bot$ is a ready for computation clause. $\bot, q$ are called the heads. This clause has no body.
   - Let $A_i=(B_i\Rightarrow x_i)$, $i=1,\ldots,n$, be ready for computation clauses with bodies B_i and heads x_i (x_i is either atomic or $\bot$). Let x be either atomic or $\bot$; then $\bigwedge_i A_i\Rightarrow x$ is a ready for computation clause with body $\bigwedge_i A_i$ and head x.

2. The following is a translation $*$ of an aribtrary wff into a conjunction of ready for computation clauses (which is classically equivalent to it).[2]

   A is rewritten as A^* using the following steps:

   $$(A \Rightarrow B \wedge C)^* = (A \Rightarrow B)^* \wedge (A \Rightarrow C)^*$$
   $$(A \Rightarrow (B \Rightarrow C))^* = (A \wedge B \Rightarrow C)^*$$
   $$(A \Rightarrow q)^* = (A^* \Rightarrow q), q \text{ atomic}$$
   $$(A \Rightarrow \bot)^* = (A^* \Rightarrow \bot)$$
   $$(\neg A)^* = (A \Rightarrow \bot)^*$$
   $$(A \vee B)^* = ((A \Rightarrow \bot) \Rightarrow B)^*$$
   $$(A \wedge B)^* = A^* \wedge B^*$$

DEFINITION 4.28 (Backward computation with diminishing resource).

1. A database is a list of clauses annotated with numbers 0 and 1; 1 means available for computation and 0 means not available.

   We present the list as

   $$\mathcal{P} = ((\alpha_1, A_1), \ldots, (\alpha_n, A_n))$$

   where A_i is a clause and $\alpha_i \in \{0, 1\}$.

2. Let $\mathcal{P}$ be an annotated database as above and A a conjunction of clauses of the form[3]

   $$A = \bigwedge_{i=1}^{k} (B_i \Rightarrow x_i)$$

   where x_i is either atomic or $\bot$. We let $\mathcal{P} + A$ mean the annotated database

   $$((\alpha_1, A_1), \ldots, (\alpha_n, A_n), (1, B_1 \Rightarrow x_1), \ldots, (1, B_k \Rightarrow x_k))$$

3. A goal list is a list of the form $H = (x_1, \ldots, x_n)$ where x_i are atoms or $\bot$.

4. A *computation* state has the form $\langle \mathcal{P}, H, G \rangle$, where $\mathcal{P}$ is an annotated database, H is a goal list and G a clause called the goal or query.

DEFINITION 4.29 (Diminishing resource computation procedures). The following are recursive definitions of the notion of success or finite failure of a computation state.

---

[2]The translation A^* of A is classically equivalent to A. It is *not* intuitionistically equivalent to A, because of the way we translate disjunction. Thus for example in Exercise 4.2.18 item 8, $B \vee (B \Rightarrow C)$ is not an intuitionistic theorem but its translation $(B \Rightarrow \bot) \Rightarrow (B \rightarrow C)$ is an intuitionistic theorem and indeed in the solution at the end of the book, restart is not used.

[3]We can view the conjunction as a list $((B_1 \Rightarrow x_1), \ldots, (B_k \Rightarrow x_k))$. Although in classical logic the order of the conjuncts is not important, the computation can take account of the order if necessary.

1. *G atomic or $\perp$, immediate success*

   - $\langle \mathcal{P}, H, x \rangle$ succeeds immediately *without restart* for x atomic or $\perp$ if for some $i, (\alpha_i, y) \in \mathcal{P}$ and $\alpha_i = 1$ and either $y = x$ or $y = \perp$.

   - It succeeds immediately *with bounded restart* if for some $a_i \in H$, $a_i = x$ and for some $a_j \in H$, $j \geq i$ and $(1, a_j) \in \mathcal{P}$.

   - It succeeds immediately *with restart* if for some $a \in H$, $(1, a) \in \mathcal{P}$.

   - It succeeds immediately if it succeeds according to one of the above.[4]

2. *Case G = atom or $\perp$, immediate failure*
   $\langle \mathcal{P}, H, x \rangle$ fails immediately *without restart* if for all the clauses $B \Rightarrow y$ such that $(1, B \Rightarrow y) \in \mathcal{P}$, we have $y \neq \perp$ and $y \neq x$.

   - It fails immediately even *with bounded restart* if for any $a_i = x, a_i \in H$ and any $a_j, i \leq j, a_j \in H$, there is no clause B with head a_j such that $(1, B) \in \mathcal{P}$.

   - It fails immediately even *with restart* if for any $a \in H$, there is no clause B with head a such that $(1, B) \in \mathcal{P}$.

3. *Case of success of G atom or $\perp$, using a clause in the data*
   $\langle \mathcal{P}, H, y \rangle$, $y =$ atom or $\perp$, succeeds (succeeds with bounded restart, succeeds with restart) if for some $(\alpha_i, A_i) \in \mathcal{P}$ we have $\alpha_i = 1$, and $A_i = (\bigwedge_j (B_j \Rightarrow x_j)) \Rightarrow x$ and either $x = \perp$ or $x = y$ and for each j, the following succeeds (succeeds with bounded restart, succeeds with restart, respectively)

$$\langle \mathcal{P}'_j, H + y, x_j \rangle$$

   where $\mathcal{P}'_j$ is obtained from $\mathcal{P} + B_j$ by changing $\alpha_i = 1$ to $\alpha'_i = 0$, and where $H + y$ is the result of appending y to the end of the list H.

4. *Case of failure of G atom or $\perp$ using a clause in the data*

   - We say $\langle \mathcal{P}, H, y \rangle$ above fails for the choice of (α_i, A_i) if at least one of $\langle \mathcal{P}'_j, H + y, x_j \rangle$ fails (respectively with or without restart or bounded restart).

   - We say $\langle \mathcal{P}, H, y \rangle$ fails if for all (α, A) in $\mathcal{P}$ such that $\alpha = 1$ and A has head $x = \perp$ or $x = y$, $\langle \mathcal{P}, H, y \rangle$ fails for the choice of (α, A).

5. $\langle \mathcal{P}, H, A \Rightarrow y \rangle$ succeeds (resp. fails) iff $\langle \mathcal{P} + A, H, y \rangle$ succeeds (resp. fails).

---

[4]If the current query is x and the history of previous queries is $(a_1, \ldots, a_k = x)$ then restart allows to be asked any previous query a_j. Bounded restart allows to be asked any a_j, which is 'trapped' between 'now' (i.e. $a_k = x$) and a previous occurrence of x (e.g. $a_i = x$ and $i < j < k$).

6. $\langle \mathcal{P}, H, A_1 \wedge A_2 \rangle$ succeeds (resp. fails) iff both (resp. at least one) of $\langle \mathcal{P}, H, A_i \rangle$ succeed (resp. fail).

REMARK 4.30.

It is possible to show that (compare with Exercise 4.3.8)

- $\mathcal{P} \vdash A$ in classical logic iff $\langle \mathcal{P}, \varnothing, A \rangle$ succeeds with restart.

- $\mathcal{P} \vdash A$ in intuitionistic logic iff $\langle \mathcal{P}, \varnothing, A \rangle$ succeeds with bounded restart.

Let us redo some of the examples using restart and diminishing resource. What we shall do is take some of the examples in the previous section and add 0 or 1 annotations and remember the history H of previous goals. We are not writing the history H as a sequence since it can be seen from the record of the computation on the page. The initial list is of course empty since obviously there are no previous goals.

EXAMPLE 4.31.

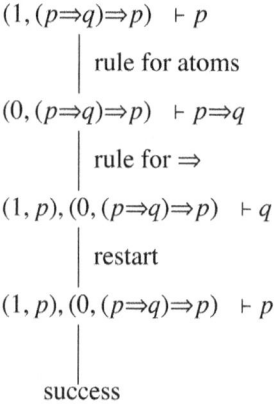

$(1, (p \Rightarrow q) \Rightarrow p) \vdash p$

    rule for atoms

$(0, (p \Rightarrow q) \Rightarrow p) \vdash p \Rightarrow q$

    rule for $\Rightarrow$

$(1, p), (0, (p \Rightarrow q) \Rightarrow p) \vdash q$

    restart

$(1, p), (0, (p \Rightarrow q) \Rightarrow p) \vdash p$

    success

EXAMPLE 4.32.

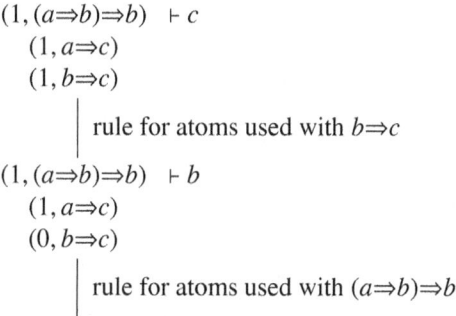

$(1, (a \Rightarrow b) \Rightarrow b) \vdash c$
  $(1, a \Rightarrow c)$
  $(1, b \Rightarrow c)$

    rule for atoms used with $b \Rightarrow c$

$(1, (a \Rightarrow b) \Rightarrow b) \vdash b$
  $(1, a \Rightarrow c)$
  $(0, b \Rightarrow c)$

    rule for atoms used with $(a \Rightarrow b) \Rightarrow b$

$(0, (a{\Rightarrow}b){\Rightarrow}b) \quad \vdash a{\Rightarrow}b$
$\quad (1, a{\Rightarrow}c)$
$\quad (0, b{\Rightarrow}c)$

$\qquad$ | $\quad$ rule for $\Rightarrow$

$(0, (a{\Rightarrow}b){\Rightarrow}b) \quad \vdash b$
$\quad (1, a{\Rightarrow}c)$
$\quad (0, b{\Rightarrow}c)$
$\qquad (1, a)$

$\qquad$ | $\quad$ Notice here that we cannot use the rule for atoms for b with $(a{\Rightarrow}b){\Rightarrow}b$ because it is annotated 0. Thus we not only get that the databases decrease, but also cannot loop! Let us use restart.

$\qquad$ | $\quad$ restart

$(0, (a{\Rightarrow}b){\Rightarrow}b) \quad \vdash c$
$\quad (1, a{\Rightarrow}c)$
$\quad (0, b{\Rightarrow}c)$
$\qquad (1, a)$

$\qquad$ | $\quad$ Notice now that we can only use $a{\Rightarrow}c$.

$\qquad$ | $\quad$ rule for atoms with $a{\Rightarrow}c$

$(0, (a{\Rightarrow}b){\Rightarrow}b) \quad \vdash a$
$\quad (0, a{\Rightarrow}c)$
$\quad (0, b{\Rightarrow}c)$
$\qquad (1, a)$

$\qquad$ |

$\qquad$ success

EXAMPLE 4.33.

$(1, (a{\Rightarrow}b){\Rightarrow}b) \quad \vdash (b{\Rightarrow}a){\Rightarrow}a$

$\qquad$ | $\quad$ rule for $\Rightarrow$

$(1, (a{\Rightarrow}b){\Rightarrow}b) \quad \vdash a$
$\quad (1, b{\Rightarrow}a)$

$\qquad$ | $\quad$ rule for atoms for $b{\Rightarrow}a$

$(1, (a{\Rightarrow}b){\Rightarrow}b) \quad \vdash b$
$\quad (0, b{\Rightarrow}a)$

$\qquad$ | $\quad$ rule for atoms using $(a{\Rightarrow}b){\Rightarrow}b$

$(0, (a \Rightarrow b) \Rightarrow b) \quad \vdash a \Rightarrow b$
$\quad (0, b \Rightarrow a)$

> Note that at this stage the database is empty—no active (anno-tated with 1) data. However, we do have the history which is $H = (a, b)$.
>
> We now use rule for $\Rightarrow$.

$(0, (a \Rightarrow b) \Rightarrow b) \quad \vdash b$
$\quad (0, b \Rightarrow a)$
$\quad\quad (1, a)$

> restart

$(0, (a \Rightarrow b) \Rightarrow b) \quad \vdash a$
$\quad (0, b \Rightarrow a)$
$\quad\quad (1, a)$

success

EXERCISE 4.34 (Soundness of the diminishing resource computation procedure). Show
that if $\langle \mathcal{P}, H, B \rangle$ succeeds with restart then $\bigwedge \mathcal{P} \Rightarrow B \vee \bigvee H$ is a classical tautology, where $\bigwedge \mathcal{P}$ means $\bigwedge_{(1,A) \in \mathcal{P}} A$.

4   Abduction

Given a logic with a notion of $\Delta \vdash ?G$, where Δ is a database and G is a goal formula, the following is the abduction problem for Δ and G.

1. Assume $\Delta \nvdash G$

2. We are looking for a hypothesis H such that

   (a) $H \nvdash G$

   (b) $\Delta + H \vdash G$.

   We require $H \nvdash G$ so that we do not simply hypothesize G itself

3. Write $\mathbf{Ab}(\Delta, G) = H$

EXAMPLE 4.35. Let Δ be *sick* $\Rightarrow$ *coughs*. Let G be *coughs*.

So we observe that John is coughing a lot and we are looking for a hypothesis to explain this.

From what is given we can take *sick* as a hypothesis. Formally we have $\Delta = \{p \Rightarrow q\}$ and $G = q$. We abduce p. Thus $\mathbf{Ab}(p \Rightarrow q, q) = p$.

EXAMPLE 4.36.

$$\Delta : \qquad\qquad a \wedge b \Rightarrow c$$
$$G : a \Rightarrow c$$

What do we abduce?

Method 1: Truth tables
Let us do truth tables:

	a	b	c	$a \wedge b \Rightarrow c$	$a \Rightarrow c$
1	$\top$	$\top$	$\top$	$\top$	$\top$
2.	$\top$	$\top$	$\bot$	$\bot$	$\bot$
3.	$\top$	$\bot$	$\top$	$\top$	$\top$
4.	$\top$	$\bot$	$\bot$	$\top$	$\bot$
5.	$\bot$	$\top$	$\top$	$\top$	$\top$
6.	$\bot$	$\top$	$\bot$	$\top$	$\top$
7.	$\bot$	$\bot$	$\top$	$\top$	$\top$
8.	$\bot$	$\bot$	$\bot$	$\top$	$\top$

We see from the table that $a \wedge b \Rightarrow c$ is true and $a \Rightarrow c$ is false only in row 4. Hence a reasonable hypothesis is to add to Δ the negation of what row 4 says, namely $\neg(a \wedge \neg b \wedge \neg c)$ or $a \Rightarrow b \vee c$.

So $H_{\text{Tables}} = a \Rightarrow (b \vee c)$.

Another commonsense option is to look at $a \wedge b \Rightarrow c$ and observe that if we have $b = \top$ then it becomes $a \Rightarrow c$, which is what we want. So $H_{\text{guess}} = b$.

The process for finding H_{guess} was not systematic. The truth table method is systematic. Given $\mathbf{Ab}(\Delta, G)$, we do the following steps to find a hypotheis H.

1. Construct a full truth table for all elements of Δ and for G. Sicne $\Delta \nvdash G$, there will be some rows in the table, say $h_1, \ldots, h_k$ such that h_i makes all members of Δ to be $\top$ and makes G to be $\bot$ for $i = 1, \ldots, k$.

2. Now let H be a formula which says that all of these rows are impossible. Let $E_1, \ldots, E_k$ be the conjunctive form of rows $h_1, \ldots, h_k$. That is for each atom q, if h_i says $q = \top$, we put q in the conjunction E_i and if h_i says $q = \bot$ we put $\neg q$ in the conjunct E_i.

Now let H be

$$H = \bigwedge_{i=1}^{k} \neg E_i$$

clearly $\Delta + H \vdash G$.

Method 2: Semantic Tableaux

We now solve the problem using a proof theory approach. The idea is to try and prove $a \Rightarrow c$ from $a \wedge b \Rightarrow c$ and whenever we get stuck we add (or *abduce*) the needed assumptions to continue. Thus what we abduce will depend on the method of proof used.

Let us try a semantic tableaux:

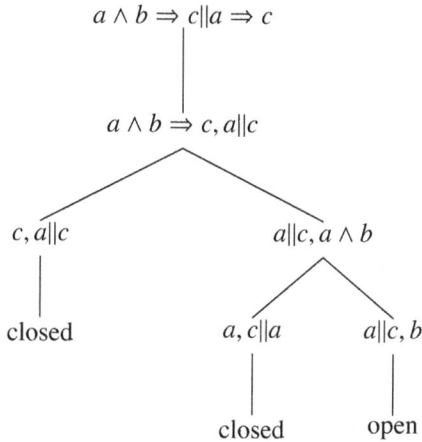

$$a \wedge b \Rightarrow c \| a \Rightarrow c$$

$$a \wedge b \Rightarrow c, a \| c$$

$$c, a \| c \qquad a \| c, a \wedge b$$

closed

$$a, c \| a \qquad a \| c, b$$

closed   open

We get that the only open endpoint in the tableaux is $a \| c, b$. To make it closed we have three options.

1. Abduce a on the right, i.e. assume $\neg a$.

2. Abduce c on the left, i.e. assume c

3. Abduce b on the left, i.e. assume b.

One of our conditions for a hypothesis H is that it does not prove the goal.Thus since $c \vdash a \Rightarrow c$ and $\neg a \vdash a \Rightarrow c$, the only hypothesis left is $H = b$.

Thus we see that actually $H_{\text{guess}} = H_{\text{tableaux}}$.

Method 3: Goal Directed Computation

$$a \wedge b \Rightarrow c ? a \Rightarrow c$$

$$a \wedge b \Rightarrow c ? c$$

a

$$a \wedge b \Rightarrow c ? a \qquad\qquad a \wedge b \Rightarrow c ? b$$

a $\qquad\qquad\qquad\qquad$ a

success $\qquad\qquad\qquad\qquad$ fail

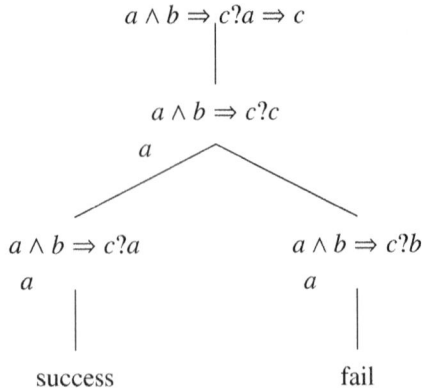

We need to add b in order to succeed. Since b is added under the new additional assumption a, we abduce $a \Rightarrow b$.

So $H_{\text{goal-directed}} = a \Rightarrow b$.

Note that b was added under the assumption of the database $\Delta = a \wedge b \Rightarrow c$ as well as the assumption a. So we could take the weaker hypothesis

$$(a \wedge b \Rightarrow c) \wedge a \Rightarrow b,$$

which is equivalent to

$$(b \Rightarrow c) \wedge a \Rightarrow b$$

which is equivalent to[5]

$$a \Rightarrow b.$$

So no gain this time by including Δ in the antecedent but see next example!

EXAMPLE 4.37.

$$\Delta = a \Rightarrow b \text{ and } G = \neg a.$$

We are looking for a hypothesis H such that $\Delta + H \vdash G$.

---

[5]If $c = \top$ we get $(b \Rightarrow \top) \wedge a \Rightarrow b$ which is equivalent to $a \Rightarrow b$. If $c = \bot$ we get $(b \Rightarrow \bot) \wedge a \Rightarrow b$ which is equivalent to $a \Rightarrow (\neg b \Rightarrow b)$ which is equivalent to $a \Rightarrow b$.

Method 1: Truth tables

	a	b	$a \Rightarrow b$	$\neg a$
1.	$\top$	$\top$	$\top$	$\bot$
2.	$\top$	$\bot$	$\bot$	$\bot$
3.	$\bot$	$\top$	$\top$	$\top$
4.	$\bot$	$\bot$	$\top$	$\top$

The only row which allows for $a \Rightarrow b = \top$ and $\neg a = \bot$ is row 1. So our hypothesis will negate it.

$$H_{\text{tables}} \equiv \neg(a \wedge b) \equiv \neg a \vee \neg b$$

Method 2: Tableaux

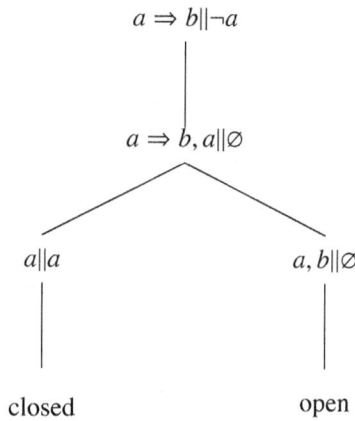

To close the right-hand side we have two options

1. Put a on the right, i.e. add $\neg a$

2. Put b on the right, i.e. add $\neg b$.

The first option, $\neg a$ is the goal, so it cannot be taken and we are left with

$$H_{\text{tableaux}} = \neg b$$

Method 3: Goal directed

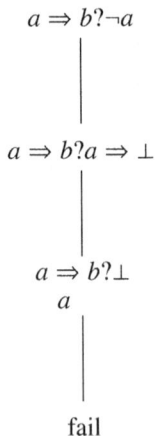

$$a \Rightarrow b?\neg a$$

$$a \Rightarrow b?a \Rightarrow \perp$$

$$a \Rightarrow b?\perp$$
$$a$$

fail

So according to our rules we need to add $\perp$ and the abduced sentence is $a \Rightarrow \perp$, i.e. $\neg a$. But this is the goal itself, so this is not acceptable. We notice that Δ itself i.e. $a \Rightarrow b$ itself is also an assumption, so let us add $(a \Rightarrow b) \wedge a \Rightarrow \perp$. We thus get $(a \Rightarrow b) \Rightarrow \neg a$ which is equivalent to

$$(a \wedge \neg b) \vee \neg a$$

or equivalently

$$(a \vee \neg a) \wedge (\neg b \vee \neg a)$$

which is equivalent to

$$\neg b \vee \neg a.$$

EXAMPLE 4.38. Let $\Delta = \{(a \Rightarrow b) \Rightarrow b, a \Rightarrow c\}$ and let $G = c$. What do we abduce?

Method 1: Truth tables

	a	b	c	$(a \Rightarrow b) \Rightarrow b$	$a \Rightarrow c$
1.	$\top$	$\top$	$\top$	$\top$	$\top$
2.	$\top$	$\top$	$\perp$	$\top$	$\perp$
3.	$\top$	$\perp$	$\top$	$\top$	$\top$
4.	$\top$	$\perp$	$\perp$	$\top$	$\perp$
5.	$\perp$	$\top$	$\top$	$\top$	$\top$
6.	$\perp$	$\top$	$\perp$	$\top$	$\top$
7.	$\perp$	$\perp$	$\top$	$\top$	$\top$
8.	$\perp$	$\perp$	$\perp$	$\perp$	$\top$

Looking at the table, the only row for which $\Delta = \top$ and $G = \bot$ is row 6, namely $\neg a \wedge b \wedge \neg c$.

So we abudce

$$
\begin{aligned}
H_{\text{tables}} \quad &\equiv \quad \neg(\neg a \wedge b \wedge \neg c) \\
&\equiv \quad a \vee \neg b \vee c \\
&\equiv \quad b \Rightarrow a \vee c
\end{aligned}
$$

Method 2: Semantic Tableaux

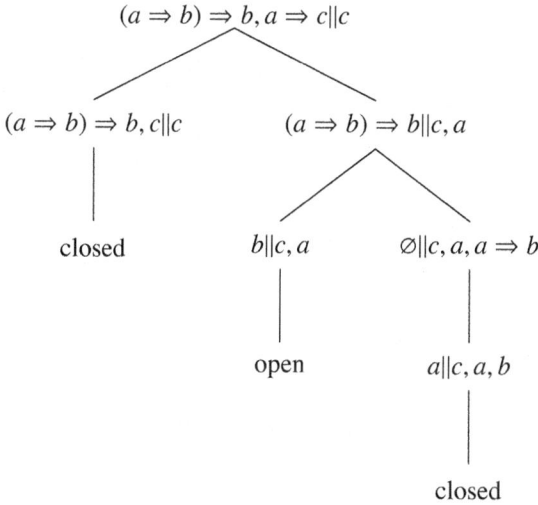

$$(a \Rightarrow b) \Rightarrow b, a \Rightarrow c \| c$$

$(a \Rightarrow b) \Rightarrow b, c \| c \qquad\qquad (a \Rightarrow b) \Rightarrow b \| c, a$

closed

$b \| c, a \qquad\qquad \varnothing \| c, a, a \Rightarrow b$

open

$a \| c, a, b$

closed

The only open tableau is $b \| c, a$.

We have three options:

1. add c to the left, i.e. make c true.

2. add a to the left, i.e. make a true.

3. add b to the right i.e make $\neg b$ true.

The first option is not acceptable as it proves the goal.
Thus we can take H_{tableaux} to be $\neg b$ or to be a.

Method 3: Goal Directed

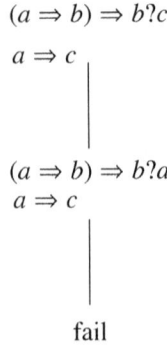

$$(a \Rightarrow b) \Rightarrow b?c$$

$$a \Rightarrow c$$

$$(a \Rightarrow b) \Rightarrow b?a$$
$$a \Rightarrow c$$

fail

We therefore abduce a.

PROPOSITION 4.39. *Let Δ be a database and let G be a goal such that $\Delta \nvdash G$. Assume that $H_1, \ldots, H_n$ are hypotheses abduced by a variety of possibly differnet methods such that*

1. $\Delta + H_i \vdash G$

2. $H_i \nvdash G$.

Then the new hypothesis

$$H = \bigwedge \Delta \Rightarrow \bigvee_{i=1}^{n} H_i$$

is also an acceptable hypothesis satisfying (1) and (2) above.

Proof.

1. First we show $\Delta + H \vdash G$. This follows because $\Delta + H$ proves $\bigvee_i H_i$ and $\Delta \vdash H_i \Rightarrow G$ for each i, and so $\Delta \vdash \bigvee_i H_i \Rightarrow G$.

2. We now show $H \nvdash G$. Otherwise we get

$$\vdash (\bigwedge \Delta \Rightarrow \bigvee H_i) \Rightarrow G$$

   or equivalently

$$\vdash (\neg \bigwedge \Delta \vee \bigvee H_i) \Rightarrow G.$$

   But

$$(X \vee Y \Rightarrow Z) \equiv (X \Rightarrow Z) \wedge (Y \Rightarrow Z)$$

Therefore we get

$$\vdash (\neg \bigwedge \Delta \Rightarrow G) \wedge \bigwedge_i (H_i \Rightarrow G)$$

In particular, we get

$$\vdash H_i \Rightarrow G.$$

A contradiction

■

DEFINITION 4.40 (Abduction algorithm for the goal directed computation).
Consider an abduction problem $\Delta \nvdash G$. The algorithm we have in mind is to compute $\Delta?G$ and whenever we get stuck with a query $?q$ to abduce q. When we are in the middle of the computation we have the then current database Δ, the local goal A and the history of the previous goals $\mathbb{H}$, for the purpose of the restart rule. Thus we define the functional $\mathbf{Ab}(\Delta, A, \mathbb{H})$ by induction as follows:

For convenience we abduce truth $\top$ in the case that $\Delta \vdash G$. This way our algorithm always comes with an answer. If $\Delta \nvdash G$, we get an H such that $\Delta + H \vdash G$ and when $\Delta \vdash G$, we get $\top$ such that $\Delta + \top = \Delta \vdash G$.

1. $\mathbf{Ab}(\Delta, q, \mathbb{H}) = q$, if neither q nor any element of $\mathbb{H}$ is a head of any clause in Δ.

2. $\mathbf{Ab}(\Delta, A \Rightarrow B, \mathbb{H}) = A \Rightarrow \mathbf{Ab}(\Delta + A, B, \mathbb{H})$.

3. $\mathbf{Ab}(\Delta, A \wedge B, \mathbb{H}) = \mathbf{Ab}(\Delta, A, \mathbb{H}) \wedge \mathbf{Ab}(\Delta, B, \mathbb{H})$.

4. $\mathbf{Ab}(\Delta, q, \mathbb{H}) = \mathbf{Ab}(\Delta, A, \mathbb{H} + q)$ if $A \Rightarrow q$ is a clause in Δ or $A \Rightarrow \bot$ is a clause in Δ.

5. $\mathbf{Ab}(\Delta, q, \mathbb{H}) = \top$ if $q \in \Delta$

6. $\mathbf{Ab}(\Delta, q, \mathbb{H}) = \mathbf{Ab}(\Delta, p, \mathbb{H} + q)$ if $p \in \mathbb{H}$ (this is the use of the restart rule).

7. We take as hypothesis H for the abduction probem $\Delta \nvdash G$ the value

$$H = \mathbf{Ab}(\Delta, G, \varnothing)$$

EXAMPLE 4.41. We know that in classical logic $(a \Rightarrow b) \Rightarrow a \vdash a$ but not in intuitionistic logic. So let us see how our abduction algorithm treats the problem.

Note that the goal directed computation for classical logic has restart but not for intuitionistic logic.[6]

$$\mathbf{Ab}(\{(a \Rightarrow b) \Rightarrow a\}, a, \varnothing) =$$
$$\mathbf{Ab}(\{(a \Rightarrow b) \Rightarrow a\}, a \Rightarrow b, \{a\}) =$$
$$a \Rightarrow \mathbf{Ab}(\{(a \Rightarrow b) \Rightarrow a, a\}, b, \{a\}) =$$
$$a \Rightarrow b$$

if we do not have restart, since b is not the head of any of the clauses $(a \Rightarrow b) \Rightarrow a, a$.

When we have restart, we continue

$$= a \Rightarrow \mathbf{Ab}(\{(a \Rightarrow b) \Rightarrow a, a\}, a, \{a, b\})$$
$$= a \Rightarrow \top = \top$$

DEFINITION 4.42. We now define what to abduce in the case of the tableaux.

Let $\mathbf{Ab}(\Delta \| \Theta)$ be the value of what to add to Δ and to Θ to make the tableaux close. We write $\mathbf{Ab}(\Delta \| \Theta) = (\Delta', \Theta')$. Thus we add Δ' to Δ and Θ' to Θ. There are two rules

1. If $\Delta \| \Theta$ has all atoms in it and it is not closed, then we can add any $x \in \Theta$ to Δ and or any $y \in \Delta$ to Θ. Let (Δ', Θ') be one of these options.

2. If $\Delta \| \Theta$ splits into $\Delta_1 \| \Theta_1$ and $\Delta_2 \| \Theta_2$ and (Δ'_1, Θ'_1) and (Δ'_1, Θ'_2) are the abduced additions for each respectively, then let $(\Delta', \Theta') = (\Delta'_1 \cup \Delta'_2, \Theta'_1 \cup \Theta'_2)$.

3. For each combination of options from (1), we get a final option for the original problem $\Delta \| G$. An option is not acceptable if $\Delta' \vdash \Theta' \vee G$.

Note that for the abduction probem $\Delta \nvdash G$, we form the tableau $\Delta \| G$, find the abduced additions (Δ', Θ') and the hypotheses H is

$$H = \bigwedge \Delta' \wedge \neg \bigvee \Theta'.$$

---

[6]To make it clear, let $\Delta ? G$ be a ready for computation problem: goal directed with restart yields classicallgoic and goal directed without restart yields intuitionistic logic.

CHAPTER 5

Non-classical boxes

This chapter defines a box discipline suitable for non-classical logics. The basic idea is that a proof is now being observed and controlled. When we say that from $A_1, \ldots, A_n$ we can prove B (i.e. $A_1, \ldots, A_n \vdash B$) in a logic, we want to know exactly *how* B was derived. For example, we can ask which of the A_i were used in the derivation, which rules were used and in what form. When we perform *modus ponens* A, $A{\Rightarrow}B \vdash B$, then A and $A \Rightarrow B$ are used, A is the minor premise, and $A{\Rightarrow}B$ is the major premise.

In order to follow what assumptions are used in proofs, we annotate all formulae appearing in the proof. New assumptions are annotated (labelled) by new atomic labels and the labelling is propagated through the deduction. Here is how we do it. We need a stock of atomic labels, which is a set (or a multiset, as defined later) $\mathbb{A} = \{a_1, a_2, a_3, \ldots\}$. The labels can be finite subsets of this set, or sequences of elements from this set. If α, β are set labels, then we can perform the operations $\alpha \cup \beta$ to get new labels. If α, β are sequence labels, we can perform the operation $\beta * \alpha$ to get new labels (where '$*$' denotes concatenation of sequences). Assume we defined what our labels are and some operation $f_i(\beta, \alpha)$, $i = 1, 2, \ldots$, giving new labels from old. We can agree on how to label our assumptions and as we progress in the proof we can create new labels using the operation f_i.

Modus ponens will take the following form:

$$\frac{\alpha : A; \quad \beta : A \Rightarrow B}{f_{\text{MP}}(\beta, \alpha) : B}$$

We now present the natural deduction rules of Chapter 3 for labelled formulae.

1   Labelled deduction rules

The labelled rules for $\Rightarrow$

Recall the rules for introducing and eliminating implication in Chapter 3:

$$(\Rightarrow E) \quad \frac{\begin{array}{c} A \\ A \Rightarrow B \end{array}}{B}$$

and

$(\Rightarrow I)$: If $\dfrac{\Delta, A}{B}$ is shown to be valid then $\dfrac{\Delta}{A \Rightarrow B}$ is also valid

The labelled versions of these rules are as follows: (we assume labels are sets α, β of atomic labels and the operation on labels is union $\cup$; we write $a : A$ instead of $\{a\} : A$, for a atomic).

$$(\Rightarrow E) \quad \frac{\begin{array}{c} \alpha : A \\ \beta : A \Rightarrow B \end{array}}{\alpha \cup \beta : B}$$

and

$(\Rightarrow I)$: If $\dfrac{\Delta, a : A}{\alpha \cup \{a\} : B}$ is shown to be valid with a not in α then

$$\frac{\Delta}{\alpha : A \Rightarrow B} \quad \text{is also valid}$$

The labelled rules for $\wedge$

We can use the rules below for introducing and eliminating conjunctions:

$$(\wedge I) \quad \frac{\begin{array}{c} \alpha : A \\ \alpha : B \end{array}}{\alpha : A \wedge B} \qquad (\wedge E) \quad \frac{\alpha : A \wedge B}{\alpha : A}$$

but note that the introduction rule can be applied only when both formulae in the conjunction rely on exactly the same set of assumptions. Another possibility exists for conjunction, which (since the new labelling rule makes it different from $\wedge$) we might denote by $\sqcap$:

$$(\sqcap I) \quad \frac{\begin{array}{c} \alpha : A \\ \beta : B \end{array}}{\alpha \cup \beta : A \sqcap B} \qquad (\sqcap E) \quad \frac{\begin{array}{c} \gamma : A \sqcap B \\ \hline \alpha : A \\ \beta : B \\ \alpha \cup \beta = \gamma \end{array}}{}$$

where α, β are new variable labels, satisfying $\alpha \cup \beta = \gamma$. Here when we eliminate $\sqcap$ we obtain *both* $\alpha : A$ and $\beta : B$, $\alpha \cup \beta$ being a decomposition of γ whose exact value is to be determined later in the proof.

The labelled rules for ∨

There are no special changes necessary to the natural deduction rules for disjunction, except to add the labels:

$$(\vee I) \frac{\alpha : A}{\alpha : A \vee B} \qquad (\vee E) \frac{\begin{array}{c}\alpha : A \Rightarrow C \\ \beta : B \Rightarrow C \\ \gamma : A \vee B\end{array}}{\alpha \cup \beta \cup \gamma : C}$$

The labelled rules for ¬

When we turned the forward natural deduction rules into the backward automated rules, we showed that we could use $A \Rightarrow \bot$ instead of $\neg A$, provided we had a rule for $\bot$. Thus we need

$$\frac{\alpha : \bot}{\alpha : B}$$

We can also add the classical rule:

$$\frac{\alpha : (A \Rightarrow \bot) \Rightarrow \bot}{\alpha : A}$$

As a consequence of the above rules, $\bot$ can be derived from different parts of the database; in particular we may be able to derive several of the $\bot$, each labelled differently.

EXAMPLE 5.1. Suppose we have a labelled database:

$$\begin{array}{ll}(i) & \alpha : A \\ (ii) & \beta : A \Rightarrow B \\ (iii) & \gamma : A \Rightarrow \bot \\ (iv) & \delta : B \Rightarrow \bot\end{array}$$

Using ($\Rightarrow$E) on (i) and (ii), and on the results of that and (iv), we derive $\alpha \cup \beta \cup \delta : \bot$. By using ($\Rightarrow$E) on (i) and (iii), we again derive falsity, but with a different label, i.e. $\alpha \cup \gamma : \bot$.

The usual classical negation rules can be written as

$$(\neg I) \frac{\alpha : A \Rightarrow B, \beta : A \Rightarrow \neg B}{\gamma : \neg A} \qquad (\neg E) \frac{\alpha : \neg A \Rightarrow B, \beta : \neg A \Rightarrow \neg B}{\gamma : A}$$

but we have to decide what the label of the deduction, γ, will be. The simplest choice is to take $\gamma = \alpha \cup \beta$.

We now have two label disciplines for negation, one through the use of $\bot$, and one through $\neg$. The two disciplines are in agreement. This we can verify by deriving the labelled ($\neg$I) and ($\neg$E) in the $\bot$ discipline. We translate $\neg A$ as $A \Rightarrow \bot$. Thus the premises for the ($\neg$I) rule are

$$\alpha : A{\Rightarrow}B, \beta : A{\Rightarrow}(B{\Rightarrow}\perp)$$

Using the ($\Rightarrow$I) rule and two applications of *modus ponens*, we can derive the conclusion $\alpha \cup \beta : A{\Rightarrow}\perp$, which is what our $\neg$ discipline would require. Let us now repeat this same proof for $A = (A'{\Rightarrow}\perp)$. We get

$$\frac{\alpha : (A'{\Rightarrow}\perp){\Rightarrow}B \qquad \beta : (A'{\Rightarrow}\perp){\Rightarrow}(B{\Rightarrow}\perp)}{\alpha \cup \beta : (A'{\Rightarrow}\perp){\Rightarrow}\perp}$$

Note that we have the expected $\alpha \cup \beta$ as the label on the conclusion. This second rule really says

$$\frac{\gamma : (A{\Rightarrow}\perp){\Rightarrow}\perp}{\gamma : A}$$

EXAMPLE 5.2.   Let us redo Example 3.14 using the labels. We had to show that $B{\Rightarrow}(A{\Rightarrow}C)$ follows from the assumption $A{\Rightarrow}(B{\Rightarrow}C)$. We therefore label the data with $\{a_1\}$. We want to show $B \Rightarrow (A \Rightarrow C)$. We have to say with which label. An obvious choice is $\{a_1\}$. The first two lines of the proof will be

$$
\begin{array}{lll}
(1) & \{a_1\} : A{\Rightarrow}(B{\Rightarrow}C) & \text{data} \\
(2) & \text{Show } \{a_1\} : B{\Rightarrow}(A{\Rightarrow}C) &
\end{array}
$$

We proceed as we did originally, by assuming that B is true, and attempting to show that $A{\Rightarrow}C$ is true. We have to decide what labels to attach to each formula. The B is a new assumption, with no past dependencies, so it should have a new label, a_2, say. The choice of label to be placed on our goal of $A{\Rightarrow}C$ is slightly more complicated. The labelled version of the implication introduction rule indicates that if we can show $\alpha \cup \{c\} : D$ by assuming $\{c\} : C$, with c not in α, then we can show $\alpha : C{\Rightarrow}D$. Thus if we are assuming $\{a_2\} : B$, then we show $\{a_1\} : B{\Rightarrow}(A{\Rightarrow}C)$ by showing $\alpha \cup \{a_2\} : A{\Rightarrow}C$, i.e. our label is $\{a_1\} \cup \{a_2\}$, which is $\{a_1, a_2\}$.

$$
\begin{array}{lll}
(2.1) & \{a_2\} : B & \text{assumption with a new label} \\
(2.2) & \text{Show } \{a_1, a_2\} : A{\Rightarrow}C &
\end{array}
$$

We show $\{a_1, a_2\} : A{\Rightarrow}C$ by going to another subcomputation in which we assume A, and show C with the appropriate labels. Again we give the assumption a new label, a_3 say, and give the goal C the label which is the union of the label of the new assumption and the end goal, $\{a_1, a_2\}$. We can now proceed to complete the proof:

$$
\begin{array}{lll}
(2.2.1) & \{a_3\} : A & \text{assumption for subcomputation } (2.2) \\
(2.2.2) & \{a_1, a_3\} : B{\Rightarrow}C & (2.2.1) \text{ and from } (1) \text{ and } (\Rightarrow\text{E}) \\
(2.2.3) & \{a_1, a_2, a_3\} : C & \text{from } (2.1) \text{ and } (2.2.2) \text{ and } (\Rightarrow\text{E})
\end{array}
$$

Note that in steps (2.2.2) and (2.2.3) we constructed the label for the formula obtained by implication elimination from the union of the labels on the premises to the elimination.

As with the non-labelled formulae, we can draw the subcomputations as nested boxes:

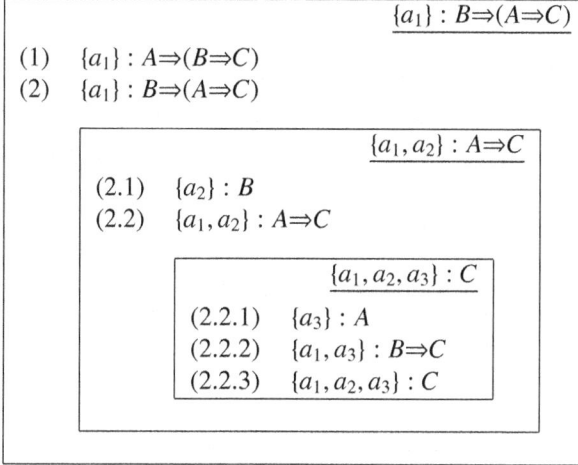

$$\boxed{\begin{array}{ll}
& \hspace{5cm}\underline{\{a_1\} : B{\Rightarrow}(A{\Rightarrow}C)} \\
(1) & \{a_1\} : A{\Rightarrow}(B{\Rightarrow}C) \\
(2) & \{a_1\} : B{\Rightarrow}(A{\Rightarrow}C) \\
& \boxed{\begin{array}{ll}
& \hspace{3cm}\underline{\{a_1, a_2\} : A{\Rightarrow}C} \\
(2.1) & \{a_2\} : B \\
(2.2) & \{a_1, a_2\} : A{\Rightarrow}C \\
& \boxed{\begin{array}{ll}
& \hspace{1.5cm}\underline{\{a_1, a_2, a_3\} : C} \\
(2.2.1) & \{a_3\} : A \\
(2.2.2) & \{a_1, a_3\} : B{\Rightarrow}C \\
(2.2.3) & \{a_1, a_2, a_3\} : C
\end{array}}
\end{array}}
\end{array}}$$

2 Non-classical use of labels

We shall illustrate the use of the labels to perform computations in non-classical logics such as those introduced in Chapter 2. Our labels are multisets as defined in Definition 5.2.1 below. Multisets are like sets except that elements may appear in them more than once. The use of multisets allows us to keep track of how many times an assumption is used in *modus ponens*.

DEFINITION 5.3 (Multisets). Let $\mathbb{A}$ be a set of atoms. A multiset based on $\mathbb{A}$ is a function α on $\mathbb{A}$ giving for each element $a \in \mathbb{A}$ a natural number $\alpha(a) \geq 0$. $\alpha(a)$ tells us how many copies of a we have in the multiset α. Let $\gamma = \alpha \cup \beta$ be defined as the function $\gamma = \alpha + \beta$ (i.e. for each a, $\gamma(a) = \alpha(a) + \beta(a)$). Let $\gamma = \alpha \dot{-} \beta$ be the function defined for each a by $\gamma(a) = 0$, if $\alpha(a) \leq \beta(a)$, and $\gamma(a) = \beta(a) - \alpha(a)$, otherwise.

We shall consider a propositional language with implication only, and reason forwards using *modus ponens*. The proof will be of $(B{\Rightarrow}A){\Rightarrow}((A{\Rightarrow}B){\Rightarrow}(A{\Rightarrow}B))$. We have two options for the labels: we can regard them either as sets or as multisets.

In the derivation with labels as sets, we will end up with the empty label $\varnothing$, showing the formula to be a theorem. If the labels are multisets, we do not end up

with the empty label; hence the formula is not a theorem of the logic whose labels
are multisets.

We begin by using the ($\Rightarrow$I) rule to assume $\{a_1\}$: $B \Rightarrow A$ and try to show $\{a_1\}$:
$(A \Rightarrow B) \Rightarrow (A \Rightarrow B)$. This will succeed only when the labels are sets, not when they
are multisets. However, let us go on. Further assume $\{a_2\}$: $A \Rightarrow B$ and show
$\{a_1, a_2\}$: $A \Rightarrow B$. Further assume $\{a_3\}$: A and show $\{a_1, a_2, a_3\}$: B. We thus end
up with the following problem (the strange line numbers have to do with the box
proof later on):

Assumptions

1. $\{a_1\}$: $B \Rightarrow A$

2.2 $\{a_2\}$: $A \Rightarrow B$

2.2.1 $\{a_3\}$: A

show $\{a_2, a_1, a_2, a_3\}$: B

Derivation

2.2.2 $\{a_2, a_3\}$: B by *modus ponens* from lines (2.1) and (2.2.1).

2.2.3 $\{a_1, a_2, a_3\}$: A from (2.2.2) and (1).

2.2.4 $\{a_2, a_1, a_2, a_3\}$: B from (2.2.3) and (2.1),
                                                        note a_2 is used twice.

2.2 $\{a_2, a_1, a_2\}$: $A \Rightarrow B$ from (2.2.1) and (2.2.4) by ($\Rightarrow$I).

2. $\{a_2, a_1\}$: $(A \Rightarrow B) \Rightarrow (A \Rightarrow B)$ from (2.1) and (2.2) by ($\Rightarrow$I).

0. $\{a_2\}$: $(B \Rightarrow A) \Rightarrow ((A \Rightarrow B) \Rightarrow (A \Rightarrow B))$ from (1) and (2).

Note the following three conventions:

1. Each new assumption is labelled by a new atomic label. An ordering on the
   labels can be imposed, namely $a_1 < a_2 < a_3$. This is to reflect the fact that
   the assumptions arose from our attempt to prove $(B \Rightarrow A) \Rightarrow ((A \Rightarrow B) \Rightarrow (A \Rightarrow B))$
   and not for example from $(A \Rightarrow B) \Rightarrow ((B \Rightarrow A) \Rightarrow (A \Rightarrow B))$ in which case the ordering would be $a_2 < a_1 < a_3$. The ordering can affect the proofs in certain
   logics. Some logics allow us to bring in, anywhere in the proof, theorems of
   the logic with the empty label and allow their use in the proof. Other logics
   do not allow this.

2. If in the proof A is labelled by the multiset α and $A \Rightarrow B$ is labelled by β then
   B can be derived with a label $\alpha \cup \beta$ where $\cup$ denotes multiset union.

3. If B was derived using A as evidenced by the fact that the label α of A is a singleton $\{a\}$, a atomic and a is in the label β of $B(\alpha \subseteq \beta)$ then we can derive $A \Rightarrow B$ with the label $\beta \dot{-} \alpha$ ('$\dot{-}$' is multiset subtraction).

In case our labels are sets, we use $\beta - \alpha$, where '$-$' is set subtraction. The labels of the derivation above become, in this case, the following:

$$
\begin{array}{ll}
2.2.4 & \{a_1, a_2, a_3\} \\
2.2 & \{a_1, a_3\} \\
2 & \{a_1\} \\
0 & \varnothing
\end{array}
$$

The derivation of 2 from 1 can be represented in a more graphical way:

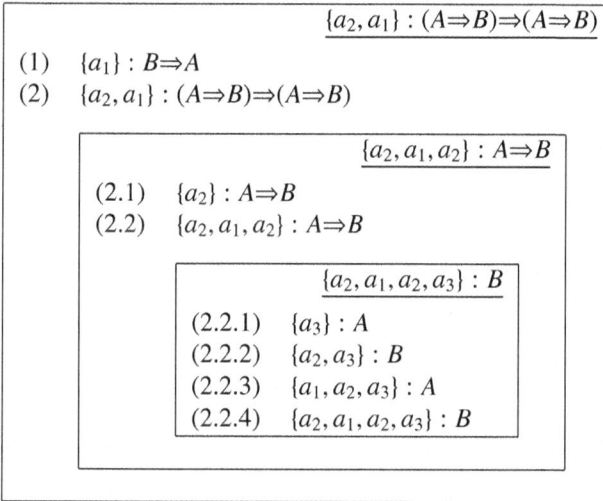

$$\{a_2, a_1\} : (A \Rightarrow B) \Rightarrow (A \Rightarrow B)$$

(1) $\{a_1\} : B \Rightarrow A$
(2) $\{a_2, a_1\} : (A \Rightarrow B) \Rightarrow (A \Rightarrow B)$

$$\{a_2, a_1, a_2\} : A \Rightarrow B$$

(2.1) $\{a_2\} : A \Rightarrow B$
(2.2) $\{a_2, a_1, a_2\} : A \Rightarrow B$

$$\{a_2, a_1, a_2, a_3\} : B$$

(2.2.1) $\{a_3\} : A$
(2.2.2) $\{a_2, a_3\} : B$
(2.2.3) $\{a_1, a_2, a_3\} : A$
(2.2.4) $\{a_2, a_1, a_2, a_3\} : B$

The above is the box method of representing the deduction. Note that in leaving the inner box for $\{a_2, a_1, a_2\} : A \Rightarrow B$, multiset subtraction was used and only one copy of the label a_2 was taken out. The other copy of a_2 remains and cannot be cancelled, so that the entire computation finishes with the label of $\{a_2\}$. We thus have scope here to define different logics by saying when a labelled proof is acceptable. For linear logic, the final label at the end of the computation must be empty, signifying that formulae have only been used once. Hence this formula is not a theorem of linear logic because the outer box does not exit with label $\varnothing$. In relevance logic, the discipline uses sets and not multisets. Thus the label upon leaving the inner box in this case would be $\{a_1\}$ and that upon leaving the outermost box would be $\varnothing$.

Note that different conditions on labels correspond to different logics, given informally in the following table:

condition:	logic:
ignore the labels	intuitionistic logic
accept only the derivations which use all the assumptions	relevance logic
accept derivations which use all assumptions exactly once	linear logic

The conditions on the labels can be translated into reasoning rules.

EXERCISE 5.4.   Construct box derivations for the formulae below and indicate which logic (linear, relevance or intuitionistic) allows a derivation with the empty label.

1. $A \Rightarrow A$

2. $(A \Rightarrow (A \Rightarrow B)) \Rightarrow (A \Rightarrow B)$

3. $(C \Rightarrow A) \Rightarrow ((B \Rightarrow C) \Rightarrow (B \Rightarrow A))$

4. $(C \Rightarrow A) \Rightarrow ((A \Rightarrow B) \Rightarrow (C \Rightarrow B))$

5. $(A \Rightarrow (B \Rightarrow C)) \Rightarrow ((A \Rightarrow B) \Rightarrow (A \Rightarrow C))$

6. $A \Rightarrow (B \Rightarrow A)$

7. $((A \Rightarrow A) \Rightarrow A) \Rightarrow A$

3   The theory of labelled deductive systems

Previous sections have only touched slightly on the powerful use of labels in logic. We used the labels to control the forward proofs of a given system. Labels can have many roles and this section will hint at some of them. First note that by using sequences as labels we can have a better control of the proof. Thus $a : A$, $b : A \Rightarrow B$ should yield $(b, a) : B$ and not $\{b, a\} : B$. From the sequence (b, a) we know that b was the label of the ticket $A \Rightarrow B$ and a was the label of the minor premise.

Consider the following argument:

EXAMPLE 5.5 (Labels as resource).

> Assumptions:
> $a_1 : A$
> $a_2 : A \Rightarrow B$
> $a_3 : C$
> $a_4 : C \Rightarrow B$
> $a_5 : D \Rightarrow \neg B$
> $a_6 : B \Rightarrow E$
> $a_7 : D$

The labels just name the assumptions. We perform deduction with the rule of *modus ponens*, ($\Rightarrow$ elimination rule). We use the labels to record the sequence of deduction steps. For example, from these assumptions we can deduce E in two different ways. We can record that by concatenating the labels in the following way:

$$\beta : X \Rightarrow Y; \gamma : X$$
$$(\beta * \gamma) : Y$$

where $*$ is concatenation. Notice that we put β first; it labels the 'ticket'.

We can get

> $a_2 * a_1 : B$
> $a_4 * a_3 : B$
> $a_5 * a_7 : \neg B$

and therefore by another step of *modus ponens*:

> $a_6 * (a_2 * a_1) : E$
> $a_6 * (a_4 * a_3) : E$

Note that by looking at the labels we can tell exactly how each formula is derived. We can also determine from which parts of the data an inconsistency is derived. Thus B and $\neg B$ can be obtained either from $\{a_1, a_2, a_5, a_7\}$ or from $\{a_3, a_4, a_5, a_7\}$. We can double check those assumptions for errors.

The $\Rightarrow$ introduction rule has the following form:

> To introduce $t : A \Rightarrow B$ we further assume (add to our assumptions) the labelled formula $y : A$, where y is a *new* arbitrary label, and show $t * y : B$.

The above used the labels as names used for resource considerations. However, we can use labels in much more profitable ways. The labels can be more complex annotations of the assumptions. For example, the labels can be names of the persons putting forward the assumptions together with a measure (number?) of their reliability, such as (john, 0.7). The label can be an entire chain of reasoning justifying the assumption. For example, the context of the argument of the previous example may be legal:

A = The prisoner has terminal cancer.
B = The prisoner should be freed.

In this case the label a_2 of $A \Rightarrow B$ can be a reference $a_2 = l_1$ to some legislation or precedent and the label a_1 of A can be a medical file $a_1 = m$ which involves medical evidence and argument.

In fact, C may be:

C = The prisoner was illegally arrested.

The label for $a_3 = r$ for C could be a report r from an internal investigative body of the police and the label $a_4 = l_2$ of $C \Rightarrow B$, another legal reference. We can thus write:

$m : A$
$l_1 : A \Rightarrow B$
$r : C$
$l_2 : C \Rightarrow B$

and B can be derived in two ways with two labels. '$\cup$' reads union of databases, giving the cumulative support of what is deduced:

$l_1 \cup m : B$
$l_2 \cup r : B$

A person wishing to attack the conclusion B will have to attack the derivation. In the labelled deductive system (LDS) where the labels are names or people who recorded the assumptions, there is no recourse. In the LDS where the labels are themselves justifications to the assumptions, one can 'attack' the label. Thus one can question the medical argument which supports A, or the police report which supports C. Note that it is convenient to put the medical and police support in the label and not as further data because their reasoning is different in nature from the master deduction.

There are practical examples such as arguments having to do with abortion, where one cannot label the data so easily. Medical, religious, social, legal and political considerations all intermingle. However, a neat theory of labelling can help the practical reasoner in presenting and studying the arguments and counterarguments.

There is much more to be done with labels as the next example shows.

EXAMPLE 5.6 (Aggregation, priorities and flattening). Assume that in the previous example we have another implication

$$b_1 : C \Rightarrow \neg E$$
$$b_2 : D$$

We can now derive $\neg E$ with the label

$$b_1 * a_3 : \neg E$$

and derive $\neg B$ with $a_5 * b_2 : \neg B$.

The data may appear inconsistent. Certainly without the labels we get an inconsistent set of assumptions and in many logics nothing can be done.[1] In the LDS what we do depends on the nature of the labels. First we must aggregate labels supporting the same formula. Let $\uplus$ be the aggregation symbol. We thus have

$$(a_2 * a_1) \uplus (a_4 * a_3) : B$$
$$a_5 * b_2 : \neg B$$
$$(a_6 * (a_2 * a_1)) \uplus (a_6 * (a_4 * a_3)) : E$$
$$b_1 * a_3 : \neg E$$

Obviously $\uplus$ must be associative and commutative and $*$ must distribute over plus.

In practice *modus ponens* may have compatibility restrictions. For example, the b_1, b_2 labels may be political files and we may not wish to intermingle political and legal considerations. Thus we need a predicate $\mathcal{F}(\beta, \gamma)$, which, when it holds, licenses the *modus ponens* between $\gamma : X; \beta : X \Rightarrow Y$.

In general, there is no way to decide whether to accept B over $\neg B$ or E over $\neg E$ and with what label, without more information about the labels. For example, if we give general priority to b_1, b_2 labels over $a_1, \ldots, a_6$ labels, we get priority for deriving $\neg B$ over B and $\neg E$ over E.

However, if the labels are reliability numbers then since B can be derived in two different ways it might end up with a higher reliability than $\neg B$. Everything depends on our policy.

A policy of deciding with which label and which X or $\neg X$ to emerge given a variety of derivations of $t_i : X$ and $s_j : \neg X$ is called a *flattening policy*.

For mathematical clarity we must now give a formal definition.

DEFINITION 5.7 (An algebraic LDS for implication and negation). Let **L** be a propositional language with $\Rightarrow, \neg$ and atoms. Let $\mathcal{A}$ be an algebra of labels with relations $x < y$ for priority among labels, $\mathcal{F}(x, y)$ of compatibility among labels and functions, $f(x, y)$ for propagating labels and $\uplus$ for aggregating labels.

1. A *declarative unit* is a pair $t : A$, where A is a formula and t a term on the algebra of labels (built up from atomic labels and the functions f and $\uplus$).

---

[1]Recall that in our system for classical logic, any goal succeeds immediately if $\bot$ is in the database. This is not realistic. A practical database may contain data on several individuals. Getting the address of one individual wrong should not logically imply any statement about any other individual.

2. A *database* is a set containing declarative units and formulae of the form $t_i < s_i$ and $\mathcal{F}(t_i, s_i)$ for some labels $t_1, \ldots, s_i, \ldots$.

3. The $\Rightarrow$ elimination rule, *modus ponens*, has the form

$$\frac{t : A; s : A \Rightarrow B; \mathcal{F}(s, t)}{f(s, t) : B}$$

4. The $\Rightarrow$ introduction rule has the form

   - To introduce $t : A \Rightarrow B$
     Assume $x : A$, for x arbitrary in the set $\{y \mid \mathcal{F}(t, y)\}$, and show $f(t, x) : B$.

5. Negation rules have the form

$$\frac{t : B; s : \neg B}{r : C}$$

We are not writing any specific rules because there are so many options for negation.

6. A family of *flattening rules* **Flat** of the form

$$\frac{t_1 : A, \ldots, t_k : A; s_1 : \neg A, \ldots, s_m : \neg A; y_i < y_j, i = 1, 2, \ldots, j = 1, 2, \ldots}{\mathsf{Flat}(\{t_1, \ldots, t_k, s_1, \ldots, s_m\})}$$

where γ is the result of applying the function **Flat** on the set containing t_i, s_j and where y_j, y_i range over $\{t_1, \ldots, t_k, s_1, \ldots, s_m\}$.[2]

7. *Aggregation rule*

$$\frac{t : A; s : A}{t \uplus s : A}$$

8. $\uplus$ is associative, commutative and f is distributive over $\uplus$.

9. A proof is a sequence of expressions which are of the form $t < s$, $\mathcal{F}(t, s)$ or $t : A$ such that each element of the sequence is either an assumption or is obtained from previous elements in the sequence by an elimination rule or is introduced by a subcomputation via the $\Rightarrow$ introduction rule. Flattening rules are to be used last.

---

[2]**Flat** is a function defined on any set of labels and giving as value a new label. To understand this, recall another function on numbers which we may call **Sum**. It adds any set of numbers to give a new number: their sum!

REMARK 5.8. Note that since $<$ is an ordering appearing positively in a database we can always consistently lower the priority of any label in the database.

EXAMPLE 5.9. Consider the following database

1. $m : A$ 5. $r < m$
2. $l_1 : A \Rightarrow B$ 6. $\mathcal{F}(l_1, m)$
3. $r : X$ 7. $\mathcal{F}(l_2, r)$
4. $l_2 : X \Rightarrow \neg B$

where A, B mean as before and $<$ says that medical support for assumptions has higher priority (probably because it can more easily be reconfirmed) and the labelling propagation function is $\cup$.

$$\frac{\gamma : A; \beta : A \Rightarrow B; \mathcal{F}(\beta, \gamma)}{\beta \cup \gamma : B}$$

$\mathcal{F}$ is the compatibility function saying something like the supports γ, β are of a compatible kind, e.g. legal–medical, etc.

We can take the flattening rule

$$\frac{t : \neg B; s : B; t < s}{\mathsf{Flat}(t, s) : B}$$

and can thus prove $\mathsf{Flat}(l_2 \cup r; l_1 \cup m) : B$ from our data. If, however, the credibility of the label m is attacked (i.e. $r < m$ is questioned) then B may no longer be provable.

EXAMPLE 5.10 (Flattening examples). We give more examples where flattening occurs.

1. Imagine the label α lists the independent sources confirming a statement A. Thus $\alpha : A$ means that A is confirmed by the sources in α. Then $\alpha_1 : A, \ldots, \alpha_n : A$ can be consolidated into $\alpha = \mathsf{Flat}(\{\alpha_1, \ldots, \alpha_n\})$. The consolidation process will take into account connections between the sources, etc.

2. Imagine we are dealing with a medical diagnosis system. $\alpha : A$ can mean that A is true with likelihood α, α being a number. There are various considerations involved in obtaining such numbers and we may have estimates $\alpha_1 : A, \ldots, \alpha_n : A$ coming from various directions. These can be flattened into $\alpha : A$ according to some statistical or probabilistic model [Gabbay, 1996].

The reader can find more on the LDS in my book *Labelled Deductive Systems*, [Gabbay, 1996].

CHAPTER 6

Probabilistic Logic

1 Discrete probability

This section presents just enough probability theory to enable us to introduce probabilistic logic. We begin with a simple example. Imagine we are dealing with an important political issue and that the government (comprised of one Prime Minister and nine other ministers) wants to leave the deliberation and decision to a subcommittee of ministers. Of course, the composition of the committee is important. Some people (voters) think that the entire government should be involved. Some may think that the Prime Minister should be involved in any committete, others insist on certain ministers whom they trust. The government decided to put the matter to the public for a vote. How can they do that?

The simplest way is to list all possible committees (i.e. list all subsets of ministers (there are 2^{10} such subsets where voting for the empty subset can mean voting that the matter can be dropped), and asking each voter to choose one.[1]

So, for example, for three poeple, $\{a, b, c\}$ the subsets are:

$$
\begin{array}{ll}
x_1 : & \{a, b, c\} \\
x_2 : & \{a, b\} \\
x_3 : & \{a, c\} \\
x_4 : & \{a\} \\
x_5 : & \{b, c\} \\
x_6 : & \{b\} \\
x_7 : & \{c\} \\
x_8 : & \{\varnothing\}
\end{array}
$$

So the ballot would look like:

---

[1] In practice, one can have a voting ballot containing 10 names and two boxes next to each name, one for "in" and one for "out". Each voter has to tick one of each pair.

Name	In	Out
a	✓	
b		✓
c	✓	

So, suppose that out of 10,000 voters we got 500 votes voting for x_8, 3500 voting for x_1 and 1000 voters voting for each of the other alternatives. In percents, we get the following numbers $\pi(x)$ for case x:

$$
\begin{aligned}
\pi(x_1) &= 0.35 \\
\pi(x_2) &= 0.1 \\
\pi(x_3) &= 0.1 \\
\pi(x_4) &= 0.1 \\
\pi(x_5) &= 0.1 \\
\pi(x_6) &= 0.1 \\
\pi(x_7) &= 0.1 \\
\pi(x_8) &= 0.05
\end{aligned}
$$

Note that $\sum_{i=1}^{8} \pi(x_i) = 1$.

Now suppose we pick up a voter at random and ask what is the chance (probability) that he voted for say x_5? The answer is $\pi(x_5) = 0.1$, which is the percent which voted for x_5.

There is another way of doing this. In case all the ministers have differnt talents and the inclusion of one minister does not influence the inclusion of another, we can ask for each minister, how many voters want him/her in and how many want him out. Thus each minister a will get a number $\eta(a)$ in percents of the proportion of the voters who want him/her in. For a given committee, the percents of people who want exactly that committee is the product of the percents of the members who are voted in multiplied by the product of the (1–percents) of the ministers who are voted out. For the case of three ministers a, b, c, let $\eta(a), \eta(b), \eta(c)$ be the proportion of voters who want them in respectively. Then

$\pi(x_1)$ for $\{a, b, c\}$ will have $\eta(a) \times \eta(b) \times \eta(c)$
$\pi(x_5)$ for $\{b, c\}$ will have $(1 - \eta(a)) \times \eta(b) \times \eta(c)$
and $\pi(x_9)$ for $\varnothing$ will have $(1 - \eta(a)) \times (1 - \eta(b)) \times (1 - \eta(c))$.

We have motivated the following definition.

DEFINITION 6.1.

1. A discrete base for a (logic) probability space is any finite set $S \neq \varnothing$.

2. A π probability distribution on S is a function π giving a value $\pi(X) \in [0, 1]$ for any subset $X \subseteq S$. We assume that $\sum_{X \subseteq S} \pi(X) = 1$.

3. An η probability distribution on S is a function η on S giving values $\eta(a)$ in $[0, 1]$ for any $a \in S$.

4. An η-distribution induces a π distribution by letting, for $X \subseteq S$

$$\pi(X) = (\prod_{s\in X} \eta(s)) \times \prod_{s\notin X}(1 - \eta(s))$$

We assume the emtpy product is to be 1 by agreement.

So for example, $\eta(S) = \prod_{s\in S} \eta(s)$ and $\eta(\varnothing) = \prod_{s\in S}(1 - \eta(s))$.

5. An event $\mathbb{E}$ is a family of subsets of S. Thus $\mathbb{E} \in 2^{2^S}$.

An atomic even is an element $q \in S$, regarded as a sbuset of 2^S. Thus

$$\mathbb{E}_q = \{X \subseteq S | q \in X\}.$$

It is easy to calculate that under the η-probability $\eta(\mathbb{E}_q) = \eta(q)$.

2 Probabilistic models

2.1

This section presents a general discussion on how to impose external probability on a logic.

Let $\mathbb{L}$ be a logic with a conseqeunce relation $\vdash$. $\mathbb{L}$ can be presented to us either syntactically through some proof theoretic system or semantically through a class of models S and a semantic consequence $\vDash$.

We begin with the semantic approach. We assume that we have the notion of satisfaction, $\mathbf{m} \vDash A$, for a model $\mathbf{m} \in S$ and a wff A of $\mathbb{L}$, and that we have

$$A \vdash_{\mathbb{L}} B \text{ iff for all } \mathbf{m} \in S, \text{ if } \mathbf{m} \vDash A \text{ then } \mathbf{m} \vDash B. \tag{*}$$

The π-external probability approach endows the set of models S with a probability measure π and defines

$$\pi(A) = \pi(\{\mathbf{m}|\mathbf{m} \vDash A\}) \tag{**}$$

It is convenient for this approach to restrict the language to n atomic propositions $Q = \{q_1, \ldots, q_n\}$. For many logics this restriction allows us to consdier only a finite set S of models $\{\mathbf{m}_1, \ldots, \mathbf{m}_k\}$ and then our π approach simply gives values $x_i = \pi(\mathbf{m}_i)$ such that $\sum_i x_i = 1$.

Note that for $\mathbb{L}$ there may be several possible semantics $S_1, S_2, \ldots$ which characterise it (i.e. for which (*) holds). It is not clear whether for any given π_1 on S_1 we can have a π_2 on S_2 such that for any wff A we have $\pi_1(A) = \pi_2(A)$.

The η-approach works on the syntax of $\mathbb{L}$. Schematically it works as follows.

First we give independent probability values to all atoms of the language (or of Q if we deal with only n atoms). Then we propagate the probability to all complex formulas A by using $\vdash$ and by using induction on the complexity of A.

So we may have an inductive clause of the form

$\eta(A) =$ Some linear combination function on $\eta(X)$ for X a less
complex formula related to A, where we use the $\vdash$ $(* * *)$
relation in choosing such Xs and in deciding how to
combine their η values to get the η value of A

This definition is so general that we hasten to give an immediate example.

In classical propositional logic, let $\eta(q_i) = x_i, 0 \leq x_i \leq 1, q_i \in Q$. Let

$$
\begin{aligned}
\eta(A(q_i)) &= \eta(A(q_i/\top))\eta(q_i) + \eta(A(q_i/\bot))\eta(\neg q_i) \\
&= x_i\eta(A(q_i/\top) + (1 - x_i)\eta(A/q_i/\bot))
\end{aligned}
$$

where $A(q/\bot)$ and $Q(q/\top)$ are the result of substituting $\bot$ and $\top$ respectively for q in A.

Note that this definition is different from the traditional recursive definition of a truth table for many valued logic, where for each connective $\sharp(A_1, \ldots, A_n)$, we have a function $f_\sharp$ on truth values such that

$$
V(A = \sharp(A_1, \ldots, A_n)) = f_\sharp(V(A_1), \ldots, V(A_n)).
$$

Note that in $(***)$ we may use details of the proof theory of $\mathbb{L}$ in case $\vdash$ is presented proof theoretically rather than as an axiomatic consequence relation.

Of course, the two approaches can be related and for a logic with both semantics and proof theory a combination of the two approaches may be used.

2.2   Labelled Deductive Systems and Probability Logic

This section will introduce a new method for constructing probability logics within the framework of Labelled Deductive Systems (LDS) of [Gabbay, 1996]. This construction is more general than currently known probability logics as well as Bayesian networks. It can be used to develop probabilistic logics based on logics other than classical logic, or its extensions (such as modal logic).

We begin by introducing the version of LDS required for our construction. We shall motivate it step by step.

Consider a propositional language with the binary connective $\rightarrow$ alone. Consider a natural deduction proof system for this language containing two rules only, $\rightarrow I$ and $\rightarrow E$. Let us state these rules:

$$
\rightarrow E : \qquad \frac{A \rightarrow B; A}{B}
$$

The → *I* rule says that to show $A \rightarrow B$, we need to assume A and show B. We write it schematically as

$$→ I :$$

A
...
B

Exit : $A \rightarrow B$

The box indicates that we are dealing with a subcomputation, beginning with the assumption A and ending with B. There are further hidden procedural agreements here. These are:

1. The background data (theory), Δ is a *set* of wffs.

2. Adding the assumption A to Δ means that we form $\Delta' = \Delta \cup \{A\}$.

3. In the proof inside the box (from A to B) all of Δ is accessible to be used.

Different logics may vary on (1)–(3) above, especially on the meaning of a database Δ and on the meaning of "adding" an assumption to Δ.

EXAMPLE 6.2. To show $\Delta = \{A \rightarrow (A \rightarrow B)\} \vdash A \rightarrow B$.
The proof is as follows:

1. $A \rightarrow (A \rightarrow B)$, data

2. $A \rightarrow B$ from box using → *I*

2.1	A, assumption
2.2	$A \rightarrow B$, from 1 and 2.1 using → *E*
2.3	B, from 2.1, 2.2 using → *E*

Exit : $A \rightarrow B$

It is well known that the above proof theory characterises intuitionistic implication.

Our first step in introducing LDS is to introduce labels into the system. Let $\mathcal{A}$ be a set of labels and let **f** be a binary operation on $\mathcal{A}$ and let φ be a binary predicate on $\mathcal{A}$. We also need a function $\delta = (\mathbf{Exit}\,x)\gamma(x)$ yielding a term $\delta \in \mathcal{A}$ from any term $\gamma(x)$ with free variable x. We allow for $(\mathbf{Exit}\,x)\gamma(x)$ to be undefined. So it is a partial function.

We define a declarative unit as a pair $t : A$, where t is a label and A a wff. A database Δ is a set of declarative units with possibly some conditions on their labels and to add an assumption $x : A$ to Δ, take $\Delta' = \Delta \cup \{x : A\}$, with possbily some conditions on x relating it to existing labels in Δ.

The two rules become the following in our labelled system:

Labelled $\rightarrow E$:

$$\frac{\beta : A \rightarrow B; \alpha : A; \varphi(\beta, \alpha)}{\mathbf{f}(\beta, \alpha) : B}$$

Note that $\mathbf{f}$ is used to give the new label for the result of the modus ponens, and φ is the condition on the labels that will enable the modus ponens. Different φ and $\mathbf{f}$ will give different rules. This kind of rule is not the most general rule we need; we shall see later that it needs to be generalised. But we are presenting and motivating our system in stages.

We now give the introduction rule:

Labelled $\rightarrow I$

$x : A,$	assumption, where x is a free new
$\vdots$	labelling variable, satisfying the
$\vdots$	prescribed relationship to other labels
$\gamma(x) : B$	with $(\mathbf{Exit}\, x)\gamma(x)$ defined!

Exit : $(\mathbf{Exit}\, x)\gamma(x) : A \rightarrow B$

We now have to explain in general terms what we mean by "$(\mathbf{Exit}\, x)\gamma(x)$ defined". Suppose we are advancing in the proof line by line and we are now at line 99 of the proof. At line 99 we want to introduce the labelled formula

99. $y : A \rightarrow B$

We need to give an argument justifying the introduction of $y : A \rightarrow B$. The justification is a subcomputation, starting with the assumption $x : A$, where x is an arbitrary *new* atomic label, possibly satisfying some standard constraints defined by our logic, and proceeding to prove B with some label $\gamma(x, a_i) : B$, where a_i are some parameters accumulated during the proof. This can schematically be written as

99. $y : A \rightarrow B$, from box subcomputation

99.1	$x : A$, assumption
$\vdots$	
99.??	$\gamma(x, a_i) : B$, where $(\mathbf{Exit}\, x)\gamma(x)$ is defined and $y = (\mathbf{Exit}\, x)\gamma(x)$

$$\mathbf{Exit} : y : A \rightarrow B$$

How do we find y?

Well, at line 99 we claim that we have buried in our proof the information $y : A \rightarrow B$. OK. If this is the case, let us pretend we do have

(*) $y : A \rightarrow B, \varphi(y, x)$ holds

(**) $x : A, x$ atomic new label

and prove using the modus ponens rules of our logic the formula B. If executing the modus ponens gives us a label $\mathbf{f}(y, x, b_j)$, b_j being some parameters, then we must have that the following **Exit** equation must hold:

$$(\mathbf{Exit} \text{ equation}) : \gamma(x, a_i) = \mathbf{f}(y, b_j).$$

If we can solve this equation for y, then we say that "$(\mathbf{Exit}\, x)\gamma(x)$ is defined".

EXAMPLE 6.3. Let $\mathcal{A}$ be the free algebra on atomic generators $\{t_1, t_2, t_3, \ldots\}$. Let $\mathbf{f}(\beta, \alpha)$ be $\beta\alpha$, the concatenation of β and then α. Let us assume that concatenation is associative. Let φ be *Truth*. Let $(\mathbf{Exit}\, x)\gamma(x)$ be the result of deleting the single occurrence of x from $\gamma(x)$ if x occurs in $\gamma(x)$ exactly once and otherwise let it be undefined.

Let us now check the proof of the previous example, namely,

$$t : A \rightarrow (A \rightarrow B) \vdash ? : A \rightarrow B$$

here is an attempt at the proof:

1. $t : A \rightarrow (A \rightarrow B)$, data

2. any label: $A \rightarrow B$, from box below:

> 2.1 $x : A$, assumption
> 2.2 $(tx) : A \rightarrow B$, from 1 and 2.1 using $\rightarrow E$
> 2.3 (txx), from 2.1 and 2.2
>
> We cannot exit because $(\mathbf{Exit}\, x)(txx)$ is not defined!

Thus $A \rightarrow B$ cannot be proved from $t : A \rightarrow (A \rightarrow B)$ with any label.

The reader will note that A was used twice in the box!

EXAMPLE 6.4. Let the labels be numbers and define a database to be of the form $\{t_1 : A_1, \ldots, t_k : A_k\}$ with $t_1 < t_2 < \ldots < t_k$.

Let $f(\beta, \alpha) = \beta\alpha$. Let $\varphi(\beta, \alpha)$ mean $\max(\beta) < \max(\alpha)$. Let $(\mathbf{Exit}\, x)\gamma(x)$ be the result of deleting x from $\gamma(x)$.

Define input into Δ only with a label x bigger than all labels of Δ.
Define modus ponens as

$$\frac{s : A \to B; x : A; x \text{ atomic and } s < x}{sx : B}$$

Consider now the database

$$\Delta = \{t : A \to (B \to C); s : B, t < s\}.$$

We ask: can we prove $A \to C$ with any label? To check this we assume $x : A$.
The rules are that x has to be atomic and we need to assume $s < x$. Under this
assumption we can do modus ponens with $t : A \to (B \to C)$ and get $tx : B \to C$,
but we cannot continue and do modus ponens with $s : B$.

REMARK 6.5. The previous example can be used to make some theoretical points.
Imagine we are given as before the two assumptions

1. $t : A \to (B \to C)$

2. $s : B$

3. $t < s$

It is clear that if a new item of data $r : A$ presents itself with $t \leq r \leq s$, then we
can get $(trs) : C$. We now ask: can we do some sort of modus ponens and get
something like

4. $(t, s) : A \to B^2$

With the understanding that the modus ponens rule governing 4 is

$$\to E_1 : \frac{(t, s) : A \to B; \gamma : A; t \leq r \leq s}{(trs) : B}$$

Compare this with our ordinary $\to E$ rule

$$\to E : \frac{y : A \to B; x : A; y \leq x}{yx : B}$$

This means that we can have partial modus ponens rule yielding as results some
new and different modus ponens. We would need to reconfigure our labelling
system so that we can write down the new rules in a systematic way.

Here is how we do it. Let A be any formula of the logic. It has the form
$A = (A_1 \to (A_2 \to \ldots \to A_n \to q)\ldots)$ where q is atomic. When A is an

---

[2]Note we are writing (t, s) rather than ts because we are going to impose some additional conditions
on the labelling.

item of data in the datbase with label β, then successive modus ponens with labels $x_1, \ldots, x_n$ in that order will yield

$$(\beta x_1 x_2 \ldots x_k) : A_{k+1} \to (\ldots \to (A_n \to q) \ldots).$$

So let us give A the label $(\lambda x_1, \ldots, x_n(\beta x_1, \ldots, x_n)$ and if $\alpha_k : A_k$ presents itself we can substitute at the right place and get $(\lambda x_1, \ldots, x_{k-1} \alpha_k x_{k+1}, \ldots, x_n) : A_1 \to \ldots \to (A_{k-1} \to (A_{k+1} \ldots \to A_n \to q) \ldots)$. This means that we need a new kind of modus ponens rule, which we call *hyper modus ponens*.It has the form of a family of rules, dependent on the formulas in question of the form

$$\to E_{A \to B} \frac{\beta : A \to B; \alpha : A, \varphi(\beta, \alpha)}{\mathbf{f}(\beta, \alpha) : B; \varphi'}$$

Thus if $B = B_1 \to B_2$ then its modus ponens rule will use φ' as a condition and will induce a new φ'' for B_2.

The moral of this example is the following. Suppose we have a complex network with wffs in it and a clear concept of how to prove things in the right order from data coming in. We can now form a complex label for the network and write new rules of how to reduce the network to a smaller one with the right correct label, no matter in what order the data arrives.

Basically we shall need to be using a λ-term system for the logic.

2.3 Classical probabilistic tables

Consider a truth table for a formula A built up from the atoms $q_1, \ldots, q_n$. Consider an assignment h giving values $h(q_1) = x_1, \ldots, h(q_n) = x_n$ to the atoms. For this assignment we get that the truth value of A is $y = h(A)$. If $q_1, \ldots, q_n$ have some meaning, i.e. if they formalise some meaningful sentences, then we can ask what is the chance that $h(q_i) = x_i$ in the certain situation under consideration. For example, $A(p, q)$ may be $p \wedge \neg q$, with

- $p = $ I use my visa card to buy this camera over the internet

- $q = $ the visa number is secure.

What are the chances for $p = \top$ and $q = \bot$?

In this case we can get something like the following:

If $p = \top$ (i.e. I do buy the camera over the net) then the probability that my visa number is secure is 80% (0.8). Of course if I don't buy the camera over the net then the probabilty that my visa number is secure is 98% (0.98). Now, the next question to ask is what is the probability that I do buy the camera? That, of course, depends on me. So suppose I can't make up my mind and decide to flip a coin. Then the probability is 50% (0.5). So the probabilities associated with each option are as follows:

- $p = \top$ and $q = \top$ is $\frac{1}{2} \times 0.8 = 0.4$

- $p = \top$ and $q = \bot$ is $\frac{1}{2} \times -0.2 = 0.1$.

- $p = \bot$ and $q = \top$ is $\frac{1}{2} \times 0.98 = 0.49$

- $p = \bot$ and $q = \bot$ is $\frac{1}{2} \times 0.02 = 0.01$.

What we get here is a probability number associated with each row of the truth table for p and q, as in the diagram (Figure 6.1).

probability	p	q	$A = p \wedge \neg q$
$\pi_1 = 0.4$	$\top$	$\top$	$\bot$
$\pi_2 = 0.1$	$\top$	$\bot$	$\top$
$\pi_3 = 0.49$	$\bot$	$\top$	$\bot$
$\pi_4 = 0.01$	$\bot$	$\bot$	$\bot$

Figure 6.1.

The sum of all probabilities must add up to 1.

We can now give any formula B with atoms p and q, a probability value. We look at all the rows which give A the value $\top$ and sum up the probabilities. We thus get for $A = p \wedge \neg q, \pi(A) = \pi_2 = 0.1$.

The above described how propositional probability logic works for the case of classical logic. Given atoms $q_1, \ldots, q_n$ we have 2^n rows in the truth table which we can denote by $h_1, \ldots, h_{2^n}$. For each row h_i, we are also given a probability π_i, such that the sum of all probabilites is 1. (i.e. $\sum_{i=1}^{2^n} \pi_i = 1$). Given any wff B, the probability $\pi(B)$ of B under the above situation is

$$\pi(B) = \sum_{i, h_i(B) = \top} \pi_i$$

For big practical problems the diffculity is in calculating $\pi(B)$.

Note that the above approach, which we call the π-approach, assumes that the models (or assignments) are independent of each other and thus get independent probability values. The values of formulas are calculated according to what assignments make them true.

Thus for example in Figure 6.1 we get

$$\pi(p) = \pi_1 + \pi_2 = 0.4 + 0.1 = 0.5$$
$$\pi(q) = \pi_1 + \pi_3 = 0.4 + 0.49 = 0.89$$

Another approach, the η-approach, is to use a probability function $\eta(q)$ giving each atom q a probability $\eta(q)$ for being true. This approach assumes the atoms (as opposed to the models) to be independent. For any model h we can calculate its η value, $\eta(h)$ by

$$\eta(h) = \varepsilon_1 \times \cdots \times \varepsilon_n$$

where

$$\varepsilon_j = \begin{cases} \eta(q_j) \text{ if } h(q_j) = \top \\ 1 - \eta(q_j) \text{ if } h(q_j) = \bot \end{cases}$$

The two approaches are not the same. The π approach does not make the atoms necessarily independent of each other, for example, compare the π of Figure 6.1 with the following η defined by letting

$$\eta(p) = \pi(p) = 0.5$$

and

$$\eta(q) = \pi(q) = 0.89$$

Consider η as a new probability function of the second approach, then we have:

$$\pi(p \wedge q) = \pi_1 = 0.4$$

but

$$\pi(p) \times \pi(q) = 0.5 \times 0.89 = 0.445.$$

This also means that we cannot derive/calculate $\pi(p \wedge q)$ from $\pi(p)$ and $\pi(q)$. So the π value of each formula has to be calculated directly from the probabilities of the assignments which make it true and not recursively from the values of its components.

The π approach and the η approach are fully compatible. π gives probability to models or assignment h. So for a language based on n atoms $Q = \{q_1, \ldots, q_n\}$, we have 2^n models and therefore we have 2^n degrees of freedom assigning arbitrary probability values to these models, the only restriction is that the values all sum to 1. In the η approach we assume the values that the atoms q_i get are independent. So once we give the probabilities of the atoms, the probabilities of the models can be derived from that. We therefore have only n degrees of freedom in the η-case as compared to 2^n degrees in the π case.

We can also have a mixed approach. We can have, for example, that q_1 is independent and therefore received η probability, while $q_2, \ldots, q_n$ receive probability according to the π approach. So any model h of $q_1, \ldots, q_n$ can be split into a model $h'(q_1)$ and a model h'' of $q_2, \ldots, q_n$. So the probability of h, which we can denote by $Pr(h)$ is comprised of the probability of $h(q_1)$ multiplied by the probability of the rest $(h(q_2), \ldots, h(q_n))$. Thus

$$Pr(h) = \eta(q_1^{h(q_1)}) \times \pi(h(q_2), \ldots, h(q_n))$$

where we use the notation

$$q^\top = q \text{ and } q^\perp = \neg q.$$

EXAMPLE 6.6 (Comparing π and η probability). Consider the following database (a, b are atomic).

$$\alpha : a \lor b$$
$$\beta : a \land b$$

Is it consistent? I.e. is it π consistent or η consistent?

Let us examine η consistency. We get

$$
\begin{aligned}
\alpha &= \eta(a) + \eta(b) - \eta(a \land b) \\
&= \eta(a) + \eta(b) - \beta
\end{aligned}
$$

Thus we have

1. $\eta(a) + \eta(b) = \alpha + \beta$

2. $\eta(a)\eta(b) = \beta$

Consider the quadratic equation

$$
\begin{aligned}
(z - \eta(a))(z - \eta(b)) &= 0 \\
z^2 - (\eta(a) + \eta(b))z + \eta(a)\eta(b) &= 0 \\
z^2 - (\alpha + \beta)z + \beta &= 0 \\
z = \tfrac{1}{2}(+\alpha + \beta \pm \sqrt{(\alpha + \beta)^2 - 4\beta^2} \\
= \tfrac{1}{2}(+\alpha + \beta + \sqrt{\alpha^2 + 2\alpha\beta - 3\beta^2}
\end{aligned}
$$

This will have real solutions only if $(\alpha + \beta)^2 \geq 4\beta^2$ or
$\alpha + \beta \geq 2\beta$ or
$\alpha \geq \beta$.

Otherwise we need to take the square root of a negative number.

To make it concrete, let $\beta = \tfrac{1}{2}, \alpha = \tfrac{5}{6}$.

$$
\begin{aligned}
z &= \tfrac{1}{2}(+\tfrac{8}{6} \pm \sqrt{\tfrac{25}{36} + \tfrac{5}{6} - \tfrac{3}{4}} \\
&= \tfrac{1}{2}(\tfrac{+8}{6} \pm \sqrt{\tfrac{50}{36} - \tfrac{27}{36}} \\
&= \tfrac{1}{2}(\tfrac{+8}{6} \pm \sqrt{\tfrac{13}{36}} \\
&= \tfrac{1}{2} \frac{+8 \pm \sqrt{13}}{6} \\
&= \frac{+8 \pm \sqrt{13}}{12}
\end{aligned}
$$

Since $3 \leq \sqrt{13} \leq 4$, we get two solutions z_1, z_2 for z, between $\frac{1}{3} \leq z \leq 1$.

These two solutions comprise essentially one solution for η because of the symmetry of a and b. So either $\eta(a) = z_1$ and $\eta(b) = z_2$ or $\eta(a) = z_1$ and $\eta(b) = z_2$.

On the other hand, there are many possibilities for the π solution. $\pi(a \wedge b) = \beta$ but $x_1 = \pi(a \wedge \neg b)$, $x_2 = \pi(\neg a \wedge b)$ and $x_3 = \pi(\neg a \wedge \neg b)$ can be any numbers such that

$$x_1 + x_2 + x_3 = 1 - \beta$$

and

$$\tfrac{1}{2} + x_1 + x_2 = \alpha.$$

So

$$\alpha + \beta - 1 = \tfrac{1}{2} - x_3$$

and so $x_3 = \frac{3}{2} - \alpha - \beta$.

If $\alpha = \frac{5}{6}, \beta = \frac{1}{2}$, we get $x_3 = \frac{3}{2} - \frac{5}{6} - \frac{1}{2} = \frac{1}{6}$.

This is also clear since x_3 is the probability of $\neg a \wedge \neg b$ which is $\neg(a \vee b)$ and the probability of $a \vee b$ is $\alpha = \frac{5}{6}$.

So for example we can let

$$\pi(a \wedge b) = \beta = \tfrac{1}{2}$$
$$\pi(a \wedge \neg b) = \pi(\neg a \wedge b) = \pi(\neg a \wedge \neg b) = \tfrac{1}{6}$$

The notion of probabilistic logic just introduced is only one of many. This is a very large and active area which has many applications. Let us now look at the problem of deduction, namely the question of does $A_1, \ldots, A_n$ imply B? or equivalently, in classical logic, is $D = \bigwedge_i A_i \Rightarrow B$ a tautology?

We can certainly compute the probability $\pi(D)$ of D. Is this the answer to the question of what is the probability that $A_1, \ldots, A_n$ imply B? Do we say that $A_1, \ldots, A_n$ imply B with probability $\pi(D)$? Call this option α.

We now consider another option, let us look at our definition of the notion that $A_1, \ldots, A_n$ imply B. We said that $A_1, \ldots, A_n$ imply B if under any situation (i.e. row in the truth table) in which all A_i are true we must have that also B is true.

So the probability of this happening is the frequency of the cases that B is true from among the cases where all the A_i are true. Thus we get the number

$$\beta = \frac{\pi(B \wedge A_1 \wedge \cdots \wedge A_n)}{\pi(A_1 \wedge \cdots \wedge A_n)}$$

This is the conditional probability of B relative to $A_1 \wedge \cdots \wedge A_n$; call this option β.

David Lewis has shown that these two options α and β are not the same. We can illustrate this from our own example.

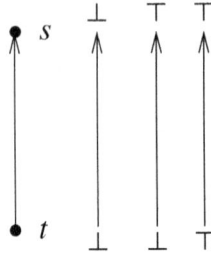

Figure 6.2.

Consider $B = (p \Rightarrow q)$. The probability number

$$\beta = \frac{\pi(p \wedge q)}{\pi(p)} = \frac{0.4}{0.5} = 0.8$$

while

$$\alpha = \pi(p \Rightarrow q) = 0.9$$

as calculated from the table of Figure 6.1.

2.4   Intutionistic probabilistic models

Let us now introduce probability to intuitionistic models. Our starting point is the Kripke models of Definition 2.2.3. To explain our ideas let us look at a concrete example, as given in Figure 6.2. We have only two possible worlds, t and s with $t \leq s$.

The option of truth values for an atom q at (t, s) are:

1. $(\perp, \perp)$,

2. $(\perp, \top)$, and

3. $(\top, \top)$.

The option $(\top, \perp)$ is not allowed by the conditions on the semantics.

As in the classical case, we have two approaches of giving probabilities. The π approach and the η approach. The π approach for one atomic letter q is to give probability for each of the options π_1 for option 1. $(\perp, \perp)$, π_2 for option 2. $(\perp, \top)$ and π_3 for option 3. $(\top, \top)$, with $\pi_1 + \pi_2 + \pi_3 = 1$. For further example, let us look at the π approach for two atomic letters p and q. Table 6.3 gives all possible options, and the associated probabilities.

The assignment $h_{2,3}$ for example, gives p the value $\perp$ at t and $\top$ at s and gives q the values $\top$ at t and $\top$ at s. This means it takes option 2 for p, $(\perp, \top)$ and option

	q at (t, s)		
p at (t, s)	1. $(\bot, \bot)$	2. $(\bot, \top)$	3. $(\top, \top)$
1. $(\bot, \bot)$	$h_{1,1}$	$h_{1,2}$	$h_{1,3}$
2. $(\bot, \top)$	$h_{2,1}$	$h_{2,2}$	$h_{2,3}$
3. $(\top, \top)$	$h_{3,1}$	$h_{3,2}$	$h_{3,3}$

Figure 6.3.

option	p	r
1. $(\bot, \bot)$	$x_1 = (1 - x_t) \times (1 - x_s)$	$y_1 = (1 - y_t) \times (1 - y_s)$
2. $(\bot, \top)$	$x_2 = (1 - x_t) \times x_s$	$y_2 = (1 - y_t) \times y_s$
3. $(\top, \top)$	$x_3 = x_t \times x_s$	$y_3 = y_t \times y_s$

Figure 6.4.

3 for q, $(\top, \top)$. Each of $h_{i,j}(1 \leq i, j \leq 3)$ is a model (for 2 points t and s) and so we can give it probabiliity $\pi_{i,j}$ with $$\sum_{\substack{i = 1,\ldots,3 \\ j = 1,\ldots,3}} \pi_{i,j} = 1.$$

The η approach gives probabilites to the atoms. There are two ways of doing it, going inductively up the tree denoted by the η^+ approach and going inductively down the tree, denoted by the η^- approach. We start with the η^+ approach.

Let the value of p at t be $\top$ with probability $\eta^+(t, p) = x_t$ and $\bot$ with probability $1 - x_t$. Similarly $\eta^+(t, q) = y_t$ for $q = \top$ and $1 - y_t$ for $1 = \bot$ at t.

The conditions on the model require that if an atom gets $\top$ at t it must also have $\top$ at s, since $t \leq s$. Thus the only additional probability we need to have is the probability of a $\bot$ at t changing to a $\top$ at s.

Let $\eta^+(s, p) = x_s$ the probability for $p = \bot$ at t changing to $p = \top$ at s. Similarly let $\eta^+(s, q) = y_s$.

Thus the probabilities of the model option 1,2,3 for p and for q, at (t, s) are as in Figure 6.4

So the probability of the model $h_{i,h}$ is $\eta_{i,j}^+ = x_i \times y_j$. This should be compared with $\pi_{i,j}$ of the π approach.

There is another way of looking at the η models, namely the η^- approach. We can start with the point s and let $\eta^-(s) = w_s$ be the probability of the atom p getting $\top$ at s. Therefore the probability of it getting $\bot$ is $1 - w_s$. If the atom is $\bot$ at s then it must also be $\bot$ at t, since $t \leq s$. but if the atom is $\top$ at s, it may be $\top$ or $\bot$ at t. Let $\eta^-(t) = w_t$ be the probability of the atom being $\top$ at t and $1 - w_t$ of it being $\bot$. Then we have for option 1. $(\bot, \bot)$, 2. $(\bot, \top)$ and 3. $(\top, \top)$, the following probabilities respecitvely:

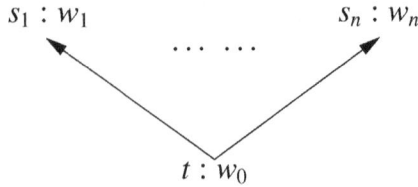

Figure 6.5.

1. $(1 - w_s)$

2. $w_s \times (1 - w_t)$,

3. $w_s \times w_t$.

This point of view allows us to assign probabilities to any tree Kripke model in a comutationally convenient way. Consider the situation in Figure 6.5

We can read the numbers in the Figure 6.5 in two different ways, as η^+ numbers or as η^- numbers. We start with the η^- reading.

w_i is the probability that the atom gets $\top$ at s_i. Hence the probability that the atom gets $\top$ at all s_i is $w = \prod_i w_i$.

Hence the probability that the atom gets at leat one $\bot$ for some s_i is $1 - w$. In this case the atom must get $\bot$ at t. Let w_0 be the probability of getting $\top$ at t in case the atom gets all $\top$ at s_i. Then the probability of getting $\bot$ at t is $w \times (1 - w_0)$.

So the probability of getting $\bot$ at t is $(1 - w) + w \times (1 - w_0)$ and the probability of getting $\top$ at t is $w \times w_0$.

Adding them up, we get

$$1 - w + w - w \times w_0 + w \times w_0 = 1.$$

We now read the numbers in Figure 6.5 in the η^+ approach. In this case w_0 is the probability of the atom getting $\top$ at t. We know that in this case the atom must continue to get $\top$ at all points s_i. However, in case the atom gets $\bot$ at t (with probability $1 - w_0$) then at s_i the atom might get either $\top$ or $\bot$. We interpret in the η^+ approach the number w_i as the probability that the atom gets $\top$ at s_i given that the atom got $\bot$ at t. Thus the probability that the atom gets $\bot$ at s_i is $(1-x) \times (1-w_i)$. The probability that it gets $\top$ at s_i is $w_0 + (1 - w_0) \times w_i$.

Summing up, we get

$$(1 - w_0)(1 - w_i) + w_0 + (1 - w_0)w_i = 1.$$

We assumed here that the nodes s_i get their probabilities independently of one another.

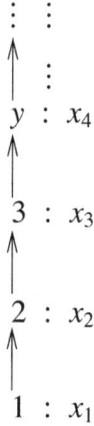

$$\vdots \quad \vdots$$

$$\uparrow \quad \vdots$$

$$y \;:\; x_4$$

$$\uparrow$$

$$3 \;:\; x_3$$

$$\uparrow$$

$$2 \;:\; x_2$$

$$\uparrow$$

$$1 \;:\; x_1$$

Figure 6.6.

The η^+ approach has its advantages. Consdier an infinite linear chain as in Figure 6.6.

Adopting the η^+ approach, let x_1 be the probability of the atom getting $\top$ at 1. Let x_2 be the probability of the atom getting $\top$ at 2 assuming it got $\bot$ at x_1. Let x_{n+1} be the probability of the atom getting $\top$ at $(n+1)$ given it got $\bot$ at x_n. Then the probability that the atom starts getting $\top$ at node n is $y_n = \prod_{i=1}^{n} x_i$. If we choose $x = \frac{1}{2}$ then $y_n = \frac{1}{2^n}$. We have $\sum_{n=1}^{\infty} \frac{1}{2^n} = 1$. This means that the atom will get $\top$ at some point with probability $\alpha = 1$. If we want $\alpha \neq 1$, we need to let $x_n = \alpha/2$.

The above discussion presented probabilistic semantics for the case of Gödel's logic.

3   Probabilistic Proof

In Section 2 we introduced probability into the truth table semantics, and showed how to compute the probability of $\pi(D)$ of a wff D getting a value $\top$. In this section we examine a syntactical approach.

We begin with a more general problem of how to propagate numbers associated with formulas through the proof process. These numbers can be anything, including probabilities.

Consider the rule of modus ponens:

$$\frac{\begin{array}{c} A \\ A \Rightarrow B \end{array}}{B}$$

If we assign numerical values α for A and β for $A \Rightarrow B$, we ask what is the value we propagate to B?

The first point to observe is that α and β may not be arbitrary. They may be connected. We have to ask where these numbers come from. Let us take for example the semantical probability model of Section 2.6. Assume A and B are built up from the atoms $q_1, \ldots, q_m$. We can now give probabilites to either each row in the truth table (the π approach) or to each atom q_i (the η approach giving each q_i the probability of its being true), and calculate the probabilites of A and $A \Rightarrow B$.

Assume that $\alpha : A$ and $\beta : A \Rightarrow B$ are probabilities which are properly calculated, namely for some function π on assignments we have

$$\pi(A) = \alpha$$
$$\pi(A \Rightarrow B) = \beta$$

and that in general for any D we have

$$\pi(D) = \sum_{h_i(D)=\top} \pi(h_i)$$

where $h_1, \ldots, h_{2^m}$ are all the rows (assigments) of the truth table.

Then the probability $x = \pi(B)$ satisfies

$$
\begin{aligned}
\beta &= \pi(A \Rightarrow B) = \pi(\neg A \vee B) \\
&= \pi(\neg A) + \pi(B) - \pi(\neg A \wedge B) \\
&= 1 - \alpha + x - \pi(\neg A \wedge B).
\end{aligned}
$$

So $x = \beta + \alpha - 1 + \pi(\neg A \wedge B)$

Only if $\neg A$ and B are independent can we calculate the value of x. In this case we have

$$x = \beta + \alpha - 1 + (1 - \alpha)x$$

Therefore

$$x = \frac{\beta + \alpha - 1}{\alpha} \qquad\qquad (*)$$

In general we cannot calculate x directly from α and β.

EXAMPLE 6.7. Consider the following model for two atoms a and c. Let the probability $\eta(a) = 0.5$ and $\eta(c) = 0.3$. Thus $\eta(\neg a) = 0.5$ and $\eta(\neg c) = 0.7$.

We get the following probabiliteis for the rows of the truth table.

probability	a	c
0.15	$\top$	$\top$
0.35	$\top$	$\bot$
0.15	$\bot$	$\top$
0.35	$\bot$	$\bot$

The probability of $c \Rightarrow a$ is calculated by adding the probabilites of the rows in the truth table which make $c \Rightarrow a$ true.

Thus

$$\eta(c \Rightarrow a) = 0.15 + 0.35 + 0.35 = 0.85$$

The probability of $(c \Rightarrow a) \Rightarrow c$ is the same as the probability of c since the two are equivalent.

Consider now the database Δ with

$$0.3 : B = ((c \Rightarrow a) \Rightarrow c)$$
$$0.85 : A = (c \Rightarrow a)$$

If we derive c by modus ponens and try to use formula (*) we get:

$$\eta(c) = \frac{0.85 + 0.3 - 1}{0.85} = \frac{0.15}{0.85} \neq 0.3$$

Thus we get the wrong number. This is because $\neg A$ and B are not independent. $\neg A$ is $c \wedge \neg a$ and B is equivalent to c.

Let us do modus ponens the other way by replacing in the database Δ the assumption $0.3 : B$ by its logical equivalent $0.3 : c$. We have

$$0.3 : c \text{ (equivalent to } B)$$
$$0.85 : c \Rightarrow a$$

We get using (*): :

$$\eta(a) = \frac{0.3 + 0.85 - 1}{0.3} = 0.5$$

This is OK since c and a are independent.

Let us now consider a proof of a from the database using a goal directed proof.

EXAMPLE 6.8. Consider the following goal directed problem:

1. $(c \Rightarrow a) \Rightarrow c$?a

2. $c \Rightarrow a$

Let us proceed with the computation of the goal ?a.

$$?c$$

This is because we used the second clause

$$?c \Rightarrow a$$

because we used the first clause.

We now have to add c into the database. So we continue:

c

$$?a$$

ask for c from clause 2

$$?c,$$

$$\text{success.}$$

because of c.

REMARK 6.9.

Consider

$$\alpha : A$$
$$\beta : A \Rightarrow B$$
$$\gamma : C$$
$$\delta : C \Rightarrow B$$

with A, B, C independent atoms. We can prove B in two different ways, with different probabilities. Do we combine them?

After all, B does follow from more than one part of the database?

Note also that we can use (*) to propagate the numbers, so

$$\alpha : A$$
$$\beta : A \Rightarrow B$$

yields

$$\frac{\beta + 2 - 1}{\alpha} : B.$$

and similarly

$$\gamma : C$$
$$\delta : C \Rightarrow B$$

yields

$$\frac{\delta + \gamma - 1}{\gamma} : B$$

Any other reasonable numerical propagation formula can be used and the validity of its use depends on the application. For example, we can use the Dempster–Shafer formula of Section 2.5.2

$$\alpha \oplus \beta = \frac{\alpha\beta}{1 - \alpha - \beta + 2\alpha\beta}$$

4 LDS and probabilistic proof

We now introduce the LDS proof method appropriate for probabilistic classical logic.

4.1 Cut rule

Consider the Gentzen sequent method for classical logic. The basic syntactical structures have the form

$$\Gamma \vdash \Delta$$

where Γ is a set of formulas $A_1, \ldots, A_n$ and Δ is a set of formulas $B_1, \ldots, B_m$. The intended meaning of the above is that $\bigwedge_k A_i \vDash \bigvee_j B_j$, where $\vDash$ is the classical semantic consequence.

The proof rules have the form in Figure 6.7

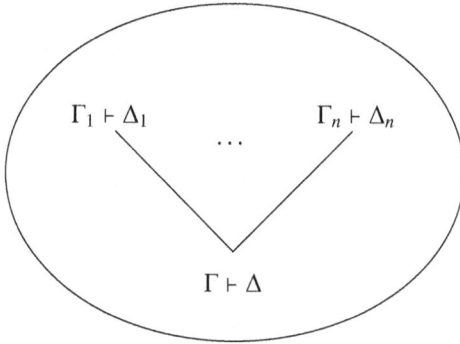

Figure 6.7.

For example, here is a version of the cut rule Figure 6.8 and of a negation rule Figure 6.9.

The way we would view the above rules is that we are just manipulating syntactically several pairs of databases of the logic, all in parallel.

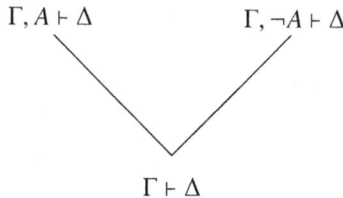

Figure 6.8. Cut rule

$$\Gamma, \neg A \vdash \Delta$$

$$\Gamma \vdash \Delta, A$$

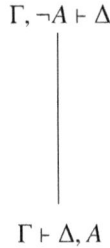

Figure 6.9. Negation rule

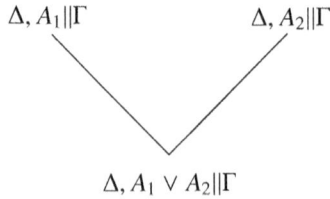

$$\Delta, A_1 \| \Gamma \qquad\qquad \Delta, A_2 \| \Gamma$$

$$\Delta, A_1 \vee A_2 \| \Gamma$$

Figure 6.10.

Tableaux is no different. The basic structures have the form

$$\Delta \| \Gamma$$

where the semantic meaning is that there exists an assignment h to the atoms such that $h(A) = \top$ for all $A \in \Delta$ and $h(B) = \perp$ for all $B \in \Gamma$. The tableaux rules are again manipulations of pairs of databases. For example,the rule for disjunction on the left is seen in Figure 6.10

Now in LDS the notion of a declarative unit is not just a formula A but a formula and a label of the form, $t : A$. A database has the form

$$\Delta = \{t_i : A_i, \textbf{Equations}\}$$

where **Equations** is a general set of formulas giving relationships about the labels. For example, $t_1 \leq t_2$ or $t_1^2 = t_2 + t_3$, or whatever. The language in which these relationships are expressed can be metalevel, and part of the presentation of an LDS system is to specify this language, as well as many other notions (consistency, manipulation rules, input into databases, etc).

Given this point of view, the LDS proof rules will have the form in Figure 6.11, or, more generally, since we may have constants everywhere, we can have $\mathbf{E}_i = \mathbf{E}'$ and $\mathbf{E}'$ talks about all constants appearing in any of $\Delta_i, \Gamma_i, i = 1, \dots, n$. A simple example will illustrate the idea. Consider a classical proof of $A, A \to B, A \to C \vdash B \wedge C$. The natural way to prove this is to split into two cases as in Figure 6.12

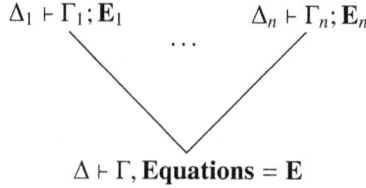

Figure 6.11.

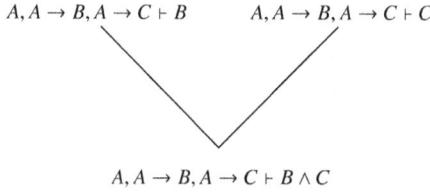

Figure 6.12.

The left branch succeeds becasue of modus ponens

$$A \rightarrow B, A \vdash B$$

and the right hand branch succeeds because of modus ponens $A \rightarrow C, A \vdash C$.

This proof will not be acceptable in linear logic because the assumption A is used twice in modus ponens. So the left branch must tell the right branch that it is using A. Also in linear logic all assumptions must be used and so we need to communicate beween branches to verify that $A \rightarrow B$ is used and that $A \rightarrow C$ is used. Thus the LDS way of writing this rule is in Figure 6.13. where $\mathbf{E}, \mathbf{E}'$ are in a metalanguage recording what is being used.

We get similar proof rules for probability logics where $\Delta = \{x_i : A_i\}, \Gamma = \{y_j : B_j\}$ and x_i, y_j are probabilities and $\mathbf{E}$ is a set of global equations on $\{x_i, y_j\}$.

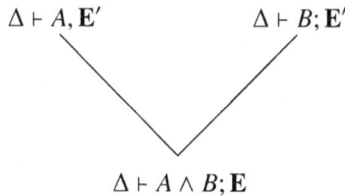

Figure 6.13.

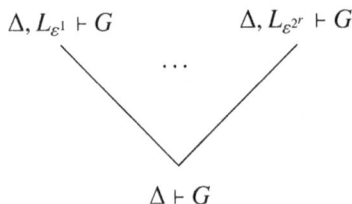

Figure 6.14.

We shall use in the case of classical logic a special case of the cut rule.

Let Δ, G be wffs built up from the atoms $\{q_1, \ldots, q_k\}$ and let $r \leq k$. Let $\varepsilon = (\varepsilon_1, \ldots, \varepsilon_r)$ be a sequence of $\{\top, \bot\}$. Understand $q^\top = q$ and $q^\bot = \neg q$. Let $L_\varepsilon = \bigwedge_{j=1}^{r} q_j^{\varepsilon_j}$.

Let $\varepsilon^i = (\varepsilon_1^i, \ldots, \varepsilon_r^i), i = 1, \ldots, 2^r$, range over all possible sequences of elements from $\{\top, \bot\}$.

Then we have the rule of Figure 6.14.

Note that if we take $r = k$ then L_ε (if true) gives a complete assignment of truth values to all atoms of Δ and G and hence both Δ and G get their own truth values immediately. In this case the cut rule becomes a full truth table case by evaluation.

If we take a smaller $r < k$ we are using a mixture of truth tables and proof theory. The reason is that in the presence of say $q_1 \wedge \neg q_2$, the problem

$$\Delta(q_1, q_2), q_1 \wedge \neg q_2 \vdash ?G(q_1, q_2)$$

is equivalent to

$$\Delta(q_1/\top, q_2/\bot), q_1 \wedge \neg q_2 \vdash ?G(q_1/\top, q_2/\bot)$$

where q/x means that we substitute x for q. The substitution simplifies the problem.

Our probabilistic proof theory will rely on the above rule.

4.2   Probabilistic modus ponens

Section 6.2.2 discussed various options for the rule of modus ponens in LDS. There is still a more general option (to that of Remark 6.5). Consider the two formulas A and $A \to B$. Let Ω be a finite set of formulas closed under Boolean combinations of subformulas and containing A and B. So for example $\neg A \wedge B \in \Omega$. For every $E_i \in \Omega$, let e_i be a lable for E_i. Then a labelled modus ponens rule suirable for probabilistic proof is the following:

$$\frac{\alpha : A; \beta : A \to B, \varphi_\Omega}{\mathbf{f}(\alpha, \beta, \{e_i\}) : B, \varphi'_\Omega}$$

where $\varphi_\Omega, \varphi'_\Omega$ is some condition on the labels of Ω and $\mathbf{f}$ is an expression dependent on α, β and all or some of e_i.

This is best illustrated by an example.

We know that $A \rightarrow B$ is equivalent to $\neg A \vee B$ and hence

$$p(A \rightarrow B) = 1 - p(A) + p(B) - p(\neg A \wedge B)$$

Therefore

$$p(B) = p(A \rightarrow B) + p(A) - 1 + p(\neg A \wedge B).$$

we thus have the rule:

$$\frac{p(A \rightarrow B) : A \rightarrow B; p(A) : A}{p(A \rightarrow B) + p(A) - 1 + p(\neg A \wedge B) : B}$$

The label of B contains $p(\neg A \wedge B)$ as a parameter.

EXAMPLE 6.10. Suppose we have $p(a) = \omega, p(a \wedge \neg b) = \beta$ and $p(b \rightarrow (a \rightarrow c)) = \alpha$. So our probabilistic database is:

1. $\omega : a$

2. $\beta : a \rightarrow b$

3. $\alpha : b \rightarrow (a \rightarrow c)$

We want to prove (find the value of) $x : a \rightarrow c$, i.e. the probability $x = p(a \rightarrow c)$. We get in LDS:

4. $\beta + \omega - 1 + p(\neg a \wedge b) : b$, from (1) and (2)

5. $\alpha + \beta + \omega - 1 + p(\neg a \wedge b) - 1 + p(\neg b \wedge (a \rightarrow c)) : a \rightarrow c$, from (3) and (4).

6. $\alpha + \beta + \omega - 1 + p(\neg a \wedge b) - 1 + p(\neg b \wedge (a \rightarrow c)) + \omega - 1 + p(\neg a \wedge c) : c$, from (1) and (5).

We can simplify a bit the label of $a \rightarrow c$ in (5), as follows:

$$
\begin{aligned}
p(\neg a \wedge b) + p(\neg b \wedge (a \rightarrow c)) &= p(\neg a \wedge b) + p((\neg b \wedge \neg a) \vee (\neg b \wedge c)) \\
&= p(\neg a \wedge b) + p(\neg b \wedge \neg a) + \\
&\quad p(\neg b \wedge c) - p(\neg a \wedge \neg b \wedge c) \\
&= p(\neg a) + p(\neg b \wedge c) - p(\neg a \wedge \neg b \wedge c) \\
&= 1 - \omega + p(\neg b \wedge c) - p(\neg a \wedge \neg b \wedge c)
\end{aligned}
$$

The last equality is because $\omega = p(a)$.

We also have

$$p(\neg b \wedge c) = p(\neg b \wedge c \wedge \neg a) + p(\neg b \wedge c \wedge a).$$

Hence we can continue our equation and get:

$$p(\neg a \wedge b) + p(\neg b \wedge (a \rightarrow c)) = 1 - \omega + p(a \wedge \neg b \wedge c).$$

Therefore

$$
\begin{aligned}
p(a \rightarrow c) &= \text{label of } a \rightarrow c \text{ in (5)} \\
&= \alpha + \beta + \omega - 2 + 1 - \omega + p(a \wedge \neg b \wedge c) \\
&= \alpha + \beta - 1 + p(a \wedge \neg b \wedge c).
\end{aligned}
$$

We therefore have

$$
\begin{aligned}
p(c) &= \text{label of } c = \\
&\quad \alpha + \beta - 1 + p(a \wedge \neg b \wedge c) + \omega - 1 + p(\neg a \wedge c) \\
&= \alpha + \beta + \omega - 2 + p(\neg a \wedge c) + p(a \wedge \neg b \wedge c).
\end{aligned}
$$

EXAMPLE 6.11. Consider the database

1. $p(a \rightarrow b) = \alpha : a \rightarrow b$

2. $p(a \wedge c) = \beta : a \wedge c$

3. $p(d) = \gamma : d$

4. $p(d \rightarrow c) = \delta : d \rightarrow c.$

We want to find $p(b)$.

This database obviously proves b. We make use of that.

5. $1 : a \wedge c \rightarrow a$, tautology

6. $\beta + p(\neg c \wedge a) : a$, from (2) and (5) by modus ponens and then some simplification,

7. $\alpha + \beta + p(\neg c \wedge a) - 1 + p(\neg a \wedge b) : b$, from (1) and (6).

8. $\gamma + \delta - 1 + p(\neg d \wedge c) : c$, from (3) and (4)

We cannot go any further without further assumptions. For example about the independence of a, b, c, d.

5   Probabilistic labels and proof for the η-approach

We saw in Section 6.2.1 how to give probability values to statements of classical propositional logic. The η-approach was to give probability values to all the atoms of a formulae and then propagate the values to all assignments. So if $Q = \{q_1, \ldots, q_n\}$ are all the atoms of a formula E, then any assignment h for E will give values $h(q_1), \ldots, h(q_n)$, to the atoms where $h(q_i)$ are either $\top$ or $\bot$. If $\eta(q_i)$ is the probability of q_i getting $\top$ and $1 - \eta(q_i)$ is the probability of q_i getting $\bot$,then the probability of h, denoted by $\eta(h)$ is given by

$$\eta(h) = \prod_{\substack{i \\ h(q_i) = \top}} \eta(q_i) \times \prod_{\substack{j \\ h(q_j) = \bot}} (1 - \eta(q_j))$$

Let us use the notation of $q^{h(q)}$, where

$$q^\top = q$$

and

$$q^\bot = \neg q.$$

In this case

$$\eta(q^{h(q)}) = \eta(q) \text{ if } h(q) = \top = \eta(\neg q) = 1 - \eta(q) \text{ if } h(q) = \bot.$$

Therefore we can write

$$\eta(h) = \prod_{i=1}^{n} \eta(q_i^{h(q_i)})$$

The probability $\eta(E)$ of E is

$$\sum_{\substack{h \\ h(E) = \top}} \eta(h)$$

being the sum of all probabilities of assignments h making E true.

The π approach gives probabilities directly to assignments h and therefore we can write

$$\pi(E) = \sum_{\substack{h \\ h(E) = \top}} \pi(h)$$

Consider the atoms $q_1, \ldots, q_n$ and consider an arbitrary disjunct of the form $L = \bigwedge_{i=1}^{n} q_i^{\varepsilon_i}$, where $\varepsilon_i \in \{\top, \bot\}$. Denote this disjunct by L_ε, where $\varepsilon = (\varepsilon_1, \ldots, \varepsilon_n)$.

Every formula E built up from $\{q_1, \ldots, q_n\}$ can be written as a disjunction of the form $E \equiv \bigvee_j L_{\varepsilon^j}$ for some $\varepsilon^j = (\varepsilon_1^j, \ldots, \varepsilon_n^j)$, $j = 1, 2, \ldots$. Clearly $\eta(E) = \sum_j \eta(L_{\varepsilon^j})$ and $\pi(E) = \sum_j \pi(L_{\varepsilon^j})$.

Consider now the rule of modus ponens, $A \Rightarrow B, A \vdash B$. Now suppose we don't know exactly the full picture of the probability distribution η for the atoms of Q. We do know however that the probability of A is α and the probability of $A \Rightarrow B$ is γ. Can we say anything about the probability β of B? If we could write $\beta = f(\gamma, \alpha)$ for some function f that would be nice because then we would be providing an LDS proof theory for probabilistic logic.

In fact, even a simpler condition will do. LDS allows for databases of the form

$$\Delta = \{\alpha_i : A_i, \text{ equations on } \alpha_i\}.$$

So a proof rule moving from Δ to Δ' with new labels and new equations will be satisfactory.

So if

$$\alpha : A,$$
$$\gamma : A \Rightarrow B$$

is in Δ, with α, γ satisfying some interconditions with the rest of the labels in Δ, we can move to

$$\Delta' = \Delta \cup \{\beta : B \text{ more equations involving } \beta\}.$$

Let us check a few facts. We have

$$(A \Rightarrow B) \equiv (\neg A \vee B)$$

So

$$(\#) : \quad \eta(A \Rightarrow B) = \eta(\neg A \vee B) = \eta(\neg A) + \eta(B) - \eta(\neg A \wedge B).$$

Now if A and B have no atoms in common, they would be independent of each other in the η-approach and we will have

$$\eta(\neg A \wedge B) = \eta(\neg A)\eta(B).$$

We can therefore continue in this case:

$$\eta(A \Rightarrow B) = \eta(\neg A) + \eta(B) - \eta(\neg A)\eta(B)$$

and so

$$\eta(B) = \frac{\eta(A \Rightarrow B) - \eta(\neg A)}{1 - \eta(\neg A)}$$

This means that in this case

$$\beta = \frac{\gamma + \alpha - 1}{\alpha}$$

So we have a modus ponens rule of the form

$$\frac{\gamma : A \Rightarrow B; \alpha : A; \alpha \neq 0; A \text{ and } B \text{ have no atom in common}}{\frac{\gamma + \alpha - 1}{\alpha} : B}$$

Note that the above steps go through only in the η approach, where all the atoms are independent and therefore formulas not sharing any atoms are also independent.

In the π approach two different atoms may be dependent because the π probabilites are assigned to models h and not to atoms.[3]

Suppose A and B have one atom in common, say q_1, what do we do?

In this case, we use the cut rule. We formulate the cut rule in a convenient way.

Let Δ be a database of formulas containing the atom q and $G(q)$ be a goal to prove, also containing q. Then

$$\Delta(q) \vdash G(q)$$

iff both 1. and 2. below hold:

    1. $\Delta(q), q \vdash G(q)$

and

    2. $\Delta(q), \neg q \vdash G(q)$

iff both 1. and 2. below hold:

    1. $\Delta(q/\top), q \vdash G(q/\top)$

and

    2. $\Delta(q/\bot), \neg q \vdash G(q/\bot)$

The reader can check that this holds since any assignment h either makes $h(q) = \top$ or $h(q) = \bot$.

Consider the truth table for any formula E built up from $q_1, \ldots, q_n$. It has all rows of the form

$$h(q_1), \ldots, h(q_n)$$

Let us divide the rows into the part where $h(q_1) = \top$ and the part where $h(q_1) = \bot$. The probability of $E(q_1)$ is the sum of all the probabilites of the rows h which make $E(q_i)$ $\top$. Let us write it again explicitly.

$$\eta(E(q_1, \ldots, q_n)) = \sum_{\substack{h \\ h(E) = \top}} \prod_{i=1}^{n} \eta(q_i^{h(q_i)})$$

$$= \sum_{\substack{h \\ h(E) = \top \\ h(q_1) = \top}} \eta(q_1) \prod_{i=2}^{n} \eta(q_i^{h(q_i)}) + \sum_{\substack{h \\ h(E) = \top \\ h(q_1) = \bot}} \eta(\neg q_1) \eta(q_i^{h(q_i)}).$$

---

[3] Strictly speaking any probability assignment which allows to solve equation (#) for $\eta(B)$ can allow for modus ponens to go through. Note also the slightly puzzling result that if $\gamma = 1$ and $\alpha \neq 0$, we get B with probability 1.

Let $E(q_1/\top)$ denote the result of substituting $\top$ for q_1 in E. This yields a formula with $q_2, \ldots, q_n$ only. Similarly let $E(q_1/\bot)$ be the resultof substituting $\bot$ for q_1 in E.

Let h^1 be the same as h restricted to $q_2, \ldots, q_n$. Then we can cotinue and write

$$
\begin{aligned}
\eta(E(q_1, \ldots, q_n)) &= \eta(q_1) \sum_{\substack{h_1 \\ h_1(E(q_1/\top)) = \top}} \prod_{i=1}^{n} \eta(q_i^{h_1(q_i)}) \\
&\quad + \eta(\neg q_1) \sum_{\substack{h_1 \\ h_1(E(q_1/\bot)) = \top}} \eta(q_i^{h_1(q_i)}) \\
&= \eta(q_1)\eta(E(q_1/\top)) + \eta(\neg q_1)\eta(E(q_1/\bot)).
\end{aligned}
$$

Notation: If $y = \eta(E(q_1, \ldots, q_n))$ **then let** $y_1^\top = \eta(E(q_1/\top))$ **and** $y_1^\bot = \eta(E(q_1/\bot))$.

We have
$$
y = y_1^\top \eta(q_1) + y_1^\bot \eta(\neg q_1)
$$

The above does not work for the π approach. We have

$$
\begin{aligned}
E(q_1, \ldots, q_n) &\equiv [E(q_1, \ldots, q_n) \wedge q_1] \vee [E(q_1, \ldots, q_n) \wedge \neg q_1] \\
&\equiv [E(q_1/\top, q_2, \ldots, q_n) \wedge q_1] \vee [E(q_1/\bot, q_2, \ldots, q_n) \wedge \neg q_1]
\end{aligned}
$$

Therefore, since the two disjuncts are independent, we get

$$
\pi(E) = \pi(E(q_1/\top) \wedge q_1) + \pi(E(q_1/\bot) \wedge \neg q_1)
$$

We cannot go any further, as the following example shows:

EXAMPLE 6.12. Let $E = (p \wedge q) \vee (p \wedge \neg q) \vee (\neg p \wedge q)$ we have

$$
\begin{aligned}
E(p/\top) &= q \vee \neg q \vee (\neg p \wedge q) = \top \\
E(p/\bot) &= q
\end{aligned}
$$

We have
$$
\begin{aligned}
\pi(E) &= 0.99, \\
\pi(E(p/\top)) &= 1, \\
\pi(E(p/\bot)) &= \pi(q) = 0.53, \\
\pi(p) &= 0.5
\end{aligned}
$$
and
$$
\pi(\neg p) = 0.5.
$$

We have

$$\pi(E(p/\top))\pi(p) + \pi(E(p/\bot))\pi(\neg p) = 1 \times 0.5 + 0.53 \times 0.5 = 0.765.$$

EXAMPLE 6.13. Consider the database Δ:

1. $\gamma : (c \Rightarrow a) \Rightarrow c$

2. $\alpha : c \Rightarrow a.$

Here $A = c \Rightarrow a, B = c$. So they have c in common. We use the cut rule for c.
Cut rule says
We have:

$$\Delta(c) \vdash c$$

iff

1. $\Delta(\top), c \vdash \top$

and

2. $\Delta(\bot), \neg c \vdash \bot.$

$\Delta(\top), c$ is

1. $\gamma_c^\top : \top$

2. $\alpha_c^\top : a$

3. $\eta(c) : c$

and $\Delta(\bot), \neg c$ is

1*. $\gamma_c^\bot : \bot$

2*. $\alpha_c^\bot : \top$

3*. $\eta(\neg c) : c \Rightarrow \bot$

Indeed

$$\Delta(\top), c \vdash \top$$
$$\Delta(\bot), \neg c \vdash \bot.$$

From the two databases we get equations

1. $\gamma_c^\top = 1$

2. $\alpha_c^\top = \eta(a)$

3. $\gamma_c^\bot = 0$

1*. $\alpha_c^\perp = 1$

2*. $\gamma = \gamma_c^\top \eta(c) + \gamma_c^\perp \eta(\neg c)$

3*. $\alpha = \alpha_c^\top \eta(c) + \alpha_c^\perp \eta(\neg c)$

Simplifying, we get

   5. $\gamma = \eta(c)$

   6. $\alpha = \eta(a)\eta(c) + 1 - \eta(c)$

Therefore

$$\eta(a) \;=\; \frac{\alpha + \eta(c) - 1}{\eta(c)}$$

$$=\; \frac{\alpha + \gamma - 1}{\gamma}$$

Indeed, since $(c \Rightarrow a) \Rightarrow c$ is equivalent to c, clearly $\eta(c) = \gamma$.

To check the other equation for $\eta(c)$, observe that $c \Rightarrow a$ is equivalent to $\neg c \lor a$ and hence

$$
\begin{aligned}
\alpha = -\eta(\neg c \lor a) \;&=\; \eta(\neg c) + \eta(a) - \eta(\neg c \land a) \\
&=\; 1 - \eta(c) + \eta(a) - (1 - \eta(c))\eta(a) \\
&=\; 1 - \eta(c) + \eta(a) - n/a) + \eta(a)\eta(c) \\
&=\; 1 - \eta(c) + \eta(a)\eta(c)
\end{aligned}
$$

Hence

$$\eta(a) = \frac{\alpha + \gamma - 1}{\gamma}$$

What we see here is that the cut rule gives us equations to solve and find the probabilities.

EXAMPLE 6.14. The database is:

   1. $\alpha : (a \Rightarrow b) \Rightarrow b$

   2. $\beta : b \Rightarrow a$

and the goal G is

$$\delta : (a \Rightarrow c) \Rightarrow c.$$

Let's do cut on a, which is common to the data and the goal.

We have $\Delta(a) \vdash G(a)$ iff $\Delta(a/\top), a \vdash G(a/\top)$ and $\Delta(a/\perp), \neg a \vdash G(a/\perp)$.

For $a = \top$ we get

1. $\alpha_a^\top : \top$

2. $\beta_a^\top : \top$

3. $\eta(a) : a$

and the goal is $\vdash \delta_a^\top : \top$.

For $a = \bot$ we get

1*. $\alpha_a^\bot : b$

2*. $\beta_a^\bot : \neg b$

3*. $\eta(\neg a) : \neg a$

and the goal is $\vdash \delta_a^\bot : c$

We get the following equations:

1. $\alpha_a^\top = 1$

2. $\beta_a^\top = 1$

3. $\delta_a^\top = 1$

1*. $\alpha_a^\bot = \eta(b)$

2*. $\beta_a^\bot = 1 - \eta(b)$

3*. $\delta_a^\bot = \eta(c)$

We also have

4. $\alpha = \alpha_a^\top \eta(a) + \alpha_a^\bot \eta(\neg a)$

5. $\beta = \beta_a^\top \eta(a) + \beta_a^\bot \eta(\neg a)$

6. $\delta = \delta_a^\top \eta(a) + \delta_a^\bot \eta(\neg a)$.

Simplifying

4*. $\alpha = \eta(a) + \eta(b)(1 - \eta(a))$

5*. $\beta = \eta(a) + (1 - \eta(b))(1 - \eta(a))$

6*. $\delta = \eta(a) + \eta(c)(1 - \eta(a))$

Adding 4* and 5* we get

$$\alpha + \beta \;=\; 2\eta(a) + 1 - \eta(a)$$
$$=\; 1 + \eta(a)$$

Hence

$$\eta(a) = \alpha + \beta - 1$$

From 4* we get

$$\eta(b) \;=\; \frac{\alpha - \eta(a)}{1 - \eta(a)}$$
$$=\; \frac{\alpha - \alpha - \beta + 1}{1 - \alpha - \beta + 1}$$
$$=\; \frac{1 - \beta}{(1 - \alpha) + (1 - \beta)}$$

From 6* we get

$$\eta(c) \;=\; \frac{\delta - \eta(a)}{1 - \eta(a)}$$
$$=\; \frac{\delta - \alpha - \beta + 1}{(1 - 2) + (1 - \beta)} \;.$$

EXAMPLE 6.15. Consider the following database

1. $a_1 : v_1 \wedge \neg v_2$

2. $a_2 : \neg v_4 \wedge v_3 \Rightarrow v_2.$

3. $a_3 : v_5 \vee v_3$

4. $a_4 : v_4$

The goal is $y : v_5 \Rightarrow v_1.$

We want to find y.

Let us use the cut rule on v_3.

For $v_3 = \top$ we get:

1. $a_1 : v_1 \wedge \neg v_2.$

2. $a_2^\top : \neg v_4 \Rightarrow v_2$

3. $a_3^\top : \top$

4. $a_4 : v_4$

The goal is $y : v_5 \Rightarrow v_2$. Let us leave it for the moment.

For $v_3 = \bot$ we get:

1*. $a_1 : v_1 \wedge \neg v_2$

2*. $a_2^{\perp} : \top$

3*. $a_3^{\perp} : v_5$

4*. $a_4 : v_4$

The goal remains the same, $y : v_5 \Rightarrow v_1$.

We get the following equations from the above:

1. $\eta(v_1)(1 - \eta(v_2)) = a_1$

2. Since $\neg v_4 \Rightarrow v_2$ is $v_4 \vee v_2$ we get

$$a_2^{\top} = \eta(v_4) + \eta(v_2) - \eta(v_4)\eta(v_2)$$

3. $a_3^{\top} = 1$

4. $\eta(v_4) = a_4$

2*. $a_2^{\perp} = 1$

3*. $a_3^{\perp} = \eta(v_5)$

We also have the following:

5. $a_2 = a_2^{\top}\eta(v_3) + a_2^{\perp}(1 - \eta(v_3))$

6. $a_3 = a_3^{\top}\eta(v_3) + a_3^{\perp}(1 - \eta(v_3))$.

Simplifying:

5*. $a_2 = [\eta(v_4) + \eta(v_2) - \eta(v_4)\eta(v_2)]\eta(v_3) + 1 - \eta(v_3)$.

6*. $a_3 = \eta(v_3) + \eta(v_5)(1 - \eta(v_3))$.

Let us solve what we can. We get

4. $\eta(v_4) = a_4$, from 4.

1. $\eta(v_1)(1 - \eta(v_2)) = a_1$.

From 5* we get

$$
\begin{aligned}
a_2 &= [a_4 + \eta(v_2)(1 - a_4)]\eta(v_3) + 1 - \eta(v_3) \\
&= -\eta(v_3)[+(1 - a_4) - \eta(v_2)(1 - a_4)] + 1 \\
&= -\eta(v_3)(1 - a_4)(1 - \eta(v_2)) + 1
\end{aligned}
$$

Therefore we get:

5*. $\dfrac{(1 - a_2)}{(1 - a_4)} = \eta(v_3)(1 - \eta(v_2))$

6* becomes after simplification

6*. $(a_3 - \eta(v_3)) = \eta(v_5)(1 - \eta(v_3))$

Of course any solution will depend on the numbers $a_1, \ldots, a_4$.
We need to find the probability y of $v_5 \Rightarrow v_1$.
We have

7. $\begin{aligned} y &= \eta(\neg v_5 \vee v_1) = 1 - \eta(v_5) + \eta(v_1) - \eta(v_1)(1 - \eta(v_5)) \\ &= 1 - \eta(v_5) + \eta(v_1) - \eta(v_1) + \eta(v_1)\eta(v_5) \end{aligned}$

Hence

7. $y = 1 - \eta(v_5)(1 - \eta(v_1))$.

This is as far as we can go algebraically.

Let us assume $\eta(v_3) = a_3$. This will simplify the calcuations.

case $a_3 \neq 1$
In this case we get from 6* that $\eta(v_5) = 0$ and we get $y = 1$.

case $a_3 = 1$
In this case $\eta(v_3) = 1$ and we get

5**. $\dfrac{1 - a_2}{1 - a_4} = 1 - \eta(v_2)$

Hence

$$
\eta(v_2) = \frac{1 - a_4 - 1 + a_2}{1 - a_4} = \frac{a_2 - a_4}{1 - a_4}
$$

From equation 1. we get

$$
\eta(v_1) = \frac{a_1}{1 - \eta(v_2)}
$$

Using 5** we get

$$\eta(v_1) = \frac{a_1(1 - a_4)}{(1 - a_2)}$$

Therefore

$$
\begin{aligned}
y &= 1 - \eta(v_5)(1 - \eta(v_1)) \\
&= 1 - \eta(v_5)\left(\frac{1 - a_2 - a_1 + a_1 a_4}{1 - a_2}\right)
\end{aligned}
$$

We are free to choose $\eta(v_5)$.

EXAMPLE 6.16. This example shows we can get equations on the probabilities when the same conclusion can be derived in more than one way.

Consider the database

1. $x : A$

2. $y : A \Rightarrow B$

3. $u : C$

4. $z : C \Rightarrow B$.

A, B, C are independent atoms. We get

$$\eta(B) = \frac{y + x - 1}{x} \qquad \text{from 1 and 2}$$

$$\eta(B) = \frac{z + u - 1}{u} \qquad \text{from 3 and 4}$$

Hence we get

$$
\begin{aligned}
(z + u - 1)x &= (y + x - 1)u \\
zx + ux - x &= uy + ux - u \\
zx - x &= uy - u \\
x(1 - z) &= u(1 - y)
\end{aligned}
$$

$$\frac{x}{1 - y} = \frac{u}{1 - z}$$

We can see from the data that $\eta(A) = x$ and $\eta(C) = u$.

Let us express y in terms of $\eta(B)$.

$$
\begin{aligned}
y = \eta(\neg A \vee B) &= (1 - x) + \eta(B) - (1 - x)\eta(B) \\
&= 1 - x + \eta(B)x \\
&= 1 - x(1 + \eta(B))
\end{aligned}
$$

DEFINITION 6.17. Let Δ be a database of the form $\Delta = \{x_i : A_i, \text{Equations}\}$ where x_i are atomic indefinite probability labels and "Equations" are some equations involving x_i. Let Q be the set of atoms of the language. We say that Δ is η-consistent if for some η probability assignment to the atoms of Q we have for all $x : A \in \Delta$ that if we set $\eta(A) = x$, then all the equations hold. We say such an η is a model of Δ.

We say that $\Delta \vdash^P y : G$, for a wff G (in words: $y : G$ is a probabilistic consequence of Δ) iff for any probability assignment η which is a model of Δ we have that $\eta(G) = y$. y may appear in Δ, in which case it will have to satisfy all the equations of Δ.

Other notions of consequence are possible for example we can have $\Delta \vdash^{\mathbb{C}_1}_{\mathbb{C}_2} y : A$ iff by definition for any η-model whose labels sastisfy $\mathbb{C}_1$, the label y satisfies condition $\mathbb{C}_2$ with the labels of Δ.

For example we can require that if the probabilities in Δ approach 1 then y does not approach 0.

We now summarise our proof theory for this probabilistic consequence. We saw how to deal with modus ponens. So let us now see how to handle $\Rightarrow$ introduction. The idea is standard in LDS.

To say in LDS that

$$\Delta \vdash \gamma : A \Rightarrow B$$

is to claim that Δ contains inside it the information equivalent to $\gamma : A \Rightarrow B$. So to show that this is indeed the case we put a "test" assumption $x : A$ into Δ (x atomic label) and expect to derive B with a label $y_1 = \mathbf{g}(x)$. The value y_1 must be the same as the value $y = \mathbf{f}(x, \gamma)$ we would get by performing the modus ponens with $\gamma : A \Rightarrow B$ and $x : A$.

This means that

$$\mathbf{f}(x, \gamma) = y = \frac{\gamma + x - 1}{x} = y_1 = \mathbf{g}(x) \tag{*}$$

where A and B have no atoms in common. In the case that A and B have some atoms in common, say the atom q, then the calculation of $\mathbf{f}(x, \gamma)$ is more complex, using the cut rule but the equation (*) still holds and we use it to solve for γ.

Let us illustrate this idea in an example

EXAMPLE 6.18 (Probabilistic $\Rightarrow$ introduction rule). Consider the database

1. $\alpha : a \Rightarrow b$

2. $\beta : a \wedge c$

and the goal b.

Method 1: Calculating probabilites

From 1 we get

$$\alpha = (1 - \eta(a)) + \eta(b) - (1 - \eta(a))\eta(b) = 1 - \eta(a) + \eta(a)\eta(b)$$

From 2 we get

$$\beta = \eta(a)\eta(c)$$

Therefore solving for $\eta(b)$ in terms of α, β and $\eta(c)$ we get

$$\eta(b) = \frac{1 + (\alpha - 1)\eta(c)}{\beta}$$

note that $0 \le \alpha \le 1$ and so $\eta(b) \le 1$.

Method 2: Using cut

We use cut on c

Case $c = \top$:
We get the following equations

   1. $\alpha : a \Rightarrow b$

   2. $\beta^\top : a$

The goal remains b
   From the above we get

   3. $\eta(b) = \dfrac{\alpha + \beta^\top - 1}{\beta^\top}$
   and

   4. $\beta^\top = \eta(a)$

Case $c = \bot$:
We get the equations

   1*. $\alpha : a \Rightarrow b$

   2*. $\beta^\bot : \bot$

We therefore get

   3*. $\beta^\bot = 0$.

From the cut rule on item 2 we get

5.

$$\begin{aligned} \beta &= \beta^{\top}\eta(c) + \beta^{\perp}\eta(\neg c) \\ &= \beta^{\top}\eta(c) \end{aligned}$$

Hence

$$\beta^{\top} = \frac{\beta}{\eta(c)}$$

Substituting in 3 we get

6.

$$\eta(b) = \frac{\alpha + \beta/\eta(c) - 1}{\beta/\eta(c)}$$

$$\eta(b) = \frac{1 + (\alpha - 1)\eta(c)}{\beta}$$

Same as in method 1.

We now see how to do $\Rightarrow$ introduction.
Consider the problem

$$\alpha : a \Rightarrow b \vdash ?x : a \wedge c \Rightarrow b.$$

We want to find x. According to our LDS method, as discussed above, we put
a test $\beta : a \wedge c$ in the database and derive b with some label $y = \mathbf{f}(\beta)$ and we
must have the equation ($\sharp$) below (because $a \wedge c$ and b have no atoms in common,
otherwise the equations get more complicated):

$$y = \frac{x + \beta - 1}{\beta} . \qquad\qquad (\sharp)$$

Well, we know what y is because we have already calculated that

$$y = \frac{1 + (\alpha - 1)\eta(c)}{\beta}$$

we therefore get an equation for x.

$$\frac{x + \beta - 1}{\beta} = \frac{1 + (\alpha - 1)\eta(c)}{\beta}$$

hence

$$x + \beta - 1 = \beta + (\alpha - 1)\eta(c)$$

and so
$$x = 1 + (\alpha - 1)\eta(c).$$

Note that if $c = \top$, $\eta(c) = 1$ and we get $x = \alpha$ as expected, because our problem becomes
$$\alpha : a \Rightarrow c \vdash ?x : a \wedge \top \Rightarrow c$$

which is the same as
$$\alpha : a \Rightarrow c \vdash ?x : a \Rightarrow c.$$

Summary of the method:

Given the problem
$$B?x : A \Rightarrow B$$

put in the database $\beta : A$ and get a value $y = \mathbf{f}(\beta)$ for the probability of B. In parallel to the abvove calcuation, calculate the value $y_1 = \eta(B)$ from the datbase

$$x : A \Rightarrow B$$
$$\beta : A$$

If A and B have no atoms in common, then we know that $y_1 = \dfrac{x + \beta - 1}{\beta}$.

Then solve x in the equation

$$y_1 = \frac{x + \beta - 1}{\beta} = \mathbf{f}(\beta) = y.$$

If A and B do have some atoms in common, we must find y_1 as a function of x by using the cut rule for the common atoms. Suppose we get eventually that $y_1 = \mathbf{g}(x, \beta)$, then we solve again

$$\mathbf{f}(\beta) = y = y_1 = \mathbf{g}(x, \beta)$$

We cannot ensure that the equation can be solved for x.

EXAMPLE 6.19. Let us do the previous problem using the cut rule. The problem is:

1. $\alpha : a \Rightarrow b \vdash ?x : a \wedge c \Rightarrow b$

use cut on c.

Case $c = \top$

1. $\alpha : a \Rightarrow b \vdash ?x^\top : a \Rightarrow b$

Case $c = \bot$

1*. $\alpha : a \Rightarrow b \vdash ?x^\perp : \top$.

we get from the equations that

2. $x^\top = \alpha$
   (we have checked that this is the case)
and

2*. $x^\perp = 1$.

We also have

3.

$$
\begin{aligned}
x &= x^\top \eta(c) + x^\perp \eta(\neg c) \\
  &= \alpha \eta(c) + 1 - \eta(c)
\end{aligned}
$$

and hence

$$x = 1 + (\alpha - 1)\eta(c)$$

which is the same result as before in the previous example.

EXAMPLE 6.20 (Probabilistic modus ponens in general). This example calculates the case of modus ponens in general, when A and B have atoms in common.
    Assume we have

1. $\alpha : A \Rightarrow B$

2. $\beta : A$

We want to calculate the exit label $\gamma : B$. We know if A and B have no atoms in common then

$$\gamma = \frac{\beta + \alpha - 1}{\beta}$$

The question is what is γ in the case that A and B share the atoms $q_1, \ldots, q_k$ in common?
    We use the cut rule.
    Let $\varepsilon = (\varepsilon_1, \ldots, \varepsilon_k)$ be a sequence of $\top$ or $\perp$. For a formula $E(q_1, \ldots, q_k)$ let E^ε be $E(q_1/\varepsilon_1, \ldots, q_k/\varepsilon_k)$. Consider now the modus ponens of the form:

Case ε

$$
\frac{\alpha^\varepsilon : A^\varepsilon \Rightarrow B^\varepsilon \qquad \beta^\varepsilon : A^\varepsilon}{\gamma^\varepsilon : B^\varepsilon}
$$

Since A^ε and B^ε have no atoms in common, we have

3. $\gamma^{\varepsilon} = \dfrac{\alpha^{\varepsilon} + \beta^{\varepsilon} - 1}{\beta^{\varepsilon}}$

Let $\varepsilon^i = (\varepsilon^i_1, \ldots, \varepsilon^i_k), i = 1, \ldots, 2^k$ be all possible sequences of elements from $\{\top, \bot\}$. then we have for any E.

$$E \equiv \bigvee_{i=1}^{2^k} \left(B^{\varepsilon^i} \wedge \bigwedge_{j=1}^{k} q_j^{\varepsilon^i_j} \right)$$

Hence we have the following equation

4. $\gamma = \eta(B) = \sum_{i=1}^{2^k} \eta(B^{\varepsilon^i}) \prod_{j=1}^{k} \eta(q_j^{\varepsilon^i_j})$

From equation 3 we have that $\eta(B^{\varepsilon^i}) = \gamma^{\varepsilon^i}$.

We also have

5. $\alpha = \sum_{i=1}^{2^k} \beta^{\varepsilon^i} \prod_{j=1}^{k} \eta(q_j^{\varepsilon^i_j})$

6. $\beta = \sum_{i=1}^{2^k} \beta^{\varepsilon^i} \prod_{j=1}^{k} \eta(q_j^{\varepsilon^i_j}))$

We have above only few equations and lots of unknowns, namely all the α^{ε} and β^{ε}. The thing is we may get values if A^{ε} or $A^{\varepsilon} \Rightarrow B^{\varepsilon}$ are either tautologies or contradictions or are known from other parts of the database.

If A and B have all their atoms in common then always $A^{\varepsilon}, B^{\varepsilon}$ are either $\top$ or $\bot$ and so $\alpha^{\varepsilon}, \beta^{\varepsilon}$ are either 0 or 1.

When we want to use the $\Rightarrow$ introduction rule for a database

$$\Delta \vdash ?\alpha : A \Rightarrow B$$

We assume $\beta : A$ and try and prove B with some label $\mathbf{g}(\beta)$. We also do the calculation above of the modus ponens

$$\alpha : A \Rightarrow B$$
$$\beta : A$$

and get (if we can) γ as a function of β and α. We can use the probabilies in Δ as additional equations to solve for $\alpha^{\varepsilon}, \beta^{\varepsilon}$. Then we write the equation

$$\mathbf{g}(\beta) = \gamma(\beta, \alpha)$$

and hope to solve for α as a function of β. Of course we further hope that β will not show in the solution, i.e. α will not really depend on β.

REMARK 6.21. The $\Rightarrow$ introduction method is a general one for any labelled logic. In general we get a label which is a function. More precisely to show

$$\Delta \vdash ?x : A \Rightarrow B$$

assume $\beta : A$ prove $\mathbf{f}(\beta) : B$ and therefore x is $\lambda\beta\mathbf{f}(\beta)$.

It is always a special case when we can find an acutal label (not a function) which realises $\lambda\beta\mathbf{f}(\beta)$.

If the modus ponens rule has the form

$$\frac{\beta : A, x : A \Rightarrow B}{\mathbf{g}(x,\beta) : B}$$

then we need to solve x in the equation

$$\mathbf{g}(x,\beta) = \mathbf{f}(\beta).$$

If we are lucky it can be solved and in a manner *not dependent on β*!

EXAMPLE 6.22 (Connection with abduction). Consider the database Δ as follows:

1. $\alpha : a \wedge b \Rightarrow c$

2. $\beta : a$

We ask does Δ prove c?

$$\Delta \vdash ?c$$

Even if $\alpha = \beta = 1, c$ does not follow. Abduction is a process whereby we find what additional assumptions we need (other than adding c itself) to add to Δ to be able to prove c. Abduction is a complex concept and for our purpose let us say that we follow a proof process for proving c and when we hit upon steps that require missing assumptions, we put them into Δ or 'abduce' them. This procedure depends on the proof procedure we use. In this simple example it is clear that we need to add b.

Let us try another way. Let us compute the probability $\eta(c)$ and see how to maximise it and make it $\eta(c) = 1$.

We use the cut rule on b:

The query $\Delta \vdash ?c$ reduces to $\Delta(b = \top), b \vdash ?c$ and $\Delta(b = \bot), \neg b \vdash ?c$. Let us check.

Case $b = \top$:
We get for the database

1. $\alpha^\top : a \Rightarrow c$

2. $\beta : a$

3. $\eta(b) : b$

The goal is c.

Case $b = \bot$
We get the database

1*. $\alpha^{\bot} : \top$

2*. $\beta : a$

3*. $1 - \eta(b) : b \Rightarrow \bot.$

the goal is c.
   We have one more equation.

   4. $\alpha = \alpha^{\top}\eta(b) + \alpha^{\bot}(1 - \eta(b)).$

   We simplify:
From 1* we get
$$\alpha^{\bot} = 1.$$

From 1 and 2 we get

$$\eta(c) = \frac{\alpha^{\top} + \beta - 1}{\beta} \ , \text{ assuming } \beta \neq 0.$$

From 4 we get

$$\alpha = \alpha^{\top}\eta(b) + 1 - \eta(b)$$

Hence

$$\alpha^{\top} = \frac{\alpha + \eta(b) - 1}{\eta(b)} \ , \text{ assuming } \eta(b) \neq 0.$$

Hence

$$\eta(c) \ = \ \frac{\alpha + \eta(b) - 1}{\eta(b)\beta} + \frac{\beta - 1}{\beta}$$

$$\eta(c) \ = \ \frac{\alpha + \eta(b) - 1 + \eta(b)\beta - \eta(b)}{\eta(b)\beta}$$

$$\eta(c) \ = \ \frac{\alpha - 1}{\eta(b)\beta} + 1$$

$$\ = \ 1 - \frac{(1 - \alpha)}{\eta(b)\beta}$$

for $\beta = 1$ we get

$$\eta(c) = \frac{\eta(b) + \alpha - 1}{\eta(b)}$$

To maximise $\eta(c)$ we need to minimise

$$\frac{(1 - \alpha)}{\eta(b)\beta}$$

and so we need to maximise $\eta(b)$. Thus we take $\eta(b) = 1$ and get $\eta(c) = \alpha$.

Let us look at it another way.

$$(a \wedge b \Rightarrow c)$$

is

$$\neg a \vee \neg b \vee c.$$

So

$$\eta(\neg a \vee \neg b \vee c) = \eta(\neg b) + \eta(\neg a \vee c) - \eta(\neg b)\eta(\neg a \vee c).$$
$$\eta(\neg a \vee c) = \eta(\neg a) + \eta(c) - \eta(\neg a)\eta(c)$$

Therefore

$$\begin{aligned}
\alpha &= \eta(\neg b) + \eta(\neg a) + \eta(c) \\
&\quad -\eta(\neg a)\eta(c) - \eta(\neg b)(\eta(\neg a) \\
&\quad +\eta(c) - \eta(\neg a)\eta(c)). \\
&= \eta(\neg b) + \eta(\neg a) + \eta(c) - \eta(\neg a)\eta(c) \\
&\quad -\eta(\neg b)\eta(\neg a) - \eta(\neg b)\eta(c) + \eta(\neg b)\eta(\neg a)\eta(c)
\end{aligned}$$

Therefore

$$\alpha - \eta(\neg b) - \eta(\neg a) + \eta(\neg b)\eta(\neg a) = \eta(c)[1 - \eta(\neg a) - \eta(\neg b) + \eta(\neg b)\eta(\neg a)]$$

Hence since $\eta(a) = \beta$

$$\alpha - 1 + \eta(b) - 1 + \beta + (1 - \eta(b))(1 - \beta) = \eta(c)[1 - 1 + \beta - 1 + \eta(b) + (1 - \eta(b)(1 - \beta))]$$

Hence

$$\alpha - 1 + \eta(b) - 1 + \beta + 1 - \eta(b) - \beta_\eta(b)\beta = \eta(c)[\beta - 1 + \eta(b) + 1 - \eta(b) - \beta + \eta(b)\beta].$$

Hence

$$\alpha - 1 + \eta(b)\beta = \eta(c)\eta(b)\beta$$

Hence

$$\begin{aligned}
\eta(c) &= \frac{\alpha - 1 + \eta(b)\beta}{\eta(b)\beta} \\
&= 1 - \frac{1 - \alpha}{\eta(b)\beta}
\end{aligned}$$

as we obtained before.

6 Bayesian net approach and its proof theory

We begin with an extended case study. We choose a simple meaningful problem and solve it in three different ways, the π-approach, the η-approach and the Bayesian net approach. The discussion that follows will make our point clear. We shall call the proof theoretical Bayesian approach the β-approach.

Our *Case Study* has the database Δ with

1. $\alpha : a \wedge b \Rightarrow c$

2. $\beta : a \Rightarrow b$

and the goal is to find x in the goal

3. $x : a \Rightarrow c$

When both $\alpha = 1$ and $\beta = 1$ we essentially get a familiar classical case study and the question is to show $x = 1$, i.e. prove or show that $a \Rightarrow c$ follows from $a \wedge b \Rightarrow c$ and $a \Rightarrow b$.

In the classical case, we recall three methods of showing that $x = 1$.

1. *Truth table method*
    Construct the full 8 rows truth table based on the atoms $\{a, b, c\}$ and show that all rows which make both $(a \wedge b \Rightarrow c) = \top$ and $(a \Rightarrow b) = \top$ make also $(a \Rightarrow c) = \top$.

2. $\Rightarrow$ *Introduction and* $\Rightarrow$ *Elimination method*
    We prove the conclusion from the assumptions:

    (1) $A1 : a \wedge b \Rightarrow c$, assumption

    (2) $A2 : a \Rightarrow b$, assumption

    We want to show the conclusion

    (3) $C : a \Rightarrow c$

    We proceed as follows:

    (4) $W : a$, temporary assumption

    (5) $(A2, W) : b$, from (2) and (3)

    (6) $(A2, W) : a \wedge b$, from (5) and (4)

    (7) $(A1, A2, W) : c$, from (6) and(1)

    We now discharge assumption (4) and get

    (8) $(A1, A2) : a \Rightarrow c$, from the proof in lines (4)–(7)

3. *Cut Rule method*
   The cut rule says that $\Delta \vdash G$ iff both

$$\Delta(a = \top), a \vdash G(a = \top)$$

and

$$\Delta(a = \bot), \neg a \vdash G(a = \bot).$$

We do cut on a

Case $a = \top$
The database and goal become

$$b \Rightarrow c, b, a \vdash c$$

Case $a = \bot$
The database and goal become

$$\top, \top, a \vdash \top.$$

Clearly both cases are valid.

EXAMPLE 6.23 (Case Study: η-approach using cut).   Consider the database Δ

1. $\alpha : a \wedge b \Rightarrow c$

2. $\beta : a \Rightarrow b$

The goal is

3. $x : a \Rightarrow c$

Option a: use cut on a
We begin by performing cut on a.
Case $a = \top$
We get the following:

4. $\alpha^\top : b \Rightarrow c$

5. $\beta^\top : b$

The goal is

6. $x^\top : c$

By modus ponens we get, assuming $\beta^\top \neq 0$

7. $x^\top = \dfrac{\alpha^\top + \beta^\top - 1}{\beta^\top}$

Case a = ⊥

We get

8. $\alpha^\perp : \top$

9. $\beta^\perp : \top$

The goal is

10. $x^\top : \top$

We get the equations

11. $\alpha^\perp = \beta^\perp = x^\perp = 1$

We also have

12. $x = x^\top \eta(a) + x^\perp(1 - \eta(a))$

We therefore have (from ((7))

12* $x = \dfrac{(\alpha^\top + \beta^\top - 1)\eta(a)}{\beta^\top} + 1 - \eta(a)$

We also have

13. $\beta = \beta^\top \eta(a) + \beta^\perp(1 - \eta(a))$

From (5) we know that $\beta^\top = \eta(b)$, therefore

13* $\beta = \eta(b)\eta(a) + 1 - \eta(a)$

Therefore

14. $\beta^\top = \dfrac{\eta(a) + \beta - 1}{\eta(a)}$

We also have

15. $\alpha = \alpha^\top \eta(a) + \alpha^+(1 - \eta(a))$

and therefore from (11) and (15) we solve for $\alpha^\top$ and get

16. $\alpha^\top = \dfrac{\alpha + \eta(a) - 1}{\eta(a)}$

We now look at equation (12*) and simplify

$$x = \frac{(\alpha^\top + \beta^\top - 1)\eta(a)}{\beta^\top} + 1 - \eta(a)$$

$$12* \quad = \frac{(\alpha^\top - 1)\eta(a)}{\beta^\top} + \eta(a) + 1 - \eta(a)$$

$$= \frac{(\alpha^\top - 1)\eta(a)}{\beta^\top} + 1$$

Substituting $\alpha^\top$ from (16) we get

$$= \frac{\alpha + \eta(a) - 1 - \eta(a)}{\beta^\top} + 1$$

$$= \frac{\alpha - 1}{\beta^\top} + 1$$

We now substitute for $\beta^\top$ from (14). We get the final solution:

$$= \frac{(\alpha - 1)\eta(a)}{\eta(a) + \beta - 1} + 1$$

Let us call this solution for x - the solution according to the η approach. We can denote it by x_η Let us write it nicely:

17. $x_\eta = 1 - \dfrac{(1 - \alpha)\eta(a)}{\eta(a) + \beta - 1}$

Option b: use cut on b
It is instructive to solve the problem by using cut on b. When we use the Bayesian approach to solve this case study, only cut on a will be possible.
Case $b = \top$

4. $\alpha^\top : a \Rightarrow c$

5. $\beta^\top : \top$

6. $x : a \Rightarrow c$

Case $b = \perp$

We get

7. $\alpha^\perp : \top$

8. $\beta^\perp : \neg a$

9. $x : a \Rightarrow c$

We get the following equations:

10. $x = \alpha^\top$

11. $\beta^\top = 1$

12. $\alpha^\perp = 1$

13. $\beta^\perp = 1 - \eta(a)$

14. $\alpha = \alpha^\top \eta(b) + \alpha^\perp(1 - \eta(b))$

15. $\beta = \beta^\top \eta(b) + \beta^\perp(1 - \eta(b))$

Substituting $\alpha^\perp =?$ in (14) we get

$$\alpha = \alpha^\top \eta(b) + (1 - \eta(b))$$

therefore

16. $\alpha^\top = \dfrac{\alpha + \eta(b) - 1}{\eta(b)} = \dfrac{\alpha - 1}{\eta(b)} + 1$

Substituting in (15) we get

17. $\beta = \eta(b) + (1 - \eta(a))(1 - \eta(b)) = 1 - \eta(a) \vdash \eta(a)\eta(b)$

Therefore

18. $\eta(b) = \dfrac{\beta + \eta(a) - 1}{\eta(a)}$

From (10), (16) and (18) we get

19. $$x = 1 + \dfrac{\alpha + 1}{\eta(b)} =$$
$$= 1 + \dfrac{(\alpha - 1)\eta(a)}{\beta + \eta(a) - 1}$$

EXAMPLE 6.24 (Case study: η approach; $\Rightarrow$ introduction).   We can now use the $\Rightarrow$ Introduction rule. We have

1. $\alpha : a \wedge b \Rightarrow c$

2. $\beta : a \Rightarrow b$

We are looking for

3. $x : a \Rightarrow c$.

Recall the probabilistic η-rule for modus ponens

$$\frac{\begin{array}{c} d : A \Rightarrow B \\ e : A \end{array}}{\dfrac{d+e-1}{e} : B}$$

When A and B are independent!
    To show 3, temporarily assume

4. $\eta(a) : a$

We get from (2) and (4)

5. $\dfrac{\beta + \eta(a) - 1}{\eta(a)} : b$

6. We get from (4) and (5)
   $\beta + \eta(a) - 1 : a \wedge b$.

7. We get from (1) and 6)

8. $\dfrac{\beta + \eta(a) - 1 + \alpha - 1}{\beta + \eta(a) - 1} : c$

   or

   $\dfrac{\beta + \eta(a) + \alpha - 2}{\beta + \eta(a) - 1} : c$

Doing modus ponens with $x : a \Rightarrow c$ and $\eta(a) : a$ would give the value

$$\frac{x + \eta(a) - 1}{\eta(a)} : c$$

These two values are the same, hence

$$\frac{x + \eta(a) - 1}{\eta(a)} = \frac{\beta + \eta(a) + \alpha - 2}{\beta + \eta(a) - 1}$$

Solving or x we get:

$$x = 1 - \frac{(1 - \alpha)\eta(a)}{\beta + \eta(a) - 1}$$

this is the same result as we saw in Example 6.23.

REMARK 6.25 (Discussion of the η solution). If we are looking for a mathematical solution to the problem, then we have been successful with the η-approach. We found a choice of a probability distribution of the more restrictive η-approach with only three degrees of freedom (a, b, c are completley independent) using our proof theory for the η-approach.

Whether this solution is acceptable for an application area depends on the meaning of a, b and c.

Consider a university situation where students need to submit a thesis and pass an oral examination in order to get a PhD.

Here we have

a =   John submits a good thesis by 2007
b =   John does well in the oral viva by 2007
c =   The univesity awards John a PhD by 2008.

Then

$$\alpha : a \wedge b \Rightarrow c$$

gives the probability that the above process works. We must bear in mind that we are dealing with a system that might get stuck on various issues, such as fulfillment of other conditions (foreign language, fees issues, lost library books, staff strikes, disciplinary actions, etc).

So probability α need not be 1.

The item

$$\beta : a \Rightarrow b$$

also makes sense, because we might think that if the thesis is good, then chances are the oral exam will be good, though we cannot be certain.

The η-approach makes a, b, c all independent.

So with probability $\eta(c)$, we may have $c = \top$, i.e. the university might award the title of PhD anyway, indpendently of what John does!

Let us now examine the π-approach where no independence of the atoms a, b and c is assumed.

EXAMPLE 6.26 (Case study: π-approach). We now examine our case study problem seeking a π-approach solution. We have again

1. $\alpha : a \wedge b \Rightarrow c$

2. $\beta : a \Rightarrow b$

We are seeking x

3. $x : a \Rightarrow c$.

model	π-probability
$a \wedge b \wedge c$	x_1
$a \wedge b \wedge \neg c$	x_2
$a \wedge \neg b \wedge c$	x_3
$a \wedge \neg b \wedge \neg c$	x_4
$\neg a \wedge b \wedge c$	x_5
$\neg a \wedge b \wedge \neg c$	x_6
$\neg a \wedge \neg b \wedge c$	x_7
$\neg a \wedge \neg b \wedge \neg c$	x_8

Figure 6.15.

The way to handle the problem is to assign probability variables to all classical models for the triple $\{a, b, c\}$, and then look for a probability assignment π satisfying the constraints (1) and (2).

One well known feature of the π-approach is that usually there will be many probability options to choose from and we will need to invoke additional metalevel principles (such as the Maximum Entropy Principle) to make a choice.

We have the followng models, see Figure 6.15

According to Figure 6.15, we have, since $(a \wedge b \Rightarrow c) \equiv \neg(a \wedge b \wedge \neg c)$ and $(a \Rightarrow b) \equiv \neg(a \wedge \neg b)$, that:

4. $\alpha = 1 - x_2$

5. $\beta = 1 - x_3 - x_4$

and for $x : a \Rightarrow c$, we get, since $(a \Rightarrow c) \equiv \neg(a \wedge \neg c)$:

6. $x = 1 - x_2 - x_4$

Therefore

7. $x = \alpha + \beta - 1 + x_3$

So we need to see if it is possible to assign probabilities $x_1, \ldots, x_8$ under the π approach such that the constraints equation (4) and (5) hold, as well as (8) below

8. $x_1 + \ldots + x_8 = 1$

Once we find x_3, we can solve for x according to (7).

So we use the Maximus Entropy Principle.

We want to maximise

$$H = -\sum_{i=1}^{8} x_i \log x_i$$

under the constraints (4), (5) and (8).

Consider the function

$$G = -\sum_{i=1}^{8} x_i \log x_i + \lambda_1(x_1 + \ldots + x_8 - 1)$$
$$+ \lambda_2(\alpha + x_2 - 1) +$$
$$+ \lambda_3(1 - x_3 - x_4 - \beta).$$

Here we are going to use the method of Lagrange multipliers. The partial derivatives

$$\frac{\partial G}{\partial x_i}, i = 1, \ldots, 8$$

must all be zero to give the maximum solution for $x_i, i = 1, \ldots, 8$.

We get

From

$$\frac{\partial G}{\partial x_1} = 0$$

we get

$$-\log x_1 - 1 + \lambda_1 = 0$$

and hence

(9.1) $x_1 = e^{\lambda_1 - 1}$

Similarly from $\dfrac{\partial G}{\partial x_2} = 0$ we get

$$-\log x_2 - 1 + \lambda_1 + \lambda_2 = 0$$

and hence

(9.2) $x_2 = e^{\lambda_1 + \lambda_2 - 1}$

and continuing in this manner we get

(9.3) $x_3 = e^{\lambda_1 - \lambda_3 - 1}$

(9.4) $x_4 = e^{\lambda_1 - \lambda_3 - 1}$

(9.5) $x_5 = e^{\lambda_1 - 1}$

(9.6) $x_6 = e^{\lambda_1 - 1}$

(9.7) $x_7 = e^{\lambda_1 - 1}$

(9.8) $x_8 = e^{\lambda_1 - 1}$

We immediatley see from the above equations that[4]

(10.1) $x_1 = x_5 = x_6 = x_7 = x_8$

(10.2) $x_3 = x_4$

We recall equations (4) and (5) and get

(10.3) $x_2 = 1 - \alpha$

(10.4) $x_3 = x_4 = \dfrac{1 - \beta}{2}$

From (8) and (10) we get

11. $5x_1 + 1 - \alpha + 1 - \beta = 1$

and therefore

12. $x_1 = x_5 = x_6 = x_7 = x_8 = \dfrac{\beta + \alpha - 1}{5}$

and from (7) we get

13.

$$
\begin{aligned}
x_\pi &= 1 - (1 - \alpha) - \frac{1 - \beta}{2} \\
&= \frac{2 - 2 + 2\alpha - 1 + \beta}{2} \\
&= \frac{\beta + 2\alpha - 1}{2}
\end{aligned}
$$

Note that if $\alpha = \beta = 1$ we get $x_\pi = 1$.
    Let us calculate $\pi(a)$. It is

14. $\pi(a) = x_1 + x_2 + x_3 + x_4 = \dfrac{\beta + \alpha - 1}{5} + 1 - \alpha + 1 - \beta = \dfrac{9 - 4(\alpha + \beta)}{5}$

Note that if $\alpha = \beta = 1$, we get $\pi(a) = 1/5$.
    Let us calculate $\pi(b)$.

---

[4]Note that if we have no constraints beyond $\sum_{i=1}^{8} x_i = 1$, then all the x_i end up equal to $e^{\lambda_1 - 1}$. This shows that the Maximum Entropy Principle assigns equal proabilites as much as possible to all variables, subject to constraints.

15.

$$\pi(b) \quad = x_1 + x_2 + x_5 + x_6 =$$

$$= \frac{3(\beta + \alpha - 1)}{5} + 1 - \alpha$$

$$= \frac{3\beta + 3\alpha - 3 + 5 - 5\alpha}{5}$$

$$= \frac{3\beta + 2(1 - \alpha)}{5}$$

If $\alpha = \beta = 1$, we get $\pi(b) = 3/5$.

Let us calcualte $\pi(c)$.

16.

$$\pi(c) \quad = x_1 + x_3 + x_5 + x_7 =$$

$$= \frac{3(\beta + \alpha - 1)}{5} + \frac{1 - \beta}{2} = \frac{6\beta + 6\alpha - 6 + 5 - 5\beta}{10}$$

$$= \frac{6\alpha + \beta - 1}{10}$$

If $\alpha = \beta = 1$, we get

$$\pi(c) = 6/10 = 3/5$$

REMARK 6.27 (Discussion of the π-solution). Obviously, the π solution is really just a mathematical solution. If we go to the thesis–viva–PhD example, we get for $\alpha = \beta = 1$, that indeed $x = 1$ but the underlying model π allows for $\pi(c)$ to be 60% while the chance that a thesis is produced is only 20%!

Note also that we can solve the problem in the η-approach by doing a full case analysis like in the π-approach. In the η-approach we ahve for example

$$x_1 = \eta(a)\eta(b)\eta(c)$$
$$x_2 = \eta(a)\eta(b)\eta(\neg c)$$
$$x_3 = \eta(a)\eta(\neg b)\eta(c)$$
$$x_4 = \eta(a)\eta(\neg b)\eta(\neg c)$$

We also have

$$\alpha = 1 - x_2 = 1 - \eta(a)\eta(b)\eta(\neg c)$$
$$\beta = 1 - x_3 - x_4 = 1 - \eta(a)\eta(\neg b)$$
$$x = 1 - x_2 - x_4 = 1 - \eta(a)\eta(\neg c)$$

Solving for x we get

$$x = 1 - \frac{1-\alpha}{\eta(b)} = 1 - \frac{(1-\alpha)\eta(a)}{\eta(a)+\beta-1}$$

which is the same value as in Examples 6.23 and 6.24.

EXAMPLE 6.28 (Case study: π-approach $\Rightarrow$ Introduction rule). Let us solve the problem using modus ponens and $\Rightarrow$ introduction rule.

Our original database is

1. $\alpha : a \wedge b \Rightarrow c$

2. $\beta : a \Rightarrow b$

and our goal is

3. $x : a \Rightarrow c.$

Let us rewrite the implication of the form $D \Rightarrow E$ as $D \Rightarrow D \wedge E$, when convenient. The two wffs are equivalent. Thus we formulate our database as

1. $\alpha : a \wedge b \Rightarrow b \wedge c$

2. $\beta : a \Rightarrow a \wedge b$

and our goal is

3. $x : a \Rightarrow a \wedge c$

To show $a \Rightarrow a \wedge c$, let us use $\Rightarrow$ introduction.

4. Assume temporarily
   $w : a$ (so $w = \pi(a)$)

5. From (2) we calculate

$$\beta = \pi(\neg a \vee (a \wedge b)) \quad \begin{aligned} &= \pi(\neg a) + \pi(a \wedge b) - \pi(\neg a \wedge a \wedge b)\\ &= \pi(\neg a) + \pi(a \wedge b)\\ &= 1 - w + \pi(a \wedge b) \end{aligned}$$

Therefore

6. $\pi(a \wedge b) = \beta + \omega - 1$

Similarly

7.

$$\begin{aligned}
\alpha\ &= \pi(\neg(a \wedge b) \vee (a \wedge c)) = \pi(\neg(a \wedge b)) + \pi(a \wedge c) - \pi(\neg(a \wedge b) \wedge a \wedge c) \\
&= 1 - \pi(a \wedge b) + \pi(a \wedge c) - \pi((\neg a \vee \neg b) \wedge a \wedge c) \\
&= 1 - \pi(a \wedge b) + \pi(a \wedge c) - \pi(\neg a \wedge a \wedge c) - \pi(\neg b \wedge a \wedge c)
\end{aligned}$$

We use (6) and note that $\neg a \wedge a \wedge c \equiv \perp$, and get

8. $\alpha = 1 - \beta - \omega + 1 + \pi(a \wedge c) - x_3$

Since $x_3 = \pi(a \wedge \neg b \wedge c)$, see Figure 6.15

Thus

9. $\pi(a \wedge c) = \alpha + \beta + \omega - 2 + x_3.$

Now let us do modus ponens with $x : a \Rightarrow a \wedge c$.
   So we have

$$x : a \Rightarrow a \wedge c$$
$$\omega : a$$

We get

10. $x = \pi(\neg a) + \pi(a \wedge c) - \pi(\neg a \wedge a \wedge c)$

and hence

11. $\pi(a \wedge c) = x + \omega - 1$

The two values for $\pi(a \wedge c)$ from (9) and (11) must be equal

12. $x + \omega - 1 = \alpha + \beta + \omega - 2 + x_3$

Hence

13. $x = \alpha + \beta - 1 + x_3.$

Thus we obtained an answer using proof theory and a clever trick. To check that
   what we give is correct, we go back to Example 6.26.
   Recall from the table of Figure 6.15, that

14. $\beta = 1 - x_3 - x_4$

15. $\alpha = 1 - x_2$

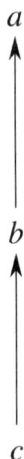

$$a$$

$$\uparrow$$

$$b$$

$$\uparrow$$

$$c$$

Figure 6.16.

We therefore get

$$x = \alpha - x_4 = 1 - x_2 - x_4$$

which is exactly what we get for x from Figure 6.15 directly, given that $\neg(a \Rightarrow c) \equiv a \land \neg c$.

EXAMPLE 6.29 (Case study: Bayesian β approach). In the Bayesian net approach we take into account reasonable dependencies among the atoms, depending on the application. In our case, we need dependencies of the form

- The viva depends on the thesis

- The PhD depends on both the viva and the thesis or (since the viva already depends on the thesis) on the viva alone.

This is also in line with the data itself, namely

1. $\alpha : a \land b \Rightarrow c$

2. $\beta : a \Rightarrow b$

We can therefore form the Bayesian net of Figure 6.16
   In this figure we need the following dependent probabilities

$$p(a),\ p(b|\pm a)\ \text{and}\ p(c|\pm b).$$

This requires 5 parameters, i.e. 5 degrees of freedom.

Figure 6.17 gives the parameters involved.
The parameters are

$$\omega, u^+, u^-, v^+, v^-$$

namely:

$$\omega = p(a), u^\pm = p(b|\pm a), v^\pm = p(c|\pm b)$$

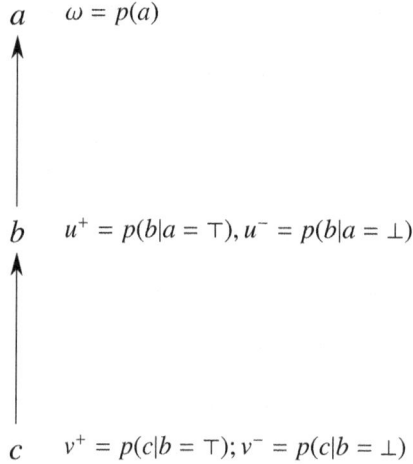

$$a \qquad \omega = p(a)$$

$$b \qquad u^+ = p(b|a = \top), u^- = p(b|a = \bot)$$

$$c \qquad v^+ = p(c|b = \top); v^- = p(c|b = \bot)$$

Figure 6.17.

Figure 6.18 below gives the values obtained for $x_1, \ldots, x_8$ according to the net of Figure 6.17.

model	symbolic value
x_1	$\omega u^+ v^+$
x_2	$\omega u^+ (1 - v^+)$
x_3	$\omega (1 - u^+) v^-$
x_4	$\omega (1 - u^+)(1 - v^-)$
x_5	$(1 - \omega) u^- v^+$
x_6	$(1 - \omega) u^- (1 - v^+)$
x_7	$(1 - \omega)(1 - u^-) v^-$
x_8	$(1 - \omega)(1 - u^-)(1 - v^-)$

Figure 6.18.

The constraints we have give us equations on the parameters $\omega, u^\pm, v^\pm$. We get

3. $\alpha = 1 - x_2$

4. $\beta = 1 - x_3 - x_4$

and we want to find $x : a \Rightarrow c$, namely

5. $x = 1 - x_2 - x_4$

We get the following equations for our parameters

3*. $\alpha = 1 - \omega u^+(1 - v^+)$

4*. $\beta = 1 - \omega(1 - u^+).$

We can now find the values of u^+, v^+, in terms of α, β.
From 4* we get

4**. $u^+ = \dfrac{\omega + \beta - 1}{\omega}$

and now from 3* we get

3**. $v^+ = 1 - \dfrac{1 - \alpha}{\omega + \beta - 1}$

We want to find the value of

5*.

$$
\begin{aligned}
x &= 1 - \omega u^+(1 - v^+) - \omega(1 - u^+)(1 - v^+) \\
  &= 1 - \omega u^+ + \omega u^+ v^+ - \omega + \omega u^+ - \omega u^+ v^+ + \omega v^+ \\
  &= 1 - \omega + \omega v^+
\end{aligned}
$$

From 3* we get

$$ x = \alpha - \omega(1 - u^+)(1 - v^+) $$

and from 4* and 3** we get

$$
\begin{aligned}
x &= \alpha - (1 - \beta)(1 - v^+) \\[2mm]
x &= \alpha - \frac{(1 - \beta)(1 - \alpha)}{\omega + \beta - 1} = 1 - \frac{(1 - \alpha)\omega}{\omega + \beta - 1}
\end{aligned}
$$

Note that $1 - v^+$ is the probability of a PhD not being awarded, given that the viva was successful.

Again note that if $\alpha = \beta = 1$ we get $x = 1$.

Let us see what values we get if we assume $\alpha = \beta = 1$. We get

3***. $1 = 1 - \omega u^+(1 - v^+)$

therefore

$$0 = \omega u^+(1 - v^+)$$

4***. $1 = 1 - \omega(1 - u^+)$

therefore

$$0 = \omega(1 - u^+)$$

Option 1 $\omega = 0$
This is the choice of $a = \perp$

Option 2 $w \neq 0$
then the only other option is $u^+ = 1$ and $v^+ = 1$.
   This means that the probability of $p(b|a = \top) = 1$ and $p(c|b = \top) = 1$.

Let us calculate $p(a), p(b), p(c)$.
It is easy to see that (using 3*** and 4***):

• $p(a) = \omega$

•

$$
\begin{aligned}
p(b) &= x_1 + x_2 + x_5 + x_6 \\
&= \omega u^+ + (1 - \omega)u^- \\
&= \omega + \beta - 1 + (1 - \omega)u^-
\end{aligned}
$$

•

$$
\begin{aligned}
p(c) &= x_1 + x_3 + x_5 + x_7 \\
&= \omega u^+ v^+ + \omega(1 - u^+)v^- + (1 - \omega)u^- v^+ + \\
&\quad + (1 - \omega)(1 - u^-)v^- \\
&= \text{(we can substitute } u^+, v^+ \text{ in here and get an expression with } \omega, u^-, v^-)
\end{aligned}
$$

If $\omega \neq 0$ and $\alpha = \beta = 1$, we have as we saw $u^+ = v^+ = 1$ and therefore we have for this case:

• $p(a) = \omega \neq 0$

• $p(b) = \omega + (1 - \omega)uu^-$

• $p(c) = \omega + (1 - \omega)u^- + (1 - \omega)(1 - u^-)v^-$

Note that a maximising entropy condition might require that $v^- = u^-$, in which case $p(c)$ simplifies to

• $p(c) = \omega + (1 - \omega)u^-(2 - u^-)$

REMARK 6.30. It is obvious from the calculations of the previous example that we have some choice of proabilities here despite the constraints. We need some additional principles to help us choose. We can use the maximum entropy principle or any other principle.

Let us not do any calculations now but turn towards proof theory. I think the need for proof theory is obvious given the complexity of computation involved. So let us now do the proof theory and see how to make choices during the proof.

EXAMPLE 6.31 (Case study: Bayesian proof approach). Let us look at the net of Figure 6.16. This gives us the depenency between the variables. So we observe that a is an independent variable and so let us use the cut rule on a as if we are in the η-approach. In fact we can use cut only on independent variables.

So we have again

1. $\alpha : a \wedge b \Rightarrow c$

2. $\beta : a \Rightarrow b$

and we are trying to find

3. $x : a \Rightarrow c$

We perform cut on a

Case $a = \top$

4.

$$
\begin{aligned}
(a \wedge b \Rightarrow c) &\equiv [(b \Rightarrow c) \wedge a] \vee [\top \wedge \neg a] \\
&\equiv ((b \Rightarrow c) \wedge a) \vee \neg a
\end{aligned}
$$

Therefore

5. $\alpha = p(a \wedge b \Rightarrow c)p((b \Rightarrow c) \wedge a) + 1 - p(a)$

The problem is that we cannot know the value of $p((b \Rightarrow c) \wedge a)$ in terms of $p(b \Rightarrow c)$ and $p(a)$ because we are not in the η approach where a, b and c are independent.We are in the Bayesian approach relative to the net of Figure 6.16 and according to this figure b is dependent on a. So we need to do cut again. The net for the case of $a = \top$ is just in Figure 6.19.

So we carry on with cut on b.

6. $(b \Rightarrow c) \wedge a \equiv (c \wedge a \wedge b) \vee (a \wedge \neg b)$

Therefore

7. $p((b \Rightarrow c) \wedge a) = p(c \wedge a \wedge b) + p(a \wedge \neg b)$

$$b|(a = \top)$$

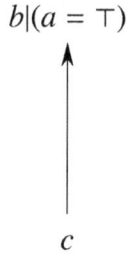

$$c$$

Figure 6.19.

and hence

8. $p(a \wedge b \Rightarrow c) = p(c \wedge a \wedge b) + p(a \wedge \neg b) + p(\neg a)$

We can continue by looking at Figure 6.17

9.

$$
\begin{aligned}
p(a \wedge b \Rightarrow c) = \alpha &= \omega u^+ v^+ + \omega(1 - u^+) + 1 - \omega \\
&= \omega u^+ v^+ + 1 - \omega u^+
\end{aligned}
$$

Let us do the same for the second clause

10.

$$
\begin{aligned}
\beta = p(a \Rightarrow b) &= p((b \wedge a) \vee (\top \wedge \neg a)) \\
&= p(b \wedge a) \vee p(\neg a) \\
&= \omega u^+ + 1 - \omega
\end{aligned}
$$

We therefore get

11. $\beta = \omega u^+ + 1 - \omega$

Note that the cut rules we use follow the Bayesian net of Figure 6.16 and the conditional probabilities of Figure 6.17

We do not need Figure 6.18. To compare with non-probabilistic classical logic, Figure 6.18 is like a fully fledged truth table analysis while the proof theory using cut we propose is like guided tableaux method which may be much simpler than a full case analysis.

So compare equations (11) and (9) above with equation (3*) and (4*) of Example 6.28. They give identical results. The proof theory however was quicker and more importantly, we followed the rationale of hte application.

Let us now calculate $x : a \Rightarrow c$.

We must start with cut on a.

12.

$$\begin{aligned}(a \Rightarrow c) &\equiv (c \wedge a) \vee (\top \wedge \neg a) \\ &\equiv c \wedge a \vee \neg a\end{aligned}$$

Hence

13. $x = p(a \Rightarrow c) = p(c \wedge a) + p(\neg a)$

c is dependent on b which depends on a, so we do cut on b

14. $c \wedge a \equiv (c \wedge a \wedge b) \vee (c \wedge a \wedge \neg b)$

Hence

$$\begin{aligned}p(c \wedge a) &= p(c \wedge a \wedge b) + p(c \wedge a \wedge \neg b) \\ &= \omega u^+ v^+ + \omega(1 - u^+)v^-\end{aligned}$$

Thus

15.

$$\begin{aligned}x &= p(c \wedge a \wedge b) + p(c \wedge a \wedge \neg b) + p(\neg a) \\ &= \omega u^+ v^+ + \omega(1 - u^+)v^+ + 1 - \omega \\ &= \omega v^+ + 1 - \omega\end{aligned}$$

Compare (15) with equation 5* of Example 6.28.

7 Further Exercises

We begin by summarising our probability options for propositional classical logic with three atomic letters $\{a, b, c\}$.

The possible models (rows in the truth table) for three letters are listed as follows:

$\mathbf{m}_1 : a \wedge b \wedge c$
$\mathbf{m}_2 : a \wedge b \wedge \neg c$
$\mathbf{m}_3 : a \wedge \neg b \wedge c$
$\mathbf{m}_4 : a \wedge \neg b \wedge \neg c$
$\mathbf{m}_5 : \neg a \wedge b \wedge c$
$\mathbf{m}_6 : \neg a \wedge b \wedge \neg c$
$\mathbf{m}_7 : \neg a \wedge \neg b \wedge c$
$\mathbf{m}_8 : \neg a \wedge \neg b \wedge \neg c$

The π approach gives probabilities to the models directly. These values, which we denote by $x_i = \pi(\mathbf{m}_i), i = 1, \ldots, 8$ are arbitrary and the only restriction is that they should all sum up to 1. Thus

$$x_1 + \ldots + x_8 = 1 \tag{$*$}$$

We thus have 7 degrees of freedom here. We can choose seven of these number as we wish and the eighth number is determined by (*).

The probability of any formula A is the sum of the probabilities of the models which satisfy A. Thus

$$\pi(A) = \sum_{i, \mathbf{m}_i \models A} \pi(\mathbf{m}_i).$$

Note that if $A \equiv B$ (i.e. A and B are logically equivalent, then they have the same truth table and therefore have the same probability.

EXAMPLE 6.32.

1. The probability of $a \Rightarrow b$ is the same as the probability of $\neg a \vee b$ which is

$$x_1 + x_2 + x_5 + x_6 + x_7 + x_8 = 1 - x_3 - x_4$$

2. The probability of a is $x_1 + x_2 + x_3 + x_4$

3. The probability of $b \Rightarrow c$ is the same as the probability of $\neg b \vee c$, which is

$$x_1 + x_3 + x_4 + x_5 + x_7 + x_8 = 1 - x_2 - x_6.$$

The other extreme approach for giving probability is the η-approach, which regards a, b, c as independent and have their own probabilities for being $\top$ or $\perp$.

Let
$$\eta(a) = \text{probability of } a = \top$$
$$\eta(b) = \text{probability of } b = \top$$
$$\eta(c) = \text{probability of } c = \top$$

Since a, b, c are independent, the probability of $a \wedge b$ is the product of their probabilities.[5]

Thus we have for example:

$$\eta(\mathbf{m}_1) = \eta(a)\eta(b)\eta(c)$$

The full table is:

$$\eta(\mathbf{m}_1) = \eta(a)\eta(b)\eta(c)$$
$$\eta(\mathbf{m}_1) = \eta(a)\eta(b)(1 - \eta(c))$$
$$\eta(\mathbf{m}_3) = \eta(a)(1 - \eta(b))\eta(c)$$
$$\eta(\mathbf{m}_4) = \eta(a)(1 - \eta(b))(1 - \eta(c))$$
$$\eta(\mathbf{m}_5) = (1 - \eta(a))\eta(b)\eta(c)$$
$$\eta(\mathbf{m}_6) = (1 - \eta(a))\eta(b)(1 - \eta(c))$$
$$\eta(\mathbf{m}_7) = (1 - \eta(a))(1 - \eta(b))\eta(c)$$
$$\eta(\mathbf{m}_8) = (1 - \eta(a))(1 - \eta(a))(1 - \eta(c))$$

---

[5]The definition of A and B being independent is (in the theory of probability) that the probability of $A \wedge B$ is the product of probability of A times the probability of B, i.e. $\pi(A \wedge B) = \pi(A) \times \pi(B)$.

Note that we do indeed have that

$$\eta(\mathbf{m}_1) + \ldots + \eta(\mathbf{m}_8) = 1 \qquad (**)$$

Note that the η-approach allows for 3 degrees of freedom, namely the three numbers $\eta(a), \eta(b), \eta(c)$.

EXAMPLE 6.33. Suppose we are given that the probability of $a \Rightarrow b$ is α and that of a is β, what can we say about the probability y of b?

We begin by adopting a point of view about the database

1. $\alpha : a \Rightarrow b$

2. $\beta : a$

These are considered as data items with probabilities. In the most general case (i.e. the π approach with 7 degrees of freedom) the probability of $a \Rightarrow b$ is $1 - x_3 - x_4$ and the probability of a is $x_1 + x_2 + x_3 + x_4$. Therefore the database is saying that all we know is

1* $\alpha = 1 - x_3 - x_4$

2* $\beta = x_1 + x_2 + x_3 + x_4$

We also know that the probability of b is determined by all the models where b is true, therefore

3* $y = x_1 + x_2 + x_5 + x_6$

From equations 1* and 2* we get

$$\alpha + \beta = 1 + x_1 + x_2$$

and therefore we get

$$y = \alpha + \beta - 1 + x_5 + x_6$$

Obviously we cannot determine y without additional equations, or additional assumptions, on x_5 and x_6.

So we view the database as giving us some equations on $x_1 \ldots x_8$ and we can try and find solutions for some of them, as we may be asked (in our case we were asked what was the probability of b).

Suppose now that we assume that a, b, c are independent. This assumption allows us to assume only 3 unknowns $\eta(a), \eta(b)$ and $\eta(c)$.

The equations become

1** $\alpha = 1 - \eta(a)(1 - \eta(b))\eta(c) - \eta(a)(1 - \eta(b))(1 - \eta(c))$

2** $\beta = \eta(a)\eta(b)\eta(c) + \eta(a)\eta(b)(1 - \eta(c)) + \eta(a)(1 - \eta(b))\eta(c)+$
$\eta(a)(1 - \eta(b))(1 - \eta(c))$
$= \eta(a)\eta(b) + \eta(a)(1 - \eta(b))$
$= \eta(a)$

We should have known that the probability of a is $\eta(a)$ in the η approach but it was interesting to calculate it directly from the models.

Substituting from equation 2** into 1** we get

$$\begin{aligned} \alpha &= 1 - \beta(1 - \eta(b))\eta(c) - \beta(1 - \eta(b))(1 - \eta(c)) \\ &= 1 - \beta(1 - \eta(b)) = 1 - \beta + \beta\eta(b) \end{aligned}$$

Therefore

♯ $\eta(b) = \dfrac{\alpha + \beta - 1}{\beta}$

Assuming $\beta \neq 0$

We have thus learnt how to do modus ponens for independent atoms a and b. It looks like the following:

$\alpha : a \Rightarrow b$

$\dfrac{\beta : a}{}$

•

$\dfrac{\alpha + \beta - 1}{\beta} : b$

provided $\beta \neq 0$

We can get this result directly by syntactical manipulation as follows.

EXAMPLE 6.34. *Assume Data*:

$\alpha : A \Rightarrow B$

$\beta : A$

Question

What is the probability y of B under the assumption that A and B are independent?

We use the following probability axioms

- If $X \equiv Y$ then $\text{prob}(Y) = \text{prob}(X)$

- $\text{prob}(X \vee Y) = \text{prob}(X) + \text{prob}(Y) - \text{prob}(X \wedge Y)$

- For X and Y independent
  $\text{prob}(X \wedge Y) = \text{prob}(X) \times \text{prob}(Y)$

- $\text{prob}(\neg X) = 1 - \text{prob}(X)$

- prob($\top$) = 1

- prob($\bot$) = 0

We have

$$
\begin{aligned}
\alpha &= \text{prob}(A \Rightarrow B) = \text{prob}(\neg A \vee B) \\
&= \text{prob}(\neg A) + \text{prob}(B) - \text{prob}(\neg A \wedge B) \\
&= 1 - \text{prob}(A) + \text{prob}(B) - \text{prob}(\neg A)(\text{prob}(B) \\
&= 1 - \text{prob}(A) + \text{prob}(B) - (1 - \text{prob}(A))\text{prob}(B) \\
&= 1 - \beta + y - (1 - \beta)y
\end{aligned}
$$

Solving for y

$$
\begin{aligned}
\alpha + \beta - 1 &= y - (1 - \beta)y \\
&= \beta y
\end{aligned}
$$

hence

$$
y = \frac{\alpha + \beta - 1}{\beta}
$$

provided $\beta \neq 0$. We got the same as before!

Chaining of Modus ponens

Under the assumption of a, b, c being independent, we saw that we can perform modus ponens with probabilities.

So

$$
\frac{\begin{array}{c} \alpha : a \Rightarrow b \\ \beta : a \end{array}}{y = \dfrac{\alpha + \beta - 1}{\beta} : b}
$$

Suppose we also have

$$
\gamma : b \Rightarrow c.
$$

We can now do chaining and get

$$
\frac{\gamma + y - 1}{y} : c
$$

or

$$
\frac{\gamma + \dfrac{\alpha + \beta - 1}{\beta} - 1}{\dfrac{\alpha + \beta - 1}{\beta}} : c
$$

or equivalently

$$
\frac{\gamma\beta + \alpha + \beta - 1 - \beta}{\alpha + \beta - 1} : c
$$

or

$$\frac{\gamma\beta + \alpha - 1}{\alpha + \beta - 1} : c$$

In the general case, under the π-approach, we do not know whether a, b, c are independent. So we need to go back and look at the models of $a, a \Rightarrow b, b, b \Rightarrow c$ and c and see what can be calculated.

We already calculated in our first examples 1 and 2 that given

$$\alpha : a \Rightarrow b$$
$$\beta : a$$
$$\gamma : b \Rightarrow c$$

we have that

$$\alpha = 1 - x_3 - x_4$$
$$\beta = x_1 + x_2 + x_3 + x_4$$
$$\gamma = 1 - x_2 - x_6$$

Adding them all up we get

$$\alpha + \beta + \gamma = 2 + x_1 - x_6$$

The probability z of c is

$$z = x_1 + x_3 + x_5 + x_7$$

Obviously we need more equations to find z.

EXAMPLE 6.35. Given

$$\alpha : a \Rightarrow b$$
$$\beta : a$$
$$\gamma : b \Rightarrow c$$

We ask for the probability of $a \wedge b \wedge c$? This means that we want to know the value of x_1. This is slightly easier. We get from our earlier calculations that

$$x_1 = \alpha + \beta + \gamma - 2 + x_6$$

We don't know the value of x_6.

x_6 is the probability of $\neg a \wedge b \wedge \neg c$.

Suppose we are given for example am additional item of data

$$\delta : b \Rightarrow (a \vee c)$$

Since x_6 is the probability of $\neg(b \Rightarrow a \vee c) = \neg a \wedge b \wedge \neg c$. We know that $x_6 = 1 - \delta$ and so

$$x_1 = \alpha + \beta + \gamma - 1 - \delta$$

To summarise we found without any assumptions that

$$\alpha : a \Rightarrow b$$
$$\beta : a$$
$$\gamma : b \Rightarrow c$$
$$\delta : b \Rightarrow a \vee c$$

can prove that

$$\alpha + \beta + \gamma - 1 - \delta : a \wedge b \wedge c.$$

EXAMPLE 6.36. We have seen that the database

1. $\alpha : a \Rightarrow b$

2. $\beta : a$

3. $\gamma : b \Rightarrow c$

4. $\delta : b \Rightarrow a \vee c$

is able to force the result

$$\alpha + \beta + \gamma - \delta - 1 : a \wedge b \wedge c$$

the question we ask is can we go forward using modus ponens and get to this result?

Our previous calculation was looking at the models for the formulas above. This is like reasoning using full truth tables. It is computationally expensive. We prefer to use proof theory. We have a problem. The modus ponens rules we know we can use, work only under the assumption that a, b, c are independent. We cannot assume this for our example. So, what shall we do?

In this particular case we use a trick. Instead of $X \Rightarrow Y$, we write $X \Rightarrow X \wedge Y$. These two formulas are equivalent. So

$$\text{prob}(X \Rightarrow Y) = \text{prob}(X \Rightarrow X \wedge Y) = \text{prob}(\neg X \vee (X \wedge Y)) =$$
$$\text{prob}(\neg X) + \text{prob}(X \wedge Y) - \text{prob}(\neg X \wedge X \wedge Y)$$

but $\text{prob}(\neg X \wedge X \wedge Y) = \text{prob}(\bot) = 0$

So we get

$$\text{prob}(X \Rightarrow Y) = 1 - \text{prob}(X) + \text{prob}(X \wedge Y).$$

and so

$$\text{prob}(X \wedge Y) = \text{prob}(X) + \text{prob}(X \Rightarrow Y) - 1$$

We thus have the following modus ponens rule, requiring no independence assumptions:

$$\frac{\alpha : X \Rightarrow X \wedge Y}{\alpha + \beta - 1 : X \wedge Y}$$

So from our assumptions we can get (from 1 and 2)

 5. $\alpha + \beta - 1 : a \wedge b$

Consider

 6. $y : b$

y is the probability of b. We do not know what y is but we can use it in our reasoning, and hope it will help and we will not need a value for it.

So to carry on, from 6 and 3, we get

 7. $\gamma + y - 1 : b \wedge c$

and from 6 and 4 we get

 8. $\delta + y - 1 : (a \vee c) \wedge b$.

But $(a \vee c) \wedge b \equiv (a \wedge b) \vee (c \wedge b)$ and so

$$\delta + y - 1 = \text{prob}(a \wedge b) + \text{prob}(c \wedge b) - \text{prob}(a \wedge b \wedge c)$$

and so

$$(\delta + y - 1) = (\alpha + \beta - 1) + (\gamma + y - 1) - \text{prob}(a \wedge b \wedge c)$$

Hence

$$
\begin{aligned}
\text{prob}(a \wedge b \wedge c) &= \alpha + \beta - 1 + \gamma + y - 1 \\
&\quad -\delta - y + 1 \\
&= \alpha + \beta + \gamma - \delta - 1
\end{aligned}
$$

Maximum entropy principle

We have seen in the previous example that the data

$$
\begin{aligned}
\alpha &: a \Rightarrow b \\
\beta &: a \\
\gamma &: b \Rightarrow c
\end{aligned}
$$

is not sufficient to determine the probability z of c. In ordinary logic we can use modus ponens to get c. Ordinary logic operates on the assumption that the probability of the data is 1. So $\alpha = \beta = \gamma = 1$. In this case, if we look at equation for z from our discussion of chaining of modus ponens, we have

$$
\begin{aligned}
z &= x_1 + x_3 + x_5 + x_7 \\
\alpha + \beta + \gamma &= 2 + x_1 - x_6
\end{aligned}
$$

If $\alpha = \beta = \gamma = 1$ we get $x_1 - x_6 = 1$ or $x_1 = 1 + x_6$. Now since x_1 can be at most 1, we must have $x_1 = 1$ and $x_6 = 0$. If $x_1 = 1$, then since $\sum x_i = 1$ we must have $x_2 = x_3 = x_4 = x_5 = x_6 = x_7 = x_8 = 0$ and so

$$z = 1 + 0 + \ldots + 0 = 1.$$

What do we do in general when we do not have enough equations? We invoke the principle which says all things being equal, the probabilities of the variables we do not know about are all equal, given the constraints, (this is called the maximum entropy principle). So, for example, if the database is empty, no data is given, we assume $x_1 = x_2 = x_8$ and so $x_i = 1/8$.

In the case z, we an assume $x_3 = x_4$ and $x_1 = x_2$ since they all appear symmetrically in the equations. We get

$$\alpha = 1 - 2x_3$$

So

$$x_3 = \frac{1 - \alpha}{2} = x_4$$

$$\beta = 2x_1 + 1 - \alpha$$

So

$$x_1 = \frac{\alpha + \beta - 1}{2} = x_2$$

We can now solve for x_6:

$$
\begin{aligned}
x_6 &= 1 - x_2 - \gamma = 1 - \frac{\alpha + \beta - 1}{2} - \gamma \\
&= \frac{2 - \alpha + \beta - 1}{2} - \gamma \\
&= \frac{1 - \alpha + \beta}{2} - \gamma
\end{aligned}
$$

We can also assume that $x_5 = x_7 = x_8$ since they are symmetrically not mentioned in any equation.

So since $x_1 + \ldots + x_8 = 1$ we get

$$
\begin{aligned}
3x_5 &= 1 - x_1 - x_2 - x_3 - x_4 - x_6 \\
&= 1 - (\alpha + \beta - 1) - (1 - \alpha) \\
&\quad - \left(\frac{1 - \alpha + \beta}{2} - \gamma\right) \\
&= 1 - \alpha - \beta + 1 - 1 + \alpha - \frac{1}{2} + \frac{\alpha}{2} - \frac{\beta}{2} + \gamma = \\
&= \frac{1}{2} - \frac{3}{2}\beta + \frac{\alpha}{2} + \gamma
\end{aligned}
$$

So

$$x_5 = x_7 = x_8 = \frac{1 - 3\beta + \alpha + 2\gamma}{6}$$

CHAPTER 7

Methodology and metatheorems

In previous chapters we encountered several kinds of logics defined in a variety of ways. It is time for a methodological discussion about logics and their properties in general, and some metatheorems about classical logic in particular.

In Chapter 2 we said that to present a logical system we need three components:

- A formal language **L** defining the well-formed formulae of the logic.

- A semantic interpretation for the language.

- A family of reasoning rules.

We proceeded to define classical logic in this way. The formulae of the language were built up from atomic propositions and the connectives $\{\neg, \wedge, \vee, \Rightarrow, \top, \bot\}$. The semantic interpretation was given through the classical truth tables. We had several options for reasoning rules: forward rules was one and backward rules was another. We also saw how to define our logics by changing the semantic interpretation (defining many-valued logics), or the language (adding modality $\Box$), or modifying the reasoning rules (adopting the policy of diminishing resource). All of these different definitions actually define different consequence relations for the language of the logics. We now need to study this notion in the abstract.

1 Consequence relations and Hilbert systems

Let **L** be a language. This section will briefly outline several syntactical methods for defining logical systems for **L**.

DEFINITION 7.1. We define a (transitive) logic (or consequence relation) as any relation $\vdash$ between well-formed formulae satisfying the following:

Identity:

$$A \vdash A$$

Transitivity:

$$\frac{A \mathrel{\vdash} B; B \mathrel{\vdash} C}{A \mathrel{\vdash} C}$$

Equivalence:[1]

$$\frac{A \mathrel{\vdash} B; B \mathrel{\vdash} A; C \mathrel{\vdash} A}{C \mathrel{\vdash} B}$$

$$\frac{A \mathrel{\vdash} B; B \mathrel{\vdash} A; A \mathrel{\vdash} C}{B \mathrel{\vdash} C}$$

Such systems can be extended to relations between sets $\mathcal{P}$ of wffs (including the empty set) and single wff, satisfying:

Reflexivity:

$$\mathcal{P} \mathrel{\vdash} A, \text{ if } A \in \mathcal{P}$$

Restricted monotonicity:

$$\frac{\mathcal{P} \mathrel{\vdash} A; \mathcal{P} \mathrel{\vdash} B}{\mathcal{P}, A \mathrel{\vdash} B}$$

Cut:

$$\frac{\mathcal{P}, A \mathrel{\vdash} B; \mathcal{P} \mathrel{\vdash} A}{\mathcal{P} \mathrel{\vdash} B}$$

A rule ρ for $\vdash$ has the form

$$\rho: \quad \frac{\mathcal{P}_i \mathrel{\vdash} A_i, i = 1, \ldots, k}{\mathcal{P} \mathrel{\vdash} A}$$

A consequence relation $\vdash$ is said to satisfy (or be closed under) the rule ρ if for any substitution instance $\mathcal{P}', A_i', A'$ of $\mathcal{P}, A_i$ and A respectively obtained by substituting B_j for q_j, $j = 1, \ldots$, we have that if $\mathcal{P}_i' \mathrel{\vdash} A_i'$ holds for $i = 1, \ldots, k$ then $\mathcal{P}' \mathrel{\vdash} A'$ holds.

A logic is defined by a set of rules $\{\rho_i\}$ if it can be presented as the smallest consequence relation closed under these rules.

EXAMPLE 7.2. Consider a language with the connectives $\{\wedge, \Rightarrow, \bot\}$. Consider the smallest consequence relation $\vdash$ for this language satisfying the following.

- $A \wedge B \mathrel{\vdash} A$

- $A \wedge B \mathrel{\vdash} B$

---

[1]*Equivalence* is derivable from *transitivity* and so can be eliminated. However, equivalence is more basic than transitivity. Some notions of a (non-monotonic) logical system do not include transitivity. See, for example, the systems $>_N$ of Theorem 11.6 and $\vdash$ of Definition 11.9.

- $C \wedge A \vdash B$ iff $C \vdash A \Rightarrow B$

- $\perp \vdash A$

- $A \wedge B \vdash B \wedge A$

- $$\dfrac{A \vdash B_1, A \vdash B_2}{A \vdash B_1 \wedge B_2}$$

- $$\dfrac{A \vdash B; C \wedge B \vdash D}{C \wedge A \vdash D}$$

We now show that this consequence relation gives intuitionistic logic for this fragment of the language. We prove

EXERCISE 7.3. Let $\vDash_I$ be the consequence relation of Definition 2.6. Show that $\vDash_I$ is the same as $\vdash$ of the previous example.

Hints

1. First show that $\vDash_I$ satisfies the conditions on $\vdash$. This will show that $\vdash \subseteq \vDash_I$.

2. To show that $\vDash_I \subseteq \vdash$, construct a Kripke model as follows.

   Let $A \equiv B$ mean $A \vdash B$ and $B \vdash A$.

   - Let T = the set of all equivalence classes of wffs over $\equiv$, *except* the class of $\perp$. We denote such a class by $A/ \equiv$.

   - Let $A/ \equiv \ \leq \ B/ \equiv$ be defined as $B \vdash A$. Show that this relation is well defined; in other words, show that $A \equiv A_1, B \equiv B_1$ imply $B_1 \vdash A_1$ iff $B \vdash A$.

   - Let $h(A/ \equiv, q)$ be defined as holding iff $A \vdash q$.

   Show that in the model $(T, \leq, h)$ we have

$$h(A/ \equiv, B) = 1 \text{ iff } A \vdash B$$

In particular the definition of h does not depend on the representative $A \in A/ \equiv$. The above shows that if $A \nvdash B$ then $A \nvDash_I B$, as we have $h(A/ \equiv, B) = 0$ in the above model. For a solution see the proof of Theorem 7.29.

Some logics can be completely characterized by the set of theorems, i.e. by $\{A \mid \varnothing \vdash A\}$. This leads us to a Hilbert formulation of a logic, and to the next section.

2 Hilbert formulation of a logic

We saw in previous sections that different logics for the same language, say for $\rightarrow$, have different sets of tautologies. There is a way of characterizing a logic by generating its tautologies. We need some definitions.

DEFINITION 7.4. Consider a propositional language with atomic propositions and the single binary connective $\rightarrow$.

1. We define the set of wffs in the usual way, namely:

    - Let q be atomic; then 'q' is a wff based on $\{q\}$.
    - If $A(q_1, \ldots, q_n)$, $B(p_1, \ldots, p_k)$ are wffs based on $\{q_1, \ldots, q_n\}$ and $\{p_1, \ldots, p_k\}$ respectively then $(A \rightarrow B)$ is a wff based on $\{p_1, \ldots, p_k, q_1, \ldots, q_n\}$.

2. Assume C is based on $q_1, \ldots, q_n$, then C' is said to be a substitution instance of C if for some $A_i, i = 1, \ldots, n$, we have $C' = C(q_i/A_i), i = 1, \ldots, n$. Recall Definition 1.1.2.

DEFINITION 7.5. A set $\mathcal{P}$ of wffs in a language with a binary connective $\rightarrow$ is said to be *generated* as a Hilbert system from the formulae (called *Hilbert axioms*) $C_1, \ldots, C_k$ if $\mathcal{P}$ is the smallest set of wffs, such that

- $C_1, \ldots, C_k \in \mathcal{P}$.

- If $C \in \mathcal{P}$ and C' is a substitution instance of C then $C' \in \mathcal{P}$.

- If $A \in \mathcal{P}$ and $(A \rightarrow B) \in \mathcal{P}$ then also $B \in \mathcal{P}$.

It is customary to compare logics by generating their set of tautologies. The stronger logics will have more axioms.

EXAMPLE 7.6.

It is possible to generate all intuitionistic implicational tautologies by substitution, and the rule of *modus ponens*, namely

$$\frac{A, A \Rightarrow B}{B}$$

and the Hilbert axioms

$$A \Rightarrow (B \Rightarrow A)$$

and

$$(A \Rightarrow (B \Rightarrow C)) \Rightarrow ((A \Rightarrow B) \Rightarrow (A \Rightarrow C))$$

The following additional tautology, taken as an additional axiom and known as Peirce's rule, helps generate all classical implicational tautologies, i.e. turns $\Rightarrow$ into classical implication

$$((A \Rightarrow B) \Rightarrow A) \Rightarrow A$$

EXERCISE 7.7. **Glivenko theorem**

1. Show that A is a classical tautology, if and only if $\neg\neg A$ is an intuitionistic tautology.

2. Show that if $A \equiv B$ in classical logic, then $\neg\neg A \equiv \neg\neg B$ in intuitionistic logic.

EXERCISE 7.8.

1. Prove (generate) $A \Rightarrow A$ from the two Hilbert axioms of intuitionistic $\Rightarrow$, and the rule of *modus ponens*.

2. Show that Peirce's rule cannot be generated from the intuitionistic axioms, and *modus ponens*.

EXAMPLE 7.9 (A Hilbert formulation for classical logic). The following is a sample of a Hilbert formulation of classical logic, taken from [Nidditch, 1962].
The axioms are (all substitution instances of)

1. $p \Rightarrow (q \Rightarrow p)$

2. $(p \Rightarrow (q \Rightarrow r)) \Rightarrow ((p \Rightarrow q) \Rightarrow (p \Rightarrow r))$

3. $p \Rightarrow p \vee q$

4. $q \Rightarrow p \vee q$

5. $(p \Rightarrow r) \Rightarrow ((q \Rightarrow r) \Rightarrow (p \vee q \Rightarrow r))$

6. $p \wedge q \Rightarrow p$

7. $p \wedge q \Rightarrow q$

8. $(r \Rightarrow p) \Rightarrow ((r \Rightarrow q) \Rightarrow (r \Rightarrow p \wedge q))$

9. $(p \Rightarrow q) \Rightarrow (\neg q \Rightarrow \neg p)$

10. $p \Rightarrow \neg\neg p$

11. $\neg\neg p \Rightarrow p$

The above axioms together with *modus ponens* generate all classical tautologies. In fact, if we drop axiom 11, the remaining axioms together with *modus ponens* constitute a *Hilbert formulation for intuitionistic logic* and generate all intuitionistic theorems.[2]

---

[2]This axiom system is *separated*; that is, any formula A built up from $\Rightarrow$ and other connectives is provable only from the axioms about $\Rightarrow$ and these other connectives.

A consequence relation $\sim$ can be defined from the Hilbert system by letting $A_1, \ldots, A_n \sim B$ iff the formula $A_1 \Rightarrow (A_2 \Rightarrow \cdots \Rightarrow (A_n \Rightarrow B) \cdots)$ is generated.

EXAMPLE 7.10 (A Hilbert formulation of three-valued logic). For comparison with the classical two-valued case, the following is a Hilbert axiom system for Łukasiewicz three-valued logic, for the language with $\{\neg, \wedge, \vee, \Rightarrow\}$.

1. $A \Rightarrow (B \Rightarrow A)$

2. $(A \Rightarrow B) \Rightarrow ((B \Rightarrow C) \Rightarrow (A \Rightarrow C))$

3. $(A \Rightarrow (B \Rightarrow C)) \Rightarrow (B \Rightarrow (A \Rightarrow C))$

4. $((A \Rightarrow B) \Rightarrow B) \Rightarrow ((B \Rightarrow A) \Rightarrow A)$

5. $((((A \Rightarrow B) \Rightarrow A) \Rightarrow A) \Rightarrow (B \Rightarrow C)) \Rightarrow (B \Rightarrow C)$

6. $A \wedge B \Rightarrow A$

7. $A \wedge B \Rightarrow B$

8. $(A \Rightarrow B) \Rightarrow ((A \Rightarrow C) \Rightarrow (A \Rightarrow (B \wedge C)))$

9. $A \Rightarrow A \vee B$

10. $B \Rightarrow A \vee B$

11. $(A \Rightarrow C) \Rightarrow ((B \Rightarrow C) \Rightarrow (A \vee B \Rightarrow C))$

12. $(\neg B \Rightarrow \neg A) \Rightarrow (A \Rightarrow B)$

The inference rule is *modus ponens*.

See [Avron, 1988] for more details.

DEFINITION 7.11 (Consequence relations associated with Hilbert systems). Let H be a Hilbert system, as defined in Definition 7.5. We define a consequence relation $\sim_H$ as follows: $A_1, \ldots, A_n \sim_H B$ iff there exists a (proof) sequence of formulae $(D_1, \ldots, D_k)$ such that the following hold.

1. $D_k = B$.

2. For each element D_m in the sequence, one of the following cases holds:

   (a) $D_m = A_i$, for some $1 \le i \le n$.

   (b) D_m is a theorem of (i.e. is generated by) the Hilbert system H.

   (c) For some $m_1, m_2 < m$ we have that $D_{m_2} = (D_{m_1} \twoheadrightarrow D_m)$.[3]

---

[3] Note that for the Hilbert systems of Example 7.9, the natural rules for the other connectives can be derived; for example, using instances of axiom 8 we can get that $D_1, D_2 \vdash D_1 \wedge D_2$.

3 Metatheorems about classical logic consequence

At the start of Chapter 3, we encountered the cut rule, which we restate as a theorem below:

THEOREM 7.12 (Cut theorem). *If $\mathcal{P} \vDash \varphi$ and $\mathcal{P}, \varphi \vDash \psi$ then $\mathcal{P} \vDash \psi$.*

Proof. Suppose that $\mathcal{P} \vDash \varphi$ and $\mathcal{P}, \varphi \vDash \psi$, and draw a truth table for $\mathcal{P}$, φ and ψ. Each row in the table which has all the formulae in $\mathcal{P}$ true, and also has φ true, will have ψ true (because $\mathcal{P}, \varphi \vDash \psi$). But every row with all of the formulae in $\mathcal{P}$ true will have φ true (because $\mathcal{P} \vDash \varphi$). Therefore every row with all of the formulae in $\mathcal{P}$ true will also have ψ true. Hence $\mathcal{P} \vDash \psi$. ∎

We can see the cut theorem in action as follows. Let $\mathcal{P} = \{a \Rightarrow b, a \wedge c\}$, and let $\varphi = a$ and $\psi = b$. Now $\mathcal{P} \vDash a$ because whenever all of $\mathcal{P}$ is true, $a \wedge c$ must be true, and thus a must be true. Moreover, $\mathcal{P}, a \vDash b$ because whenever $a \Rightarrow b$ and a are true together, b must be true. Hence by the cut theorem, we must have $\mathcal{P} \vDash b$. This is indeed the case, as can be seen from the truth table below. Each row which makes all of $\mathcal{P}$ true has b true.

a	b	c	$a \Rightarrow b$	$a \wedge c$	$\mathcal{P}$	$\mathcal{P} \Rightarrow a$	$\mathcal{P}, a \Rightarrow b$
T	T	T	T	T	T	T	T
T	T	⊥	T	⊥	⊥	T	T
T	⊥	T	⊥	T	⊥	T	T
T	⊥	⊥	⊥	⊥	⊥	T	T
⊥	T	T	T	⊥	⊥	T	T
⊥	T	⊥	T	⊥	⊥	T	T
⊥	⊥	T	T	⊥	⊥	T	T
⊥	⊥	⊥	T	⊥	⊥	T	T

Towards the end of Chapter 1 we stated that logical consequence possessed the property of monotonicity, namely that if a conclusion from a set of assumptions is valid, then the same conclusion is valid from the set of assumptions with some additional formulae added.

THEOREM 7.13 (Monotonicity). *Let $\mathcal{P}$ and Q be sets of formulae, and φ be a formula. If $\mathcal{P} \vDash \varphi$ then $\mathcal{P} \cup Q \vDash \varphi$ for any Q.*

Proof. If $\mathcal{P} \cup Q \nvDash \varphi$ then we would have a row in the truth table in which all of $\mathcal{P} \cup Q$ was true, but φ was false. But for every such row, it is the case that $\mathcal{P}$ would be all true, and φ would be false, and thus $\mathcal{P} \nvDash \varphi$. ∎

We can now use these two theorems to prove the transitivity theorem presented earlier.

THEOREM 7.14 (Transitivity). *For any three propositional formulae α, β and γ, if $\alpha \vDash \beta$ and $\beta \vDash \gamma$ then $\alpha \vDash \gamma$.*

Proof. Suppose that $\alpha \vDash \beta$ and $\beta \vDash \gamma$. From the latter, by using the monotonicity theorem we can show that $\alpha, \beta \vDash \gamma$. The cut theorem on this and $\alpha \vDash \beta$ then gives us $\alpha \vDash \gamma$ as required.   ∎

THEOREM 7.15 (Substitution). *If φ is a tautology which contains a particular proposition p, and we simultaneously replace p with some formula ψ (which does not contain p) throughout φ to get a new formula φ', then the new formula φ' is also a tautology.*

Proof. See Example 1.3.3.   ∎

A somewhat surprising theorem about propositional logic shows that if one formula is a logical consequence of another, and there is a subset of propositions common to both formulae, then there is a third formula involving just the common propositions which is a consequence of the first formula, and which in turn has the second formula as a consequence. This is perhaps easier to present symbolically:

THEOREM 7.16 (Interpolation). *For any two formulae of propositional logic φ and ψ such that $\varphi \vDash \psi$, with φ and ψ having some common atomic propositions, then there exists a formula θ built up solely of the common atomic propositions, such that $\varphi \vDash \theta$ and $\theta \vDash \psi$.*

Proof. Draw up a truth table for the propositions common to both φ and ψ. For each row in the truth table which can be expanded to make ψ false (i.e. by adding the propositions private to ψ to values that make ψ false), let the row have the truth value $\bot$, otherwise let the row have the value $\top$. A formula θ can then be constructed for this table (see Section 1.2). It is not possible for a row to be expanded to make φ true and ψ false (since $\varphi \vDash \psi$); hence there is no conflict as to which value to give to θ. Now all the rows in which θ is true are rows in which ψ cannot be made false; hence $\theta \vDash \psi$. All the rows which can be expanded to make φ true have θ true; hence $\varphi \vDash \theta$.   ∎

See also Remark 6.7.3.

4   Propositional soundness and completeness

It is important that any procedure purporting to be a theorem prover for a logical system should possess the property of *soundness*; that is, any formula which the procedure indicates is a theorem of the logical system actually is a theorem of the system. In addition, our theorem prover should be *complete*. This means that if a formula is a theorem of the logical system, then our procedure will indicate that. In Figure 7.1 we illustrate the four possible interesting relationships between the set of formulae that our procedure indicates is a theorem ($\vdash$) and the set of theorems of the system (taut). As you can see from Figure 7.1, the possibilities are:

(a) there is no subset relationship between ⊢ and taut and so some of the formulae that the theorem prover claims are valid are theorems, and some are not. Hence the theorem prover is neither sound nor complete. (The intersection of the two sets may be empty — in which case every answer produced by the theorem prover is wrong.)

(b) the formulae that the theorem prover claims are valid are a proper subset of the theorems of the system, and so the theorem prover is sound (although because there are theorems which lie outside ⊢, it is not complete).

(c) the theorems of the system are a proper subset of the formulae that the theorem prover claims are valid, so the theorem prover is complete (it proves all valid tautologies) but not sound (there are formulae it claims are tautologies, but which are not).

(d) the set of formulae that the theorem prover claims are valid is equal to the set of theorems of the system, and thus the theorem prover is both sound and complete.

For some logical systems it is not possible to build theorem provers which have the completeness property. Fortunately, for the propositional logic we have been dealing with, it is possible to have theorem-proving procedures which are both sound and complete — the use of truth tables is one such procedure. In this chapter we will show that the backward rules procedure is also sound and complete. From now on every definition and so forth in this chapter should be taken as being with respect to propositional logic.

DEFINITION 7.17. We shall write $\vdash_\Gamma A$ to mean that the procedure Γ indicates that A is a theorem. We say that the Γ-computation of A *succeeds*. A procedure Γ is said to have the *soundness* property iff

$$\vdash_\Gamma A \text{ implies that } A \text{ is a tautology}$$

for every wff A. A procedure Γ is said to have the *completeness* property iff

$$A \text{ is a tautology implies } \vdash_\Gamma A$$

for every wff A. These can alternatively be written as

$$\vdash_\Gamma A \text{ implies that } \vDash A \qquad \text{and} \qquad \vDash A \text{ implies } \vdash_\Gamma A$$

If we denote our backward rules procedure by the symbol $\mathcal{B}$, then we need to show that for any wff A,

$$\vdash_{\mathcal{B}} A \quad \text{iff} \quad A \text{ is a tautology}$$

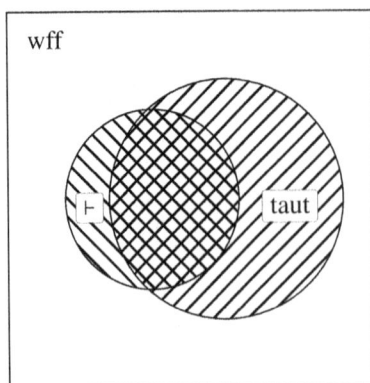

(a) neither sound nor complete

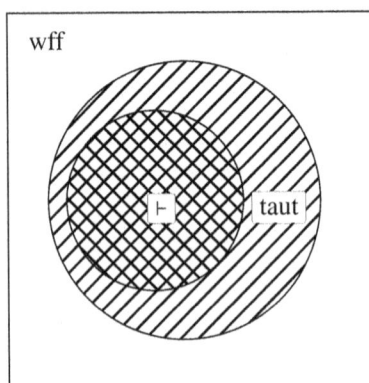

(b) sound but not complete

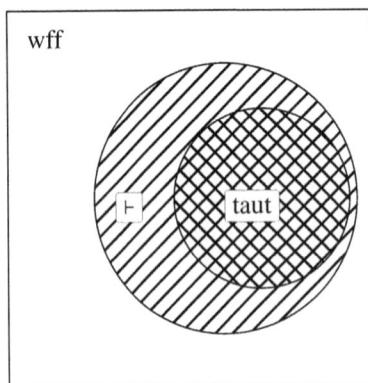

(c) complete but not sound

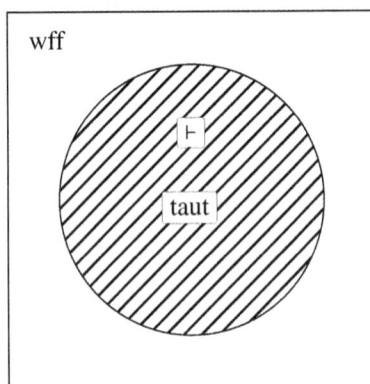

(d) both sound and complete

Figure 7.1. Combinations of soundness and completeness

in order to prove that the backward rules procedure is both sound and complete. To carry out the proof, we shall need a formal definition of the backward rules procedure for propositional logic.

We agreed in Chapter 4 that all our formulae shall be written using $\wedge$, $\Rightarrow$ and $\perp$ only, and that all the rules will have atomic heads so that each rule has the form $A \Rightarrow q$, with q being atomic. We saw that this can be done using the rules

$$
\begin{aligned}
\neg A &= A \Rightarrow \perp \\
A \vee B &= (A \Rightarrow \perp) \Rightarrow B \\
A \Rightarrow x \wedge y &= (A \Rightarrow x) \wedge (A \Rightarrow y) \\
\text{and} \quad A \Rightarrow (x \Rightarrow y) &= A \wedge x \Rightarrow y.
\end{aligned}
$$

The following is an inductive definition of the notion of a $\mathcal{B}$-clause (i.e. the type of clause we are dealing with).

DEFINITION 7.18 (Propositional $\mathcal{B}$-clauses).

1. An atom q is a propositional $\mathcal{B}$-clause, as is $\perp$.

2. If $A_1, \ldots, A_n$ are $\mathcal{B}$-clauses and q is an atom then

$$
A_1 \wedge \cdots \wedge A_n \Rightarrow q \text{ and } A_1 \wedge \cdots \wedge A_n \Rightarrow \perp
$$

are propositional $\mathcal{B}$-clauses.

3. A query is a conjunction of propositional $\mathcal{B}$-clauses, e.g.

$$
A_1 \wedge \cdots \wedge A_n
$$

where $A_1, \ldots, A_n$ are propositional $\mathcal{B}$-clauses.

The discussion in Chapter 4 showed that any formula of propositional logic can be rewritten as a conjunction of propositional $\mathcal{B}$-clauses. Let us state this formally.

LEMMA 7.19. *Any formula A of propositional classical logic can be equivalently written as a conjunction of $\mathcal{B}$-clauses.*

The general form of asking a query from a set of data using backward computation is $\mathcal{P} \vdash_\mathcal{B} A$ where $\mathcal{P}$ is a set of $\mathcal{B}$-clauses and A is a conjunction of $\mathcal{B}$-clauses. For example,

$$
\left\{
\begin{array}{l}
(a \Rightarrow b) \Rightarrow b \\
(c \wedge b) \Rightarrow \perp \\
b \Rightarrow \perp
\end{array}
\right\} \vdash_\mathcal{B} (a \Rightarrow \perp) \Rightarrow c
$$

We extend the notion of a computation succeeding and write $\mathcal{P} \vdash_\mathcal{B} A$ to mean A succeeds from $\mathcal{P}$. Recall that for the purposes of the restart rule, the backward computation is performed relative to the original goal, so we should write

$\langle \mathcal{P}, G \rangle \vdash_{\mathcal{B}} A$ where $\langle \mathcal{P}, G \rangle$ means $\mathcal{P}$ is the data and G is the original goal. The following definition is a summary of the computation rules. Remember, the clauses in $\mathcal{P}$ are always of the form $B \Rightarrow q$. Thus when we write $\mathcal{P} \cup \{D\}$ and D is $(B_1 \Rightarrow q_1) \wedge (B_2 \Rightarrow q_2)$ we mean $\mathcal{P} \cup \{B_1 \Rightarrow q_1, B_2 \Rightarrow q_2\}$.

DEFINITION 7.20 (Backward computation rules). We define $\langle \mathcal{P}, G \rangle \vdash_{\mathcal{B}} A$ by induction over the structure of the $\mathcal{B}$-clause A, and the restart rule.

1. When A is an atom q we have $\langle \mathcal{P}, G \rangle \vdash_{\mathcal{B}} q$ iff either

    (a) $q \in \mathcal{P}$ or $\bot \in \mathcal{P}$, or

    (b) for some $B \Rightarrow q \in \mathcal{P}$ or $B \Rightarrow \bot \in \mathcal{P}$ we have $\langle \mathcal{P}, G \rangle \vdash_{\mathcal{B}} B$.

2. When A is a conjunction $B \wedge C$, we have $\langle \mathcal{P}, G \rangle \vdash_{\mathcal{B}} B \wedge C$ iff $\langle \mathcal{P}, G \rangle \vdash_{\mathcal{B}} B$ and $\langle \mathcal{P}, G \rangle \vdash_{\mathcal{B}} C$.

3. When A is an implication $B \Rightarrow q$ we have $\langle \mathcal{P}, G \rangle \vdash_{\mathcal{B}} B \Rightarrow q$ iff $\langle \mathcal{P} \cup \{B\}, G \rangle \vdash_{\mathcal{B}} q$.

4. The restart rule states that $\langle \mathcal{P}, G \rangle \vdash_{\mathcal{B}} q$ for an atom q if $\langle \mathcal{P}, G \rangle \vdash_{\mathcal{B}} G$, where G is the original goal of the computation.

5. We sometimes abbreviate $\langle \mathcal{P}, Q \rangle \vdash_{\mathcal{B}} Q$ by $\mathcal{P} \vdash_{\mathcal{B}} Q$.

6. Let us write $\mathcal{P} \vdash_I Q$ if $\mathcal{P} \vdash_{\mathcal{B}} Q$ *without* use of the restart rule (clause 4 above).

Our use of the backward rules procedure has generally been to show that a formula Q is a tautological consequence of a set of formulae $\mathcal{P}$. Thus the tautology that we are interested in is not Q, but $\bigwedge \mathcal{P} \Rightarrow Q$, where $\bigwedge \mathcal{P}$ is the conjunction of all the formulae in $\mathcal{P}$ (see Definition 1.10). Hence in showing the soundness and completeness of the backward rules procedure, we are concerned with showing that

$$\langle \mathcal{P}, Q \rangle \vdash_{\mathcal{B}} Q \text{ iff } \bigwedge \mathcal{P} \Rightarrow Q \text{ is a tautology}$$

5   Proof of soundness

The proof of the soundness of the backward computation rules is fairly simple. We show that for each type of query Q that the procedure can claim to follow from a given set of data $\mathcal{P}$, the query is a tautological consequence of the data.

THEOREM 7.21 (Soundness of the backward computation rules). *If $\langle \mathcal{P}, G \rangle \vdash_{\mathcal{B}} Q$ then $\bigwedge \mathcal{P} \Rightarrow Q \vee G$ is a tautology.*

Proof. We shall deal with each computation rule in turn. Assume that $\langle \mathcal{P}, G \rangle \vdash_{\mathcal{B}} Q$.

1. If $Q = q$ where q is an atom, then we have one of the following cases:

(a) $q \in \mathcal{P}$, in which case q cannot be false without $\bigwedge \mathcal{P}$ being false; hence the only situation which could falsify $\bigwedge \mathcal{P} \Rightarrow q$ cannot arise, so that $\bigwedge \mathcal{P} \Rightarrow q \vee G$ is a tautology.

(b) $\bot \in \mathcal{P}$. This means that $\bigwedge \mathcal{P}$ must be false and therefore $\bigwedge \mathcal{P} \Rightarrow q \vee G$ must be a tautology.

(c) For some $A \Rightarrow q \in \mathcal{P}$ we have $\langle \mathcal{P}, G \rangle \vdash_{\mathcal{B}} A$. Now if the subcomputation of A succeeds, then we have $\bigwedge \mathcal{P} \Rightarrow A \vee G$ as a tautology. Hence whenever $\bigwedge \mathcal{P}$ is true, $A \vee G$ must be true, and by the clause $A \Rightarrow q$ we must have $q \vee G$ true. Therefore $\bigwedge \mathcal{P} \Rightarrow q \vee G$ is true.

(d) For some $A \Rightarrow \bot \in \mathcal{P}$ we have $\langle \mathcal{P}, G \rangle \vdash_{\mathcal{B}} A \vee G$. If the subcomputation of A succeeds, then we have $\bigwedge \mathcal{P} \Rightarrow A \vee G$ as a tautology.

Assume that $\bigwedge \mathcal{P}$ is true, then $A \vee G$ is true. But $A \Rightarrow \bot \in \mathcal{P}$ and thus $A \Rightarrow \bot$ is true, i.e. A is false. Then G must be true, and hence $q \vee G$ is true.

Therefore $\bigwedge \mathcal{P} \Rightarrow q \vee G$ is true.

2. If $Q = A \wedge B$ then we know that $\langle \mathcal{P}, G \rangle \vdash_{\mathcal{B}} A$ and $\langle \mathcal{P}, G \rangle \vdash_{\mathcal{B}} B$ and thus we have $\bigwedge \mathcal{P} \Rightarrow A \vee G$ and $\bigwedge \mathcal{P} \Rightarrow B \vee G$ as tautologies.

Assume that $\bigwedge \mathcal{P}$ is true; then $A \vee G, B \vee G$ are true. Now there are two cases:

- If G is true then $(A \wedge B) \vee G$ is true.
- If G is false then A, B must be true; hence $(A \wedge B)$ is true, and again $(A \wedge B) \vee G$ is true.

So we must have $\bigwedge \mathcal{P} \Rightarrow ((A \wedge B) \vee G)$ as a tautology.

3. If $Q = A \Rightarrow B$ then we know that $(\mathcal{P} \cup \{A\}, G) \vdash_{\mathcal{B}} B$, and thus we know that $(\bigwedge \mathcal{P}) \wedge A \Rightarrow B \vee G$ is a tautology. Assume $\bigwedge \mathcal{P}$ is true; hence we know that $A \Rightarrow B \vee G$ is also true; therefore $\bigwedge \mathcal{P} \Rightarrow (A \Rightarrow B) \vee G$ is also true, since $((A \Rightarrow B) \vee G) \equiv (A \Rightarrow B \vee G)$.

Thus $\bigwedge \mathcal{P} \Rightarrow (A \Rightarrow B) \vee G$ is a tautology.

4. The soundness of the restart rule follows from the following: G is equivalent to $\neg G \Rightarrow G$, which is equivalent to $(G \Rightarrow \bot) \Rightarrow G$ (which can be checked via truth tables). Thus when we start our computation with $(\mathcal{P}, G) \vdash_{\mathcal{B}} G$ we can write $\langle \mathcal{P}, G \rangle \vdash_{\mathcal{B}} (G \Rightarrow \bot) \Rightarrow G$ instead, since $[(G \Rightarrow \bot) \Rightarrow G] \equiv G$. Using the rule for $\Rightarrow$, we add the antecedent to the data, and ask $\langle \mathcal{P} \cup \{G \Rightarrow \bot\}, G \rangle \vdash_{\mathcal{B}} G$. If in the course of the computation we want to restart and ask G again, we can use the rule for $\bot$, since $G \Rightarrow \bot$ is available, so we have $\langle \mathcal{P} \cup \{G \Rightarrow \bot\}, G \rangle \vdash_{\mathcal{B}} q$ whenever $\langle \mathcal{P} \cup \{G \Rightarrow \bot\}, G \rangle \vdash_{\mathcal{B}} G$.

Thus $\langle \mathcal{P}, G \rangle \vdash_{\mathcal{B}} G$ succeeds with the use of restart iff $\mathcal{P} \cup \{G \Rightarrow \bot\} \vdash_{\mathcal{B}} G$ succeeds, even without restart. If the latter succeeds then $[(\bigwedge \mathcal{P}) \wedge (G \Rightarrow \bot)] \Rightarrow G$ is a tautology, and thus $\bigwedge \mathcal{P} \Rightarrow G \vee Q$ is a tautology.   ■

6   Proof of completeness

Proving completeness is much more tricky than proving soundness. When we prove soundness, we have to show that each 'positive' usage of the computation rules maintains the property of tautological consequence. The computation rules are a small set of ideas to work with. In contrast, when we prove completeness, we have to show that each tautological consequence is demonstrated by the computation rules. In order to be able to work from the rules for the proof procedure, instead of showing that

$$\bigwedge \mathcal{P} \Rightarrow \varphi \text{ is a tautology implies } \mathcal{P} \vdash_{\mathcal{B}} \varphi$$

we will show the equivalent

$$\mathcal{P} \nvdash_{\mathcal{B}} \varphi \text{ implies } \bigwedge \mathcal{P} \Rightarrow \varphi \text{ is not a tautology}$$

This means that we have to work with the cases in which our proof procedure fails to show φ from $\mathcal{P}$, and prove that φ is then not a tautological consequence of $\mathcal{P}$. The drawback with this approach is due to the difficulty of identifying the cases when the proof procedure fails to show φ from $\mathcal{P}$. The proof of Theorem 7.22 is therefore rather drawn out, and so we sketch the proof in broad outline, before filling in the details.

THEOREM 7.22 (Completeness of the backward computation rules). *If $\mathcal{P} \nvdash_{\mathcal{B}} \varphi$, then $\bigwedge \mathcal{P} \Rightarrow \varphi$ is not a tautology.*

Proof sketch: Assume that the proof procedure fails, i.e. $\mathcal{P} \nvdash_{\mathcal{B}} \varphi$. We will show from this that there are truth values which can be assigned to the atoms which make $\bigwedge \mathcal{P}$ true and φ false, and hence that $\bigwedge \mathcal{P} \Rightarrow \varphi$ is not a tautology.

     Proving this is much more complicated than proving soundness, and so we shall proceed in comprehensible stages. We begin by defining the notion of a computation tree which records the progress of the proof of a query, and what it is for such a tree to be 'successful'. We illustrate some of the properties of the trees which we shall use, including replacing branches of the tree with other, equivalent, branches.

     Next we show that a version of the cut theorem holds for computation trees, i.e. if we have trees for $\mathcal{P} \vdash_{\mathcal{B}} \varphi$ and $\mathcal{P} \cup \{\varphi\} \vdash_{\mathcal{B}} q$ then we have a tree for $\mathcal{P} \vdash_{\mathcal{B}} q$, where q is an atomic proposition. Then we show how we include restart into the trees. As the final part of the preparation, we prove that if we have a tree for $\mathcal{P} \cup \{R\} \vdash_{\mathcal{B}} \varphi$ and $\mathcal{P} \cup \{\neg R\} \vdash_{\mathcal{B}} \varphi$ then we have a tree for $\mathcal{P} \vdash_{\mathcal{B}} \varphi$.

DEFINITION 7.23 (Computation trees without restart). We define the notion of a successful computation tree of a proof of a formula φ from a set of assumptions $\mathcal{P}$.

The tree is for a proof without the restart rule. A basic tree structure is described by three components: $\mathcal{T} = \langle T, <, 0 \rangle$. T is a set of nodes which make up the tree, $<$ is a binary relation which describes the ordering of nodes in the tree, and 0 is the node which is the root of the tree. The following hold:[4]

- $<$ is an irreflexive and transitive relation.

- Let $x <^0 y$ be $x = y$ and $x <^{n+1} y$ iff for some z, $x < z$ and $z <^n y$.

  Let $T_t = \{ y \mid \text{for some } n, t <^n y \}$. Then we require that $T = T_0$ and for all $t \in T$, $t < x$ and $t < y$ and $x \neq y$ imply $T_x \cap T_y = \varnothing$.

- Let $\mathcal{T}_t$ be the tree $\langle T_t, <, t, g \rangle$, where g is defined below.

To turn the basic tree structure into a computation tree, we need a labelling function, which associates information with each node in the tree. Let g be this function. For each $t \in T$, $g(t) = \langle \mathcal{P}(t), G(t) \rangle$, i.e. g labels each node with a set of assumptions $\mathcal{P}(t)$ and a goal formula $G(t)$. The system $\langle T, <, 0, g \rangle$ must satisfy the following conditions:

1. $g(0) = \langle \mathcal{P}, \varphi \rangle$ where $\mathcal{P}$ is the initial set of assumptions, and φ is the initial goal formula.

2. If $t \in T$ and $g(t) = \langle \mathcal{P}(t), G(t) \rangle$ and if $G(t) = A_1 \wedge \cdots \wedge A_n$, then the node t has exactly n immediate successors in the tree ($s_1, \ldots, s_n$, say) with $g(s_i) = \langle \mathcal{P}(t), A_i \rangle$.

3. If $t \in T$ and $g(t) = \langle \mathcal{P}(t), G(t) \rangle$ and if $G(t) = B \Rightarrow C$, then the node t has one immediate successor s in the tree with $g(s) = \langle \mathcal{P}(t) \cup \{B\}, C \rangle$.

4. If $t \in T$ and $g(t) = \langle \mathcal{P}(t), G(t) \rangle$ and if $G(t) = q$ (an atom), then there are several subcases:

   (a) $q \in \mathcal{P}(t)$ or $\bot \in \mathcal{P}(t)$ and t has no successors;

   (b) t has one immediate successor s, and for some formula $A \Rightarrow x \in \mathcal{P}(t)$ (called the *transition formula* of node t) we have $x = q$ or $x = \bot$, and that $g(s) = \langle \mathcal{P}(t), A \rangle$. Note that in this case we may still have either $q \in \mathcal{P}(t)$ or $\bot \in \mathcal{P}(t)$.

LEMMA 7.24 (Tree properties).   *A computation tree has the following properties:*

1. *It computes the proof* $\mathcal{P}(0) \vdash_I G(0)$.

2. *Any point in the tree, with the label* $\langle \mathcal{P}(t), G(t) \rangle$, *is the root of a computation tree* $\mathcal{T}_t$ *for the proof* $\mathcal{P}(t) \vdash_I G(t)$,

---

[4]The tree is imagined to be 'growing' downwards, with the root 0 at the top.

3. *If $t < s$, i.e. s is a successor (not necessarily immediate) to t, then $\mathcal{P}(t) \subseteq \mathcal{P}(s)$ (formulae are never removed from the assumptions as we move down the tree).*

4. *Suppose that $\mathcal{P}'$ is an additional set of assumptions, and that $(T, <, 0, g)$ is a successful computation tree for the proof $\mathcal{P}(0) \vdash_I G(0)$, with $g(t) = \langle \mathcal{P}(t), G(t) \rangle$ for each node t. Suppose that we define g' such that $g'(t) = \langle \mathcal{P}(t) \cup \mathcal{P}', G(t) \rangle$; in other words, we add the assumptions $\mathcal{P}'$ to all the nodes in the tree, even though we do not need them, and do not use them. Then $\mathcal{T} = \langle T, <, 0, g' \rangle$ is a successful computation tree for the proof $\mathcal{P}(0) \cup \mathcal{P}' \vdash_I G(0)$.*

5. *We call the tree $\mathcal{T}'$ of (4) above the tree of $\mathcal{T}' + \mathcal{P}'$ obtained by adding $\mathcal{P}'$ to the data of $\mathcal{T}'$.*

Proof. Straightforward from the definitions.   ∎

Notice that a successful tree must be finite. An important operation is the grafting of one tree onto another. We will use grafts to prove a lemma below, by replacing part of a computation tree with another with different properties.

DEFINITION 7.25 (Grafting). Let $\mathcal{T} = \langle T, <_T, 0, g \rangle$ and $\mathcal{S} = \langle S, <_S, 1, h \rangle$ be two successful computation trees with only one point 1 in common, and for some B we have $g(1) = \langle \mathcal{P}(1), B \rangle$ and $h(1) = \langle Q(1), B \rangle$. Note that 1 is the root of $\mathcal{S}$. We construct a new tree which is the result of grafting $\mathcal{S}$ onto $\mathcal{T}$ at the point 1.

1. The set of points in the new tree is $T - \{t \in T \mid 1 <_T t\} \cup S$ so that we have all of S, plus all of T except those points below the common point.

2. The ordering relation over the new tree is given by

$$x < y \quad \text{if} \quad x \in T \text{ and } y \in T \text{ and } x <_T y$$
$$\text{or} \quad x \in S \text{ and } y \in S \text{ and } x <_S y$$
$$\text{or} \quad x \in T \text{ and } x <_T 1 \text{ and } y \in S \text{ and } 1 <_S y$$

3. The labelling function f for the new tree is defined for $x \in T$ by

$$f(x) = \langle \mathcal{P}(x) \cup Q(1), G(x) \rangle$$

and for $x \in S$ by

$$f(x) = \langle \mathcal{P}(1) \cup Q(x), H(x) \rangle$$

where $g(x) = \langle \mathcal{P}(x), G(x) \rangle$ in $\mathcal{T}$, and $h(x) = \langle Q(x), H(x) \rangle$ in $\mathcal{S}$. Notice that when $x = 1$, the two definitions agree.

The lemma we shall now prove is needed for a step in the proof of completeness. The proof of the lemma involves a three-way induction, and the simplicity of the lemma itself belies the awkwardness of its proof. Readers who wish to may omit the proof without hindering their reading of the rest of this book.

LEMMA 7.26 (Tree cut). *If there exist computation trees for $\mathcal{P} \vdash_I A_i$ for $i = 1, \ldots, n$ and there exists a computation tree for $\mathcal{P} \cup \{A_1\} \cup \cdots \cup \{A_n\} \vdash_I q$, then there exists a computation tree for $\mathcal{P} \vdash_I q$.*

Proof: The proof is a complicated induction on the complexity of the A_i and on the number n and on the maximum number of nested uses of the A_i in the computation of q (which number we shall denote by m).

Base case: All the A_i are atomic propositions; n and m take arbitrary values. Assume that we have a computation tree for $\mathcal{P} \cup \{A_1\} \cup \cdots \cup \{A_n\} \vdash_I q$ in which $t_1, \ldots, t_k$ are the highest points in the tree which involves the A_i in the computation. Since the A_i are atomic, the only way in which they can be used is to solve the goal $G(t_j) = A_i$, so that the tree rooted at t_j is for $\mathcal{P}(t_j) \vdash_I A_i$ for some A_i. Now we are given that $\mathcal{P} \vdash_I A_i$, and from Lemma 7.24 we know that $\mathcal{P} \subseteq \mathcal{P}(t_j)$ and further that we have computation trees for $\mathcal{P}(t_j) - \{A_1\} - \cdots - \{A_n\} \vdash_I A_i$.

Hence we can replace the subtrees rooted at each of the $t_1, \ldots, t_k$ with the appropriate subtrees which do not have $A_1, \ldots, A_n$ as assumptions by means of grafting. Thus we have $\mathcal{P}(t_j) - \{A_1\} - \cdots - \{A_n\} \vdash_I G(t_j)$, and therefore $\mathcal{P} \vdash_I q$ (since $A_1, \ldots, A_n$ are not used in the reconstructed tree for $\mathcal{P} \cup \{A_1, \ldots, A_n\} \vdash_I q$).

Induction step: Assume that we have computation trees for $\mathcal{P} \vdash_I A_i \Rightarrow x_i$ for $i = 1, \ldots, n$ (so that we have trees for $\mathcal{P} \cup \{A_i\} \vdash_I x_i$) and a computation tree for $\mathcal{P} \cup \{A_1 \Rightarrow x_1\} \cup \cdots \cup \{A_n \Rightarrow x_n\} \vdash_I q$. Assume that m is the maximum number of nested uses of any $A_i \Rightarrow x_i$ in the tree.

Let $\mathcal{T} = \langle T, <, 0, g \rangle$ be a computation tree for $\mathcal{P} \cup \{A_1 \Rightarrow x_1\} \cup \cdots \cup \{A_n \Rightarrow x_n\} \vdash_I q$ and let $t_1, \ldots, t_k$ be the lowest points in the tree in which any of the $A_i \Rightarrow x_i$ are used in the computation, so that below each t_j none of the $A_i \Rightarrow x_i$ are used. Therefore each of the $t_1, \ldots, t_k$ is labelled such that $\mathcal{P}(t_j) \supseteq \mathcal{P}$ and intersects $\{A_1 \Rightarrow x_1\} \cup \cdots \cup \{A_n \Rightarrow x_n\}$ and $G(t_j) = y$ for some proposition y. The single immediate successor to t_j, say t'_j, is derived by the use of one of the $A_i \Rightarrow x_i$, say $A \Rightarrow x$, and must therefore compute the goal $G(t'_j) = A$ from $\mathcal{P}(t'_j) = \mathcal{P}(t_j)$. x might be equal to y, or alternatively be $\bot$.

Now we know that the subtree rooted at t'_j does not use any of the $A_i \Rightarrow x_i$ (by definition) so we know that we have a computation tree for

$$\mathcal{P}(t_j) - \{A_1 \Rightarrow x_1\} - \cdots - \{A_n \Rightarrow x_n\} \vdash_I A$$

Now we are given that $\mathcal{P} \cup \{A\} \vdash_I x$ and since $\mathcal{P}(t_j) \supseteq \mathcal{P}$, by Lemma 7.24 we have $\mathcal{P}(t_j) \cup \{A\} - \{A_1 \Rightarrow x_1\} - \cdots - \{A_n \Rightarrow x_n\} \vdash_I x$.

By the induction hypothesis, from the existence of computation trees for $\mathcal{P}(t_j) - \{A_1 \Rightarrow x_1\} - \cdots - \{A_n \Rightarrow x_n\} \vdash_I A$ and for $\mathcal{P}(t_j) \cup \{A\} - \{A_1 \Rightarrow x_1\} - \cdots - \{A_n \Rightarrow x_n\} \vdash_I x$

we get a computation tree for $\mathcal{P}(t_j) - \{A_1 \Rightarrow x_1\} - \cdots - \{A_n \Rightarrow x_n\} \vdash_I x$. Let S be that tree, and replace the subtree at t_j by S. Thus one nested use of one of the $A_i \Rightarrow x_i$ has been eliminated. By applying this to each of $t_1, \ldots, t_k$, we can reduce m, the maximum number of nested uses of one of the $A_i \Rightarrow x_i$, by 1.

Repeated applications of the above will eliminate all of the uses of the original $A_i \Rightarrow x_i$ from the tree for $\mathcal{P} \cup \{A_1 \Rightarrow x_1\} \cup \cdots \cup \{A_n \Rightarrow x_n\} \vdash_I q$, resulting in a tree for $\mathcal{P} \vdash_I q$. ∎

LEMMA 7.27 (Tree for restart). *If $\mathcal{P} \vdash_\mathcal{B} \varphi$ succeeds using the restart rule then there is a successful computation tree for $\mathcal{P} \cup \{\varphi \Rightarrow \bot\} \vdash_I \varphi$.*

Proof. Each time the restart rule is used in the computation of φ from $\mathcal{P}$, its use can be replaced by the use of $\varphi \Rightarrow \bot$. Thus $\mathcal{P} \cup \{\varphi \Rightarrow \bot\} \vdash_I \varphi$ succeeds without restart, and hence has a computation tree. Compare with the proof of soundness of restart in Theorem 6.5.1. ∎

LEMMA 7.28 (Cut elimination). *If $\mathcal{P} \cup \{\psi\} \vdash_\mathcal{B} A$ and $\mathcal{P} \cup \{\psi \Rightarrow \bot\} \vdash_\mathcal{B} A$ then $\mathcal{P} \vdash_\mathcal{B} A$.*

Proof. First we can assume that $\psi = (\alpha \Rightarrow y)$ and that $y \neq \bot$. Otherwise we can prove the theorem for α, since it can easily be shown that if $\mathcal{P} \cup \{(\alpha \Rightarrow \bot) \Rightarrow \bot\} \vdash_\mathcal{B} A$ then $\mathcal{P} \cup \{\alpha\} \vdash_\mathcal{B} A$.

Our proof is by induction. To explain how we do the induction we need some notation. Let $\mathcal{T} = \langle T, <_T, 0, g \rangle$ be a tree for $\mathcal{P}' \cup \{\psi \Rightarrow \bot\} \vdash_I A$, where $\mathcal{P}' = \mathcal{P} \cup \{A \Rightarrow \bot\}$. Let $S = \langle S, <_S, 1, h \rangle$ be a tree for $\mathcal{P}' \cup \{\psi\} \vdash_I A$. We assume of course that $S \cap T = \varnothing$.

We use induction on the number n, being the maximal number of nested uses of $\psi \Rightarrow \bot$ (as a transition formula) in the tree $\mathcal{T}$.

Case $n = 0$
$\psi \Rightarrow \bot$ is not used in the tree $\mathcal{T}$. Hence $\mathcal{P}' \vdash_I A$ and so $\mathcal{P} \vdash_\mathcal{B} A$, by the converse of the previous lemma.

Case n
We assume that if $\mathcal{T}$ has at most $n - 1$ nested occurrences of use of $\psi \Rightarrow \bot$ then $\mathcal{P}' \vdash_I A$. We want to show the same for case n. We accomplish this task by using the trees $\mathcal{T}$ and S and the tree cut theorem to construct a tree $\mathcal{T}^* = \langle T^*, <^*, 0, g^* \rangle$ for $\mathcal{P}' \cup \{\psi \Rightarrow \bot\} \vdash_I A$ which falls under case $n - 1$, namely the induction hypothesis. $\mathcal{T}^*$ will have at most $n - 1$ nested uses of $\psi \Rightarrow \bot$, and we will therefore conclude that $\mathcal{P} \vdash_\mathcal{B} A$.

The rest of this proof is a detailed analysis of the trees $\mathcal{T}$ and S and a grafting of various modified parts of these trees into the desired tree $\mathcal{T}^*$.

Let us begin:

Consider the tree $\mathcal{T}$. Let $t_1, \ldots, t_k \in T$ be the last points from the top in which the transition formula in the tree is $\psi \Rightarrow \bot$, i.e. $(\alpha \Rightarrow y) \Rightarrow \bot$. Assume that at the node t_j the goal is a_j; that is, we have $g(t_j) = \langle \mathcal{P}'(t_j) \cup \{(\alpha \Rightarrow y) \Rightarrow \bot\}, a_j \rangle$. The transition formula is $(\alpha \Rightarrow y) \Rightarrow \bot$ for all j. We thus must have immediate successors s_j of t_j in the tree with $g(s_j) = \langle \mathcal{P}'(t_j) \cup \{(\alpha \Rightarrow y) \Rightarrow \bot\}, \alpha \Rightarrow y \rangle$ and in the trees $\mathcal{T}_{s_j}$, the wff $(\alpha \Rightarrow y) \Rightarrow \bot$ is never used!

Figure 7.2 illustrates the situation:

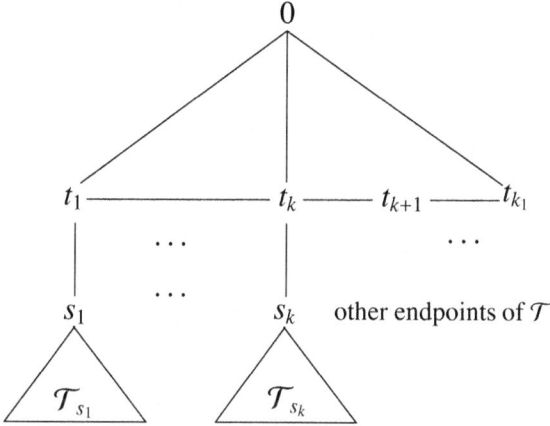

Figure 7.2.

The points $t_{k+1}, \ldots, t_{k_1}$ are endpoints of $\mathcal{T}$ where in the computation path to them, $\psi \to \bot$ is used no more $(n-1)$ nested times. Let $\mathcal{T}'$ be the part of the tree $\mathcal{T}$ down to these points.

Thus we conclude:

(*) $\quad \mathcal{P}'(t_j) \vdash_I \alpha \Rightarrow y.$

We now use the fact that $\mathcal{P}' \cup \{\alpha \Rightarrow y\} \vdash_I A$ has the tree S to conclude (**) below. First, if $\alpha \Rightarrow y$ is not used in the tree S then the tree S with $\alpha \Rightarrow y$ deleted shows that $\mathcal{P}' \vdash_I A$ succeeds. Since $\mathcal{P}' \vdash_I A$ implies $\mathcal{P}' \vdash_\mathcal{B} A$ and $\mathcal{P}' \vdash_\mathcal{B} A$ implies $\mathcal{P} \vdash_\mathcal{B} A$, we get that $\mathcal{P} \vdash_\mathcal{B} A$ succeeds and there is nothing to prove.

If $\alpha \Rightarrow y$ is used in the tree S, let $r_1, \ldots, r_{k^*}$ be the top (i.e. first) nodes in S in which $\alpha \Rightarrow y$ is used. We thus have that (since $y \neq \bot$)

$$f(r_j) = \langle \mathcal{P}'(r_j) \cup \{\alpha \Rightarrow y\}, y \rangle$$

We can assume that $\alpha \Rightarrow y$ is not a member of $\mathcal{P}'(r_j)$. Thus

(**) $\quad \mathcal{P}'(r_j) \cup \{\alpha \Rightarrow y\} \vdash_I y.$

We also recall that we assumed that the nodes r_j, $j = 1, \ldots, k^*$, are the first nodes (from the root $1 \in S$) in which $\alpha \Rightarrow y$ is used. Thus the computation path down to r_j uses transition formulae from $\mathcal{P}'(r_j)$ only.

Let $S' = \{s \in S \mid$ there is no point $s' \in S, s' <_S s$ and $\alpha \Rightarrow y$ is used at $s'\}$. Thus $r_1, \ldots, r_{k^*} \in S^*$ as well as possibly many other points. Let $<'$ be the inherited ordering on S' (inherited from $\langle S, <_S \rangle$). Copies of $\langle S', <' \rangle$ as well as a suitable g^* will be defined later and used as building blocks to construct the desired tree $\mathcal{T}^*$. The nodes $r_1, \ldots, r_{k^*}$ are not endpoints since ψ is used at these nodes so the computation must proceed. Let $\bar{r}_1, \ldots, \bar{r}_{k^*}$ be their immediate successors and let $S_{\bar{r}_1}, \ldots, S_{\bar{r}_{k^*}}$ be the trees below these successors. See Figure 6.3.

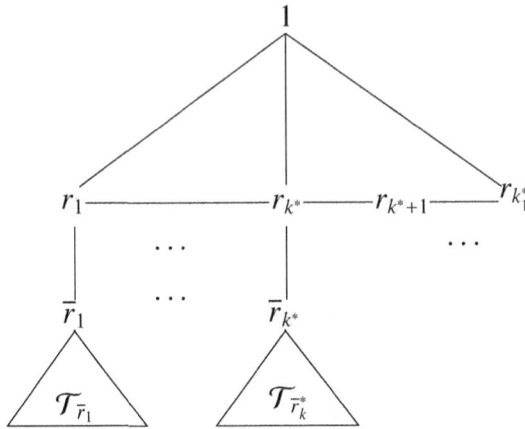

Figure 7.3.

The points $r_1, \ldots, r_{k^*}$ in Figure 7.3 are the first points where ψ is used. The points $r_{k^*+1}, \ldots, r_{k_1^*}$ are endpoints. In the path leading to $r_1, \ldots, r_{k_1^*}$, ψ is not used. Thus S' is the set of all points in S above $\{r_1, \ldots, r_{k_1^*}\}$.

We shall make use later of the trees $S_{\bar{r}_j}$.

Consider now the tree $\mathcal{T}$ and the node t_j. We have $g(t_j) = \langle \mathcal{P}'(t_j) \cup \{(\alpha \Rightarrow y) \Rightarrow \bot\}, a_j \rangle$ at node t_j; $(\alpha \Rightarrow y) \Rightarrow \bot$ was used to move to node s_j. We want to succeed with a_j at node t_j by using other clauses from the data and not the clause $(\alpha \Rightarrow y) \Rightarrow \bot$. The clause we want to use is $A \Rightarrow \bot \in \mathcal{P}'(t_j)$. If we do that we will have to ask next for a tree for $\mathcal{P}'(t_j) \vdash_I A$.

Since $\mathcal{P}' \subseteq \mathcal{P}'(t_j)$, we can follow the computation steps of the tree S (with initial goal A), down to the points $r_1, \ldots, r_{k^*}$ (where $\alpha \Rightarrow y$ is first used) but no further because $\alpha \Rightarrow y$ is not available. At the points $r_1, \ldots, r_{k^*}$ the data is $\mathcal{P}'(t_j) \cup \mathcal{P}'(r_1)$, $\ldots, \mathcal{P}'(t_j) \cup \mathcal{P}'(r_{k^*})$, respectively, and the goal is y. From (*) and (**) above we get for each j and i that

- $\mathcal{P}'(t_j) \cup \mathcal{P}'(r_i) \cup \{\alpha \Rightarrow y\} \vdash_I y$

- $\mathcal{P}'(t_j) \cup \mathcal{P}'(r_i) \vdash_I \alpha \Rightarrow y$.

Hence by Lemma 6.6.5 we get

(***) $\mathcal{P}'(t_j) \cup \mathcal{P}'(r_i) \vdash_I y$.

Let $\overline{\mathcal{T}}_{t_j,r_i}$ be a tree for (***).

We now have all the components to construct a tree for $\mathcal{P}' \cup \{\psi \Rightarrow \bot\} \vdash_I A$, which uses $\psi \Rightarrow \bot$ not more than $n-1$ nested times. We now define the various pieces:

1. Let $T' = \{x \in T \mid x$ is above or equal to any of $t_1, \ldots, t_{k_1}\}$. T' is the tree T less all points strictly below $t_1, \ldots, t_{k_1}$. Recall that $t_1, \ldots, t_{k_1}$ are the last points in which $(\alpha \Rightarrow y) \Rightarrow \bot$ is used at most $(n-1)$ nested times. If we can continue the computation at $t_1, \ldots, t_k$, without using $(\alpha \Rightarrow y) \Rightarrow \bot$, we will have reduced the nested number of uses of this formula.

2. For each t_j, $j = 1, \ldots, k$, form a copy of $(S', <')$ which we denote by S'_{t_j}. We let $S'_{t_j} = \{(t_j, s) \mid s \in S'\}$ and let $(t_j, s_1) <'_{t_j} (t_j, s_2)$ iff $s_1 <' s_2$.

   The above means that we made a special copy of S' for the point t_j in the tree, for $j = 1, \ldots, k$.

3. Among the points of S'_{t_j} are the endpoints $(t_j, r_1), \ldots, (t_j, r_{k^*})$. We graft at these points the trees $\bar{\mathcal{T}}_{t_j,r_1}, \ldots, \bar{\mathcal{T}}_{t_j,r_{k^*}}$ respectively, where $\bar{\mathcal{T}}_{t_j,r_i} = \langle \bar{T}_{t_j,r_i}, <_{t_j,r_i}, (t_j, r_i), g_{t_j,r_i} \rangle$. We now have T^* as

$$ T^* = T' \cup \bigcup_{j \le k} \left(S'_{t_j} \cup \bigcup_{i \le k^*} \bar{T}_{t_j,r_i} \right) $$

The ordering $<^*$ on T^* is defined as follows: $x <^* y$ iff

1. $x, y \in T'$ and $x <_T y$

2. $x, y \in S'_{t_j}$ and $x <'_{t_j} y$

3. $x, y \in \bar{T}_{t_j,r_i}$ and $x <_{t_j,r_i} y$

4. $t_j < (t_j, 1)$

5. $x \in T, x <_T t_j$, and $y \in S'_{t_j} \cup \bigcup_{i \le k^*} \bar{T}_{t_j,r_i}$

6. $x \in S'_{t_j}, x <'_{t_j} (t_j, r_i)$, and $y \in \bigcup_{i \le k^*} \bar{T}_{t_j,r_i}$.

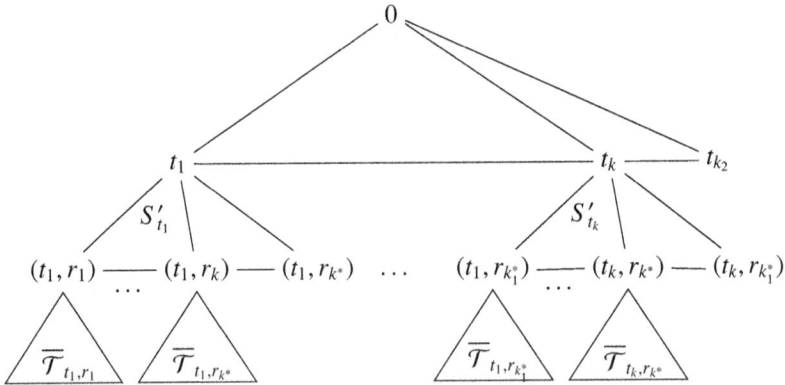

Figure 7.4.

Note that (t_j, r_i) is in both $\bar{T}_{t_j,r_i}$ and S'_{t_j}.

Figure 7.4 describes the tree T^*.

The root of $\mathcal{T}^*$ is 0 and the function g^* of $\mathcal{T}^*$ is as follows:

$$g^*(y) = \text{(1) } g(y), \text{ for } y \in T'$$
$$\text{(2) } \langle \mathcal{P}'(t_j) \cup \mathcal{P}(s), a_s \rangle, \text{ for } y \in S'_{t_j}, y = (t_j, s) \text{ and } h(s) = \langle \mathcal{P}(s), a_s \rangle$$
$$\text{(3) } g_{t_j,r_i}(y), \text{ for } y \in \bar{T}_{t_j,r_i}$$

The function g^* shows that we start at 0 and compute according to the tree $\mathcal{T}$ down to the points $t_1, \ldots, t_k, t_{k+1}, \ldots, t_{k_1}$. At the points $t_1, \ldots, t_k$, $\psi \Rightarrow \bot$ is used in the tree $\mathcal{T}$ for the nth nested time. The goal at t_j is a_j. We cannot use $\psi \Rightarrow \bot$ any more for the goal a_j. We therefore use $A \Rightarrow \bot$ instead and the next goal is A. To compute A we proceed as in the tree S which at the point t_j we rename as the copy S'_{t_j}, down to the points $r_1, \ldots, r_{k^*}, \ldots, r_{k_1^*}$, renamed $(t_j, r_1), \ldots, (t_j, r_{k_1^*})$. The tree S'_{t_j} is used for the data $\mathcal{P}' \cup \{\psi\}$. $\mathcal{P}'$ is available at points t_j of the tree $\mathcal{T}$ but not ψ, but we can continue up to $r_1, \ldots, r_{k^*}, r_{k^*+1}, \ldots, r_{k_1^*}$ (named $(t_j, r_i), i = 1, \ldots, k_1^*$) because ψ is not used. At the points $(t_j, r_1), \ldots, (t_j, r_{k_1^*})$, ψ is used for the first time and the goal is y. We cannot continue as in S but we continue as in $\mathcal{T}_{(t_j,r_i)}$ and succeed.

The above construction of $\mathcal{T}^*$ completes the inductive step and the lemma is proved. ∎

Final proof of Theorem 7.22. Let $\psi_1, \psi_2, \psi_3, \ldots$ be a list of the wffs of the logic. Define a set of assumptions $\mathcal{P}_\infty$ by induction as follows:

$$\mathcal{P}_0 = \mathcal{P}$$

$$\mathcal{P}_{i+1} \quad = \quad \mathcal{P}_i \cup \{\psi_i\} \text{ if } \mathcal{P}_i \cup \{\psi_i\} \nvdash_\mathcal{B} \varphi$$
$$\mathcal{P}_i \cup \{\psi_i \Rightarrow \bot\} \text{ otherwise}$$

Note that if both $\mathcal{P}_i \cup \{\psi_i \Rightarrow \bot\} \vdash_\mathcal{B} \varphi$ and $\mathcal{P}_i \cup \{\psi\} \vdash_\mathcal{B} \varphi$ then $\mathcal{P}_i \vdash_\mathcal{B} \varphi$. This was shown in Theorem 6.6.7.

Let

$$\mathcal{P}_\infty \quad = \quad \bigcup_{i=0}^{\infty} \mathcal{P}_i$$

Now we know that if $\mathcal{P}_i \nvdash_\mathcal{B} \varphi$ (which is certainly true for $i = 0$), then $\mathcal{P}_{i+1} \nvdash \varphi$ also. By induction we have that $\mathcal{P}_\infty \nvdash_\mathcal{B} \varphi$. Success in the computation of φ from $\mathcal{P}_\infty$ will only involve a *finite* part of $\mathcal{P}_\infty$, and hence will be successful from some $\mathcal{P}_i$. If we define an assignment h on the atoms by

$$h(a) = \top \quad \text{iff} \quad \mathcal{P}_\infty \vdash_\mathcal{B} a$$

we can show by induction on the structure of the wffs φ that under the assignment h, we have for any φ

$$h(\varphi) = \top \quad \text{iff} \quad \mathcal{P}_\infty \vdash_\mathcal{B} \varphi$$

There are three cases to be considered:

1. φ is atomic
   This is given by definition.

2. $\varphi = \alpha \wedge \beta$
   $h(\varphi) = \top$ iff $h(\alpha) = \top$ and $h(\beta) = \top$ (from Definition 1.2). Now by induction, $h(\alpha) = \top$ iff $\mathcal{P}_\infty \vdash_\mathcal{B} \alpha$, and $h(\beta) = \top$ iff $\mathcal{P}_\infty \vdash_\mathcal{B} \beta$. Hence $h(\varphi) = \top$ iff $\mathcal{P}_\infty \vdash_\mathcal{B} \alpha$ and $\mathcal{P}_\infty \vdash_\mathcal{B} \beta$. Now $\mathcal{P}_\infty \vdash_\mathcal{B} \alpha$ and $\mathcal{P}_\infty \vdash_\mathcal{B} \beta$ iff $\mathcal{P}_\infty \vdash_\mathcal{B} \alpha\wedge\beta$. Thus $h(\varphi) = \top$ iff $\mathcal{P}_\infty \vdash_\mathcal{B} \alpha\wedge\beta$.

3. $\varphi = \alpha \Rightarrow q$
   We prove the two directions of the 'iff' separately.

   (a) Assume that $\mathcal{P}_\infty \vdash_\mathcal{B} \alpha\Rightarrow q$; then certainly if $\mathcal{P}_\infty \vdash_\mathcal{B} \alpha$ then $\mathcal{P}_\infty \vdash_\mathcal{B} q$ by Lemma 7.26. Hence by the induction hypothesis, $h(\alpha) = \top$ implies $h(q) = \top$, i.e. $h(\alpha\Rightarrow q) = \top$.

   (b) Now assume that $\mathcal{P}_\infty \nvdash \alpha\Rightarrow q$, i.e. that $\mathcal{P}_\infty \cup \{\alpha\} \nvdash q$. We know that $\mathcal{P}_\infty$ either contains α or $\alpha\Rightarrow\bot$. If $\mathcal{P}_\infty$ contains α then we get $\mathcal{P}_\infty \vdash_\mathcal{B} \alpha$ and $\mathcal{P}_\infty \nvdash q$, i.e. $h(\alpha\Rightarrow q) = \bot$. The other possibility, that $\mathcal{P}_\infty$ contains $\alpha\Rightarrow\bot$, cannot arise since $\mathcal{P}_\infty\cup\{\alpha\}$ would be inconsistent and that would imply that $\mathcal{P}_\infty \cup \{\alpha\} \vdash_\mathcal{B} q$.

Now—provided that $\mathcal{P}_\infty$ is consistent—every assignment h that is a model for $\bigwedge \mathcal{P}$ (which of course assigns $\top$ to all the atoms provable from $\mathcal{P}$ by the backward rules) assigns $\bot$ to all the formulae which are not provable from $\mathcal{P}$. Thus whenever $\mathcal{P}_\infty \nvdash \varphi$, there is an assignment h for which $h(\bigwedge \mathcal{P} \Rightarrow \varphi) = \bot$, i.e. $\bigwedge \mathcal{P} \Rightarrow \varphi$ is not a tautology.   ∎

7   Properties of intuitionistic logic fragment of $\{\wedge, \Rightarrow, \bot\}$

We saw in the previous section that the backward computation without restart satisfies the cut rule, namely

$$\mathcal{P} \vdash_I A_i, i = 1, \ldots, k, \text{ and } \mathcal{P} \cup \{A_1, \ldots, A_n\} \vdash_I q \text{ imply } \mathcal{P} \vdash_I q$$

We can also prove by induction on the structure of the goal B that

$$\mathcal{P} \vdash_I B \text{ if } B \in \mathcal{P}$$

It is also clear that $\vdash_I$ is monotonic and that it satisfies the deduction theorem (by definition) since the rule

$$\mathcal{P} \vdash_I B \Rightarrow q \text{ iff } \mathcal{P} + B \vdash_I q$$

is one of the computation rules.

$\vdash_I$ is also clearly transitive (transitivity follows, in fact, from the cut elimination theorem). It is therefore clear that we have that $\vdash \subseteq \vdash_I$, where $\vdash$ is the consequence relation of Example 7.2.

THEOREM 7.29 (Axiomatization of $\vdash_I$). *Let $\vdash$ be the system of Example 7.2. Then $\vdash_I = \vdash$.*

Proof. We show that if $\mathcal{P} \nvdash_I B$ then there exists an intuitionistic Kripke model (see Definition 2.2.3) in which $\mathcal{P}$ holds but not B. Define $\mathcal{P}_1 \equiv \mathcal{P}_2$ if for all $A \in \mathcal{P}_2$, $\mathcal{P}_1 \vdash_I A$ and for all $A \in \mathcal{P}_1, \mathcal{P}_2 \vdash_I A$.

Let $\mathcal{P}/\equiv$ be the equivalence class of $\mathcal{P}$. Let $\mathcal{P}_1/\equiv \ \leq \mathcal{P}_2/\equiv$ be defined as for all $A \in \mathcal{P}_1, \mathcal{P}_2 \vdash_I A$ (we also write it as $\mathcal{P}_2 \vdash_I \mathcal{P}_1$). It is easy to show that $\leq$ is well defined. Let $T = \{\mathcal{P}/\equiv | \mathcal{P} \nvdash_I \bot \text{ and } \mathcal{P} \text{ a set of wffs}\}$.

Define $h(\mathcal{P}/\equiv, q)$ to be 1 iff $\mathcal{P} \vdash_I q$. Again one can show h is well defined.

Consider now the model $(T, \leq, h)$.

We show that for any $B, \mathcal{P}$ we have that $h(\mathcal{P}/\equiv, B) = 1$ iff $\mathcal{P} \vdash_I B$. The proof is by structural induction on B.

The crucial case is that of $B \Rightarrow C$.

1. Assume $\mathcal{P} \vdash_I B \Rightarrow C$. Then of course $\mathcal{P} \cup B \vdash_I C$.

    We show that for any $\mathcal{P}'/\equiv \ \geq \mathcal{P}/\equiv$ such that $\mathcal{P}' \vdash_I B$, we have $\mathcal{P}' \vdash_I C$. But if $\mathcal{P}' \vdash_I B$ then $\mathcal{P}' \vdash \mathcal{P} \cup \{B\}$ and hence $\mathcal{P}' \vdash_I C$. Hence $h(\mathcal{P}/\equiv, B \Rightarrow C) = 1$.

2. Assume $h(\mathcal{P}/ \equiv, B \Rightarrow C) = 1$. Then, for any $\mathcal{P}'/ \equiv \; \geq \mathcal{P}'/ \equiv$ and, in particular, for $\mathcal{P}' = \mathcal{P} \cup \{B\}$ we have (by the induction hypothesis) that if $\mathcal{P}' \vdash_I B$ then $\mathcal{P}' \vdash_I C$. Therefore $\mathcal{P} \cup \{B\} \vdash_I C$ and so $\mathcal{P} \vdash_I B \Rightarrow C$.

Thus we have seen that if $\mathcal{P} \nvdash_I B$ then there is a Kripke countermodel and so by Exercise 6.1.3, $\mathcal{P} \nvdash B$.   ■

The above theorem is very strong. If the database $\mathcal{P}$ is comprised of clauses of the form $A_i \Rightarrow q_i$ and we know that if $\mathcal{P} \vdash q$ then by the theorem we also have $\mathcal{P} \vdash_I q$, but for the computation to succeed, it *must* be the case that $q = q_i$ for some i and $\mathcal{P} \vdash_I A_i$.

This is not true in classical logic. For example, we have $(a \Rightarrow b) \Rightarrow a \vdash a$ in classical logic but we do *not* have $(a \Rightarrow b) \Rightarrow a \vdash a \Rightarrow b$.

The above strong cut property can be used to prove interpolation for intuitionistic logic.

THEOREM 7.30 (Interpolation). *The following holds for the fragment of intuitionistic logic with* $\{\wedge, \Rightarrow, \perp\}$. *If* $A \vdash B$ *then there is a* C *built up from the common atoms of* A *and* B *and* $\perp$ *such that* $A \vdash C$ *and* $C \vdash B$.

Proof. We prove that, for a finite database $\mathcal{P}$ of the fragment and for a formula B, if $\mathcal{P} \vdash_I B$ then for some $C, \mathcal{P} \vdash_I C$ and $C \vdash_I B$.

We already know that $\vdash_I$ is the same as $\vdash$ of Example 7.2 (Theorem 7.29).

To find C, we use induction on the complexity of the computation.

Length 1
If $B = q$ is atomic, then $q \in \mathcal{P}$ or $\perp$ is in $\mathcal{P}$ and the interpolant is $C = q$, or $C = \perp$ respectively.

Length $n + 1$

1. Assume $\mathcal{P}$ is the set of clauses $\{A_j \Rightarrow p_j\}$ and the goal is

$$B = \bigwedge_k (B_k \Rightarrow y_k) \Rightarrow q$$

Then $\mathcal{P} \vdash_I B$ iff $\{A_j \Rightarrow p_j\} \cup \{B_k \Rightarrow y_k\} \vdash_I q$.

Since the goal-directed computation succeeds, the computation must go through one of the clauses. This clause is of the form either $B_m \Rightarrow y_m$ or $A_m \Rightarrow p_m$. We check each case.

Case 1: q is equal to y_m or $y_m = \perp$, for some m. Clearly $y_m \vdash q$ in this case. Since the computation succeeds and continues by having B_m as a goal, we get

$$\mathcal{P} \vdash_I \bigwedge_k (B_k \Rightarrow y_k) \Rightarrow B_m$$

B_m is a conjunction, say $B_m = \bigwedge_j B_{m,j}$.

Hence, for each j

$$\mathcal{P} \vdash_{\mathcal{I}} \bigwedge_k (B_k \Rightarrow y_k) \Rightarrow B_{m,j}$$

By the induction hypothesis there exists a C_j in the common language such that

$$\mathcal{P} \vdash_{\mathcal{I}} C_j \text{ and } C_j \vdash_{\mathcal{I}} \bigwedge_k (B_k \Rightarrow y_k) \Rightarrow B_{m,j}$$

Let $C = \bigwedge_j C_j$.

We have $\mathcal{P} \vdash_{\mathcal{I}} C$ and $C \vdash_{\mathcal{I}} \bigwedge_k (B_k \Rightarrow y_k) \Rightarrow B_m$. But $\bigwedge_k (B_k \Rightarrow y_k) \vdash_{\mathcal{I}} B_m \Rightarrow y_m$ since $B_m \Rightarrow y_m$ is one of the conjuncts; therefore we get $C \vdash_{\mathcal{I}} y_m$ and since $y_m \vdash q$ we get $C \vdash_{\mathcal{I}} B$.

Case 2: $q = p_m$ or $p_m = \bot$ for some m. Again the computation succeeds with A_m. We note that in this case p_m is in the common language. We can therefore rewrite what we have into

$$\bigwedge_k (B_k \Rightarrow y_k) \vdash \bigwedge \mathcal{P} \Rightarrow A_m$$

Therefore there exists an interpolant C_1 such that

$$\bigwedge_k (B_k \Rightarrow y_k) \vdash_{\mathcal{I}} C_1 \text{ and } \mathcal{P}, C_1 \vdash_{\mathcal{I}} A_m$$

Therefore, since $p_m \vdash q$ we get

$$(*) \quad (C_1 \Rightarrow p_m) \vdash_{\mathcal{I}} \bigwedge_k (B_k \Rightarrow y_k) \Rightarrow q$$

On the other hand, since $\mathcal{P} \vdash A_m \Rightarrow p_m$ and we get

$$\mathcal{P}, C_1 \vdash_{\mathcal{I}} p_m$$

then

$$(**) \quad \mathcal{P} \vdash_{\mathcal{I}} C_1 \Rightarrow p_m$$

Thus from (*), (**) it is clear that $C = C_1 \Rightarrow p_m$ is the desired interpolant.

2. If B is a conjunction $B = B_1 \wedge \cdots \wedge B_n$ then we find interpolant C_i for B_i and the interpolant for B is $\bigwedge_i C_i$.

This completes the induction and the theorem is proved. ∎

REMARK 7.31 (Interpolation for classical logic). The previous theorem can be used to give us a syntactical proof of interpolation for classical logic. We can use interpolation for the intuitionistic fragment, since we have: $A \vdash B$ in classical logic iff $A \nvdash \neg B \Rightarrow B$ in the intuitionistic fragment.

8 Summary of systems and completeness theorems

We now list in Table 7.1 the logical systems we have so far considered, together with their various presentations.

9 Worked examples

EXAMPLE 7.32 (Independence of Hilbert axioms). Show independence of each of the axioms of classical propositional logic (Example 7.9). This means that for each of axioms 1–11 show that it is not provable in the logic defined by *modus ponens* and the remaining axioms.

Solution [cf. [Novikov, 1964]]

Independence of axioms 3–11 is proved by making non-standard (but still two-valued) interpretations of some logical connectives.

The argument is as follows:

(I) We show that all axioms except one (say, A) are true under any assignment.

(II) We show that A is not true under some assignment.

(III) We show that if formulae $X, X \Rightarrow Y$ are always true then Y is always true.

Then we obtain that what is provable without A is always true, whereas A is sometimes false. Therefore A is independent.

When showing independence of 3–11, we will interpret only one connective in a non-standard way. Implication will be standard, and thus (III) holds trivially.

In Example 1.3.3.4 we showed that all substitution instances of tautologies are also tautologies. The same proof applies to any many-valued tautologies used in this independence proof.

Now let us describe particular interpretations and check (I), (II).

- Axiom 6. Only $\wedge$ will be non-standard.
  Axioms 1–5, 9–11 remain true, because $\Rightarrow$ is not involved there.
  Axiom 7: $(p \wedge q) \Rightarrow q$ is true because $p \wedge q \equiv q$. But axiom 6: $(p \wedge q) \Rightarrow p$ fails when $p = \perp, q = \top$.
  Axiom 8: $(r \Rightarrow p) \Rightarrow ((r \Rightarrow q) \Rightarrow (r \Rightarrow p \wedge q))$ becomes equivalent to $(r \Rightarrow p) \Rightarrow ((r \Rightarrow q) \Rightarrow (r \Rightarrow q))$, which is also $\top$.

p	q	$p \wedge q$
$\top$	$\top$	$\top$
$\perp$	$\top$	$\top$
$\top$	$\perp$	$\perp$
$\perp$	$\perp$	$\perp$

Table 7.1.

Logic	Language	Semantic interpretation	Reasoning rules	Comments
Classical propositional logic	Connectives $\neg, \wedge, \vee, \Rightarrow, \top, \bot$	Two-valued truth tables Consequence relation defined in Definition 1.2	Forward reasoning rules in Chapter 3 Box consequence in Definition 3.4.5	Exercise 3.4.6 gives soundness
As above	As above	As above	Backward reasoning rules in Section 4.2 with restart	Rules described intuitively with examples
As above	As above	As above	Diminishing resource backward reasoning rules of Section 4.3, with restart	Soundness described in Exercise 4.3.8
Fragment of classical logic without disjunction and negation	$\wedge, \Rightarrow, \top, \bot$	As above	The relevant rules for the connectives present in the fragment	Section 7.6 proves completeness
The $\{\wedge, \Rightarrow, \bot\}$ fragment of Intuitionistic logic	Connectives are $\wedge, \Rightarrow, \bot$	Kripke models given in Definition 2.2.3 semantic consequence $\vdash_I$	Backward rules for the language without restart	Section 7.6 gives completeness
As above	As above	As above	Diminishing resource for the fragment with bounded restart	Completeness proved in [Gabbay and Olivetti, ta]
As above	As above	As above	As in Example 7.2	Completeness proved in Exercise 7.3 and Theorem 7.29
Many-valued logic L_n or L_∞	Connectives $\wedge, \vee, \Rightarrow, \neg$	As in Definition 2.1.2	Not given in this book	
Temporal many-valued logic	$\wedge, \vee, \twoheadrightarrow, \neg$	As in Definition 2.2.1	Not known	
Classical logic	$\wedge, \vee, \neg, \Rightarrow$	As above	Hilbert formulation Section 7.2	See [Niddich, 1962]
Intuitionistic logic	As above	As above	Hilbert formulation	As above
Many-valued logic	As above	As above	As above	As above
Classical logic	$\wedge, \vee, \rightarrow, \neg$	As above	As above	As above

- Axiom 7. Similarly, take the interpretation

p	q	$p \wedge q$
$\top$	$\top$	$\top$
$\bot$	$\top$	$\bot$
$\top$	$\bot$	$\top$
$\bot$	$\bot$	$\bot$

Now $p \wedge q \equiv p$, and axiom 6 becomes always true, and axiom 7 is sometimes false.

Axiom 8 is equivalent to

$$(r \Rightarrow p) \Rightarrow ((r \Rightarrow q) \Rightarrow (r \Rightarrow p))$$

which is a particular case of axiom 1, and thus it is true.

- Axiom 8. Take the interpretation in which $p \wedge q \equiv \bot$. Then axioms 6, 7 are obviously true.

  Axiom 8 becomes

  $$(r \Rightarrow p) \Rightarrow ((r \Rightarrow q) \Rightarrow (r \Rightarrow \bot))$$

  and this can be made $\bot$, if $p = q = r = \top$.

- Axiom 3 is dual to axiom 6. Take the interpretation $p \vee q \equiv q$ leaving other connectives unchanged. Then axiom 4 is equivalent to $q \Rightarrow q$, which is true. Axiom 5 is equivalent to $(p \Rightarrow r) \Rightarrow ((q \Rightarrow r) \Rightarrow (q \Rightarrow r))$ which is also $\top$. But $p \Rightarrow p \vee q$ is $\bot$, when $p = \top, q = \bot$.

- Axiom 4 is dual to axiom 7. Then we interpret $p \vee q$ as p. Axiom 3 becomes $p \Rightarrow p$, axiom 5 becomes $(p \Rightarrow r) \Rightarrow ((q \Rightarrow r) \Rightarrow (p \Rightarrow r))$ which is $\top$. But $q \Rightarrow p \vee q$ is $\bot$, if $p = \bot, q = \top$.

- Axiom 5 is dual to axiom 8. Now we interpret $(p \vee q)$ as $\top$.

  Then Axioms 3, 4, are obviously $\top$ and axiom 5 becomes $(p \Rightarrow r) \Rightarrow ((q \Rightarrow r) \Rightarrow (\top \Rightarrow r))$.

  This can be made $\bot$, if $p = q = r = \bot$.

- Axiom 9. Now we interpret $\neg p$ as p. Then axioms 1–8 remain true. Axioms 10, 11 become $p \Rightarrow p$, which is $\top$. Axiom 9 is equivalent to $(p \Rightarrow q) \Rightarrow (q \Rightarrow p)$, and it is $\bot$, if $p = \bot, q = \top$.

- Axiom 10. Now we interpret $\neg p$ as $\bot$. Axiom 9 is equivalent to $(p \Rightarrow q) \Rightarrow (\bot \Rightarrow \bot)$, which is $\top$. Axiom 11 is obviously true. Axiom 10 becomes $p \Rightarrow \bot$, which is $\bot$ if $p = \top$.

- Axiom 11. In this case we interpret $\neg p$ as $\top$. Axiom 9 is equivalent to

$$(p \Rightarrow q) \Rightarrow (\top \Rightarrow \top) \equiv \top$$

Axiom 10 is obviously $\top$.

Axiom 11 is equivalent to $\top \Rightarrow p$, and it is $\bot$ if $p = \bot$.

- Axiom 2. This case is more difficult. Now we interpret our connectives in Łukasiewicz three-valued logic. Axioms 3, 4, 6, 7, 10, 11 are obviously true. Axiom 1 is also true:

if $q \leq p$ then $(p \Rightarrow p) = 1$ and so $p \Rightarrow (q \Rightarrow p) = 1$;
if $q > p$ then $(q \Rightarrow p) = 1 - q + p \geq p$, and thus $p \Rightarrow (q \Rightarrow p) = 1$.

It is also easy to check axiom 9:

if $p \leq q$ then $\neg q \leq \neg p$, and so $(\neg q \Rightarrow \neg p) = 1$, $(p \Rightarrow q) \Rightarrow (\neg q \Rightarrow \neg p) = 1$;
if $p > q$ then $1-q > 1-p$, $p \Rightarrow q = 1-p+q$, $\neg q \Rightarrow \neg p = 1-(1-q)+(1-p) = 1 + q - p$, and thus $(p \Rightarrow q) = (\neg q \Rightarrow \neg p)$, and the axiom is true.

Axiom 2 can be made non-true if we take $p = q = 1/2, r = 0$.

Indeed, then $(p \Rightarrow q) = 1, (p \Rightarrow r) = (q \Rightarrow r) = 1/2$, $p \Rightarrow (q \Rightarrow r) = (1/2) \Rightarrow (1/2) = 1$, $(p \Rightarrow q) \Rightarrow (p \Rightarrow r) = 1 \Rightarrow (1/2) = (1/2)$, and the whole formula is $1 \Rightarrow (1/2) = 1/2$.

Axioms 5, 8 can be examined via truth tables but there are $3^3 = 27$ rows to check, and we leave this to the reader. It turns out that these axioms are always true. Finally, *modus ponens* derives tautologies from tautologies, because in Łukasiewicz logic $A = A \Rightarrow B = 1$ only if $B = 1$.

- Axiom 1. Now to show independence we can take four truth values $\{0, 1/3, 2/3, 1\}$ where $\wedge, \vee, \neg$ are interpreted in the same way as in Łukasiewicz logic:

$$x \wedge y = \min(x, y), x \vee y = \max(x, y),$$
$$\neg x = 1 - x$$

and

$$x \Rightarrow y = \begin{cases} 1, & \text{if } x \leq y \\ 0, & \text{if } x > y \end{cases}$$

Obviously, axioms 3, 4, 6, 7, 10, 11 are true in this interpretation.

To check axiom 5, note that implication takes values 1 or 0, and thus either $(q \Rightarrow r) \Rightarrow (p \vee q \Rightarrow r) = 1$, in which case the axiom is true, or $(q \Rightarrow r) \Rightarrow$

$(p \vee q \Rightarrow r) = 0$. The latter is the case only if $q \Rightarrow r = 1, p \vee q \Rightarrow r = 0$, i.e. if $q \leq r$, $\max(p, q) > r$. Hence in this case $p = \max(p, q) > r$, and $p \Rightarrow r = 0$. The whole implication is again $0 \Rightarrow 0 = 1$.

To check axiom 8, we use a similar argument. If $(r \Rightarrow q) \Rightarrow (r \Rightarrow p \wedge q) = 0$, then $r \Rightarrow q = 1, r \Rightarrow p \wedge q = 0$, and thus $r \leq q, r > \min(p, q)$. Hence $p = \min(p, q) < r$, and $r \Rightarrow p = 0$. Therefore the whole implication is $0 \Rightarrow 0 = 1$.

For axiom 9 we notice that $p \Rightarrow q = \neg q \Rightarrow \neg p$, because $p \leq q$ iff $1 - q \leq 1 - p$.

Now consider axiom 2:

$$(p \Rightarrow (q \Rightarrow r)) \Rightarrow ((p \Rightarrow q) \Rightarrow (p \Rightarrow r))$$

First, note that if $p \leq q \leq r$, then the consequent is 1, and the whole implication is 1.

If $p > q$, then $p \Rightarrow q = 0$, and again the consequent is 1.

If $q > r$, then $q \Rightarrow r = 0$, and the premise becomes 0, except the only case when $p = 0$. If the premise is 0, the whole implication is 1. If $p = 0$ then the consequent is $(0 \Rightarrow q) \Rightarrow (0 \Rightarrow r) = 1 \Rightarrow 1 = 1$, and again the whole is 1.

Axiom 1 can be made non-true if we put $p = 1/3$, $q = 1$: then $q \Rightarrow p = 0, p \Rightarrow (q \Rightarrow p) = 0$.

Finally we observe that *modus ponens* when applied continues to derive tautologies, because $A = 1$ and $A \Rightarrow B = 1$ only if $B = 1$.

EXAMPLE 7.33 (Consequence relation for a Hilbert system). Let H be a Hilbert system and let $\vdash_H$ be the consequence relation defined in Definition 7.2.8. Show it has the following properties:

1. $A_1, \ldots, A_n, B \vdash_H B$.

2. If $A_1, \ldots, A_n \vdash_H B$ then $A_1, \ldots, A_n, X \vdash_H B$.

3. If $A_1, \ldots, A_n, X \vdash_H B$ and $C_1, \ldots, C_m \vdash_H X$ then $A_1, \ldots, A_n, C_1, \ldots, C_m \vdash_H B$.

Solution

1. To prove this we use the single proof sequence (B).

2. Use the same proof sequence in this case.

3. Let $(D_1, \ldots, D_k)$ with $D_k = B$ be the proof sequence for proving B and let $(D'_1, \ldots, D'_k)$ be the sequence for proving X; then $(D'_1, \ldots, D'_k, D_1, \ldots, D_k)$ is a proof sequence for B from $A_1, \ldots, A_n, C_1, \ldots, C_m$.

EXAMPLE 7.34 (The deduction theorem for a Hilbert system).   Let H be a
Hilbert system and let $\vdash_H$ be the consequence relation defined in Definition 7.2.8.
  Show that $\vdash_H$ satisfies the *deduction theorem*:

$$A_1, \ldots, A_n, B \vdash_H C \text{ iff } A_1, \ldots, A_n \vdash_H B \twoheadrightarrow C$$

if and only if the following formulae are theorems of H:

$$A \twoheadrightarrow (B \twoheadrightarrow A)$$
$$(A \twoheadrightarrow (B \twoheadrightarrow C)) \twoheadrightarrow ((A \twoheadrightarrow B) \twoheadrightarrow (A \twoheadrightarrow C))$$

Solution

1. Assume $\vdash_H$ satisfies the deduction theorem. Then since $A, B \vdash_H A$ we get
   that

   $$\emptyset \vdash_H A \twoheadrightarrow (B \twoheadrightarrow A)$$

   and similarly since

   $$A, A \twoheadrightarrow B, A \twoheadrightarrow (B \twoheadrightarrow C) \vdash_H C$$

   we get

   $$\emptyset \vdash_H (A \twoheadrightarrow (B \twoheadrightarrow C)) \twoheadrightarrow ((A \twoheadrightarrow B) \twoheadrightarrow (A \twoheadrightarrow C))$$

   Thus both of these formulae are generated by H.

2. Assume the above formulae are in H. We show the deduction theorem for
   $\vdash_H$.

   (a) Assume $A_1, \ldots, A_n \vdash_H B \Rightarrow C$, and show that $A_1, \ldots, A_n, B \vdash_H C$.
       Let $(D_1, \ldots, D_k)$ be a proof sequence for $B \twoheadrightarrow C$; then the following is
       a proof sequence for C:

       $$(D_1, \ldots, D_k, B, C)$$

   (b) Assume $A_1, \ldots, A_n, B \vdash_H C$; we show that $A_1, \ldots, A_n \vdash_H B \twoheadrightarrow C$. Let
       $(D_1, \ldots, D_k)$ be a proof sequence for C. We use induction on k.

   Case $k = 1$
   In this case $D_k = C$ and hence one of the following subcases holds:

   (a) C is a theorem of H.
   (b) $C = B$.
   (c) $C = A_i$, for some $0 \leq i \leq n$.

For (a) and (c) the proof sequence for $B \twoheadrightarrow C$ is $(C, C \twoheadrightarrow (B \twoheadrightarrow C), B \twoheadrightarrow C)$.

For (b) the proof sequence is $(B \twoheadrightarrow C)$. We use the fact that $B \twoheadrightarrow B$ is a theorem of H as shown in Exercise 7.2.5.

Case $k > 1$

In this case we have four possibilities for $D_k = C$, (a), (b) and (c): as before and the following case:

(d) For some $k_1, k_2 < k$ we have $D_{k_2} = D_{k_1} \twoheadrightarrow C$.

By the induction hypothesis we have proof sequences $(E^i_1, \ldots, E^i_{m_i})$ for proving $B \Rightarrow D_{k_i}$ from $A_1, \ldots, A_n$, for $i = 1, 2$.

The following is a proof sequence for $B \twoheadrightarrow C$.

$$E^1_1, \ldots, E^1_{m_1}, E^2_1, \ldots, E^2_{m_2},$$
$$(B \twoheadrightarrow (D_{k_1} \twoheadrightarrow C)) \twoheadrightarrow ((B \twoheadrightarrow D_{k_1}) \twoheadrightarrow (B \twoheadrightarrow C)),$$
$$(B \twoheadrightarrow D_{k_1}) \twoheadrightarrow (B \twoheadrightarrow C), B \twoheadrightarrow C$$

EXAMPLE 7.35. Let $\vdash$ be the consequence relation defined at the end of Example 6.2.6, namely $A_1, \ldots, A_n \vdash B$ iff $A_1 \Rightarrow \ldots \Rightarrow (A_n \Rightarrow B) \ldots)$ is generated. Show that $\vdash$ satisfies the conditions listed in Example 7.33.

Solution

$\vdash$ satisfies the deduction theorem by Example 7.34, since the needed axioms are available. Hence $A_1 \Rightarrow \cdots \Rightarrow (A_n \Rightarrow B) \ldots)$ is generated iff $A_1, \ldots, A_n \vdash_H B$ and therefore by the proof in Example 7.34 the properties are satisfied.

CHAPTER 8

Introducing predicate logic

So far in this book we have concentrated on the classical *propositional* logic, with some deviations along the way to show the possibilities offered by changing the interpretation placed on the truth functors, especially implication ($\Rightarrow$). This has meant that we have only considered perhaps half of the functionality of logics, since the power of a logic may be considered to lie in two distinct aspects. The first is its expressiveness as a language for stating assumptions and conclusions. The second is the set of rules it has for checking whether the conclusions follow from the assumptions. The first part of this book concentrated on the latter.

The propositional logics we have dealt with so far are weak in *expressive power* — the smallest semantic units which can receive truth values in propositional logic are *sentences*. Yet we are often concerned with the various pieces of information which make up a sentence. For example, 'the boy with the bicycle was Bethan's brother' contains several data which cannot be represented distinctly in propositional logic. We would be reduced to using a single proposition, b say, to represent the entire sentence. To increase the expressive power of the logic, we need to add the means to talk about the semantic units contained within sentences — this entails using a *predicate* logic. Fortunately, we do not have to abandon the work we have already done, since all the rules of propositional logic concerning connectives and reasoning are valid for predicate logic.

1 Simple sentences

The language of predicate logic has a much richer syntax than that of propositional logic. Consider the following deduction:

$$\frac{\text{all girls are good}}{\frac{\text{Ann is a girl}}{\text{Ann is good}}}$$

In propositional logic we would represent each of the three sentences of the deduction by a proposition such as p, q and r, as the smallest units to which we can assign a truth value. Thus our deduction must be written as

$$\frac{p, q}{r}$$

which of course is not valid. We need to use predicate logic to represent the structure of the sentences, and thus indicate the connection (the property of someone being a girl) between the sentence about Ann, and the sentence about being good.

As its name might suggest, predicate logic enables us to describe properties of individual objects, and the relationship between several objects. Thus we can encode the English sentence 'Ann is a girl' by identifying the property ('is a girl') and the object which possesses that property ('Ann'). We might write this as is-a-girl(Ann) in predicate logic, or possibly just girl(Ann), to distinguish the predicate—which is outside the brackets—from its arguments which are within the brackets. The English sentence 'Ian loves Ann' with a predicate of 'loves' denoting the relationship between the two objects 'Ian' and 'Ann' might be encoded as loves(Ian,Ann).[1]

Just as we can increase our expressive power by moving from propositional logic to the predicate logic we will consider in the rest of this book, we can further increase the expressive power to reach what are known as higher order logics. To distinguish it from these even more powerful logics, the predicate logic we shall be dealing with is also known as *first-order logic*.

1.1 Building simple sentences

The basic building blocks of a predicate language are the set of names of the objects we shall talk about (the *constants*), and the set of names of relationships which we shall use to connect the constants (the *predicates*). Let us take as an example a predicate language describing a classroom of children. The set of constants is {Ann, Brenda, Carol, David, Edward}, and the set of predicates is {boy, girl, sits-next-to}. We need to know how many arguments each relationship has, i.e. how many objects are involved in the relationship. This is sometimes known as the *arity* of the relationship. boy and girl name unary relationships; thus they describe a property of a single object. sits-next-to names a binary relationship, which means that it describes a relationship between two objects.

With this knowledge we can write atomic sentences about the classroom, e.g. boy(David) and sits-next-to(Ann, Carol). An atomic sentence consists of a predicate applied to as many arguments, taken from the set of constants, as the predicate's arity. Thus the following are all well formed atomic sentences in our predicate logic of the classroom:

---

[1] Notice that 'Ann is a girl' might also be represented by a binary relationship, such as is-a(Ann, girl).

boy(Edward)

sits-next-to(Brenda, David)

girl(Carol)

boy(Ann)

We said above that all the connective rules of propositional logic are valid for predicate logic. Thus we can combine atomic sentences into more complex compound sentences using the same connectives ($\land$, $\lor$, $\neg$, $\Rightarrow$) as we did in propositional logic with the atomic propositions. So the following sentences are all well formed in predicate logic:

¬boy(David)

girl(Carol) $\lor$ boy(Carol)

sits-next-to(Ann, Brenda) $\Rightarrow$ girl(Brenda)

¬(¬boy(Edward) $\land$ ¬girl(Edward))

Predicates and constants cannot be used in place of each other. Furthermore, as mentioned above, the number of arguments must be the same as the arity of the predicate. The following sentences are therefore *not* well formed, for the reasons given:

Ann(Carol)	(constant Ann used as predicate)
boy(girl)	(predicate girl used as constant)
boy(David, Edward)	(incorrect number of arguments)
Brenda(girl)	(constant used as predicate and vice versa)
sits-next-to(Edward)	(incorrect number of arguments)

We can express functional relationships between objects by applying a *function name* to the objects' names. Like predicates, function names have a specific arity. For example, if best-friend is a function of arity 1, then best-friend(Ann) is another object, functionally dependent on Ann. Functions can be applied repeatedly, e.g. best-friend(best-friend(Carol)). Because the result of applying a function to an object (or group of objects) is another object, they can be used in the arguments to predicates, such as sits- next-to(Ann,best-friend(Ann)). The same division between predicates and constants also applies to function names, namely that they may not be used in place of each other. Notice that best-friend (Ann) is not an atomic sentence but an object, and must have a predicate applied to it, such as girl(best-friend(Ann)).

EXERCISE 8.1.

1. Translate the following English sentences about the classroom into predicate logic:

   (a) Brenda is a girl and she sits next to Ann.

   (b) Ann doesn't sit next to Edward.

   (c) David is either a boy or a girl.

2. Translate the following predicate logic sentences into English:

   (a) girl(Carol) $\Rightarrow$ ¬boy(Carol)

   (b) sits-next-to(Ann, Brenda) $\wedge$ sits-next-to(Brenda, Ann)

   (c) ¬(boy(David) $\wedge$ girl(David))

1.2   Truth of simple sentences

So far we have only talked about sentences being well formed. Without some way of determining the truth of sentences, predicate logic would only be of limited interest. For propositional logic we used the notion of an interpretation which stated which of the atomic sentences (i.e. the propositions) were true or false, and then extended the interpretation to deal with the various connectives. That is basically what we shall do for predicate logic, but since our atomic sentences are no longer propositions but have structure of their own, we will have to change how we assign truth values to them. The extension of the assignment to cover compound sentences, constructed using the connectives, remains the same as for propositional logic.

The basic elements of an interpretation are a *domain*—a non-empty set of objects—and a set of *relationships* over the domain. (Contrast this with the definition of the predicate language, which is concerned with the *names* of objects and relationships.) We may also have a set of functions over the domain. The domain can be any non-empty set. Often well-understood sets such as the natural numbers ($\mathbb{N}$) are used. For our example we shall use 'real' children, i.e. the objects are the children in our hypothetical classroom. We define an interpretation which maps every element of our set of names to a child in the classroom. We are at liberty to do this in any way we please—the children may not be called Ann, Brenda, Carol, David and Edward. There may only be one child in the class, in which case our interpretation would map all the names to that child. Alternatively we could define an interpretation mapping the names to a completely different domain—such as the dates of birth of British prime ministers, or the cities of the United States.

(As a brief aside, consider the problems facing authors who need to distinguish between the names of objects and the objects themselves, when they have only symbols (i.e. names) at their disposal. In an attempt to stave off confusion, we will write the names of objects thus: pen, book, easel; and refer to the objects themselves thus: *pen, book, easel.* We also assume that each name refers to a unique object.)

For entirely subjective reasons, let us map the names to a set of five children, whom we shall label *A, B, C, D* and *E*:

$$
\begin{array}{rcl}
\text{Ann} & \mapsto & A \\
\text{Brenda} & \mapsto & B \\
\text{Carol} & \mapsto & C \\
\text{David} & \mapsto & D \\
\text{Edward} & \mapsto & E
\end{array}
$$

Just as we map names of objects to objects in the domain, we map names of relationships to relationships over the domain. For example, we map

$$
\begin{array}{rcl}
\text{boy} & \mapsto & \{D, E\} \\
\text{girl} & \mapsto & \{A, B, C\} \\
\text{sits-next-to} & \mapsto & \{(A, C), (D, E)\}
\end{array}
$$

To interpret a sentence such as boy(David), we look at the predicate boy, and see whether the mapping of the argument (David) of the predicate is a member of the map of the predicate. In other words, is the map of David a member of the map of boy, i.e. is $D \in \{D, E\}$? Of course it is; therefore boy(David) is true in this interpretation.

sits-next-to(Ann, Carol) is interpreted by seeing if the mapping of the pair of objects (Ann, Carol) is a member of the mapping of sits-next-to. This reduces to seeing if $(A, C) \in \{(A, C), (D, E)\}$. Hence sits-next-to(Ann, Carol) is also true in this interpretation. However, girl(Edward) is false in the interpretation, because the mapping of Edward (i.e. E) is not a member of the mapping of girl (i.e. $\{A, B, C\}$).

Finding the truth of boy(Carol) $\lor$ girl(Carol) requires us to use the extended interpretation which handles connectives. Recall from Chapter 1 that $A \lor B$ is interpreted as true if either A or B is interpreted as true. This is valid for predicate logic as well, so boy(Carol) $\lor$ girl(Carol) is interpreted as true if either boy(Carol) or girl(Carol) is interpreted as true. This reduces to C being a member of either $\{A, B, C\}$ or $\{D, E\}$, which it is.

Suppose that we have the following function over the domain:

$$\{A \mapsto B,\ B \mapsto C,\ C \mapsto A,\ D \mapsto E,\ E \mapsto D\}$$

we can use this as the mapping of the function best-friend thus:

$$\text{best-friend} \mapsto \{A \mapsto B,\ B \mapsto C,\ C \mapsto A,\ D \mapsto E,\ E \mapsto D\}$$

The interpretation of the sentence girl(best-friend(Ann)) depends therefore on whether the mapping of best-friend(Ann) is a member of the mapping of

girl. The mapping of best-friend(Ann) is found by taking the mapping of
Ann and applying the mapping of the function best-friend to it. The mapping
of Ann is A, and under the mapping of best-friend given above, A becomes
B; hence the mapping of best-friend(Ann) is B. Therefore the interpretation
of the sentence girl(best-friend(Ann)) reduces to whether B is a member of
the mapping of girl, which it is. Thus girl(best-friend(Ann)) is true in the
example interpretation.

Note that formally we can interpret syntactical expressions like 'sit next to'
as any set of pairs in the domain. However, since 'sit next to' has a meaning in
English and it implies symmetry, it is unwise to ignore that and not interpret it as
a symmetrical relation.

EXERCISE 8.2.

1. Evaluate the truth value of the following sentences using the interpretation
    above, together with the extensions to the interpretation to deal with con-
    nectives:

    (a) girl(Brenda) $\Rightarrow$ ¬boy(Brenda)

    (b) boy(David) $\wedge$ girl(David) $\Rightarrow$ sits-next-to(David, Edward)

    (c) sits-next-to(Edward, David)

    (d) sits-next-to(best-friend(Edward), Edward)

2. Does the truth value of sentence (a) above change if the interpretation is
    changed so boy maps to $\{B, D, E\}$ leaving girl still mapped to $\{A, B, C\}$?

3. How many atomic sentences can one construct in our classroom language
    with five constants and three predicates?

4. How many interpretations can be distinguished by our language? (Two in-
    terpretations are distinguishable if there is a sentence which is true in one
    case and false in the other.)

2   Variables and quantifiers

Recall the argument with which we began this chapter:

all girls are good

Ann is a girl
_____

Ann is good

While we can now happily write predicate sentences for 'Ann is a girl' and 'Ann
is good', we do not yet have enough notation in the language to translate 'all girls
are good'. Each atomic sentence we have written so far has been about a specific

object name, or a coupling of specific object names. We lack the ability to describe general cases.

Suppose we wish to state that every child in our classroom was good. We introduce a new predicate good, and write

$$\text{good(Ann)} \wedge \text{good(Brenda)} \wedge \text{good(Carol)} \wedge$$
$$\text{good(David)} \wedge \text{good(Edward)}$$

This can get quite cumbersome, so let us introduce a shorthand:

$$\bigwedge\nolimits_{\text{x} \in \{\text{Ann, Brenda, Carol, David, Edward}\}} \text{good(x)}$$

where the large conjunction symbol behaves in a similar way to the $\sum$ summation symbol in mathematics. The variable x stands for each of the elements of the indicated set. Let us suppose that a new child joins the class, with the name of Fred. We must therefore write

$$\bigwedge\nolimits_{\text{x} \in \{\text{Ann, Brenda, Carol, David, Edward, Fred}\}} \text{good(x)}$$

This would become increasingly tiresome as George, Harry, Ian and friends all join the class, so we make a final notation change and write

$$\forall \text{x}. \quad \text{good(x)}$$

This is read as good(x) for every object name in the language. The $\forall$ (pronounced 'for all') is called the *universal quantifier*. Now we can change the set of object names as often as we wish without changing the sentence describing the property. Let us return to our sentence 'all girls are good'. For our original class we could write

$$
\begin{array}{lll}
& (\text{ girl(Ann)} & \Rightarrow & \text{good(Ann))} \\
\wedge & (\text{ girl(Brenda)} & \Rightarrow & \text{good(Brenda))} \\
\wedge & (\text{ girl(Carol)} & \Rightarrow & \text{good(Carol))} \\
\wedge & (\text{ girl(David)} & \Rightarrow & \text{good(David))} \\
\wedge & (\text{ girl(Edward)} & \Rightarrow & \text{good(Edward))}
\end{array}
$$

We write the implication for David and Edward as well, because our interpretation may map these 'boys' names' to girls in the real classroom. This large conjunction can be written more compactly using the quantifier $\forall$:

$$\forall \text{x}. \quad \text{girl(x)} \Rightarrow \text{good(x)}$$

Recall that when we originally introduced the connectives, we agreed a precedence hierarchy which allowed us to omit many brackets from our logical sentences. We add $\forall$ at the bottom of the hierarchy so that it is below $\Rightarrow$. Therefore the sentence above is syntactically equivalent to

$$\forall \text{x}. \quad (\text{ girl(x)} \Rightarrow \text{good(x))}$$

The universal quantifier ∀ has a counterpart ∃, known as the *existential quantifier*. Just as ∀x. good(x) takes each object name, puts it as an argument to good and makes one *conjunction*, ∃x. good(x) puts each object name as an argument to good and makes one *disjunction*. In the classroom example, ∃x. good(x) would produce

good(Ann)∨ good(Brenda)∨ good(Carol)∨
good(David)∨ good(Edward)[2]

The interpretation of a predicate formula is extended to evaluate the truth or falsity of quantifier sentences very simply. ∀x. φ(x), where φ(x) stands for some (possibly complex) sentence involving the variable x, is true in an interpretation if and only if φ(x) is true in the interpretation *for all* replacements of x in φ(x) by an object name. Similarly, ∃x. φ(x) is true in an interpretation if and only if φ(x) is true in the interpretation *for some* (i.e. at least one) replacement of x in φ(x) by an object name. We are assuming that every object has a syntactical name.

Let $\varphi(z)$ be a formula with the free variable z and assume x and y do not appear in φ. It is clear from our interpretation that $\forall x.\varphi(x)$ and $\forall y.\varphi(y)$ mean the same. This means that we can change bound variables to completely new ones.

EXAMPLE 8.3. In our classroom interpretation, ∀x.boy(x) is not true, since there are names (Ann, Brenda and Carol) which can replace x in boy(x) which would make boy(x) false in the given interpretation. On the other hand, ∃x.boy(x) is true, since replacing x with either David or Edward would make boy(x) true.

2.1 Scope of quantifiers

Sentences can have more than one quantifier in them. Since the x in ∀x is simply a variable, we can use symbols other than x. Thus we can write ∀y, ∃z and so forth. Hence

    (∀x. boy(x)) ∨ (∃y. girl(y))

is a well-formed sentence. As in mathematics, variables can be renamed at will, provided we obey certain *scoping* rules.

In formulae such as $\forall x.\varphi$, the subformula φ is the *scope* of the quantifier ∀x. Suppose that φ contains no other occurrence of ∀x. Then if x occurs in φ, then x is said to be *free* in φ. However, it becomes *bound* by the ∀x, so that it is not free in $\forall x.\varphi$. For example, in ∀x. boy(x), the variable x is free in the subformula boy(x), but bound in the formula as a whole. If the scope of a quantifier for variable x contains another quantifier for x, e.g. ∀x.(boy(x)∧∀x.girl(x)) then the free/bound status of x within the subformula boy(x)∧∀x.girl(x) depends on where it occurs in the subformula. Any occurrence within the scope of the

---

[2]If the domain is infinite, we cannot replace ∀ and ∃ by ordinary ∧ and ∨ as we are doing here, unless we allow infinitely long sentences.

subformula's quantifier is bound; otherwise it is free. Thus the x which is the argument to boy is free within the subformula, and the x which is the argument to girl is bound. The x which is the argument to boy is bound by the outer ∀x so that it is not free in the formula as a whole.

The scoping rules do not depend on which quantifier is used, so that for example,

> ∃x. (boy(x) ∧ ∀x. girl(x))

still has the x in boy(x) bound by the outer quantifier (now ∃x) and the x in girl(x) bound by the inner quantifier ∀x. In the following formulae, x is bound, but y is free.

> boy(y) ∧ ∀x. good(x)
> ∃x. (good(x) ∧ girl(y))

We need to clarify a point about the meaning of the quantifiers. Consider the formula

> ∀x. girl(x) ⇒ ∃x. good(x)

From what we have already said, this is true if and only if for every replacement of x in the subformula girl(x) ⇒ ∃x. good(x) the subformula is true. In fact, if we were to replace every occurrence of x, we would override the ∃x quantifier, and distort the intended meaning of the sentence. We instead replace only the *free* occurrences of x in the subformula. Thus ∀x. girl(x) ⇒ ∃x. good(x) is true (for the original class) iff

$$
\begin{array}{ll}
 \ (\, \mathrm{girl(Ann)} & \Rightarrow \quad \exists \mathrm{x. good(x)}\,) \\
\wedge \ (\, \mathrm{girl(Brenda)} & \Rightarrow \quad \exists \mathrm{x. good(x)}\,) \\
\wedge \ (\, \mathrm{girl(Carol)} & \Rightarrow \quad \exists \mathrm{x. good(x)}\,) \\
\wedge \ (\, \mathrm{girl(David)} & \Rightarrow \quad \exists \mathrm{x. good(x)}\,) \\
\wedge \ (\, \mathrm{girl(Edward)} & \Rightarrow \quad \exists \mathrm{x. good(x)}\,)
\end{array}
$$

is true.

To decide the truth of the subformula ∃x. good(x) we need to expand the subformula to a disjunction by replacing each *free* occurrence of x by an object name. Thus the entire formula is equivalent to

$$
\begin{array}{ll}
 \ (\, \mathrm{girl(Ann)} & \Rightarrow \quad (\mathrm{good(Ann) \vee good(Brenda) \vee \cdots \vee good(Edward))}\,) \\
\wedge \ (\, \mathrm{girl(Brenda)} & \Rightarrow \quad (\mathrm{good(Ann) \vee good(Brenda) \vee \cdots \vee good(Edward))}\,) \\
\wedge \ (\, \mathrm{girl(Carol)} & \Rightarrow \quad (\mathrm{good(Ann) \vee good(Brenda) \vee \cdots \vee good(Edward))}\,) \\
\wedge \ (\, \mathrm{girl(David)} & \Rightarrow \quad (\mathrm{good(Ann) \vee good(Brenda) \vee \cdots \vee good(Edward))}\,) \\
\wedge \ (\, \mathrm{girl(Edward)} & \Rightarrow \quad (\mathrm{good(Ann) \vee good(Brenda) \vee \cdots \vee good(Edward))}\,)
\end{array}
$$

If we have a formula ∀x. $\varphi(x)$ and we wish to replace the x with y, we can do so provided we only change the *free* occurrences of x in $\varphi(x)$ with y. For example,

∀x. (good(x) ∨ boy(x)) is syntactically equivalent to ∀y. (good(y) ∨ boy(y)). The formula (∀x. girl(x)) ∨∃x. boy(x) cannot be changed to use y throughout in one step, as the x in boy(x) is not free in girl(x) ∨ ∃x. boy(x). We must first change the subformula ∃x. boy(x) to ∃y. boy(y), and then change (∀x. girl(x)) ∨∃y. boy(y) to (∀y. girl(y)) ∨ ∃y. boy(y).

EXERCISE 8.4.   Consider a language with the following predicates: friend(x,y), (meaning x is a friend of y), beautiful(x), man(x), and woman(x) and just one constant which is John.

1. Write the following English sentences in predicate logic:

   (a) No one is both a man and a woman

   (b) There are beautiful women

   (c) No friend of John is beautiful

   (d) John is a beautiful man

   (e) No one is a friend of anyone who is not a friend of himself

   (f) Every man is a friend of some beautiful woman but not vice versa

   (g) A friend of a friend is a friend

   (h) If all one's friends are beautiful then one is a woman

   (i) Everyone is either a man or a woman.

2. Translate the following predicate logic sentences into English:

   (a) ∃x. ∃x. [woman(x)] ⇒ woman(x)]

   (b) ∀x. ∃y. [friend(x, y) ⇒ friend(y, x)]

   (c) ∀x. [∃y. [friend(y, y)] ⇒ man(x)].

3. Find the free and bound variables of the following expression:

   ∃x.[[[∃x. friend(x, y)] ⇒ friend(y, y)] ∧
   friend(x,y) ∧ woman(x) ∧ [woman(y) ⇒ woman(x)] ∧
   ∀y. friend(y, y)]

4. Consider the language with the numbers as constants {0, 1, 2, 3, . . .} and the predicates x<y (x is smaller than y) and prime(x) (x is a prime number). Express the following (if possible):

   (a) there is no greatest number

   (b) there exists no greatest prime number

   (c) there exists a first element

    (d) y is a prime number

    (e) z does not divide 9

    (f) John loves a prime number.

5. Paradox of the barber
   In a certain village, there is a barber who shaves all those in the village who do not shave themselves. Is this possible, i.e. is it consistent?

2.2   Quantifier rules and equivalences

We are finally in a position to represent the argument at the start of the chapter. The English sentence 'all girls are good' can be written in predicate logic as $\forall x. (\text{girl}(x) \Rightarrow \text{good}(x))$. Thus the whole argument can be written

$$\frac{\begin{array}{c} \forall x. (\text{girl}(x) \Rightarrow \text{good}(x)) \\ \text{girl(Ann)} \end{array}}{\text{good(Ann)}}$$

Remember that $\forall x.\varphi(x)$ means (the possibly infinite expression) $\varphi(a_1) \wedge \varphi(a_2) \wedge \varphi(a_3) \wedge \ldots$ where $a_1, a_2, a_3, \ldots$ are the object names we are dealing with. So since Ann is one of the names we are dealing with, the $\forall x. \varphi(x)$ in the argument above means

$$\varphi(\text{Ann}) \wedge \varphi(a_1) \wedge \varphi(a_2) \wedge \varphi(a_3) \wedge \ldots$$

So we have

$$
\begin{array}{rll}
 & (\,\text{girl(Ann)} & \Rightarrow & \text{good(Ann)}\,) \\
\wedge & (\,\text{girl}(a_1) & \Rightarrow & \text{good}(a_1)\,) \\
\wedge & (\,\text{girl}(a_2) & \Rightarrow & \text{good}(a_2)\,) \\
\wedge & (\,\text{girl}(a_3) & \Rightarrow & \text{good}(a_3)\,) \\
 & & \vdots &
\end{array}
$$

The $(\wedge E)$ rule which we used when we introduced the forward propositional rules is still valid here, and allows us to split up the big conjunction, so that we have

$$
\begin{array}{lll}
\text{girl(Ann)} & \Rightarrow & \text{good(Ann)} \\
\text{girl}(a_1) & \Rightarrow & \text{good}(a_1) \\
\text{girl}(a_2) & \Rightarrow & \text{good}(a_2) \\
\text{girl}(a_3) & \Rightarrow & \text{good}(a_3) \\
 & \vdots & \\
\multicolumn{3}{c}{\text{girl(Ann)}}
\end{array}
$$

as the assumptions. The $(\Rightarrow E)$ rule now allows us to deduce

$$\frac{\text{girl(Ann)} \Rightarrow \text{good(Ann)} \qquad \text{girl(Ann)}}{\text{good(Ann)}}$$

So we can see that our argument is valid.

In the above we went from $\forall x.\ \varphi(x)$ to $\varphi(\text{Ann})$, by means of the ($\wedge$E) rule. We can write this as a forward deduction rule in its own right, namely ($\forall$E):

$$\frac{\forall x.\ \varphi(x)}{\varphi(a)}$$

where a is some object name in the language. There is a deduction rule for the existential quantifier as well, based on the ($\vee$I) rule:

$$\frac{A}{A \vee B}$$

Recall that $\exists x.\ \varphi(x)$ is syntactically equivalent to (the possibly infinite expression) $\varphi(\text{Ann}) \vee \varphi(a_1) \vee \varphi(a_2) \vee \varphi(a_3) \vee \dots$. Therefore if we know $\varphi(a_i)$ for some name a_i, by ($\vee$I) we know $\varphi(a_1) \vee \varphi(a_2) \vee \dots \vee \varphi(a_i) \vee \dots$ and thus we know $\exists x.\ \varphi(x)$. This is the ($\exists$I) rule:

$$\frac{\varphi(a)}{\exists x.\ \varphi(x)}$$

The existential quantifier is known as the 'dual' of the universal quantifier because $\forall x.\ \neg\varphi(x)$ is equivalent to $\neg\exists x.\ \varphi(x)$. To see this, remember that $\neg(A \vee B)$ is equivalent to $\neg A \wedge \neg B$. Hence $\neg\exists x.\ \varphi(x)$, which can be expanded to $\neg(\varphi(a_1) \vee \varphi(a_2) \vee \varphi(a_3) \vee \dots)$, is equivalent to $\neg\varphi(a_1) \wedge \neg\varphi(a_2) \wedge \neg\varphi(a_3) \wedge \dots$. This, of course, is $\forall x.\ \neg\varphi(x)$. Hence

$$\forall x.\ \neg\varphi(x) \equiv \neg\exists x.\ \varphi(x)$$

By a similar argument, we have

$$\neg\forall x.\ \varphi(x) \equiv \exists x.\ \neg\varphi(x)$$

Further manipulation of the expansions of $\forall$ and $\exists$ gives us a set of equivalences which can be used to move quantifiers around in formulae without changing the meaning; some of these equivalences are presented in Figure 8.1. Note that we assume that the variable being quantified over (for illustration purposes in Figure 8.1 we use x) does not appear as a free variable in the formula γ.

We shall give an illustration of how to show that the equivalences of Figure 8.1 are valid. Take for example the formula $\forall x.\ [\varphi(x) \vee \gamma]$, where γ contains no free occurrences of x. This formula can be written (by expanding the $\forall x$) as

$$[\varphi(a_1) \vee \gamma] \wedge [\varphi(a_2) \vee \gamma] \wedge [\varphi(a_3) \vee \gamma] \wedge \dots$$

$$\forall x. \ \neg\varphi(x) \quad \equiv \quad \neg\exists x. \ \varphi(x)$$
$$\neg\forall x. \ \varphi(x) \quad \equiv \quad \exists x. \ \neg\varphi(x)$$
$$\forall x. \ [\varphi(x) \lor \gamma] \quad \equiv \quad [\forall x. \ \varphi(x)] \lor \gamma$$
$$\exists x. \ [\varphi(x) \lor \gamma] \quad \equiv \quad [\exists x. \ \varphi(x) \lor \gamma]$$
$$\forall x. \ [\varphi(x) \land \gamma] \quad \equiv \quad [\forall x. \ \varphi(x)] \land \gamma$$
$$\exists x. \ [\varphi(x) \land \gamma] \quad \equiv \quad [\exists x. \ \varphi(x)] \land \gamma$$
$$\forall x. \ [\varphi(x) \Rightarrow \gamma] \quad \equiv \quad [\exists x. \ \varphi(x)] \Rightarrow \gamma$$
$$\exists x. \ [\varphi(x) \Rightarrow \gamma] \quad \equiv \quad [\forall x. \ \varphi(x)] \Rightarrow \gamma$$
$$\forall x. \ [\gamma \Rightarrow \varphi(x)] \quad \equiv \quad \gamma \Rightarrow \forall x. \ \varphi(x)$$
$$\exists x. \ [\gamma \Rightarrow \varphi(x)] \quad \equiv \quad \gamma \Rightarrow \exists x. \ \varphi(x)$$
$$\forall x. \ [\varphi(x) \land \psi(x)] \quad \equiv \quad [\forall x. \ \varphi(x)] \land [\forall x. \ \psi(x)]$$
$$\exists x. \ [\varphi(x) \lor \psi(x)] \quad \equiv \quad [\exists x. \ \varphi(x)] \lor [\exists x. \ \psi(x)]$$

Figure 8.1. Quantifier equivalences

for each object $a_1, a_2, a_3, \ldots$ in the domain. Now recall the propositional equivalence

$$[p \lor r] \land [q \lor r] \quad \equiv \quad [p \land q] \lor r$$

This enables us to write the expansion of the $\forall x$ as

$$[\varphi(a_1) \land \varphi(a_2) \land \varphi(a_3) \land \ldots] \lor \gamma$$

which can be compressed by contracting back to the $\forall x$

$$[\forall x. \ \varphi(x)] \lor \gamma$$

as required. Similar proofs hold for the remaining equivalences. Note that the following are *inequivalences*:

$$\forall x. \ [\varphi(x) \lor \psi(x)] \quad \not\equiv \quad [\forall x. \ \varphi(x)] \lor [\forall x. \ \psi(x)]$$
$$\exists x. \ [\varphi(x) \land \psi(x)] \quad \not\equiv \quad [\exists x. \ \varphi(x)] \land [\exists x. \ \psi(x)]$$

Consider the first inequivalence, and consider the following concrete example:

$$[\forall x. \ \text{man}(x) \ \lor \ \forall x. \ \text{woman}(x)] \quad \Rightarrow \quad \forall x. \ [\text{man}(x) \ \lor \ \text{woman}(x)]$$

It is clearly true. If every person is a man or every person is a woman, then every person is either a man or a woman. The converse is not, however, true—if every person is a man or a woman, there is no basis for concluding that every person is a man or every person is a woman. Therefore

∀x. [man(x) ∨ woman(x)]   ⇒   [∀x. man(x) ∨ ∀x. woman(x)]

A similar argument can be made for the second inequivalence—if there is a man, and there is a woman, one cannot conclude that there is someone who is both a man and a woman.

EXERCISE 8.5.   Prove that these two quantifier equivalences from Figure 8.1 are true:

1. $\forall x. [\varphi(x) \wedge \psi(x)] \equiv [\forall x. \varphi(x)] \wedge [\forall x. \psi(x)]$

2. $\exists x. [\varphi(x) \vee \psi(x)] \equiv [\exists x. \varphi(x)] \vee [\exists x. \psi(x)]$.

3. Use quantifier equivalences from Figure 8.1 to show that the formula $\exists x. \forall y. (\varphi(x) \Rightarrow \varphi(y))$ is always true.

2.3   Prenex normal form

The importance of the quantifier equivalences is that they enable us to write every wff in an equivalent form with all the quantifiers on the outside. Thus a formula such as

∀x. [p(x) ⇒ ∃y. [q(y) ∧ ∀z. r(y,z)]]

can be rewritten as the equivalent formula

∀x.∃y.∀z. [p(x) ⇒ q(y) ∧ r(y,z)]

Formulae with all their quantifiers grouped together outside the propositional connectives are said to be in *prenex* normal form. The prenex formula can be abstractly presented as

$$Q_1 x_1. Q_2 x_2. \cdots . Q_n x_n. \varphi(x_1, x_2, \ldots, x_n)$$

where each Q_i is either ∀ or ∃, and $\varphi(x_1, x_2, \ldots, x_n)$ is a quantifier-free formula, known as the *matrix*, involving the variables $x_1, x_2, \ldots, x_n$. It is usual for the matrix to be in disjunctive normal form (Definition 1.7). The quantifiers $Q_1 x_1. Q_2 x_2. \cdots . Q_n x_n$ are known as the *prefix*. It is permissible for n to be zero, so that quantifier-free formulae are in prenex normal form. We now show that there is an equivalent prenex formula for each predicate formula.

THEOREM 8.6.   *Every formula α of predicate logic can be transformed to another formula β in prenex normal form such that $\alpha \Leftrightarrow \beta$ is valid.*

Proof: The proof is an induction over the structure of the formula α. There are two base cases, when α is atomic or α is $\bot$; in either case α is quantifier free and hence by definition in prenex normal form. α is thus its own prenex equivalent.

There are six induction cases, although four of these are redundant, being definable from the two we deal with here, and the base cases:

$\alpha = \varphi \Rightarrow \psi$. By the induction hypothesis we can assume that φ and ψ are already in prenex normal form, or have been replaced by their prenex equivalents. If necessary we can further rewrite the formulae to ensure that the sets of variables $\{x_1, \ldots, x_n\}$ and $\{y_1, \ldots, y_m\}$ are disjoint. Hence

$$\varphi \;=\; Q_1 x_1.Q_2 x_2. \cdots .Q_n x_n.\varphi'$$
$$\psi \;=\; R_1 y_1.R_2 y_2. \cdots .R_m y_m.\psi'$$

where the Q_i and R_j are quantifiers. By repeated application of the following equivalences from Figure 8.1

$$\forall x. \, [\varphi(x) \Rightarrow \gamma] \;\equiv\; [\exists x. \, \varphi(x)] \Rightarrow \gamma$$
$$\exists x. \, [\varphi(x) \Rightarrow \gamma] \;\equiv\; [\forall x. \, \varphi(x)] \Rightarrow \gamma$$

we can move all the quantifiers $Q_1, \ldots, Q_n$ from under the $\Rightarrow$ to outside it (as ψ contains none of the variables $x_1, \ldots, x_n$). We now have

$$Q_1' x_1.Q_2' x_2. \cdots .Q_n' x_n.[\varphi' \Rightarrow R_1 y_1.R_2 y_2. \cdots .R_m y_m.\psi']$$

where Q_i' is $\forall$ if Q_i is $\exists$ and vice versa. By use of two more equivalences from Figure 8.1

$$\forall x. \, [\gamma \Rightarrow \varphi(x)] \;\equiv\; \gamma \Rightarrow \forall x. \, \varphi(x)$$
$$\exists x. \, [\gamma \Rightarrow \varphi(x)] \;\equiv\; \gamma \Rightarrow \exists x. \, \varphi(x)$$

we can move $R_1, \ldots, R_m$ from under the $\Rightarrow$ as well, leaving only the quantifier-free formulae φ' and ψ' under the $\Rightarrow$:

$$Q_1' x_1.Q_2' x_2. \cdots .Q_n' x_n.R_1 y_1.R_2 y_2. \cdots .R_m y_m.[\varphi' \Rightarrow \psi']$$

which is the prenex equivalent for α. (The R quantifiers are not changed by the equivalences.)

$\alpha = \exists x.\varphi$. We assume that φ is of the form $Q_1 x_1.Q_2 x_2. \cdots .Q_n x_n.\varphi'$, by the induction hypothesis. Hence $\alpha = \exists x.Q_1 x_1.Q_2 x_2. \cdots .Q_n x_n.\varphi'$ which is in prenex normal form. ∎

Many automatic theorem-proving techniques rely on formulae being in prenex normal form, and we shall also exploit it. Once we have translated a set of formulae into this form, we can then convert the matrix for each formula into the $\mathcal{B}$-clausal form of Definition 7.18, because each matrix is simply atoms joined together by propositional connectives, and thus all the familiar manipulations that we used to transform arbitrary propositional formulae into $\mathcal{B}$-clauses can be used on the matrix.

EXERCISE 8.7. Write the following formulae in prenex normal form (p, q are predicate symbols):

1. $\exists x.\forall y.p(x, y) \wedge \exists x.\forall y.q(x, y)$

2. $\exists x.\forall y.p(x, y) \Rightarrow \forall x.\exists y.q(x, y)$

2.4   Equality

There is a special predicate, $x \approx y$, which is interpreted as identity. Thus $a \approx b$ if and only if they name the same element in the domain. The symbol '$\approx$' is a formal symbol for equality. From now on we use the more common '$=$' symbol.

3   Formal definitions

We have now completed the informal presentation of predicate logic, and we now provide formal definitions of the material covered above. Because of the interdefinability of the various connectives, the following definition provides a minimal set of connectives. Exercise 8.10 involves the derivation of some of the other connectives.

DEFINITION 8.8 (Syntax of predicate logic). The formulae of the predicate logic language $\mathcal{L}$ are built up from the following symbols:

- a set $\mathcal{L}_{pred}$ of predicate symbols, each with an associated arity, which is a positive integer,

- a set $\mathcal{L}_{cons}$ of constant symbols,

- a set $\mathcal{L}_{var}$ of variable symbols,

- a set $\mathcal{L}_{func}$ of function symbols, each with an associated arity, which is a positive integer,

- a quantifier $\exists$,

- classical connectives $\perp$ and $\Rightarrow$. The other classical connectives are definable from $\perp$ and $\Rightarrow$.

The set of terms $\mathcal{L}_{term}$ is given by the following rules:

- any member of $\mathcal{L}_{\text{cons}}$ is a term in $\mathcal{L}_{\text{term}}$, with no variables;

- any member x of $\mathcal{L}_{\text{var}}$ is a term in $\mathcal{L}_{\text{term}}$, with variable x (itself);

- if f is a member of $\mathcal{L}_{\text{func}}$ with arity n, and $t_1, \ldots, t_n$ are terms in $\mathcal{L}_{\text{term}}$, then $t = f(t_1, \ldots, t_n)$ is a term in $\mathcal{L}_{\text{term}}$. The set of variables of t is the union of all the sets of variables of $t_1, \ldots, t_n$.

We can now define the well-formed formulae (wffs) of $\mathcal{L}$ by the rules:

- $\perp$ is a wff of $\mathcal{L}$, with no free variables;

- if p is a member of $\mathcal{L}_{\text{pred}}$ with arity n, and $t_1, \ldots, t_n$ are terms in $\mathcal{L}_{\text{term}}$, then $p(t_1, \ldots, t_n)$ is a wff in $\mathcal{L}$, with the free variables being all the variables of $t_1, \ldots, t_n$;

- if φ and ψ are wffs in $\mathcal{L}$ then so is $\varphi \Rightarrow \psi$, with the free variables being the union of those free in φ and ψ;

- if v is a variable in $\mathcal{L}_{\text{var}}$ and φ is a wff in $\mathcal{L}$, then $\exists v.\varphi$ is a wff in $\mathcal{L}$. The free variables of $\exists v.\varphi$ are those of φ less the variable v.

Each symbol in $\mathcal{L}$ must be interpreted in order for wffs of $\mathcal{L}$ to be given a truth value. For propositional logic, we simply assigned truth values to the propositions via a function h, and then extended h to propagate the truth values from the propositions through the formulae. As outlined in Section 1.2, the change from atomic propositions to predicates with structured terms being the simplest wffs means that the basic model becomes more complicated.

DEFINITION 8.9 (Semantics of predicate logic). The formulae are given truth values with respect to an *interpretation* or a *model* $\mathcal{M} = \langle \mathcal{D}, \pi_{\text{cons}}, \pi_{\text{func}}, \pi_{\text{pred}} \rangle$, with the four components:

- $\mathcal{D}$, a non-empty domain of objects,

- π_{cons}, a mapping from members of $\mathcal{L}_{\text{cons}}$ to $\mathcal{D}$,

- π_{func}, mapping each member of $\mathcal{L}_{\text{func}}$ to a function mapping $\mathcal{D}^n$ to $\mathcal{D}$, for each $p \in \mathcal{L}_{\text{func}}$ $\pi_{\text{func}}(p) : \mathcal{D}^n \mapsto \mathcal{D}$, where n is the arity of the member of $\mathcal{L}_{\text{func}}$, and

- π_{pred}, mapping each member of $\mathcal{L}_{\text{pred}}$ to $\mathcal{D}^n \mapsto \{\top, \perp\}$, where n is the arity of the member of $\mathcal{L}_{\text{pred}}$.

We also need to interpret the free variables in the formulae. This is done by defining a *variable assignment* V, which is a mapping from $\mathcal{L}_{\text{var}}$ to $\mathcal{D}$. We need the notation $V_{[v \mapsto d]}$ to mean the assignment V' satisfying $V'(x) = V(x)$, for $x \neq v$ and

$V'(v) = d$. Given this, we can interpret all the terms of $\mathcal{L}$ by means of a term mapping π_{term}, based on V, π_{cons} and π_{func}, which maps all members of $\mathcal{L}_{\text{term}}$ to $\mathcal{D}$. For t in $\mathcal{L}_{\text{term}}$:

- for all members c of $\mathcal{L}_{\text{cons}}$, $\pi_{\text{term}}(c) = \pi_{\text{cons}}(c)$;

- for all members v of $\mathcal{L}_{\text{var}}$, $\pi_{\text{term}}(v) = V(v)$;

- for all members f of $\mathcal{L}_{\text{func}}$ with arity n, $\pi_{\text{term}}(f(t_1, \ldots, t_n)) = \pi_{\text{func}}(f)(\pi_{\text{term}}(t_1), \ldots, \pi_{\text{term}}(t_n))$;

- $\pi_{\text{term}}(t)$ is called the value of t in the model, under the assignment V.

Finally we can define the truth of a wff φ of $\mathcal{L}$, with respect to an interpretation $\mathcal{M}$ and a variable assignment V. This is written as $\langle \mathcal{M}, V \rangle \vDash \varphi$, read as '$\varphi$ holds in $\langle \mathcal{M}, V \rangle$', or '$\langle \mathcal{M}, V \rangle$ is a model of φ' and given by

$$\langle \mathcal{M}, V \rangle \nvDash \bot$$
$$\langle \mathcal{M}, V \rangle \vDash p(t_1, \ldots, t_n) \quad \text{iff} \quad \pi_{\text{pred}}(p)(\pi_{\text{term}}(t_1), \ldots, \pi_{\text{term}}(t_n)) = \top$$
$$\langle \mathcal{M}, V \rangle \vDash \varphi \Rightarrow \psi \quad \text{iff} \quad \langle \mathcal{M}, V \rangle \vDash \varphi \text{ implies } \langle \mathcal{M}, V \rangle \vDash \psi$$
$$\langle \mathcal{M}, V \rangle \vDash \exists v.\, \varphi \quad \text{iff} \quad \text{there exists } d \in \mathcal{D} \text{ and } \langle \mathcal{M}, V_{[v \mapsto d]} \rangle \vDash \varphi$$

Let $\varphi(x_1, \ldots, x_n)$ be a formula with the free variables $x_1, \ldots, x_n$. It is common to use the notation $\mathcal{M} \vDash \varphi(a_1, \ldots, a_n)$ to represent $\langle \mathcal{M}, V_{[x_i \mapsto a_i | i = 1, \ldots, n]} \rangle \vDash \varphi$.

If the formula contains no free variables, then an arbitrary mapping (sometimes called *empty* mapping) can be used as the initial variable assignment. We use the notation [ ] for such a mapping and we write $\langle \mathcal{M}, [\,] \rangle \vDash \varphi$.

We write $\vDash \varphi$ to indicate that 'φ holds in all models $\langle \mathcal{M}, V \rangle$'.

EXERCISE 8.10.

1. Given that $\neg \alpha \equiv \alpha \Rightarrow \bot$, $\alpha \vee \beta \equiv (\alpha \Rightarrow \bot) \Rightarrow \beta$, $\alpha \wedge \beta \equiv (\alpha \Rightarrow (\beta \Rightarrow \bot)) \Rightarrow \bot$ and $\forall x.\, \varphi \equiv (\exists x.\, (\varphi \Rightarrow \bot)) \Rightarrow \bot$, derive definitions for

    (a) $\langle \mathcal{M}, V \rangle \vDash \neg \varphi$

    (b) $\langle \mathcal{M}, V \rangle \vDash \varphi \vee \psi$

    (c) $\langle \mathcal{M}, V \rangle \vDash \varphi \wedge \psi$

    (d) $\langle \mathcal{M}, V \rangle \vDash \forall x.\, \varphi$

2. Let the language be based on the following sets:

    - $\mathcal{L}_{\text{cons}} = \{\text{a, b, c, d}\}$

    - $\mathcal{L}_{\text{var}} = \{\text{x, y, z}\}$

    - $\mathcal{L}_{\text{func}} = \{\text{f}, \text{g}\}$, f with arity 1 and g with arity 2

- $\mathcal{L}_{\text{pred}} = \{p, q, r\}$, p with arity 2, q with arity 1 and r with arity 3.

Let the model be given by $\mathcal{M} = \langle \mathcal{D}, \pi_{\text{cons}}, \pi_{\text{func}}, \pi_{\text{pred}} \rangle$:

- $\mathcal{D} = \{1, 2, 3, 4, 5, 6, 7\}$,

- π_{cons}: $\{a \mapsto 1, b \mapsto 3, c \mapsto 5, d \mapsto 7\}$

- π_{func}: $\{f \mapsto \{1 \mapsto 2, 2 \mapsto 3, 3 \mapsto 5, 4 \mapsto 7, 5 \mapsto 7, 6 \mapsto 7, 7 \mapsto 7\}, g \mapsto \{(u, v) \mapsto u + v \text{ if } u + v \leq 7, \text{ otherwise } (u, v) \mapsto 1\}\}$

- π_{pred}:

$$
\{ \begin{array}{rl}
p \mapsto & \{(2, 3) \mapsto \top, (3, 2) \mapsto \top\}, \\
q \mapsto & \{2 \mapsto \top, 4 \mapsto \top, 6 \mapsto \top\}, \\
r \mapsto & \{(1, 3, 5) \mapsto \top, (2, 4, 6) \mapsto \top\} \}
\end{array}
$$

All other combinations are assigned $\bot$ by π_{pred}.

Work out which of the following formulae are true in the above model, with the initial variable assignment [ ]:

(a) p(f(a),b)

(b) r(a,f(b),c)

(c) ∃x.(¬q(x) ⇒ p(f(a),g(x,2)))

(d) ∀x.(¬q(x) ⇒ p(f(a),g(x,2)))

EXERCISE 8.11. Consider the language based on the following sets:

- $\mathcal{L}_{cons} = \emptyset$
- $\mathcal{L}_{var} = \{x, y, z\}$
- $\mathcal{L}_{func} = \emptyset$
- $\mathcal{L}_{pred} = \{s, p\}$, both with arity 3.

Let the model be given by $\mathcal{N} = \langle \mathbb{N}, \pi_{cons}, \pi_{func}, \pi_{pred} \rangle$ where

- $\mathbb{N} = \{0, 1, 2, \ldots, \}$ is the set of natural numbers
- π_{cons}, π_{func} are empty
- $\pi_{pred}(s)(a, b, c) = \top$ iff $a + b = c$,
  $\pi_{pred}(p)(a, b, c) = \top$ iff $a \cdot b = c$.

(a)–(f): Write down a formula with a single free variable x stating that

(a) $x = 0$ (d) x is even

(b) $x = 1$ (e) x is prime

(c) $x = 2$ (f) $x > 27$.

(g), (h): Write down a formula with two free variables x, y stating that

(g) $x = y$

(h) $x < y$

(i) Write down a sentence stating that there are infinitely many primes.

EXERCISE 8.12. Check whether the following formulae have models:

(a) $\exists x. \forall y.(Q(x, x) \wedge \neg Q(x, y))$

(b) $\exists x. \exists y.(P(x) \wedge \neg P(y))$

(c) $\exists x. \forall y.(Q(x, y) \Rightarrow \forall z.R(x, y, z))$

(d) $P(x) \Rightarrow \forall y.P(y)$.

EXERCISE 8.13. Check whether the following formulae are valid:

(a) $\exists x.P(y) \Rightarrow \forall x.P(x)$

(b) $\neg(\exists x.P(x) \Rightarrow \forall x.P(x))$

(c) $\exists x. \forall y.Q(x, y) \Rightarrow \forall y. \exists x.Q(x, y)$

(d) $\forall x. \exists y.Q(x, y) \Rightarrow \exists y. \forall x.Q(x, y)$.

4   Worked examples

The purpose of the worked examples of this section is to demonstrate the expressive power of predicate logic as a language for specification. This capability plays a crucial role in all computer science applications.

EXAMPLE 8.14 (Euler's problem 1782). There are 36 officers of six regiments (nos $1, 2, \ldots, 6$) and of six ranks (nos $1, 2, \ldots, 6$), so that every pair of numbers is presented by some officer. The problem is to arrange them in a 6×6 square, such that at every row and at every column ranks and regiments of officers are different. This means that we have to find a six-element model of some set of sentences. This example presents a simple set of sentences for which it is difficult to check whether it has a model.

1. Write down these sentences, using the following language:

    - $\mathcal{L}_{cons} = \varnothing$
    - $\mathcal{L}_{var} = \{x, y, z, t, u, v, w\}$
    - $\mathcal{L}_{func} = \{rk, rg\}$
    - $\mathcal{L}_{pred} = \{ \ = \ \}$.

    ($rk(a, b)$ means the rank of the officer standing at the a-th row and at the b-th column, $rg(a, b)$ means the regiment of this officer.)

    [Euler's conjecture was that such models do not exist. This was proved over a century later, in 1900.]

2. Construct a three-element model of the same set of sentences.

Solution

1. $\varphi_1 : \forall x.\forall y.\exists z.\exists t.(rk(z, t) = x \land rg(z, t) = y)$

    This means: 'every pair (rank, regiment) is presented by some officer'.

    $\varphi_2 : \forall x.\forall y.\forall z.(rk(x, y) = rk(x, z) \Rightarrow y = z)$

    this means: 'ranks at every row are distinct'.

    $\varphi_3 : \forall x.\forall y.\forall z.(rk(y, x) = rk(z, x) \Rightarrow y = z)$

    ('Ranks at every column are distinct').

    $\varphi_4 : \forall x.\forall y.\forall z.(rg(x, y) = rg(x, z) \Rightarrow y = z)$

    $\varphi_5 : \forall x.\forall y.\forall z.(rg(y, x) = rg(z, x) \Rightarrow y = z)$

    (φ_4 and φ_5 are similar to φ_2, φ_3).

2. One of the possible solutions is

1, 1	2, 3	3, 2
3, 3	1, 2	2, 1
2, 2	3, 1	1, 3

(The pair of elements in the above square in the third row and first column (i.e. position (3, 1)) is '2,2'. This means that $rk(3, 1) = 2, rg(3, 1) = 2$. Similarly, $rk(1, 2) = 2, rg(1, 2) = 3$, etc.)

EXAMPLE 8.15 (Affine planes). Consider the language with

- $\mathcal{L}_{cons} = \emptyset$

- $\mathcal{L}_{var} = \{x, y, \ldots\}$

- $\mathcal{L}_{func} = \emptyset$

- $\mathcal{L}_{pred} = \{=, P, L, \in\}$ with unary P, L, binary $=, \in$.

$P(x)$ is read as 'x is a point', $L(x)$ as 'x is a line'; $\in (x, y)$ is read as 'x belongs to y', or as 'y contains x'.
  Write down sentences, stating that

(α)   Everything is either a point or a line, but not both.

(β)   Every line contains at least two points.

(γ)   Everything containing a point is a line.

(δ)   Everything belonging to a line is a point.

(ε)   Every two distinct points belong to some line, and this line is unique.

(ξ)   Given a point x and a line y, not containing x, one can find a unique line containing x which has no common points with y.

(ζ)   There exist at least two lines.

Solutions

(α) $\forall x.[(P(x) \vee L(x)) \wedge \neg(P(x) \wedge L(x))]$

(β) $\forall x.(L(x) \Rightarrow \exists y.\exists z.(\in (y, x) \wedge \in (z, x) \wedge \neg y = z))$

(γ) $\forall x.\forall y.(P(x) \wedge \in (x, y) \Rightarrow L(y))$

(δ) $\forall x.\forall y.(L(x) \wedge \in (y, x) \Rightarrow P(y))$

(ε) $\forall x.\forall y.(P(x) \land P(y) \land \neg x = y \Rightarrow \exists z.[L(z)\land \in (x,z)\land \in (y,z) \land \forall t.(L(t)\land \in (x,t)\land \in (y,t) \Rightarrow t = z)])$

(ξ) $\forall x.\forall y.[P(x) \land L(y) \land \neg \in (x,y) \Rightarrow \exists z.[L(z)\land \in (x,z) \land \neg \exists t.(\in (t,z)\land \in (t,y)) \land \forall u[L(u)\land \in (x,u) \land \neg \exists t.(\in (t,u)\land \in (t,y)) \Rightarrow u = z]]]$

(ζ) $\exists x.\exists y.(L(x) \land L(y) \land \neg x = y).$

EXAMPLE 8.16 (Affine planes, continued[3]).   A model of the set of formulae $\Delta = \{\alpha, \beta, \gamma, \delta, \varepsilon, \xi, \zeta\}$ of the previous example is called an *affine plane*.

1. Construct an affine plane with four points.

2. Show that in every finite affine plane all lines contain an equal number of points.

3. Show that in any affine plane containing a line with n points, every point belongs to exactly $n + 1$ lines.

4. Show that the number of points in any finite affine plane is a full square.[4]

Solutions
Here is the picture:

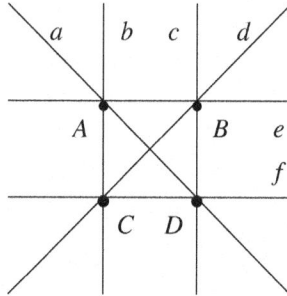

There are four points (A, B, C, D) and six lines (a, b, c, d, e, f).
Here is the description of the model according to Definition 7.3.1

$D = \{A, B, C, D, a, b, c, d, e, f\}$;
$\pi_{\text{pred}}(P)(X) = \top$ iff $X \in \{A, B, C, D\}$;
$\pi_{\text{pred}}(L)(X) = \top$ iff $X \in \{a, b, c, d, e, f\}$;
$\pi_{\text{pred}}(\in)(X, y) = \top$ iff
   $(X, y) \in \{(A, a), (D, a), (A, b), (C, b), (B, c), (D, c), (B, d), (C, d), (A, e), (B, e), (C, f), (D, f)\}$;
$\pi_{\text{pred}}(=)(X, Y) = \top$ iff $X = Y.$

---

[3] For more information on the logical approach to affine geometry, see [Blumenthal, 1980].
[4] However, it is not yet known completely which full squares can occur as numbers of points of affine planes. Nobody knows, for example, if there exist affine planes with 100 points.

The truth of formulae (α), (β), (γ), (δ), (ζ) in this model is quite clear. (ε) holds because for any two distinct points there is a unique line containing them, namely:

$$a \text{ for } A, D; \quad d \text{ for } B, C;$$
$$b \text{ for } A, C; \quad e \text{ for } A, B;$$
$$c \text{ for } B, D; \quad f \text{ for } C, D.$$

(ξ) can be checked for all possible values x, y for which the premise is true:

$$\text{if } x = A, y = d \quad \text{then } z = a,$$
$$\text{if } x = A, y = c \quad \text{then } z = b,$$
$$\text{if } x = A, y = f \quad \text{then } z = e,$$
$$\text{if } x = B, y = a \quad \text{then } z = d,$$
$$\text{if } x = B, y = b \quad \text{then } z = c,$$
$$\text{if } x = B, y = f \quad \text{then } z = e,$$
$$\text{if } x = C, y = a \quad \text{then } z = d,$$
$$\text{if } x = C, y = c \quad \text{then } z = b,$$
$$\text{if } x = C, y = e \quad \text{then } z = f,$$
$$\text{if } x = D, y = e \quad \text{then } z = f,$$
$$\text{if } x = D, y = d \quad \text{then } z = a,$$
$$\text{if } x = D, y = b \quad \text{then } z = c.$$

2. To deal with affine planes, we somewhat simplify our notations. According to tradition, we will denote lines by small letters, and points by capitals. We write $B \in a$ instead of $\in (B, a)$ and $B \notin a$ instead of $\neg \in (B, a)$, as is usually done.

Also we write $a\|b$ (read as 'a is parallel to b') instead of

$$\neg \exists X.(X \in z \wedge X \in b)$$

Now consider an affine plane $\mathcal{M}$; let a, a' be two distinct lines in $\mathcal{M}$.

First we notice that there exists A_1' such that

$$\mathcal{M} \vDash A_1' \in a' \wedge A_1' \notin a \tag{2.1}$$

To show this, assume the contrary. Since $\mathcal{M} \vDash (\beta)$, one can find two points (say, B_1, B_2) such that $\mathcal{M} \vDash B_1 \neq B_2 \wedge B_1 \in a' \wedge B_2 \in a'$.

By our assumption, we also have that

$$\mathcal{M} \vDash B_1 \in a \wedge B_2 \in a$$

Now the formula (ε) provides that $a = a'$, which is a contradiction. Thus (2.1) holds for some A_1'. Likewise, there exists A_1 such that

$$\mathcal{M} \vDash A_1 \in a \wedge A_1 \notin a' \tag{2.2}$$

Now let $A_1, \ldots, A_n$ be all points of a, and let us show that a' contains exactly n points.

Owing to (ε), there exists a unique line b_1, such that

$$\mathcal{M} \vDash A_1 \in b_1 \wedge A_1' \in b_1 \tag{2.3}$$

($A_1 \neq A_1'$ is clear from (2.1).)

Then if we take any A_i, $1 < i \leq n$, it follows that

$$\mathcal{M} \vDash A_i \notin b_1 \tag{2.4}$$

because otherwise

$$\mathcal{M} \vDash A_1 \in b_1 \wedge A_i \in b_1 \wedge A_1 \in a \wedge A_i \in a \wedge A_1 \neq A_i$$

which implies $a = b_1$, owing to (ε). but $a \neq b_1$, because $A_1' \in b_1, A_2' \notin a$. So (2.4) holds.

Now since $\mathcal{M} \vDash (\xi)$, there exists a unique line b_i such that

$$\mathcal{M} \vDash A_i \in b_i \wedge b_i \| b_1 \tag{2.5}$$

Further on, we observe that

$$\mathcal{M} \nvDash b_i \| a' \tag{2.6}$$

Indeed, suppose the contrary; then (by (2.1), (2.5), (2.3))

$$\mathcal{M} \vDash a' \| b_i \wedge b_i \| b_1 \wedge A_1' \in a' \wedge A_1' \in b_1 \wedge A_1' \notin a$$

Hence by (ξ) we get that $a' = b_1$. But this is impossible because $A_1 \in b_1, A_1 \notin a'$ (by (2.2), (2.3)).

Thus (2.6) holds.

From (2.6) it follows that a', b_i have a common point. This point is unique, because otherwise $a' = b_i$ (owing to (ε)), which is impossible, because $b_i \| b_1$, $a' \nparallel b_1$ (since they have a common point A_1').

So let A_i' be this point:

$$\mathcal{M} \vDash A_i' \in b_i \wedge A_i' \in a'$$

In this way each point at a corresponds to a unique point at a', and it remains to prove that $A_i \mapsto A_i'$ is a one-to-one correspondence.

This is clear if we find the inverse function. But we can construct it in the same way. Namely, given a point D, such that $D \in a'$, $D \neq A_1'$, we can construct a unique line l, such that $\mathcal{M} \vDash D \in l \wedge l \| b_1$.

This gives us the unique C, such that

$$\mathcal{M} \vDash C \in l \wedge C \in a$$

Since $C \in a$, it follows that $C = A_j$, for some j. But then $l = b_j$, because

$$\mathcal{M} \vDash l \| b_1 \wedge b_j \| b_1 \wedge C \in l \wedge C \in b_j$$

And therefore $D = A'_j$, because

$$\mathcal{M} \vDash D \in l \wedge D \in a'$$

This mapping, $A_i \mapsto A'_i$, is one-to-one, implying that $A'_1, \ldots, A'_n$ are exactly all points of a'.

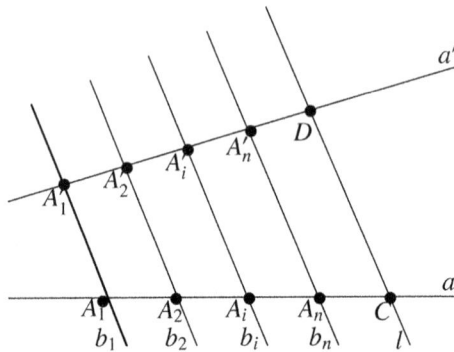

3. First we prove that in any affine plane $\mathcal{M}$

$$\mathcal{M} \vDash \forall A . \exists a . A \notin a \tag{3.1}$$

In fact, by (ζ) we can find two different lines (say, b and c) in $\mathcal{M}$.

If $A \notin b$ or $A \notin c$, there is nothing to prove. If $A \in b$ and $A \in c$, we take B, C such that

$$\mathcal{M} \vDash B \in b \wedge C \in c \wedge B \neq A \wedge C \neq A \tag{3.2}$$

Such B, C exist because $\mathcal{M} \vDash (\varepsilon)$. Then $B \neq C$ because otherwise we had

$$\mathcal{M} \vDash A \in b \wedge A \in c \wedge B \in b \wedge B \in c \wedge A \neq B \wedge b \neq c$$

which contradicts (ε). Applying (ε) again, we find a line a, such that

$$\mathcal{M} \vDash B \in a \wedge C \in a$$

Then $A \notin a$ because otherwise $A \in a \wedge B \in a \wedge A \in b \wedge B \in b$ which implies $a = b$, owing to (ε); likewise, we obtain that $a = C$, and then $b = c$, which is a contradiction.

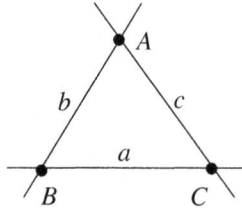

Now we can prove the main statement. By item (2), the line a contains exactly n points, say $A_1, \ldots, A_n$. Obviously for every i, $A \neq A_i$ (since $A \notin a$). Then we can use (ε) again and get that for any i ($1 \leq i \leq n$)

$$\mathcal{M} \models \exists a_i.(A \in a_i \wedge A_i \in a_i) \tag{3.3}$$

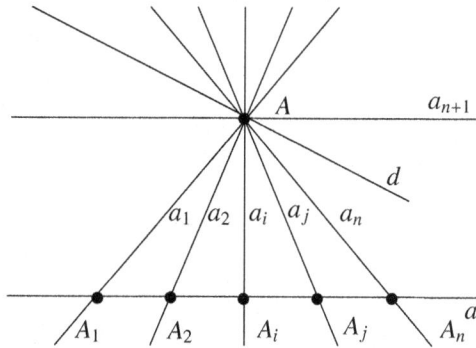

Next, we notice that

$$\text{if } i \neq j \text{ then } a_i \neq a_j \tag{3.4}$$

In fact, $a_i = a_j$ implies (by (3.3))

$$\mathcal{M} \models A_i \in a_i \wedge A_j \in a_i \wedge A_i \in a \wedge A_j \in a$$

and thus $a_i = a$ by (ε), since $A_i \neq A_j$. But then $A \in a$, which brings us to a contradiction. Thus (3.4) holds.

So we have found n different lines containing A. There is also a line a_{n+1}, such that $A \in a_{n+1}, a_{n+1} \| a$ (by (ξ)). Obviously, $a_{n+1} \neq a_i$ for any $i \leq n$ because a_i and a have a common point A_i.

It remains to show that

$$\mathcal{M} \models \forall d.(A \in d \Rightarrow d = a_1 \vee d = a_2 \vee \cdots \vee d = a_{n+1}) \tag{3.4}$$

Really, if $A \in d$ and $d \parallel a$ then $d = a_{n+1}$, owing to (ξ). And if $A \in d$ and $d \nparallel a$ then d and a must have a common point, so for some $i \le n$

$$\mathcal{M} \vDash A_i \in d \wedge A \in d \wedge A_i \in a_i \wedge A \in a_i$$

This implies $a_i = d$ (by (ε)), because $A_i \ne A$.

Therefore $a_1, \ldots, a_{n+1}$ are exactly all lines containing A.

4. Let $\mathcal{M}$ again be an affine plane, with a line a, containing exactly n points: $A_1, \ldots, A_n$. As above, we can construct a line b_1, such that

$$\mathcal{M} \vDash A \in b_1 \wedge a \ne b_1 \tag{4.1}$$

Then by (ξ) we get for any $i > 1$

$$\mathcal{M} \vDash \exists b_i.(A_i \in b_i \wedge b_i \parallel b_1) \tag{4.2}$$

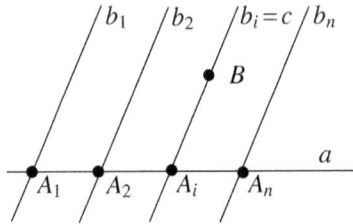

We notice that $b_i \parallel b_j$ whenever $i \ne j$, because otherwise for some C we had

$$\mathcal{M} \vDash C \in b_i \wedge C \in b_j \wedge b_i \ne b_j \wedge b_i \parallel b_1 \wedge b_j \parallel b_1$$

in contradiction with (ξ).

By item (2) each b_i consists of n points, and in total we get $n \cdot n = n^2$ distinct points in $\mathcal{M}$.

Finally, we observe that we have calculated all points in $\mathcal{M}$. In fact, if we take any point $B \notin a$, and if $B \notin b_1$, then by (ξ) there exists a line c, such that

$$\mathcal{M} \vDash B \in c \wedge c \parallel b_1 \tag{4.3}$$

Hence $c \parallel a$, because otherwise we had

$$\mathcal{M} \vDash b_1 \parallel c \wedge a \parallel c \wedge A_1 \in b_1 \wedge A_1 \in a \wedge b_1 \ne a$$

in contradiction with (ξ).

Thus c and a have a common point, i.e. for some i,

$$\mathcal{M} \vDash A_i \in c$$

Now (ξ) yields that $b_i = c$, because

$$\mathcal{M} \vDash A_i \in b_i \wedge A_i \in c \wedge b_i \| b_1 \wedge c \| b_1$$

Therefore, every point belongs to some of the lines $b_1, \ldots, b_n$.

EXAMPLE 8.17. Show that the following formula φ is false in any finite model, but is true in some infinite model:

$$\varphi = \forall x.\neg Q(x, x) \wedge \forall x.\forall y.\forall z.(Q(x, y) \wedge Q(y, z) \Rightarrow Q(x, z)) \wedge \forall x.\exists y.Q(x, y)$$

Solution

1. Assume that φ is true in some model $\mathcal{M}$ with the domain D. We have to show that D is infinite.

   First take any $d_0 \in D$. Since $\mathcal{M} \vDash \varphi$, it follows that $\mathcal{M} \vDash \forall x.\exists y.Q(x, y)$ and hence (by Exercise 8.3.3) $\mathcal{M} \vDash \exists y.Q(d_0, y)$. Then $\mathcal{M} \vDash Q(d_0, d_1)$ for some $d_1 \in D$.

   Now we can find a sequence $d_0, d_1, \ldots \in D$ by induction as follows. If $d_0, \ldots, d_n$ are already chosen, we note that $\mathcal{M} \vDash \exists y.Q(d_n, y)$. And then $\mathcal{M} \vDash Q(d_n, d_{n+1})$ for some $d_{n+1} \in D$. Finally we notice that all elements d_n in the sequence are different. In fact $d_n \neq d_{n+1}$ because otherwise we had $\mathcal{M} \vDash Q(d_n, d_n)$ which contradicts $\mathcal{M} \vDash \forall x.\neg Q(x, x)$. Also $d_n \neq d_{n+m}$ for any $m > 1$.

   To see this, it is sufficient to show that for any $m \geq 1$

   (a) $\mathcal{M} \vDash Q(d_n, d_{n+m})$, and recall that $\mathcal{M} \vDash \neg Q(d_n, d_n)$. The claim (a) is proved by induction over m:

   - $Q(d_n, d_{n+1})$ by our construction.
   - If $\mathcal{M} \vDash Q(d_n, d_{n+m})$ is proved, we notice that $\mathcal{M} \vDash Q(d_{n+m}, d_{n+m+1})$ by the construction. Since $\mathcal{M} \vDash \varphi$, we have also that

     $$\mathcal{M} \vDash \forall x.\forall y.\forall z.(Q(x, y) \wedge Q(y, z) \Rightarrow Q(x, z))$$

     and thus

   (b) $\mathcal{M} \vDash Q(d_n, d_{n+m}) \wedge Q(d_{n+m}, d_{n+m+1}) \Rightarrow Q(d_n, d_{n+m+1})$, by Exercise 8.3.3.

     The premise in (b) is true by our construction and the inductive hypothesis, and therefore $\mathcal{M} \vDash Q(d_n, d_{n+m+1})$.

     This completes the proof of (a), and therefore we have found an infinite subset in D.

2. Consider a model $\mathcal{M}$ with the domain $\mathbb{N}$ and π_{pred} such that $\pi_{\text{pred}}(Q)(a, b) = \top$ iff $a < b$. Then

   - $\mathcal{M} \models \forall x.\neg Q(x, x)$, because $\neg a < a$ holds for any a.
   - $\mathcal{M} \models \forall x \forall y.\forall z.(Q(x, y) \wedge Q(y, z) \Rightarrow Q(x, z))$, because '$<$' is a transitive relation in $\mathbb{N}$.
   - $\mathcal{M} \models \forall x.\exists y.Q(x, y)$, because for any a we have $\mathcal{M} \models \exists y.Q(a, y)$, and the latter holds because we can take, say, $y = a + 1$.

EXAMPLE 8.18. Find a formula with equality which holds in a model iff

1. the domain is one-element;

2. the domain is more than n-element;

3. the domain is n-element for some finite n.

Solution

1. Consider the formula $\varphi_1 : \forall x.\forall y.(x = y)$.

   We have
   $$\mathcal{M} \models \varphi_1 \text{ iff for any } a \in D, \ \mathcal{M} \models \forall y.(a = y)$$

   iff for any $a, b \in D$, $\mathcal{M} \models a = b$. The latter means that all elements of the domain coincide, i.e. that the domain is one-element.

2. We have to say that there exist at least $(n+1)$ distinct elements in the domain. Consider the formula
   $$\psi_{n+1} : \exists x_1.\exists x_2.\cdots.\exists x_{n+1}.\left(\bigwedge_{i \neq j} \neg(x_i = x_j) \right)$$

   In fact, $\mathcal{M} \models \psi_{n+1}$ iff there exist $d_1, \ldots, d_{n+1} \in D$ such that $d_i \neq d_j$ whenever $i \neq j$, i.e. all $d_1, \ldots, d_{n+1}$ are different.

3. Let φ_n be the formula
   $$\exists x_1.\cdots.\exists x_n.\left[\left(\bigwedge_{i \neq j} \neg(x_i = x_j) \right) \wedge \forall y.\left(\bigvee_{i=1}^{n} (y = x_i) \right) \right]$$

   Then $\mathcal{M} \models \varphi_n$ iff there exist $d_1, \ldots, d_n \in D$ such that
   $$\mathcal{M} \models \bigwedge_{i \neq j} \neg(d_i = d_j) \wedge \forall y.\left(\bigvee_{i=1}^{n} (y = d_i) \right)$$

The first conjunct says that all the d_i are distinct, and the second holds iff for any $d \in D$

$$\mathcal{M} \vDash (d = d_1 \vee \cdots \vee d = d_n)$$

i.e. iff every $d \in D$ is among $d_1, \ldots, d_n$.

Thus $\mathcal{M} \vDash \varphi_n$ iff $D = \{d_1, \ldots, d_n\}$ for some $d_1, \ldots, d_n$.

EXAMPLE 8.19.

1. Show that the following formula is false in any two-element model, but true in some three-element model:

$$\exists x. \exists y. \exists z. (P(x) \wedge Q(x) \wedge P(y) \wedge \neg Q(y) \wedge \neg P(z))$$

2. Find a formula without equality which is false in some five-element model, but true in any model of less number of elements.

Solution

1.

$$\mathcal{M} \vDash \exists x. \exists y. \exists z. (P(x) \wedge Q(x) \wedge P(y) \wedge \neg Q(y) \wedge \neg P(z))$$

iff for some $d_1, d_2, d_3 \in D$

$$\mathcal{M} \vDash P(d_1) \wedge Q(d_1) \wedge P(d_2) \wedge \neg Q(d_2) \wedge \neg P(d_3)$$

Then

$$
\begin{array}{lll}
d_1 \neq d_3 & \text{since} & \mathcal{M} \vDash P(d_1) \wedge \neg P(d_3) \\
d_1 \neq d_2 & \text{since} & \mathcal{M} \vDash Q(d_1) \wedge \neg Q(d_2) \\
d_2 \neq d_3 & \text{since} & \mathcal{M} \vDash P(d_2) \wedge \neg P(d_3)
\end{array}
$$

Thus the formula cannot be true in a two-element model.

On the other hand, it has a three-element model. That is, we can take $\mathcal{M}_0$ with the domains $\{d_1, d_2, d_3\}$ such that:

$\pi_{\text{pred}}(P)(d) = \top$ iff $d = d_1$ or $d = d_2$;

$\pi_{\text{pred}}(Q)(d) = \top$ iff $d = d_1$.

Then obviously

$$\mathcal{M}_0 \vDash P(d_1) \wedge Q(d_1) \wedge P(d_2) \wedge \neg Q(d_2) \wedge \neg P(d_3)$$

and thus the formula is true.

2. The idea is the same. We can write a formula saying that a model contains at least five different elements, and then take its negation. So let

$$\varphi = \exists x_1.\exists x_2.\exists x_3.\exists x_4.\exists x_5.(P(x_1) \wedge Q(x_1) \wedge R(x_1) \wedge$$
$$\neg P(x_2) \wedge Q(x_2) \wedge R(x_2) \wedge P(x_3) \wedge \neg Q(x_3) \wedge R(x_3) \wedge$$
$$\neg P(x_4) \wedge \neg Q(x_4) \wedge R(x_4) \wedge \neg R(x_5))$$

Similarly to (a) we have:

$\mathcal{M} \vDash \varphi$ only if D has at least five elements. Now take the formula $\neg \varphi$. Then $\mathcal{M} \vDash \neg \varphi$ if $card\ D < 5$ ('$card\ D$' means 'the number of elements in D'). On the other hand, $\neg \varphi$ is false (i.e. φ is true) in some five-element model. That is, let $D = \{d_1, d_2, d_3, d_4, d_5\}$

$$\pi_{\text{pred}}(P)(d) = \top \text{ iff } d = d_1 \text{ or } d = d_3; \pi_{\text{pred}}(Q)(d) = \top$$
$$\text{iff } d = d_1 \text{ or } d = d_2; \pi_{\text{pred}}(R)(d) = \top \text{ iff } d \neq d_5$$

and consider a model $\mathcal{M}_0$ with these D, π_{pred}.

Then

$$\mathcal{M}_0 \vDash P(d_1) \wedge Q(d_1) \wedge R(d_1) \wedge \neg P(d_2) \wedge Q(d_2) \wedge R(d_2) \wedge$$
$$P(d_3) \wedge \neg Q(d_3) \wedge R(d_3) \wedge \neg P(d_4) \wedge \neg Q(d_4) \wedge R(d_4) \wedge \neg R(d_5)$$

Hence $\mathcal{M}_0 \vDash \varphi$.

EXAMPLE 8.20. Let $\varphi(x_1, \ldots, x_n)$ be a quantifier-free formula in a language without functional symbols and constants. Prove that if $\forall x_1. \ldots. \forall x_n. \varphi(x_1, \ldots, x_n)$ holds in any n-element model, then it holds in any model.

Solution
Assume that $\forall x_1. \cdots. \forall x_n. \varphi(x_1, \ldots, x_n)$ holds in any n-element model. Consider an arbitrary model $\mathcal{M}$, such that $card\ \mathcal{M} \neq n$, and show that $\mathcal{M} \vDash \forall x_1. \cdots. \forall x_n. \varphi(x_1, \ldots, x_n)$ as well. Then two cases are possible, (1) and (2) below.

1. $card\ \mathcal{M} < n$. Let $D = \{a_1, \ldots, a_m\}$ ($m < n$) be the domain of $\mathcal{M}$. Then we can put $(n - m)$ new elements into D, in such a way that our formula would keep its truth value. So we introduce new elements $b_1, \ldots, b_{n-m}$ and make them behave in the same way as a_1, say. That is, we do the following:

   - Take $D' = \{a_1, \ldots, a_m, b_1, \ldots, b_{m-n}\}$.
   - Define the mapping $c \mapsto c^0$ from D' to D sending every b_j to a_1 and every a_i to itself.
   - If $\pi_{\text{pred}}(P)$ is an interpretation of a k-place predicate symbol P in $\mathcal{M}$, we define its new interpretation $\pi'_{\text{pred}}(P)$:

(a1) $\pi'_{\text{pred}}(P)(c_1, \ldots, c_k) = \pi_{\text{pred}}(P)(c_1^0, \ldots c_k^0)$.

Now let $\mathcal{M}'$ be the model based on D', π'_{pred}. Then for any $c_1, \ldots, c_s \in D'$, and for any quantifier-free formula $\psi(x_1, \ldots, x_s)$, we have

(a2) $\mathcal{M}' \vDash \psi(c_1, \ldots, c_s)$ iff $\mathcal{M} \vDash \psi(c_1^0, \ldots, c_s^0)$.

This is proved by induction on ψ. The base is given by (a1) because

$$\mathcal{M}' \vDash P(c_1, \ldots, c_k) \text{ iff } \pi'_{\text{pred}}(P)(c_1, \ldots, c_k) = \top \text{ iff}$$
$$\pi_{\text{pred}}(P)(c_1^0, \ldots, c_k^0) = \top \text{ iff } \mathcal{M} \vDash P(c_1^0, \ldots, c_k^0)$$

Other cases are all alike, so we consider only $\psi = \psi_1 \vee \psi_2$:

$$\mathcal{M}' \vDash \psi_1(c_1, \ldots, c_k) \vee \psi_2(c_1, \ldots, c_k)$$
$$\text{iff } \mathcal{M}' \vDash \psi_1(c_1, \ldots, c_k) \text{ or } \mathcal{M}' \vDash \psi_2(c_1, \ldots, c_k)$$
$$\text{iff } \mathcal{M} \vDash \psi_1(c_1^0, \ldots, c_k^0) \text{ or } \mathcal{M} \vDash \psi_2(c_1^0, \ldots, c_k^0)$$
$$\text{iff } \mathcal{M} \vDash \psi_1(c_1^0, \ldots, c_k^0) \vee \psi_2(c_1^0, \ldots, c_k^0)$$

From (a2) we obtain

$$\mathcal{M} \vDash \forall x_1 . \cdots . \forall x_n . \varphi(x_1, \ldots, x_n)$$

iff for any $c_1, \ldots, c_n \in D$, $\mathcal{M}' \vDash \varphi(c_1, \ldots, c_n)$ (since $c_i^0 = c_i$).

But the latter holds because $\mathcal{M}' \vDash \forall x_1 . \cdots . \forall x_n . \varphi(x_1, \ldots, x_n)$ by our assumption.

Therefore $\mathcal{M} \vDash \forall x_1 . \cdots . \forall x_n . \varphi(x_1, \ldots, x_n)$.

2. *card* $\mathcal{M} > n$. Let D again be the domain of $\mathcal{M}$, π_{pred} be the interpretation function. To show that $\mathcal{M} \vDash \forall x_1 . \cdots . \forall x_n . \varphi(x_1, \ldots, x_n)$ we have to consider arbitrary $d_1, \ldots, d_n \in D$ and show

(b1) $\mathcal{M} \vDash \varphi(d_1, \ldots, d_n)$.

We take these $d_1, \ldots, d_n$ and restrict our $\mathcal{M}$ to the new domain $D' = \{d_1, \ldots, d_n\}$. More precisely, we define

(b2) $\pi'_{\text{pred}}(P)(c_1, \ldots, c_k) = \pi_{\text{pred}}(P)(c_1, \ldots, c_k)$ (for any $c_1, \ldots, c_k \in D'$). Let $\mathcal{M}'$ be the model formed by D', π'_{pred}. Take any quantifier-free $\psi(x_1, \ldots, x_s)$. Then the following holds:

(b3) for any $c_1, \ldots, c_s \in D'$, $\mathcal{M}' \vDash \psi(c_1, \ldots, c_s)$ iff $\mathcal{M} \vDash \psi(c_1, \ldots, c_s)$.

This is proved by induction on ψ similarly to (a2), with (b2) as a starting point.

Now $\mathcal{M}' \vDash \forall x_1 . \cdots . \forall x_n . \varphi(x_1, \ldots, x_n)$ by (1) because *card* $\mathcal{M}' \leq n$ (note that some of the $d_1, \ldots, d_n$ may be identical).

Hence $\mathcal{M}' \vDash \varphi(d_1, \ldots, d_n)$ and thus $\mathcal{M} \vDash \varphi(d_1, \ldots, d_n)$ by (b3). That is, we have proved (b1).

CHAPTER 9

Forward and backward predicate rules

Let us summarize our knowledge so far. In propositional logic we can use backward rules to answer the question

$$\text{data} \quad \vdash \quad \text{query}$$

i.e. does the query follow logically from the data? We have seen three techniques for solving this problem. In Chapter 1, we used an automatable method based on constructing a truth table for an implication from the data to the query, and checking that the implication was a tautology. In Chapter 3, we presented the 'natural deduction' forward reasoning rules, which require that one make guesses when reasoning, and are hence not easily automatable. These forward rules were then developed into the backward rules for the propositional logic, in Chapter 4.

The truth table method always gives us an answer. We also know how many steps we need to get the answer. The backward method may loop but is in principle as mechanical as the truth table method. The forward rules method requires ingenuity and one is not guaranteed to find an answer. The following basic notions are shared by all three methods:

- Consistency of a set of formulae (same as satisfiability), meaning all formulae in the set can be made true in a single interpretation.

- Tautology (or logical theorem), meaning a formula which is always true.

These notions carry over to the predicate logic of the previous chapter. As we stated there, all the propositional rules of reasoning are valid in predicate logic, since predicate logic extends propositional logic with richer means of expression. The basis of this greater expressiveness is the use of quantifiers, for which we require additional reasoning rules. In the previous chapter we encountered some quantifier rules, mainly having to do with pulling quantifiers out of a formula. This chapter will introduce further quantifier reasoning rules, so that we are able to get an answer to a question from data, this time expressing both the data and the query in predicate logic:

$$\text{predicate data} \quad \vdash \quad \text{predicate query}$$

This will require a combination of the quantifier rules, together with the rules at the end of Chapter 4.

1   Reasoning with variables

Our first step is to rewrite the data and query in a ready to compute form. We have to do the translation of $A \lor B$ as $(A \Rightarrow \bot) \Rightarrow B$, and $\neg A$ as $A \Rightarrow \bot$ as we did for the propositional case. We can also translate $\exists x.\ A(x)$ as $\neg \forall x.\ \neg A(x)$ but still the presence of quantifiers everywhere in the formula of the database is not good enough for ease of computation. Our first task is to stylize all data and queries into the prenex normal form, by putting all quantifiers at the front:

$$(\forall x. \exists y. \forall z. \ldots)[\text{matrix}]$$

with no quantifiers in the matrix. Recall that the string of quantifiers is called the prefix. In the previous chapter we looked at rules which allow us to rewrite any formula into the prenex normal form, with all quantifiers at the front. We can use the propositional rewrite rules to write the quantifier-free matrix in a form ready for computation, i.e. in the form of $\mathcal{B}$-clauses (with atomic heads etc.) Thus for example we can have a database such as

1. $\forall x. \exists y.\ [A(x,\ y) \Rightarrow Q(x,\ x)]$

2. $A(a,\ a)$

with a query of $[\exists z.\ A(z,\ a)] \Rightarrow Q(a,\ a)$. The above is the best formulation we can give using our rewrite rules. All quantifiers are at the front, and the quantifier-free matrix is rewritten in $\mathcal{B}$-clausal form with atomic heads. For computing purposes this is not enough. The existential quantifiers present in the prefix are a big nuisance. We would like to be able to write the data with *universal* quantifiers only. Now we know that $\exists y.\ \varphi(y) \Leftrightarrow \neg \forall y.\ \neg \varphi(y)$, so we might replace each existential quantifier in the prefix by a negated universal quantifier. In the case of sentence 1 above we could write

$\forall x.\ \neg \forall y.\ \neg [A(x,\ y) \Rightarrow Q(x,\ x)]$

This does not solve the problem because we now have a negation stuck in the middle of the quantifier prefix. We want to have a *universal prenex* form of

$$(\forall x. \forall y. \forall z. \ldots)[\text{matrix}]$$

We shall achieve this by using *Skolem functions*, which we shall cover later in this chapter.

Let us assume for a moment that we can always rewrite data in the above universal prenex form. The big advantage, as far as computation is concerned, is that theoretically it allows us to reduce the problem of whether a query succeeds from some data from predicate logic into propositional logic. Here is an example of how it is done, which should give an intuitive notion of what happens.

EXAMPLE 9.1.   From the items of data:

1. A person is happy if he loves someone

2. Carol loves David

we must show that the query 'Carol is happy' follows. We translate the English sentences into predicate logic, using the predicates loves(x,y) for x loves y and happy(x) for x is happy. The data becomes:

1. ∀x. [[∃y. loves(x, y)] ⇒ happy(x)]

2. loves(Carol, David)

and we must show the sentence happy(Carol). To begin computation we have to rewrite, and first we push the quantifiers outside. The first sentence in the data becomes

∀x.∀y. [loves(x, y) ⇒ happy(x)]

by applying the quantifier rule

$$\forall x.[\varphi(x) \Rightarrow \gamma] \equiv [\exists x.\varphi(x)] \Rightarrow \gamma$$

from Figure 8.1 to move the ∃y from the antecedent to become ∀y outside the implication, since y does not appear in happy(x). We are fortunate that we now have this sentence in the universal prenex form, and we do not need to concern ourselves with Skolem functions for now. The second sentence in the data contains no quantifiers, and is thus already in the universal prenex form, as is the conclusion we wish to prove. The data is thus

1. ∀x.∀y. [loves(x, y) ⇒ happy(x)]

2. loves(Carol, David)

and we must show the sentence happy(Carol).

The reduction of this predicate formula to the propositional case is done by substituting all the possible constant names that we have, for the universally quantified variables in the first formula in the data.

Thus since the data contains only universal quantifiers

$$\forall x.\forall y.[\text{matrix}]$$

we write down all the possible combinations $\theta_1, \ldots, \theta_n$ of names in the data and replace the universally quantified sentence with

$$[\text{matrix}]\theta_1 \wedge \cdots \wedge [\text{matrix}]\theta_n$$

where θ_i is a variable assignment such as $[x \mapsto \text{David}, y \mapsto \text{Carol}]$. Our first data sentence therefore is replaced by n variable-free sentences—in this case, since there are just two names in the example, there are four different ways to assign the names to the two variables; hence $n = 4$:

		$x \mapsto$	$y \mapsto$	
	1	Carol	Carol	loves(Carol, Carol) $\Rightarrow$ happy(Carol)
1.	2	Carol	David	loves(Carol, David) $\Rightarrow$ happy(Carol)
	3	David	Carol	loves(David, Carol) $\Rightarrow$ happy(David)
	4	David	David	loves(David, David) $\Rightarrow$ happy(David)

2. loves(Carol, David)

The question then is whether we can use propositional rules, especially backward ones, to get happy(Carol). Clearly in this case we can, by matching the query with the head of implication 1.2, and asking for loves(Carol, David) which succeeds.

The process of replacing variables by constants, as seen in the preceding example, and by other variables, is known as *substitution*. In Definition 8.9, variable assignments were defined as mappings from $\mathcal{L}_v$ to $\mathcal{D}$. Substitutions are a little more general than that, being *syntactic* rather than semantic operations.

DEFINITION 9.2 (Substitution).   A *substitution* is a finite set of pairs (*bindings*) of the form v/t where v is a variable and t is a term. A typical substitution is thus

$$\sigma = \{v_1/t_1, \ldots, v_n/t_n\}$$

We also write $\sigma(v_i) = t_i$, $i = 1, \ldots, n$.

The *application* of a substitution σ to a formula A is the simultaneous replacement of every free occurrence of each v_i in σ by t_i, denoted $A\sigma$ and known as a *substitution instance*.

In order for the substitution to be done correctly, we must assume that the free variables in the terms t_i are different from the bound variables of the formula A, otherwise the bound variables of A need to be renamed.

There are a number of properties of substitutions which we shall either require or prefer. A required property is that the substitution be *functional*. This means that the variables v_i in the substitution are distinct. Thus $\sigma_1 = \{x/a, y/b, x/c\}$ is not functional, whereas $\sigma_2 = \{x/a, y/b, z/c\}$ is. A preferred property is that of *idempotency*, where for any formula A, we have $A\sigma = (A\sigma)\sigma$. For this to be the case, none of the variables v_i may appear in any of the terms t_j, unless $v_i \mapsto v_i$. Thus $\sigma_1 = \{x/a, y/b\}$ is idempotent, whereas $\sigma_2 = \{x/a, y/x\}$ is not.

Substitutions may be joined together, by means of a composition operator $\circ$, defined as follows. Given two substitutions, both functional and idempotent,

$$\sigma_1 = \{u_1/s_1, \ldots, u_m/s_m\}$$
$$\sigma_2 = \{v_1/t_1, \ldots, v_n/t_n\}$$

the composition of σ_1 and σ_2, written $\sigma_1 \circ \sigma_2$, is given by

$$\sigma_1 \circ \sigma_2 = \{u_1/s_1\sigma_2, \ldots, u_m/s_m\sigma_2\} \cup \{v_j/t_j \mid v_j/t_j \in \sigma_2$$
$$\text{and } v_j \notin \{u_1, \ldots, u_m\}\}$$

Composition possesses the following properties:

1. $\sigma_1 \circ \sigma_2$ is functional

2. $A(\sigma_1 \circ \sigma_2) = (A\sigma_1)\sigma_2$ for any formula A

3. $(\sigma_1 \circ \sigma_2) \circ \sigma_3 = \sigma_1 \circ (\sigma_2 \circ \sigma_3)$.

Because of the asymmetric definition of $\circ$, note, however, that in general $\sigma_1 \circ \sigma_2 \neq \sigma_2 \circ \sigma_1$, i.e. $\circ$ is not commutative.

1.1 Introduction to unification

Returning to the problem of computing from predicate sentences, the next step is to ask: if we have several clauses in the universal prenex form, each with a number of universally quantified variables, and many constants in the language, do we have to write a possibly (or practically) infinite list of clauses just to perform the computation?

The answer is no. Any proof that a query follows from some data must contain a finite number of inferences, or applications of rules, so that in any proof, we can only use a finite number of the possibly infinite number of substitutions of constants for variables. In fact, we need only substitute exactly those constants which we will need to carry out the proof. To do this we do not begin by making substitutions, but retain the universal prenex form of the clauses until the moment during the proof when we discover that we need to use the clause. It is only at this stage that we generate an instance of the clause with constants substituted for the variables.

This process is best illustrated by an example, so let us check again whether Carol is happy. Our data is

1. `loves(x, y) ⇒ happy(x)`

2. `loves(Carol, David)`

We have chosen to omit the universal quantifiers from the first clause, since all variables appearing in the data clauses must be universally quantified. There is an implicit agreement that any possible combination of constants can be substituted for the variables x and y in the clause. To demonstrate that happy(Carol) follows from the data, we again try to match the query against the head of some rule in the data. There is only one head which could match the query, namely happy(x), provided that the variable x was substituted for by Carol. We make that substitution, but leave the choice of the substitution for y until later. The new clause is added to the data

> `loves(Carol, y) ⇒ happy(Carol)`

and is used as before, generating a subquery `loves(Carol, y)` which, we must demonstrate, follows from the extended data. This new query is different from all the others we have previously seen, in that it contains a variable, y. Without worrying about the meaning of this variable for the moment, let us continue with the proof. We need to find a head in the data which will match `loves(Carol, y)`. Fortunately such a head exists, `loves(Carol, David)`, provided we can make a substitution of David for y. Because we left the choice of a substitution for y open when we generated the new clause `loves(Carol, y) ⇒ happy(Carol)`, we may now generate a further clause

> `loves(Carol, David) ⇒ happy(Carol)`

as a retrospective justification of our choice to substitute David for y now. Our proof is complete, so we have demonstrated happy(Carol) by only making the substitution $[x \mapsto \text{Carol}, y \mapsto \text{David}]$.

The process of generating the substitutions $[x \mapsto \text{Carol}]$ and $[y \mapsto \text{David}]$ is known as *unification*, because when we have two sentences such as happy(Carol) and happy(x), we wish to blend (or unify) the two sentences together, so that they may be regarded as identical. Once the two sentences are unified, we may use the propositional reasoning rules on them, so that being able to unify sentences is important. Unification is at the heart of almost all the reasoning methods for first-order logic.

Although the two examples of unification in the illustration above involved just making one variable substitution in one sentence to make it identical to the other, ground, sentence, there is much more to unification. Suppose that we have the two sentences

> `loves(x, Brenda)`   and   `loves(brother-of(y), y)`.

By means of unification, we can make substitutions in these sentences so that they turn into a single unified sentence. Informally, unification proceeds as follows. The only constant we have is `Brenda`, which is the second argument to `loves` in the first sentence. If the two sentences are to be unified, the second argument to `loves` in the second sentence must become equal to `Brenda`; hence we can generate the substitution [y ↦ `Brenda`]. Now we substitute throughout the two sentences for y, generating:

> `loves(x, Brenda)` and `loves(brother-of(Brenda), Brenda)`.

Now we have unified the second arguments of `loves`, we move to the first arguments. In the first sentence the first argument is a variable, x, and in the second sentence it is the term `brother-of(Brenda)`. We must therefore generate the substitution [x ↦ `brother-of(Brenda)`] and replace x throughout the sentences, leaving us with

> `loves(brother-of(Brenda), Brenda)` and
> `loves(brother-of(Brenda), Brenda)`.

By means of the combined substitution [x ↦ `brother-of(Brenda)`, y ↦ `Brenda`], we have unified the two sentences into a single unified sentence.

DEFINITION 9.3 (Unifiers). A substitution σ is a *unifier* of two atomic sentences A and B iff $A\sigma = B\sigma$. A substitution σ is a *most general unifier* of two atomic sentences A and B iff it is a unifier of A and B, and for any other unifier σ' of A and B, there is a substitution θ such that $\sigma' = \sigma \circ \theta$.

1.2 A unification algorithm

The algorithm that we shall give is just one of many for computing unifiers. The idea is to work through the syntactic construction of two atomic sentences to see where they differ, and whether the differences can be overcome by making substitutions for the variables. Should a difference be found which cannot be overcome by a set of variable substitutions, then the sentences are not unifiable, otherwise a set of variable substitutions (the most general unifier) is output.

The unification algorithm works on a stack S of pairs of terms, and goes through one cycle for each pair on the stack. A unifier θ is used to store the substitutions as they arise. We present the algorithm in an informal pseudo-code in Figure 9.1. We assume that the algorithm is to work on two atomic sentences A_1 and A_2. The algorithm begins by placing the pairs of corresponding terms from A_1 and A_2 onto the stack S. The unifier θ is initialized to the empty substitution.

The algorithm proceeds to cycle through the following steps for each pair on the stack, until a failure point is reached, or the stack becomes empty: (i) the top pair of terms is popped from S, and the latest version of θ is applied to them, yielding terms e_1 and e_2; (ii) the terms are compared and if there is no way of matching

begin
  S := empty stack
  put all the term pairs from A_1 and A_2 on S
  θ := {}
  while S is not empty
    pop the term pair $\langle s_1, s_2 \rangle$ from S
    $e_1 = s_1\theta;\ e_2 = s_2\theta$
    if e_1 and e_2 are both constants and $e_1 \neq e_2$
      then fail
    else if e_1 and e_2 are both functions and e_1 and e_2 have different functors
      then fail
    else if either e_1 or e_2 is a function and the other is a constant
      then fail
    else if e_1 and e_2 are both functions and e_1 and e_2 have the same functor
      then push pairs of their corresponding arguments onto S
    else if e_1 and e_2 are both variables
      then θ := $\theta \circ \{e_1/e_2\}$
    else if either e_1 or e_2 is a variable which occurs strictly within the other
      then fail
    else if e_1 is a variable
      then θ := $\theta \circ \{e_1/e_2\}$
    else if e_2 is a variable
      then θ := $\theta \circ \{e_2/e_1\}$
  end while
  return θ
end

Figure 9.1. The unification algorithm

them, failure is generated, otherwise an appropriate binding is added to θ. If e_1 and e_2 are functional terms which might unify, their term pairs are added onto the stack for further comparison.

EXAMPLE 9.4.   We will unify the atomic sentences $p(x,f(x),a)$ and $p(y, f(g(z),z))$. The initial stack is

x, y
f(x), f(g(z))
a, z

The stack is not empty, so we pop the top pair off the stack, and apply θ (currently empty) to the pair, getting x and y. The terms are compared, and since both are variables, we add {x/y} to θ. The bottom of the cycle is reached, so we again see that the stack is not empty, and pop the top pair of terms off the stack, and apply θ. This time θ is not empty, so applying it to the top pair, $f(x)$ and $f(g(z))$, yields $f(y)$ and $f(g(z))$. These terms can now be compared, and as they are functional terms with the same functor (f), the term pair y and $g(z)$ are pushed onto the stack:

y, g(z)
a, z

Going back to the beginning of the cycle, we pop the top pair of terms off the stack, and apply θ, which has no effect, so we are left with comparing y and $g(z)$. Since y is a variable and $g(z)$ is not, the binding {y/g(z)} is added to θ. In the final run through the cycle, the pair of terms a and z are popped off the stack, θ is applied, and the terms compared. Since z is a variable and a is not, the binding {z/a} is added to θ. The stack is now empty, and the algorithm ends, returning the composition θ = {x/y} ∘ {y/g(z)} ∘ {z/a}, which is indeed the following simultaneous substitution {x/g(a), y/g(a), z/a}.

EXERCISE 9.5.   For each of the following pairs of atomic sentences, decide whether or not they unify, and if the latter, what the most general unifier is.

1. $p(a,f(z))$ and $p(x,f(b))$

2. $q(f(g(x)))$ and $r(c)$

3. $r(x,x,f(b))$ and $r(g(f(b)),g(y),y)$

4. $p(a,f(g(x)))$ and $p(y,g(z))$

5. $q(b,x)$ and $q(y,f(x))$

6. $q(f(a,x))$ and $q(f(y,f(z)))$

1.3   The meaning of variables in clauses

When we were demonstrating by means of unification that Carol was happy, we generated a subquery which contained a variable, loves(Carol, y). Although we did not concern ourselves with y's nature then, we should do so now. Is y a universal or existential variable in loves(Carol, y)? It was generated from the clause

loves(Carol, y)⇒happy(Carol)

which is in the data as a universal prenex form clause. Hence there is an implicit universal quantifier on y:

(9.1) ∀y. [loves(Carol, y) ⇒ happy(Carol)]

so one might assume that y is a universally quantified variable in the query loves (Carol, y). However, one would be wrong. The clause (9.1) can be rewritten via the quantifier equivalences to

(9.2) [∃y. loves(Carol, y)] ⇒ happy(Carol)

so that when the query happy(Carol) is asked, we must demonstrate that ∃y. loves(Carol, y) holds. From this we can see that the variables in the query are, in fact, *existentially* quantified.

The general form of the data and the query, and the variables they contain, is therefore:

Universal sentences (query):   Existential sentence (query):
A(x) ⇒ B(x)
                                                    C(y)
B(x) ⇒ C(x)

The convention is that the data clauses and query are regarded as having the following quantification:

∀x. [A(x) ⇒ B(x)]
                                                    ∃y. C(y)
∀x. [B(x) ⇒ C(x)]

Remember that because the x is quantified for each clause, the x in A(x) ⇒ B(x) is not the same as the x in B(x) ⇒ C(x).

The distinction becomes more central when we add clauses to the database from the goal. Consider the following example:

Universal sentence (data)
$A(x) \Rightarrow B(x)$
$B(x) \Rightarrow C(x)$
Existential sentence (query)
$A(y) \Rightarrow C(y)$.

Since the query is an implication, we need to add $A(y)$ to the database and ask the query $C(y)$. Our database is now

1. $A(x) \Rightarrow B(x)$

2. $B(x) \Rightarrow C(x)$

3. $A(y)$

and the query is $C(y)$.

The original logical meaning was whether

$$\models \forall x.(A(x) \Rightarrow B(x)) \land \forall x.(B(x) \Rightarrow C(x)) \Rightarrow \exists y.(A(y) \Rightarrow C(y))$$

The same meaning must be retained after we put $A(y)$ into the database.

To see what we have to do let us pull $\exists y$ up front. We get

$$\models \exists y.[\forall x.(A(x) \Rightarrow B(x)) \land \forall x.(B(x) \Rightarrow C(x)) \Rightarrow (A(y) \Rightarrow C(y))]$$

which is equivalent to

$$\models \exists y.[\forall x.(A(x) \Rightarrow B(x)) \land \forall x.(B(x) \Rightarrow C(x)) \land A(y) \Rightarrow C(y)]$$

The last formula is the conjunction of the data implying ($\Rightarrow$) the goal.

We thus need to agree on two types of variables: universal variables (like the variable x) and existential variables (like the variable y). A database may have both kinds of variables. The goal has only existential variables. Assuming that Data $= \{A_1, \ldots, A_n\}$ then success in computation of Data $\vdash$? Goal means: $\models$ ($\exists$ existential variables) $[\bigwedge_i (\forall$ universal variables$) A_i \Rightarrow$ Goal $]$.

What do we do then when we want to show a query of the form $\forall z. Q(z)$, in which we must show that $Q(z)$ follows from the data for all possible values of z? The way to do this is to choose a new constant say, k, which has not been mentioned anywhere before, in either the data or the query, and try to show that $Q(k)$ follows from the data. If we succeed, then we have shown that

$$\frac{\mathcal{P}}{Q(k)}$$

where $\mathcal{P}$ represents the data, is logically valid. This means that all models for $\mathcal{P}$ are models for $Q(k)$. Now since k is not mentioned anywhere in $\mathcal{P}$, any model for $\mathcal{P}$ is a model for $Q(k)$, no matter what element in the domain k is mapped to. Hence any model for $\mathcal{P}$ is a model for $Q(k)$ for all values of k; thus any model for $\mathcal{P}$ is a model for $\forall z. Q(z)$. This gives us

$$\frac{\mathcal{P}}{\forall z.\, Q(z)}$$

as required. Therefore we have a new forward rule known as *universal generalization*:

If $\dfrac{\mathcal{P}}{Q(k)}$ and k is not mentioned in $\mathcal{P}$, then $\dfrac{\mathcal{P}}{\forall z.\, Q(z)}$

See the soundness theorem, 8.3.6.

1.4   Skolemization

We will now deal with *Skolem functions*. Earlier in this chapter we said that we would need such functions to eliminate existential quantifiers from clauses such as

$$\forall x.\, \exists y.\, [A(x,\, y) \Rightarrow Q(x,\, x)]$$

so as to present all clauses in the universal prenex form. Consider the formula $\phi = \forall x.\exists y.R(x,y)$. In every model in which this formula is true, for every name a, there must exist a y such that R(a,y) is true. Expanded out, this is

$$[\exists y.\, R(a_1,y)] \wedge [\exists y.\, R(a_2,y)] \wedge \, \cdots$$

Of course the y promised by $[\exists y.\, R(a_i, y)]$ depends on a_i. Let $f(a_i)$ be a function to choose such a y. The function f is known as a Skolem choice function; for each x it chooses $y = f(x)$ such that R(x,y) holds.

We can thus write $\varphi = \forall x.\, R(x,f(x))$. The relationship between φ and ϕ is that

1. $\varphi \Rightarrow \phi$ is a theorem of logic,

2. in any model in which ϕ is true, f can be chosen in such a way that φ is true.

The second property yields

For every formula ψ, $\dfrac{\phi}{\psi}$ succeeds if and only if $\dfrac{\varphi}{\psi}$ succeeds

We really should write $\varphi = \forall x.\, R(x, f_\phi(x))$, since the Skolem function is introduced especially for the formula ϕ. If we had a further formula θ to Skolemize, we would introduce a new Skolem function f_θ.

In practice, the predicate R will have an intended meaning and so the Skolem function f will also be endowed with a meaning. For example, ϕ might mean 'every man is married to some woman', i.e.

$$\phi = \forall x.\, [\mathtt{man}(x) \Rightarrow \exists y.\, (\mathtt{woman}(y) \wedge \mathtt{married}(x,\, y))]$$

If we pull the quantifiers to the front, we get

$$\phi = \forall x. \exists y. [\texttt{man(x)} \Rightarrow (\texttt{woman(y)} \wedge \texttt{married(x, y))}]$$

Taking the Skolem function f, we have

$$\varphi = \forall x. [\texttt{man(x)} \Rightarrow (\texttt{woman(f(x))} \wedge \texttt{married(x, f(x)))}]$$

We can read $\texttt{f(x)}$ as 'the first wife of x'. In fact there is nothing to stop us from using $\texttt{wife-of(x)}$ instead of $\texttt{f(x)}$:

$$\varphi = \forall x. [\texttt{man(x)} \Rightarrow (\texttt{woman(wife-of(x))} \wedge \texttt{married(x, wife-of(x)))}]$$

When we have an existential quantifier within the scope of more than one universal quantifier, the Skolem function takes all of the universally quantified variables as its arguments. So that to eliminate the existential quantifiers from ϕ where

$$\phi = \forall x. \forall y. \exists z. [\texttt{R(x, y)} \wedge \texttt{Q(z)}]$$

we do this by taking a function $g(x, y)$ to replace z, giving us

$$\varphi = \forall x. \forall y. [\texttt{R(x, y)} \wedge \texttt{Q(g(x, y))}]$$

This example shows that wholesale automatic Skolemization loses information present in the original formula. We can rewrite ϕ to be

$$\phi' = \forall x. \forall y. [\texttt{R(x, y)} \wedge \exists z. \texttt{Q(z)}]$$

since the z does not appear in $\texttt{R(x, y)}$. Similarly, we can remove $\texttt{Q(z)}$ from the scope of the $\forall x$ and $\forall y$ because neither x nor y appears in $\texttt{Q(z)}$. Hence

$$\phi'' = [\forall x. \forall y. \texttt{R(x, y)}] \wedge [\exists z. \texttt{Q(z)}]$$

We can now see that the existential variable does not depend on x or y at all, and if Skolemization were to take place on this rewritten version of ϕ, we could use a 0-place function, i.e. a constant h to replace the quantifier, yielding

$$\varphi'' = [\forall x. \forall y. \texttt{R(x, y)}] \wedge [\texttt{Q(h)}]$$

This second Skolem formula, φ'', contains the information that the formula is satisfiable in a model with only one element for which Q is true. The original Skolem formula, φ, did not. The information was lost when the original Skolemization took place. This is why we stated above that $\varphi \Rightarrow \phi$ is a theorem of logic, and not that $\varphi \Leftrightarrow \phi$ is a theorem of logic.

EXERCISE 9.6.

1. Skolemize this prenex normal form sentence:

$$\forall x. \exists y. \forall z. \forall u. \exists v. [R(x, z) \Rightarrow \neg Q(u, v)]$$

2. Where necessary, pull the quantifiers out of, and Skolemize, the following sentences:

   (a) $\forall x. [\exists y. A(x, y) \Rightarrow B(x)]$

   (b) $\neg[\forall x. A(x) \wedge \forall y. B(y)]$

   (c) $\exists x. \exists y. [A(x) \wedge \forall z. B(z, y)]$

   (d) $\forall x. \forall y. \exists z. \forall u. \forall v. \exists t. [A(x, y) \Rightarrow B(x, t) \wedge C(z)]$

The above discussion showed essentially how to eliminate existential quantifiers from a formula: put it in prenex normal form and then Skolemize.

Thus, given the query

$$\gamma \vdash ?\alpha$$

we can Skolemize γ into a formula $\gamma^\forall$ in universal normal form, i.e. $\gamma = \forall x_1. \cdots,$ $\forall x_n. \gamma_0$ where γ_0 is a formula without quantifiers, such that the following holds:

$$(*) \quad \gamma \vdash \alpha \text{ iff } \gamma^\forall \vdash \alpha$$

Our next question is what is the desired ready for computation form of the formula α?

We want to rewrite α into a formula $\alpha^\exists$ of the form $\alpha^\exists = \exists x_1. \cdots. \exists x_n. \alpha_0$, where α_0 is without quantifiers, such that for all wffs β we have

$$(**) \quad \beta \vdash \alpha \text{ iff } \beta \vdash \alpha^\exists$$

To do this, observe that

$$\beta \vdash \alpha \text{ iff } \neg \alpha \vdash \neg \beta$$

Skolemize $\neg \alpha$ into a formula $\alpha' = \forall x_1. \cdots. \forall x_n. \alpha_0'$.

Thus we have for all β,

$$\alpha' \vdash \neg \beta \text{ iff } \neg \alpha \vdash \neg \beta$$

and hence for all β

$$\beta \vdash \neg \alpha' \text{ iff } \beta \vdash \alpha$$

but $\neg \alpha' \equiv \exists x_1. \cdots. \exists x_n. \neg \alpha_0'$.

Hence let $\alpha^\exists = \neg \alpha'$ and this is the formula we are looking for.

EXAMPLE 9.7 (Preparing for computation). In Section 8.3 we shall define the notion of $\mathcal{B}$-computation, for checking whether $A \vdash ?B$, for arbitrary formulae of predicate logic A and B. The $\mathcal{B}$-computation procedure requires that A and B have the form of $\mathcal{B}$-clauses (Definition 8.3.1) and A is universally quantified and B is existentially quantified. We therefore need to know how to rewrite an arbitrary problem $A \vdash ? B$ into an equivalent problem $A^{*\forall} \vdash ? B^{*\exists}$ such that $A^{*\forall}$ is a universally quantified $\mathcal{B}$-clause and $B^{*\exists}$ is an existentially quantified $\mathcal{B}$-clause.

We already know how to do this, as follows:

1. Skolemize A into A' of the form $\forall x_1. \cdots . \forall x_n. A_0'$ where A_0' contains no quantifiers.

2. A_0' can be rewritten using propositional translation $*$ into A_0^* as in Definition 4.3.1.

   $A^{*\forall}$ can now be defined as $A^{*\forall} = \forall x_1. \cdots . \forall x_n. A_0^*$.

3. Find $B_1 = (\neg B)^{*\forall} = \forall y_1. \cdots . \forall y_m. B_0^*$ using steps (1) and (2) above.

   Let $B^{*\exists} = \neg B_1 = \exists y_1. \cdots . \exists y_m. \neg B_0^*$.

We have

$$A \vdash B \text{ iff } A^{*\forall} \vdash B^{*\exists}$$

Here is an example:

$$\forall x. \exists u. R(x, u) \vdash ? \exists u. \forall x. R(x, u)$$

becomes

$$\forall x. R(x, f(x)) \vdash ? \exists u. R(g(u), u)$$

where f and g are Skolem functions.

In comparison

$$\exists u. \forall x. R(x, u) \vdash ? \forall x. \exists u. R(x, u)$$

becomes

$$\forall x. R(x, c) \vdash ? \exists u. R(d, u)$$

where c, d are constants.

2   Reasoning forwards

We are now in a position to produce proofs in predicate logic that a conclusion follows from some assumptions (or equivalently, that a query succeeds from some data) using forward reasoning rules. We make use of all the forward reasoning rules for propositional logic, as presented in Chapter 3, as well as the quantifier equivalences of Figure 8.1 of the preceding chapter. The additional rules of reasoning that we have introduced in this chapter are:

- Universal instantiation ($\forall$ elimination)

$$\frac{\forall x.\ A(x)}{A(c)}$$

where c is a constant in the language.

- Universal generalization (∀ introduction)

  If $\dfrac{\mathcal{P}}{Q(c)}$ and c is not mentioned in $\mathcal{P}$, then $\dfrac{\mathcal{P}}{\forall z.\ Q(z)}$

- ∃ introduction

  $$\frac{A(t)}{\exists x.\ A(x)}\ ,\ \text{t a term of the language}$$

  where c is a constant in the language.

- Skolemization (∃ elimination)

  If $\dfrac{\mathcal{P}}{\exists x.\ A(x)}$ and k is not mentioned in $\mathcal{P}$, then $\dfrac{\mathcal{P}}{A(k)}$

  We annotate the constant k as being introduced as a Skolem constant and we do not allow the use of the (∀ introduction) rule to it.

We shall work with Skolemized sentences, so that there are no existentially quantified variables in the data. Recall that variables in the query are existentially quantified, however. The query is not to be Skolemized in the same way as the data. The universal generalization rule (∀I) gives a hint as to how we remove quantifiers from queries. The (∀I) states that if we can prove a sentence about an individual whose name does not appear in the data, then we can prove the same sentence about all individuals. This leads to the idea of using Skolem constants and functions in the query to represent *universally* quantified variables. This can easily be done by the Skolemization method we have already presented, but by applying it to a negated form of the query, and subsequently negating the Skolemized formula again. For example, suppose that we have the data ∀z. loves(Bethan,z) and we ask the query ∃x.∀y. loves(x,y). The data contains no existential quantifiers, and so is represented by the clause

1. loves(Bethan,z)

The query, on the other hand, contains both existential and universal quantifiers, and so must be Skolemized. As it is a query, we first negate it, to get ∀x.∃y. ¬loves(x,y), so that the universal quantifiers become existential, and vice versa. We can now Skolemize, getting ∀x. ¬loves(x,f(x)). This can then be negated again, to get ∃x. loves(x,f(x)), and thus we have a query in which the universally quantified variable has been replaced by a Skolem function. By convention, we can now omit the existential quantifier from the query, and understand that all variables in the query are existentially quantified. A simple unification between loves(Bethan,z) and loves(x,f(x)) yields the unifier {x/Bethan, z/f(x)} which is our answer.

EXAMPLE 9.8.   Using these rules, we shall attempt to show that the following argument is valid:

> Some logicians teach at Imperial College. Anyone who teaches at
> Imperial College lives in London. All logicians who live in London
> are good. All good logicians support logic programming. Therefore
> some good logicians support logic programming.

We must first translate the sentences above into logic, resulting in

1. ∃x.[logician(x) ∧ teaches-at(x,Imperial-College)]
2. ∀x.[teaches-at(x,Imperial-College) ⇒ lives-in-London(x)]
3. ∀x.[logician(x) ∧ lives-in-London (x) ⇒ good(x)]
4. ∀x.[logician(x) ∧ good(x) ⇒ support-LP(x)]

5. ∃x.[logician(x) ∧ good(x) ∧ support-LP(x)]

These logic sentences are in prenex normal form, but sentence 1 in the data and sentence 5 (the query) are not in universal prenex form. Only sentences in the data must be in universal prenex form, so sentence 1 must be Skolemized, introducing the Skolem constant **k**.

> 6.   logician(k) ∧ teaches-at(k,Imperial-College)

Now we may begin reasoning. We use universal instantiation for **k** in sentences 2, 3 and 4, which produces the following new sentences:

> 7.   teaches-at(k,Imperial-College) ⇒ lives-in-London(k)
> 8.   logician(k) ∧ lives-in-London (k) ⇒ good(k)
> 9.   logician(k) ∧ good(k) ⇒ support-LP(k)

Using the now familiar propositional forward rules we can reason from 6, 7, 8 and 9 that

> 10.   logician(k) ∧ good(k) ∧ support-LP(k)

Finally, by applying existential introduction to sentence 10 we reach

> 5.   ∃x. [logician(x) ∧ good(x) ∧ support-LP(x)]

EXAMPLE 9.9.   Here is another example of reasoning with forward rules. Is the following argument valid?

Everything pleasant is either illegal or immoral. Programming in Pascal is unpleasant. Therefore programming in Pascal is neither illegal nor immoral.

As for the good logicians above, we must translate the argument into logical form, giving us

> 1. ∀x. [pleasant(x) ⇒ illegal(x) ∨ immoral(x)]
> 2. ¬pleasant(Pascal)
> _____
> 3. ¬illegal(Pascal) ∧ ¬immoral(Pascal)

These sentences are already in universal prenex form, so we can start to compute straight away. Using universal instantiation for the constant Pascal in sentence 1 we get

> 4. pleasant(Pascal) ⇒ illegal(Pascal) ∨ immoral(Pascal)

By now you should have realized that the conclusion *does not* follow from the assumptions. One of the drawbacks of the forward reasoning rules method is that it does not indicate when the conclusion does not follow from the assumptions. To prove that the argument is not valid, we must provide a model to serve as a counterexample, i.e. a model which satisfies all the assumptions, but not the conclusion. In the propositional case, using truth tables, we could find a line in the truth table to serve as the counterexample. For the time being, we shall have to guess at a counterexample for invalid predicate arguments.

Consider the model given by $\mathcal{M} = \langle \mathcal{D}, \pi_{\text{cons}}, \pi_{\text{func}}, \pi_{\text{pred}} \rangle$:

- $\mathcal{D} = \{p\}$

- π_{cons}: {Pascal $\mapsto p$}

- π_{func}: $\varnothing$

- π_{pred}: {immoral $\mapsto \{p \mapsto \top\}$ }, all other predicates are assigned $\{p \mapsto \bot\}$ by π_{pred}.

We should check the assumptions against this model. Is it true in model $\mathcal{M}$ that

> 1. ∀x. [pleasant(x) ⇒ illegal(x) ∨ immoral(x)]

is satisfied? The answer is yes, since for $x = p$ (the only element in the domain) we get $\bot \Rightarrow \bot \vee \top$, which reduces to $\top$. The second assumption,

> 2. ¬pleasant(Pascal)

is also satisfied, since the constant Pascal maps to the domain element p, which is mapped to $\bot$ by π_p. This is then changed to $\top$ by the $\neg$ connective. Finally, since the assumptions are satisfied by $\mathcal{M}$, we must demonstrate that the conclusion is not satisfied by $\mathcal{M}$:

3. ¬illegal(Pascal) ∧ ¬immoral(Pascal)

Only immoral(Pascal) maps to ⊤ in *M*, so that sentence 3 reduces to ⊤∧⊥ which further reduces to ⊥. Hence *M* is indeed a counterexample to the above argument.

EXERCISE 9.10. Demonstrate that the following argument is valid:

> All interrupt commands are undesirable. Some control commands are interrupt commands. Therefore some control commands are undesirable.

EXAMPLE 9.11.   This example indicates a common misconception about the meaning of the universal quantifier. Suppose that we have to show that the following argument is valid:

> All the lecturers like every student taking course 140. No lecturer likes John. Therefore John does not take course 140.

One translation into universal prenex form is

1. ∀x.∀y. [student(x) ∧ lecturer(y) ∧ takes(140,x) ⇒ likes(y, x)]
2. ∀x. [lecturer(x) ⇒ ¬likes(x, John)]
---
3. ¬[student(John) ∧ takes(140, John)]

To show the conclusion, we will show a rewritten form of it, namely

3′. [student(John) ∧ takes(140, John)] ⇒ ⊥

which we will attempt to show by adding the antecedent student(John) ∧ takes(140, John) to the assumptions, and try to derive ⊥:

4. student(John) ∧ takes(140, John)

Since we are interested in John we should substitute John in assumptions 1 and 2, and try to derive ⊥. Notice that assumption 2 can, like the conclusion, be written to have ⊥ as its consequent:

2′. ∀x. [lecturer(x) ∧ likes(x, John) ⇒ ⊥]

So to show ⊥, by assumption 2 it is sufficient to show that for some x, lecturer(x) ∧ likes(x, John). You can try and show this for as long as you like, but you will not succeed. The conclusion does not follow from the assumptions. To see this, take a model in which John is a student and John is taking course 140, but there are no lecturers. Assumptions 1 and 2 will be true since the lecturer(y) (in the antecedents) will be false for all y, but the conclusion 3 will be false.

A common misconception is that the statement 'every object has some property' implies the existence of at least one object. This is not the case. One might state that 'every common factor of two different prime numbers is even', despite the fact that two different prime numbers have, by definition, no common factor. You may feel that the translation of the lecturer problem from English into logic was incorrect, and that a further assumption, that there are teachers, should be added:

$$0.\quad \exists\texttt{x. lecturer(x)}$$

The argument can now be demonstrated to be valid. Skolemizing the new assumption 0, with the constant k, we get

$$5.\quad \texttt{lecturer(k)}$$

Applying universal instantiation to assumptions 1 (x=John, y=k) and 2' (x=k), we get

6. `student(John) ∧ lecturer(k) ∧ takes(140, John)`
   `⇒ likes(k, John)`
7. `[lecturer(k) ∧ likes(k, John)] ⇒ ⊥`

Again trying to show ⊥, we use the rewritten form of assumption 2, this time in its instantiated form 7, so that we must show `lecturer(k) ∧ likes(k, John)`. Now applying *modus ponens* to sentences 4, 5 and 6 gives us `likes(k, John)`. With ∧ introduction with sentence 5, we get `lecturer(k) ∧ likes(k, John)` and thus the conclusion is proved.

3   Reasoning backward

As in the propositional case, we resolve all our difficulties by using backward rather than forward reasoning; we go from the conclusion to the assumptions. The assumptions are prepared in the universal prenex form, with universal quantifiers outside a quantifier-free matrix. The matrix is in a predicate form of the propositional $\mathcal{B}$-clauses. Recall the definition of $\mathcal{B}$-clauses from Chapter 8:

1. An atom q is a $\mathcal{B}$-clause, as is ⊥.

2. If $A_1, \ldots, A_n$ are $\mathcal{B}$-clauses and q is atomic or ⊥ then

$$A_1 \wedge \cdots \wedge A_n \Rightarrow q$$

   is a $\mathcal{B}$-clause.

3. A query is a conjunction of $\mathcal{B}$-clauses, e.g.

$$A \wedge B \wedge \cdots \wedge C$$

   where A, B, C are $\mathcal{B}$-clauses.

The extension to the predicate case is simple, and involves only a change to the definition of an atomic clause. We divide our variables into two types: universal variables $\{x_1, x_2, x_3, \ldots\}$ and existential variables $\{y_1, u_1, y_2, u_2, \ldots\}$. This division is for the purpose of computation only.

DEFINITION 9.12 (Predicate $\mathcal{B}$-clauses).

1. An atom $p(t_1, \ldots, t_n)$, where p is a predicate symbol and the t_i are terms, is a $\mathcal{B}$-clause, as is $\bot$.

2. If $A_1, \ldots, A_n$ are $\mathcal{B}$-clauses and q is atomic or $\bot$ then

$$A_1 \wedge \cdots \wedge A_n \Rightarrow q$$

   is a $\mathcal{B}$-clause.

3. A query is a conjunction of $\mathcal{B}$-clauses whose free variables are all existential, e.g.
$$A \wedge B \wedge \cdots \wedge C$$

   where A, B, C are $\mathcal{B}$-clauses.

4. A database is a set of $\mathcal{B}$-clauses with possibly mixed free variables.

The propositional backward reasoning rules were formally defined in Definition 7.20 as follows:

1. When A is an atom q we have $\langle \mathcal{P}, G \rangle \vdash_{\mathcal{B}} q$ iff either

   (a) $q \in \mathcal{P}$ or $\bot \in \mathcal{P}$, or
   (b) for some $B \Rightarrow q \in \mathcal{P}$ or $B \Rightarrow \bot \in \mathcal{P}$ we have $\langle \mathcal{P}, G \rangle \vdash_{\mathcal{B}} B$.

2. When A is a conjunction $B \wedge C$, we have $\langle \mathcal{P}, G \rangle \vdash_{\mathcal{B}} B \wedge C$ iff $\langle \mathcal{P}, G \rangle \vdash_{\mathcal{B}} B$ and $\langle \mathcal{P}, G \rangle \vdash_{\mathcal{B}} C$

3. When A is an implication $B \Rightarrow q$ we have $\langle \mathcal{P}, G \rangle \vdash_{\mathcal{B}} B \Rightarrow q$ iff $\langle \mathcal{P} \cup \{B\}, G \rangle \vdash_{\mathcal{B}} q$

4. The restart rule states that $\langle \mathcal{P}, G \rangle \vdash_{\mathcal{B}} q$ for an atom q if $\langle \mathcal{P}, G \rangle \vdash_{\mathcal{B}} G$, where G is the original goal of the computation.

The predicate form of these rules is essentially the same, with a few modifications to handle variables and quantifiers. First, when we have a conjunctive goal, such as $B \wedge C$, in the predicate case B and C may have common variables, such as b(u,y) and c(y,z) where y is a common variable. We must ensure that the variable substitutions which we generate when solving the first subgoal b(u,y) are applied to the second subgoal c(y,z) before we solve it. This ensures that incorrect answers are not generated. For example, if we have the assumptions b(1,2)   b(1,3)   c(2,3)   c(1,4)

the subgoal b(u,y) will succeed with the substitutions {u/1, y/2} and {u/1, y/3}. The subgoal c(y,z) will succeed with the substitutions {y/2, z/3} and {y/1, z/4}. However, there is only one correct substitution for the whole goal b(u,y) ∧ c(y,z), which is {u/1, y/2, z/3}. By applying the two answers for the subgoal b(u,y) to the second subgoal c(y,z), we generate two new subgoals c(2,z) and c(3,z). Only the former succeeds, with answer {z/3} which, when composed with the answer to the first subgoal, gives the desired {u/1, y/2, z/3}.

When the goal is an atomic formula Q(s,t,...) where s and t etc. are terms then we have a number of possibilities:

- Q(p,q,...) is one of the assumptions, where p and q etc. are terms. Provided that Q(s,t,...) and Q(p,q,...) unify, with most general unifier θ, we succeed with answer θ.

- ⊥ is one of the assumptions, in which case we succeed with the empty unifier as the answer.

- φ(p,q,u,v...) ⇒ Q(p,q,...) is one of the assumptions, where p, q, u, v, etc. are terms. Provided that Q(s,t,...) and Q(p,q,...) unify, with most general unifier θ, and the subgoal φ(p,q,u,v...) succeeds with answer σ, we succeed with answer $\theta \circ \sigma$.

- φ(p,q,u,v...) ⇒ ⊥ is one of the assumptions, where p, q, u, v, etc. are terms. Provided that the subgoal φ(p,q,u,v...) succeeds with answer σ, we succeed with answer σ.

Finally, the restart rule must be modified to take variables into account. Recall that the variables in the goal are *existentially* quantified. When we attempt to show that a goal φ(u) succeeds, we are really showing that the goal ∃u. φ(u) succeeds. We can justify the restart rule on the basis that $\psi \equiv \neg\psi \Rightarrow \psi$, so that instead of asking the goal ψ, we ask the goal $\neg\psi \Rightarrow \psi$. The implication is checked by adding $\neg\psi$ or rather $\psi \Rightarrow \bot$ to the database, and asking for ψ. If we use the restart rule, we are attempting to show ⊥ by asking for ψ. Because in predicate logic ψ is of the form ∃u. φ(u), we add the rule (∃u. φ(u))⇒⊥ to the database and so when we restart, we are asking the goal ∃u. φ(u) again. The presence of the existential quantifier is important, as it indicates that the goal involves another new existential variable y different from the variables used so far. After all, ∃u. φ(u) is equivalent to ∃y. φ(y). Now in the computation leading up to the use of the restart rule, we may have generated bindings for u, but these bindings have no connection with the restarted goal. If we just go on using u, we might generate an incorrect answer by use of the bindings.

DEFINITION 9.13 (Predicate $\mathcal{B}$-computation). We define the success of the computation $\langle \mathcal{P}, G \rangle \vdash_{\mathcal{B}} A$ with an associated answer substitution θ. θ is a substitution of terms to the existential variables. The terms used in the substitution θ are built up from constants, function symbols and existential variables only.

1. When A is an atom $Q(s,t,...)$ where s and t etc. are terms we have $\langle \mathcal{P}, G \rangle \vdash_{\mathcal{B}} Q(s,t,...)$ with answer θ iff one of the following holds

   (a) $Q(p,q,...) \in \mathcal{P}$, where p and q etc. are terms and $Q(s,t,...)$ and $Q(p,q,...)$ unify with most general unifier (θ_1, θ), where θ_1 is the substitution to the universal variables of the data clauses, and θ is the substitution to the existential variables.

   (b) $\bot \in \mathcal{P}$, and $\theta = \{\}$.

   (c) $\varphi(p,q,u,v...) \Rightarrow Q(p,q,...) \in \mathcal{P}$, where p, q, u, v, etc. are terms and $Q(s,t,...)$ and $Q(p,q,...)$ unify with most general unifier (θ_1', θ'), and $\langle \mathcal{P}, G \rangle \vdash_{\mathcal{B}} \varphi(p,q,u,v...)$ with answer σ, and $\theta = \theta' \circ \sigma$.

   (d) $\varphi(p,q,u,v...) \Rightarrow \bot \in \mathcal{P}$, where p, q, u, v, etc. are terms and $\langle \mathcal{P}, G \rangle \vdash_{\mathcal{B}} \varphi(p,q,u,v...)$ with answer θ.

2. When A is a conjunction $B \wedge C$, we have $\langle \mathcal{P}, G \rangle \vdash_{\mathcal{B}} B \wedge C$ with answer $\theta \circ \sigma$ iff $\langle \mathcal{P}, G \rangle \vdash_{\mathcal{B}} B$ with answer θ and $\langle \mathcal{P}, G \rangle \vdash_{\mathcal{B}} C\theta$ with answer σ.

3. When A is an implication $B \Rightarrow Q(s,t,...)$ we have $\langle \mathcal{P}, G \rangle \vdash_{\mathcal{B}} B \Rightarrow Q(s, t,...)$ with answer θ iff $\langle \mathcal{P} \cup \{B\theta\}, G \rangle \vdash_{\mathcal{B}} Q(s,t,...)$ with answer θ.

4. The restart rule states that $\langle \mathcal{P}, G \rangle \vdash_{\mathcal{B}} Q(s,t,...)$ for an atom $Q(s,t,...)$ with answer θ if $\langle \mathcal{P}, G \rangle \vdash_{\mathcal{B}} G$, where G is the original goal of the computation, written with completely new existential variables $y_1, ..., y_k$ and with θ extended to $y_1, ..., y_k$ as $\theta(y_j) = y_j$.

5. Another way of looking at the restart rule is that every time we use the rule, we restart with new variables $y_1, ..., y_k$ and a new substitution for them, obtained by extending θ. Thus assume that at the start of the computation the goal is assumed to be $A(x,t,...)$ with the free existential variables $u_1, ..., u_k$. We start with the substitution $\theta^1(u_i) = y_i^1, i = 1, ..., k$ where y_i^1 are also existential variables. θ^1 can be refined to an answer θ_*^1 at some stage of the computation in which we choose to restart. We restart with the original goal but with completely new substitution $\theta^2(u_i) = y_i^2$, with completely new existential $y_i^2, i = 1, ..., k$.

   We continue until we succeed. We shall have on record, at the moment of success, variables $y_1^1, ..., y_k^1, ..., y_1^n, ..., y_k^n$ and an extended substitution θ for these variables. If we regard $\theta(y_i^m)$ as a substitution $\theta_*^m(u_i)$ for the variable u_i, we can say we have got n different substitutions $\theta_*^1, \ldots, \theta_*^n$ for the variables $u_1, \ldots, u_k$. We shall see from the soundness theorem that this means that the formula $\bigvee_{i=1}^n G\theta_*^n$ successfully follows from $\mathcal{P}\theta$.

EXAMPLE 9.14. We shall illustrate the use of the rules by redoing Example 9.8 using the backward reasoning method. The argument, when Skolemized, can be represented by

1. `logician(k)`
2. `teaches-at(k,Imperial-College)`
3. `teaches-at(x,Imperial-College)` $\Rightarrow$ `lives-in-London(x)`
4. `logician(x)` $\wedge$ `lives-in-London(x)` $\Rightarrow$ `good(x)`
5. `logician(x)` $\wedge$ `good(x)` $\Rightarrow$ `support-LP(x)`

---

6. `logician(u)` $\wedge$ `good(u)` $\wedge$ `support-LP(u)`

The goal is conjunctive, so we must ensure that we solve all three conjuncts with the correct answer substitution. We begin by asking the subgoal `logician(u)` which succeeds immediately from sentence 1, with the substitution {u/k}, i.e. $\theta(u) = k$. This substitution is then applied to the remaining goal, `good(u)` $\wedge$ `support-LP(u)`, giving `good(k)` $\wedge$ `support-LP(k)`. Again we have a conjunctive goal, so we ask the first subgoal of the conjunction, `good(k)`. This will unify with the head of sentence 4. Notice that sentence 4, like the other sentences in the database, uses the variable `x`. Because each sentence is universally quantified, the `x` in sentence 4 is distinct from each of the `x` in the other sentences. (To avoid confusion, we can rename the variable in sentence 4 at this point, to `y`, say.) Thus the unification with the goal produces the substitution $\theta_1(x) = k$ which is composed with the earlier substitution. We generate the new subgoal from the antecedent of sentence 4, and apply the substitution, getting `logician(k)` $\wedge$ `lives-in-London(k)`. The first part of this will succeed from sentence 1, and the second part will unify with the head of sentence 3 and generate the subgoal `teaches-at(k,Imperial-College)`, which will succeed from sentence 2.

This only leaves the third of the original conjuncts, `support-LP(k)` which unifies with the head of sentence 5, generating the subgoal `logician(k)` $\wedge$ `good(k)`. These can be solved as we have just seen, so that the entire goal succeeds, with the answer substitution {u/k}, i.e. $\theta(u) = k$. (We omit the bindings for variables generated during the course of the computation.)

EXAMPLE 9.15. Let us illustrate all features involved with an example. Let the data be

$$\forall x_1, x_2.(R(x_1, x_2) \Rightarrow Q(x_2))$$

and the goal be

$$\exists u, y.[\neg\neg R(u, y) \Rightarrow Q(y)]$$

We first rewrite the data and goal as $\mathcal{B}$-clauses. We get the problem

$$R(x_1, x_2) \Rightarrow Q(x_2) \vdash_\mathcal{B}?((R(u, y) \Rightarrow \bot) \Rightarrow \bot) \Rightarrow Q(y)$$

which becomes using the $\Rightarrow$ rule

1. $R(x_1, x_2) \Rightarrow Q(x_2)$

2. $(R(u, y) \Rightarrow \bot) \Rightarrow \bot$

with the query $\vdash_\mathcal{B}?Q(y)$.

We use clause 1. We substitute $\theta_1(x_1) = y_1, \theta_1(x_2) = y, \theta(y) = y$.

We get the goal $\vdash_\mathcal{B}?R(y_1, y)$ with answer substitution θ. Note that θ_1 had to substitute existential variable terms for the universal variables x_1, x_2 in clause 1.

Using clause 2 we ask for the goal $\vdash_\mathcal{B}?R(u, y) \Rightarrow \bot$. We add the antecedent to the data as clause 3 and ask for $\bot$

3. $R(u, y)$

with the query $\vdash_\mathcal{B}?\bot$.

We now choose to restart. We ask the original query with completely new existential variables u', y'

$$\vdash_\mathcal{B}?((R(u', y') \rightarrow \bot) \Rightarrow \bot) \Rightarrow Q(y')$$

We add the antecedent to the data as clause 4 and ask for the head

4. $(R(u', y') \rightarrow \bot) \Rightarrow \bot$

with the query $\vdash_\mathcal{B}?Q(y')$.

We now substitute in clause 1 $\theta_2(x_1) = z_1, \theta_2(x_2) = y'$ and $\theta(y') = y'$ and get

$$\vdash_\mathcal{B}?R(z_1, y')$$

Substitute $\theta(z_1) = u, \theta(y') = y$ and we can succeed.

Success means that

$$\vdash \exists u, y.[\forall x_1, x_2.(R(x_1, x_2) \Rightarrow Q(x_2)) \Rightarrow (\neg\neg R(u, y) \Rightarrow Q(y)]$$

EXERCISE 9.16. Decide, using the predicate backward rules, whether the following arguments are valid. See Example 8.1.7 on how to rewrite the formulae into $\mathcal{B}$-clauses.

1. $\forall x. (a(x) \lor b(x))$
$\underline{\qquad \neg\exists x. \ a(x) \qquad}$
$\forall x. \ b(x)$

2. $$\frac{\exists x.\ (a(x)\ \Rightarrow\ b(x))}{(\exists x.\ a(x))\ \Rightarrow\ \exists x.\ b(x)}$$

3. $$\frac{\exists x.\forall y.\ a(x,y)}{\forall y.\exists x.\ a(x,y)}$$

4. $$\frac{\begin{array}{c}\exists x.\exists y.\ r(x,y)\\ \forall x.\forall y.\ r(x,y)\ \Rightarrow\ r(y,x)\\ \forall x.\forall y.\forall z.\ r(x,y)\ \wedge\ r(y,z)\ \Rightarrow\ r(x,z)\end{array}}{\forall x.\ r(x,x)}$$

5. $$\frac{\forall x.\exists y.R(x,\ y)}{\exists y.\forall x.R(x,\ y)}$$

THEOREM 9.17 (Soundness of the predicate $\mathcal{B}$-computation).   *Consider the $\mathcal{B}$-computation with restart and assume that at some stage we have the query $\langle \mathcal{P}, G\rangle \vdash_{\mathcal{B}}?A$ and a history of restart substitutions $\theta_*^1, \ldots, \theta_*^n$. Assume that this query now succeeds with substitution θ. Then we have that $\models ((\forall \text{ universal variables})(\bigwedge \mathcal{P}) \Rightarrow \bigvee_{i=1}^{n} G\theta_*^n \vee A\theta)$, i.e. it is true in every classical interpretation, under any assignment.*

Proof. By induction on the computation.

We first show that for a computation without restart we have $\langle \mathcal{P}, G\rangle \vdash_{\mathcal{B}} A$ iff $\models ((\forall \text{ universal variables}) \bigwedge \mathcal{P} \Rightarrow A\theta)$.

Our proof reduces the predicate case to the propositional case. Let $u_1, \ldots, u_k$ be the existential variables of A and let $t_i = \theta(u_i)$. Let $\mathcal{P}'$ be the result of substituting for the universal variables of the clauses of $\mathcal{P}$ all possible combinations of $t_1, \ldots, t_n$. $\mathcal{P}'$ can be regarded as a finite propositional database and $A\theta$ succeeds propositionally from it.

Hence by propositional soundness we have $\bigwedge \mathcal{P}' \vdash A\theta$.

Hence

$(\forall \text{ universal variables}) \bigwedge \mathcal{P} \vdash A\theta)$ and so $\models ((\forall \text{ universal variables}) \bigwedge \mathcal{P} \Rightarrow A\theta)$

Assume now that A succeeds with n uses of the restart rule and that the existential variables involved are $y_1^1, \ldots, y_k^1, \ldots, y_1^n, \ldots, y_k^n$. Consider the new computation of $A\theta$ from the new database $\mathcal{P}_1$ where

$$\mathcal{P}_1 = \mathcal{P}\theta \cup \{G(y_1^m, \ldots, y_k^m) \Rightarrow \bot \mid m \le n\}\theta$$

$A\theta$ can succeed without restart from this database, because at the mth trigger of restart, we do not use the restart rule but use the clause

$$G(y_i^m)\theta \Rightarrow \bot$$

We therefore get that $\vDash ((\forall \text{ universal variables}) \wedge \mathcal{P} \wedge \bigwedge_m (G(y_i^m)\theta \Rightarrow \bot) \Rightarrow A\theta)$.
Since

$$\bigwedge \mathcal{P} \wedge \bigwedge_m (G(y_i^m)\theta \Rightarrow \bot) \Rightarrow A\theta$$

is equivalent to

$$\bigwedge \mathcal{P} \Rightarrow \bigvee_m G(y_i^m)\theta \vee A\theta$$

our inductive case is proved.

Thus the theorem is proved. ∎

REMARK 9.18 (Completeness, Herbrand theorem). We are not going to prove completeness in this book. See [Gabbay and Olivetti, 2000].

The following well-known theorem follows from the soundness of completeness of our computation.

Herbrand theorem

Let A be a formula of the form $\exists u_1, \ldots, u_n \cdot A_0$, where A_0 is quantifier free and assume that $\vDash A$ in classical logic. Then for some substitutions $\theta^1, \ldots, \theta^m$ of terms to the variables $u_1, \ldots, u_n$ we have $\vDash \bigvee_j A_0 \theta^j$.

See also Example 8.5.2.

REMARK 9.19 (Hilbert formulation). It is possible to give a Hilbert formulation for classical and for intuitionistic predicate logics by adding the following schemas for quantifiers to the schemas in Examples 7.2.6 and 7.2.7.

12. $\forall x.A(x) \Rightarrow A(t)$, t arbitrary term.

13. $A(t) \Rightarrow \exists x.A(x)$, t arbitrary term.

14. $\dfrac{\vdash A \Rightarrow B(x)}{\vdash A \Rightarrow \forall x.B(x)}$ x not free in A.

15. $\dfrac{\vdash B(x) \Rightarrow A}{\vdash \exists x.B(x) \Rightarrow A}$ x not free in A.

3.1 Connection with resolution

In this book we have concentrated on reasoning via a set of simple rules, from assumptions to conclusions (reasoning forwards) and from conclusions back to assumptions (reasoning backwards). Another well-known method of checking whether a query follows from a database is *resolution*.

We know that if A follows logically from $\mathcal{P}$, i.e. $\mathcal{P} \vdash A$ succeeds, then any interpretation which makes all the formulae of $\mathcal{P}$ true must also make A true. In other words $\wedge\mathcal{P}\Rightarrow A$ is a predicate tautology. Thus we cannot make $\mathcal{P}$ true and A false, or in other words we cannot make $\mathcal{P} \cup \{\neg A\}$ all true, i.e. $\mathcal{P} \cup \{\neg A\}$ is not consistent. In our case $\mathcal{P}$ contains universal formulae of the form $\forall x.\ B(x)$. The query A is an existential formula of the form $\exists y.\ C(y)$. If we negate the query, we get $\neg A = \forall y.\ \neg C(y)$, which is a universal formula, like those in $\mathcal{P}$. Therefore if we have a computation for checking whether a set of universal sentences is consistent or not, then we can check whether a query A follows from data $\mathcal{P}$. If $\mathcal{P} \cup \{\neg A\}$ can be shown to be inconsistent, then $\mathcal{P} \vdash A$.

Resolution is a method for checking inconsistency. For the purposes of this method it is convenient to write the clauses of $\mathcal{P} \cup \{\neg A\}$ in conjunctive normal form. So for example the acceptable (to our backward computation) clause

$$(A \wedge B \Rightarrow C) \Rightarrow D$$

will have to be rewritten for resolution as

$$(A \vee D) \ \wedge \ (B \vee D) \ \wedge \ (\neg C \vee D)$$

which becomes the set of assumptions

$$A \vee D$$
$$B \vee D$$
$$\neg C \vee D$$

Suppose we have two clauses in the database of the form

$$\neg A \vee p$$
$$\neg q \vee A'$$

They are logically equivalent to

$$A \Rightarrow p$$
$$q \Rightarrow A'$$

If we can unify A with A' we can get, by transitivity of $\Rightarrow$,

$$q\theta \Rightarrow p\theta$$

where θ is the substitution which makes $A'\theta = A\theta$. This can be rewritten as

$$\neg q\theta \vee p\theta$$

Thus the basic computation of resolution is: if the set to be tested contains the formulae

$$\neg A \vee p$$
$$\neg q \vee A'$$

and A and A' can be unified with most general unifier θ, we can add a new clause, the *resolvent*

¬q$\theta\lor$pθ

to the set.

When we have formulae in the set of the form

¬A∨p
A′

the resolvent is just pθ. In this way, the formulae

¬C
C

resolve to the *empty clause*, written □. As one might expect from having both C and ¬C, the empty clause indicates the presence of an inconsistency. Now ¬C is equivalent to C⇒⊥, so that in the backward reasoning method, we would have

C⇒⊥
C

as assumptions, so that the query ⊥ would succeed from the formulae, and hence we would deduce that the assumptions were inconsistent.

Resolution is a powerful technique, with many variations having been designed to cope with different logics and applications, and is worthy of a book in its own right. For further details, see [Goubault-Larrecq and Mackie, 1997; Gallier, 1986].

4 Decidability

A logic (see Definition 7.1.1) is said to be decidable iff there exists an algorithm (which always terminates) to decide for any two wffs A, B whether $A \mathrel{\vdash\!\!\sim} B$ holds or not.

According to this definition, classical propositional logic is decidable. For any A, B we can check by truth tables whether $A \Rightarrow B$ is a tautology, as explained in Section 1.1.2. In fact, all the propositional systems mentioned in the table of Section 7.8 are decidable.

The decidability of the classical propositional calculus can also be seen from the diminishing resource backward computation algorithm of Definition 4.3.3. This algorithm is terminating, as the database gets smaller and smaller. The restart rule involves only one scan of the history and needs to be applied only once. Remark 4.3.4 quotes completeness of the algorithm for classical propositional logic (with restart) and for intuitionistic propositional logic (with bounded restart); therefore these logics are decidable.[1]

Classical predicate logic, however, is undecidable. Although there are many algorithms for checking whether $A \vdash B$ holds in classical predicate logic, they are

---

[1] At this point it is worthwhile to take another look at Example 4.2.5.

not guaranteed to terminate for arbitrary $A \vdash ?B$. Such systems are called *semi-decidable* or *recursively enumerable*.

Thus classical predicate logic and intuitionistic predicate logic are semi- decidable but not decidable.

5   Worked examples

EXAMPLE 9.20.

Data

If everybody buys Jane Fonda's *Quick Slimming* book, then someone is bound to follow the programme successfully, and be liked by all her friends, envied by her neighbours and generally feel more self-confident and loving towards her children.

Anyone liked by all her friends must be good natured.

Goal

Therefore if everybody buys Jane Fonda's book then someone is good natured.

Let us translate, using the obvious predicates:

Data

(1) $\forall x.\ \text{Buy}(x, J) \quad \rightarrow \quad \exists y.\ [\text{Follow}(y) \wedge$
$\forall z.\ [\text{Friend}(z, y) \Rightarrow \text{Like}(z, y)] \wedge$
$\forall z.\ [\text{Neighbour}(z, y) \Rightarrow \text{Envy}(z, y)] \wedge$
$\text{Confident}(y) \wedge$
$\forall z.\ [\text{Child}(z, y) \Rightarrow \text{Love}(y, z)]]$

(2) $\forall x.[\forall y.\ [\text{Friend}(y, x) \Rightarrow \text{Like}(y, x)]. \Rightarrow \text{Good}(x)]$.

Goal

(3) $\forall x.\text{Buy}(x, J) \Rightarrow \exists x.\text{Good}(x)$

We need a ready for computation form. We pull the quantifiers out and get the (*) formulation as follows:

(1*) $\exists x.\exists y.\forall z_1.\forall z_2.\forall z_3.\text{Buy}(x, J) \quad \Rightarrow \quad (\text{Follow}(y) \wedge$
$[\text{Friend}(z_1, y) \Rightarrow \text{Like}(z_1, y)] \wedge$
$[\text{Neighbour}(z_2, y) \Rightarrow \text{Envy}(z_2, y)]$
$\wedge \text{Confident}(y) \wedge$
$[\text{Child}(z_3, y) \Rightarrow \text{Love}(y, z_3)])$

(2*) $\forall x.\exists y.[(\text{Friend}(y, x) \Rightarrow \text{Like}(y, x)) \Rightarrow \text{Good}(x)]$

and the Goal is

(3*) $\exists x.\exists y.[\mathrm{Buy}(x, J) \Rightarrow \mathrm{Good}(y)]$.

The above equivalences are valid in classical logic. In intuitionistic logic we cannot rewrite as we did.

Skolemizing and decomposing (1*) into several clauses we get the final (#) formulation:

Data

(1#)   1. $\mathrm{Buy}(c_1, J) \Rightarrow \mathrm{Follow}(c_2)$

   2. $\mathrm{Buy}(c_1, J) \Rightarrow (\mathrm{Friend}(x, c_2) \Rightarrow \mathrm{Likes}(x, c_2))$

   3. $\mathrm{Buy}(c_1, J) \Rightarrow (\mathrm{Neighbour}(x, c_2) \Rightarrow \mathrm{Envy}(x, c_2))$

   4. $\mathrm{Buy}(c_1, J) \Rightarrow \mathrm{Confident}(c_2)$

   5. $\mathrm{Buy}(c_1, J) \Rightarrow (\mathrm{Child}(x, c_2) \Rightarrow \mathrm{Love}(c_2, x))$.

(2#) $[\mathrm{Friend}(f(x), x) \Rightarrow \mathrm{Like}(f(x), x)] \Rightarrow \mathrm{Good}(x)$.

Goal

(3#) $\mathrm{Buy}(x, J) \Rightarrow \mathrm{Good}(y)$.

The above is ready for computation. Notice that after Skolemizing and rewriting we lost a bit of the natural linguistic structure.

The computation

Data#	$\vdash_\mathcal{B}$?	**Goal#**
which reduces to		
(1#), (2#)	$\vdash_\mathcal{B}$?	(3#)
which reduces to		
(1#), (2#)	$\vdash_\mathcal{B}$?	Buy$(u, J) \Rightarrow$ Good(v)
where u, v are existential variables.		
This reduces to		
(4#), (1#), (2#)	$\vdash_\mathcal{B}$?	Good(v)
where (4#) = Buy(u, J)		
Unify with (2#) and get		
	$\vdash_\mathcal{B}$?	Friend$(f(v), v) \Rightarrow$ Like$(f(v), v))$
which reduces to		
(1#), (2#), (4#), (5#)	$\vdash_\mathcal{B}$?	Like$(f(v), v))$

where (5#) Friend$(f(v), v)$ was added to the database.

Unify with (1#.2). Choose $c_2 = v$. Thus everywhere where v appears it becomes c_2, including the database.

We now get

Current data		**Current goal**
(1#)	?	Friend$(f(c_2), c_2)$
(2#)		
(4#) Buy(u, J)		
(5#) Friend$(f(v), v))$, for $v = c_2$		
i.e. Friend$(f(c_2), c_2)$		
Therefore success.		

EXAMPLE 9.21. Using *backward rules* for classical logic provide formal proofs for the following:

$$\exists x.(A(x) \Rightarrow A(a) \wedge A(b))$$

Solution

$$\varnothing \vdash \exists x\, [A(x) \Rightarrow A(a) \wedge A(b)]$$
$$\varnothing \vdash A(u) \Rightarrow A(a) \wedge A(b)$$
where u is an existential variable to be instantiated
$$\vdash A(u) \Rightarrow A(a) \wedge A(b)$$

$$A(u) \vdash A(a) \qquad\qquad A(u) \vdash A(b)$$

choose $u = a$ and
left branch succeeds

because of the choice of $u = a$ in
the left branch, the right branch becomes

$$A(a) \vdash A(b)$$

restart with new variable

$$A(a) \vdash A(u_1) \Rightarrow A(a) \wedge A(b)$$

$$\begin{matrix} A(a) \\ A(u_1) \end{matrix} \vdash A(a) \wedge A(b)$$

$$\begin{matrix} A(a) \\ A(u_1) \end{matrix} \vdash A(a) \qquad\qquad \begin{matrix} A(a) \\ A(u_1) \end{matrix} \vdash A(b)$$

left subbranch
succeeds

right subbranch
succeeds
with $u_1 = b$

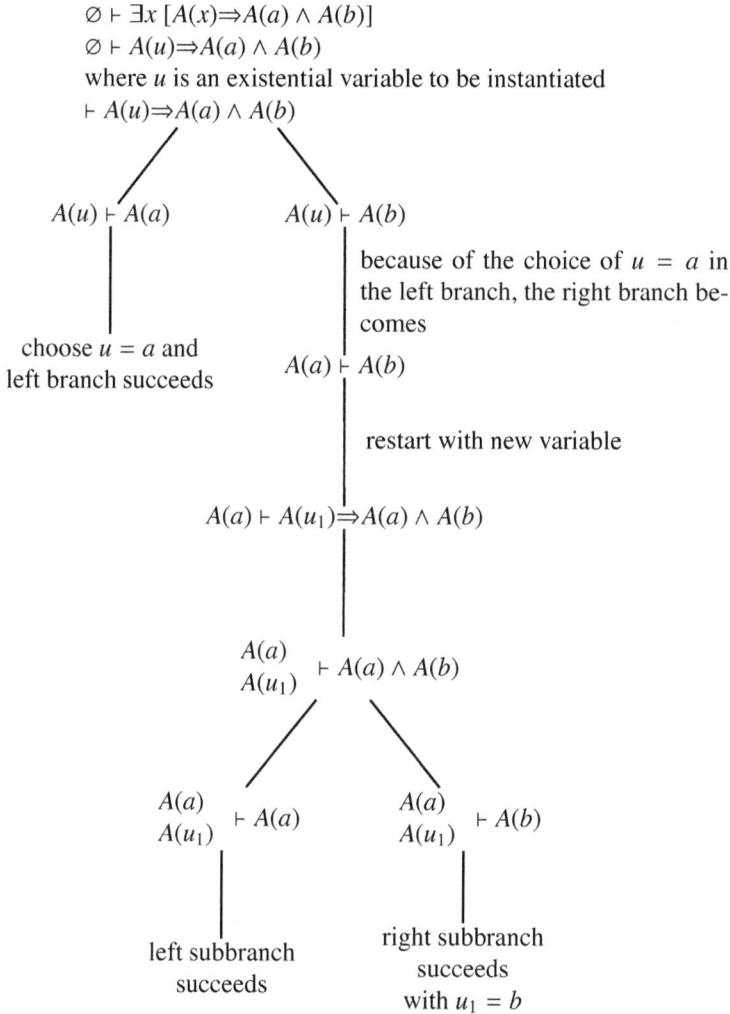

Using the soundness theorem, Theorem 8.3.6, we get that the success of the
goal $A(u) \Rightarrow A(a) \wedge A(b)$ with $\theta_1(u) = a, \theta_2(u) = b$ means that

$$\vDash (A(a) \Rightarrow A(a) \wedge A(b)) \vee (A(b) \Rightarrow A(a) \wedge A(b))$$

CHAPTER 10

Elements of modal and temporal logics

This chapter gives more details on modal and temporal logics. These logics were briefly mentioned in Chapter 2 in the context of other non-classical logics. We now look at modal logic more closely.

1 Modal logic

The basic language of modal propositional logic with one modality (which could be temporal) is the extension of the language of classical propositional logic with the unary modal connective $\Box$. Thus our language contains $\neg, \wedge, \vee, \Rightarrow$ and $\Box$, and a non-empty set of atomic propositions.

DEFINITION 10.1. The notion of a well-formed formula, or *formula*, is defined by induction as follows:

1. Any atomic proposition q is a formula: an *atomic formula*.

2. If A and B are formulae then so are $(A \wedge B), (A \vee B), (A \Rightarrow B), (\neg A)$ and $(\Box A)$.

   Recall from Chapter 2 that we denote $\Box(A \Rightarrow B)$ by $A \twoheadrightarrow B$.

The brackets are needed, as without them a string such as $A \wedge B \vee C$ would be ambiguous. We usually omit the brackets where there is no ambiguity.

$\Box A$ is read 'box A'. We know the meaning of $\wedge, \vee, \Rightarrow$ and $\neg$. The intended meaning of $\Box$ is

'A is necessarily true' or

'A will always be true' or

'A is believed to be true', etc.

At this stage we do not have to be committed to any one meaning.

1.1 Semantics

In classical propositional logic an assignment h assigned a truth value true ($\top$) or false ($\bot$) to each atomic formula. Then we computed the truth value of the complex non-atomic formulae using the truth tables.

In modal logic, a model is built up from a family S of ordinary classical propositional assignments. The elements of S are usually called *possible situations*, or *possible worlds*. The job of the modal model S is to give every modal formula a truth value *at each situation*.

Thus the assignment h becomes dependent on the worlds $t \in S$ as is written $h(t, q)$, for q atomic.

EXAMPLE 10.2. Consider the formula $A = (p \Rightarrow \neg q) \wedge q$. The language has atoms p, q only.

1. *Classical logic*
   A model h is a row in the truth table, assigning values to p and q. So a model is just an interpretation function $h : \{p, q\} \Rightarrow \{\top, \bot\}$, e.g.

$$h(p) = \top, \ h(q) = \bot$$

   We can extend h in the usual way to a truth valuation defined on the set of all formulae, using the standard classical propositional definitions; so $h(A \wedge B) = \top$ iff $h(A) = \top$ and $h(B) = \top$, etc. The value of A can be computed as $(\top \Rightarrow \neg\bot) \wedge \bot = \bot$. So $h(A) = \bot$ (computed).

2. *Modal logic*
   Here we have a non-empty set S of possible situations. For each situation $t \in S$ we assign truth values to the atoms. So a modal model gives a truth value in $\{\top, \bot\}$ to each *pair*: (situation in S, atom).

For example, let $S = \{o, t, s\}$. So a modal model is *in part* a function $h : S \times \{p, q\} \Rightarrow \{\top, \bot\}$.

$$\text{Let} \quad \left. \begin{array}{l} h(o, p) = \top \\ h(o, q) = \bot \end{array} \right\} \text{world } o$$
$$\left. \begin{array}{l} h(t, p) = \top \\ h(t, q) = \top \end{array} \right\} \text{world } t$$
$$\left. \begin{array}{l} h(s, p) = \bot \\ h(s, q) = \top \end{array} \right\} \text{world } s$$

Computing the value of A we get

$$h(o, A) = \bot$$
$$h(t, A) = \bot$$
$$h(s, A) = \top$$

What about $h(o, \Box A)$? It is up to us to decide how to compute the truth value of $\Box A$. The way we compute it will determine the meaning of $\Box$.

An interesting and useful meaning of $\Box$ is as follows. Let us imagine that S is a set of databases, o, t, s. Further assume, just to give an example, that there are connections between the databases, as illustrated in Figure 10.1.

M

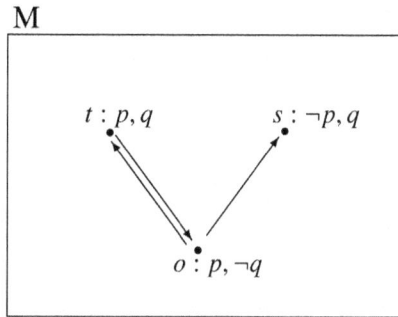

Figure 10.1.

If xRy denotes that there is a connection '$x \rightsquigarrow y$', then we have

$$oRs, oRt, tRo$$

We can now give a meaning to $h(x, \Box A)$ as follows:

DEFINITION 10.3.

$$h(x, \Box A) = \top \text{ iff } \forall y[\text{if } xRy \text{ then } h(y, A) = \top]$$

The way we view the meaning of $\Box$ is that each database x in S can 'talk' about whether A is true in databases 'accessible' from x. We introduce the relation R as the *accessibility relation on* S: the databases accessible to x are deemed to be those databases y in S such that xRy. So the meaning of $\Box$ is: $\Box A$ *is true in database* x *iff* A *is true in all databases* y *accessible to* x. (Thus if no databases are accessible, $\Box A$ is always true.)

According to the above:

$$h(o, \Box A) = \bot$$
$$h(t, \Box A) = \bot$$
$$h(s, \Box A) = \top$$

DEFINITION 10.4. A possible world Kripke model for the modal language with $\Box$ is a 4-tuple (S, R, o, h), where S is a non-empty set (the set of possible worlds), $R \subseteq S \times S$ is the accessibility relation, $o \in S$ is the *actual world* and h is the assignment (interpretation) function giving truth values $h(x, q)$ for each $x \in S$ and each atom q.

The truth value for each formula is defined by induction as follows:

$$h(x, A \wedge B) = \top \text{ iff } h(x, A) = \top \text{ and } h(x, B) = \top$$
$$h(x, A \vee B) = \top \text{ iff } h(x, A) = \top \text{ or } h(x, B) = \top$$
$$h(x, \neg A) = \top \text{ iff } h(x, A) = \bot$$
$$h(x, A \Rightarrow B) = \top \text{ iff } h(x, A) = \bot \text{ or } h(x, B) = \top$$
$$h(x, \Box A) = \top \text{ iff } \forall y (xRy \Rightarrow h(y, A) = \top)$$

Notice that the computation reduces the truth value of a complex formula to a smaller (simpler) one.

DEFINITION 10.5.

$$\Diamond A =_{\text{def}} \neg \Box \neg A$$

So $h(x, \Diamond A) = \top$ iff $\exists y (xRy \wedge h(y, A) = \top)$. We pronounce $\Diamond A$ as *diamond A*.

EXAMPLE 10.6.

1. Let $S = \{0, 1, 2, 3, \ldots\}$.

   Define $R \subseteq S \times S$ by: xRy iff $y = x + 1$.

   Then if we understand S as representing time in days (day 0, day 1, ...), and o is the actual world, $\Box A$ would mean 'A is true tomorrow'.

2. Let S be $\{0, 1, 2, 3, \ldots\}$ and let xRy iff $x < y$. Then $\Box A$ means 'A will always be true'.

DEFINITION 10.7. A formula A is *true* in a Kripke model (S, R, o, h) iff $h(o, A) = \top$.

We notice that certain formulae always get value $\top$ in any Kripke model (S, R, o, h), no matter what h is. These are:

1. All classical tautologies, e.g. $\Box A \Rightarrow \Box A$ (this has the form $q \Rightarrow q$)

2. $\Box(A \Rightarrow B) \Rightarrow (\Box A \Rightarrow \Box B)$

3. $\Box(A \wedge B) \Leftrightarrow (\Box A \wedge \Box B)$.

Formulae that always get value $\top$ are called *valid formulae*, or sometimes just *(modal) tautologies*.

1.2   Proof theory

We consider the following problem

Given a set of formulae $\mathcal{P}$ true at o, and a query G, must G also be true at o (in any model)? That is, does G logically follow from $\mathcal{P}$?

We denote this using the notation: $\mathcal{P} \vdash ?G$.

EXAMPLE 10.8.

1. $a \Rightarrow \Box b$

2. $(a \Rightarrow b) \Rightarrow a$

3. $\Diamond(b \Rightarrow c)$.

Does $\Diamond c$ *follow from* the data (1)–(3)? That is, $\{1,2,3\} \vdash ?\Diamond c$.
The semantical meaning of the above is the following: for any model (S,R,o,h),

if $h(o,(a \Rightarrow \Box b)) = \top$,
and $h(o,(a \Rightarrow b) \Rightarrow a) = \top$,
and $h(o,\Diamond(b \Rightarrow c)) = \top$,
must we also have $h(o,\Diamond c) = \top$?

REMARK 10.9.   Different *restrictions* on (S,R,o,h) give rise to different sets of modal tautologies and different systems of logic. Examples of such conditions are:

1. R reflexive (the logic **T**) (xRx holds for all x), corresponding to the axiom $\Box A \Rightarrow A$.

2. R transitive (the logic **K4**) (xRy and yRz imply xRz), corresponding to the axiom $\Box A \Rightarrow \Box\Box A$.

3. (S,R,o) is a finite tree (the logic **G** of modal provability), axioms $\Box A \Rightarrow A$ and $\Box(\Box A \Rightarrow A) \Rightarrow \Box A$.

4. R symmetric (xRy implies yRx) and reflexive (the logic **B**), corresponding to $\Diamond\Box A \Rightarrow A$.

5. R reflexive and transitive (the logic **S4**), axioms $\Box A \Rightarrow A$ and $\Box A \Rightarrow \Box\Box A$.

6. R reflexive, symmetric and transitive (the logic **S5**), axioms $\Box A \Rightarrow A, \Box A \Rightarrow \Box\Box A$ and $\Diamond\Box A \Rightarrow A$.

The general case described here, i.e. *no restrictions*, gives rise to the modal logic **K**.

In the case of classical logic we used forward reasoning and/or backward reasoning to check whether the query G followed from the data $\mathcal{P}$. We need to find a similar algorithm here. Note again that the data describes the relationships of other databases to the database o, as well as some information about database o itself. The query may be a question about this information, of global interest to the database designer!

EXAMPLE 10.10 (Example 10.8 continued). Proof of the query in the example:

4. $[(a \Rightarrow b) \Rightarrow a] \Rightarrow a$ (classical tautology)

5. a from (2) and (4) using *modus ponens*

6. $\Box b$ from (1) and (5) using *modus ponens*.

We now see that we have 6 saying that *in all worlds accessible from o, b is true* and we have 3 saying that *in at least one such world $x(b \Rightarrow c)$ is true*.

Let us look at world x.

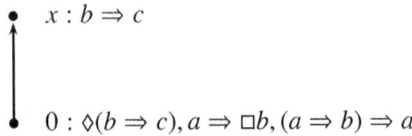

$$x : b \Rightarrow c$$

$$0 : \Diamond(b \Rightarrow c), a \Rightarrow \Box b, (a \Rightarrow b) \Rightarrow a$$

Figure 10.2.

Thus since b and $b \Rightarrow c$ are true at x, we get c is true at x. But we found a world x in which c is true. Hence:

7. $\Diamond c$ is true at o (from the reasoning and Figure 10.2).

How do we make our reasoning more formal? We can adopt a rule: $\Box A \wedge \Diamond B \Rightarrow \Diamond(A \wedge B)$. So from $\Box b$ and $\Diamond(b \Rightarrow c)$ we get $\Diamond[b \wedge (b \Rightarrow c)]$.

How do we get $\Diamond c$ from the above? $\Diamond A \wedge \Diamond(A \Rightarrow B)$ *does not imply* $\Diamond B$. However, $\Diamond[b \wedge (b \Rightarrow c)]$ does imply $\Diamond c$. What is the difference? The difference is that $[b \wedge (b \Rightarrow c)] \Rightarrow c$ is a tautology of classical logic. Thus we have a rule:

$$\Diamond A \text{ and } \vDash A \Rightarrow B \text{ imply } \Diamond B$$

$\vDash A \Rightarrow B$ means: $A \Rightarrow B$ is always true in any model.

We have to guess a set of rules for proving queries (goals) from assumptions.

EXAMPLE 10.11.

1. $a \Rightarrow \Box[\Diamond(b \Rightarrow c) \wedge d]$

2. $(a \Rightarrow \Diamond b) \Rightarrow a$

3. $\Diamond(b \wedge \Box b)$.

The query is $\{1, 2, 3\} \vdash ? \Diamond \Diamond c$.

This example is more complicated. First from (2) and the tautology

4. $[(a \Rightarrow \Diamond b) \Rightarrow a] \Rightarrow a$

we get by *modus ponens*:

5. a.

So from 1 by *modus ponens*, we get

6. $\Box[\Diamond(b \Rightarrow c) \wedge d]$.

From 6 and 3 we get

7. $\Diamond[\Diamond(b \Rightarrow c) \wedge d \wedge b \wedge \Box b]$.

We want to show $\Diamond \Diamond c$. Since 7 promises a world in which $\Diamond(b \Rightarrow c) \wedge d \wedge b \wedge \Box b$ is true, maybe $\Diamond c$ is true in this world?

Let us try then the subproblem:

1^*. $\Diamond(b \Rightarrow c)$

2^*. b

3^*. d.

The query is $\{1^*, 2^*, 3^*\} \vdash ? \Diamond c$

4^*. $\Box b$.

This will indeed succeed because of 1^* and 4^*.

We are thus led to:

Forward computation rules

1. *Modus ponens*, rule for $\Rightarrow$ elimination, familiar from classical logic:

   line n: A

   $\vdots$

   line m: $A \Rightarrow B$
   _____
   line k B

2. Rule for $\Rightarrow$ introduction:

   line n: $A \Rightarrow B$ because of box:

	Show B
(n.1)	Assume A
(n.2)	Assume whatever has already been proved
	$\vdots$
	B

3. Rule for $\Diamond$ introduction:

   line k: $\Diamond A$

   $\vdots$

   line n: $\Diamond C$, because of box:

	Show C
(n.1)	Assume A
(n.2)	Assume all B such that $\Box B$ has been proved.
	$\vdots$
	C

EXAMPLE 10.12.

1. $a \Rightarrow \Box b$

2. $(a \Rightarrow b) \Rightarrow a$

3. $\Diamond(b \Rightarrow c)$.

The query is $\{1, 2, 3\} \vdash ?\Diamond c$.

We continue our proof in lines 4 to n below, giving a proof of 'a' from 2 using rules of classical logic.

4.

$$\vdots$$
$$\vdots$$

n. a

$n + 1.$ $\Box b$ from (n) and (1)

$n + 2.$ $\Diamond c$ from box via rule 3:

$(n + 2).1$	$b \Rightarrow c$	from 3
$(n + 2).2$	b	from $n + 1$
$(n + 2).3$	c	from $(n + 1).1$ and $(n + 2).2$

We are now ready to give a formal definition of the forward computation rules. Since we are going to have many boxes, one inside the other, rather than drawing them we are better off naming the boxes and just listing the clauses inside the boxes.

DEFINITION 10.13 (Modal forward computation rules). A state in the computation is a sequence of lines. Associated with each line are a label, a formula, a graph and a justification. So:

Line #: label, formula, graph, justification.

Lines can be obtained from previous lines as follows:

1. The line can be a *tautology*.[1] The label can be any label. The justification is 'tautology'. The graph is the same as the previous line.

2. The line can be an *assumption*. The label is o, the graph is $\{o\}$ (one-point graph), the justification is 'assumption'.

---

[1] Our discussion in this chapter so far was of *classical modal logic*, i.e. adding a modality $\Box$ to classical logic. Thus by 'tautology' we mean 'classical tautology'. We can also base our modal logic on other non-classical logics, say intuitionistic logic. In this case we can take 'tautology' to mean 'intuitionistic tautology'. We have to make a similar change in item 8 below in this definition. See also Definition 10.15 'Intuitionistic modal logic'.

3. *Modus ponens*: a line can be obtained from two previous lines of the form

m: a: $A \Rightarrow B$
n: a: A

where a is the label. We can then get a new line as follows:

Current line k : $a : B$.

It is assumed that the two previous lines m, n have the same label. The new label for line k is also the same label—a. The graph is the same as the previous line $(k - 1)$. The justification is '*modus ponens* from m, n'.

4. $\Diamond$-*elimination*: if $m < k$ and line m is $a : \Diamond X$ then line k can be $a_1 : X$ where a_1 is a *new* label not used so far in the proof. The new graph is the old graph together with a new node a_1 and the new connection aRa_1. The justification is 'from line m by creating a_1'.

5. $\Diamond$-*introduction*: the current *line k* : a_1 : $\Diamond X$ is obtained from a previous *line* $m : a : X$ with $m < k$. The graph of line k is the same as the graph of the previous line; the label a_1 is already in the graph, and a_1Ra. The justification is 'from line m by accessibility'.

6. $\Box$-*elimination*: the current line is k : a_2 : X, obtained from an earlier *line* $m : a : \Box X$, if in the graph of line $k - 1$ we have aRa_2. The new graph is the same as the graph of line $k - 1$ and the justification is 'from line m via accessibility'.

7. Rule for falsity $\bot$. Obtain the *line k* : a : $\bot$ from any previous *line* $m : a_1$: $\bot$.

8. Use all classical box rules for $\wedge, \Rightarrow$ and $\bot$, retaining the same label and graph with the justification being the 'classical box rule'.

9. To prepare for computation write any $\neg A$ as $A \Rightarrow \bot$. In the query, write any $\Box A$ as $\Diamond(A \Rightarrow \bot) \Rightarrow \bot$.

We say that *assumptions* $A_1, \ldots, A_n$ *prove* B (notation $A_1, \ldots, A_n \vdash B$) if there is a proof of the form:

1) o : A_1 assumption

$\vdots$

n) o : A_n assumption

$\vdots$

k) o: B.

EXAMPLE 10.14.

1. $o : \Box A$

2. $o : \Box(A \Rightarrow B)$.

The query is $\{1, 2\} \vdash ?o : \Box B$.

We first rewrite the goal as $\Diamond(B \Rightarrow \bot) \Rightarrow \bot$. We then obtain:

3. $o : \Diamond(B \Rightarrow \bot) \Rightarrow \bot$ from 'box':

3.1	$o : \Diamond(B \Rightarrow \bot)$	assumption	(box is to show $o : \bot$)
3.2	$a : B \Rightarrow \bot$	by creating from 3.1 a new label a with oRa	
3.3	$a : A$	from 1 by rule 6	
3.4	$a : A \Rightarrow B$	from 2 by rule 6	
3.5	$a : B$	from 3.3 and 3.4	
3.6	$a : \bot$	from 3.2 and 3.5	
3.7	$o : \bot$	from 3.6 by rule 7.	

With the forward rules one has to guess how to go forward. We want a backward computation. Here is the definition.

DEFINITION 10.15 (Challenge: intuitionistic modal logic). Consider a language with $\land, \Diamond, \Rightarrow$ and $\bot$, and atoms $p, q, \dots$. Define the notion of a *clause* as follows:

1. $\bot$ is a clause and an atom.

2. If A_i are clauses then $(\bigwedge A_i \Rightarrow \text{atom})$ is a clause.

3. If A_i are clauses then $\Diamond \bigwedge A_i$ is a clause.

4. Nothing else is a clause.

Define the following algorithmic system for this modal language: the basic predicate is $\mathbf{S}(D, T, R, t, Q)$ (**S** stands for 'success'), where

- D is a set of labelled clauses of the form $s : A$, where A is a clause and s is a label.

- T is the set of labels.

- $R \subseteq T \times T$ represents the accessibility relation.

- $t \in T$.

- Q is the current goal to prove.

Rule 1

$\mathbf{S}(D, T, R, t, Q)$ if Q is atomic and for some $t : A \Rightarrow Q$ or $t : A \Rightarrow \bot$ in D we have $\mathbf{S}(D, T, R, t, A)$.

Rule 2

$\mathbf{S}(D, T, R, t, Q)$ 　　　　if Q is atomic and $t : Q \in D$ or if $s : \bot \in D$ for any s.

Rule 3

$\mathbf{S}(D, T, R, t, Q \wedge Q')$ 　if $\mathbf{S}(D, T, R, t, Q)$ and $\mathbf{S}(D, T, R, t, Q')$.

Rule 4

$\mathbf{S}(D, T, R, t, Q \Rightarrow Q')$ 　if $\mathbf{S}(D \cup \{t : Q\}, T, R, t, Q')$.

Rule 5

$\mathbf{S}(D, T, R, t, \Diamond Q)$ 　　　if for some $s \in T$ such that tRs, $\mathbf{S}(D, T, R, s, Q)$.

Rule 6

$\mathbf{S}(D, T, R, t, \Diamond Q)$ 　　　if for some $(t : \Diamond \bigwedge A_i) \in D$ and some new label r,
　　　　　　　　　　　　$\mathbf{S}(D \cup \{r : A_i\}, T \cup \{r\}, R \cup \{(t, r)\}, r, Q)$.

Rule 7

$\mathbf{S}(D, T, R, t, Q)$ 　　　　if for some $(s : B \Rightarrow \bot) \in D$, $\mathbf{S}(D, T, R, s, B)$.

Rule 8

$\mathbf{S}(D, T, R, t, Q)$ 　　　　if $\mathbf{S}(D, T, R, s, \bot)$ for any s.

EXERCISE 10.16.

(a) (Challenge) Show that the relation defined by

$$\{A_i\} \vdash B \text{ iff } \mathbf{S}(\{t : A_i\}, \{t\}, \varnothing, t, B) \text{ succeeds}$$

　　is a consequence relation.

(b) (Challenge) Write a Prolog interpreter for the above algorithmic system.

REMARK 10.17. We can add the restart rule:

Rule 9

$\mathbf{S}(D, T, R, t, Q)$ if $\mathbf{S}(D, T, R, t, Q')$, when Q' is the original query associated with the label t when it was introduced.[2]

With the restart rule we get the modal logic **K**. (Challenge exercise: prove it.)

EXAMPLE 10.18.
   Show

   1. $\Box a$

   2. $\Box(A \Rightarrow B)$

The query is $\vdash ?\Box b$.
   We have to translate $\Box a$ as $\Diamond(a \Rightarrow \bot) \Rightarrow \bot$.
   The problem in translation becomes
   Data:
     (0) *Now:* $\Diamond\bot \Rightarrow \bot$ (we add this 'axiom' to all databases)
     (1) *Now:* $\Diamond(a \Rightarrow \bot) \Rightarrow \bot$
     (2) *Now:* $\Diamond[(a \Rightarrow b) \Rightarrow \bot] \Rightarrow \bot$
   Query:
     (3) $\vdash$? *Now:* $\Diamond(b \Rightarrow \bot) \Rightarrow \bot$
Now is the label for the actual world.

Computation
Ask for ? (3) at *now* and get from rule 4 the new database and query as indicated below:
     (0) *Now*   as above
     (1) *Now*   as above
     (2) *Now*   as above
     (4) *Now* $\Diamond(b \Rightarrow \bot)$
   with the query $\vdash ?\bot$ at *now*.

   From (0) (by rule 1 or 7) we ask $?\Diamond\bot$. From (4) and rule 6 we ask at t :$?\bot$, where t is a new label, with (*now* Rt), and where we add to the database clause 5 with label t:

$$(5)\, t : b \Rightarrow \bot$$

We continue from (5). Using rule 1 or 7 we ask at t, $?b$.

   We cannot go on, so we try to get a contradiction from rule 8, and hence our query becomes

$$?\bot \text{ at } now$$

---

[2]To do this right we must add a history H to the predicate $\mathbf{S}$ (i.e. turning it into the predicate $\mathbf{S}(D, T, R, t, Q, H)$, recording previous '$(t, Q)$'s of the computation).

and then by rule 1 from (2),

$$?\Diamond[(a \Rightarrow b) \Rightarrow \perp] \text{ at } now$$

We now have enough labels to use rule 5. We get

$$?(a \Rightarrow b) \Rightarrow \perp \text{ at } t$$

Add

(6) $t : a \Rightarrow b$ to data, and use rule 4 to ask
$?\perp$ at t

Using (5) we get at t, $?b$, and then by (6) we get at t, $?a$.
   Again we try to get a contradiction from rule 8 and (1)

$$?\Diamond(a \Rightarrow \perp) \text{ at } now$$

Continue by rule 5:

$$?a \Rightarrow \perp \text{ at } t$$

At last we can use rule 4 to add to the data $t : (7)a$. We now ask:

$$? \vdash \text{ at } t$$

From (5) ask $?b$ at t.
From (6) ask $?a$ at t.
From (7) we succeed.

EXERCISE 10.19.

1. Let $A = (p \Rightarrow \neg q) \wedge q, B_1 = \Box\neg A \Rightarrow \neg\Box q, B_2 = \neg\Box\Box(\Box q \vee p)$. Let M be the modal structure of Figure 9.1.

   The accessibility relation R is shown by the arrows, and the truth values of p, q in each world are as marked, i.e.

$$
\begin{array}{ll}
h(0, p) = \top & h(0, q) = \perp \\
h(t, p) = \top & h(t, q) = \top \\
h(s, p) = \perp & h(s, q) = \top
\end{array}
$$

   Calculate the truth values of B_1 and B_2 in each world in M.

2. Now define a new modal structure M'. M' has the same worlds as M, and p, q have the same truth values in each world as in M; however, R', the accessibility relation in M', is such that for any worlds $a, b, R'(a, b)$ iff $R(a, b)$ or $a = b$ (i.e. R' is the reflexive closure of R). What are the truth values of B_1 and B_2 in the worlds in M'?

2 Modal quantifiers

In this section we briefly discuss some of the aspects of predicate logics being given non-classical semantics. We will look in particular at how different ways of interpreting variables in temporal logics can radically alter the meaning of formulae. Recall the temporal logic of Definition 2.4, specialized for two truth values $\{0, 1\}$ in which we allowed $A \rightarrowtail B$ to be true only if A and $\neg B$ are never true together along a flow of time. Suppose now that A and B are predicate formulae, such as $A(x, y) \rightarrowtail B(y, z)$, so that x is a variable which only appears in $A(x, y)$, and z only appears in $B(y, z)$. y is shared by A and B.

The nature of each of the variables x, y and z depends on several factors, including the relative positioning of their respective quantifiers with respect to operators such as the temporal $\rightarrowtail$. For example, consider the formula

$$\forall x. \forall y. \forall z. \ A(x,y) \rightarrowtail B(y,z)$$

Now let us suppose that we have a domain which consists of the natural numbers. By the meaning of $\forall$ given earlier, we can expand this formula to (the possibly infinite)

$$(\forall y. \forall z. \ A(1,y) \rightarrowtail B(y,z)) \ \wedge \ (\forall y. \forall z. \ A(2,y) \rightarrowtail B(y,z)) \ \wedge \ \ldots$$

which can be further expanded to

$$(\forall z. \ (A(1,1) \rightarrowtail B(1,z)) \ \wedge \ (A(1,2) \rightarrowtail B(2,z)) \ \wedge \ \ldots) \ \wedge$$
$$(\forall z. \ (A(2,1) \rightarrowtail B(1,z)) \ \wedge \ (A(2,2) \rightarrowtail B(2,z)) \ \wedge \ \ldots) \ \wedge \ \ldots$$

and finally we get to

$$(((A(1,1) \rightarrowtail B(1,1)) \ \wedge \ (A(1,1) \rightarrowtail B(1,2)) \ \wedge \ \ldots) \ \wedge$$
$$((A(1,1) \rightarrowtail B(1,1)) \ \wedge \ (A(1,1) \rightarrowtail B(1,2)) \ \wedge \ \ldots) \ ) \ \wedge$$
$$(((A(2,1) \rightarrowtail B(1,1)) \ \wedge \ (A(2,1) \rightarrowtail B(1,2)) \ \wedge \ \ldots) \ \wedge$$
$$((A(2,1) \rightarrowtail B(1,1)) \ \wedge \ (A(2,1) \rightarrowtail B(1,2)) \ \wedge \ \ldots) \ ) \ \wedge \ \ldots$$

Thus we end up with a conjunction of formulae of the form $A(i, j) \rightarrowtail B(j, k)$ with i, j and k being given values of each of the natural numbers. Thus we have a typical implication such as $A(3,7) \rightarrowtail B(7,16)$ to check. Now the truth of this is decided by checking whether $B(7,16)$ is true at each time when $A(3,7)$ is true. This is essentially the same as classical predicate logic — the quantifiers can be eliminated to reach a (possibly infinite) propositional formula, which can be interpreted by the propositional rules.

Matters become more interesting when the quantifiers only take effect at the future moments. For example, consider the formula

$$\forall x. \forall y. \ A(x,y) \rightarrowtail \exists z. \ B(y,z)$$

We can expand the $\forall x$ and $\forall y$ to reach a conjunction with the typical member

$$A(5,2) \twoheadrightarrow \exists z.\ B(2,z) \qquad\qquad (*)$$

Now this is true provided that for each moment of time in which $A(5,2)$ is true, $\exists z.\ B(2,z)$ is true—in other words, there is an element in the domain which z can be mapped to which makes $B(2,z)$ true. Now consider the formula

$$\forall x. \forall y. \exists z.\ A(x,y) \twoheadrightarrow B(y,z)$$

Again, we can expand this formula to a conjunction, which this time has typical member

$$\exists z.\ A(5,2) \twoheadrightarrow B(2,z) \qquad\qquad (\dagger)$$

This formula is true as long as there is an element in the domain which z can be mapped onto such that for all moments in time in which $A(5,2)$ is true, $B(2,z)$ is true. This differs from the meaning of $(*)$ in that only a single selection of an element from the domain is allowed for $(\dagger)$, which must make $B(2,z)$ true whenever $A(5,2)$ is true, for all times. For $(*)$, z can be mapped to a different element in the domain at each time, provided that $B(2,z)$ is true whenever $A(5,2)$ is true. In effect, the $\twoheadrightarrow$ is acting in part as a universal quantifier *over time points*, so that $(*)$ is of the form $\forall\exists$, roughly meaning 'for all times, there exists an element...', whereas $(\dagger)$ is of the form $\exists\forall$, 'there exists an element such that for all times...'. Now by the basic classical quantifier equivalences of Figure 8.1, $(*)$ and $(\dagger)$ are equivalent,

$$[A(5,2) \twoheadrightarrow \exists z.\ B(2,z)] \quad \twoheadleftarrow\twoheadrightarrow \quad [\exists z.\ A(5,2) \Rightarrow B(2,z)]$$

but as we have seen, in the temporal logic they are not. Just as $\forall x. \exists y.\ \varphi(x,y)$ is not equivalent to $\exists y. \forall x.\ \varphi(x,y)$ in classical logic, because the y in the former depends on the x whereas in the latter it does not, so the z in $(*)$ depends on the moment of time being considered but in $(\dagger)$ it does not.

Returning to the formula $\forall x. \forall y. \forall z.\ A(x,y) \twoheadrightarrow B(y,z)$, we might ask whether it is equivalent to $\forall x. \forall y.\ A(x,y) \twoheadrightarrow \forall z.\ B(y,z)$, or by expanding out the $\forall x$ and $\forall y$,

$$[A(5,2) \twoheadrightarrow \forall z.\ B(2,z)] \quad \twoheadleftarrow\twoheadrightarrow \quad [\forall z.\ A(5,2) \twoheadrightarrow B(2,z)]$$

Both formulae are of the form $\forall\forall$, roughly meaning 'for all times, for all elements', and adjacent universal quantifiers can be swapped around without altering the meaning, so that we can state 'for all elements, for all times...' and have the same meaning.

3   Domains

For the classical predicate logic, we had a single domain $\mathcal{D}$ in our interpretations, $\mathcal{M} = \langle \mathcal{D}, \pi_{cons}, \pi_{func}, \pi_{pred} \rangle$, and for some of our non-classical logics, that will still be the case. The temporal logic we have just used was interpreted against a single domain, although it can be argued that the time flow itself is a second domain, and we have seen how the $\twoheadrightarrow$ acted as a quantifier over the time flow. For the moment we shall regard the time flow as a different class of domain from those which the variables are mapped to.

To keep close to real applications we must suppose that different domains are used for each moment of time, so that a member of the domain at one particular moment of time may not be a member of the domain at the next moment of time. However, temporal logic is complex and in this introductory section we want to simplify and assume that domains increase with time, i.e. elements do not die. This is not so counterintuitive, if we bear in mind that although elements die, we continue to talk about them. Let T be a set of moments of time, ordered by the binary relation $\leq$. The model then becomes

$$\mathcal{M} = \langle \mathcal{D}^T = \{\mathcal{D}_t \mid t \in T\}, \{\pi^t_{\text{cons}} \mid t \in T\}, \{\pi^t_{\text{func}} \mid t \in T\}, \{\pi^t_{\text{pred}} \mid t \in T\}\rangle$$

with each of the mappings being altered to depend on the moment of time at which the mapping is applied. We assume for simplicity that there exists a non-empty core set $\mathcal{D}$ of elements that always exist, namely

$$\mathcal{D} = \bigcap_{t \in T} \mathcal{D}_t$$

Therefore

- π^t_{cons} is a mapping from members of $\mathcal{L}_{\text{cons}}$ to $\mathcal{D}_t$,

- π^t_{func} is a mapping from members of $\mathcal{L}_{\text{func}}$ to a function mapping $\mathcal{D}^n$ to $\mathcal{D}$, for each $p \in \mathcal{L}_{\text{func}}, \pi_{\text{func}}(p): \mathcal{D}^n_t \mapsto \mathcal{D}_t$, where n is the arity of the member of $\mathcal{L}_{\text{func}}$, and

- π^t_{pred} is a mapping from members of $\mathcal{L}_{\text{pred}}$ to $\mathcal{D}^n_t \mapsto \{\top, \bot\}$, where n is the arity of the member of $\mathcal{L}_{\text{pred}}$.

As for classical logic, we have a variable assignment, but this time it is a mapping V from $\mathcal{L}_{\text{var}}$ to the core set $\mathcal{D}$ (this will ensure that all assignments are well defined in each possible world). Given this, we can interpret all the terms of $\mathcal{L}$ by means of a term mapping π^t_{term}, based on V, π^t_{cons} and π^t_{func}, which maps all members of $\mathcal{L}_{\text{term}}$ to $\mathcal{D}_t$. For terms t in $\mathcal{L}_{\text{term}}$:

- for all members c of $\mathcal{L}_{\text{cons}}$, $\pi^t_{\text{term}}(c) = \pi^t_{\text{cons}}(c)$

- for all members v of $\mathcal{L}_{\text{var}}$, $\pi^t_{\text{term}}(v) = V(v)$

- for all members f of $\mathcal{L}_{\text{func}}$ with arity n, $\pi^t_{\text{term}}(f(t_1, \ldots, t_n)) = \pi^t_{\text{func}}(f)(\pi^t_{\text{term}}(t_1), \ldots, \pi^t_{\text{term}}(t_n))$.

The reader should note that we can still allow for varying domains with elements dying provided we understand $\Box A(a)$ as true in all future worlds in which a exists. As an example, consider a model of time in which the moments of time are the natural numbers, and the domains are letters of the alphabet—the entire alphabet for even-numbered times, and just the consonants for the odd-numbered times. Now we return to the formula $\forall x. \forall y. \quad A(x,y) \twoheadrightarrow \forall z. \ B(y,z)$. We expand out the $\forall x$ and $\forall y$ as before, but over our new model, assuming that we are at the start of time so that $t = 0$. Because 0 is even, the domain over which x and y range is the entire alphabet $\{a, \ldots, z\}$. Hence our formula is equivalent to

$$(A(a,a) \twoheadrightarrow \forall z. \ B(a,z)) \ \wedge \ \cdots \ \wedge \ (A(a,z) \twoheadrightarrow \forall z. \ B(z,z)) \ \wedge$$
$$\vdots$$
$$(A(z,a) \twoheadrightarrow \forall z. \ B(a,z)) \ \wedge \ \cdots \ \wedge \ (A(z,z) \twoheadrightarrow \forall z. \ B(z,z))$$

Again we can illustrate our point by considering a typical member of this conjunction, namely

$$A(m,n) \twoheadrightarrow \forall z. \ B(n,z)$$

The meaning of this formula is that in every time in the future in which $A(m,n)$ is true must have $\forall z. \ B(n,z)$. Now when $A(m,n)$ is true in even moments of time, the $\forall z$ is expanded out over the domain of the entire alphabet, as for $\forall x$ and $\forall y$. For these times,

$$[A(m,n) \twoheadrightarrow \forall z. \ B(n,z)] \quad \longleftrightarrow \quad [\forall z. \ A(m,n) \twoheadrightarrow B(n,z)]$$

However, when $A(m,n)$ is true in odd moments of time, the $\forall z$ is expanded out over the domain of only the consonants, so that we only have one direction of the $\longleftrightarrow$ holding:

$$[A(m,n) \twoheadrightarrow \forall z. \ B(n,z)] \quad \longleftarrow \quad [\forall z. \ A(m,n) \twoheadrightarrow B(n,z)]$$

4 Modal temporal logic

In Chapter 2, we introduced the $\Box$ and $\Diamond$ modalities, with $\Box A$ meaning that A will always be true, and $\Diamond A$ meaning that A will be true at some (unknown) future moment. These two modalities were defined by means of the temporal $\twoheadrightarrow$. We now directly define $\Box$ and $\Diamond$ as parts of the language in their own right, and use classical $\Rightarrow$. The modalities are interdefinable, so only one ($\Diamond$) is included as part of the definition.

DEFINITION 10.20 ((Modal) Temporal predicate many-valued logic).   A formula
φ is true in interpretation $\mathcal{M}$ with respect to a time t and variable assignment V, to the non-empty core $\mathcal{D} = \bigcap_t \mathcal{D}_t$, written $\langle \mathcal{M}, V \rangle \vDash^t \varphi$, according to this definition:

$\langle \mathcal{M}, V \rangle \nvDash^t \bot$

$\langle \mathcal{M}, V \rangle \vDash^t p(t_1, \ldots, t_n)$ iff $\pi^t_{\text{pred}}(p)(\pi^t_{\text{term}}(t_1), \ldots, \pi^t_{\text{term}}(t_n)) = \top$

$\langle \mathcal{M}, V \rangle \vDash^t \varphi \Rightarrow \psi$ iff $\langle \mathcal{M}, V \rangle \vDash^t \varphi$ implies $\langle \mathcal{M}, V \rangle \vDash^t \psi$

$\langle \mathcal{M}, V \rangle \vDash^t \exists v. \, \varphi$ iff   there exists $d \in \mathcal{D}_t$ and $(\mathcal{M}, V_{[v \mapsto d]}) \vDash^t \varphi$

$\langle \mathcal{M}, V \rangle \vDash^t \Diamond \varphi$ iff   there exists $s \in T$ such that $t \le s$ and
$\langle \mathcal{M}, V \rangle \vDash^s \varphi$

In this definition, the only real changes from the classical definition are to the condition for $\vDash$ for atomic sentences, where the appropriate time point is used in the predicate and term mappings, and in the condition for $\Diamond$. Notice that the definition of the meaning of $\Diamond$ is not concerned simply with finding a future time s, but an s in which the terms of φ all refer to members of the domain of s. Without this restriction, we might have to evaluate the truth of a formula which had been mapped onto members of another domain entirely. For example, the sentence 'in the future, Dylan gets married' requires us to evaluate the truth of 'Dylan gets married' at all the future points. However, at those future points at which Dylan no longer exists (i.e. after his death) there will be no domain individual for Dylan to refer to, and hence the sentence 'Dylan gets married' will have no determinable truth value. Thus we will have violated one of the basic assumptions that we have made in this book: that each sentence can receive a truth value of some sort.

To illustrate this logic, let us have a (function-free) language based on the following sets:

- $\mathcal{L}_{\text{cons}} = \{a, b, c, d, e\}$

- $\mathcal{L}_{\text{var}} = \{x, y, z\}$

- $\mathcal{L}_{\text{pred}} = \{p, q\}$, p with arity 2, and q with arity 1.

Let the model based on two moments of time $0 \le 1$ be given by

$$\mathcal{M} = (\{\mathcal{D}_0, \mathcal{D}_1\}, \pi^t_{\text{cons}}, \pi^t_{\text{func}}, \pi^t_{\text{pred}}) :$$

$$
\begin{aligned}
\mathcal{D}_0 &= \{a, b, c, d\} \\
\mathcal{D}_1 &= \{a, b, c, d, e\} \\
\pi^0_{\text{cons}} &\text{ is } \{a \mapsto a, b \mapsto b, c \mapsto c, d \mapsto d\} \\
\pi^1_{\text{cons}} &\text{ is } \{c \mapsto c, d \mapsto d, e \mapsto e\} \\
\pi^0_{\text{pred}} &\text{ is } \{p \mapsto \{(a, b) \mapsto \top, (b, c) \mapsto \top\}, \\
&\qquad q \mapsto \{a \mapsto \top, c \mapsto \top\} \\
\pi^1_{\text{pred}} &\text{ is } \{p \mapsto \{(c, d) \mapsto \top, (c, e) \mapsto \top\}, \\
&\qquad q \mapsto \{c \mapsto \top, e \mapsto \top\}
\end{aligned}
$$

all other combinations being assigned $\perp$ by π^0_{pred} and π^1_{pred}. Let $\mathcal{D}_1 = \mathcal{D}_0$, $\pi^i_{\text{cons}} = \pi^0_{\text{cons}}$ and $\pi^i_{\text{pred}} = \pi^0_{\text{pred}}$ when i is even, and $\mathcal{D}_i = \mathcal{D}_1$, $\pi^i_{\text{cons}} = \pi^1_{\text{cons}}$ and $\pi^i_{\text{pred}} = \pi^1_{\text{pred}}$ when i is odd.

We can evaluate formulae in this model with respect to time 0 and with the initial variable assignment V. For example, suppose we have the formula $\exists x.\; q(x) \wedge \Diamond \neg q(x)$.

$$\langle \mathcal{M}, V \rangle \vDash^0 \exists x.\; q(x) \wedge \Diamond \neg q(x)$$

iff   there exists $d \in \mathcal{D}_0$ and $\langle \mathcal{M}, V_{[x \mapsto d]} \rangle \vDash^0 q(x) \wedge \Diamond \neg q(x)$

iff $\langle \mathcal{M}, V_{[x \mapsto a]} \rangle \vDash^0 q(x) \wedge \Diamond \neg q(x)$

iff $\langle \mathcal{M}, V_{[x \mapsto a]} \rangle \vDash^0 q(x)$ and $\langle \mathcal{M}, V_{[x \mapsto a]} \rangle \vDash^0 \Diamond \neg q(x)$

iff $\pi^0_{\text{pred}}(q)(\pi^0_{\text{term}}(x)) = \top$ and there exists $s \in T$ and $0 \le s$ and
$\langle \mathcal{M}, V_{[x \mapsto a]} \rangle \vDash^s \neg q(x)$

iff $\langle \mathcal{M}, V_{[x \mapsto a]} \rangle \nvDash^1 q(x)$

iff $\pi^1_{\text{pred}}(q)(\pi^1_{\text{term}}(x)) = \perp$

iff   true

EXERCISE 10.21.

1. Using the model just given, establish the truth value of the sentences:

$$\varphi_1 = \forall x. \forall y.\; (p(x,y) \Rightarrow \Diamond q(y))$$
$$\varphi_2 = \forall x. \forall y.\; (p(x,y) \Rightarrow \exists z.\; \Diamond q(z))$$

2. Given that $\Box A \equiv \neg \Diamond \neg A$, establish the truth value of the sentences:

$$\varphi_3 = \exists y.\; \Box q(y)$$
$$\varphi_4 = \Box \exists x. \exists y.\; p(x,y) \wedge \neg q(y)$$

Over increasing or varying domains, the Barcan formula is not necessarily true — as we have seen, we can have a domain $\mathcal{D}$ now and a domain $\mathcal{D} \cup \{a\}$ in the future, where $a \notin \mathcal{D}$. Suppose that for all times, all members of $\mathcal{D}$ possessed the property φ, but that a did not possess that property. This would make the condition of the Barcan formula true. Yet there would be a time in the future, when there was an object in the domain (namely a) for which φ was false. Hence the Barcan formula would be false.

The converse of the Barcan formula is tautological, however:

$$[\Box \forall x.\; \varphi(x)] \; \Rightarrow \; [\forall x.\; \Box \varphi(x)]$$

must be true in all situations, because whenever the condition is true, all objects in all future worlds possess the property φ, and hence all the objects which possess the property φ now must possess it in all future worlds (in which they exist—recall the extra restriction on the meaning of the modal operator).

EXERCISE 10.22.   Decide whether the following are tautologies of the modal temporal logic presented above.

1. $[\Diamond \forall x.\ \varphi(x)] \Rightarrow [\forall x.\ \Diamond \varphi(x)]$

2. $[\exists x.\ \Box \varphi(x)] \Rightarrow [\Box \exists x.\ \varphi(x)]$

3. $[\forall x.\ \Diamond \varphi(x)] \Rightarrow [\Diamond \forall x.\ \varphi(x)]$

4. $[\Box \exists x.\ \varphi(x)] \Rightarrow [\exists x.\ \Box \varphi(x)]$

5   Worked examples

EXAMPLE 10.23 (Domains).   Consider a temporal flow of time with the natural numbers as the moments of time: $1 \le 2, \le 3, \le 4 \le \cdots \le n \le \ldots$.
   The domains are as follows

$$\mathcal{D}_n = \{a_1, \ldots, a_n\},\ n = 1, 2, 3, \ldots$$

Note that at time n, a_n is the person 'just born'.
   Consider the constants $\mathbf{c}$, $\mathbf{b}$ of the predicate language (think of $\mathbf{c}$ as the local congressman and $\mathbf{b}$ as the local baker on duty) and suppose they may change every year. $\pi_{cons}^n(\mathbf{c})$ gives the local congressman of the year n, and similarly $\pi_{cons}^n(\mathbf{b})$ gives the baker. Variable assignments $V(x)$ are fixed and do not change with time. Thus $\mathcal{D} = \bigcap_n \mathcal{D}_n = \mathcal{D}_1$ is the core domain and $V(x) \in \mathcal{D}$ for all variables x. Recall that

$$n \vDash \Box \varphi \text{ iff for all } m \ge n, m \vDash \varphi$$
$$n \vDash \Diamond \varphi \text{ iff for some } m \ge n, m \vDash \varphi$$

Express the following in temporal logic (assume evaluation at $n = 1$):

1. Eventually the congressman will be the same every year.

2. Sometimes the baker and congressman are the same.

3. Everybody becomes the congressman sooner or later.

4. The congressman is always the person 'just born'.

5. Someone will repeatedly become the congressman.

6. A baker never becomes a congressman.

Solutions

1. $\Diamond\Box(\exists x.(\Box(x = \mathbf{c})))$

2. $\forall x.\Diamond(x = \mathbf{c})$

3. $\Diamond(\mathbf{b} = \mathbf{c})$

4. $\forall x.\Box(x = \mathbf{c} \rightarrow \Box(x \neq \mathbf{c}))$. This one is tricky. At time 1, there is only one element a_1 so it must be $\mathbf{c}$. If at any time the local congressman can never be a congressman again, then at time 2 the only available option is a_2 etc.

   Sentence 4 means what it means only in this particular model!

5. $\Diamond\exists x.\Box\Diamond(x = \mathbf{c})$

6. $\Box\forall x.(x = \mathbf{b} \rightarrow \Box(x \neq \mathbf{c}))$.

Summary

The reader is warned that the area of modal and temporal logics is very wide and complex. See [Gabbay *et al.*, 1994] and [Gabbay, 1976]. This chapter just gave a taste of it.

6   Two dimensional temporal logic

Classical propositional logic can be viewed as describing the state of affairs at a single moment of time. If q_i are atomic then any assignment h (row in the truth table) giving a value $\top$ or $\bot$ to each q_i is simply saying what the truth value of q_i is at that state. The different rows in the truth table are all the possibilities for h. When we present a database $\Delta = \{A_1, \ldots, A_n\}$ and ask whether $\Delta \vdash G$ for some goal G, we similarly deal with a single state, a single moment of time (say *now*) and ask whether, if Δ is true, so must be G.

When we have variation over time, we need another parameter, the time t, and the assignment h also depends on t. Thus we write $h(t, q_i) = \top$ or $\bot$. We have to say what kind of flow of time we have.

In this case a database will involve statement true at different times and the goal also be a statement about a moment of time.

Let us assume that we have a tree T flow of time as in Figure 10.3.

now is the present. We assume that the future is not known and we consider several options for tomorrow. At option t_1 we go to the office. At option t_2 we stay home, etc. We will actually take one of these options when tomorrow comes. Say we take option t_3 (that is at tomorrow what will happen will be as in t_3). Then the day after tomorrow will have several options, $t_{3,1}, t_{3,2}, \ldots$. We can carry on in this manner and get a tree for the open future as in Figure 10.3. Real history, what actually happens, will be a path in this tree. For example the path described in Figure 10.4.

The indices tell you which option did actually occur.

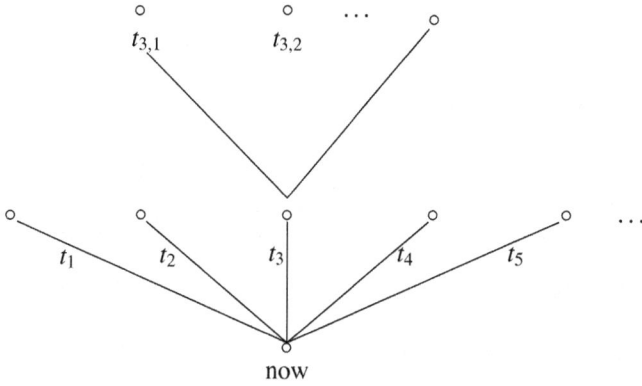

Figure 10.3.

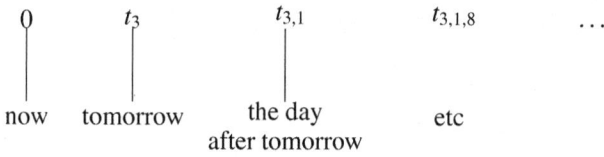

Figure 10.4.

If we rise above the system and look at the path as history, we get that time is linear.

$$0, 1, 2, 3, 4, \ldots$$

and at each moment of time m, $h(m, q)$ tells you whether $q = \top$ or $\bot$ at time m.

Now imagine we are at time $0 = now$ and we want to say that $A = \top$ tomorrow. How will you say it? There are two main options.

1. Use time as a label, and write

$$1 : A$$

According to this point of view a temporal database will have the form $\Delta = \{t_1 : A_1, \ldots, t_k : A_k\}$ and a goal has the form $s : G$, where $t : A$ means A is true at t. t may be a point of time or an interval. For example

$$[1980 - 2010] : A \Rightarrow B$$
$$2000 : A$$

imply

$$2000 : B$$

2. Have a special connective $\bigcirc A$, for tomorrow. So

- $\bigcirc A$ is true at time m iff A is true at time $m + 1$.

This is how natural language refers to time when convenient.

The simplest temporal logic uses the second option with the following connectives:

1. The usual connectives of classical logic $\neg, \wedge, \vee \Rightarrow, \top, \bot$

2. The temporal connectives
   $\bigcirc A$ (A is true tomorrow)
   YA (A was true yesterday)
   FA (A will be true at some day in the future)
   PA (A was true at some day in the past).

   We can also use
   GA (A will always be true)
   HA (A has always been true)
   We have
   $GA \equiv \neg F \neg A$
   $HA \equiv \neg P \neg A$
   $A \equiv \bigcirc Y A \equiv Y \bigcirc A$

DEFINITION 10.24 (Formal definition of one dimensional temporal logic).

1. We are given a *flow of time*) $(T, <, now)$ which is a set T of moments of time, with an irreflexive and transitive relation $<$ on T. This means that $t < s$ satisfies

   1.1. $\neg(t < t)$ for any t

   1.2. $t < s \wedge s < r \Rightarrow t < r$.
   $<$ is the earlier–later relation and $t < s$ means that s is in the future of t.
   We also need a name for "now" say $now \in T$.

2. We need an assignment h to the atoms, of the form $h(t, q) \in \{\top, \bot\}$ saying for each atomic q and each $t \in T$ whether q is true at t or not.

3. Now we can define the truth value of any temporal formula at any t as follows. ($t \vDash A$ says A is true at t).

   3.1. $t \vDash q$ iff $h(t, q) = \top$

   3.2. $t \vDash A \wedge B$ iff $t \vDash A$ and $t \vDash B$

   3.3. $t \vDash A \vee B$ iff $t \vDash A$ or $t \vDash B$

   3.4. $t \vDash \neg A$ iff $t \nvDash A$

   3.5. $t \vDash A \Rightarrow B$ iff either $t \nvDash A$ or $t \vDash B$

   3.6. $t \vDash FA$ iff for some $s, t < s$ and $s \vDash A$

   3.7. $t \vDash PA$ iff for some $s, s < t$ and $s \vDash A$

   3.8. When time is the numbers $0, 1, 2, 3, \ldots$, we can also write

      - $t \vDash \bigcirc A$ iff $t + 1 \vDash A$
      - $t \vDash YA$ iff $t - 1 \vDash A$ (provided $t \neq 0$)

   3.9. A formula is said to be a temporal tautology iff for any $(T, <, now)$ and any h. We have $now \vDash A$.

EXAMPLES 10.25.

1. For any tautology E of classical logic and any $t \in T$ we have $t \vDash E$. Here are some such tautologies.

   - $FB \vee \neg FB$
   - $FA \Rightarrow FA$

The following are temporal tautologies having to do with the meaning of P and F and the nature of the flow of time:

   - $FFA \Rightarrow FA$

- $A \Rightarrow PFA$

- $A \Rightarrow FPA$

EXERCISE 10.26. Show that for any $t, t \vDash FFA \Rightarrow FA$.

Solution

- $t \vDash FFA$ iff for some $s, t < s$ and $s \vDash FA$.

- $s \vDash FA$ iff for some $r, s < r$ and $r \vDash A$

- But $t < s \wedge s < r \Rightarrow t < r$,
  hence we have that $t \vDash FA$, because for some point (i.e. r) we have $t < r$ and $r \vDash A$.

Thus $t \vDash FFA \Rightarrow FA$ because if $t \vDash FFA$ then $t \vDash FA$.

EXERCISE 10.27.

1. Similarly show that for any $t, t \vDash A \Rightarrow FPA$

2. Show that if time is linear,
    i.e. we have $(t < s) \vee (t = x) \vee (s < t)$,
    then $t \vDash FA \wedge FB \Rightarrow F(A \wedge B) \vee F(A \wedge FB) \vee F(FA \wedge B)$, for any t.

The above treatment of time is one dimensional, i.e. we use only one index for time when we write

$$t \vDash A.$$

To express in logic the use of temporal expression in English the above is not sufficient.

Consider the following examples:

1. You will be glad in the future that I am helping you *now*.

If we analyse this sentence as;

- *now* $\vDash F$ (glad that help *now*)

then when we get to t in the future when we are glad we no longer 'remember' when *now* was!

Consider further:

2. John will find out that Mary betrayed him.

If we write the above as

- *now* $\vDash F$ find out (P betray)

We must have a t for "find out" such that $now < t$ and an s for "betray" such that $s < now$. The current logic can find an $s < t$ but not necessarily $s < now$, because by the time we get to t, we forget about where now was.

Consider

3. 'A child was born that will be king.'

The child was born in the past of *now*. He will be king in the future of *now*.

Take the English sentence:

4. 'John told me that he will not come to the meeting'.

This sentence means that at some time in the past t of *now*, John said that he will not come at some time s *in the future of now*.

Compare (4) with the following

5. 'Why didn't John come?'
   'Well, he told me he would be busy'.

There is a certain ambiguity here (we will have better examples later), but by and large, if the meeting has already taken place, one would use 'would' and if not — 'will'.

The iteration FPA has similar properties. Consider the following

6. 'If you will not be generous with your child, he will hate you for the hard time you will have given him'.

7. 'If you will not compensate your child, he will hate you for the hard time you gave him'.

In (6) the future perfect is used to indicate that the 'hard time' is in the past of 'hate' but still in the future of 'now'. While ordinary past takes us back to the past of 'now'.

Notice that both the 'future perfect' and the 'would', although they do not 'jump' over 'now', do not go all the way but still remain *bounded* by the present (compare with 11 below).

Consider more complex examples:

8. 'I knew that by the time the criminal is brought to trial, he will have realised that his best policy will be to deny that he owned the gun'.

9. 'I will not admit that it was I who told him that the price would change'.

The above examples show that there are two types of temporal operators involved

(a) $F_w A$ (A will be true)

(b) $F_d A$ (A would be true)

(c) $P_w A$ (A was true)

(d) $P_d A$ (A will have been true) (i.e. future perfect).

The examples suggest that the truth values of the tense operators cannot be evaluated simple mindedly 'at point s', i.e. 'the value of A at s').

    because:

1. The present *now*, is involved (i.e. with F_w and P_w that jump).

2. We have to know the point of reference of time that preceded s.

To understand (2), look at the following example:

10. 'He will realise, that by the time he will graduate, the draft will have been cancelled'.

By the way, compare (10) with

11. 'He will realise that the draft was cancelled'.

In (10) the 'will have been' refers to the time between his 'realisation' and 'graduation'. So we must keep a record of the time of his 'realisation'.

The above discussion indicates that we need to evaluate formulas at two points, the old evaluation point t and an additional reference point which we remember and use when we look for the next evaluation point, i.e. we write $(t, s) \vDash A$.

So suppose we start with evaluating at (now, now) when we apply F or P.

We move to a point (t, now) where t is the new evaluation point and *now* remains as the reference point. We have $t < now$ if we use P, and $t > now$ if we use F.

If we continue to apply F or P in the same direction (i.e. we have FF or PP) we continue to find a $t' > t$ (for F) or a $t' < t$ (for P) but keep the reference as *now*.

The minute we change direction, we have two possible situations either

- (Future perfect), 'will have'
  $(t, now) \vDash PA$, with $t > now$

or

- 'would' or 'will'
  $(t, now) \vDash FA$, with $t < now$.

In this case we can either ask for a point *s* 'trapped' between *t* and *now* and take the new reference point as *t* (as in 'would' or 'will have' or we jump over *now* and keep the reference point as now.

Further examples from English.

Up until now we mostly assumed that the only point that needs to be kept on record through the sequences is the *now* point, along with the immediately preceding point. There are, however, grounds for supposing that even this added feature will not take care of all of the complexities of iteration. (To be sure, we must be careful when we talk of iteration in this context. We don't have English sentences like: "it is the case that it will be the case that it was the case that ... etc." Rather, the tenses affect a sequence of events. In this respect the tense operators in English differ from the modal operators.)

We shall now consider sentences that seem to involve the consideration of points that are not *now*, or are immediately preceding the point to be computed. For example:

12. 'She regretted that she married the man who was to become an officer of the bank where she had had her account.'

The regret was prior to the time of utterance, the marriage prior to the regret, the promotion to the status of officer of the bank came after the marriage but prior to the point of utterance. Still, the period during which she had her account with the bank must have been prior to the marriage. Thus in order to calculate the last temporal reference point we must jump back to the last past, which is neither the starting point, nor the immediately preceding temporal point. (We are jumping over a future, so to speak.)

It is far from clear what sort of rule would take care of this phenomenon. For one thing, it is not clear that the interpretation of the sequence of temporal references is independent of the particular verbs used. Let us consider

11a. She regretted that she married the man who was to become an officer of the bank where she had opened her account'.

Syntactically and referentially we have the same structure; but the substitution of the verb 'open' seems to cast doubt on whether the last event must be prior to the marriage, or merely prior to the point of utterance.

Perhaps a clearer example would be

12. 'She will go to the school, that was her mothers' alma mater, and it will become better than Harvard'.

Here the going to school is in the future of the point of utterance, the mother's attendance is in the past of the point of utterance, but in order to calculate the time at which the school overtake Harvard we must consider the last future reference, and thus we jump over one point, the past reference to mother's attendance, without going all the way back to the original point of utterance.

Cases like (12) might be explained on syntactic grounds. We have here a coordinate structure, and what we 'jump over' is a relative clause off a first conjunct. Thus one explanation for the 'jumpings' might be that in a sequence of conjunctions the temporal reference points form a sequence that bypasses the sequence built into any possible relative clause. If this is so, it would show that one cannot formulate detailed rules for the complete semantics of tense iterations without taking into account the syntactic structures that make up the sequence. This is suggested also by

11b. 'She regretted that the man who was to become an officer of the bank where she had had her account married her'.

Clearly here too, the having of the account must be prior to the marriage even though the latter is only mentioned at the end of the sentence. We can explain this by pointing out that (11b) is transformationally related to (11). Once more we see that syntactic structure other than mere left-to-right ordering must be taken into account in the computation of the tense sequence.

In the meantime, the tentative conclusion is that we must keep record of the entire sequence of points and not only that, but also keep track of the kind of operators used (i.e. whether t_3 was introduced because of an F or not, because if we have another F, the next point may have to be chosen in the future of t_3!

Doubts:

1. We must make sure that in the examples above we use only the structure of the sequence of Ps and Fs and not the meaning of the verbs.

2. We don't naturally speak like $PFPA$ but introduce an event with each tense operator. E.g. he *thought* I will *find out* that she was *killed*. Is this significant for our purposes?

Do we take truth values at points?

Up to now we evaluated A either at a point of time or a sequence of points of time. The original underlying flow of time was not changed. $h(t, p)$ gave for each t and p the value of p at t. Is this OK?

13. 'Yesterday she worked in the garden for ten hours'.

14. 'This castle was built during the 17th Century'.

15. 'He won the game in the 17th Century'.

We see that some verbs can be evaluated at a moment of time (e.g. win) while others need a period of time! This means that $h(t, p)$ should be replaced by $h(I, p)$. I is an interval. We have no idea what table to give to the tense operators F, P, etc.

Conclusions

The preceding discussion showed that in order to present an adequate semantics and syntax for tensed English one must go beyond one dimensional logics. We have also seen, however, that the complications arising with regard to certain types of sentences as of now resist adequate treatment. Even so, our explorations at least helped to set the level of adequacy for the treatments of tense in English. For only a system that can fully account for the data surveyed briefly here we can claim descriptive adequacy. At the same time, the data in question indicate the possibility of uncovering interesting results concerning the interaction of the tense system with prior syntactic structure and analysis, as well as possible criteria of complexity of the semantics of natural languages.

EXERCISE 10.28. Analyse the sentences below

(*) The day after tomorrow John will deny he accepted the contract the day before.

(**) The day after tomorrow John will deny he accepted the contract tomorrow.

Can you explain why (**) sounds odd or even unacceptable?

Solution

We start analysing the English sentence by letting $now = 0 = x = y$.

The day after tomorrow takes us from $(0, 0)$ to $(2, 0)$. The denial of contract is the day before, namely at $(1, 0)$.

That is $1 = 2 - 1$, and is described relative to the evaluation point, namely the day after tomorrow.

If we describe 1 as $0 + 1$ (i.e. 'tomorrow'), we are using the reference point to describe an evaluation point and this is not allowed. This is why (**) sounds odd to unacceptable.

EXERCISE 10.29. Analyse the time sequence of the sentence below. How many dimensions do you need?

(***) When I made the arrest I knew that by the time the criminal is brought to trial he will have realised that his best policy would be to deny that he bought the gun.

Solution

Diagram 10.5 shows the sequence of events of (***)

We need two reference points and one evaluation point, i.e. we need three dimensions. We start at $(0, 0)$ and go to the time x_1 of the arrest in the past. We

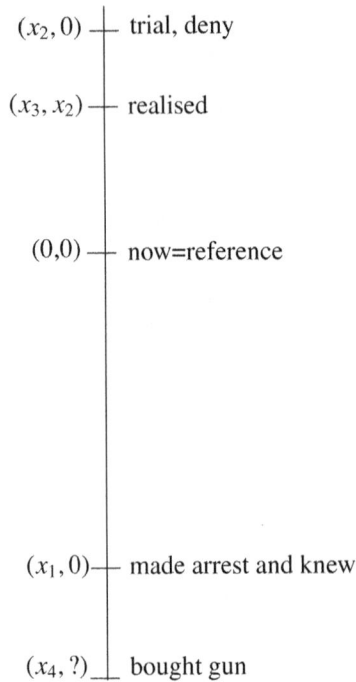

$(x_2, 0)$ ┼ trial, deny

(x_3, x_2) ┼ realised

$(0,0)$ ┼ now=reference

$(x_1, 0)$┼ made arrest and knew

$(x_4, ?)$ ┴ bought gun

Figure 10.5.

remember 0 as a reference because the trial at x_2 must be in the future of 0. 'He will have realised' is future perfect and so the realisation point x_3 is before x_2 and in the future of 0. By now the reference changes to x_2, as it should do with any future perfect. The deny is at x_2 but buying the gun is before the arrest at x_1 and so we must remember x_1. Thus we need three dimensions.

It is now time to give a formal definition for 2 dimensions.

DEFINITION 10.30. Let $(T, <, now)$ be a linear flow of time. It is convenient to assume that $(T, <)$ is the integers and $now = 0$. The propositional language has the atomic sentences $p, q, r, \ldots$ and the classical connectives $\neg, \wedge, \vee \Rightarrow$ together with the temporal connectives F and P. We evaluate at two indices (t, s), where t is the evaluation point and s is the reference point.

Let $h(t, q)$ be an assignment giving for each moment of time t and each atomic q a truth value $\top$ or $\bot$.

We now give the inductive definition for $t, s \vDash A$.

1. $t, s \vDash q$, for q atomic, iff $h(t, q) = \top$.

2. $t, s \vDash A \wedge B$ iff $t, s \vDash A$ and $t, s \vDash B$
   $t, s \vDash A \vee B$ iff $t, s \vDash A$ or $t, s \vDash B$
   $t, s \vDash \neg A$ iff $t, s \nvDash A$.

3. $t, s \vDash FA$
   depends on case analysis

   3.1 $t \geq s$
       $t, s \vDash FA$ iff for some $u > t, u, t \vDash A$
       Here we go to the future of t but keep s as the reference point.

   3.2 $t < s$
       Subcase F = would
       $t, s \vDash FA$ iff for some $u, t < u < s$
       $u, v \vDash A$.
       Here we trap the evaluation point between t and s.
       The new reference point is v.

       We have three possibilities for the choice of v.
       $v = s$ or $v = u$ or $v = t$.
       In the case of *would* $v = t$ is reasonable.

       Subcase F = will
       In this case we require F to jump over the reference point. So we have
       $t, s \vDash FA$ iff for some us, we have $u, v \vDash A$
       Again there are three choices for v, $v = t, v = u$ or $v = s$.

       In case of *will* it is reasonable to let $r = s$.

       To summarise, we have 6 possibilities for F when $t < s$.
       $t, s \vDash FA$ iff for some u, v, we have $u, v \vDash A$.
       The possibilities are

$$
\begin{array}{ll}
t < u < s & v = t \\
t < u < s & v = u \\
t < u < s & v = s \\
s < u & v = t \\
s < u & v = u \\
s < u & v = s
\end{array}
$$

The case of PA is symmetrical in its options

$$(t, s) \vDash PA \text{ iff for some } (u, r), u, r \vDash A.$$

The table is:

1. if $t \leq s$ then $u < t$ and $v = s$.

2. if $t > s$ then either $[s < u < t$ and $(v = s$ or $v = u$ or $v = t)$, this is the case of the future perfect] or $[u < s$ and $(v = s$ or $v = u$ or $v = t)$, this is the case of 'had'.]

EXAMPLE 10.31. $0,0 \vDash$ by the time the train arrives a taxi will have been ordered.
iff
$t, 0 \vDash P$ order taxi
iff
$u, v \vDash$ order taxi, $0 < u < t$, and $v = 0$ or $v = t$.

If we had in the sentence 'a taxi had been ordered', this would have forced $u < 0$ and $v = 0$ or $v = t$.

7   Examples in planning

Consider the blocks world problem. We have several blocks on the table and a robot can move the blocks around. We need a language for describing the states the blocks can be in, and a language for the actions of the robot. We give the robot a goal and the robot can use various algorithms to string a sequence of actions to achieve his goal.

Language for states

We have a table t and blocks named A, B, C, D, etc. The state is a configuration where some blocks are on top of others and some are on the table. Figure 10.6 is an example of a state

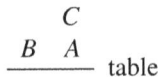

$$
\begin{array}{c}
C \\
B \quad A \\
\hline
\end{array} \quad \text{table}
$$

Figure 10.6.

B and A are on the table and C is on A. So we have a predicate on(x, y) which we use to specify what is on top of what and names for the blocks. The situation in Figure 10.6 can be described by the database Δ containing: {on(B, t), on(C, A), on(A, t)}. We agree that the following are constraints for the blocks world

1. on(x, y) $\wedge$ on(x, y') $\Rightarrow$ y = y'. A block cannot be on top of two different blocks.

2. on(x, y) $\wedge$ on(x', y) $\Rightarrow$ (x = x') $\vee$ y = t. A block can have at most one other block on top of it. The table can have as many blocks as we want on it.

3. $\forall x(x \neq t \Rightarrow \exists y \, on(x,y))$. A block which is not on the table is always on something.

4. We call a block (which is not on the table) Free if it has nothing on top of it. Thus

$$\text{Free}(x) \equiv \neg \exists y \, on(y,x). \text{ for } x \neq t$$

So a state Δ is a set of formulas saying which block is on top of which block.

EXAMPLE 10.32. Suppose we let $\Delta_1 = \{on(C,A), on(B,t)\}$.

We ask: is this a state?

Well, it doesn't say where A is. Do we have $on(A,B)$? Do we have $on(A,t)$?

Since we know that any $x \neq t$ must be on something, we want a state to tell us completely where (on what) everything is. So Δ_1 is a theory of blocks but not a fully specified state.

Actions

Actions can operate on states and change them to new states. Actions denoted by **a, b**, etc. have two components. The precondition of **a**, α_a, and the post-condition for **a**, β_a. Thus $\mathbf{a} = (\alpha_a, \beta_a)$. To enable the actions on Δ α_a must be true in Δ (in logic this means $\Delta \vdash \alpha_a$). Once the action is executed (we must have an algorithm for the robot to execute the action) then we get a new state and we are assured that the post-condition holds in the new state. In our case we have all actions of moving one block from one place to another.

So the preconditions for moving block x on top of block y are:

$\alpha 1$:   Free(x); i.e. nothing on top of x.

$\alpha 2$: $x \neq t$; we do not move the table.

$\alpha 3$:   (Free(y); nothing on top of y) or $y = t$. (We can put as many blocks as we want on the table).

$\alpha 4$: $on(x,z)$, x is on some z. Of course, we know that x has to be on something, but if we know that it is on z and that $z \neq t$, then when we move x and put it on y, then z becomes free. So we need z mentioned i the precondition to enable the new information we need to put in the post-condition.

Having executed the action, we are assured that

$\beta 1$: z is free (when $z \neq t$).

$\beta 2$: x is free.

$\beta 3$: x is on y.

So here is a summary of the action. We call it **Move(x, y)** :

Precondition
$x \neq t \wedge$ Free(x) $\wedge$ [Free(y) $\vee$ y = t] $\wedge$ on(x, z).

Post condition
Free(x) $\wedge$ on(x, y) $\wedge$ [Free(z) $\vee$ z = t].

If a state Δ proves the precondition, then the algorithm for executing the action says how to obtain the new state Δ' as follows.

1. Delete "on(x, z)" from Δ, to obtain Δ_1.

2. Insert "on(x, y)" into Δ_1 to obtain Δ'.

Clearly $\Delta' \vdash$ Free(x) since there is nothing on top of x listed in Δ'. Also $\Delta \vdash$ on(x, y), since we put it there.

Also if $z \neq t$, then z is free again because there is nothing listed as being on top of it.

Note that the logic we use to prove what follows from states is not ordinarily classical consequence. We made two assumptions:

1. If two different constants are used as names of blocks or table then they are different.

2. If an atom on(x, y) is not in the database (the state description) then it is false. This is what we called "civil servant logic". So for example

$$\Delta = \{on(A, B)\} \vdash \neg on(C, D),$$

because we do not have on(C, D) mentioned explicitly in Δ.

EXAMPLE 10.33.

1. If A is on B, can we move A and put it back on B?

2. If A is on the table, can we move A and put it back on the table?

EXAMPLE 10.34 (The Sussmann anomaly). Assume we have the situation in Figure 10.6. So our state is

$$\Delta = \{on(A, t), on(B, t), on(C, A)\}$$

Our goal is to have a tower

$$\Delta' = \{on(A, B), on(B, C), on(C, t)\}$$

We give the goal to the robot to achieve. This means that the robot must make a sequence of actions moving from the initial state $\Delta_0 = \Delta$ into $\Delta_1, \Delta_1, \ldots, \Delta_n$ until he gets $\Delta_n = \Delta'$.

Each action $\mathbf{a}_i, i = 1, \ldots, n$ takes the state Δ_{i-1} to Δ_i in the way specified before. How can we do it?

There are two major ways of searching for the goal state.

1. Breadth first search

2. Depth first search

The first option is to apply all admissible actions to the initial state Δ_0, to get the new states $\Delta_{0,1}, \Delta_{0,2}, \ldots, \Delta_{0,k}$. Then again apply all possible actions to each $\Delta_{0,i}$ to get $\Delta_{0,i,1}, \Delta_{0,i,2}, \ldots$ and so on.we continue until we hit upon the desired final state.

Figure 10.7 shows what we can get if we adopt this search. We partially developed the tree (going downwards) to the point where the goal is achieved.

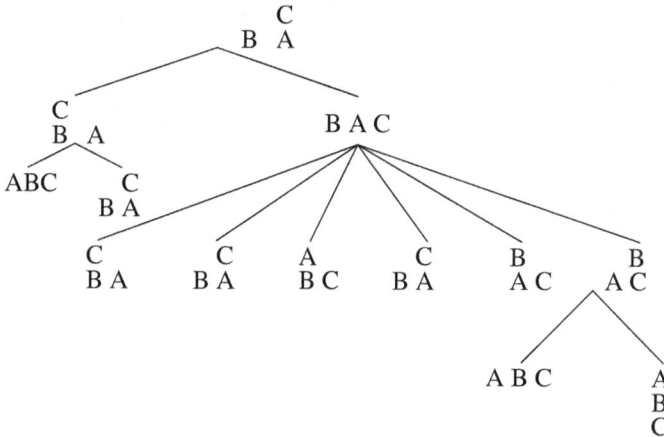

Figure 10.7.

The second method, the depth first is where we get the anomaly. In the depth first approach we choose one of the goals, say on(A, B) and pursue it until it is achieved. When we finish with it we start working on the next goal (e.g. on(B, C)) and so on.

So to achieve on(A, B) we must free A. So we must move C off A. Say we put C either on B or on the table. The robot might or might not realise that it is better to put C on the table than on B because we want to put A on B. So anyway, let us assume the robot puts C on the table. So the sequence of actions to achieve on(A, B) is as in Figure 10.8

```
          C
       B  A
          |
          |
          |
       C B A
          |
          |
          |
          A
       C B
```

Figure 10.8.

Having achieved the goal on(A, B), we now turn to the next goal on(B, C). Our current state is with A on top of B and so we must free B to be able to move it.

This means that to achieve the second goal on(B, C), we must *undo* the actions we did to achieve the first goal.

This is part of the anomaly. What we do now is described in Figure 10.9

```
          C
       B  A
          ↑
          |
          |
       C B A
          |
          |
          |
          A
       C B
```

Figure 10.9.

OK, maybe if we were to start with on(B, C) as our first depth-first goal, we would not need to undo it? Figure 10.10 shows the steps

Figure 10.10 achieves the goal on(B, C) but now to achieve on(A, B) we have to undo it again, see Figure 10.11

The best way is to start with on(C, t) then on(B, C) and then on(A, B), see Figure 10.12.

Consider Figure 10.6 again. Suppose the robot insists on moving A to put it on top of B. The precondition does not hold because C is on top of A. So instead of

Figure 10.10.

Figure 10.11.

moving C to the table to free A, the robot simply pulls A from underneath C and puts it on B.

One would expect now that the new situation is as in Figure 10.13

The reason is gravity. The robot pulls A from under C and puts it on top of B. So C slides down onto the table.

However, we have to check in detail how the robot updates and changes its data; i.e. check what his program does!

We shall see that the result is different.

The initial database is

$$\Delta = \{on(B, t), on(C, A), on(A, t)\}$$

The robot performed the action **Move(A, B)**, even though he was not allowed. Part

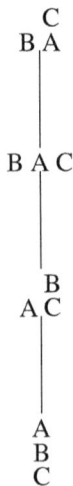

```
        C
      B A
        |
        |
        |
      B A C
        |
        |
        |
          B
      A C
        |
        |
        |
      A
      B
      C
```

Figure 10.12.

```
      A
    B   C
```

Figure 10.13.

of his program is to take on(A, t) out of Δ and insert on(A, B) into the database to form the new database Δ'. We get

$$\Delta' = \{\text{on}(B, t), \text{on}(A, B), \text{on}(C, A)\}.$$

Thus the entire tower resting on *A* has also moved. We get Figure 10.14

```
      C
      A
      B
```

Figure 10.14.

The post condition Free(A) is not satisfied.

Let us look at a more complicated example. Consider Figure 10.15.

$$
\begin{array}{cc}
 & U \\
 & Y \\
X & Z \\
 & W
\end{array}
$$

Figure 10.15.

Assume and the robot moves (illegally) Z onto X then we get Figure 10.16 instead of Figure 10.17

$$
\begin{array}{cc}
 & U \\
 & Y \\
 & Z \\
W & X
\end{array}
$$

Figure 10.16.

$$
\begin{array}{cc}
 & U \\
Z & Y \\
X & W
\end{array}
$$

Figure 10.17.

The problem is that if we look at Figure 10.16 with the comment that Z should be free, the simplest correction is to put Y and U on the table, not on W. we also know that W should be free because what is on top of it has moved. So what do we do? Do we aim for Figure 10.17? In which case, the robot pulled out Z very carefully or do we aim at Figure 10.18 in which case the robot was not careful and just let the entire tower fall on the table?

Obviously we need an algorithm that does the following

1. Given a consistent and acceptable database Δ and a consistent input β such that $\Delta + \beta$ is not acceptable (inconsistent) then the algorithm can insist on adding β to Δ and restore acceptability in some rasonable way.

2. The algorithm may need to know what were the last few moves that gave rise to the unacceptable situation $\Delta + \beta$.

$$Z$$
$$X \quad W \quad Y \quad U$$

Figure 10.18.

$$Z \qquad U$$
$$X \quad W \quad Y$$

Figure 10.19.

3. It is customary to denote the result Δ' of the algorithm by $\Delta' = \Delta \circ \beta$.

The following are the properties of the revision process (called AGM axioms).

1. $\Delta \circ \beta$ is consistent and acceptable

2. $\Delta \circ \beta = \Delta$ if $\Delta \vdash \beta$

3. $\Delta \circ \beta \vdash \beta$

4. If $\Delta \nvdash \neg\beta$ then $\Delta \circ \beta = \Delta + \beta$

CHAPTER 11

Elements of non-monotonic logics

This chapter introduces non-monotonic deduction. We recall that the basic theme of the book so far was to examine whether a conclusion A follows from a set of assumptions (database) $\mathcal{P}$. We studied various methods for proving A from $\mathcal{P}$, including forward rules, box computation and goal-directed computation, using several options for the underlying logics involved. All the logics involved were *monotonic*. They have the property that conclusions can be derived from any subset of assumptions in the database using agreed rules. Any other database (larger or smaller) which still contains all the assumptions participating in the proof can also prove the conclusion. With this understanding, *monotonicity* holds, namely:

$$\text{If } \mathcal{P} \vdash A \text{ then } \mathcal{P} \cup \mathcal{P}' \vdash A.$$

The logical systems which satisfy monotonicity are called *monotonic logics*. In practical reasoning situations, there are other rules at play. There is a variety of *non-monotonic* rules, which consider the database $\mathcal{P}$ as a whole and derive conclusions from it. A simple example of such a mechanism at work is a database $\mathcal{P}$ of airline flights. If a flight A to London on Christmas day is not listed, then we can conclude that there is no such flight. This assumes that we have examined the *entire* list of flights and not just part of it. Thus we have $\mathcal{P} \mathrel{\mid\!\sim} A$ but we certainly may also have $\mathcal{P} \cup \mathcal{P}' \vdash A$, since $\mathcal{P}'$ may be $\{A\}$. See also Section 11.4.

Given a database $\mathcal{P}$, we can deduce conclusions from it using two kinds of rules: monotonic rules and non-monotonic rules. When we allow deduction from $\mathcal{P}$ using nonmonotonic rules as well as monotonic ones we write $\mathcal{P} \mathrel{\mid\!\sim} A,$[1] to distinguish it from the monotonic $\mathcal{P} \vdash A$.

The exact formal form of this kind of reasoning will be discussed in the next section. Chapter 11 will discuss some typical practical non-monotonic rules (also sometimes called non-monotonic *mechanisms*) that are commonly used in practical human reasoning.

---

[1] I introduced this notation in [Gabbay, 1982] and it seems to have caught on. Note that in Section 6.1 we use the notation $\mathrel{\mid\!\sim}$ for consequence relations, since monotonicity was not necessarily required.

The non-monotonic rules are divided into two main groups: the *expectation rules* and the *scenario* (or *default*) *rules*. The difference between the two groups is conceptual.[2]

Expectation rules ($\mathbb{E}$ rules) arise in situations where there are regulations, laws, conventions, agreed procedures and the like, which may or may not be followed, but in the absence of contrary information, we can assume they are followed. Thus if our data is $\mathcal{P}$, then depending on the particular meaning of the formulae in $\mathcal{P}$, extra deduction can be made of the expectation type. The list of flights example is one case where there is a convention that what is not listed does not exist, but there are many others. If an accident occurs at some place then the ambulance is likely to take the injured to the nearest hospital. This may be a matter of common sense and even a recommended procedure. In fact, a huge part of our everyday lives is regulated in this way.

The scenario rules ($\mathbb{S}$ rules) arise in situations of uncertainty where several possible futures (outcomes, diagnoses) are possible. They also arise in arguments for and against something (action, legislation, verdict) where several scenarios are possible for the consequences and we are trying to build a plausible scenario in full detail.

The main mechanism in such rules is consistency. The rules say that if it is consistent on the basis of the situation described in $\mathcal{P}$ to expect A then we can choose to assume it (or add it to $\mathcal{P}$) and see what kind of scenario we get.

The next section will give formal definitions for these two kinds of rules. In general non-monotonic reasoning both kinds of rules play an interactive part.

The plan of the chapter is as follows.

Section 1 will discuss informally the machinery of non-monotonic deduction $\mathcal{P} \mathrel{|\!\sim} A$ as compared with the monotonic deduction $\mathcal{P} \vdash A$ of previous chapters.

Section 2 will define the formal proof systems. Section 3 will present worked examples. Chapter 12 will complement the formal machinery and will intuitively examine various non-monotonic principles and the contexts in which they arise.

For a more in-depth study of the subject the reader is referred to [Antoniou, 1996; Besnard, 1989; Brewka *et al.*, 1997] and [Brewka, 1991].

1   Principles of non-monotonic deduction

Let $\mathcal{P}$ be a set of formulae (perceived as a database) and let A be a formula (perceived as a query). We would like to formalize the distinction between monotonic deduction and expectation and scenario non-monotonic deduction of A from $\mathcal{P}$, written as $\mathcal{P} \vdash A$ and $\mathcal{P} \mathrel{|\!\sim} A$ respectively.

---

[2]This terminology is introduced in this book for the first time. In the literature the community recognizes major non-monotonic methodologies such as default, inheritance, circumscription, etc., on the one hand and the methodology of classifying non-monotonic systems according to properties of their consequence relations on the other hand.

We start with an example which will introduce the expectation kind of rules ($\mathbb{E}$ rules).

EXAMPLE 11.1. Let $\mathcal{P}$ be the database, in a language with $\Rightarrow$ and $\neg$, with the items

1. $A \Rightarrow (B \Rightarrow C)$

2. $\neg D \Rightarrow B$

3. A.

Assume we are dealing with intuitionistic logic with the connectives $\neg$ and $\Rightarrow$, and that we are using the forward rules of Chapter 3. More specifically, assume we have the rules ($\Rightarrow$ E), ($\Rightarrow$ I), ($\Rightarrow$ I2), ($\neg$2) and ($\neg$I) of Section 4. Assume A, B, C, D are atomic.

If $\vdash$ denotes the monotonic deduction of this system, then we have

$$\mathcal{P} \vdash B \Rightarrow C$$
$$\mathcal{P} \vdash \neg D \Rightarrow C$$
$$\mathcal{P} \nvdash C.$$

If we want to be very explicit about the use of our rules we can write the derivation step by step in a box, as we learnt in Chapter 3.

			$\neg D \Rightarrow C$
(1)	$A \Rightarrow (B \Rightarrow C)$	data	
(2)	$\neg D \Rightarrow B$	data	
(3)	A	data	
(4)	$\neg D \Rightarrow C$	subcomputation	

			$\underline{C}$
(4.1)	$\neg D$	assumption	
(4.2)	$B \Rightarrow C$	($\Rightarrow$ E) from (1) and (3)	
(4.3)	B	($\Rightarrow$ E) from (4) and (4.1)	
(4.4)	C	($\Rightarrow$ E) from (4.2) and (4.3)	

We can now write

$$\mathcal{P} \vdash_{(\Rightarrow E),(\Rightarrow I)} \neg D \Rightarrow C$$

where we record as subscript to ' $\vdash$ ' the rules actually used in the proof.

We now turn our proof system into an $\mathbb{E}$-type non-monotonic one by adding an additional non-monotonic $\mathbb{E}$ rule:

(N1) If X is atomic and X is not a head of any clause in $\mathcal{P}$, then deduce $\neg X$ (where $\mathcal{P}$ is the whole database at the time the rule is applied).

Note that this rule needs to know, for its successful application, the entire database $\mathcal{P}$. In our case it needs to check each of the clauses (1)–(3) to see if X is a head of the clause. We have to define what we mean by 'X is a head of a clause'. This we define similarly to Definition 4.27, with a slight change. The following defines what we need:

DEFINITION 11.2 (*N*-clauses[3]).

- If A is atomic then A is an N-clause with head A.

- If A is a clause then A and $\neg A$ are N-bodies.

- If $A_1, \ldots, A_n$ are N-bodies and B is an N-clause with head q then

$$C = A_1 \Rightarrow (\ldots \Rightarrow (A_n \Rightarrow B)\ldots)$$

  is an N-clause with head q.

- Note that all N-clauses have atomic heads, and so no formula of the form $A \Rightarrow \neg B$ can be an N-clause.

- A database $\mathcal{P}$ is a set of clauses.

EXAMPLE 11.3.
    We can now continue the previous example. Using the rule (N1) we can prove $\mathcal{P} \vdash C$. In fact we can write

$$\mathcal{P} \vdash_{(\Rightarrow E),(\Rightarrow I),(N1)} C$$

The following is a proof of C from $\mathcal{P}$.

---

[3]We call these *N*-clauses because of the connection with *N*-Prolog; see [Gabbay and Reyle, 1984].

(1) $A \Rightarrow (B \Rightarrow C)$ data

(2) $\neg D \Rightarrow B$ data

(3) A data

(4) $B \Rightarrow C$ derived data from (1) and (3) using ($\Rightarrow$ E).

(5) $\neg D$ derived data using ($\mathbb{N}$1), since D is atomic and it is not the head of (1)–(4).

(6) B derived data from (2) and (5) using ($\Rightarrow$ E).

(7) C derived data from (4) and (6) using ($\Rightarrow$ E).

Note that in line (5), when we applied rule ($\mathbb{N}$1), we considered the new bigger database which includes the new derived data item (4). This is because ($\mathbb{N}$1) is a non-monotonic rule which must scan the complete database as it is at the moment ($\mathbb{N}$1) is applied.

The reader can see that although $\mathcal{P} \mathrel{\vdash\mkern-7mu\sim} C$ holds, we have $\mathcal{P} \cup \{D\} \mathrel{\not\vdash\mkern-7mu\sim} C$, because ($\mathbb{N}$1) can no longer be used.

Our example so far dealt with expectation ($\mathbb{E}$-type) rules. This means that our perception of a rule deriving more data from a database $\mathcal{P}$ is that there exists some coherent situation which $\mathcal{P}$ describes and that all the possible derivations from $\mathcal{P}$ give us more and more information about what the database is describing. We have an underlying monotonic logic $\vdash$ which we use to prove conclusions from $\mathcal{P}$ and we also have some additional non-monotonic rules. The non-monotonic rules, which scan and assess the entire database $\mathcal{P}$ to give us conclusions, are just a matter of abbreviation and technical convenience. In our flight example, we make a full list of what flights are available and make the convention that what is not listed is not available. In Section 7 we shall see more examples of conventions of this type, relating to databases of time-dependent data. The rules of the game, for this type of coherent databases, are that the data is supplemented and enhanced by various conventions, regulations, agreements and so on, which save us from explicitly listing a great amount of additional data. This keeps the official database small and manageable. The conventions may not be explicit but may rely on the vast common sense practical experience of human everyday life. The rules of type

ℕ need not be schematic rules. They may be given for some particular formulae. For example, imagine that it is raining heavily and an umbrella is available and I am going out; then it is expected that I take the umbrella. This is just a common sense rule. We can therefore expect for such databases that the set $\{A \mid \mathcal{P} \mathrel{\vdash\!\!\!\vdash} A\}$ is consistent.

It is now time to address the other kinds of non-monotonic rules, namely the default or scenario rules (𝕊 rules).

Consider the following well-known example of heuristic rules:

1. Quakers (typically) are pacifists.

2. Republicans (typically) are not pacifists.

3. Nixon is a quaker and a republican.

What conclusion can we draw from the above?

Here we have to choose a scenario. We can consistently go on to conclude that Nixon is a pacifist but equally consistently conclude that he is not. We cannot have both.

This is a case where the database $\mathcal{P}$ has several optional scenarios for extensions and they are not compatible.

Another area where such rules arise is medical diagnosis (see Section 10). We may have a database $\mathcal{P}$ of symptoms and some rules telling us that illness A is likely as a diagnosis but it is also possible that it is illness B. We cannot have both and we have to act immediately. So we choose one of the options and administer medication or possibly run more tests, which may also depend on our choice of scenario.

For such a set **N** of rules, what can we mean by $\mathcal{P} \mathrel{\vdash\!\!\!\vdash_N} A$?

If we have different possible scenarios for extending $\mathcal{P}$ to complete theories $\mathcal{P}_1, \mathcal{P}_2 \dots$, then what can $\mathcal{P}$ prove?

We can adopt a sceptical approach:

- $\mathcal{P} \mathrel{\vdash\!\!\!\vdash_N} A$ iff for all i, $\mathcal{P}_i \vdash \perp$.[4]

However, this may not always be meaningful in practical applications because the different scenarios $\mathcal{P}_i$ may not have much in common. If, for example, $\mathcal{P}_1$ and $\mathcal{P}_2$ are scenarios for different illnesses, then they themselves deserve our interest and not necessarily what they have in common, which may be obvious anyway (cost and suffering?).

The following is a typical scenario rule:

Default scenario rule. (𝔻𝕊 rule)
(We assume $\mathcal{P} \cup \{\beta, \gamma\}$ is consistent):

---

[4]Note that we use '⊢' because $\mathcal{P}_i$ are complete.

- $\mathbb{S} = (\mathcal{P} : \frac{\beta}{\gamma})$ If the current database is $\mathcal{P}$ and β is consistent with $\mathcal{P}$ in the underlying logic then we can add γ to $\mathcal{P}$.

In the literature (see [Besnard, 1989]) default rules have the form $\delta = (\alpha : \frac{\beta}{\gamma})$ meaning as follows:

- If the current database is $\mathcal{P}$ and $\mathcal{P} \vdash \alpha$ and β is consistent with $\mathcal{P}$ then add γ.

In this form the default rule is a schema applicable to any database and has a tinge of monotonicity to it. It satisfies the following.

If $\delta = (\alpha : \frac{\beta}{\gamma})$ is applicable to $\mathcal{P}$ (i.e. $\mathcal{P} \vdash \alpha$ and $\mathcal{P}$ is consistent with β) then it is applicable to any $\mathcal{P}' \supseteq \mathcal{P}$ which is consistent with β.

In our formulation this cannot happen since each rule is specific to its $\mathcal{P}$. Of course we can read $\delta = (\alpha : \frac{\beta}{\gamma})$ as a family of scenario rules of the form $(\mathcal{P} \cup \{\alpha\} : \frac{\beta}{\gamma})$ for any $\mathcal{P}$ for which $\mathcal{P} \cup \{\alpha, \beta, \gamma\}$ is consistent. Even so, the two notions are still not the same.[5]

Let us refer to our defaults as scenario rules and to the traditional defaults (of the form $\delta = (\alpha : \frac{\beta}{\gamma})$) as Reiter defaults. (Ray Reiter invented this area in 1980.)

We have to be careful with our notation. We can write $\mathcal{P} \vdash_{\mathbb{S}} \gamma$ when the rule $\mathbb{S} = (\mathcal{P} : \frac{\beta}{\gamma})$ is applicable. We can read the above as: in the scenario $\mathbb{S}$, starting with $\mathcal{P}$ we get γ. We can similarly write $\mathcal{P}_0 \vdash_{(\mathbb{S}_1, \ldots, \mathbb{S}_n)} \gamma_n$, to mean that for each $i = 1, \ldots, n$ the rule $\mathbb{S}_i = (\mathcal{P}_i : \frac{\beta_i}{\gamma_i})$ is applicable to $\mathcal{P}_{i-1}$ and that $\mathcal{P}_{i+1} = \mathcal{P}_i + \gamma_i$. It is more transparent to present $\mathcal{P}_i$ as $\mathcal{P}_{(\mathbb{S}_1, \ldots, \mathbb{S}_i)}$. Since the scenario rules must allow for possibly conflicting scenarios, we may have $\mathcal{P} \vdash_{\mathbb{S}_1} A$ and $\mathcal{P} \vdash_{\mathbb{S}_2} B$ and yet $\mathcal{P} + A + B$ is not consistent.

The $\mathbb{DS}$ rule as we stated it is more compatible with the non-monotonic nature of the $\mathbb{E}$ rules and is more suitable for a mixed reasoning environment, where both expectation rules and scenario rules are at play interactively. For example, we may

---

[5]Given a consistent set $\mathcal{P}$ and several defaults $\delta_i = (\alpha_i : \frac{\beta_i}{\gamma_i})$, $i = 1, \ldots, k$, the intention is to identify all extensions Q of $\mathcal{P}$ which are closed under the application of all the defaults δ_i. Thus, for example, if $\mathcal{P} = \{a\}$ and $\delta_1 = (a : \frac{\neg b}{d})$, $\delta_2 = (\top : \frac{c}{b})$ then $Q = \{a, b\}$ (obtained by applying δ_2 first and then δ_1 is not applicable). This extension is closed under δ_2, and δ_1 is not applicable. If we apply δ_1 first and then δ_2 we get $\mathcal{P}_1 = \{a, d, b\}$. δ_1 is no longer applicable to $\mathcal{P}_1$ and so there is no longer a justification for $d \in \mathcal{P}_1$. Default theory will not accept $\mathcal{P}_1$.

Now, to consider these rules as scenario rules, we need to read δ_1 and δ_2 as families of scenario rules. In this case we get the scenarios

$$\mathcal{P}_1 = \{a, d, b\} \text{ and } \mathcal{P}_2 = \{a, b\}$$

We cannot apply δ_2 to $\mathcal{P}_1$ (even though it is applicable, i.e. $a \in \mathcal{P}_1$) because the result is not consistent. This actually means that $(\mathcal{P}_1 : \frac{c}{b})$ is not a member of our scenario rules. In contrast, default theory requires d to be justified and therefore cannot accept $\mathcal{P}_1$ as an extension. See [Antoniou, 1996] for an excellent coverage of default theory.

To summarize, even if Reiter default can be presented as a family of scenario rules, we use the rules differently.

start with an initial database $\mathcal{P}_1$, apply some monotonic and $\mathbb{E}$ rules to get to a new database $\mathcal{P}_2$ and now be in a position where some default rules give us a choice of two scenarios. We can choose one of them, i.e. use a default rule to get $\mathcal{P}_3$ and then go on with the chosen scenario, using further non-monotonic $\mathbb{E}$ rules.[6]

Let us consider an example.

EXAMPLE 11.4 (WTA example for $\mathbb{E}$ and $\mathbb{S}$ rules).   The World Travel Agency (WTA) offers package tours from New York to Prague via Paris. Every Sunday a group of New Yorkers board a WTA plane in New York, some get off at Paris and the rest continue to Prague. The Prague office arranges for hotels and tours in Europe. The WTA is a small company facing tough competition. In fact, it is being squeezed out by the big airlines. It cannot afford the cost of the high standards of maintenance and safety required. Therefore management tends to cut corners systematically. WTA planes don't carry enough reserve fuel and their captains fly too many hours. The captains are not happy with this practice. They are worried about possible 'problems' so they use any possible excuse to land during a long flight or take short flights. In parallel they try to save the company money in all other 'legitimate' ways. They are very alert and sensitive to any 'odd' behaviours of their planes, as they have very little margin of safety. Our non-monotonic reasoning example takes place at Prague.

At 13.00 Prague time, 3 hours after the scheduled New York take-off of the WTA group, the Prague office learns that a terrorist attack has taken place in Paris airport. The airport is not closed but there are delays for all incoming and outgoing flights. All flights nearing France are asked to circle and wait or go to another airport.

Prague has to decide what to do with the WTA group. Telephone lines to New York are busy and no communication is available with the plane itself. The only established fact is that the plane did take off in New York.

The database in Prague at 13.00 hours is the following:

1. Group flight took off.

2. Paris airport offers delays.

3. Delays $\Rightarrow$ big fuel consumption.

We have three non-monotonic rules:

$\mathbb{S}$1. If it is consistent to shorten a trip or split it, a WTA captain will do it.

$\mathbb{S}$2. Of two possible actions the captain will choose the one that saves money.

$\mathbb{E}$1. The standard regulation for rerouting from Paris is to go to London.

---

[6]Practical applications may also involve actions, as discussed in Section 6.

Thus at 13.00 Prague can reason as follows:

> The captain will be offered either to circle or to go to London. We don't know what the captain will choose.

Scenario 1

The captain chooses to circle Paris and land in Paris, in which case the captain might spend the night there, using the turmoil as an excuse. In this case Prague-bound passengers remain is Paris.

Scenario 2

The captain chooses to be rerouted to London. In this case, following regulations, Prague-bound passengers will take other flights and arrive tonight in Prague from London. Paris passengers will stay in London overnight.

Two hours later, Prague manages to establish contact with New York. It learns the extra information that the plane from New York was 2 hours late in taking off. We now have a new database. It is not known what the captain actually decided to do when hearing about the trouble in Paris. However, company regulations for saving money, as well as the $S1, S2$ rules, all yield that the captain will return to New York and let the passengers sleep at home.

Therefore according to the latter database, Prague passengers remain in New York.

The structure of the argument in the above example was as follows.

$\mathcal{P}_1$ database at 13.00

using $\mathbb{E}$ reasoning

$\mathcal{P}_2$

split using $\mathbb{S}$ reasoning

$\mathcal{P}_{2,1}$ $\mathcal{P}_{2,2}$

Q_1 extra information creates a new database at 15.00

Q_2 $\mathbb{S}$ rules and $\mathbb{E}$ rules give only one possible scenario for Q_1, leading to Q_2.

Let us now see what kind of rationality postulates we can impose on our non-monotonic rules. We begin by looking at the case of $\mathbb{E}$ rules. We ask ourselves about what kind of properties we expect from a set **N** of $\mathbb{E}$ rules and how they relate to the monotonic ones. There are some obvious requirements.

Let $\mathcal{P}$ be a database and **N** a family of non-monotonic $\mathbb{E}$ rules. Formally **N** is just a set of pairs of the form (Q, A), where Q is a database and A is a formula. In many applications **N** is given by a group of rules $\mathbb{N}_i$, each stating some conditions defining a family of pairs to be in **N**. Thus **N** can also be perceived as a family of (families of) $\mathbb{E}$ rules $\mathbb{N}_1, \mathbb{N}_2, \ldots$. We write $\mathcal{P} \leadsto_{\mathbf{N}} A$ to mean that $(\mathcal{P}, A) \in \mathbf{N}$, or in words that A can be derived from $\mathcal{P}$ using a rule $\mathbb{N}$ in **N**. Thus in Example 11.3, we have $\mathcal{P} \leadsto_{\mathbb{N}_1} D$.

We assume the rules in **N** are compatible with $\vdash$, i.e. the following hold:

Compatibility

- $\mathcal{P} \vdash A$ implies $\mathcal{P} \leadsto A$
- If $\mathcal{P}$ is $\vdash$ equivalent to Q then $\mathcal{P} \leadsto A$ iff $Q \leadsto A$.

We need additional rationality postulates on **N**.

Another rationality requirement is of course that of

Consistency[7]

If $\mathcal{P}$ is consistent and $\mathcal{P} \rightsquigarrow_N B$ holds then $\mathcal{P} \cup \{B\}$ is also consistent.

The consistency rule applies equally to $\mathbb{E}$ rules and to $\mathbb{S}$ rules. We shall see later that if **N** is a family of $\mathbb{E}$ rules, then stronger consistency principles can be adopted.

The reader should note that ($\mathbb{N}1$) satisfies *consistency* only because we are not allowing formulae of the form $A \Rightarrow \neg C$ to appear in databases. This formula is not an *N*-clause. If we allow databases to contain arbitrary formulae we can get the consistency rule violated. Consider the database

1. $\neg D \Rightarrow \neg C$,

2. C.

This is a consistent database. Applying rule ($\mathbb{N}1$) would give $\neg D$ and cause inconsistency.

It is possible in such a case to weaken rule ($\mathbb{N}1$) into a default version ($\mathbb{DN}1$).

($\mathbb{DN}1$) If it is possible to apply rule ($\mathbb{N}1$) consistently then do so.

Note that the properties of *consistency* and of *compatibility* are also implicit in the way we proved our goal in Example 11.3. The monotonic and non-monotonic rules define the system together.

It seems that at this juncture we may wish to adopt the following stronger consistency principle, which we call coherence, for a family **N** of $\mathbb{E}$-type rules.

Coherence

- $\mathcal{P} \rightsquigarrow_N A$ and $\mathcal{P} \rightsquigarrow_N B$ imply that $\mathcal{P} \cup \{A, B\}$ is consistent.

  If we have $\wedge$ in the language we would write the rule as

- $\mathcal{P} \rightsquigarrow_N A$ and $\mathcal{P} \rightsquigarrow_N B$ iff $\mathcal{P} \rightsquigarrow_N A \wedge B$.

The rule is not suitable for application areas where scenarios are possible. These will be addressed later. They form a wide and rich research area. See for example [Besnard, 1989].

If we think of $\mathcal{P}$ as a database from which coherent and consistent information can be deduced using $\mathbb{E}$ rules, we must consider what happens when we add this deduced information into $\mathcal{P}$, i.e. we have $\mathcal{P} \vdash A$ and we consider $\mathcal{P}' = \mathcal{P} \cup \{A\}$. Do we expect that for all X, $\mathcal{P}' \vdash X$ iff $\mathcal{P} \vdash X$?

---

[7]One should not be surprised if in some applications where $\mathbb{E}$ rules are used the expectations turn out to be inconsistent. I would not insist on this postulate. See footnote 13.

The non-monotonic rules depend on the database, but $\mathcal{P}'$ is just $\mathcal{P}$ together with some of its consequences, and need not necessarily be considered a proper extension database.

It is reasonable to adopt the following principle for all the non-monotonic rules $\mathbb{E}$ involved.

Restricted monotonicity for $\mathbf{N}$[8]

$\mathcal{P} \leadsto_{\mathbf{N}} A$ and $\mathcal{P} \leadsto_{\mathbf{N}} B$ imply $\mathcal{P} \cup \{A\} \leadsto_{\mathbf{N}} B$.

There are also technical reasons for accepting this rule. Suppose we start with $\mathcal{P}$ and in one step prove A. When we continue to the next step and prove something else, we want to be able to use A (which we have just proved) and prove more. So technically we are dealing with the database $\mathcal{P} \cup \{A\}$, not the original $\mathcal{P}$. We want everything we have proved so far to be still available for our use to continue and prove more and we want everything we prove this way to be considered as following from the initial database. To have this property means that we want restricted monotonicity.

We are now almost ready for a formal definition of coherent non-monotonic systems. We first need to clarify some technical points.

Assume our language contains conjunction, and let $\mathbf{N}$ be a family of non-monotonic $\mathbb{E}$ rules satisfying coherence and restricted monotonicity. This means that for one step derivation these two principles hold. What happens if we chain them? We need the following definition.

DEFINITION 11.5 (Chaining). Let $\mathbf{N}$ be a set of expectation rules of the form $\mathcal{P} \leadsto_{\mathbf{N}} A$. Define the notions $\mathcal{P} >_m A$ by induction as follows:

- $\mathcal{P} >_1 A$ iff $\mathcal{P} \leadsto_{\mathbf{N}} A$

- $\mathcal{P} >_{m+1} A$ iff for some X, $\mathcal{P} >_1 X$ and $\mathcal{P} + X >_m A$

where we use the notation $\mathcal{P} + X$ for $\mathcal{P} \cup \{X\}$.

Define $\mathcal{P} > A$ as follows (strictly speaking $>$ depends on $\mathbf{N}$; when necessary we shall write $>_{\mathbf{N}}$):

- $\mathcal{P} > A$ iff for some m, $\mathcal{P} >_m A$.

The first property we need to worry about is whether cut and restricted monotonicity hold for $>$. The answer is yes.

THEOREM 11.6 (Properties of non-monotonic $\mathbb{E}$-deduction). *Let $\vdash$ be an underlying monotonic logic containing the classical connective $\wedge$ and let $\mathbf{N}$ be a set of expectation rules of the form $\mathcal{P} \leadsto_{\mathbf{N}} A$, in the language of $\vdash$, satisfying the following conditions:*

---

[8][Gabbay, 1985] introduced this principle but the name used now in the literature is *cautious monotony*. See also [Kraus *et al.*, 1990].

1. *If $\mathcal{P}$ is consistent and $\mathcal{P} \leadsto_N A$ then $\mathcal{P} \cup \{A\}$ is consistent.*

2. *$\mathcal{P} \leadsto_N A$ and $\mathcal{P} \leadsto_N B$ iff $\mathcal{P} \leadsto_N A \wedge B$.*

3. *$\mathcal{P} \leadsto_N A$ and $\mathcal{P} >_m X$ imply $\mathcal{P}, X \leadsto_N A$.*

4. *If $\mathcal{P} \vdash A$ then $\mathcal{P} \leadsto_N A$.*

Then the relation $>$, as defined in Definition 11.5, satisfies the following:

5. *$\mathcal{P} > A$ implies $\mathcal{P} \cup \{A\}$ is consistent (consistency).*

6. *$\mathcal{P} > A$ and $\mathcal{P} > B$ iff $\mathcal{P} > A \wedge B$ (coherence).*

7. *$\mathcal{P} > A$ and $\mathcal{P} > B$ imply $\mathcal{P}, A > B$ (restricted monotonicity).*

8. *$\mathcal{P} > A$ and $\mathcal{P}, A > B$ imply $\mathcal{P} > B$ (cut).*

Proof. See worked Example 11.15.[9]   ∎

REMARK 11.7. Note that for a given monotonic $\vdash$, an expectation consequence $>$ can always be generated by a set of pairs $\mathbf{N} = \{(\mathcal{P}, A)\}$ provided it is consistent, i.e. provided it satisfies that for all consistent $\mathcal{P}$, the set $\mathcal{P} \cup \{A \mid (\mathcal{P}, A) \in \mathbf{N}\}$ is also consistent. To generate $>$ we simply close the initial set of pairs N under the rules 1–4 of Theorem 11.6.

If $\mathbf{N}$ is finite (or recursive) then the closure can be properly recursively calculated as shown by K. Schulz. See my lecture notes [Gabbay, 1988].

Further note that for a given $\mathcal{P}$, $\mathcal{P} + X$ is not regarded as an update of $\mathcal{P}$ with X but as a new theory. Let $\mathbf{N}$ be a coherent set of $\mathbb{E}$ rules and let $Q = \{A \mid \mathcal{P} >_N A\}$. Then $\mathcal{P} \subseteq Q$. Assume $Q \nvdash X$ and let $\mathcal{P}_1 = \mathcal{P} + X$ and $Q_1 = \{A \mid \mathcal{P}_1 >_N A\}$. If we regard X as an update to $\mathcal{P}$, then we might expect that for all $Y \in Q$, if $Q_1 + Y$ is consistent then $Y \in Q_1$. This means that the input X throws out of the set of expectations Q only what is inconsistent, and does not start a completely new set of expectations. The reader should note that although we do not take this view the necessary machinery can be developed for its adoption. See Example 11.14.

2   Formal non-monotonic proof theory

This section develops natural deduction presentation of non-monotonic proofs. The basic idea behind the definitions is as follows.

We start with a language and an underlying monotonic logic $\vdash$ which already has a natural deduction formulation. For example, we may choose to start with the $\{\wedge, \Rightarrow\}$ fragment of intuitionistic logic. $\vdash$ is the first component of the intended non-monotonic system. To this we add a family $\mathbf{N}$ of $\mathbb{E}$ rules of the form $\mathcal{P} \leadsto_N A$

---

[9]Note that the proofs of items 1–4 in Example 11.15 do not make use of condition 3.

(satisfying conditions 1–4 of Theorem 11.6) and therefore the relation $\mathcal{P} > A$ can be generated and assumed to satisfy conditions 5–8 of Theorem 11.6. The relation $>$ is the second component of the intended non-monotonic system.

We now use $\vdash$ and $>$ to define the notion of $A_1, \ldots, A_n \mathrel{\vdash\!\!\!\sim} B$. We modify the proof process of $A_1, \ldots, A_n \vdash B$ by allowing in the course of the $\vdash$ proof of B from $A_1, \ldots, A_n$ the use not only of deduction rules of $\vdash$, but also $\mathbb{E}$ rules. (That is, we make use of $>$ as well.) It is best that we illustrate the process first by giving a few examples and only give the formal definition and assess its implications afterwards.

EXAMPLE 11.8 (Non-monotonic forward deduction).   Consider the intuitionistic logic fragment with $\wedge$ and $\Rightarrow$ and the monotonic rules $(\wedge I), (\wedge E), (\Rightarrow E)$ and $(\Rightarrow I)$ from Section 4. Let $\vdash$ be the monotonic intuitionistic consequence for this fragment.[10] Consider the following specific additional non-monotonic rules, for $i = 1, 2$, with $\beta = A_1 \Rightarrow (A_2 \Rightarrow C)$.

$(\mathbb{N}_1)$ $\beta \wedge A_1 \rightsquigarrow D_1$

$(\mathbb{N}_2)$ $\beta \wedge A_1 \wedge A_2 \rightsquigarrow D_2.$

We let $>$ be the closure of $\{\mathbb{N}_i\}$ under coherence, restricted monotonicity and cut.

Let $\mathrel{\vdash\!\!\!\sim}$ denote the non-monotonic consequence (which has not yet been defined formally) based on $\vdash$ and $\mathbb{N}_i$, $i = 1, 2$.

We show that $\beta \mathrel{\vdash\!\!\!\sim} \alpha$ where

$$\alpha = A_1 \Rightarrow (D_1 \wedge (A_2 \Rightarrow C \wedge D_2))$$

The following box deduction shows that $\mathcal{P} \mathrel{\vdash\!\!\!\sim} \alpha$.

---

[10]$\vdash$ can also be characterized as in Example 7.2 without the axiom for falsity $\bot$.

$$A_1 \Rightarrow (D_1 \wedge (A_2 \Rightarrow C \wedge D_2))$$

(1)	$A_1 \Rightarrow (A_2 \Rightarrow C)$	data
(2)	$A_1 \Rightarrow (D_1 \wedge (A_2 \Rightarrow C \wedge D_2))$	subcomputation

$$D_1 \wedge (A_2 \Rightarrow C \wedge D_2)$$

(2.1)	A_1	assumption
(2.2)	D_1	from (1), (2.1) and ($\mathbb{N}_1$) and ($\wedge$I)
(2.3)	$A_2 \Rightarrow C \wedge D_2$	subcomputation

$$C \wedge D_2$$

(2.3.1)	A_2	assumption
(2.3.2)	D_2	from ($\mathbb{N}_2$) and (1), (2.1) and
		(2.3.1) and ($\wedge$I)
(2.3.3)	$A_2 \Rightarrow C$	from (2.1) and (1) using ($\Rightarrow$ E)
(2.3.4)	C	from (2.3.1) and (2.3.3) using ($\Rightarrow$ E)
(2.3.5)	$C \wedge D_2$	from (2.3.2) and (2.3.3) using ($\wedge$I).

(2.4)	$D_1 \wedge (A_2 \Rightarrow C \wedge D_2)$	from (2.2) and (2.3) using ($\wedge$I).

Note that in line (2.3.2) we used rule $\mathbb{N}_2$ because the then current database was $\{A_1, A_2, (1)\}$. Also note that although D_1 was derived in (2.2), it is not considered part of the database for getting D_2 at (2.3.2), because D_1 is part of a parallel branch proof for $\wedge$. D_2 was not used inside the (2.3) box. Further note that each time ($\wedge$I) is used the two conjuncts rely on the same database.

Example 11.8 presents us with a puzzle. We have shown that $\mathcal{P} \mathrel{\vdash\mkern-7mu\sim} \alpha$. Since $\mathcal{P}, \alpha \vdash (X \Rightarrow \alpha)$, we would expect that $\mathcal{P}, \alpha \mathrel{\vdash\mkern-7mu\sim} X \Rightarrow \alpha$ and hence we get for all X, α that $\mathcal{P} \mathrel{\vdash\mkern-7mu\sim} \alpha$ implies $\mathcal{P} \mathrel{\vdash\mkern-7mu\sim} X \Rightarrow \alpha$.

Does that imply that $\mathcal{P} + X \mathrel{\vdash\mkern-7mu\sim} \alpha$? Do we have the deduction theorem for $\mathrel{\vdash\mkern-7mu\sim}$?

The answer is definitely not. If we apply our proof procedures to the database $\mathcal{P} + X$, none of the rules $\mathbb{N}_1, \mathbb{N}_2$ can be triggered because the database is *not* $\mathcal{P}$.

The following attempted proof shows what happens:

(1)	$\mathcal{P}, \alpha \vdash X \Rightarrow \alpha$	axiom
(2)	$\mathcal{P}, \alpha \rightsquigarrow X \Rightarrow \alpha$	compatibility
(3)	$\mathcal{P} > \alpha$	given
(4)	$\mathcal{P} > X \Rightarrow \alpha$	cut
(5)		we cannot deduce from (4) that $\mathcal{P}, X > \alpha$ because we do not have the deduction theorem for $>$.

We now prepare the ground for the formal definition of two possible non-monotonic computations.

Consider the language fragment of intuitionistic logic with $\wedge$ and $\Rightarrow$ and possibly $\perp$ and let **N** be a set of pairs of the form $(\mathcal{P}, A)$, where $\mathcal{P}$ is a set of formulae and A is a formula. Let $\vdash$ denote intuitionistic provability for the fragment and let $(\wedge E), (\wedge I), (\Rightarrow E)$ and $(\Rightarrow I)$ be the monotonic rules for $\wedge$ and $\Rightarrow$ as given in Section 4. If we admit $\perp$ as well we can take the rule

$(\perp)$: From $\perp$ deduce any A.

We want to explore what options we have for defining non-monotonic consequence based on $\vdash$ and **N** for the connectives $\wedge$ and $\Rightarrow$ and possibly $\perp$ as well.

We require that **N** be compatible with $\vdash$, namely that if $\mathcal{P}$ is $\vdash$ equivalent to $\mathcal{Q}$ then for all $A, (\mathcal{P}, A) \in \mathbf{N}$ iff $(\mathcal{Q}, A) \in \mathbf{N}$. Compatibility on the other coordinate will come out of the proof theory.

We shall outline two options, relating to the two ways in which the notion $\vdash$ can be presented for the intuitionistic fragment (with $\wedge, \Rightarrow$ and $\perp$). The first option for defining $\mathcal{P} \vdash A$ is by using Hilbert system proof theory as done in Definition 7.11 through the system of Example 7.9.

The second option for defining intuitionistic $\vdash$ is to use the natural deduction rules of Section 4, rules $(\Rightarrow E), (\Rightarrow I), (\Rightarrow I2), (\neg 2)$ and $(\neg I)$, and if we have $\perp$ also the rule $(\perp)$ just mentioned.

The consequence relation corresponding to the first option is the non-monotonic deduction $>_{\mathbf{N}}$ based on $\vdash$ and **N** as defined in Definition 11.5. $>_{\mathbf{N}}$ satisfies the properties mentioned in Theorem 11.6, namely

- $\mathcal{P} >_{\mathbf{N}} A$ if $\mathcal{P} \vdash A$

- $\mathcal{P} >_{\mathbf{N}} A$ and $\mathcal{P} >_{\mathbf{N}} B$ imply $\mathcal{P} >_{\mathbf{N}} A \wedge B$

- $\mathcal{P} >_{\mathbf{N}} A$ and $\mathcal{P} >_{\mathbf{N}} B$ imply $\mathcal{P} + A >_{\mathbf{N}} B$

- $\mathcal{P} + A >_{\mathbf{N}} B$ and $\mathcal{P} >_{\mathbf{N}} A$ imply $\mathcal{P} >_{\mathbf{N}} B$.

By Remark 11.7, $>_{\mathbf{N}}$ can be recursively generated from any initial set $\mathbf{N_0} = \{(\mathcal{P}, A)\}$ which is consistent (i.e. $\mathcal{P} \cup \{A \mid (\mathcal{P}, A) \in \mathbf{N_0}\}$ is consistent in the underlying logic).

The second option is to define a consequence relation $\vdash_{\mathbf{N}}$ (or just $\vdash$) through a modified non-monotonic box computation for $\Rightarrow, \wedge$ and $\perp$. We use the schema of indices as defined in Definition 3.13 and follow the clauses of Definition 3.15. The definition for the non-monotonic case makes use of $\mathbf{N}$ and is therefore slightly different from the monotonic one. We shall point out the differences after we give the formal definition.

DEFINITION 11.9 (Non-monotonic box computation).

1. Let $\mathbf{N}$ be a set of pairs $(\mathcal{P}, A)$, where $\mathcal{P}$ is a set of formulae of the fragment and A is a wff. Assume $\mathbf{N}$ is such that for each $\mathcal{P}$, the set $\mathcal{P} \cup \{X \mid (\mathcal{P}, X) \in \mathbf{N}\}$ is intuitionistically consistent. We use $\mathbf{N}$ to define a non-monotonic box natural deduction system $\vdash$.

2. Let $\mathcal{P} = \{A_1, \ldots, A_n, \ldots\}$ be a database and G a goal. We allow $\mathcal{P}$ to be possibly infinite. Consider a set of indexed formulae of the form $\pi = \{(\alpha_1, B_1, a_1), (\alpha_2, B_2, a_2), \ldots\}$. π is said to be a forward non-monotonic proof for the goal G from the data $\mathcal{P}$ iff each element $(\alpha, B, a) \in \pi$ exactly satisfies one of the following conditions:

   (a) $a =$ 'data' and $B \in \mathcal{P}$.

   (b) For some b and for some $\beta < \alpha$, $(\beta, B, b) \in \pi$ and $b =$ 'assumption' and $a =$ 'reiteration from β'.

   (c) $\alpha = \beta \oplus (k)$ and for some b_1 and some $1 \leq k_2 < k$, $(\beta \oplus (k_1), B, b_1) \in \pi$ and $a =$ 'repetition'.

   (d) $\alpha = \beta \oplus (k)$, for natural number $k \geq 1$, and for some a_i and some $1 \leq k_1, k_2 < k$, $(\beta \oplus (k_i), B_i, a_i) \in \pi$ and $B_2 = B_1 \Rightarrow B$ and $a =$ 'from $\alpha \oplus (k_1), \alpha \oplus (k_2)$, using the rule $(\Rightarrow E)$'.

   (e) $\alpha = \beta \oplus (k)$ for $k \geq 1$, and for some $1 \leq k_1 < k$ and some b we have $(\beta \oplus (k_1), B \wedge B_1, b) \in \pi$ and $a =$ 'from $\beta \oplus (k_1)$ using the rule $(\wedge E)$'.

   (f) Same as 2e above with '$B_1 \wedge B$' replacing '$B \wedge B_1$'.

   (g) B is $B_1 \Rightarrow B_2$ and $\alpha \oplus (1)$ is an index in π and $(\alpha \oplus (1), B_1, \text{assumption}) \in \pi$ and for some b and for some $k > 1$ $(\alpha \oplus (k), B_2, b) \in \pi$, and $a =$ 'subcomputation'.

   (h) $\alpha = \beta \oplus (k)$ and for some $1 \leq k_1, k_2 < k$, and for some $b_i, (\alpha \oplus (k_i), B_i, b_i) \in \pi, i = 1, 2$, and $B = B_1 \wedge B_2$ and $a = ($from $\alpha \oplus (k_1), \alpha \oplus (k_2)$ and rule $(\wedge E))$.

   (i) $a =$ 'non-monotonic deduction using $(\mathcal{P}_\alpha, B) \in \mathbf{N}$' and where $\mathcal{P}_\alpha = \mathcal{P} \cup \{X \mid$ for some $\beta < \alpha$ and $b, (\beta, X, b) \in \pi$ and $b =$ 'assumption'$\}$. In other words, $\mathcal{P}_\alpha$ is the set of all data and assumptions available at stage α.

   (j) In case we have $\perp$ in the language we can add the following rule which says that from $\perp$ we can have any formula: $\alpha = \beta \oplus (k)$ for some $k > 1$

and for some $1 \leq k_1 < k$ and some a_1 we have $(\alpha \oplus (k_1), \bot, a_1) \in \pi$ and $a = $ 'from rule $(\bot)$ for falsity'.

EXAMPLE 11.10 (Dealing with falsity).   This example will show that we need to be careful with $\bot$. Consider the formula $\alpha = (A \Rightarrow B) \wedge C \Rightarrow \bot$ and the two non-monotonic rules

$(\mathbb{N}_1)$ $\alpha \wedge A \rightsquigarrow B$

$(\mathbb{N}_2)$ $\alpha \rightsquigarrow C$.

Let $>$ be the closure of $\{\mathbb{N}_i\}$ under coherence, restricted monotonicity and cut.

The database containing α alone is intuitionistically consistent.

So is the set $Q_\alpha = \{X \mid \alpha > X\}$, because $A \Rightarrow B$ is not intuitionistically provable from it. We have $Q_\alpha = \{\alpha, C, (A \Rightarrow B) \Rightarrow \bot\}$.[11]

We also have that the database $\alpha \wedge A$ is intuitionistically consistent. It is equivalent to $A \wedge (B \wedge C \Rightarrow \bot)$. The set $Q_{\alpha \wedge A} = \{X \mid \alpha \wedge A > X\}$ is also intuitionistically consistent. We have $Q_{\alpha \wedge A} = \{\alpha, A, B, C \Rightarrow \bot\}$.

Given the above, we would expect α to be $\vdash$ consistent. However, we have $\alpha \vdash \bot$, because $\alpha \vdash A \Rightarrow B$, since $\alpha \wedge A > B$ and hence $\alpha \vdash \bot$.

The following is a box proof of $\alpha \vdash \bot$.

$$\bot$$

(1)	$(A \Rightarrow B) \wedge C \rightarrow \bot$	data
(2)	$A \Rightarrow B$	subcomputation

		$\underline{B}$
(2.1)	A	assumption
(2.2)	$\alpha \wedge A$	from (1), (2.1) and $(\wedge I)$
(2.3)	B	from (2.2) and $\mathbb{N}_1$

(3)	C	from (1) and $\mathbb{N}_2$
(4)	$(A \Rightarrow B) \wedge C$	from (2) and (3) and $(\wedge I)$
(5)	$\bot$	from (1), (4) and $(\Rightarrow E)$

Thus we have to treat falsity $\bot$ carefully in non-monotonic logics. The best approach is to use labels in the proofs, as done in Chapter 5, which will allow us to know exactly how $\bot$ is derived and deal with $\bot$ accordingly. The full treatment of negation is too advanced for this book.[12]

EXAMPLE 11.11 (Comparing $\vdash_N$ and $>_N$). Let $\mathbf{N}$ be such that $\mathbf{N} = \{(\mathcal{P}, A) \mid \mathcal{P} >_N X\}$. We can use $\mathbf{N}$ to define $\vdash_N$ as in Definition 11.9. Obviously $\mathcal{P} >_N A$

---

[11]The reader should prove this as an exercise, namely that $\{X \mid \alpha \wedge C \vdash X\} = \{X \mid \alpha > X\}$. Similalry for $Q_{\alpha \wedge A}$.

[12]I cannot resist quoting the *Holy Bible* (King James's version) at this point. *Keep thee far from a false matter* said the Lord in *Exodus*, Chapter 23, Verse 7.

implies $P \hspace{1pt}\mid\hspace{-4pt}\sim_N A$. We ask whether they are equal. The previous example 11.10 shows that they are not. If we regard $\perp$ just as another atom, we get $\alpha \hspace{1pt}\mid\hspace{-4pt}\sim_N \perp$ but *not* $\alpha >_N \perp$.

EXAMPLE 11.12 (Special characteristics of the non-monotonic deduction). We will compare the non-monotonic deduction for $\Rightarrow$ and $\wedge$ with the monotonic one. We use the box computation of Example 11.8 for comparison.

Consider line (2.3.2) in this box computation. In this line we form the conjunction of

(1) $A_1 \Rightarrow (A_2 \Rightarrow C)$

(2.1) A_1

and use rule $\mathbb{N}_2$, which is

$$A_1 \wedge (A_1 \Rightarrow (A_2 \Rightarrow C)) \rightsquigarrow D_2$$

to obtain

(2.3.2) D_2.

We have used (i.e. reiterated), in the (2.3) box subcomputation, some formulae outside the box. In the non-monotonic deduction only formulae that are data or assumptions can be reiterated. We are not allowed to use (as in the monotonic case) all the formulae which were already derived. Thus, for example,

(2.2) D_1

is not usable within the (2.3) box, although it is already derived. The reason is explained by the following schema.

Let P be a database. Let Q_P be its non-monotonic 'closure', i.e.

$$Q_P = \{X \mid P \hspace{1pt}\mid\hspace{-4pt}\sim X\}$$

Then one way to show $A \Rightarrow B \in Q_P$ is to check whether $P + A \hspace{1pt}\mid\hspace{-4pt}\sim B$, i.e. we add A to P and not to Q_P. This is exactly the nature of non-monotonicity. Once A is added to P, some previously derivable X may no longer be derivable.

Thus looking again at our example, the data of box (2) are (1) and (2.1). Thus $P = \{(2), (2.1)\}$. Item (2.2) is in Q_P. Thus when we add (2.3.1), we add it to P, not to Q_P, and so (2.2) is not available within box (2.3).

LEMMA 11.13 (Properties of $\hspace{1pt}\mid\hspace{-4pt}\sim$).

1. $P \hspace{1pt}\mid\hspace{-4pt}\sim B_1$ *and* $P \hspace{1pt}\mid\hspace{-4pt}\sim B_2$ *imply* $P \hspace{1pt}\mid\hspace{-4pt}\sim B_1 \wedge B_2$.

2. $Q_P = \{X \mid P \hspace{1pt}\mid\hspace{-4pt}\sim X\}$ *contains* P *and is consistent.*

3. $\mathcal{P} \mathrel{\vdash\!\!\!\sim} A$ and $\mathcal{P} + A \mathrel{\vdash\!\!\!\sim} B$ imply $\mathcal{P} \mathrel{\vdash\!\!\!\sim} B$.

4. $\mathcal{P} \vdash A$ implies $\mathcal{P} \mathrel{\vdash\!\!\!\sim} A$.

5. $\mathcal{P} + A \mathrel{\vdash\!\!\!\sim} B$ implies $\mathcal{P} \mathrel{\vdash\!\!\!\sim} A \Rightarrow B$.

Proof. (1) Let π_i be a box proof of $B_i, i = 1, 2$. Assume $\mathcal{P}$ is $\{A_1, \ldots, A_n, \ldots\}$. Assume the last line in π_i is $((m_i), B_{(m_i)}, b_{(m_i)})$.

All indices α in π_2 will have the form $\alpha = (k) \oplus \alpha'$ where $1 \leq k \leq m_2$, labelling the item $(\alpha, B_\alpha, b_\alpha)$.

Let α^* be $(m_1 + k) \oplus \alpha'$ for all such α.

For any b_β in π_2 let b_β^* be obtained from b_β by replacing any mention of any α in b_β by α^*.

Let $\pi^* = \pi_1 \cup \{(\alpha^*, B_\alpha, b_\alpha^*) \mid (\alpha, B_\alpha, b_\alpha) \in \pi_2\} \cup \{((m_1 + m_2 + 1), B_1 \wedge B_2,$ from (m_1) and $(m_1 + m_2)$ using $(\wedge I))\}$.

Then π^* is a proof of $B_1 \wedge B_2$ from $\mathcal{P}$, obtained by first proving B_1, then B_2 and then forming $B_1 \wedge B_2$.

(2) It is clear that $\mathcal{P} \subseteq \mathcal{Q}_\mathcal{P}$. Also $\mathcal{Q}_\mathcal{P}$ is consistent because we do not have falsity $\perp$.[13]

(3) Let π_1 be a proof of A from $\mathcal{P}$ and let $((m_1), A, b_{(m_1)})$ be its last line. Let π_2 be a proof of B from $\mathcal{P} + A$ and let $((m_2), B, b_{(m_2)})$ be its last line.

For each $((\alpha), B_\alpha, b_\alpha) \in \pi_2$ where $\alpha = (k) \oplus \alpha'$, let α^* be $(m_1 + k) \oplus \alpha'$.

Let b_α^* be the modified justification obtained from b_α by replacing any reference to any β by the same reference to β^*. Further if B_α happens to be A and b_α happens to be 'data', then replace 'data' by 'repetition from line (m_1)'.

Let b_α^* be this new justification.

Let $\pi_2^* = \{(\alpha^*, B_\alpha, b_\alpha^*) \mid (\alpha, B_\alpha, b_\alpha) \in \pi_2\}$.

Then $\pi_1 \cup \pi_2^*$ is a proof of B from $\mathcal{P}$.

(4) This follows from the fact that the proof procedure for the non-monotonic box computation includes all the rules of the monotonic computation.

(5) This follows from the definition of box computation. ∎

EXAMPLE 11.14 (Input as updates).   Consider the non-monotonic rules, $a \rightsquigarrow c \Rightarrow \perp, a \rightsquigarrow b$ and $a \wedge c \rightsquigarrow d$, for a, b, c, d atomic.

Then we have

$$a \mathrel{\vdash\!\!\!\sim} c \Rightarrow \perp$$
$$a \mathrel{\vdash\!\!\!\sim} b$$
$$a \wedge c \mathrel{\vdash\!\!\!\sim} d$$

---

[13]Even when we have falsity $\perp$ we can consider it as just another atom $q_\perp$ and add the formulae $q_\perp \Rightarrow A$ for all A to all our theories. Thus an 'inconsistent' theory is just a 'consistent' theory which happens to prove all formulae A.

This method reduces $\perp$ to the $\wedge, \Rightarrow$ fragment without it.

We cannot show $a \wedge c \mathrel{\vert\!\!\sim} b$, because the rule $a \rightsquigarrow b$ is not applicable in the presence of c in the database. However, b is consistent with d. Thus if our view of c is as an update to the theory of $Q_a = \{X \mid a \mathrel{\vert\!\!\sim} X\}$, then we should try and keep as much of Q as we can. We must throw $c \Rightarrow \perp$ out of Q, but we can assume that b can still non-monotonically follow from $a \wedge c$, because it is consistent with its consequences. Compare with Remark 11.7.[14]

3   Worked examples; preferential semantics

This section offers some worked examples and more on semantics for $\mathbb{E}$-type non-monotonic logics.

EXAMPLE 11.15 (Properties of $>$). Show by induction that the following hold; for $>$ of Definition 11.5, you can assume that any finite theory $\mathcal{P}$ is identical with any conjunction of all of its elements.

1. If $\mathcal{P} > B$ then $\mathcal{P} \cup \{B\}$ is consistent.

2. Let $X_0, \ldots, X_{m+1}$ and $Y_0, \ldots, Y_{m+1}$ be two sequences such that the following hold:

   - $X_0 = Y_0 = A$

     and for $k = 0, \ldots, m$ we have that

   - $\displaystyle\bigwedge_{i=0}^{k} X_i >_1 X_{k+1}$

   - $\displaystyle\bigwedge_{i=0}^{k} Y_i >_1 Y_{k+1}.$

   Then we have for $k = 0, \ldots, m, \quad j = 0, \ldots, m,$

   - $\displaystyle\left(\bigwedge_{i=0}^{j} Y_i \right) \wedge \left(\bigwedge_{i=0}^{k} X_i \right) >_1 X_{k+1} \wedge Y_{j+1}.$

3. If $\mathcal{P} >_n X$ and $\mathcal{P} >_m Y$ and $n \leq m$ then $\mathcal{P} >_m X \wedge Y$.

4. If $\mathcal{P} >_k A$ and $\mathcal{P} >_m X$ then $\mathcal{P} + X >_k A$.

5. *Cut property*

   $\mathcal{P} > X$ and $\mathcal{P} + X > A$ imply $\mathcal{P} > A$.

---

[14]We cannot go too far into the theory of non-monotonic reasoning in this book. The reader should note a connection with theories of updates and theories of defeasible reasoning. See [Antoniou, 1996; Gabbay and Guenthner, 1977–99].

Solutions

1. This is proved by induction on the chain.

2. By induction on j, and k.

   (a) For $j = 0$ and any k we have to show that

   $$Y_0 \wedge \bigwedge_{i=0}^{k} X_i >_1 X_{k+1} \wedge Y_1$$

   Clearly since $Y_0 >_1 Y_1$ and $Y_0 = X_0$ we can use compatibility.

   (b) For $j = 1$ and $k = 1$ we have to show that

   $X_0 \wedge X_1 \wedge Y_0 \wedge Y_1 >_1 X_2 \wedge Y_2$

   Since

   $X_0 \wedge \cdots \wedge X_k \wedge Y_0 >_1 Y_1 \wedge X_{k+1}$

   by the case $j = 0$, we get

   $X_0 \wedge X_1 \wedge Y_0 \wedge Y_1 >_1 X_2$

   We now want to show that

   $X_0 \wedge X_1 \wedge Y_0 \wedge Y_1 >_1 Y_2$

   but this follows by symmetry.

   Thus we get

   $X_0 \wedge X_1 \wedge Y_0 \wedge Y_1 >_1 X_2 \wedge Y_2$.

   (c) Assume that the claim holds for any $j' < j$, $k' < k$; we want to show it for j, k.

   We can assume

   $(X_0 \wedge \cdots \wedge X_{k'}) \wedge (Y_0 \wedge \cdots \wedge Y_{j'} >_1 X_{k'+1} \wedge Y_{j'+1}$

   We show the same for the case of $k' = k$ and any $j' \leq j$, by induction on j'.
   The case of $j' = 0$ and any k we have shown in (a).
   Assume the claim holds for $j' < j$ and k.
   Show the claim for $j' + 1 \leq j$ and k.
   We have

   (*) $X_0 \wedge \cdots \wedge X_k \wedge Y_0 \wedge \cdots \wedge Y_{j'} >_1 X_{k+1} \wedge Y_{j'+1}$
   by the induction hypothesis for j' and k.

   (**) $X_0 \wedge \cdots \wedge X_{k-1} \wedge Y_0 \wedge \cdots \wedge Y_{j'+1} >_1 X_k \wedge Y_{j'+2}$
   by the induction hypothesis (c).

   Hence from (*) and (**) resp. we get:

- $X_0 \wedge \cdots \wedge X_k \wedge Y_0 \wedge \cdots \wedge Y_{j'} \wedge Y_{j'+1} >_1 X_{k+1}$
- $X_0 \wedge \cdots \wedge X_k \wedge Y_0 \wedge \cdots \wedge Y_{j'+1} >_1 Y_{j+2}$
  and hence
- $X_0 \wedge \cdots \wedge X_k \wedge Y_0 \wedge \cdots \wedge Y_{j'+1} >_1 X_{k+1} \wedge Y_{j'+2}.$

This proves the induction case for (c).
Thus we can conclude the induction and 2 is proved.

3. Assume that $A > Y$ and $A > X$. We can assume that there are chains of the form $X_0 = A, \ldots, X_{m+1} = X$ and $Y_0 = A, \ldots, Y_{m+1} = Y$ such that the assumption of 3 holds. We can assume both chains have the length $m + 1$ because any chain $Z_0, \ldots, Z_n$ can be made longer by taking $Z_0, \ldots, Z_n, Z_n, Z_n, \ldots$. Certainly $\bigwedge_{i=1}^n Z_i >_1 Z_n$ because of the axiom $A \wedge B \Rightarrow B$, and very simple compatibility.

Now by 2 for our two chains we get for $j = k < m + 1$

$$\left(\bigwedge_{i=0}^{k} X_i\right) \wedge \left(\bigwedge_{i=0}^{k} Y_i\right) >_1 X_{k+1} \wedge Y_{k+1}$$

or in other words

$$\bigwedge_{i=0}^{k} (X_i \wedge Y_i) >_1 X_{k+1} \wedge Y_{k+1}$$

Let

$$Z_0 = X_0 \wedge Y_0 = A$$
$$Z_i = X_i \wedge Y_i, i = 1, \ldots, m$$
$$Z_{m+1} = X_{m+1} \wedge Y_{m+1} = X \wedge Y$$

Then we get that $Z_0 = A, Z_1, \ldots, Z_{m+1} = X \wedge Y$ is a chain for $A >_m X \wedge Y$. This proves 3.[15]

---

[15] Solution 3 shows that if $\mathcal{P} > A$ and $\mathcal{P} > B$ then $\mathcal{P} > A \wedge B$ and hence $\mathcal{P} + A + B$ is consistent. This means that if we start with the core information $\mathcal{P}$ and apply our chain deductions, we enlarge the body of information more and more, to bigger and bigger consistent sets $\mathcal{P}_1, \mathcal{P}_2, \mathcal{P}_3$, etc., as we apply longer and longer chains.

Let $\mathcal{P}_0 = \mathcal{P}$

$\mathcal{P}_{m+1} = \mathcal{P}_m \cup \{A | \mathcal{P} >_{m+1} A\}$

$\mathcal{P}_\infty = \bigcup^n \mathcal{P}_n$

Then we have the situation described in the figure

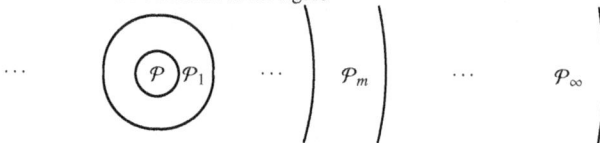

4. By induction on k.

   Case $k = 1$
   This is an assumed property of $>_1$.

   Case $k = n + 1$
   Let $A_1, \ldots, A_n$ be such that

   - $\mathcal{P} >_1 A_1$
   - $\mathcal{P} + A_1 >_1 A_2$
   - $\mathcal{P} + A_1 + \cdots + A_n >_1 A$.

   Since $\mathcal{P} + A_1 >_n A$ and $\mathcal{P} >_m X$, we have $\mathcal{P} + X + A_1 >_n A$ by the induction hypothesis.
   We also have $\mathcal{P} >_1 A_1$ and $\mathcal{P} >_m X$; hence by case 1, $\mathcal{P} + X >_1 A_1$. The two conclusions together mean $\mathcal{P} + X >_{n+1} A$.

5. Assume that $\mathcal{P} + X >_m A$ and $\mathcal{P} >_k X$. We will show that $\mathcal{P} >_{m+k} A$. We use induction on k.

   Case $k = 1$
   We have $\mathcal{P} >_1 X$ and $\mathcal{P} + X >_m A$. Clearly this implies by definition $\mathcal{P} >_{m+1} A$.

   Case $k + 1$
   Assume that $\mathcal{P} + X >_m A$ and $\mathcal{P} >_1 X_1$ and $\mathcal{P} + X_1 >_k X$.

   By the assumed property of $>$, since $\mathcal{P} >_1 X_1$ and $\mathcal{P} >_{k+1} X$, we get $\mathcal{P} + X >_1 X_1$.

   By 4 since $\mathcal{P} + X >_m A$ and $\mathcal{P} + X >_1 X_1$ we get $\mathcal{P} + X + X_1 >_m A$.

   We also have $\mathcal{P} + X_1 >_k X$.

   Hence by the induction hypothesis for k we get $\mathcal{P} + X_1 >_{m+k} A$. Since $\mathcal{P} >_1 X_1$, we finally conclude $\mathcal{P} >_{m+k+1} A$, which completes the induction case of $k + 1$ and thus proves 5.

We can now present semantics for our non-monotonic $>_N$ consequence.

DEFINITION 11.16 (Preferential semantics [Kraus *et al.*, 1990]).

1. A non-monotonic intuitionistic model has the form $\mathbf{m} = (W, <, \mathbf{l})$, where $(W, <)$ is a reflexive and symmetric ordered set and $\mathbf{l}$ is a function associating with each state s an intuitionistic Kripke model $\mathbf{l}(s) = (T_s, \leq_s, h^s)$, where $\leq_s$

is reflexive and transitive. h^s is the assignment giving for each atomic q a subset $h^s(q) \subseteq T_s$. Recall that we require that for all s and for all $t_1, t_2 \in T_s$ and for all $q, t_1 \in h^s(q)$ and $t_1 \leq_s t_2$ imply $t_2 \in h^s(q)$.

We refer to W as the set of states, $<$ is the preference relation and $\mathbf{l}$ associates with each state the set of possible worlds T_s. $\leq_s$ is the local possible worlds accessibility relation. We can consider $(T_s, \leq_s, h^s)$ as a Kripke model for intuitionistic logic as defined in Definition 2.6.

We can therefore extend h^s to all formulae of the fragment with $\Rightarrow, \wedge$ and $\perp$, as done in Definition 2.6.

2. Define satisfaction $\approx$ in $s \in W$ by

- $s \approx A$ iff $h^s(A) = T_s$.

3. Let $S \subseteq W$. A state $s \in S$ is said to be a minimum in S iff for every state $x \in S$ we have $s < x$.

4. Define a consequence $\vdash_{\mathbf{m}}$ by

- $A \vdash_{\mathbf{m}} B$ iff for the minimum state s in $\hat{A} = \{x \in W \mid x \approx A\}$ we have $s \approx B$.

5. A model is said to be strongly smooth iff for all A, $\hat{A}$ has a minimum.

EXAMPLE 11.17 (Completeness theorem for $>_N$). Prove the following theorems.

1. For any $\mathbf{N}$ there exists a strongly smooth model $\mathbf{m}$ such that for all A, B, $A \vdash_{\mathbf{m}} B$ iff $A >_N B$.

2. For any strongly smooth model $\mathbf{m}$ there exists an $\mathbf{N}$ such that for all A, B, $A \vdash_{\mathbf{m}} B$ iff $A >_N B$.

Solutions

1. Let $\mathbf{N}$ be given and consider $>_N$. First note that $>_N$ satisfies the following:

(*) $A >_N B$ and $B >_N A$ and $A >_N C$ imply $B >_N C$.

The reason is that from $A >_N B$ and $A >_N C$ we get by restricted monotonicity $B \wedge A >_N C$ and since $B >_N A$ we get by cut that $B >_N C$.

Let $A \equiv B$ be defined as for all $C, A >_N C$ iff $B >_N C$. Then $\equiv$ is an equivalence relation.

Let W be the set of all equivalence classes. Let $A/_\equiv < B/_\equiv$ be defined as for some $A_0 \equiv A$, $B >_N A_0$. The definition of $<$ does not depend on the choice representatives.

For each class $s = A/_\equiv$, let

$$Q_s = \{Y \mid A >_N Y\}$$
$$T_s = \{\mathcal{P} \mid \mathcal{P} \supseteq Q_s\}$$

and let

$$\mathcal{P}_1 \leq_s \mathcal{P}_2 \text{ iff } \mathcal{P}_1 \subseteq \mathcal{P}_2$$

Let $\mathbf{l}(s) = (T_s, \leq_s, h^s)$, where

$$h^s(q) = \{\mathcal{P} \in T_s \mid \mathcal{P} \vdash q\}$$

$(T_s, \leq_s, h^s)$ is a Kripke model.

One can show, as done in Exercise 7.3, that for all Y,

$$h^s(Y) = \{\mathcal{P} \mid \mathcal{P} \vdash Y\}$$

Consider the model $\mathbf{m} = (W, <, \mathbf{l})$.

First note that $s = A/_\equiv \approx A$ holds. This means that $h^s(A) = T_s$. It is sufficient to show that $Q_s \vdash A$. This holds since $A \in Q_s$.

We now show that $\mathbf{m}$ is strongly smooth. This holds since $A/_\equiv$ is a minimum in $\hat{A}$.

We now show that, on formulae, $>_N$ is the same as $\vdash_\mathbf{m}$.

Assume that $A >_N B$. Then $B \in Q_{A/_\equiv}$ and hence in the minimum state of $\hat{A}$, namely in $A/_\equiv$, we have $A/_\equiv \approx B$; hence $A \vdash_\mathbf{m} B$. Conversely, if it is not the case that $A >_N B$, then we cannot have $Q_{A/_\equiv} \vdash B$ because of compatibility of $>_N$ with $\vdash$. Hence $A/_\equiv \not\approx B$ and so $A \not\vdash_\mathbf{m} B$.

2. To show this direction we semantically check that $\vdash_\mathbf{m}$ satisfies all the properties of consequence listed in Theorem 11.6. The only property that requires some proof is restricted monotonicity. This follows from strong smoothness, as we are going to show. Assume $A \vdash_\mathbf{m} B$ and $A \vdash_\mathbf{m} C$. Let s_A be a minimum of $\hat{A}$. Thus we have $s_A \approx B \wedge C$. Thus certainly $s_A \approx A \wedge B$.

We now show that $A \wedge B \vdash_\mathbf{m} C$.

Let $t_{A \wedge B}$ be a minimum in $\widehat{A \wedge B}$. Hence $t_{A \wedge B} \approx A$ and so $t_{A \wedge B} \in \hat{A}$ and so $s_A < t_{A \wedge B}$. On the other hand, since $s_A \approx A \wedge B$ we have $t_{A \wedge B} < s_A$. Hence $t_{A \wedge B} = s_A$ by antisymmetry and hence $t_{A \wedge B} \approx C$.

Thus we have shown that C holds at the minimum of $\widehat{A \wedge B}$ and hence $A \wedge B \mathrel{\mid\!\sim_\mathbf{m}} C$.

Let $\mathbf{N} = \{(A, B) \mid A \vdash_\mathbf{m} B\}$. Consider $>_N$. Since $\vdash_\mathbf{m}$ satisfies the properties of Theorem 11.6 and $>_N$ is obtained as the 'closure' of $\mathbf{N}$ under these properties, we get that, on formulae, $>_N$ is equal to $\vdash_\mathbf{m}$.

This proves 2.

4   Case study: concessive clauses and tensed conditionals

This section presents a system of non-monotonic reasoning and uses it to formally analyse concessive clauses and tensed conditionals in English.

Non-monotonic reasoning is based on the notion of expectation (not in the probability sense). The basic relation involved is that of: 'on the basis of A one expects B, following knowledge of how things are in our world'. This basic relation is denoted by $A > B$. To give but a few examples:

1. When receiving a letter one is expected to reply. John received a letter > John replied.

2. When a traffic accident occurs an ambulance is expected to arirve.

3. John is offered more money > John accepts it.

4. John leaves home for the weekend > John locks his door.

Consider the following:

5.   (a) He liked the food but didn't ask for more.

  ·(b) He liked the food but asked for more.[16]

6.   (a) He married her but did not sleep with her.

  ·(b) He married her but slept with her.

  ·(c) He did not sleep with her but married her.

7.   (a) John was offered the money but did not take it.

  ·(b) John was offered the money but took it.

  ?·(c) John did not take the money but was offered it.

When using classical logic only, $\wedge$ is the only available connective to be used to formalise the word 'but'. Clearly $\wedge$ alone cannot represent (a) and (b) parts correctly.

The following are some more examples of concessive clauses:

8.   (a) Mary is beautiful but has a terrible temper.

  (b) Mary has a terrible temper but is beautful.

9.   (a) Jones is very rich but chronically ill

  (b) Jones is chronically ill but very rich.

10. · She is tall despite being religious

---

[16]The use of the dot indicate the sentence is not acceptable in English.

11. Though she did not know it, she trusted him.

12. (a) He bought a lottery ticket but he didn't win.

     ·(b) He bought a lottery ticket but he won.

13. Not a day went by but brought us news of yet another calamity.

14. Even Scrooge was not so dreadfully cut up by the sad event, but that he was an excellent man of business on the very day of the funeral.

15. She wanted to make a speech but did not know how to begin.

16. · She was already engaged but might have accepted him as a lover.

17. She was already engaged or she might have accepted him as a lover.

18. No goals were scored, though it was an exciting game.

19. Although Britain considers itself an advanced country, it has a very old-fashioned system of measurement.

20. He borrowed my mower, even though I told him not to.

21. Even if you dislike ancient monuments, Warwick Castle is worth a visit.

22. If he is poor, at least he is honest.

23. · If she is poor, at least she is ugly.

24. Though well over eighty, he can still do it.

25. Naked as I was, I braved the storm.

26. Whether or not he finds a job, he is getting married.

27. She looks pretty, whatever she wears.

28. No matter how hard I try, I can never catch up with him.

29. (a) Although we never interviewed him we were willing to offer him the position.

     ·(b) Although we never interviewed him we were not willing to offer him the position.

30. Even if you pay me, I will not like you.

It is obvious that the above examples need for their analysis the notion of expectation $A > B$ and certainly more than just Boolean connectives. Examples like A *but* B in which there is some causal or temporal relation between A and B in the sense that first A is 'done' and then B, can be analysed as follows:

31. A *but* $B \equiv A \wedge B \wedge (A > -B)$

For example, going back to (6):

6. (a) $\equiv$ (He married her) $\wedge$ (He did not sleep with her) $\wedge$ (marry her > sleep with her).

(b) $\equiv$ (He married her) $\wedge$ (He slept with her) $\wedge$ (marry her > not sleep with her).

The last clause is ridiculously false, which explains why (6)·(b) is not acceptable.

Temporal or clausal ordereed A *but* B are not always symmetrical, i.e. B *but* A may not be acceptable. Sometimes other words are used like *despite*, etc. Some *but* sentences are always symmetrical, such as (8) and (9).

The 'but' part refers to some 'common' expected X.

Thus in (9)· one may expect 'happiness' or something like that.

The representation of A *but* B in case of no temporal or causal connection between A and B can be taken as:

32. A *but* $B = A \wedge B \wedge \exists x[(A > x) \wedge B > \neg x)]$.

Another direction where non-monotonic reasoning is useful is the area of tensed conditionals. There are many theories of conditionals and many examples and problems to be resolved. Some of them, we say, involve expectation $A > B$. We shall investigate this aspect later. Meanwhile, consider:

A = I am offered the money.
B = I take the money.

Using A and B we can construct the following conditionals. The symbol $\mapsto$ is used for conditional, and PA for 'A was true' and FA for 'A will be true'. Let HA be $\neg P \neg A$, 'A was always true' and GA be $\neg F \neg A$, 'A will always be true'.

33. If I were offered the money then I would have taken it.
     notation: were $A \mapsto$ would have B

34. If I were offered the moeny then I would have not taken it.
     notation: were $A \mapsto$ would have $\neg B$.

The import of (34) is $P(A \Rightarrow \neg B)$ because $A > B$ holds.

35. If he was offered the money then he did take it.
     notation: $PA \mapsto PB$

36. ?· If he was offered the money then he did not take it.
   notation: $PA \Rightarrow P\neg B$

In view of (7)(a) and (7)·(b), we claim that the following is the correct reading of (33)–(36):

33. says $(H\neg A) \wedge H(A > B)$

34. says $H\neg A \wedge P\neg(A > B)$

35. says no more no less than $H(A > B)$

36. says $H(A \Rightarrow \neg B)$.

We suggest the following preliminary theory for analysing out some conditionals $A \Rightarrow B$ by applying a *test* of looking at $A > B$.

37. Let us use the following rules of analysis: We have four cases to analyse:

   (a) Had $A \Rightarrow$ would have B

   (b) Had $A \Rightarrow$ would have $\neg B$

   (c) Past $A \Rightarrow$ Past B

   (d) Past $A \Rightarrow$ Past $\neg B$.

We apply a test. We check for acceptance the following:

(t1) *A but B*

(t2) *A but* $\neg B$

If either *both* (t1) and (t2) are acceptable or both ·(t1) and ·(t2) are not acceptable, then the conditionals (a)–(d) should be analysed using some current theory of conditionals and not using $>$.
   If however one of (t1) and (t2) is acceptable and the other is not acceptable then we understand that some $>$ notion is involved and we analyse $\Rightarrow$ using $>$.
   The analysis is done as follows. For simplicity assume

·(t1) is not acceptable

·(t2) is acceptable

Then translate as follows:

   (a) $\equiv H\neg A \wedge H(A > B)$

   (b) $H\neg A \wedge P\neg(A > B)$

   (c) $H(A > B)$

(d) $H(A \Rightarrow \neg B)$.

38. To give examples:

(a) Had I looked through my window I would not have gone to the party.

Thus
$A =$ look through the window,
$B =$ go to the party.
   This is the case of both (37 t1) and (37 t2) being acceptable.
Example

39. Take

(c) If he received the letter he replied.

Here we have
$A =$ receive letter;
$B =$ reply.
   We have:

(t1) I received the letter but did not reply.

·(t2) I received the letter but did reply.

According to our theory

(c) reads $H(A > B)$.

Take (a): Had I received the letter I would have replied.

(a) reads $(H\neg A) \wedge H(A > B)$.

Take (d): Had I received the letter I would not have replied.

(d) reads $H\neg A \wedge \neg H(A > B)$.

EXERCISE 11.18. Investigate the following examples, (taken from Nute's paper tense and conditional) carefully:

40.   (a) If Anthony's door is unlocked then he'll be back soon.

   ·(b) Anthony's door is unlocked but he'll not be back soon.

41.   (a) If Anthony had left for the weekeend then he would have locked his door.

   (b) Anthony had left for the weekend but did not lock his door.

42. (a) If we had invited Frank he might have come.

     (b) We invited Frank but he did not come.

43. Even if we had invited Frank, he would not have come.

44. (a) If Robert had wrecked his bicycle he would have broken his arm.

     (b) Robert had wrecked his bicycle but did not break his arm.

45. (a) If an ace had not come up, Clyde would have won his wager.

     ·(b) An ace had not come up, but Clyde had not won his wager.

D 46. (a) If I had received an invcitation I would have gone to the party.

     (b) I had received an inviation but I did not go to the party.

D 47. (a) If I had looked behind my desk, I would have gone to the party.

     ·(b) I looked behind my desk, but did not go to the party.

48. (a) If Franz had broken his leg he wouldn't have played in the finals.

     (b) Franz broke his leg but he edid play in the fionals.

49. (a) If Franz had broken his leg, there would be evidence of the break in the X-rays.

     (b) Franz had broken his leg but there was no evidence ...

50. (a) If Oswald didn't shoot Kennedy, then Kennedy is alive today. $p\neg q > r$.

     (b) Oswald did not shoot Kennedy but Kennedy is not alive today.

51. (a) If Oswald hadn't shot Kennedy then Kennedy would be alive today. $P(q > r)$

52. (a) If Max missed the train then he took the bus. $Pq > Pr$

     (b) Max missed the train but did not take the bus.

53. (a) If Max had missed the train then he would have taken the bus. $P(q > Pr)$

     (b) Max had missed the train but had not taken the bus.

D 54. If Jane received an invitation then she subsequently went to the party. $P(q > Fr)$ wrong.

55. If Joe strikes this match it will light.

CHAPTER 12

Practical reasoning

1 Introduction

The previous chapter studied formal nonmonotonic reasoning. The formal machinery involved two components:

1. An underlying monotonic logic $\vdash$.

2. A family $\mathbf{N}$ of pairs $(\mathcal{P}, A) \in \mathbf{N}$ of nonmonotonic rules of the form

   - From $\mathcal{P}$ (as a whole) conclude A.

Formally any underlying monotonic logic $\vdash$ and any compatible family $\mathbf{N}$ of pairs $(\mathcal{P}, A)$ can form the basis for (i.e. can be put together to make) a nonmonotonic system (which we denote by) $\vdash\!\!\!\sim$.

However, if we want our system to be applicable to problems of everyday life we must choose a good monotonic component and let our $\mathbf{N}$ identify the various types of common sense rules arising in everyday practice. The purpose of this chapter is to discuss intuitively the practical aspects of monotonic and nonmonotonic rules, examine the contexts in which they arise and appreciate the way they interact.

We begin by setting up some terminology.

Given a database $\mathcal{P}$ and a query A, if the intention is to check whether $\mathcal{P} \mid\!\sim A$ using rules which can also be nonmonotonic, we may refer to $\mathcal{P}$ itself as a nonmonotonic database. This is to be understood as meaning a database to which we expect to apply nonmonotonic reasoning.

Given a nonmonotonic database $\mathcal{P}$, which represents some data in a familiar application area, we can ask whether $\mathcal{P} \mid\!\sim A$. This represents a query A from $\mathcal{P}$. We can on the one hand apply our nonmonotonic rules and check the answer. We can also, on the other hand, ask a typical human agent (i.e. a group of normal people with good common sense) whether the answer should be yes. If the system is such that there is a good match with the human answers in the application area for which it is intended, we can think of it as a 'logic agent'.

Thus we seek nonmonotonic rules which correspond to intuitive human practical reasoning, in order to produce logical systems that can be used as logic agents.

Let us call any system suitable for getting answers from a nonmonotonic database an *agent system*. This terminology is my own (see [Gabbay, 1996, chapter 1]) but it is compatible with the use of the word agent in the literature.[1]

The purpose of this chapter then is to look at possible good rules for data agents.

Section 12.2 sets the scene for our problem. Section 12.3 studies the role of the underlying monotonic logic component. It criticizes classical logic as a choice and recommends intuitionistic logic.

Section 12.4 introduces informally more examples of nonmonotonic rules preparing for the more specialized sections which follow. Section 12.5 studies various aspects of negation which is a major player in nonmonotonicity. Section 11.6 explains how the order of application of rules and their interaction plays a major role in nonmonotonic deduction. This aspect was not studied in detail in Chapter 11.

Section 12.7 addresses the phenomena of time and change. Many nonmonotonic rules of everyday life arise from temporal assumptions such as persistence and temporal updating and information flow.

Sections 12.8–12.11 deal with other major causes of nonmonotonicity, namely hypotheticals, contradictions and uncertainty and vagueness.

We conclude the chapter with Section 11.12, where we give a case study — a short story involving adultery and (nonmonotonic) frustration.

2   Querying a database

Suppose we are given a database $\mathcal{P}$ containing declarative information about some subject matter. For example, $\mathcal{P}$ may contain all the rules and requirements for a college degree and all the relevant information about the teachers and students. Another example for $\mathcal{P}$ is the rules and regulations of the British Nationality Act. We want to query this database. If A is the query, we symbolically write

$$\mathcal{P} \vdash ?A$$

---

[1]To be strict, we should call the above a *data agent* or an *intelligent knowledge base*. Agents in general can do many things, take actions, move around, etc. There is no clear-cut definition of the notion of an agent in the community. To quote from the literature:

H.S. Nwana and N. Azarmi say in [Nwana and Azarmi, 1997, page 5]: 'when necessary an agent is defined as referring to a component of software and/or hardware which is capable of acting exactly in order to accomplish tasks on behalf of its user. However, it would be preferable to say it is an umbrella term which covers a range of other more specific agent types, and then go on to list and define what these other agent types are.'

J. Müller, M. Wooldridge and N. Jennings in their book [Müller *et al.*, 1997] define intelligent agents as 'computer systems that are capable of flexible autonomous action in dynamic, typically multiagent domain'. Their book contains a collection of papers on the topic 'What is an agent—Definitions and Taxonomies'.

to show that we ask A of $\mathcal{P}$. An example of such a question is

Can Mr Smith become a British citizen?

An expert human agent will look at all the rules and data of the database $\mathcal{P}$, including the data relating to Mr Smith, and then come up with an answer.

The answer is given after some serious deliberation which involves various logical principles of reasoning and search strategies in manipulating the data.

The tasks of non-monotonic logic and formal practical reasoning are to analyze the logical principles involved and find an appropriate logical language in which to express these principles. Furthermore, we need to describe the principles in such a way as to enable us to replace the human agent (who answers the questions) by a computer program (agent system).

We can thus present our problem as follows:

Find a suitable logical language and construct a suitable logical system within an appropriate framework, such that for database $\mathcal{P}$ and queries A, we have

(*) The machine gives the intuitively correct answer to any query A from the database $\mathcal{P}$, in the sense that a human expert would have given the same answer!

For a given application area, any (logical) system satisfying (*) above shall be called an *agent system*.

We are assuming here that there are some underlying general, human, logical principles which are involved in getting an answer to a query from a database, which are independent of the subject matter.

The agent systems may reason differently; in fact, different agent systems may use reasoning rules which rely heavily on a particular knowledge representation, which is natural to the specific subject matter at hand. We believe, however, that different agent systems still use similar logical rules despite a wide range of differences. A top man at British Petroleum may accept the post of general manager of ITV television. He may have to learn the particular problems of the network etc., but no one will say that he has to learn a new logic.

We must clarify our use of the notion of agent system in this chapter. The term agent systems does not have a clear-cut meaning in the literature. There are various systems doing 'expert work' like solving equations or solving specific problems in some particular area. These systems rely heavily on special tricks and shortcuts characteristic to their area of application to such an extent that no logical behaviour is recognizable. It is not clear whether we should call such and such a system of reasoning. In fact one may claim that there is no logical reasoning involved at all in agent systems and each system uses its own ways of doing 'the work'.[2]

---

[2]There is a similar problem with planning and scheduling systems. Each system is designed for a specific application to such an extent that it cannot be used for even a slightly different application area.

Our perception of the notion of agent systems is slightly different. The system must reflect the logic of the human reasoner in the area of application. Changes in the human expert ways of thinking must be easily reflected in the agent system itself. We give two examples to illustrate our point of view.

Suppose we want to replace a customs officer by our agent system which can decide whether to question and search an arriving passenger. After much consultation, a set of guidelines, rules and tests is devised which can replace this customs officer (we assume here that the law gives much discretion to the officer in the field). What we get is an agent system in our sense.

A clever observer may notice that no passenger was ever questioned (possibly because the rules were too restrictive for fear of complaints). One can thus devise the 'agent system' which says '*let everyone in, freely*'. This system is probably effective in 99.9% of the cases. However, it is not an agent system in our sense. It does not reflect the reasoning of the customs officer. A change in the human attitude cannot be incrementally reflected in the machine system.

We need correct representation in the computer system and not only any black box which can give correct results.

Our second example is exactly the opposite. Suppose the customs laws really want to say: '*search everyone on any charter flight*'. The airlines may object to a law saying that explicitly. Thus the customs laws will probably be a complex set of rules designed to achieve the same effect as the single rule above. If we discover in this case that the tendency to wear jeans and a modern hairstyle can be used in 99.9% of the cases to decide whether to search the passenger or not (because that is how you can 'recognize' a charter flight passenger), then in this case this single rule may be acceptable as a basis for an agent system replacing the complex body of rules, since the 'logic' is correct.

A change in the human attitude such as '*don't search older people on charter flights*' can be incrementally reflected in the agent system itself by checking reasonably related characteristics like '*does the candidate have an advanced hotel booking*?', and using them to add a rule for exceptions.

We need to construct an abstract logical framework which will describe all the logical possibilities of inference available to us and into which we can slot any particular agent system. The field of agent systems and non-monotonic reasoning is still in an exploratory state mainly because we have not yet completely identified the reasoning principles involved and the ways in which they can be used.

In fact, people are not aware of the strong arguments which show that intuitionistic logic is better suited to underpin human reasoning. Thus many of the existing systems, we believe, are already at a serious disadvantage right at the start! See [Gabbay, 1982].

The interest in practical non-monotonic reasoning goes beyond computer science. Serious non-monotonic research will describe and analyze some of the principles involved in human reasoning and thus be of fundamental and lasting value.

The sections below describe the various abstract logical principles and computational techniques involved in arriving at an answer to a query of a database. In our view a database is comprised of three components: the main data, a module containing logical maintenance principles which can absorb new data, respond to actions and deal with data uncertainty, and a reasoning module which can answer queries.

The following figure (12.1) shows the interrelationships of the various components involved in giving answers to queries from databases.

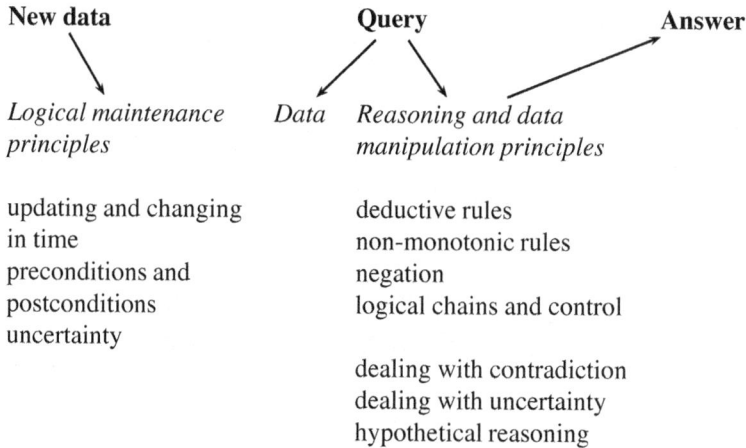

New data   **Query**   **Answer**

Logical maintenance   *Data*   *Reasoning and data*
principles   *manipulation principles*

updating and changing   deductive rules
in time   non-monotonic rules
preconditions and   negation
postconditions   logical chains and control
uncertainty

                               dealing with contradiction
                               dealing with uncertainty
                               hypothetical reasoning

Figure 12.1.

3   The underlying deductive logic

Some questions of a database can be answered immediately by direct search. For example, to the question

Is London in the UK?

one can answer immediately by searching for the datum

London is in the UK!

which may be listed in the database. Other questions may be answered only using deductive reasoning and logic as we have seen in previous chapters. No pure search of data is sufficient. The answer must be extracted from the database using rules. Figure 12.2 depicts a well-known example (Robert Moore, SRI):

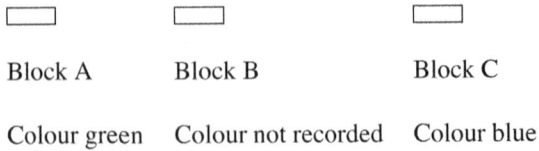

Block A   Block B   Block C

Colour green   Colour not recorded   Colour blue

Figure 12.2.

If we ask: *Is there a sequence of the blocks which are both green or both non-green?*, the answer should be *yes*. However, no search, block by block, comparing colours, will give the answer. Logic is needed here!

Another example involving a well-known logical rule is the following. Suppose the following items are in the database:

1. *The lift can carry only one person*
   (meaning the lift collapses if more than one person is in the lift).

2. *John and Mary entered the lift at 12.00 yesterday.*

The database yields the conclusion:

3. *The lift collapsed at 12.00 yesterday.*

Let us take the following symbolic representation:
  J = John entered the lift at 12.00 yesterday.
  M = Mary entered the lift at 12.00 yesterday.
  C = The lift collapsed at 12.00 yesterday.
Then the database can be taken as

1* $J \wedge M \Rightarrow C$

2* J

3* M.

The query is

4* C
      or in words:

      Did the lift collapse at 12.00 yesterday?

Any schoolchild will tell you that the answer to this questions is *yes*. The logical rules involved are simple and well known. In this case we use the rules of *modus ponens*.

The problem involved here is not of logic but of practical computation. Given a large database $\mathcal{P}$ and a query C, what manipulations shall the computer do to obtain the answer for the case where the only rules involved are deductive?

Programs for checking whether a query C follows from a database $\mathcal{P}$ by deductive rules have been presented earlier in this book. There are many other programs in the literature. They are called *automated deduction methods* and the best known of these is probably resolution (see Section 8.3.1); see [Gallier, 1986; Goubault-Larrecq and Mackie, 1997]. The well-known computer language 'Prolog' is based on resolution methods; see [Apt, 1996]. Many logic-based agent systems use resolution methods as their starting point.

We feel that unfortunately many existing resolution and theorem-proving methods are based on the wrong logic. They give the wrong answers in some cases, in the sense that they do not give the answers a human would give. Naturally, programmers may be aware of the discrepancies. They try to compensate, thus patching and obscuring the logic so that errors and their amendments multiply. Let us look at some examples of databases and queries and see what a human would reply and what resolution would reply. It is easy to point out where the fault of resolution lies.

The problem is that resolution rewrites the database in a convenient form for computation. The rewriting is logically equivalent to the original according to classical predicate logic, but is not the same in the logic of human reasoning, namely (we believe) in intuitionistic logic. Here is an example.

Consider the database we know already, namely

1* $(J \wedge M) \Rightarrow C$

2* J

3* $M.$

The above is written the way it is expressed in English. Resolution will rewrite the above as

1* $(\neg J) \vee (\neg M) \vee C$

2* J

3* $M.$

So instead of saying

1. *If John and Mary entered the lift at 12.00 yesterday then the lift collapsed at 12.00 yesterday.*

resolution will say

1#   *Either John or Mary was not in the lift at 12.00 yesterday or the lift col-
        lapsed at 12.00 yesterday.*

When we ask a query C from a database, resolution will rewrite the database and
C as shown above and will try to find out whether the answer to the query ? C is
yes by 'cancelling out' pairs of the form: $(\neg x, x)$.

In the example above we have

1# $(\neg J) \vee (\neg M) \vee C$

2# J

3# M.

The pairs
$$(J, \neg J)$$
$$(M, \neg M)$$
are cancelled out, and what remains is C. Thus the answer to C is *yes* because C
was not cancelled out.

So far we got the correct answer. We got the same answer a human would give
to the query C.

Let us now try a similar query and database, and go wrong! Let the database be

1. $J \wedge M \Rightarrow C$.

Let the query be

4. $(J \Rightarrow C) \vee (M \Rightarrow C)$.

In words, the database says that if John and Mary were in the lift at 12.00 yesterday
then the lift collapsed.

The query essentially asks: *Did one of them collapse the lift on his or her
own?* That is, either if John (alone) entered the lift at 12.00 yesterday then the
lift collapsed or if Mary (alone) entered the lift at 12.00 yesterday then the lift
collapsed.

The above query will get the answer *yes*, in classical logic, which is wrong, but
not in intuitionistic logic. One may need both John and Mary in the lift to have it
collapse.

The answer we get in this case is not what a human will answer.

Obviously we need to devise new, more human-oriented, methods of manipulating databases. We need methods based on the correct logic. The goal-directed
methods of this book operate on $\Rightarrow$ directly without rewriting it in terms of $\neg$ and
$\vee$.[3] They are more suited for human reasoning.

---

[3]It is interesting to note that the Horn clause fragment of classical logic and that of intuitionistic
logic are the same. Thus pure Prolog is intuitionistic!

Here is another example:
It may be true that

1. *If John loved Jane then John married Jane.*

And also true that

2. *If Terry loved Judith then Terry married Judith.*

It does not follow from 1 and 2 above that

3. *Either if John loved Jane then Terry married Judith or if Terry loved Judith then John married Jane.*

No human will accept the above as a valid conclusion. Resolution, however, would say *yes*, 3 does follow from 1 and 2.

A more striking example perhaps is

1. *If John is in Paris then he is in France.*

2. *If John is in London then he is in England.*

3. *Either if John is in Paris then he is in England or if John is in London then he is in France.*

Summary of this section

We saw that if the monotonic deductive component of a logic-based agent system is based on resolution methods then it is not sound for human practical reasoning. We argued in this section that our goal-directed computation (without restart) which is based on intuitionistic (implication) logic is better suited for human reasoning. It reads the way humans do. It also allows for reading $\Rightarrow$ the classical logic way (by using restart) if desired and, in such a case, the computation is the same as ordinary clausal resolution.

There is therefore a need to develop logical systems more suitable for modelling human reasoning. We refer the reader to books on non-monotonic logics. See [Antoniou, 1996; Gabbay *et al.*, 1993–95], and the books listed in the further reading section at the end of this book.

See also the discussion in Section 2.3.

4   Non-monotonic rules

Suppose our data is a table of charter flights to New York of the major airlines. It has the form shown in Figure 11.3.:

Suppose we can 'see' from the table that there are no charter flights to New York on Mondays. We mean here that we 'see' that there are no flights at all, not that the table contains no flights (which is obvious). This is a use of a non-monotonic

Airlines	Telephone numbers	List of charter
	of main booking offices	flights

Figure 12.3.

expectation rule (as discussed briefly in Chapter 10). We reason that had there been such a flight, it would have been put in the table.

Of course the table may be incomplete but we also assume, knowing how anxious airlines are in advertising their flights, that the table is complete and there are no flights at all on Monday.

Let us now see how a deductive chain of reasoning may be constructed. Suppose the law says that a businessman may deduct as expenses the cost of a flight only if he has flown British Airways. If, however, no direct British Airways flight is available on the same day, then any other airline ticket may also be deducted. Thus the database will contain the rules:

1. If a ticket is British Airways then the amount is tax deductible.

2. If British Airways has no flight to the same destination on the date of the ticket, then the amount of the ticket is tax deductible.

Let our database contain the above two rules and the table of charter flights. If one queries the database about whether a Monday charter flight ticket with TWA to New York is deductible, the answer should be *yes*. First we search the table and find no British Airways charter flight to New York on Mondays. We use next the default rule to deduce that no such flight exists. Then we use the result together with rule 2 above and give the answer *yes*. The cost of the ticket is indeed tax deductible.

Notice that the default rule is a non-monotonic rule which depends on the current state of the database. It is possible that the data is wrong and a correction may come from British Airways that indeed there is a charter flight to New York on Mondays. In this case the answer will change to *no*, the amount is not tax deductible. So in a way this rule (default rule) is a heuristic rule, based on the assumption that there is no error of omission in the table.

The following is another example of possible reasoning from a table. Suppose the airline's telephone number is listed as 432111. This is only a six-digit number and it is obvious that a digit is missing. A human would reason that the number is probably 4321111, assuming the airlines always have easy to remember telephone numbers and that the digit '1' is likely to be missed. There is only one more possibility and that is that the number is 5432111.

The above use of reasoning is very instructive, in that it applies *only* to this particular database, namely telephone numbers in London. We see that non-monotonic rules are characteristic to the database and the environment in which they apply, whereas the deductive component is comprised of general logical rules applicable to any database. What happens to our claim that there are general rules of reasoning for agent systems?

The answer is that these non-monotonic rules interact among themselves and interact with other components of the system in certain logical ways. These ways are general and independent of the environment. Thus if we code the ways in which rules chain, interact and are updated, etc., as is being done in the current literature, then we will have an abstract logical framework which will take data and the particular non-monotonic rules of the environment as further data as in the schematic diagram, Figure 11.4.

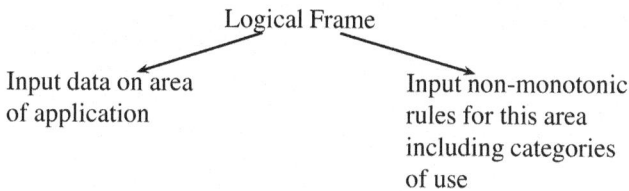

Logical Frame

Input data on area   Input non-monotonic
of application   rules for this area
                           including categories
                           of use

Figure 12.4.

The advantage of this framework is that the rules can also be changed just like the data. There could be 'grey areas' where, depending on how 'strict' we are, the answer to a query could be *yes* or *no*. The degree of 'strictness' can be put in and the system will know how to respond.

We meet here two kinds of rules: logical deductive rules of the underlying logic (as discussed in Section 12.3) and the non-monotonic, heuristic rules. Deductive rules give answers which never change in the face of an inflow of additional positive information. If non-monotonic rules are used to give an answer, then more detailed information may invalidate the answer. The additional information we are talking about is of the form of more compatible details. We are not dealing here with new information which replaces current data with new (possibly contradictory) data. We shall see that there is still a third kind of rule, discussed in Section 12.6.

Summary of this section

We saw that agent systems use non-monotonic rules for their reasoning. These rules have special characteristics and are usually tailored to specific subject matter.

Comments

There is still a feeling that something is wrong with agent systems and artificial intelligence systems even in cases where the system gives the right answer. There are cases where the 'human computer', slow as it is, gives the correct answer immediately while the agent system may take some time to find it. Something must be wrong. Why are we faster? Is it the way we perceive the rules as opposed to the way we represent them in the agent system? Do we know immediately which rule to use? We must look for the 'correct' representation in the sense that it mirrors the way we perceive and apply the rules.[4]

5   How to use negation

We are dealing here with a logically difficult concept. When a human is asked a question ? *A* and answers *no* to the question, there are complex logical principles involved in arriving at the answer. The answer *no* does not always have the same meaning in different contexts. There may be several different negations involved and the final answer *no* is a result of some complex combinations of these negations. We have already learnt in Chapter 1 the so-called classical truth functional negation. We shall analyze negation in this section by listing the main types of negation. The use of negation in agent systems is further complicated by the fact that a full logically correct treatment of negation causes a combinational explosion. Thus one cannot hope to work with negation on a computer without taking shortcuts and it is our job to make sure that these shortcuts are logically sound. This is the first time in this chapter, and indeed in this book, that we have to make 'logical concessions' owing to practical computation limitations. The challenge is, of course, to improve performance while still retaining logical control. This is an area where there is the greatest temptation for 'hacking' and *ad hoc* heuristics, and where there is the greatest danger of logical errors.

We start by arousing the reader's suspicions of the notion of negation. Suppose we ask the Council whether we can get permission to do some alterations to our house roof. Suppose the answer we get is just the word no. This will never satisfy us. We would want to know why not (i.e. by what process was the answer *no* arrived at?) and, even further, we may want to consult other authorities.

The reader may think that there is a body of specialized knowledge involved here and by asking for details on 'why not?', we are trying to learn more. This is not the main reason. We claim that what we want to know is 'what kind of *no* is involved?' Let us take a simple example. Suppose we ask a travel agent whether there is a charter flight to Timbuktu on Monday, January 1. The agent says *no*. A

---

[4]Humans use an overall impression to make decisions about how to go about finding answers to queries. Neural networks are in a better position to model this capacity. In fact we believe that every agent system must have a neural net component. See [Aleksander and Burnett, 1987; Aleksander and Morton, 1995].

rational being might wonder whether the answer is indeed correct. And if one is clever, one would ask another travel agent. No one will be surprised if the other travel agent does find a flight to Timbuktu.

We thus have the following logical types of negation.

A. Negation as default

This type of negation follows the understanding that if the information is not listed positively then it is negative. Examples of this are abundant. Any list of the winners implies that the names not on the list are the losers. A contract specifying the allowed uses of a hired computer implies that any use not specifically mentioned is forbidden. See Example 11.1.

B. Negation as inconsistency

We also answer *no* to questions because if we say *yes* then we get undesirable results. This is a dynamic sort of negation. Taking up the example of the hired computer, one may have a general clause in the contract, allowing the use of the computer in any way desired as long as the computer is not physically damaged. In this case many possible uses may be forbidden if they are thought to lead to physical damage. This use of negation assumes that there are things we do not want to have true and we say *no* to anything which may make them true.

Another example of this sort of negation is probably any general guidelines such as environment conservation laws. They do not specify what is allowed or forbidden, but any single proposal is checked for its potential for environmental damage.

This negation is rather complicated logically and needs to be carefully studied. The problem is that what we do not want depends on what we already have. In other words, if P is the current database (describing what is true now, before the next new information comes in) and if N is the set of data which we do not want to become true, then N depends on P and thus what we may negate now, we may not negate tomorrow.

For example, we may not want to work on Sunday, and thus will reject any contract which may include work on Sundays, but if our spending increases substantially, and we need more income, then we may be willing to work on Sundays.

C. Strong negation

Sometimes data is specifically negated. For example, we find written on medical bottles '*Not for internal use*', or posters like '*Do not walk on the grass*' etc. This we call strong negation, because it does not depend on any additional assumptions or information and does not change in time.

D. Informative negation

This type of negation is very common. It is not really negation but a way of giving additional information, which is contrary to what one would expect. It thus depends on and assumes a context. When we say '*the train did not leave on time*', we are adding a positive piece of information, that the train was late. Had we not volunteered this information, the hearer would have assumed that the train had left on time. Thus we say *not A* to convey the information that contrary to what one may expect (namely that *A* is true) we have that *A* is not true.

E. Negation as failure

The notion of negation as failure is more a combinatorial computational notion than a logical one. It resembles default negation in the sense that we negate *A* if we fail to affirm *A*. The difference between the two is whether we perceive the notion of failure logically or computationally. We illustrate the difference through an example.

Suppose we go to a chemist and ask for some medicine. The assistant would go and look for it. If the assistant cannot find it, the chemist will say that the assistant does not have it. We may accept this *no* at face value as negation by default. If one cannot find it then one does not have it. Suppose now that it is obvious to us that this particular assistant is new to the shop and is, furthermore, clearly incompetent. We have the feeling that the medicine is there but the assistant simply does not know where to look for it. The *no* in this case is negation as failure — the failure of the search to produce an answer *yes*. It is a computational *no*.

In general when we have an agent system searching for an answer and it fails, it is computationally very practical and convenient to say *no*. This is the use of negation as failure. This use depends on the particular search methods. It may not be logically sound. Rephrasing our query a bit differently may result in the success of the computation, because it may go along a different path. Thus the same question may get *yes* or *no* as answers, depending on the manner of asking.

Negation as failure has a serious conceptual disadvantage. We are saying *no* because we fail to say *yes*. So our *no* does not follow from some constructive (or destructive) active knowledge, but from lack of knowledge. The other negations negate from some sort of knowledge. Even negation by default uses the positive assumption that the database was carefully organized, and so if a datum is not there, then it must be negated.

Certainly strong negation, or negation as inconsistency, involves some positive action on our part, in the process of negating. The lack of positive 'action' in negation as failure surfaces when negation interacts with the quantifiers. Suppose we ask

> *Is there someone not allowed to enter the Science Museum?*
> In symbols:
> $?\exists x. \neg A(x)$

The problem is that we want to know not only that there is someone but also to get the name of such a person. We would like a more specific answer like John, e.g.

$$\neg A(\text{John})$$

Negation as failure cannot supply such a name, while other negations may be able to do that. For example, negation as inconsistency is a positive notion, it says no because it can 'show' we get things we don't want to get. The process of 'showing' will yield some names.

F. Integrity constraints

The database may come with some metalevel requirements about its contents. These are called *integrity constraints*. The following are examples:

1. Always list a telephone number with a name.

2. A name cannot be both *male* and *female*.

Some integrity constraints do not imply inconsistency, but just require adjustment or extension of the data. A statement may be 'negated' because it causes a violation of integrity constraints.

Summary of this section

We saw that there are several notions of negation used in a complex interwoven way when dealing with data. The logic involved is yet to be analyzed. Negation plays a central role in any agent system. Its use is further complicated by the fact that computationally it causes a combinatorial explosion.

Comments

The logical analysis of negation, if possible, is of immense theoretical and practical value in many fields, not only computer science. It is inherently computationally complex. It causes combinatorial explosion owing to its logical nature and not because of poor implementation. Psychologists testing human reaction time to logical queries found that the presence of negation causes complexity to go up one level higher.

6   Logical chains and control structures in logic

In the previous three sections we have met three types of logical entities involved in the process of reasoning from a database. These were:

1. deductive rules and the underlying logic;

2. the non-monotonic rules which can be regarded as additional heuristic rules, characteristic of the specific subject matter;

3. the use of negative information.

The above indicated and described only the types of rules involved. If we want a working logical framework which can successfully extract information from a database, we must indicate how these rules are used successively, i.e. how to form chain deductions. We need to specify how to obtain more information from the database using some rules and then continue and use the other rules and the extra information just obtained to answer our query. This chaining is common to any process of reasoning.

So imagine a system with a database $\mathcal{P}$ and one-step rules $R_1, R_2, R_3, \ldots$ of different types which can be used to extract more information from the database. If there are no restrictions and no special controls we can extract information in the typical way shown in Figure 12.5.

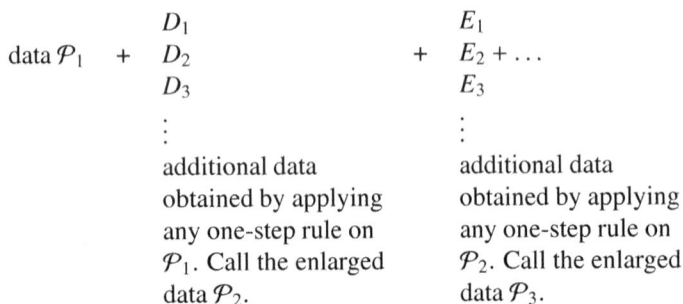

$$
\begin{array}{lll}
 & D_1 & E_1 \\
\text{data } \mathcal{P}_1 \quad + \quad & D_2 & \quad + \quad E_2 + \ldots \\
 & D_3 & E_3 \\
 & \vdots & \vdots \\
\end{array}
$$

additional data obtained by applying any one-step rule on $\mathcal{P}_1$. Call the enlarged data $\mathcal{P}_2$.	additional data obtained by applying any one-step rule on $\mathcal{P}_2$. Call the enlarged data $\mathcal{P}_3$.

Figure 12.5.

In practice the model above is too simple. What is not immediately apparent is the amount of control and common sense we exercise when we use chain reasoning in everyday life. This control must be logically analyzed and the principles incorporated into the system.

There are several types of controls on the successive use of the rules. Some of them are of logical nature and some are specific to the subject matter. Here are some typical simple control restrictions.

We may restrict the use of a rule R_1 only to certain situations. In the Nationality Act, for example, the rules of passing on citizenship to one's children depend on which rule was used in acquiring such citizenship. So we may use rule R_1 to show that Mary's father is a British citizen. Rule R_1 may say how to naturalize and we use it to show that Mary's father was naturalized. Rule R_2 may say that Mary herself can become a British citizen if her father is a British citizen, provided the father's citizenship is not because of rule R_1.

In other words, Mary can become a citizen only if her father was a British citizen through birth in the UK but not through naturalization.

The above is a 'logical' control where the 'logic' is that of the Nationality Act. We may insert controls having to do with efficiency, e.g. when either rule R_1 or R_2

can be applied, we apply R_1 first because whatever we may get using R_1 will make things more efficient for R_2.

Some restrictions on the use of the rules are given by the logical necessity of trying to make the rules mean logically what they are supposed to mean. This is especially true with negation rules. Negation rules are always restricted and tightly controlled because of the complex nature of negation.

It is not a matter of efficiency but a matter of making the system work correctly. A typical restriction is the order in which the rules may be applied and priorities among them.

Another example of heuristic control may be that when searching, for example, for a good cheap flight to the east coast of the USA, it is more efficient to look at major cities first and then airlines and flights rather than airlines first and only then look at which cities they fly to. Some of the above types of restrictions on the rules do not present any logical problems, beyond possibly the choice of a good framework in which these restrictions can be expressed. There are, however, more subtle problems which require further logical analysis.

The way the rules for negation interact with the other rules is mainly a problem of logic, but as we have seen in the last section, we may have to approximate the rules for negation in order to avoid combinatorial explosion. This must be done correctly. Furthermore, the use of non-monotonic rules together with negation is a major problem in any agent system. The way in which the problem presents itself is in the context of how to modify our thinking when a conclusion A which follows from a database is found in reality to be false.

Obviously something has gone wrong. But what exactly do we learn from this additional information (i.e. that A is false)? To be more specific suppose we have the sequence of deduction given in Figure 12.6.

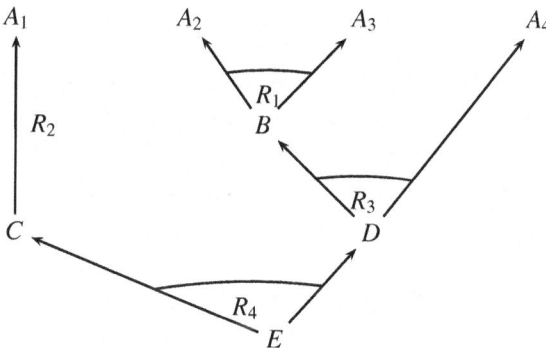

Figure 12.6.

1. E is arrived at by applying rule R_4 to C and D.

2. C was obtained from A_1 of the database using R_2.

3. D was obtained from B and A_4 using R_3.

4. A_4 is in the database but B is not in the database. B was obtained from A_2 and A_3 using rule R_1.

This is a typical situation. Suppose we check and find that E is false. How do we modify our deductions in view of this additional information? Consider the story of the yellow Rolls Royce (RR) described in Figure 12.7 which gives rise to the reasoning structure of the diagram.

Notice that the only 'observables' in this deduction are the database itself and the fact of whether the abandoned RR is found or not.

Fact A_5: No RR is found.

Our problem is now to try and rethink and examine our deduction, and more importantly, try to modify and improve our reasoning. At first glance we may think that this is a very specialized example and that no general principles of reasoning can be involved. We may believe that each practical example has its own special characteristic and 'logic'.

However, this is not the case. The police in this example will take some action which is typical of any reasoning situation.

1. They will make sure the search for the RR is exhaustive. In logical terms, this means that they verify that the negation (no RR is found) is negation of default and not negation by failure.

2. They will recheck the weakest assumptions in the chain of reasoning. In this case they will probably check how Smith knows that it was 3 o'clock. Was his alarm clock correct? How does he know it was his car he heard? Maybe it was the RR's first alarm.

3. Maybe Jones knew about Smith's hearing an alarm. Maybe Jones got into his RR and triggered his alarm by mistake. He saw Smith come to check his car but kept away. Jones himself was involved in the hit and run accident and this is his way of getting away with it, by reporting his car stolen, forgetting, or not understanding, the nature of his secondary alarm.

4. Is there another story in the database about Jones which aroused our suspicions?

5. We make a note about Jones's credibility for future reference.

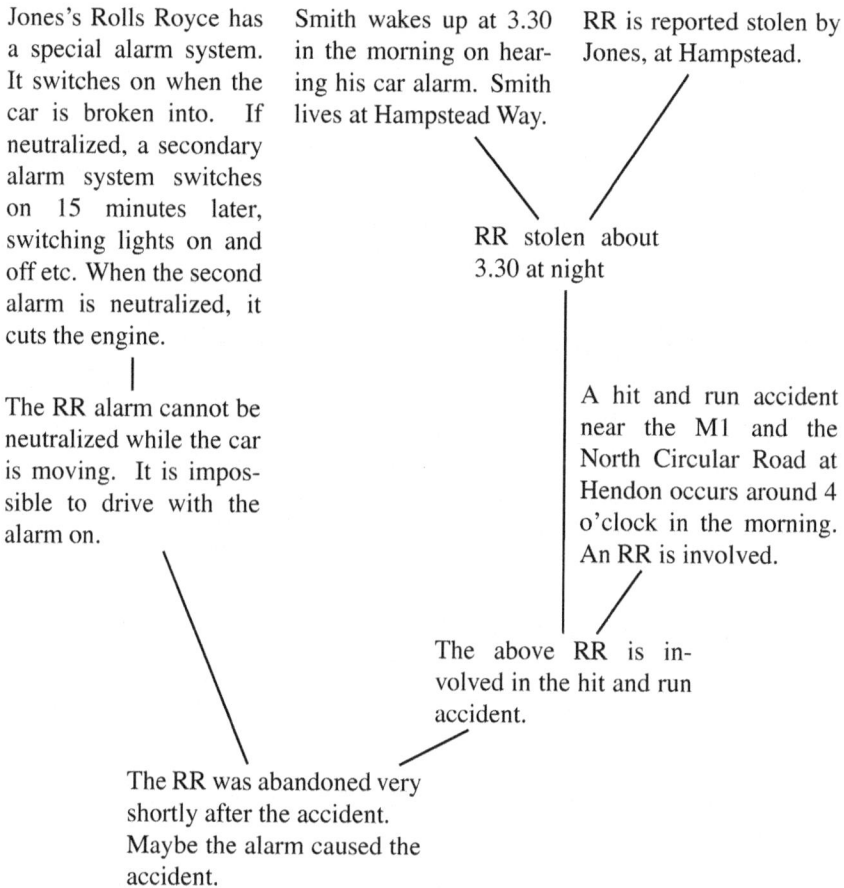

Jones's Rolls Royce has a special alarm system. It switches on when the car is broken into. If neutralized, a secondary alarm system switches on 15 minutes later, switching lights on and off etc. When the second alarm is neutralized, it cuts the engine.

The RR alarm cannot be neutralized while the car is moving. It is impossible to drive with the alarm on.

Smith wakes up at 3.30 in the morning on hearing his car alarm. Smith lives at Hampstead Way.

RR is reported stolen by Jones, at Hampstead.

RR stolen about 3.30 at night

A hit and run accident near the M1 and the North Circular Road at Hendon occurs around 4 o'clock in the morning. An RR is involved.

The above RR is involved in the hit and run accident.

The RR was abandoned very shortly after the accident. Maybe the alarm caused the accident.

Figure 12.7.

There seems to be some general principles involved:

1. With each item A in the database, we associate a 'checking' rule which says

   When you doubt the truth of A, recheck items $B_1, \ldots, B_k$ to confirm A.

2. Each rule R giving x from $y_l \ldots y_k$ is accompanied by an inverse rule of doubt which says that if x is not observed then this casts doubt about the rule R and about $y_1, \ldots, y_k$. Most importantly, this rule of doubt will recommend that we try to observe other related facts and the rule will tell us how to act on the results.

3. The system must remember for future use that R is a doubtful rule and perhaps use a measure of 'uncertainty' on rules and data.

The reader may have noticed that the above principles 1–3 are different from the reasoning principles we have discussed so far. The difference is that they involve actions! Take rule 2 for example. We start with a 'static' database, containing a certain amount of data. On the basis of this data we reason that conclusion C follows. So far everything is static; no action is taken. C, however, can be observed and tested, and so we go ahead and check C. We find that C is not true. We add $\neg C$ to the database. We can now apply the non-monotonic reasoning rules to the new database and get new conclusions. The situation could be no different from adding any new data to the database and applying the rules. But here we do more, we ask for more data, we ask to observe related facts and act upon them (maybe even modifying our rules).

There is no reason why we should allow actions in rules only when things seem wrong. We can incorporate actions into rules right from the start and have rules like

   Car won't start.
   Check headlights.
   Check electrical system.

or more direct actions like

   The carburettor is flooded.
   Depress accelerator to floor while starting.

Rules like the above make the database and the reasoning process more active, more like a human agent. We thus modify our perception of non-monotonic rules to be as follows:

- On the basis of $A_1, \ldots, A_n$, check the additional data $B_1, \ldots, B_k$, and on the basis of what is found, case by case, deduce the following $C_1, \ldots, C_m$.

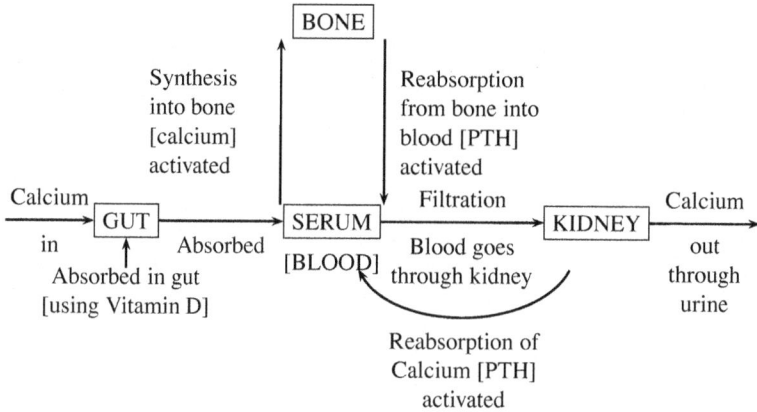

Figure 12.8.

Here is an example:

On the basis of A check B_1, B_2. If B_1 is true and B_2 false, deduce C_1. If B_1 is true and B_2 is also true, deduce C_2. Otherwise this rule is not applicable.

The rule may have only the following form:

If A check B and add the result to the database.

The above makes the inference machine interactive with the user. It behaves more like a human agent in the sense that it may answer a questions with a question.

The example given in Figures 12.8 and 12.9, shows a practical case where 'observable' items occur and where some items are 'associated' with others, though with a certain degree of uncertainty.

The analysis is courtesy of Dr T. Cory and Dr N. Bradford.

Note that in Figure 12.8, a healthy body allows for a narrow range of calcium in the blood. *Hypercalcaemia* means too much calcium in the blood. In Figure 12.9 the starred items are items that can be physically observed.

Notice that once Figure 12.8 is given it is almost automatic to build Figure 12.9 from it.

Summary of this section

Methods of chaining of rules and for rule control are at the core of any agent system. Some rules and chaining of rules have to do with the specific subject matter, others deal with negation and non-monotonic updating.

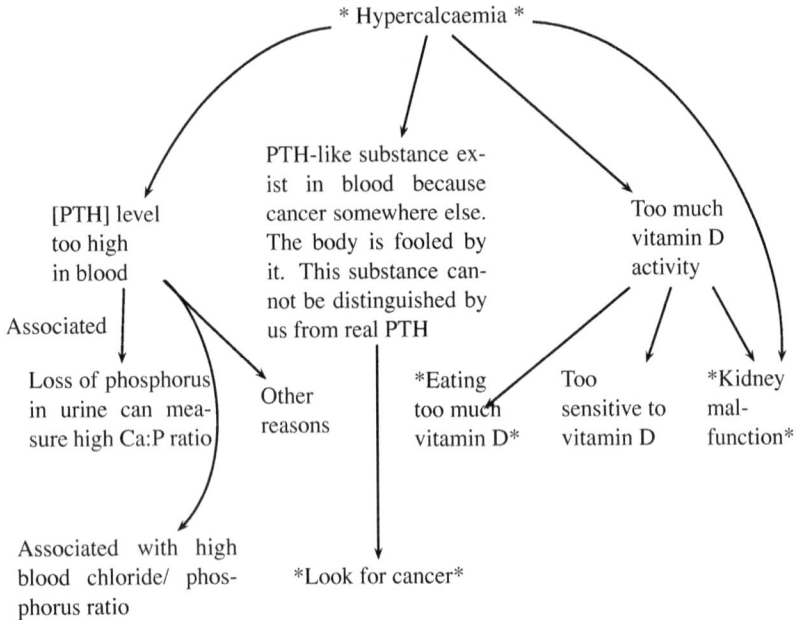

Figure 12.9.

Comments

Chaining and control rules can be very specific to the subject matter of the database. It is in this section that our hypothesis of the existence of a background logic for all reasoning from agent systems will be tested. We believe that although the chaining and control rules may be very different in different systems, the updating and re-thinking principles are very similar. Furthermore, there may be common principles having to do with handling uncertainty.

We also believe that we will find at least several large logical groupings of types of agent system even if we will not be able to find a common denominator for all agent systems.

Present-day agent systems seem to be successful without analyzing the process of chain reasoning (beyond single-step rules) at all. They rely on their ability to handle sheer bulk of information. In fact, some (e.g. E. A. Feigenbaum) hold the view that chain reasoning is not of main importance. Their argument stresses the meagre results one gets from attempted resolution reasoning in artificial intelligence. We have already discussed these methods and their limitations.

This section should be compared with the discussion and examples of scenario rules given in Section 1. Actions are particularly relevant to the quest of more inputs which can help determine whether we have chosen the right scenario.

7   How to represent changes in time and update the database

Databases are constantly changing. Information keeps coming in. The database is updated and modified. Consistency and integrity rules must be maintained. All this requires a special language and logic which can handle change and dependence on time.

We need to develop a temporal logic for representing time-dependent data and time-dependent rules. This language and logic must be expressive, must represent adequately our intuitive perception of dependence on time and change, and must properly interact and integrate with other components of our system (i.e. what we are discussing in other sections).

What are the major problems associated with our task?

A. Representation of time-dependent data

The first problem is that of choosing the correct representation language for time-dependent databases and rules. This is a serious problem. Many agent system rules work directly on a good representation language.

Here are three extreme options available to us which we will illustrate via an example.

Consider a rule A which is valid only during the period of time 1970 to 1980. The rule A itself is not time dependent. For example, A may say that a person can teach mathematics in school if they have a degree in mathematics from Oxford or Cambridge. In 1970, this rule was introduced and in 1980 it was changed. A degree in education was also required after 1980.

The problem is how to represent this rule. One way is to write the assertion below, where x stands for persons and t for a year:

1. Teach math (x) if Oxbridge (x), with a provision that this rule is valid during the period $1970 \leq t \leq 1980$.

Another way is to put time explicitly in predicates and write expression 2 below:

2. Teach math (x,t) if Oxbridge (x,t) and $1970 \leq t$ and $t \leq 1980$.

   Expression 2 is not natural for this case. We may have an entire block of rules, all valid in the period 1970–1980, and the natural way to represent these rules is as in the diagram Figure 12.10.

This is how we visualize this block of rules. It is also easy to ask from this representation which rules are valid in the period 1970–1980. If the rules are written in form 2, the answer to the latter question is not immediate. There are advantages in

Rules   *Restriction*
[not mentioning time]   use only in the period 1970–1980

Figure 12.10.

the representation of form 2, in the case where the dependence on time is not by neat large blocks of rules, but through time-interdependent rules like the following examples:

3. $Q(x, t)$ if $R(x, t + 5)$ and $S(x, t - 3)$ and $(t \leq 1991)$.

An example in English of such time dependence is a rule of the form

4. *One cannot take a holiday in Spain three years in a row.*

In natural languge we find both types of time representation available. The emphasis, however, is not to refer to time explicitly. We use words like *since, until, before, after, during,* which give relative relationships between events. For databases, we have to choose the right combination and compromise between the two representations.

There is a third way of representing time-dependent data in a database, using events. We do not mention time points (like 1970, 1980) at all. We use the events themselves as the time reference points. We thus do not talk about 1970 or 1980 but rather make references like

‘*When M. Thatcher was Prime Minister*’
‘*Before the UK joined the EEC*’
‘*When one could still be a mathematics teacher without a degree in education*’.

The database will contain the (probably partial) information of what events occurred *before, during* and *after* other events. This approach has its intuitive appeal. It does indeed contain features which are present in our everyday use of language. It may not be the predominant feature, but it could be extremely useful, especially in connection with partial information.

Researchers in temporal logic as applied to the logical and grammatical analysis of natural language do attach great importance to theories of events. The possible difficulties of such an approach for database management may be in the integration of the time component of the system (i.e. this section of the chapter) with other components (i.e. other sections of this chapter). In principle, however, a compromise of all three approaches to time descriptions can be constructed, because one can describe rules valid only if certain events (i.e. ‘*M. Thatcher is Prime Minister*’) occur, rather than rules valid at a certain time (i.e. 1970–1980). The problems of integration can be reduced to that of control (*which must be done in logic!*) of the form: ‘one can use rule A only when the answer to query ?E is yes!’, where E describes a certain event. The above amounts to saying something like

‘*The traffic restrictions below are valid when children are out of school*’.

B. Reasoning with time-dependent data

The following is a good example (based on [Kowalski and Sergot, 1986]) which we use to illustrate the interactions possible between non-monotonic reasoning and time. Take the system of registering visitors to Britannic House. When a person visits the building, the computer is informed of their entry. When that person leaves, the computer is informed of their leaving. For this type of time dependence, the best representation is form (1). We can describe schematically the presence of Mr Smith at Britannic House on Monday as in Figure 12.11.

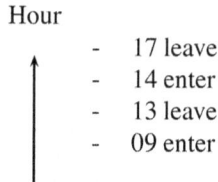

Hour

```
        -    17 leave
    ↑   -    14 enter
    |   -    13 leave
    |   -    09 enter
    |
```

Figure 12.11.

(q) *Was Mr Smith in Britannic House at 15 hours?* To answer this query we can use several possible methods of computation:

(1) We can go backwards in time until we meet *leave*, in which case we say *no*. If we meet *enter*, we say *no*. If we meet *enter*, we say *yes*. If we meet neither, we say *no*.

(2) We can go forwards in time until we meet *leave* in which case we say *yes* or meet *enter* and say *no*. If we meet neither we say *no*.

(3) We can try both directions, just to play safe.

The problem arises when something goes wrong, and the information in the database is deficient.

Consider the diagram shown in Figure 12.12, representing the information in the database.

Routine consistency checks or intergrity checks (see Section 9) would probably detect the anomaly. What the system will do to correct the above anomaly depends on the non-monotonic rules for the Britannic House system. If it is customary and routine to register leave for everyone at 17 hours, we may ignore the 17 hours leave

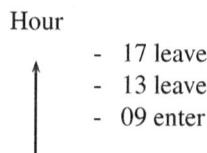

Hour

```
        -   17 leave
    ↑   -   13 leave
    |   -   09 enter
    |
```

Figure 12.12.

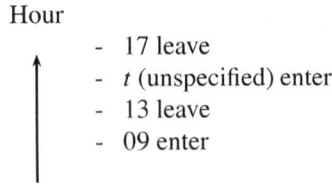

Hour

- 17 leave
- *t* (unspecified) enter
- 13 leave
- 09 enter

Figure 12.13.

for Mr Smith and decide that Mr Smith left at 13 hours. If registration is very strict and done by hand, then we may decide that an *enter* is missing and put in the extra missing *enter*, with a time *t* marked as unspecified. We thus will have the diagram of Figure 12.13 in the database. Let us follow this latter possibility. Choosing the representation above can cause trouble if we do not coordinate our time language with all the other components of the system. Depending on the way the computer conducts the search for the answer, we may have any of the following possible answers to our query (q).

(1) The answer is *yes*, because the search finds that Smith was in the building from 9 to 13 and from 13 to 15, except at 13 hours itself. The reason is that the unspecified time *t* of entry is interpreted by the computer as near to 13 as necessary. This interpretation will have the undesirable effect that Smith was out of the building at 13 hours but immediately in the building half a second past 13 hours.

(2) The answer is *no*, because the computer will interpret the time *t* of entry as near to 17 hours as necessary. Thus we have that Smith was not in the building immediately before 17 but nevertheless left it at 17.

(3) The computer may not give an answer, or saying that it cannot answer, or has to delay, until the time *t* is specified. This has the undesirable effect that when asked about Smith's presence in the building at 13.03, it will still not give an answer, even though a human would concede that it is not likely that Smith would actually register his leaving, just to come back after 3 minutes!

Another variation of (3) is that the computer, using negation as failure, will give the answer *no* to question (q) because *t* is not specified (and so it cannot succeed).

However, when asked

(q∗) '*Was Mr Smith at Britannic House at any time between 13 hours and 17 hours?*'

the computer will say *yes* (since an unspecified *t* is available). We thus have the undesirable situation that when asked about any specific time between 13 hours and 17 hours the computer will say *no*, but nevertheless the computer says *yes* to (q∗).

In the theory of events approach, the situation may be less critical. We do not

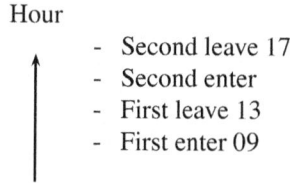

Hour

- Second leave 17
- Second enter
- First leave 13
- First enter 09

Figure 12.14.

have time points but events. Thus the scale will be as in Figure 12.14. The fact that the second enter has no time attached to it is not so important, since the 'second entry' itself is the time 'point'. The hours (09, 13, 17) are just extra details.

We may not have here the problems outlined above, other problems will arise. Unfortunately, humans make use of time in a very complex way.

(4) This possibility is the worst of all. Our system may be such that, having found an answer to a query, it records the fact explicitly in order to save computation time and not have to recompute again when the same query is asked again or used in the future.

Thus approaching the query twice in different environments, the computer may obtain and record both a yes and a no answer.

Computer consistency maintenance rules (Section 9) may be activated, and a chain reaction may be set in motion, and all of this because of a simple oversight in registering the coming of a Mr Smith!

C. Database updating

So far we have discussed representations of time-dependent data and rules in a time language. Time language is needed also for updating databases which describe static situations.

Imagine 100 boxes and 300 coloured bricks which can be distributed among the boxes. The database describes which brick is in what box. If we start moving the bricks around, we have the problem of updating the database in the most economical way. We need a time language to express the global changes and constraints on the database. We may find it convenient to regard the opertation of updating as a transition function from one database state to another. Although the particular updating operations are application specific, e.g. 'move brick no. x to box no. y', the logic involved in manipulating the updating is universal.

We also have to ensure that the time language used for time-dependent data interacts conveniently with the updating language. Updating time-dependent rules can be viewed from inside the database and from outside the database. These views must agree. For example, we do not want to say from the outside 'use this rule in 1970' and the rule to say 'I am valid only in 1980'. It is preferable to find a good common time language suitable for all time-dependent manipulations of the database.

Summary of this section

A time language is required to talk about time-dependent databases and updating. There are three extreme possibilities, none of them completely satisfactory; great care must be taken with interaction with reasoning because potentially one can get into trouble. The logic of time dependence is a 'hot' subject affording immediate possible applications to other areas of computer science as well. Possible other areas of application are object-oriented design and VLSI, where questions of synchronicity are of paramount importance. Intuitionistic implication $A \Rightarrow B$ contains in its meaning a time element. $A \Rightarrow B$ can be read as 'always in the future whenever A becomes true, B immediately follows and is also true'. This time feature of intuitionistic implication is a powerful logical tool in talking databases, and can serve as a basis for integration.

8   Hypothetical and counterfactual reasoning

We explain our problem via an example. Suppose the government is interested in raising the educational level in elementary schools in socially deprived areas. The difficulty the government faces is that good school teachers are reluctant to teach in such schools. To counter that, the government offers some inducements and fringe benefits. These include:

(a) Teachers in such schools do not have to have a full university degree to receive the full salary and benefits of degree holders. They should be good teachers with good experience. For example, missionary nuns with some experience will be considered as qualified teachers with an MA degree.

(b) Teachers with an MA degree who teach in such schools, will have their seniority increased by 10 years, and provided they teach a minimum of 2 years in such a school, they can also count this seniority towards their retirement. Thus a qualified teacher with an MA degree and seniority of 18 years can teach 2 years in such a school and retire with seniority and a pension of 30 years.

These benefits were introduced to attract good teachers to such schools. The above rules are reasonable in any environment with serious social problems. The rules are counterfactual. They say that under certain conditions, e.g. that Miss Smith teaches in a deprived children's school, the computer computes certain predicates such as the salary seniority of Miss Smith, not according to the real data in the database, but by pretending that the data was different.

Laws of the form occur in many other areas, e.g. in the British Nationality Act. To decide if a child born in the UK is a British citizen, we look at the status of the father. If the father is dead at the time of birth, but had he been alive he could have been naturalized, then the law says that the child is a citizen.

Counterfactual reasoning takes the following form (see Figure 12.15):

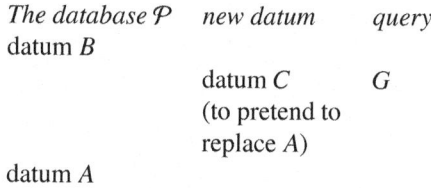

The database $\mathcal{P}$	new datum	query
datum B		
	datum C	G
	(to pretend to	
	replace A)	
datum A		

Figure 12.15.

- In the presence of B in the database, pretend A is not in the database, pretend C is in the database and then compute the answer to query G.

The problem we are faced with is that of logical control. If we pretend that A is not in the database, and we add C to the database, we may have a contradiction. Yet, we intend to compute the goal G without being worried, and apparently we intuitively know how to steer away from trouble. To take the British Nationality Act as an example, to check whether the child is a citizen today, we check the status of the father. If the father died 3 years ago, we pretend the father has not died and check whether he would have been able to be naturalized today. If the answer is yes we say that the child is a citizen. If not, we say the child is not a citizen.

It may be the case that in order for a person to be naturalized, the person must have filed all their yearly tax reports. The father, being dead, filed no reports. A human would know intuitively what is relevant and what is not. We see that there is a lot more to this counterfactual 'pretending' than the simple addition and deletion of information, and our task is to figure out its logical properties!

To give a more extreme example, consider the case of Miss Smith, the nun. She has no degree, but does have some teaching experience. She is accepted as a teacher in this special school. She is 43 years old. The computer, following the rules laid down before, considered Miss Smith as a qualified teacher with an MA degree, aged 43. Miss Smith taught for 2 years and expressed her wish to retire. The computer, when seeing the data of a 43 year old teacher with an MA (that is what the computer is supposed to see!) used the second rule, added 10 years to Miss Smith's seniority, and replied that indeed her age is 55 and she could retire!

Summary of this section

Our problem with hypothetical and counterfactual reasoning is that of logic and of control. A human knows intuitively how to play the 'pretending' game. We need to figure out the correct logic and formulate it for agent systems.

I believe the appropriate context for the study of non-monotonic reasoning systems is against a stream of inputs $A_1, A_2, \ldots$. We start with an initial database $\mathcal{P}_0$ and a non-monotonic set of rules **N**. Using it we can consider $Q_0 = \{X \mid \mathcal{P}_0 \mathrel{\vdash\!\!\!\sim} X\}$.

Then the input A_1 arrives (as a result of either further knowledge or some action). We form $\mathcal{P}_1 = \mathcal{P}_0 + A_1 +$ possibly some elements of Q_0, and consider $Q_1 = \{X \mid \mathcal{P}_1 \vdash X\}$, and so on. All the mechanisms involved in this process are the subject of non-monotonic reasoning.

9   Dealing with contradictory information, consistency and integrity of databases

The Americans are very much worried these days about computer information and technology falling into the hands of competitors. As part of their security measures, they have instructed the CIA to keep detailed files on any computer scientist making contact with major British or American companies. For individuals in Britain, both the CIA and FBI cooperate in their files and databases concerning these individuals.

In the case of Professor X an unfortunate discrepancy has occurred. The FBI had his address as Stanford University, California, and the CIA had his address as Imperial College, London. When the two databases were joined together, the union contained contradictory information. The computer, using classical logic, inferred that Professor X was none other than Public Enemy No. 1, because in classical logic a contradiction implies the truth of any statement.

There are several points of principle involved here. First, classical logic does not deal with contradictions correctly. Although it is logically correct to infer from the above contradictions that Professor X is Public Enemy No. 1, it is clearly an incorrect step in terms of human reasoning. More importantly, Professor X's address is completely irrelevant to the question of whether he is Public Enemy No. 1 or not.

Intuitionistic logic, the logic we propose to use in the solution of the problems mentioned in the previous sections, is equally useless for our problems in this section. Intuitionistic logic would make the same inference as classical logic and also conclude that Professor X is Public Enemy No. 1.

A second point of principle involved is simply the question of what to do with the contradiction itself. What do we do when we have two contradictory items of information in the database? Do we choose one of them? How do we make the choice? Do we leave them in and find a way 'around' them?

A third point is more practical. The CIA agent may investigate Professor X and find the charge the computer made to be ridiculous. The CIA may suspect that there is a contradiction in the database but how to find it? Generally the contradiction may involve several steps of reasoning and may not be as blatant as in the case of Professor X. We may have several simple and innocent-looking data items and some very reasonable rules which together give the wrong answers, but no single item is to blame. How do we debug our system in this case?

The problem of dealing with contradictions is a difficult one. We believe a solution for better handling of contradictions can be found by looking closely at the ways humans deal with them. Upon reflection we arrived at the following principles to be taken as a first attempt at a solution.

(1) We do not share the view that contradictions in a database are a 'bad' thing, and should be avoided at all costs. Contradictory information seems to be part of our lives, and sometimes we even prefer ambiguities and irreconcilable views. We must therefore seek logical principles which will allow for contradictions in the same way that we humans allow for them, and possibly even make contradictions useful.

(2) Humans seem to grasp intuitively that some information is more relevant than other information. The notion of relevance should be developed and used.

(3) There seems to be a hierarchy of rules involved here. Rules of the form

- 'When contradictory information is received about A, do B'

seemed to be used constantly. These are metarules, i.e. rules about rules. Full exploitation of these rules require our database language to be able to talk about itself. This is a requirement we have also met in previous sections, and we shall develop such a language.

(4) Never throw anything out of the database. Always keep an open mind that although A is rejected now (because of new information contradicting it), it may become useful again. Perhaps some uncertainty values may be attached to all data items. We will have to check this point of view.

(5) Despite everything we do, although we may give various heuristic rules dealing with contradictory information, there will always remain the possibility of two contradictory items of equal reliability and equal relevance and equal standing concerning which there will be no way of deciding which of the two items is the correct one. In this case, we can only wait and be suspicious of any computation involving them. The problem of contradiction is further discussed in Sections 12.11 and 12.12.1.

Summary of this section

We described the problems associated with contradictory information in a database. By contradictory we mean only logically contradictory but that the database does not satisfy some conditions it is supposed to satisfy. The main problem is how to trace and eliminate the causes of contradictions. Our view is different from the current view that contradictions are 'bad'. We think that they are an essential part of life and perhaps can even be made useful. Our slogan is

Inconsistency $\Rightarrow$ Action.

See [Gabbay and Hunter, 1991] for more details.

10   Dealing with uncertainty, vague predicates

Uncertainty arises in databases and reasoning with databases through the following reasons:

A. Lack of confidence in the data and rules

We may be uncertain about the data and the rules governing them. In a medical database, for example, results of medical tests may be only partially conclusive, and so one may find it useful to enter a datum with a certainty number between 0 and 1. Alternatively, one may assign a confidence interval for the datum. Thus A may be entered in the database as

A: 0.61

or as

A: [0.4, 0.8]

Another area of uncertainty of this type is uncertainty in the reasoning rules, especially the non-monotonic ones. It may be that from A we can deduce B only with confidence 0.75 or confidence interval [0.4, 0.7], so the rules will be written as

From A deduce B: 0.75

or as

From A deduce B: [0.4, 0.7].

Examples [Kuliakowski, 1984]

(1) *If the starter is making odd noises the probability of a bad starter is 0.75*, or equivalently:

If the starter is making odd noises the probability of a good starter is 0.25.

(2) *If a car has a bad starter then the starter will make odd noises in 0.87 of the cases.*

The above probabilities may be given by a car mechanic. We can have another rule:

(3) *The probability of a bad starter (when a car will not start) is 0.02 (before looking at any specific symptoms).*

The 2% figure was arrived at by looking at how may cars are at repair shops with starter problems relative to the total number of cars in repair shops. Here is a fourth rule, directly measured, to complete the picture:

(4) *The probability of a normal starter making odd noises is 0.07.*

There are problems with such models:

(1) It is not clear what these numbers mean. How does one get them, and how does one update them?

For instance, in the above example, if we use rules (2), (3), (4) and use Bayes's formula to compute probability (bad starter gives odd noises), we get 0.202 and not 0.25 as predicted by the expert.

We see here that the probabilities or uncertainty numbers people give do not always match.

(2) One has to figure out the correct intuitive way in which the uncertainty numbers propagate through the system. If A_i have uncertainty x_i and a deduction is used through rules R_j whose uncertainty is y_j, to give an answer to a query $?G$, then what is the uncertainty in G? Does it depend on the computation path? Does it depend on the order the rules are used?

(3) If G is now measured and found to be false or is known to be true with a high confidence number, how do we update our confidence numbers and rules? Can we let the system 'learn' automatically?

Systems used in practice usually fail on the updating and chaining of numbers. Odd results arise. Different computation paths get different numbers, to the extent that the numbers become meaningless. Agent systems have had great success with one-step predictions. That is, data A_i is entered with certainty factors and one-step rules of the form

C if D_1 and $\cdots$ and D_k

are also entered with a certainty number. The system can predict, on the basis of the A_i, which C is most likely. Since the use of confidence numbers seems problematic, researchers developed special logics, called fuzzy logics, and of course (we have already studied these in Chapter 2 of this book) many-valued logics. These logics can be described and studied in a normal way like any other logic. They offer more hope of integration into our general framework. It is possible to construct a fuzzy intuitionistic-like logic and use it fruitfully.

B. Uncertainty arising from inconsistency

We have met this phenomenon before, in the section on inconsistency. If we have conflicting information then although we may decide to ignore one item and thus avoid contradiction, we still bear in mind that we may be wrong and keep a watchful eye for more evidence. We do not have to associate numbers with data and rules, but just mark them as doubtful or very doubtful. It is important to figure out how this system interacts with updating and how it can be integrated with part A of this section. In other words, what is the meaning of 'contradiction' and doubt, in a system with confidence numbers?

C. Uncertainty due to lack of information or a simplified model

This is a simple case where the real model is causal but uncertainty is introduced because we do not know about it. If C is caused by A and B then we can write the rule

C if A and B.

If we do not know about A we will have to write C if B: 0.6, where 0.6 is the frequency with which A appears. It may be of interest to examine the thesis that all cases of uncertainty can be explained away by hidden unknown factors.

11 Human-oriented view of databases

Our human reasoning point of view leads us to adopt the human way of perceiving databases. Let us see where this view leads us.

Suppose a man wants to go abroad for a year and so wants to rent his house. He approaches an estate agent, Mr Smith, and is offered a contract for a year's lease with a family X. Our database is the static description of the contract, the house and the rent. Assume that the contract is a standard one, the house is a bit old, Mr Smith is a very busy estate agent and that the family X is a family of high-ranking diplomats. Our house owner may reject the offer on the following grounds. There may be some minor problem with the house during the year (being an old house), Mr Smith is busy (this is just small business for Mr Smith), the diplomats are certainly busy and therefore he anticipates difficulties. The tenants will be *inflexible* and insist on their rights for immediate repair. The alternative is another estate agent, as good as but less busy than Mr Smith, an ordinary family, as nice as but less busy than X, and the same contract but with the expectation of more flexibility.

We have here a case of two identical databases (contracts etc.) but different *updating rules*, one more flexible than the other. Our house owner treats the updating rule with perhaps more weight than the database itself. The moral we want to learn from this is that: a database not only is a collection of static data but also contains its own updating and consistency rules. These rules can be used in the database as ordinary data and as antecedents in other rules.

Another example to illustrate this concept is the comparison of different countries' foreign investment law. I am sure any high executive will tell you that although a body of tax benefits and inducements to invest may be wonderful in one country, the same package in another country may be unacceptable because of the other country's 'general attitude'. (Since events never go as anticipated, the general attitude is an 'updating rule'.)

We know that databases keep changing and so the 'flexibility' or 'flavour' of the updating rules is as important as the data itself. Database research has improved upon the ordinary relational database approach by stressing and promoting logic databases. This is the first step. The second step we propose is to regard the logic itself as data and as part of the database.

A further difference between our conception of human reasoning and the traditional approach is the treatment of inconsistency.

The traditional view is to talk about 'restoring consistency' as if consistency is a 'bad thing'. We take the view that it might be good and we try to 'use' inconsistencies. Certainly we may learn to live with them and we have discussed this point in Section 9. See also the story in Section 12.

Let us give here an example and see where it leads us. Mr Smith was 55 years old and wanted early retirement. He could in fact retire with a full pension if he were ill. So Mr Smith presented his employer Mr Jones with a letter certifying he had a heart condition. He was thus able to retire. His wife, Mrs Smith, however, heard of this letter and was worried. She asked Mr Smith about this letter and Mr Smith told her that he was actually quite healthy and the letter was a trick to get early retirement. Mrs Smith was relieved. Unfortunately Mr Jones overheard the conversation and very angrily confronted Mr Smith. Mr Smith was unperturbed. He explained to Mr Jones that he had had to tell his wife what he had told her in order to stop her worrying. Unfortunately Mrs Smith overheard the conversation with Mr Jones and was worried again. Mr Smith assured his wife that he was quite healthy and that he had had to tell Mr Jones what he had told him in order not to go to prison.

The circle is now complete. There is a basic inconsistency here but there is no need to'restore' consistency. In fact to restore consistency in this case is to cause disaster.

If Mr Jones meets Mrs Smith at a party, he will have to pretend that her husband is healthy in order not to worry her, or at least avoid the subject. Mrs Smith will have to pretend that her husband is not healthy in order to keep the pension. Mr Smith himself will pretend one way or the other, depending on the occasion.

The database as we described it *does not care* for the inconsistency. There are no means to resolve it and it makes no difference what 'the truth' is.

We claim the following principle. To a human, and therefore in the logic for databases, resolving inconsistencies is *not* necessarily done by 'restoring' consistency (as the traditional view would maintain) but by supplying rules telling one how to act when the inconsistency arises. One of the many possible actions could be to restore consistency but other actions are possible.

We tolerate inconsistencies because we read them as signals to take action or as signals which trigger some rules and de-activate other rules. We do not perceive ourselves as living in some platonic world contemplating for eternity which of two contradicting items to disregard.

The view of 'working with inconsistency' has been maintained by some famous logicians. H. B. Curry has said that sometimes one has to work with inconsistent systems (some of his colleagues claim Curry has to say that because so many of his combinatory logics turn out to be inconsistent). It was reported to us that T. Hoare wrote about one of his logics (shown to derive inconsistency formally) that 'indeed we must be careful how we use these rules'.

12 Case study: a story

The following story exhibits a list of nonmonotonic features, especially with regard to inconsistency. We feel it is appropriate to conclude our chapter with it.

12.1 Options by L. Rivlin

Peter had no premonition that his world was about to collapse.

A prosperous businessman who owned a Darmstadt-based company wholesaling small electrical appliances, he had every reason to be satisfied with the comfortable life he had built for himself and his family.

The opening up of Eastern Europe was good for Peter's business. In particular, a small electric toaster that previously had a steady if unspectacular market in West Germany had become a hugely popular item in East European shops, suiting the restricted family budgets and cramped kitchens which were the norm all over the lately communist world.

The Spanish manufacturers were plainly unprepared for the abrupt increase in orders and, after several hysterical telephone calls from retailers in Eastern Europe, all to do with falling stock levels, Peter decided it was time to re-negotiate the contract. This, of course, meant the personal appearance in Spain of either himself or his manager. In truth, it was more Peter's job than his manager's. But Peter was at heart a farm boy who preferred to stay at home. He felt especially unhappy about leaving his wife, on whom he relied heavily for support.

Peter had grown up helping his father run a small farm. He, too, might have continued into old age following the same hard, simple life, if his father had only lived one more year. Instead, he died suddenly when his son was only 17, leaving a boy too young to look after a farm on his own. It was sold, the money invested by sensible, if distant, relatives and in due course Peter had a legacy that started him on the successful path which he was now treading. He had been lucky enough to make a correct choice of business to start with but he considered himself even luckier to have married Ulrike.

Peter was not completely comfortable with either business or city, while his wife had been a public relations administrator until she relinquished her job on the birth of their now 3-year-old daughter. She helped him with decisions, advised him about matters of commercial etiquette, hosted flawless business dinners and acted as his ambassador at every function to which they were invited, endearing herself, and therefore himself, to all his business contacts with a seemingly effortless, unceremonious charm. Peter was so happy with his life he could not conceive that Ulrike might not feel the same way, even though he sometimes noticed that she was somewhat restless. He couldn't blame her for feeling a little isolated as a wife and mother and would have understood if she had engaged a childminder and returned to the commercial world. But Ulrike's sort of job frequently demanded irregular hours. She was the first to admit that this would have thrown too much of a strain on her and might occasionally compromise the quality of her work. In two or three years it might be easier. Meanwhile, Peter was making a determined effort to make up, as much as he could, for any lack she might feel. He took her out frequently, involved her in his business affairs and discussed plans with her in minute detail. This was the best time of his life, he acknowledged to himself. Although he was engaging Ulrike's interest as a matter of strategy, he also found that there was much personal solace for him in the attention he paid to her. He said that he didn't like to leave her alone but in reality he himself did not like to be alone.

In any case, it was too hot in Madrid. Peter had almost decided to send his manager, Rudolph Kurz, to deal with an uncomplicated situation in his usual solid, unimaginative way when a couple of disturbing letters arrived from Spain. It looked as if the manufacturers were thinking of trying to market the toaster themselves and Peter was worried that Kurz's diplomatic talents would not stretch to the circumstances.

He would have to go to Spain himself and convince the Madrid company that they were better off selling their product within his painstakingly constructed network of business and political contacts. Having done that, he would then have to re-negotiate a contract which would tie them up for a few more years. There was really no choice about it and Peter finally made up his mind to go to Madrid at the last minute.

With his mind set on the soon-to-be resolved problems involving Spanish toasters, Peter could hardly be blamed for not observing the much less manageable difficulties which were gathering, looming over his personal life like bankers over the beset owner of a precarious mortgage.

Without demur, Ulrike understood his reasons for going; after all, he had been away on business before. It might have occurred to Peter that she seemed almost relieved at the prospect of his absence but he was far too abstracted to notice.

'Yes, you should go. In fact, take the opportunity to have a rest as well', she said enthusiastically. 'You'll get a cheaper flight if you stay over Saturday, so go on Thursday and come home on Sunday. You can have your meetings and then relax by the hotel pool.'

Peter arrived at the airport on the Thursday morning to an impromptu lesson in statistics. The airlines' policy of overbooking by 5 or 10 per cent, in confident anticipation of the usual cancellations, had on this occasion backfired. Everyone turned up. Peter had the choice of waiting for the next flight—something he felt he could ill-afford to do—or he could upgrade his ticket. It was not difficult to change to Executive Class and well within his pocket. At first he grumbled a little to his fellow passengers but, when the free champagne started flowing on his side of the discreet curtain which divided the plane between those who drank beer and those who sipped something else, he stopped grumbling altogether.

Madrid turned out not to be so bad, after all. The Spanish firm had no plans to cut out his company but just wanted more money. It was all surprisingly easy and after a few hours there was no need for Peter to stay. He had an open ticket, was uncomfortable in the heat, did not like the impersonal opulence of the hotel and felt very much like going home to celebrate. In an almost euphoric mood, he requested—and instantly secured—a flight to Frankfurt via Paris. Peter telephoned home at once but there was no answer. In Paris, it was too late to ring although there was plenty of time because the connection was delayed. Very early the next morning, a travel-weary Peter arrived at Frankfurt airport, took a taxi home and arrived outside his house at 3 o'clock. The whole neighbourhood was asleep, peaceful and quiet. Peter, too, was at peace. He was home. He had negotiated a favourable and profitable contract. Inside his house lay his companion and his future: his wife and his child. Life had never been better.

Peter unlocked the door very quietly, not wanting to wake anyone. First he tiptoed to the little girl's room to kiss her damp forehead and her blue-lidded eyes. When he found her dainty bed empty, the coverlet pulled up with precision and all the stuffed toys propped neatly against the pillow, he smiled to himself. He should have realised that she would sleep with her Mummy since he was away.

Just a fraction disappointed that he would not be able to slip into bed next to his wife's warm body, Peter continued to his bedroom, planning to take a pillow out of the cupboard. He carefully switched off the hall light before he opened the bedroom door and glanced casually at the bed, his mind on the cupboard beyond.

At first, he could not believe what he saw. He was sure it must be some trick of the light that made the sleeping body lying next to Ulrike, the small body of his little girl, seem so much larger than it should have been. Banally, he blinked to clear his vision but the same picture remained stubbornly in his eyes. He stood for perhaps a full three minutes, watching his wife, lying on her back while the naked man sleeping on his belly next to her, casually rested his right arm around the gentle rise and fall of her waist. Peter looked around the room for other evidence to confirm the terrible vision on the bed. The man's trousers were so neatly folded over the chair back that Peter, having noticed them, could hardly drag his eyes away. The shoes, indisputably not his, were similarly arranged with precision under the chair. It all seemed so unremarkable, so normal, that a fleeting thought occurred to Peter that he was in the wrong house. This thought was quickly replaced with another: that, suffering a delusion of marriage, he had escaped from a mental hospital. He even speculated that he might have died and had returned to his home years later, as a ghost unconscious of its fate.

As reality finally re-asserted itself, Peter found himself surprisingly detached. He was rather surprised to find himself not particularly angry, although he was struck by an overpowering exhaustion. Slowly, heavily, he backed out of the room and retraced his steps downstairs to the kitchen where he sat, quietly thinking through his options.

Of course, he could take a long, sharp knife from the kitchen drawer and do away with both of them. The Spanish solution, he joked bitterly to himself. But he lacked the physical resources for even the twitch of a smile.

Perhaps he should confront them, make a scene and then leave, slamming the door on his way out and calling up his lawyer at a more reasonable hour. Would this be the best way? Did he really want to live the rest of his life without Ulrike? Did he really want to become a recruit to that sad army of men who turn up on their ex-wife's doorstep every second weekend? Did he really want the melancholy ritual of trips to the zoo if the weather was OK, or, if it was bad, to the cinema to see a film of no great interest to either himself or his increasingly estranged daughter?

Then again, he could be understanding and forgiving. But, even if tolerance resolved this particular crisis without splitting the family apart, what would Ulrike think of him afterwards? Indeed, if it came out in the open, would it then be talked about? Would his friends or business associates hear and laugh behind his back regarding him as legitimate prey for any other sort of cheating?

Peter sat in the kitchen for a long time. He could think of nothing at all that would honourably settle this dreadful business, except perhaps cutting his own throat over the kitchen table. Just as he was giving serious consideration to this option, another suddenly occurred to him in a glittering flash of inspiration.

Quietly, he left the house and walked to the end of the street. He telephoned for a taxi and when it arrived, took it to Frankfurt airport. Buying himself a return ticket, he flew back to Madrid. In the airport he sat at a table for a while, nursing a thick, practical cup of strong coffee and staring intermittently at the newspaper that he had been given on the plane. The words had very little significance but they restored his sense of normality. The Americans were still having problems with the Middle East. The British were still having problems with Northern Ireland. The Germans were still having problems with each other. The previous day's journey began to recede in his mind to a dream. It hardly seemed possible that he could have been in Darmstadt at all, just a few hours before.

His hand wandered to his jacket pocket and the ends of his fingers met the sharp edge of a small, folded rectangle of paper. It was the taxi driver's receipt for the journey from Frankfurt airport to his home. He crumpled it up and dropped it into his coffee. This was one tax deduction that he would never claim. He searched his other pockets for evidence of his return and having made sure there was nothing left, he walked over to the Lufthansa counter. As he did so, Peter remembered the times when his father had been tired or ill and would take him along to help with the early morning milking. It was difficult to get up in the cold and the dark and stumble out to a shed full of bad-tempered cows. As a small boy, Peter could do very little to help but even then he realised that his father was encouraging himself by chivvying his son along. As Peter crossed the polished floor of the airport, he could feel his father, urging him across the icy yard. He moved slowly and had to keep reminding himself of what he was supposed to do next, as if he were two people doggedly engaged in a disagreeable but necessary task, supporting each other, moving together clumsily.

Having assured himself of a place on the flight from Madrid to Frankfurt, Peter then rang his wife, asking her to meet his plane in.

In this way he could leave all his options open.

12.2   Logical analysis

The above is a plausible story in the life of a successful businessman. It illustrates the difficult, if not impossible, task of logic.

Ideally, artificial intelligence aims to replace Peter by a machine. To achieve this, if at all possible, we need:

1. to model conceptually and analyze Peter's mental processes;

2. to find a suitable formal representation for our model;

3. to implement the model computationally.

Logic can be the instrument for all three aims. The above story is not simple. It involves various complicated logics and models.

Let us see what kinds of logics are involved.

12.3   Temporal logic

An important component is temporal logic. We need to be able to represent time and change. We need to be able to reason about temporal patterns. In our story, time was involved in several ways:

- The development of the story was temporal. Thus at any moment of time, there were events which had happened already and events which will happen.

- When booking his return flight, Peter did some forward planning. He checked the results of various actions (booking) and checked whether he could change flights to achieve a goal (arriving home on the same day).

We thus have something like the diagram shown in Figure 12.16, as a typical temporal state of affairs.

The past can be described by what events took place and at what time. The future is branching. We have several options, e.g. to book a return flight or not, etc. Depending on that we determine the future. To represent all these possibilities we need a formal language.

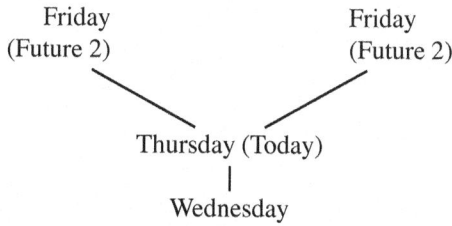

Figure 12.16.

The formal language for time and action contains special connectives for temporal patterns such as

> Fq meaning q will be true
> Pq meaning q was true
> $q\,U\,p$ meaning q until p
> $q\,S\,p$ meaning q since p.

One can also have special variables ranging over time and write

> $q(t)$ meaning q is true at time t.

There are many possible formalisms which can be used for temporal state descriptions. One possibility is a mixed formalism allowing us to write statements like

> $F^t q$ meaning q will be true in t days.

Temporal logic is an extensive area of research about the representation of and deductions with temporal information.

There are also many systems for representing actions. The most common is to use special notation for actions, say $\{a_1, a_2, \ldots\}$.

The basic notion is to apply action a to a state S and obtain the new state S^1. S, S^1 are state descriptions in some logical language. We need to write rules describing what a does. We need three languages:

- a language for the states

- a language for the actions

- a mixed language to describe the interaction between the action and the states.

In our story the action language can be taken as '*take a flight from X to Y*'. The state language can be predicates describing where Peter is and the mixed language describes the interaction. If Peter is at X at time t (i.e. state S) and he takes a flight from X to Y (i.e. takes action a) then he is at Y at time $t + n$ (i.e. state S^1).

12.4   Non-monotonic logics, knowledge and belief

Peter tried to put himself in other people's positions twice in our story. First when he assumed that the Spanish manufacturers wanted to sell his toasters directly to Eastern Europe. He was not told that. All he could see was that the Spaniards were being difficult. But he used common sense to assume that. On the basis of his assumption he flew to Madrid, only to find that it was not the case. Non-monotonic reasoning is an area of logic where additional defeasible assumptions can be made for the purpose of current reasoning at the risk that they might later be changed.

To explain this idea, let Δ be a list of outgoing flights from Madrid. We apply a non-monotonic principle, *complete*(Δ), which says the list of flights is a complete list and so since there is no Madrid–Udine flight listed, there is no such flight. Therefore from Δ we can conclude that there is no flight to Udine. Of course if Δ^1 is a bigger list, we may now conclude that there is a flight to Udine, because such a flight may now be listed. Suppose that we add the specifically negative additional information that there is no flight to Venice. This is not new information; we could have deduced it from the fact that a flight to Venice is not listed. However, we are now not sure whether indeed there is no flight to Udine. If indeed there is not, why is it not explicitly listed that there is not, in the same way that there is no flight to Venice explicitly listed? So by adding explicit information about Venice, we put in doubt the deduction about Udine.

So, in principle, non-monotonic deduction allows us to get answers from data using additional principles which use the database as a whole and are therefore not necessarily monotonic.

This is a very wide area of research in logic and AI. New types of logics have been put forward and many principles of getting new additional assumptions have been studied.

The other occasion when Peter needed non-monotonic reasoning was during his negotiations with the Spaniards. Although the story does not elaborate on that, what has happened was that each party had assumptions about the other and they tried to push the other to the limit, while still seeking agreement. There are some logics which try to negotiate automatically or act as a machine assistant to a user negotiator.

We need a special notation for agents $\{a_1, a_2, \ldots\}$ and connectives $B_a(q)$, $K_a(q)$, $W_a(q)$, reading a believes that q, and a knows that q, and a wants q. Reasoning about agents and their beliefs can be formalized in this language. For example,

$B_{\text{Peter}}(W_{\text{Spaniards}} \text{ (sell toasters direct)}) \Rightarrow F \text{ (Peter goes to Madrid)}.$

This is why Peter went to Madrid. When he met with his Spanish colleagues he found out that $\sim W_{\text{Spaniards}} \text{ (sell direct)}$.

Note for example that we can make a distinction between $B_a(p)$ and p. One is a belief, the other a fact.

12.5   Inconsistency

The most striking part of our story is inconsistency handling. We had two interesting inconsistencies in the story. A fairly simple one, the overbooking, which was solved by action, and the other one, the adultery, which was not solved but postponed. Inconsistency in logic is a state of affairs in the system which violates global conditions expected of the system (called integrity constraints in certain application areas). These conditions could range from not wanting to deduce certain conclusions (e.g. A and not A) or wanting certain axioms to hold (being faithful).

   Inconsistency can arise by design (overbooking) or by circumstances or errors (input of new data which disagrees with existing data). The framework in which inconsistency arises is the following. We have a database Δ which we use to answer queries. We externally impose restriction on such databases and the answers they give. These could be of the form:

1. certain queries should not get answer *yes*;

2. integrity constraints on the data, e.g. if an address is listed then a postal code must also be included.

Inconsistency means that the conditions we imposed on the database are not satisfied. In the case of the airline the inconsistency is that more people are booked on the flight than there are seats. In the case of the adultery certain queries should not get answer *yes* (being unfaithful).

   The logical handling of inconsistencies is a very old area of logic which has now become very active in response to needs from AI. A database may reject an input if it contradicts its existing data or if it does not fit into it. This is what Peter has done by going back to Madrid. In a sense he rejected the input. He ran away from the problem.

12.6   Automated deduction

Implicit in the story is the automatic implementation of the booking planning system and in general the implementation of logic on a machine. Generally what is happening here is that the area of logic and AI seeks ideally to replace humans by machines. This requires that we develop formalisms (logic as, for example, we discussed above) and use them to analyze and represent certain areas of human activity. This type of research is not new. Aristotle used to do it and some of the problems which we address now have been addressed or could equally have been addressed by him. The needs of AI and computer science gave a big push and urgency to this research. We still have to consider the computational aspects of the above solutions. These aspects gave rise to much fine tuning of existing logics and to the development of special proof methods and algorithms. This is the area of automated deduction in general, and in particular the area of the various 'programming in logic' languages and disciplines.

Further reading

Currently there are several main communities engaged in the study of logic.

The first community I would describe as the practical reasoning or informal logic community. Their main aim is to study human common sense day-to-day reasoning and argumentation. They see the task of formal logic to serve as a tool for checking arguments, verifying them and/or clarifying them. This community mainly resides in philosophy and humanities departments and their approach, aims and methods have roots as far back as Aristotle.

The work of this community is becoming increasingly important to computer science and artificial intelligence. As the use of computers becomes more and more widespread, a better logical analysis of human reasoning is more urgently needed, and the work of the practical reasoning and informal logic community is becoming more and more relevant and of potential use to computer applications. The reader will do well to look up some of the informal logic literature. Any basic logic textbook aimed at philosophers will do as a start. See for example [Copi, 1986; Lambert and Ulrich, 1980; Woods and Walton, 1982; Walton, 1989] and [Kahane, 1990]. See also [Gabbay and Woods, 2003; Gabbay and Woods, 2005; Gabbay et al., 2001; Gabbay et al., 2008; Gabbay et al., 2002].

A second related community where logic is used is the artificial intelligence community. A large part of this community is not using logic but many groups do pursue the development of systems of non-monotonic reasoning, temporal logics, systems of knowledge and belief and logics of action and planning.

Interesting books in this area are [Russell and Norvig, 1995; Shoham, 1988; Gillies, 1996; Copeland, 1993; Fagin et al., 1995; Marek and Truszczynski, 1993; Łukasiewicz, 1990; Brewka, 1991; Besnard, 1989; Flach, 1994; Sandewall, 1994; Hunter, 1996; Antoniou, 1996; Gabbay, 1976] and [Gabbay et al., in preparation].

The third community is the logic programming community. They use logic as a programming language, in much the same way as we use the goal-directed computation in this book. In fact, we were inspired by the logic programming approach. For further reading in this area see [Flach, 1994; Gibbins, 1988; Kowalski, 1979;

Apt, 1996] and [Hogger, 1994].

The fourth large community is the many-valued, fuzzy logic community. We quote three useful books, [Gottwald, 1993; Klir and Folger, 1988] and [Gabbay *et al.*, to appear].

The fifth community working in logic is the theoretical computer science community. In this area logic is used as a descriptive language for the purpose of specification, verification and computation. It is also used for the purpose of modelling theoretical computer science abstract notions and theories. The subareas of logic mostly needed are non-classical logics, λ-calculus and type theory and proof theory. We have touched on some of these areas in the course of this book, though not in depth. Elementary reading includes [Hankin, 2004; Hindley and Seldin, 1986; Field and Harrison, 1988; Gabbay, 1998] and [Huth and Ryan, 2004]. Advanced reading is [Barendregt, 1984].

The sixth community is the pure logic community developing formal logic for its own sake while exchanging ideas with applications of logic. References of interest to our readers are [Gabbay *et al.*, 1994; Gabbay and Guenthner, 1979–96; Chellas, 1980; Malinowski, 1993; van Dalen, 1994; Bradley and Swartz, 1979, Hughes and Cresswell, 1996] and [Chiswell and Hodges, 2007; Sainsbury, 2000; Hodges, 1977a; Gabbay, 1976; Gabbay, 1981; Gabbay *et al.*, 1994; Gabbay, 1996; Gabbay, 1998; Gabbay *et al*, 2003; Gabbay *et al.*, 2004; Gabbay and Maksimova, 2005; Gabbay *et al.*, 2007; Gabbay *et al.*, 2007a; Gabbay *et al.*, 2007b; Gabbay *et al.*, 2008].

A lot of pure logic is not directly applicable to computer science. Good general handbooks are [Barwise, 1977] and [Mendelson, 1964].

A good elementary book to read in bed is [Hodges, 1977].

The goal-directed paradigm of this book is further developed in my book [Gabbay and Olivetti, 2000].

Other automated reasoning books are [Gallier, 1986] and [Fitting, 1996].

Logic books for computer science are [Reeves and Clarke, 1990; Ben-Ari, 1993; Burke and Foxley, 1996; Broda *et al.*, 1994; Truss, 1991; Hein, 1995; Potter *et al.*, 1991] and [Lalement, 1993].

Handbooks are [Abramsky *et al.*, 1992–94] and [Gabbay *et al.*, 1993–95].

A full bibliography follows at the end of this book.

Answers to the exercises

Exercise 1.1.1

The truth values of the formulae, when p has the value $\top$, and q has the value $\bot$, are:

1. $\neg((p)\wedge(q))$ is $\top$

2. $(p)\Rightarrow(p)$ is $\top$

3. $(p)\Rightarrow(\neg(p))$ is $\bot$

4. $((q)\vee(\neg(q)))\wedge(p)$ is $\top$

Exercise 1.1.3

You were asked to find the truth tables for the following formulae:

1. $\neg A\vee B$ has the same table as $A\Rightarrow B$.

2. $\neg(\neg A\wedge\neg B)$ has the same table as $A\vee B$.

3. $A\vee\neg A$ has $\top$ in every row in its table.

4. $(A\wedge B\Rightarrow C)\Rightarrow[A\Rightarrow(B\Rightarrow C)]$ also has $\top$ in every row in its table.

5. $(A\Rightarrow B)\wedge(B\Rightarrow A)$ has the following table:

A	B	$(A\Rightarrow B)\wedge(B\Rightarrow A)$
$\top$	$\top$	$\top$
$\top$	$\bot$	$\bot$
$\bot$	$\top$	$\bot$
$\bot$	$\bot$	$\top$

6. $[A\Rightarrow(B\wedge C)]\Rightarrow[(A\Rightarrow B)\wedge(A\Rightarrow C)]$ again has $\top$ in every row in its table.

Exercise 1.1.4

1. The wff for the first table is $(p{\wedge}q){\vee}({\neg}p{\wedge}{\neg}q)$, another possibility being $(p{\Rightarrow}q){\wedge}(q{\Rightarrow}p)$. Both formulae have this table. The wff for the second table of this exercise is

$$[p{\wedge}q{\wedge}r]{\vee}[{\neg}p{\wedge}{\neg}q{\wedge}r]{\vee}[{\neg}p{\wedge}q{\wedge}{\neg}r]{\vee}[p{\wedge}{\neg}q{\wedge}{\neg}r]$$

2. Let p stand for 'the television is switched on', q stand for 'the television has power', and r for 'there is a picture'. The data to be checked for consistency is

$$p{\wedge}(p{\wedge}q{\Rightarrow}r){\wedge}{\neg}r$$

We need to draw up a truth table to see whether we can find truth values for the propositions so that the formula is true. The table is

p	q	r	$p{\wedge}q{\Rightarrow}r$	${\neg}r$	$p{\wedge}(p{\wedge}q{\Rightarrow}r){\wedge}{\neg}r$
⊤	⊤	⊤	⊤	⊥	⊥
⊤	⊤	⊥	⊥	⊤	⊥
⊤	⊥	⊤	⊤	⊥	⊥
⊤	⊥	⊥	⊤	⊤	⊤
⊥	⊥	⊤	⊤	⊥	⊥
⊥	⊥	⊥	⊤	⊤	⊥
⊥	⊥	⊤	⊤	⊥	⊥
⊥	⊥	⊥	⊤	⊤	⊥

As the third row has a ⊤ for the full conjunction, the sentences can be all true together.

Exercise 1.2.2

1. The definitions using the Sheffer stroke '|' are:

$$\neg p \stackrel{\text{def}}{=} p|p$$

$$p{\vee}q \stackrel{\text{def}}{=} {\neg}p|{\neg}q \equiv (p|p)|(q|q)$$

$$p{\wedge}q \stackrel{\text{def}}{=} {\neg}({\neg}p{\vee}{\neg}q) \equiv (p|q)|(p|q)$$

$$p{\Rightarrow}q \stackrel{\text{def}}{=} {\neg}p {\vee} q \equiv p|(q|q)$$

2. All except the third formula are tautologies.

Exercise 1.2.5

To write the disjunctive normal form equivalent to

$$A \equiv [(p\Rightarrow q)\vee r]\wedge\neg q\Rightarrow p$$

we can use two methods. One, which we have already learnt, is to find the truth table for A and then find the wff for the table. Two, use equivalences to transform A into its normal form. We start with the first method. Here is the table for A.

p	q	r	$\neg q$	$p\Rightarrow q$	$(p\Rightarrow q)\vee r$	$((p\Rightarrow q)\vee r)\wedge\neg q$	A
T	T	T	$\bot$	T	T	$\bot$	T
$\bot$	T	T	$\bot$	T	T	$\bot$	T
T	$\bot$	T	T	$\bot$	T	T	T
$\bot$	$\bot$	T	T	T	T	T	$\bot$
T	T	$\bot$	$\bot$	T	T	$\bot$	T
$\bot$	T	$\bot$	$\bot$	T	T	$\bot$	T
T	$\bot$	$\bot$	T	$\bot$	$\bot$	$\bot$	T
$\bot$	$\bot$	$\bot$	T	T	T	T	$\bot$

The wff of this table is:

$$[p\wedge q\wedge r]\vee[\neg p\wedge q\wedge r]\vee[p\wedge\neg q\wedge r]\vee[p\wedge q\wedge\neg r]\vee[\neg p\wedge q\wedge\neg r]\vee[p\wedge\neg q\wedge\neg r]$$

As we can see the wff is quite long. We can find a shorter formula if we look at the table for $B \equiv \neg A$. This table has only two Ts, in the last row (where A has $\bot$) and in the fourth row. The formula for the table for $B \equiv \neg A$ is therefore $B \equiv (\neg p\wedge\neg q\wedge r)\vee(\neg p\wedge\neg q\wedge\neg r)$, B is equivalent to $\neg p\wedge\neg q$ and so A is therefore $A \equiv \neg B \equiv \neg(\neg p\wedge\neg q)$ and hence $A \equiv p\vee q$, a much simpler formula.

We now demonstrate the second method, using equivalences. We know that $A\Rightarrow B$ is the same as $\neg A\vee B$. Hence $[(p\Rightarrow q)\vee r]$ is the same as $[\neg p\vee q\vee r]$. The expression is now

$$[\neg p\vee q\vee r]\wedge\neg q\Rightarrow p$$

We also know that

$$(A\vee B)\wedge C \equiv (A\wedge C)\vee(B\vee C)$$

Hence

$$[\neg p\vee q\vee r]\wedge\neg q \equiv (\neg p\wedge\neg q)\vee(q\wedge\neg q)\vee(r\wedge\neg q)$$

Since $q\wedge\neg q$ is a contradiction, we have for any x

$$x\vee(q\wedge\neg q) \equiv x$$

Thus we are left with

$$[\neg p\vee q\vee r]\wedge\neg q \equiv (\neg p\wedge\neg q)\vee(r\wedge\neg q)$$

The expression becomes $A \equiv [(\neg p \wedge \neg q) \vee (r \wedge \neg q)] \Rightarrow p$. Since $x \Rightarrow y \equiv \neg x \vee y$ we get $A \equiv \neg[(\neg p \wedge \neg q) \vee (r \wedge \neg q)] \vee p$. Since $\neg(x \wedge y) \equiv \neg x \vee \neg y$ and $\neg(x \vee y) \equiv \neg x \wedge \neg y$, we get

$$
\begin{aligned}
A &\equiv [\neg(\neg p \wedge \neg q) \wedge \neg(r \wedge \neg q)] \vee p \\
&\equiv [(p \vee q) \wedge (\neg r \vee q)] \vee p
\end{aligned}
$$

Distributing, we get

$$
\begin{aligned}
A &\equiv [p \wedge (\neg r \vee q)] \vee [q \wedge (\neg r \vee q)] \vee p \\
&\equiv (p \wedge \neg r) \vee (p \wedge q) \vee (q \wedge \neg r) \vee (q \wedge q) \vee p \\
&\equiv (p \wedge \neg r) \vee (p \wedge \neg q) \vee (q \wedge \neg r) \vee q \vee p
\end{aligned}
$$

This has the same truth table as $p \vee q$.

Exercise 1.2.7

1. A logically implies B iff $A \Rightarrow B$ is a tautology. $A \wedge \neg B$ is not consistent iff $\neg(A \wedge \neg B)$ is a tautology. We must therefore show the equivalence $(A \Rightarrow B) \equiv \neg(A \wedge \neg B)$, which we can do using the equivalences $p \Rightarrow q \equiv \neg p \vee q$ and $p \vee q \equiv \neg(\neg p \wedge \neg q)$.

2. Yes.

Exercise 1.2.9

1. The answer depends on whether n is even, in which case the set of sentences can be consistent, or odd, in which case it is impossible for the set to be consistent.

Exercise 1.2.10

1. The sentences translate as follows:

    (a) $p \Rightarrow q \wedge \neg s$

    (b) $r \wedge q \Rightarrow \neg s$

    (c) We cannot express that Mary loves herself. The atomic sentences given for this exercise do not contain an appropriate proposition. We would need to add a new atom, t say, to stand for 'Mary loves Mary.'

    Now we can translate as $p \wedge q \Rightarrow t$.

2. Using the equivalence rules to push all negations onto the atoms:

    (a) $\neg((a \Rightarrow b) \vee (a \Rightarrow c) \wedge \neg a)$
    $\equiv \neg(a \Rightarrow b) \wedge \neg((a \Rightarrow c) \wedge \neg a)$ ($\wedge$ binds tighter than $\vee$)
    $\equiv a \wedge \neg b \wedge (\neg(a \Rightarrow c) \vee \neg \neg a)$
    $\equiv a \wedge \neg b \wedge (a \wedge \neg c \vee a)$

(b) $\neg(a\wedge\neg b)\Rightarrow a$
$\equiv \neg\neg(a\wedge\neg b)\vee a$
$\equiv a\wedge\neg b\vee a$

3. Simply draw up the truth tables for the left and right sides of each equivalence, and it is easy to see that the sides take on the same truth values as each other, throughout the truth table.

4. The arguments translate as follows:

(a) p = it is warm
q = it is raining
r = we go outside

$p\vee q$
$\underline{\neg p\vee r}$
r

The truth table for $(p\vee q)\wedge(\neg p\vee\neg r)\Rightarrow r$ shows that it is not a tautology, and hence that this argument is not logically valid.

(b) p = the king is in the room
q = the courtiers laugh
r = the jester is in the room
s = the king laughs

$p\Rightarrow(q\Rightarrow s)$
$r\Rightarrow q$
$\underline{r\Rightarrow\neg s}$
$\neg p\vee\neg r$

The truth table for $(p\Rightarrow(q\Rightarrow s))\wedge(r\Rightarrow q)\wedge(r\Rightarrow\neg s)\Rightarrow(\neg p\vee\neg r)$ shows that it is a tautology, and hence that this argument is also logically valid.

(c) p = we are hungry
q = the food is very hot
r = we eat slowly

$\neg p\wedge q\Rightarrow r$
$\neg p\Rightarrow q\vee r$
$\underline{\neg q}$
p

This argument is not valid. If you draw up the truth table for $(\neg p\wedge q\Rightarrow r)\wedge(\neg p\Rightarrow q\vee r)\wedge(\neg q)\Rightarrow p$, the row with r true and p and q both false would have false for the implication.

(d) Let us denote 'either A or B' by $A\oplus B$. Its truth table

A	B	A ⊕ B
⊤	⊤	⊥
⊤	⊥	⊤
⊥	⊤	⊤
⊥	⊥	⊥

shows that $A \oplus B \equiv (A \wedge \neg B) \vee (\neg A \wedge B)$.

Now let

j = Jones did not meet Smith last night,
s = Smith was a murderer,
l = Jones is telling a lie,
m = the murder happened after midnight,

and consider the argument in question:

$$\frac{j \Rightarrow s \oplus l, \neg s \Rightarrow j \wedge m, m \Rightarrow s \oplus l}{s}$$

This argument is not valid, because we can take the values

j	s	l	m
⊤	⊥	⊤	⊤

Exercise 1.7.12

1.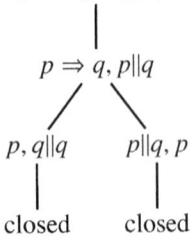

2.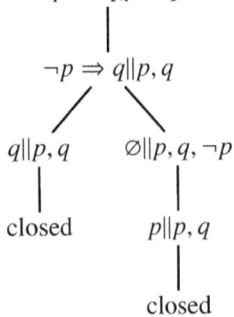

3.

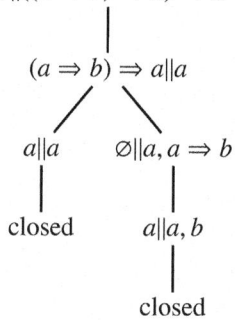

$\varnothing \| ((a \Rightarrow b) \Rightarrow a) \Rightarrow a$

$(a \Rightarrow b) \Rightarrow a \| a$

$a \| a \qquad \varnothing \| a, a \Rightarrow b$

closed $\qquad a \| a, b$

closed

4.

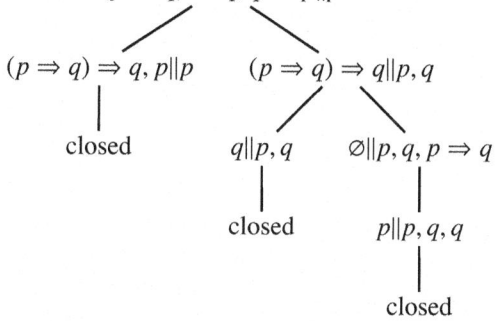

$(p \Rightarrow q) \Rightarrow q, q \Rightarrow p \| p$

$(p \Rightarrow q) \Rightarrow q, p \| p \qquad (p \Rightarrow q) \Rightarrow q \| p, q$

closed $\qquad q \| p, q \qquad \varnothing \| p, q, p \Rightarrow q$

closed $\qquad p \| p, q, q$

closed

5.

$\varnothing \| \neg (p \wedge \neg p)$

$p \wedge \neg p \| \varnothing$

$p, \neg p \| \varnothing$

$p \| p$

closed

6. $\emptyset \| \neg(p \Rightarrow q \| \Rightarrow p$

$$\big|$$

$\neg(p \Rightarrow q) \| p$

$$\big|$$

$\emptyset \| p, p \Rightarrow q$

$$\big|$$

$p \| p, q$

$$\big|$$

closed

7. $\emptyset \| \neg(p \Rightarrow q) \Rightarrow \neg q$

$$\big|$$

$\neg(p \Rightarrow q) \| \neg q$

$$\big|$$

$q \| p \Rightarrow q$

$$\big|$$

$q, p \| q$

$$\big|$$

closed

8. $\emptyset \| b \vee (b \Rightarrow c)$

$$\big|$$

$\emptyset \| b, b \Rightarrow c$

$$\big|$$

$b \| b, c$

$$\big|$$

closed

9.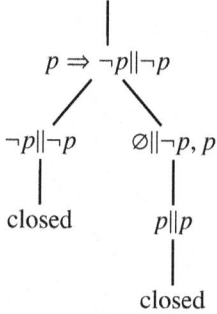

$\varnothing \| (p \Rightarrow \neg p) \Rightarrow \neg p$

$p \Rightarrow \neg p \| \neg p$

$\neg p \| \neg p \qquad \varnothing \| \neg p, p$

closed

$p \| p$

closed

10.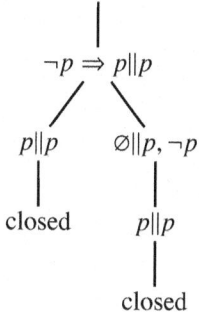

$\varnothing \| (\neg p \Rightarrow p) \Rightarrow p$

$\neg p \Rightarrow p \| p$

$p \| p \qquad \varnothing \| p, \neg p$

closed

$p \| p$

closed

11.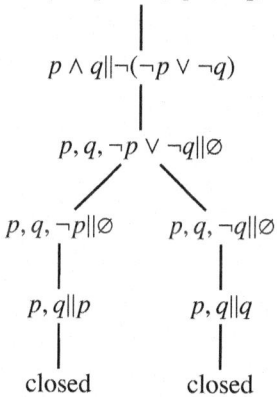

$\varnothing \| p \wedge q \Rightarrow \neg(\neg p \vee \neg q)$

$p \wedge q \| \neg(\neg p \vee \neg q)$

$p, q, \neg p \vee \neg q \| \varnothing$

$p, q, \neg p \| \varnothing \qquad p, q, \neg q \| \varnothing$

$p, q \| p \qquad p, q \| q$

closed $\qquad$ closed

12.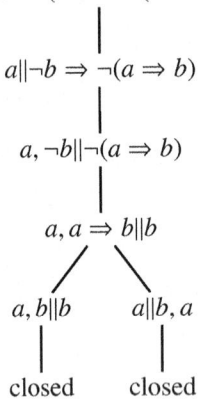

13.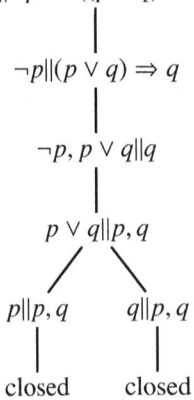

14. $a \Rightarrow ((a \wedge b) \vee (\neg a \wedge \neg b))\|b$

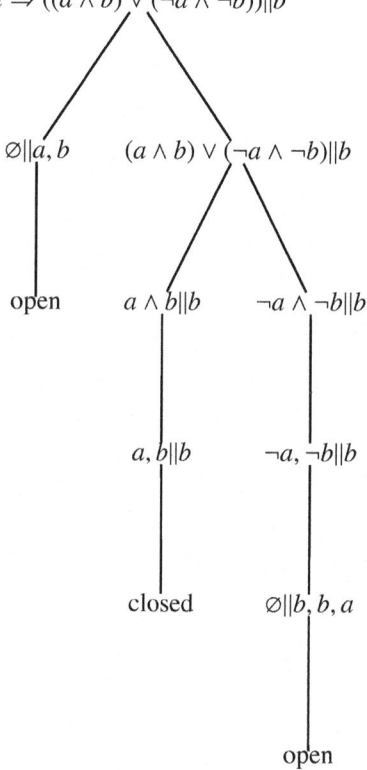

$\emptyset\|a, b$ $\qquad (a \wedge b) \vee (\neg a \wedge \neg b)\|b$

open $\qquad a \wedge b\|b \qquad \neg a \wedge \neg b\|b$

$a, b\|b \qquad \neg a, \neg b\|b$

closed $\qquad \emptyset\|b, b, a$

open

Exercise 2.1.1

1. $d_1(x) = x \Rightarrow x$

   $d_3(x) = \neg(x \Rightarrow x)$

   $d_2(x)$ does not exist because every formula gets the value 0 or 1 when each of its arguments is 0 or 1. (The latter is easily proved by induction.)

2.

A	1	1	1	1/2	1/2	1/2	0	0	0
B	1	1/2	0	1	1/2	0	1	1/2	0
$\neg A$	0	0	0	1/2	1/2	1/2	1	1	1
$\neg A \vee B$	1	1/2	0	1	1/2	1/2	1	1	1
$A \vee \neg A$	1	1	1	1/2	1/2	1/2	1	1	1
$\neg B$	0	1/2	1	0	1/2	1	0	1/2	1
$\neg A \wedge \neg B$	0	0	0	0	1/2	1/2	0	1/2	1
$A \Rightarrow B$	1	1/2	0	1	1	1/2	1	1	1
$B \Rightarrow A$	1	1	1	1/2	1	1	0	1/2	1
$(A \Rightarrow B) \wedge (B \Rightarrow A)$	1	1/2	0	1/2	1	1/2	0	1/2	1

This gives the answers for (a), (b), (c), (e). The answers for (d), (f) are given by the next table.

3.   (a) First let us show that for any k,

$$(*) \quad (\neg x)^k \Rightarrow x = \min(1, (k+1)x)$$

This comes by induction:
If $k = 0$, we have $\neg x^0 \Rightarrow x = x = \min(1, x)$.
If $(k+1)x \geq 1$, then also $(k+2)x \geq 1$, and we have $(\neg x)^{k+1} \Rightarrow x = \neg x \Rightarrow ((\neg x)^k$
$\Rightarrow x) = \neg x \Rightarrow 1$ (by the induction hypothesis) $= 1 = \min((k+2)x, 1)$.
If $(k+1)x < 1$, we have

$$(\neg x)^{k+1} \Rightarrow x \quad = \neg x \Rightarrow (k+1)x = \min(1, 1 - \neg x + (k+1)x)$$
$$= \min(1, (k+2)x)$$

Now if $k \geq n - 1$, it follows that $(k+1)x \geq 1$, unless $x = 0$ (recall that $x \in \{0, 1/n, \ldots, 1\}$). Hence $(\neg x)^k \Rightarrow x$ is either 0 or 1.

  (b) A possible example is $[(\neg x)^{n-1} \Rightarrow x] \vee \neg[(\neg x)^{n-1} \Rightarrow x]$, with x atomic. As we have proved in the solution of 3(a), $(\neg x)^{n-1} \Rightarrow x$ is either 0 or 1 in L_n; but in L_{n+1} we have $(\neg x)^{n-1} \Rightarrow x = \min(1, nx)$, and it can get also the value $n/(n+1)$ (when $x = 1/n + 1$). So

$$[(\neg x)^{n-1} \Rightarrow x] \vee \neg[(\neg x)^{n-1} \Rightarrow x] = 1$$

in L_n, but in L_{n+1} we have

$$[(\neg(1/n + 1))^{n-1} \Rightarrow 1/n + 1] \vee \neg[(\neg(1/n + 1))^{n-1} \Rightarrow 1/n + 1] =$$
$$(n/n + 1) \vee (1/n + 1) = n/n + 1.$$

4. First let us prove by induction that

$$(\#) \quad x^k \Rightarrow y = \min(1, k(1 - x) + y)$$

(in L_n). If $k = 0$ we have: $x^0 \Rightarrow y = y = \min(1, y)$. If $(\#)$ is true for k, we have

$$x^{k+1} \Rightarrow y = x \Rightarrow \min(1, k(1 - x) + y) = \min(1 - x + \min(1, k(1 - x) + y), 1).$$

Now if $k(1 - x) + y > 1$, it follows that

$$(k+1)(1 - x) + y > 1, \text{ and } x^k \Rightarrow y = 1$$

A	B	C	$A \wedge B$	$B \wedge C$	$B \Rightarrow C$	$A \Rightarrow (B \Rightarrow C)$	$A \wedge B \Rightarrow C$	(d)	$A \Rightarrow B$	$A \Rightarrow C$	$(A \Rightarrow B) \wedge (B \Rightarrow C)$	$A \Rightarrow B \wedge C$	(f)
1	1	1	1	1	1	1	1	1	1	1	1	1	1
1	1	1/2	1	1/2	1/2	1/2	1/2	1	1	1/2	1/2	1/2	1
1	1	0	1	0	0	0	0	1	1	0	0	0	1
1	1/2	1	1/2	1/2	1	1	1	1	1/2	1	1/2	1/2	1
1	1/2	1/2	1/2	1/2	1	1	1	1	1/2	1/2	1/2	1/2	1
1	1/2	0	1/2	0	0	0	0	1	1/2	0	0	0	1
1	0	1	0	0	1	1	1	1	0	1	0	0	1
1	0	1/2	0	0	1	1	1	1	0	1/2	0	0	1
1	0	0	0	0	1	1	1	1	0	0	0	0	1
1/2	1	1	1/2	1	1	1	1	1	1	1	1	1	1
1/2	1	1/2	1/2	1/2	1/2	1	1	1	1	1	1/2	1	1
1/2	1	0	1/2	0	0	0	0	1	1	0	0	0	1
1/2	1/2	1	1/2	1/2	1	1	1	1	1	1	1	1	1
1/2	1/2	1/2	1/2	1/2	1	1	1	1	1	1	1	1	1
1/2	1/2	0	1/2	0	0	0	0	1	1	0	0	0	1
1/2	0	1	0	0	1	1	1	1	0	1	0	0	1
1/2	0	1/2	0	0	1	1	1	1	0	1	0	0	1
1/2	0	0	0	0	1	1	1	1	0	0	0	0	1
0	1	1	0	1	1	1	1	1	1	1	1	1	1
0	1	1/2	0	1/2	1/2	1	1	1	1	1	1/2	1	1
0	1	0	0	0	0	1	1	1	1	1	0	1	1
0	1/2	1	0	1/2	1	1	1	1	1	1	1	1	1
0	1/2	1/2	0	1/2	1	1	1	1	1	1	1	1	1
0	1/2	0	0	0	0	1	1	1	1	1	0	1	1
0	0	1	0	0	1	1	1	1	1	1	1	1	1
0	0	1/2	0	0	1	1	1	1	1	1	1	1	1
0	0	0	0	0	1	1	1	1	1	1	1	1	1

In this case $x^{k+1} \Rightarrow y = \min(2 - x, 1) = 1$.

If $k(1 - x) + y < 1$ we get

$$x^{k+1} \Rightarrow y = \min(1 - x + k(1 - x) + y, 1) = \min((k + 1)(1 - x) + y, 1)$$

Anyway ($\sharp$) holds for $n = k + 1$.

Now in L_n we have that

$$x^n \Rightarrow y = \min(1, n(1 - x) + y) = \begin{cases} y, & \text{if } x = 1 \\ 1, & \text{if } x \neq 1 \end{cases}$$

(since $1 - x \geq 1/n$ in the latter case).

Thus $((x^n \Rightarrow y) \Rightarrow x) \Rightarrow x = (y \Rightarrow 1) \Rightarrow 1 = 1 \Rightarrow 1 = 1$ if $x = 1$,

and

$$((x^n \Rightarrow y) \Rightarrow x) \Rightarrow x = (1 \Rightarrow x) \Rightarrow x = x \Rightarrow x = 1 \text{ if } x \neq 1$$

On the other hand in L_{n+1} we have (again by ($\sharp$)):

$$(((\tfrac{1}{n+1})^n \Rightarrow 0) \Rightarrow \tfrac{1}{n+1}) \Rightarrow \tfrac{1}{n+1} = (\tfrac{n}{n+1} \Rightarrow \tfrac{1}{n+1}) \Rightarrow \tfrac{1}{n+1} =$$
$$\tfrac{2}{n+1} \Rightarrow \tfrac{1}{n+1} = \tfrac{n}{n+1}$$

5. Again we can use the equality ($*$) from the solution of 3(a).

Consider the formula $A(x) = (\neg x) \Leftrightarrow [(\neg x)^{k-2} \Rightarrow x]$. We have that $A(x) = 1$ iff $\neg x = (\neg x)^{k-2} \Rightarrow x$ iff $1 - x = \min(1, (k - 1)x)$.

Now we notice that $1 - x = (k - 1)x$ iff $1 = kx$ iff $x = 1/k$.

Thus $x = 1/k$ implies $A(x) = 1$, and also $(k - 1)x < 1$ together with $x \neq 1/k$ imply $A(x) \neq 1$. Finally, if $(k - 1)x \geq 1$ (i.e. $x \geq 1/(k - 1)$) and $1 - x = \min(1, (k - 1)x) = 1$, we obtain that $x = 0$, which is a contradiction.

Therefore $A(x)$ has the property required.

6. Assume that m is a divisor of n, and that a formula $A(p_1, \ldots, p_k)$ with atoms $p_1, \ldots,$

p_k is not an L_m-tautology. Then $A(x_1, \ldots, x_k) \neq 1$ for some values $x_1, \ldots, x_k \in \{0, 1/m, \ldots, (m-1)/m, 1\}$. But since m divides n, all the numbers $1/m, \ldots,$ $(m-1)/m$ are among $\{1/n, \ldots, (n-1)/n\}$, and thus $x_1, \ldots, x_k \in \{0, 1/n, \ldots, 1\}$.

Then $A(x_1, \ldots, x_k) \neq 1$ also in L_n because the functions $\neg, \Rightarrow, \vee, \wedge$ in L_n are computed by the same rules as in L_m. Therefore A is not an L_n-tautology.

('If') Assume that $m \leq n$. Consider an arbitrary formula A without negation, such that A is not an L_m-tautology. Let $p_1, \ldots, p_k$ be all atoms occurring in A;   then
$A(x_1, \ldots, x_k) \neq 1$ for some values $x_1, \ldots, x_k \in \{0, 1/m, \ldots, 1\}$ of these

atoms. Further on, we can assume that $x_1 \leq x_2 \leq \cdots \leq x_k$ (otherwise we make the list of atoms in a corresponding order).

Now we map the values $\{0, 1/m, 2/m, \ldots, 1\}$ into $\{0, 1/n, \ldots, (n-1)/n, 1\}$ in such a way that $1 \mapsto 1, (1 - 1/m) \mapsto (1 - 1/n), \ldots, 0 \mapsto (1 - m/n)$. This is done by the function

$$f(x) = 1 - \frac{m}{n} + \frac{m}{n}x$$

Indeed, one can observe that $f(1) = 1$ and f increases all distances by (m/n) times. Obviously f is monotonic, and thus $f(x \vee y) = f(x) \vee f(y)$, $f(x \wedge y) = f(x) \wedge f(y)$.

Moreover, f preserves the implication. For, if $x \Rightarrow y = 1$ then $x \leq y$, and so $f(x) \leq f(y)$,

$$f(x) \Rightarrow f(y) = 1 = f(x \Rightarrow y)$$

If $x \Rightarrow y \neq 1$, then

$$x > y, x \Rightarrow y = 1 - x + y,$$
$$f(x \Rightarrow y) = 1 - \frac{m}{n} - \frac{m}{n}x + \frac{m}{n}y$$

On the other hand, $f(x) > f(y)$, thanks to monotonicity, and thus

$$f(x) \Rightarrow f(y) = 1 - f(x) + f(y)$$
$$= 1 - (1 - \frac{m}{n} + \frac{m}{n}x) + (1 - \frac{m}{n} + \frac{m}{n}y)$$
$$= 1 - \frac{m}{n}x + \frac{m}{n}y.$$

Hence $f(x \Rightarrow y) = f(x) \Rightarrow f(y)$.

Since f preserves $\vee, \wedge, \Rightarrow$, we obtain that

$$f(A(x_1, \ldots, x_k)) = A(f(x_1), \ldots, f(x_k))$$

and this value is not 1, because $A(x_1, \ldots, x_k) \neq 1$ and f is monotonic.

Therefore, $A(f(x_1), \ldots, f(x_k)) \neq 1$ in L_n, which means that A is not an L_n-tautology.

Thus (in the language $\{\vee, \wedge, \Rightarrow\}$) every L_m-non-tautology is an L_n-non-tautology, i.e. $L_n \subseteq L_m$.

('Only if') Exercise 4 shows that $L_n \not\subseteq L_{n+1}$ for formulae without negation.

Hence $L_n \not\subseteq L_m$ for any $m > n$ because otherwise we had

$$L_n \subseteq L_m \subseteq L_{n+1}$$

by the 'If' part proved above.

Exercise 2.1.3

$A_1, \ldots, A_k \vdash_{L_n} B \Rightarrow C$ iff for any assignment h,

1. $h(A_1) + \cdots + h(A_k) \leq (k-1) + h(B \Rightarrow C)$.

$A_1, \ldots, A_k, B \vdash_{L_n} C$ iff for any h,

2. $h(A_1) + \cdots + h(A_k) + h(B) \leq k + h(C)$.

If $h(B) \geq h(C)$ then (1) is equivalent to (2), because $k - 1 + h(B \Rightarrow C) = k - 1 + (1 - h(B) + h(C)) = k - h(B) + h(C)$.
If $h(B) < h(C)$ then (2) is true because it is obtained by addition of inequalities $h(A_1) \leq 1, \ldots, h(A_k) \leq 1, h(B) \leq h(C)$.
(1) is also true in this case, because $h(B \Rightarrow C) = 1$, and $h(A_1) + \cdots + h(A_k) \leq \underbrace{1 + \cdots + 1}_{} = k = (k-1) + h(B \Rightarrow C)$.

So again (1) and (2) are equivalent.

Exercise 2.2.4

This is shown by induction on A (for any t, s).

- If A is an atom, A is persistent by definition;

- Suppose $A = B \wedge C$ and B, C are persistent, $t \leq s, h(t, A) = 1$. Then $h(t, B) = h(t, C) = 1$. By definition, $h(s, B) = h(s, C) = 1$ by persistence, and thus $h(s, A) = 1$ by Definition 2.2.3.

- Suppose $A = B \vee C$, with B, C persistent, $t \leq s, h(t, A) = 1$. Then $h(t, B) = 1$ or $h(t, C) = 1$ by definition; hence $h(s, B) = 1$ or $h(s, C) = 1$ by persistence, and finally, $h(s, A) = 1$ by Definition 2.2.3.

- Suppose $A = B \Rightarrow C$, with B, C persistent, $t \leq s, h(t, A) = 1$. Take any $r \geq s$; then $r \geq t$ by transitivity. Now if $h(r, B) = 1$, we have $h(r, C) = 1$ (since $h(t, A) = 1, r \geq t$). Thus $h(s, A) = 1$ because r is arbitrary. (Note that we have not used persistence of B, C at all.)

- Obviously $\perp$ is persistent.

- Suppose $A = \neg B$, with B persistent, $t \leq s, h(t, A) = 1$. Take any $r \geq s$; then $r \geq t$ by transitivity, and hence $h(r, B) = 0$ (since $h(t, A) = 1$).

This implies persistence of A (again we did not use persistence of B).

Exercise 2.2.6

1. $H_0(A \twoheadrightarrow A) = 1$ iff for any t, $H_t(A) = 1$ implies $H_{0 \otimes t}(A) = 1$. The latter is true because $0 \otimes t = t$.

   So $A \twoheadrightarrow A$ is valid.

2. $H_0(A \twoheadrightarrow (A \twoheadrightarrow A)) = 1$ iff for any t, $H_t(A) = 1$ implies $H_t(A \twoheadrightarrow A) = 1$, iff for any t, r, $H_t(A) = 1$, $H_r(A) = 1$ imply $H_{t \otimes r}(A) = 1$.

   This is not necessarily true, even in the case (a). For example, we can take A atomic, $I = \{0, a, b, 1\}$, with the operation $\otimes$ given by the following multiplication table:

$\otimes$	0	a	b	1
0	0	a	b	1
a	a	a	1	1
b	b	1	b	1
1	1	1	1	1

   (This corresponds to the operation '$\cup$' on subsets of a two-element set.) Now put

   $$H_a(A) = H_b(A) = 1$$

   and

   $$H_0(A) = H_1(A) = 0$$

   The above argument shows that

   $$H_0(A \twoheadrightarrow (A \twoheadrightarrow A)) = 1$$

   because $H_{a \otimes b}(A) = 0$.

3. $H_0[(A \twoheadrightarrow (B \twoheadrightarrow C)) \twoheadrightarrow (B \twoheadrightarrow (A \twoheadrightarrow C))] = 1$ iff for any s, $H_s(A \twoheadrightarrow (B \twoheadrightarrow C)) = 1$ only if $H_s(B \twoheadrightarrow (A \twoheadrightarrow C)) = 1$.

   In the case (a) this is true. For, assume that

   (a_1) $H_s(A \twoheadrightarrow (B \twoheadrightarrow C)) = 1$,
   and show that

   (a_2) $H_s(B \twoheadrightarrow (A \twoheadrightarrow C)) = 1$,
   i.e. that for any t, $H_t(B) = 1$ only if $H_{s \otimes t}(A \twoheadrightarrow C)$.

   So assume also

   (a_3) $H_t(B) = 1$
   and show that

(a_4) $H_{s\otimes t}(A \twoheadrightarrow C) = 1$.

To check this, assume finally that

(a_5) $H_u(A) = 1$

and show that

(a_6) $H_{(s\otimes t)\otimes u}(C) = 1$.

By our assumptions we get

(a_7) $H_{s\otimes u}(B \twoheadrightarrow C) = 1$ (by (a_1), (a_5)),

(a_8) $H_{(s\otimes u)\otimes t}(C) = 1$ (by (a_7), (a_3)).

If the operation $\otimes$ is commutative and associative, (a_8) is the same as (a_6). In the case (b) we can find a model where the formula 3 fails, i.e. we can take a three-element set with the following multiplication table:

$\otimes$	$\emptyset$	u	t
$\emptyset$	$\emptyset$	u	t
u	u	u	u
t	t	t	t

(Associativity follows because

$$(u \otimes x) \otimes y = u \otimes y = u = u \otimes (x \otimes y),$$
$$(t \otimes x) \otimes y = t \otimes y = t = t \otimes (x \otimes y),$$
$$(\emptyset \otimes x) \otimes y = x \otimes y = \emptyset \otimes (x \otimes y).)$$

Now let $H_u(C) = 1, H_t(C) = 0$,

$$H_x(A) = 1 \text{ iff } x = u$$
$$H_y(B) = 1 \text{ iff } y = t$$

Then $H_\emptyset[(A \twoheadrightarrow (B \twoheadrightarrow C)) \twoheadrightarrow (B \twoheadrightarrow (A \twoheadrightarrow C))] = 0$ because

(b_1) $H_\emptyset(A \twoheadrightarrow (B \twoheadrightarrow C)) = 1$,

(b_2) $H_\emptyset(B \twoheadrightarrow (A \twoheadrightarrow C)) = 0$,

and $\emptyset \otimes \emptyset = \emptyset$.

To show (b_1), assume

(b_3) $H_x(A) = 1$.

Then $x = u$ (by definition of H), and we have to check that

(b_4) $H_u(B \twoheadrightarrow C) = 1$

(because $\emptyset \otimes u = u$).

This means: for any y, $H_y(B) = 1$ only if $H_{u\otimes y}(C) = 1$. The latter is true since $u \otimes y = u$.

To prove (b_2) it suffices to notice that $H_t(B) = 1$, but $H_t(A \twoheadrightarrow C) = 0$. This happens since $H_u(A) = 1$, but $H_{t\otimes u}(C) = 0$.

4. First we show validity in the case (b), which means: for any s, $H_s(A \twoheadrightarrow (A \twoheadrightarrow B)) = 1$ implies $H_s(A \twoheadrightarrow B) = 1$.

So assume that

(4.1) $H_s(A \twoheadrightarrow (A \twoheadrightarrow B)) = 1$, and that

(4.2) $H_r(A) = 1$. Then we get

(4.3) $H_{s\otimes r}(A \twoheadrightarrow B) = 1$ (by (4.1), (4.2)),

(4.4) $H_{(s\otimes r)\otimes r}(B) = 1$ (by (4.2), (4.3)),

(4.5) $H_{s\otimes r}(B) = 1$ since $(s \otimes r) \otimes r = s \otimes r$.
   Thus (4.2) implies (4.5), i.e. $H_s(A \twoheadrightarrow B) = 1$.

On the other hand, the formula can be refuted in the case (a). To see this, we take the model $\langle I, \otimes, \emptyset \rangle$ in a two-element set $\{\emptyset, r\}$ with the following multiplication table:

$\otimes$	$\emptyset$	r
$\emptyset$	$\emptyset$	r
r	r	$\emptyset$

and with the assignment (for A, B atomic)

$$H_r(A) = H_\emptyset(B) = 1, H_r(B) = H_\emptyset(A) = 0$$

Now the formula 4 becomes false at $\emptyset$ because

(4.6) $H_\emptyset(A \twoheadrightarrow (A \twoheadrightarrow B)) = 1$,

(4.7) $H_\emptyset(A \twoheadrightarrow B) = 0$,
   and $\emptyset \otimes \emptyset = \emptyset$.
   (4.7) holds because $H_r(A) = 1$ but $H_r(B) = 0$. To verify (4.6) assume that

(4.8) $H_s(A) = 1$, and show that

(4.9) $H_{\emptyset\otimes s}(A \twoheadrightarrow B) = 1$.
   By definition, (4.8) can be true only for $s = r$, so (4.9) is equivalent to

(4.10) $H_r(A \twoheadrightarrow B) = 1$,
   which means that for any $u, H_u(A) = 1$ only if $H_{r\otimes u}(B) = 1$. This is true because $H_u(A) = 1$ implies
   $u = r, r \otimes u = \emptyset$.

5.   (a) The formula is valid. Assume that

(5.1) $H_s(A) = 1$,
   and prove that $H_s((A \twoheadrightarrow A) \twoheadrightarrow A) = 1$. For this, assume also

(5.2) $H_r(A \twoheadrightarrow A) = 1$,
   and show that

(5.3) $H_{s \otimes r}(A) = 1$.
   From (5.1) and (5.2) it follows that

(5.4) $H_{r \otimes s}(A) = 1$, which is equivalent to (5.3) by commutativity.

(b) The formula is non-valid. Consider the following model:

$\otimes$	$\emptyset$	s	t
$\emptyset$	$\emptyset$	s	t
s	s	s	t
t	t	s	t

with the assignment (for A atomic):

$$H_s(A) = 1, H_t(A) = H_\emptyset(A) = 0$$

Now $H_s((A \twoheadrightarrow A) \twoheadrightarrow A) = 0$ follows from $H_{s \otimes t}(A) = H_t(A) = 0$ and $H_t(A \twoheadrightarrow A) = 1$. The latter holds because $H_x(A) = 1$ only if $x = s$, only if $H_{t \otimes x}(A) = H_s(A) = 1$.
Hence $H_\emptyset(A \twoheadrightarrow ((A \twoheadrightarrow A) \twoheadrightarrow A)) = 0$.

Associativity for our operation can be checked in a similar way as in item 3 above.

Exercise 3.1.5

One way (there may be others) of proving the validity of each of the arguments is given:

1. $\dfrac{\dfrac{p \wedge q}{p} \quad (\wedge E)}{p \vee q} \quad (\vee I)$

2. $\dfrac{p \Rightarrow q \quad \dfrac{\neg q}{p \Rightarrow \neg q} \ (\Rightarrow I2)}{\neg p} \quad (\neg I)$

3. $\dfrac{p \vee r \quad r \Rightarrow q \quad \dfrac{\neg p}{p \Rightarrow q} \ (\Rightarrow I1)}{q} \quad (\vee E)$

Exercise 3.2.3

We prove the two tautologies using the forward rules.

1. We must show $\dfrac{\text{nothing}}{(p\vee q)\wedge\neg p\Rightarrow q}$ and so by $(\Rightarrow\!I)$ we have to show $\dfrac{(p\vee q)\wedge\neg p}{q}$

   which is given by $(\wedge E)$ and $(\vee E1)$.

2. We must show $\dfrac{\text{nothing}}{(\neg q\Rightarrow\neg p)\Rightarrow(p\Rightarrow q)}$

   and so by $(\Rightarrow\!I)$ we have to show $\dfrac{\neg q\Rightarrow\neg p}{p\Rightarrow q}$ and by $(\Rightarrow\!I)$ again, we have to

   show $\dfrac{\neg q\Rightarrow\neg p,\, p}{q}$ which we do by showing

   (a) $\neg q\Rightarrow p$ from $\{\neg q\Rightarrow\neg p, p\}$

   (b) $\neg q\Rightarrow\neg p$ from $\{\neg q\Rightarrow\neg p, p\}$

   and using the negation rule $(\neg E)$ to get q from $\{\neg q\Rightarrow\neg p, p\}$. To show $\neg q\Rightarrow p$, we use $(\Rightarrow I2)$. To show $\neg q\Rightarrow\neg p$, we observe that it is one of the assumptions.

Exercise 3.2.4

1. (a) Rule $(\Rightarrow I1): \neg A \vdash A \Rightarrow B$.

(b) Rule ($\Rightarrow$ I2) : $B \vdash A \Rightarrow B$.

Obviously, $B, A \vdash B$. Then we can use ($\Rightarrow$ I) to obtain $B \vdash A \Rightarrow B$.

(c) Rule ($\Rightarrow$ E1) : $A \Rightarrow B \vdash \neg A \lor B$.

			$\neg A \lor B$
(1)	$A \Rightarrow B$		data
(2)	$A \Rightarrow \neg A \lor B$		subcomputation

		$\neg A \lor B$
(2.1)	A	assumption
(2.2)	B	($\Rightarrow$ E) on (1), (2.1)
(2.3)	$\neg A \lor B$	($\lor$I) on (2.2)

(3)	$\neg A \Rightarrow \neg A \lor B$	subcomputation

		$\neg A \lor B$
(3.1)	$\neg A$	assumption
(3.2)	$\neg A \lor B$	($\lor$I) on (3.1)

(4)	$\neg A \lor B$	($\neg$2) on (2), (3)

2. (a) $p \Rightarrow (q \Rightarrow r) \vdash p \land q \Rightarrow r$.

It is sufficient to show $p \Rightarrow (q \Rightarrow r), p \land q \vdash r$, and then apply the rule ($\Rightarrow$ I).

So we proceed:

(1)	$p \Rightarrow (q \Rightarrow r)$	assumption
(2)	$p \land q$	assumption
(3)	p	($\land$E) on (2)
(4)	q	($\land$E) on (2)
(5)	$q \Rightarrow r$	($\Rightarrow$ E) on (1), (3)
(6)	r	($\Rightarrow$ E) on (4), (5)

(b) $p \lor q \Rightarrow r \vdash (p \Rightarrow r) \land (q \Rightarrow r)$.

It is sufficient to show $p \lor q \Rightarrow r \vdash p \Rightarrow r$ and $p \lor q \Rightarrow r \vdash q \Rightarrow r$, and then apply ($\land$I). Both proofs are similar, so we do the first:

$$p \Rightarrow r$$

(1)	$p \lor q \Rightarrow r$	data
(2)	$p \Rightarrow r$	subcomputation

$$\underline{r}$$

(2.1)	p	assumption
(2.2)	$p \lor q$	($\lor$I) on (2.1)
(2.3)	r	($\Rightarrow$ E) on (1), (2.2)

(c) $\vdash q \Rightarrow (p \Rightarrow q)$.

By ($\Rightarrow$ I2) we have $q \vdash p \Rightarrow q$. Then we can apply ($\Rightarrow$ I).

(d) $\vdash p \Rightarrow p$.

Immediately from $p \vdash p$ by ($\Rightarrow$ I).

(e) $\neg(p \Rightarrow q) \vdash p \land \neg q$.

$$p \land \neg q$$

(1)	$\neg(p \Rightarrow q)$	data
(2)	$\neg p \Rightarrow \neg(p \Rightarrow q)$	($\Rightarrow$ I2) on (1)
(3)	$\neg p \Rightarrow (p \Rightarrow q)$	subcomputation

$$p \Rightarrow q$$

(3.1)	$\neg p$	assumption
(3.2)	$p \Rightarrow q$	($\Rightarrow$ I1)

(4)	p	($\neg$E) on (2), (3)
(5)	$q \Rightarrow \neg(p \Rightarrow q)$	($\Rightarrow$ I2) on (1)
(6)	$q \Rightarrow (p \Rightarrow q)$	subcomputation

$$p \Rightarrow q$$

(6.1)	q	assumption
(6.2)	$p \Rightarrow q$	($\Rightarrow$ I2) on (6.1)

(7)	$\neg q$	($\neg$I) on (5), (6)
(8)	$p \land \neg q$	($\land$I) on (4), (7)

(f) $\neg p \lor q \vdash p \Rightarrow q$.

This follows by ($\lor$E) since we have

$$\vdash \neg p \Rightarrow (p \Rightarrow q) \text{ and } \vdash q \Rightarrow (p \Rightarrow q)$$

The second was proved in (c), and the first follows by ($\Rightarrow$ I1) and ($\Rightarrow$ I).

Exercise 3.3.1

1. $P \land Q \Rightarrow R \vdash P \Rightarrow (Q \Rightarrow R)$

			$P \Rightarrow (Q \Rightarrow R)$
(1)	$P \land Q \Rightarrow R$	data	
(2)	$P \Rightarrow (Q \Rightarrow R)$	subcomputation	

> | | | | $Q \Rightarrow R$ |
> |---|---|---|---|
> | (2.1) | P | assumption | |
> | (2.2) | $Q \Rightarrow R$ | subcomputation | |
>
> > | | | | R |
> > |---|---|---|---|
> > | (2.2.1) | Q | assumption | |
> > | (2.2.2) | $P \land Q$ | $(\land I)$ on (2.1),(2.2.1) | |
> > | (2.2.3) | R | $(\Rightarrow E)$ on (1),(2.2.2) | |

2. $(P \Rightarrow Q) \land (Q \Rightarrow R) \vdash P \Rightarrow R$

			$P \Rightarrow R$
(1)	$(P \Rightarrow Q) \land (Q \Rightarrow R)$	data	
(2)	$P \Rightarrow R$	subcomputation	

> | | | | R |
> |---|---|---|---|
> | (2.1) | P | assumption | |
> | (2.2) | $P \Rightarrow Q$ | $(\land E)$ on (1) | |
> | (2.3) | Q | $(\Rightarrow E)$ on (2.1),(2.2) | |
> | (2.4) | $Q \Rightarrow R$ | $(\land E)$ on (1) | |
> | (2.5) | R | $(\Rightarrow E)$ on (2.3),(2.4) | |

3. $P{\Rightarrow}R,\ Q{\Rightarrow}S \vdash P{\wedge}Q{\Rightarrow}R{\wedge}S$

$$\boxed{\begin{array}{lll}
\multicolumn{3}{r}{\underline{P{\wedge}Q{\Rightarrow}R{\wedge}S}} \\
(1) & P{\Rightarrow}R & \text{data} \\
(2) & Q{\Rightarrow}S & \text{data} \\
(3) & P{\wedge}Q{\Rightarrow}R{\wedge}S & \text{subcomputation} \\[4pt]
\multicolumn{3}{l}{\boxed{\begin{array}{lll}
\multicolumn{3}{r}{\underline{R{\wedge}S}} \\
(3.1) & P{\wedge}Q & \text{assumption} \\
(3.2) & P & ({\wedge}\text{E}) \text{ on } (3.1) \\
(3.3) & R & ({\Rightarrow}\text{E}) \text{ on } (1),(3.2) \\
(3.4) & Q & ({\wedge}\text{E}) \text{ on } (3.1) \\
(3.5) & S & ({\Rightarrow}\text{E}) \text{ on } (2),(3.4) \\
(3.6) & R{\wedge}S & ({\wedge}\text{I}) \text{ on } (3.3),(3.5)
\end{array}}}
\end{array}}$$

Exercise 3.3.2

1. $\neg(P{\wedge}\neg Q) \vdash P{\Rightarrow}Q$

$$\boxed{\begin{array}{lll}
\multicolumn{3}{r}{\underline{P{\Rightarrow}Q}} \\
(1) & \neg(P{\wedge}\neg Q) & \text{data} \\
(2) & P{\Rightarrow}Q & \text{subcomputation} \\[4pt]
\multicolumn{3}{l}{\boxed{\begin{array}{lll}
\multicolumn{3}{r}{\underline{Q}} \\
(2.1) & P & \text{assumption} \\
(2.2) & Q & \text{subcomputations} \\[4pt]
\multicolumn{3}{l}{\boxed{\begin{array}{lll}
\multicolumn{3}{r}{\underline{P{\wedge}\neg Q}} \\
(2.2.1.1) & \neg Q & \text{assumption} \\
(2.2.1.2) & P{\wedge}\neg Q & ({\wedge}\text{I}) \text{ on } (2.1),(2.2.1.1)
\end{array}}} \\[4pt]
\multicolumn{3}{l}{\boxed{\begin{array}{lll}
\multicolumn{3}{r}{\underline{\neg(P{\wedge}\neg Q)}} \\
(2.2.2.1) & \neg Q & \text{assumption} \\
(2.2.2.2) & \neg(P{\wedge}\neg Q) & \text{from } (1)
\end{array}}}
\end{array}}}
\end{array}}$$

2. $\vdash ((P \Rightarrow Q) \Rightarrow P) \Rightarrow P$

$$\underline{((P \Rightarrow Q) \Rightarrow P) \Rightarrow P}$$

(1) $((P \Rightarrow Q) \Rightarrow P) \Rightarrow P$ subcomputation

$$\underline{P}$$

(1.1) $(P \Rightarrow Q) \Rightarrow P$ assumption

(1.2) P subcomputations using the $(\neg 2)$ rule

$$\underline{P}$$

(1.2.1.1) $P \Rightarrow Q$ assumption

(1.2.1.2) P $(\Rightarrow E)$ on (1.1),(1.2.1.1)

$$\underline{P}$$

(1.2.2.1) $\neg(P \Rightarrow Q)$ assumption

(1.2.2.2) P subcomputation

$$\underline{P \Rightarrow Q}$$

(1.2.2.2.1.1) $\neg P$ assumption

(1.2.2.2.1.2) $P \Rightarrow Q$ subcomputation

$$\underline{Q}$$

(1.2.2.2.1.2.1) P assumption

(1.2.2.2.1.2.2) Q $(\neg 2)$ on (1.2.2.2.1.1) and (1.2.2.2.1.2.1)

$$\underline{\neg(P \Rightarrow Q)}$$

(1.2.2.2.2.1) $\neg P$ assumption

(1.2.2.2.2.2) $\neg(P \Rightarrow Q)$ from (1.2.2.1)

3. $\vdash \neg(P\Rightarrow Q)\Rightarrow P$

$$\frac{}{\neg(P\Rightarrow Q)\Rightarrow P}$$

(1) $\neg(P\Rightarrow Q)\Rightarrow P$ subcomputation

$$\frac{}{P}$$

(1.1) $\neg(P\Rightarrow Q)$ assumption
(1.2) P subcomputations

$$\frac{}{P\Rightarrow Q}$$

(1.2.1.1) $\neg P$ assumption
(1.2.1.2) $P\Rightarrow Q$ subcomputation

$$\frac{}{Q}$$

(1.2.1.2.1) P assumption
(1.2.1.2.2) Q subcomputations

$$\frac{}{P}$$

(1.2.1.2.2.2.1.1) $\neg Q$ assumption
(1.2.1.2.2.2.1.2) P from (1.2.1.2.1)

$$\frac{}{\neg P}$$

(1.2.1.2.2.2.2.1) $\neg Q$ assumption
(1.2.1.2.2.2.2.2) $\neg P$ from (1.2.1.1)

$$\frac{}{\neg(P\Rightarrow Q)}$$

(1.2.2.1) $\neg P$ assumption
(1.2.2.2) $\neg(P\Rightarrow Q)$ from (1.1)

Exercise 4.1.3

To show $(A\Rightarrow B), \neg B \vdash \neg A$ we show

$$\frac{A\Rightarrow B, \neg B}{A\Rightarrow x} \quad \text{and} \quad \frac{A\Rightarrow B, \neg B}{A\Rightarrow \neg x}$$

for $x = B$. Therefore, we must show

$$\frac{A\Rightarrow B, \neg B}{A\Rightarrow B} \quad \text{and} \quad \frac{A\Rightarrow B, \neg B}{A\Rightarrow \neg B}$$

both of which we can obviously do.

Exercise 4.1.14

1. After rewriting, the problem is reduced to $p \Rightarrow q, q \Rightarrow r, r \Rightarrow \bot \vdash p \Rightarrow \bot$.

    We rewrite the assumption as a set of wffs.

    By **H2**, this is reduced to $p \Rightarrow q, q \Rightarrow r, r \Rightarrow \bot, p \vdash \bot$.
    To show this it is sufficient to show $p \Rightarrow q, q \Rightarrow r, r \Rightarrow \bot, p \vdash r$
    and then apply $(\Rightarrow E)$.
    The same argument reduces our question to $p \Rightarrow q, q \Rightarrow r, r \Rightarrow \bot, p \vdash q$
    and then to $p \Rightarrow q, q \Rightarrow r, r \Rightarrow \bot, p \vdash p$
    which succeeds.

2. First we do rewriting: $(p \Rightarrow \bot) \Rightarrow \bot \vdash p$.
    It is sufficient to show $(p \Rightarrow \bot) \Rightarrow \bot \vdash p \Rightarrow \bot$,
    which reduces (by **H2**) to $(p \Rightarrow \bot) \Rightarrow \bot, p \vdash \bot$.
    Now we come into a loop,
    so we restart and ask for $(p \Rightarrow \bot) \Rightarrow \bot, p \vdash p$,
    which succeeds.

3. By rewriting this is reduced to $(p \Rightarrow \bot) \Rightarrow p \vdash p$.
    Now we can follow the argument of Example 4.1.9, with q replaced by $\bot$.

4. After rewriting we have $(p \Rightarrow \bot) \Rightarrow q, p \Rightarrow \bot \vdash q$.
    This comes by $(\Rightarrow E)$.
    But to get the result automatically,
    we ask for $(p \Rightarrow \bot) \Rightarrow q, p \Rightarrow \bot \vdash p \Rightarrow \bot$
    which reduces to $(p \Rightarrow \bot) \Rightarrow q, p \Rightarrow \bot, p \vdash \bot$.
    Now we ask for $(p \Rightarrow \bot) \Rightarrow q, p \Rightarrow \bot, p \vdash p$
    which succeeds.

5. First we rewrite: $q \wedge r \Rightarrow s, ((p \Rightarrow \bot) \Rightarrow r) \Rightarrow q, p \Rightarrow \bot \vdash r \Rightarrow s$.
    By **H2** this is reduced to $q \wedge r \Rightarrow s, ((p \Rightarrow \bot) \Rightarrow r) \Rightarrow q, p \Rightarrow \bot, r \vdash s$.
    Now we can ask for $q \wedge r \Rightarrow s, ((p \Rightarrow \bot) \Rightarrow r) \Rightarrow q, p \Rightarrow \bot, r \vdash q \wedge r$.
    By **H1** we reduce the problem to two questions:
    (a) $q \wedge r \Rightarrow s, ((p \Rightarrow \bot) \Rightarrow r) \Rightarrow q, p \Rightarrow \bot, r \vdash q$,
    (b) $q \wedge r \Rightarrow s, ((p \Rightarrow \bot) \Rightarrow r) \Rightarrow q, p \Rightarrow \bot, r \vdash r$.
    (b) is trivial.
    (a) can be obtained from
              $q \wedge r \Rightarrow s, ((p \Rightarrow \bot) \Rightarrow r) \Rightarrow q, p \Rightarrow \bot, r \vdash (p \Rightarrow \bot) \Rightarrow r$,
    which is reduced (by **H2**) to
              $q \wedge r \Rightarrow s, ((p \Rightarrow \bot) \Rightarrow r) \Rightarrow q, p \Rightarrow \bot, r, p \Rightarrow \bot \vdash r$,
    which succeeds.

6. First we rewrite by **H5**: $(p \Rightarrow \bot) \Rightarrow q, p \Rightarrow r, q \Rightarrow r \vdash r.$

Now we may try to get $(p \Rightarrow \bot) \Rightarrow q, p \Rightarrow r, q \Rightarrow r \vdash p,$

but then we are stuck,

so we ask for $(p \Rightarrow \bot) \Rightarrow q, p \Rightarrow r, q \Rightarrow r \vdash q,$

which follows from $(p \Rightarrow \bot) \Rightarrow q, p \Rightarrow r, q \Rightarrow r \vdash p \Rightarrow \bot.$

By **H2** this reduces to $(p \Rightarrow \bot) \Rightarrow q, p \Rightarrow r, q \Rightarrow r, p \vdash \bot.$

We fail again,

but now we can restart and ask for $(p \Rightarrow \bot) \Rightarrow q, p \Rightarrow r, q \Rightarrow r, p \vdash r.$

Then we come to $(p \Rightarrow \bot) \Rightarrow q, p \Rightarrow r, q \Rightarrow r, p \vdash p,$

which succeeds.

Exercise 4.2.12

1. $p \Rightarrow q, \neg q \vdash \neg p \quad \vdash$

    | rewrite

$p \Rightarrow q, q \Rightarrow \bot \vdash p \Rightarrow \bot \quad \vdash$

    | rule for $\Rightarrow$

$p \Rightarrow q, q \Rightarrow \bot, p \vdash \bot \quad \vdash$

    | rule for atoms
    | using $q \Rightarrow \bot$

$p \Rightarrow q, q \Rightarrow \bot, p \vdash q \quad \vdash$

    | rule for atoms
    | using $p \Rightarrow q$

$p \Rightarrow q, q \Rightarrow \bot, p \vdash p \quad \vdash$

    success

2. $\neg p \Rightarrow q \vdash p \vee q \quad \vdash$

    | rewrite

$(p \Rightarrow \bot) \Rightarrow q \vdash (p \Rightarrow \bot) \Rightarrow q$
$\vdash$

    | rule for $\Rightarrow$

$(p \Rightarrow \bot) \Rightarrow q, p \Rightarrow \bot \vdash q$
$\vdash$

    | rule for atoms using
    | $(p \Rightarrow \bot) \Rightarrow q$

$(p \Rightarrow \bot) \Rightarrow q, p \Rightarrow \bot \vdash p \Rightarrow \bot$
$\vdash$

    | rule for $\Rightarrow$

$(p \Rightarrow \bot) \Rightarrow q, p \Rightarrow \bot, p \vdash \bot$
$\vdash$

    | rule for atoms using $p \Rightarrow \bot$

$(p \Rightarrow \bot) \Rightarrow q, p \Rightarrow \bot, p \vdash p$
$\vdash$

    success

3. $\vdash ((a \Rightarrow b) \Rightarrow a) \Rightarrow a \;\; \vdash$

   rule for $\Rightarrow$

$(a \Rightarrow b) \Rightarrow a \vdash a \;\; \vdash$ $(a \Rightarrow b) \Rightarrow a, a \vdash b \;\; \vdash$

   rule for atoms   restart

$(a \Rightarrow b) \Rightarrow a \vdash a \Rightarrow b \;\; \vdash$ $(a \Rightarrow b) \Rightarrow a, a \vdash a \;\; \vdash$

   rule for $\Rightarrow$

                                                 success

Remark: It is more convenient to use restart not with the original goal, but with the second goal (a).

4. $(p \Rightarrow q) \Rightarrow q, q \Rightarrow p \vdash p \;\; \vdash$ 5. $\vdash \neg(p \wedge \neg p) \;\; \vdash$

   rule for atoms using $q \Rightarrow p$ rewrite

$(p \Rightarrow q) \Rightarrow q, q \Rightarrow p \vdash q \;\; \vdash$ $\vdash p \wedge (p \Rightarrow \bot) \Rightarrow \bot \;\; \vdash$

   rule for atoms using $(p \Rightarrow q) \Rightarrow q$ rule for $\Rightarrow$

$(p \Rightarrow q) \Rightarrow q, q \Rightarrow p \vdash p \Rightarrow q \;\; \vdash$ $p \wedge (p \rightarrow \bot) \vdash \bot \;\; \vdash$

   rule for $\Rightarrow$ rewrite

$(p \Rightarrow q) \Rightarrow q, q \Rightarrow p, p \vdash q \;\; \vdash$ $p, p \Rightarrow \bot \vdash \bot \;\; \vdash$

   restart   rule for atoms

$(p \Rightarrow q) \Rightarrow q, q \Rightarrow p, p \vdash p \;\; \vdash$ $p, p \Rightarrow \bot \vdash p \;\; \vdash$

   success   success

Remark: We have used restart, because the original goal appeared as an assumption.

6.　$\vdash \neg(p \Rightarrow q) \Rightarrow p\ \vdash$

　　| rewrite

　$\vdash ((p \Rightarrow q) \Rightarrow \bot) \Rightarrow p\ \vdash$

　　　| rule for $\Rightarrow$

　$(p \Rightarrow q) \Rightarrow \bot \vdash p\ \vdash$

　　　| rule for atoms

　$(p \Rightarrow q) \Rightarrow \bot \vdash p \Rightarrow q\ \vdash$

　　　| rule for $\Rightarrow$

　$(p \Rightarrow q) \Rightarrow \bot, p \vdash q\ \vdash$

　　　| restart

　$(p \Rightarrow q) \Rightarrow \bot, p \vdash p\ \vdash$

　　　|

　　success

7.　$\vdash \neg(p \Rightarrow q) \Rightarrow \neg q\ \vdash$

　　| rewrite

　$\vdash ((p \Rightarrow q) \Rightarrow \bot) \Rightarrow (q \Rightarrow \bot)\ \vdash$

　　　| rule for $\Rightarrow$

　$(p \Rightarrow q) \Rightarrow \bot \vdash q \Rightarrow \bot\ \vdash$

　　　| rule for $\Rightarrow$

　$(p \Rightarrow q) \Rightarrow \bot, q \vdash \bot\ \vdash$

　　　| rule for atoms

　$(p \Rightarrow q) \Rightarrow \bot, q \vdash p \Rightarrow q\ \vdash$

　　　| rule for $\Rightarrow$

　$(p \Rightarrow q) \Rightarrow \bot, q, p \vdash q\ \vdash$

　　　|

　　success

8.　$\vdash b \vee (b \Rightarrow c)\ \vdash$

　　| rewrite

　$\vdash (b \Rightarrow \bot) \Rightarrow (b \Rightarrow c)\ \vdash$

　　　| rule for $\Rightarrow$

　$b \Rightarrow \bot \vdash b \Rightarrow c\ \vdash$

　　　| rule for $\Rightarrow$

　$b \Rightarrow \bot, b \vdash c\ \vdash$

　　　| rule for atoms

　$b \Rightarrow \bot, b \vdash b\ \vdash$

　　　|

　　success

9.　$\vdash (p \Rightarrow \neg p) \Rightarrow \neg p\ \vdash$

　　| rewrite

　$\vdash (p \Rightarrow (p \Rightarrow \bot)) \Rightarrow (p \Rightarrow \bot)\ \vdash$

　　　| rule for $\Rightarrow$

　$p \Rightarrow (p \Rightarrow \bot) \vdash p \Rightarrow \bot\ \vdash$

　　　| rule for $\Rightarrow$

　$p \Rightarrow (p \Rightarrow \bot), p \vdash \bot\ \vdash$

　　　| rewrite

　$p \wedge p \Rightarrow \bot, p \vdash \bot\ \vdash$

　　　| rule for atoms

　$p \wedge p \Rightarrow \bot, p \vdash p \wedge p\ \vdash$

　　　| rule for $\wedge$

　$p \wedge p \Rightarrow \bot, p \vdash p\ \vdash$

　　　|

　　success

10.　$\vdash (\neg p \Rightarrow p) \Rightarrow p\ \vdash$

$$\Big|\ \text{rewrite}$$

$$\vdash ((p \Rightarrow \bot) \Rightarrow p) \Rightarrow p \quad \vdash$$

$$\Big|\ \text{rule for} \Rightarrow$$

$$(p \Rightarrow \bot) \Rightarrow p \vdash p \quad \vdash$$

$$\Big|\ \text{rule for atoms}$$

$$(p \Rightarrow \bot) \Rightarrow p \vdash p \Rightarrow \bot \quad \vdash$$

$$\Big|\ \text{rule for} \Rightarrow$$

$$(p \Rightarrow \bot) \Rightarrow p, p \vdash \bot \quad \vdash$$

$$\Big|\ \text{restart}$$

$$(p \Rightarrow \bot) \Rightarrow p, p \vdash p \quad \vdash$$

$$\Big|$$

$$\text{success}$$

11.

$$\vdash p \wedge q \Rightarrow \neg(\neg p \vee \neg q)$$

rewrite

$$\vdash p \wedge q \Rightarrow ((((p \Rightarrow \bot) \Rightarrow \bot) \Rightarrow (q \Rightarrow \bot)) \Rightarrow \bot)$$

rule for $\Rightarrow$

$$p \wedge q \vdash (((p \Rightarrow \bot) \Rightarrow \bot) \Rightarrow (q \Rightarrow \bot)) \Rightarrow \bot$$

rewrite

$$p, q \vdash (((p \Rightarrow \bot) \Rightarrow \bot) \Rightarrow (q \Rightarrow \bot)) \Rightarrow \bot$$

rule for $\Rightarrow$

$$p, q, ((p \Rightarrow \bot) \Rightarrow \bot) \Rightarrow (q \Rightarrow \bot) \vdash \bot$$

rewrite

$$p, q, ((p \Rightarrow \bot) \Rightarrow \bot) \wedge q \Rightarrow \bot \vdash \bot$$

rule for atoms

$$p, q, ((p \Rightarrow \bot) \Rightarrow \bot) \wedge q \Rightarrow \bot \vdash ((p \Rightarrow \bot) \Rightarrow \bot) \wedge q$$

rule for $\wedge$

$$p, q, ((p \Rightarrow \bot) \Rightarrow \bot) \wedge q \Rightarrow \bot \vdash (p \Rightarrow \bot) \Rightarrow \bot$$

rule for $\Rightarrow$

$$p, q, ((p \Rightarrow \bot) \Rightarrow \bot) \wedge q \Rightarrow \bot, p \Rightarrow \bot \vdash \bot$$

rule for atoms using $p \Rightarrow \bot$

$$p, q, ((p \Rightarrow \bot) \Rightarrow \bot) \wedge q \Rightarrow \bot \vdash p$$

success

$$p, q, ((p \Rightarrow \bot) \Rightarrow \bot) \wedge q \Rightarrow \bot \vdash q$$

success

12. $\vdash a \Rightarrow (\neg b \Rightarrow \neg(a \Rightarrow b)) \;\; \vdash$

     | rewrite

$\vdash a \Rightarrow ((b \Rightarrow \bot) \Rightarrow \;\; \vdash$
$((a \Rightarrow b) \Rightarrow \bot))$

     | rule for $\Rightarrow$

$a \vdash (b \Rightarrow \bot) \Rightarrow ((a \Rightarrow b) \Rightarrow \bot) \;\; \vdash$

     | rule for $\Rightarrow$

$a, b \Rightarrow \bot \vdash (a \Rightarrow b) \Rightarrow \bot \;\; \vdash$

     | rule for $\Rightarrow$

$a, b \Rightarrow \bot, a \Rightarrow b \vdash \bot \;\; \vdash$

     | rule for atoms
     | using $b \Rightarrow \bot$

$a, b \Rightarrow \bot, a \Rightarrow b \vdash b \;\; \vdash$

     | rule for atoms
     | using $a \Rightarrow b$

$a, b \Rightarrow \bot, a \Rightarrow b \vdash a \;\; \vdash$

     |

    success

13. $\vdash \neg p \Rightarrow ((p \vee q) \Rightarrow q) \;\; \vdash$

     | rewrite

$\vdash (p \Rightarrow \bot) \Rightarrow \;\;\;\;\;\; \vdash$
$(((p \Rightarrow \bot) \Rightarrow q) \Rightarrow q)$

     | rule for $\Rightarrow$

$p \Rightarrow \bot \vdash ((p \Rightarrow \bot) \Rightarrow q) \Rightarrow q \;\; \vdash$

     | rule for $\Rightarrow$

$p \Rightarrow \bot, (p \Rightarrow \bot) \Rightarrow q \vdash q \;\; \vdash$

     | rule for atoms
     | using $(p \Rightarrow \bot) \Rightarrow q$

$p \Rightarrow \bot, (p \Rightarrow \bot) \Rightarrow q \vdash p \Rightarrow \bot \;\; \vdash$

     | rule for $\Rightarrow$

$p \Rightarrow \bot, (p \Rightarrow \bot) \Rightarrow q, p \vdash \bot \;\; \vdash$

     | rule for atoms
     | using $p \Rightarrow \bot$

$p \Rightarrow \bot, (p \Rightarrow \bot) \Rightarrow q, p \vdash p \;\; \vdash$

     |

    success

14. $a \Leftrightarrow ((a \wedge b) \vee (\neg a \wedge \neg b)) \vdash b \;\; \vdash$

     | rewrite

$(a \Rightarrow (a \wedge b) \vee (\neg a \wedge \neg b)) \wedge ((a \wedge b) \vee (\neg a \wedge \neg b) \Rightarrow a) \vdash b \;\; \vdash$

     | rewrite

$a \Rightarrow (a \wedge b) \vee ((a \Rightarrow \bot) \wedge (b \Rightarrow \bot)), \;\; \vdash \vdash b$
$((a \wedge b) \vee ((a \Rightarrow \bot) \wedge (b \Rightarrow \bot)) \Rightarrow a)$

     | rewrite

$a \Rightarrow ((a \wedge b \Rightarrow \bot) \Rightarrow (a \Rightarrow \bot) \wedge (b \Rightarrow \bot)) \;\; \vdash \vdash b$
$(((a \wedge b) \Rightarrow \bot) \Rightarrow (a \Rightarrow \bot) \wedge (b \Rightarrow \bot)) \Rightarrow a$

     | rewrite

$a \wedge (a \wedge b \Rightarrow \bot) \Rightarrow (a \Rightarrow \bot)$

$a \wedge (a \wedge b \Rightarrow \bot) \Rightarrow (b \Rightarrow \bot)$ $\vdash \vdash b$

$((a \wedge b \Rightarrow \bot) \Rightarrow (a \Rightarrow \bot)) \wedge ((a \wedge b \Rightarrow \bot) \Rightarrow (b \Rightarrow \bot)) \Rightarrow a$

$\Big|$ rewrite

$a \wedge (a \wedge b \Rightarrow \bot) \wedge a \Rightarrow \bot$

$a \wedge (a \wedge b \Rightarrow \bot) \wedge b \Rightarrow \bot$ $\vdash \vdash b$

$((a \wedge b \Rightarrow \bot) \wedge a \Rightarrow \bot) \wedge ((a \wedge b \Rightarrow \bot) \wedge b \Rightarrow \bot) \Rightarrow a$

$\Big|$ rule for atoms using $a \wedge (a \wedge b \Rightarrow \bot) \wedge a \Rightarrow \bot$

$a \wedge (a \wedge b \Rightarrow \bot) \wedge a \Rightarrow \bot$

$a \wedge (a \wedge b \Rightarrow \bot) \wedge b \Rightarrow \bot$ $\vdash a \wedge (a \wedge b \Rightarrow \bot) \wedge a$

$((a \wedge b \Rightarrow \bot) \wedge a \Rightarrow \bot) \wedge ((a \wedge b \Rightarrow \bot) \wedge b \Rightarrow \bot) \Rightarrow a$

$\Big|$ rule for $\wedge$

$\vdash$

Branch I   Branch II

   $\mathcal{P} \vdash a$ $\mathcal{P} \vdash a \wedge b \Rightarrow \bot$

($\mathcal{P}$ denotes the set of assumptions in the previous step.)

Now we consider each branch separately.

(I)

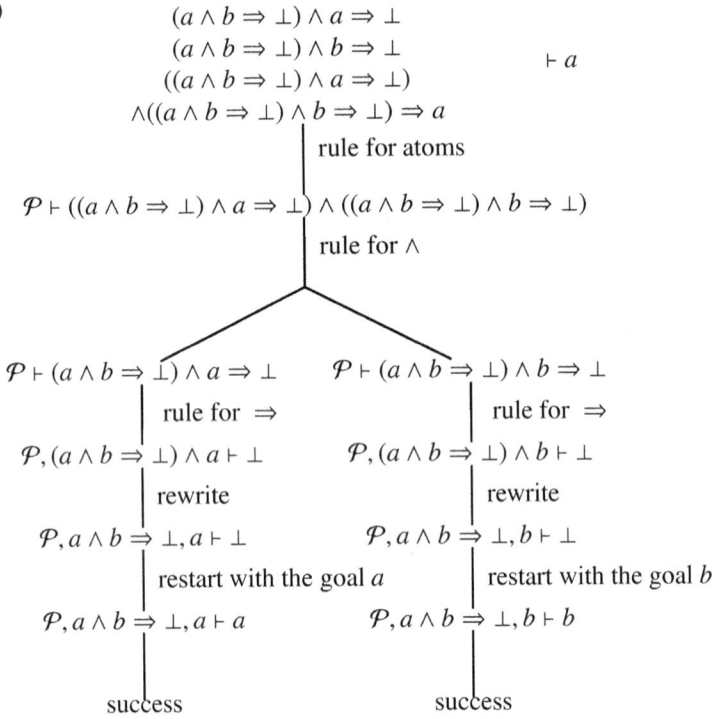

$$(a \wedge b \Rightarrow \bot) \wedge a \Rightarrow \bot$$
$$(a \wedge b \Rightarrow \bot) \wedge b \Rightarrow \bot \qquad \vdash a$$
$$((a \wedge b \Rightarrow \bot) \wedge a \Rightarrow \bot)$$
$$\wedge((a \wedge b \Rightarrow \bot) \wedge b \Rightarrow \bot) \Rightarrow a$$

rule for atoms

$$\mathcal{P} \vdash ((a \wedge b \Rightarrow \bot) \wedge a \Rightarrow \bot) \wedge ((a \wedge b \Rightarrow \bot) \wedge b \Rightarrow \bot)$$

rule for ∧

$$\mathcal{P} \vdash (a \wedge b \Rightarrow \bot) \wedge a \Rightarrow \bot \qquad\qquad \mathcal{P} \vdash (a \wedge b \Rightarrow \bot) \wedge b \Rightarrow \bot$$

rule for ⇒   rule for ⇒

$$\mathcal{P}, (a \wedge b \Rightarrow \bot) \wedge a \vdash \bot \qquad\qquad \mathcal{P}, (a \wedge b \Rightarrow \bot) \wedge b \vdash \bot$$

rewrite   rewrite

$$\mathcal{P}, a \wedge b \Rightarrow \bot, a \vdash \bot \qquad\qquad \mathcal{P}, a \wedge b \Rightarrow \bot, b \vdash \bot$$

restart with the goal a restart with the goal b

$$\mathcal{P}, a \wedge b \Rightarrow \bot, a \vdash a \qquad\qquad \mathcal{P}, a \wedge b \Rightarrow \bot, b \vdash b$$

success   success

(II) $\mathcal{P} \vdash a \wedge b \Rightarrow \bot \;\; \vdash$

     | rule for $\Rightarrow$

$\mathcal{P}, a \wedge b \vdash \bot \;\; \vdash$

     | rewrite

$\mathcal{P}, a, b \vdash \bot \;\; \vdash$

     | restart

$\mathcal{P}, a, b \vdash b \;\; \vdash$

     |

    success

Exercise 4.3.8

By induction over the length of computation procedure (cf. the proof of Theorem 6.5.1 below). If x is atomic or $x = \bot$ and $\langle \mathcal{P}, H, x \rangle$ succeeds immediately with restart, then $(1, a) \in \mathcal{P}$ for some $a \in H$. In this case a is a conjunct in $\bigwedge \mathcal{P}$ and a disjunct in $\bigvee H$.

Thus $\bigwedge \mathcal{P} = \top$ only if $a = \top$, only if $\bigvee H = \top$, and so $\bigwedge \mathcal{P} \Rightarrow x \vee \bigvee H$ is always true.

- If y is atomic or $y = \bot$ and $\langle \mathcal{P}, H, y \rangle$ succeeds with restart, then $\bigwedge \mathcal{P}$ contains the following conjunct A_i:

$$\left(\bigwedge_j (B_j \Rightarrow x_j) \right) \Rightarrow x, \text{ with } x = y \text{ or } x = \bot$$

and every $\langle \mathcal{P}'_j, H + y, x_j \rangle$ succeeds with restart (Definition 4.3.3). $\bigwedge \mathcal{P} \equiv A_i \wedge Q$ for some formula Q (Q is the conjunction of all the other available formulae in $\mathcal{P}$; we take $Q = \top$ if A_i is the only one available). From the definition it follows that

$$\bigwedge \mathcal{P}'_j \equiv Q \wedge B_j$$

and thus each formula

$$Q \wedge B_j \Rightarrow x_j \vee \bigvee H \vee y$$

is a tautology.

We have to show that

$$\bigwedge \mathcal{P} \Rightarrow y \vee \bigvee H$$

is a tautology. So we choose arbitrary truth assignment, and assume that $\bigwedge \mathcal{P}$ is $\top$. We will prove that $y \vee \bigvee H$ is $\top$. For this, we assume the contrary and come to a contradiction.

(a) $x = y$. Recall that

$$\bigwedge \mathcal{P} \equiv \left[\left(\bigwedge_j (B_j \Rightarrow x_j) \right) \Rightarrow x \right] \wedge Q$$

by our assumptions,

(a1) $(\bigwedge_j (B_j \Rightarrow x_j)) \Rightarrow y$ is $\top$, and also Q is $\top$, y, $\bigvee H$ are $\perp$.

On the other hand, $Q \wedge B_j \Rightarrow x_j \vee \bigvee H \vee y$ is a tautology, and thus under our assignment we get that $B_j \Rightarrow x_j$ is $\top$.

This holds for each j, so $\bigwedge_j (B_j \Rightarrow x_j)$ is $\top$, and then $y = \top$ by (a1), which gives a contradiction.

(b) $x = \perp$. The argument can be the same as in (a), because if $\bigwedge \mathcal{P}$ is $\top$ and $\bigwedge \mathcal{P}$ contains the conjunct $(\bigwedge_j (B_j \Rightarrow x_j)) \Rightarrow \perp$, then (a1) holds as well.

- If $\langle \mathcal{P}, H, A \Rightarrow y \rangle$ succeeds with restart, then by Definition 4.3.3, $\langle \mathcal{P}+A, H, y \rangle$ succeeds with restart. Thus we already know that $\bigwedge (\mathcal{P} + A) \Rightarrow y \vee \bigvee H$ is a tautology, and it follows from the definition that $\bigwedge (\mathcal{P} + A) \equiv (\bigwedge \mathcal{P}) \wedge A$.

   Now assume that $\bigwedge \mathcal{P}$ is true. Hence we know that $A \Rightarrow y \vee \bigvee H$ is true, and the latter is equivalent to $(A \Rightarrow y) \vee \bigvee H$. $((A \Rightarrow B \vee C) \equiv (A \Rightarrow B) \vee C$ can be checked by truth tables or by equivalences from 1.2.1.) Therefore $\bigwedge \mathcal{P} \Rightarrow (A \Rightarrow y) \vee \bigvee H$ is a tautology.

- If $\langle \mathcal{P}, H, A_1 \wedge A_2 \rangle$ succeeds with restart, then by Definition 4.3.3, $\langle \mathcal{P}, H, A_1 \rangle$, $\langle \mathcal{P}, H, A_2 \rangle$ also do, and we have $\bigwedge \mathcal{P} \Rightarrow A_1 \vee \bigvee H$ and $\bigwedge \mathcal{P} \Rightarrow A_2 \vee \bigvee H$ as tautologies. Assume that $\bigwedge \mathcal{P}$ is true; then $A_1 \vee \bigvee H$, $A_2 \vee \bigvee H$ are true, i.e. $(A_1 \vee \bigvee H) \wedge (A_2 \vee \bigvee H)$ is true. By equivalences from 1.2.1 it follows that $(A_1 \wedge A_2) \vee \bigvee H$ is true.

   Therefore $\bigwedge \mathcal{P} \Rightarrow (A_1 \wedge A_2) \vee \bigvee H$ is a tautology.

Exercise 5.2.2

1.

The proof is in linear logic.

2.

The proof is in relevance logic. It does not fit for linear logic, because if labels are multisets we obtain (1.2.3) $\{a_1, a_2, a_2\} : B$ in the innermost box, which provides only (1.2) $\{a_1, a_2\} : A \Rightarrow B$ in the next box, and then (1) $\{a_2\}$: $(A \Rightarrow (A \Rightarrow B)) \Rightarrow (A \Rightarrow B)$ in the outermost box. This happens because the assumption (1.2.1) is used twice in this proof.

3.

(1) $\varnothing : (C \Rightarrow A) \Rightarrow ((B \Rightarrow C) \Rightarrow (B \Rightarrow A))$ subcomputation

$\{a_1\} : (B \Rightarrow C) \Rightarrow (B \Rightarrow A)$

(1.1) $\{a_1\} : C \Rightarrow A$ assumption
(1.2) $\{a_1\} : (B \Rightarrow C) \Rightarrow (B \Rightarrow A)$ subcomputation

$\{a_1, a_2\} : B \Rightarrow A$

(1.2.1) $\{a_2\} : B \Rightarrow C$ assumption
(1.2.2) $\{a_1, a_2\} : B \Rightarrow A$ subcomputation

$\{a_1, a_2, a_3\} : A$

(1.2.2.1) $\{a_3\} : B$ assumption
(1.2.2.2) $\{a_1, a_3\} : C$ by (1.2.2.1), (1.2.1)
(1.2.2.3) $\{a_1, a_2, a_3\} : A$ by (1.2.2.2), (1.1)

The proof is in linear logic.

4. Similarly to 3 the proof is in linear logic.

(1) $\varnothing : (C \Rightarrow A) \Rightarrow ((A \Rightarrow B) \Rightarrow (C \Rightarrow B))$ subcomputation

$\{a_1\} : (A \Rightarrow B) \Rightarrow (C \Rightarrow B)$

(1.1) $\{a_1\} : C \Rightarrow A$ assumption
(1.2) $\{a_1\} : (A \Rightarrow B) \Rightarrow (C \Rightarrow B)$ subcomputation

$\{a_1, a_2\} : C \Rightarrow B$

(1.2.1) $\{a_2\} : A \Rightarrow B$ assumption
(1.2.2) $\{a_1, a_2\} : C \Rightarrow B$ subcomputation

$\{a_1, a_2, a_3\} : B$

(1.2.2.1) $\{a_3\} : C$ assumption
(1.2.2.2) $\{a_1, a_3\} : A$ by (1.2.2.1), (1.1)
(1.2.2.3) $\{a_1, a_2, a_3\} : B$ by (1.2.2.2), (1.2.1)

5.

(1)	$\varnothing : (A \Rightarrow (B \Rightarrow C)) \Rightarrow ((A \Rightarrow B) \Rightarrow (A \Rightarrow C))$	subcomputation

$\{a_1\} : (A \Rightarrow B) \Rightarrow (A \Rightarrow C)$

| (1.1) | $\{a_1\} : A \Rightarrow (B \Rightarrow C)$ | assumption |
| (1.2) | $\{a_1\} : (A \Rightarrow B) \Rightarrow (A \Rightarrow C)$ | subcomputation |

$\{a_1, a_2\} : A \Rightarrow C$

| (1.2.1) | $\{a_2\} : A \Rightarrow B$ | assumption |
| (1.2.2) | $\{a_1, a_2\} : A \Rightarrow C$ | subcomputation |

$\{a_1, a_2, a_3\} : C$

(1.2.2.1)	$\{a_3\} : A$	assumption
(1.2.2.2)	$\{a_1, a_3\} : B \Rightarrow C$	by (1.1), (1.2.2.1)
(1.2.2.3)	$\{a_2, a_3\} : B$	by (1.2.1), (1.2.2.1)
(1.2.2.4)	$\{a_1, a_2, a_3\} : C$	by (1.2.2.2), (1.2.2.3)

The proof is in relevance logic. It does not fit for linear logic, because the assumption (1.2.2.1) is used twice (cf. the solution to item 2).

6.

(1)	$A \Rightarrow (B \Rightarrow A)$	subcomputation

$B \Rightarrow A$

| (1.1) | A | assumption |
| (1.2) | $B \Rightarrow A$ | subcomputation |

A

| (1.2.1) | B | assumption |
| (1.2.2) | A | by (1.1) |

The proof is in intuitionistic logic. It cannot be transferred to relevance logic by introducing labels because the label for B in (1.2.1) does not disappear in the outermost box.

7.

(1)	$\varnothing : ((A \Rightarrow A) \Rightarrow A) \Rightarrow A$	subcomputation

$\{a_1\} : A$

(1.1)	$\{a_1\} : (A \Rightarrow A) \Rightarrow A$	assumption
(1.2)	$\varnothing : A \Rightarrow A$	subcomputation

$\{a_2\} : A$

(1.2.1)	$\{a_2\} : A$	assumption
(1.2.2)	$\{a_2\} : A$	by (1.2.1)

(1.3)	$\{a_1\} : A$	by (1.1), (1.2)

This proof is *not* in relevance logic, because (1.2) is proved as a 'lemma' with label $\varnothing$. Relevance logic does not allow for such labelling: you should not forget assumptions while making a proof, so $A \Rightarrow A$ should be proved with a label $\{a_1\}$, which is impossible.

Of course, by deleting all labels we get an intuitionistic proof.

Exercise

1. ('Only if') Assume that $\neg\neg A$ is not in an intuitionistic tautology, and show that A is not a classical tautology. The assumption means that there exists a Kripke model $(T, \leq, h)$, such that $h(t, \neg\neg A) = 0$ for some $t \in T$.

Hence (by Definition 2.2.3)

$$h(r, \neg A) = 1 \text{ for some } r \geq t \qquad (1.1)$$

Let $p_1, \ldots, p_n$ be all atoms occurring in A. We construct the sequence $r_0 = r \leq r_1 \leq \cdots \leq r_n$ as follows.

Consider the atom p_1 at r_0. There are two options:

- $h(r_0, \neg p_1) = 1$. Then we put $r_1 = r_0$.
- $h(r_0, \neg p_1) = 0$. Then there exists $r_1 \geq r_0$ such that $h(r_1, p_1) = 1$.

Thus we have found $r_1 \geq r_0$ such that $h(r_1, p_1) = 1$ or $h(r_1, \neg p_1) = 1$, i.e. the truth value of p_1 does not change after r_1.

Similarly, if $r_1, \ldots, r_i$ are already constructed, $i < n$, we construct $r_{i+1} \geq r_i$ such that $h(r_{i+1}, p_{i+1}) = 1$ or $h(r_{i+1}, \neg p_{i+1}) = 1$.

Eventually, we reach $r_n \geq r_0$ such that

$$\text{for every } s \geq r_n, \text{ for any } i \leq n, h(s, p_i) = h(r_n, p_i) \qquad (1.2)$$

That is because the truth value of p_i becomes constant after we reach r_i.

Now we make a classical (two-valued) assignment k for atoms $p_1, \ldots, p_n$:

$$k(p_i) = h(r_n, p_i)$$

We claim that for any B built from atoms $p_1, \ldots, p_n$, for any $s \geq r_n$,

$$k(B) = h(s, B) \tag{1.3}$$

This is proved by induction on the length of B.

- If B is an atom, this is by (1.2) and the choice of k.
- If $B = C \wedge D$, then
  $k(B) = 1$ iff $k(C) = k(D) = 1$
  iff $(h(s,C) = 1$ and $h(s,D) = 1)$
  (by the inductive hypothesis)
  iff $h(s, C \wedge D) = 1$ (by Definition 2.2.3).
  The case $B = C \vee D$ is considered similarly.
- If $B = C \Rightarrow D$, then
  $k(B) = 1$ iff $k(C) = 0$ or $k(D) = 1$
  iff $(h(s,C) = 0$ or $h(s,D) = 1)$
  (by the inductive hypothesis).

Now $h(s, C \Rightarrow D) = 1$ implies $h(s,C) = 0$ or $h(s,D) = 1$ by Definition 2.2.3. The other way round, if $h(s,C) = 0$ or $h(s,D) = 1$ then also $h(s',C) = 0$ or $h(s',D) = 1$ for any $s' \geq s$ (by the inductive hypothesis), and thus $h(s, C \Rightarrow D) = 1$ by Definition 2.2.3.

Hence $k(B) = 1$ iff $h(s, B) = 1$ in this case too.

- If $B = \bot$, (1.3) is obvious.
- If $B = \neg C$, we can rewrite it as $(C \Rightarrow \bot)$ and use the argument for implication.

From (1.3) we obtain that

$$h(r_n, \neg A) = k(\neg A)$$

but $h(r_n, \neg A) = h(r, \neg A) = 1$ by persistence (Exercise 2.2.4) and (1.1). Therefore $k(\neg A) = 1$ and so $k(A) = 0$.

Thus A is not a classical tautology.

('If') We will show first that every intuitionistic tautology is a classical tautology. So let B be an intuitionistic tautology, and consider an arbitrary classical assignment k. We have to prove that $k(B) = 1$. For this, we take a Kripke model $(T, \leq, h)$ in which $T = \{t_0\}$ is one element and $h(x) = k(x)$ for any atom x.

We claim that

$$h(t_0, C) = k(C) \text{ for any formula } C \qquad (1.4)$$

This is checked easily by induction on C. The base follows from the definition of h, and let us consider the case $C = D \Rightarrow E$.

$h(t_0, C) = 1$ iff for any $t \geq t_0$ $(h(t, D) = 0$ or $h(t, E) = 1)$
iff $(h(t_0, D) = 0$ or $h(t_0, E) = 1)$
(since $T = \{t_0\}$)
iff $(k(D) = 0$ or $k(E) = 1)$
(by the inductive hypothesis)
iff $k(C) = 1$.

The cases of $\wedge, \vee$ are even simpler. Now from $\vDash_I B$ and (1.4) we obtain that $k(B) = 1$.

Returning to the original question, we observe that if $\neg\neg A$ is an intuitionistic tautology then $\neg\neg A$ is a classical tautology. But $\neg\neg A \equiv A$ in classical logic, and therefore A is also a tautology.

2. Assume that $A \equiv B$ classically. Then both $A \Rightarrow B, B \Rightarrow A$ are classical tautologies. By the previous item,

$$\vDash_I \neg\neg(A \Rightarrow B), \neg\neg(B \Rightarrow A)$$

Let us consider an arbitrary Kripke model $(T, \leq, h)$, and show that for any $t \in T$

$$h(t, \neg\neg A) = 1 \text{ iff } h(t, \neg\neg B) = 1$$

We show 'only if', and then 'if' follows by symmetry.

So, by assumptions, we have

$$h(t, \neg\neg A) = h(t, \neg\neg(A \Rightarrow B)) = 1 \qquad (2.1)$$

and we are going to prove that $h(t, \neg\neg B) = 1$, i.e. that for any $s \geq t$

$$H(s, \neg B) = 0 \qquad (2.2)$$

Take an arbitrary $s \geq t$. By (2.1), $h(s, \neg(A \Rightarrow B)) = 0$. Then for some $r \geq s$

$$h(r, A \Rightarrow B) = 1 \qquad (2.3)$$

Since $h(t, \neg\neg A) = 1$ by (2.1) and $r \geq t$ by transitivity, it follows that $h(r, \neg A) = 0$ and thus there exists $u \geq r$ such that

$$h(u, A) = 1 \qquad (2.4)$$

Since $u \geq r$ by transitivity, (2.3) and (2.4) yield

$$h(u, B) = 1$$

This proves (2.2) because $u \geq s$.

Exercise 7.3

1. We show $A \Rightarrow A$ is generated.

   (a) $(A \Rightarrow (B \Rightarrow C)) \Rightarrow ((A \Rightarrow B) \Rightarrow (A \Rightarrow C))$, axiom.

   (b) $(A \Rightarrow (B \Rightarrow A)) \Rightarrow ((A \Rightarrow B) \Rightarrow (A \Rightarrow A))$, from (a), substituting A for C.

   (c) $A \Rightarrow (B \Rightarrow A)$, axiom.

   (d) $(A \Rightarrow B) \Rightarrow (A \Rightarrow A)$, from (c) and (b), using *modus ponens*.

   (e) $(A \Rightarrow (D \Rightarrow A)) \Rightarrow (A \Rightarrow A)$, from (d), substituting $D \Rightarrow A$ for B.

   (f) $A \Rightarrow (D \Rightarrow A)$, axiom.

   (g) $A \Rightarrow A$, from (f) and (e), using *modus ponens*.

2. First let us prove that everything derivable from the intuitionistic axioms is an intuitionistic tautology.

   - $A \Rightarrow (B \Rightarrow A)$ is a tautology (Example 2.4.2.1(a)).
   - To show that $(A \Rightarrow (B \Rightarrow C)) \Rightarrow ((A \Rightarrow B) \Rightarrow (A \Rightarrow C))$ is a tautology, consider a Kripke model $(T, \leq, h)$. Let $t \in T$; we have to verify that $h(t, (A \Rightarrow (B \Rightarrow C)) \Rightarrow ((A \Rightarrow B) \Rightarrow (A \Rightarrow C))) = 1$, i.e. that for any $b \geq t$, $h(s, A \Rightarrow (B \Rightarrow C)) = 1$ only if $h(s, (A \Rightarrow B) \Rightarrow (A \Rightarrow C)) = 1$.

   So assume that

   (2.1) $h(s, A \Rightarrow (B \Rightarrow C)) = 1$
   and show that

   (2.2) $h(s, (A \Rightarrow B) \Rightarrow (A \Rightarrow C)) = 1$.
   To prove (2.2) we take any $r \geq s$, assume that

   (2.3) $h(r, A \Rightarrow B) = 1$
   and show that

(2.4) $h(r, A \Rightarrow C) = 1$.
Further on, we take any $u \geq r$, assume

(2.5) $h(u, A) = 1$
and show that

(2.6) $h(u, C) = 1$.
In fact, we have that $u \geq r \geq s$, so from (2.5) and (2.1) we get

(2.7) $h(u, B \Rightarrow C) = 1$,
and from (2.5) and (2.3) we get

(2.8) $h(u, B) = 1$.
(2.8) and (2.7) yield (2.6).

Thus (2.5) implies (2.6) under assumptions (2.1), (2.3), and therefore (2.1) implies (2.2)

- *Modus ponens* derives tautologies from tautologies, because in any Kripke model, if $h(t, A) = -1$ and $h(t, A \Rightarrow B) = 1$ then $h(t, B) = 1$.

Second, let us show that

$$((A \Rightarrow B) \Rightarrow A) \Rightarrow A$$

is not an intuitionistic tautology. Take A, B atomic, and consider the following Kripke model:

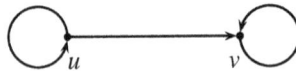

$h(u, A) = h(u, b) = h(v, B) = 0, h(v, A) = 1$.

Then $h(v, A \Rightarrow B) = 0$, and thus $h(u, A \Rightarrow B) = 0$.

This implies $h(u, (A \Rightarrow B) \Rightarrow A) = 1$. On the other hand, $h(u, A) = 0$, which yields

$$h(u, ((A \Rightarrow B) \Rightarrow A) \Rightarrow A) = 0$$

Therefore, Peirce's rule is not an intuitionistic tautology, and thus it is not derivable from the intuitionistic axioms.

Exercise 8.1

1. The translations into predicate logic of the English sentences are:

(a) girl(Brenda) ∧ sits-next-to(Brenda, Ann)

(b) ¬sits-next-to(Ann,Edward)

(c) boy(David) ∨ girl(David)

2. The translations into English of the predicate logic formulae are:

(a) If Carol is a girl then Carol is not a boy.

(b) Ann and Brenda sit next to each other.

(c) David is not both a boy and a girl.

Exercise 8.2

1. The truth values of the sentences in the given interpretation are as follows:

(a) girl(Brenda) is true and so is ¬boy(Brenda) and thus girl(Brenda) ⇒ ¬boy(Brenda) is also true

(b) boy(David) is true but girl(David) is false and so the antecedent is false, thus boy(David) ∧ girl(David) ⇒ sits-next-to(David,Edward) is also true

(c) sits-next-to(Edward,David) is false

(d) best-friend(Edward) is D, and thus sits-next-to(best-friend(Edward), Edward) is true.

2. The truth value of sentence (a) does change if the interpretation is changed so boy maps to $\{B, D, E\}$, because while the truth value of the antecedent is unaffected, the consequent's truth value becomes false, and so the implication as a whole becomes false as well.

3. Five sentences with the predicate boy plus five sentences with the predicate girl plus $5 \times 5 = 25$ sentences with the predicate sits-next-to give us 35 sentences in total.

4. If every atomic sentence has the same truth value in two interpretations, then every sentence has equal truth values in both interpretations. So we have to find the number of all possible combinations of truth values of atomic sentences. Since there are 35 atomic sentences (by the previous exercise), we obtain 2^{35} distinguishable interpretations.

However, this number decreases greatly, if we take only 'natural' interpretations into account, i.e., those in which girl(c) ⇔ ¬boy(c) is true for any constant c and in which sits-next-to is interpreted as a symmetrical relation, such that everyone has a single neighbour, and nobody can be a neighbour of him- or herself. In this case we have to indicate only boys (or girls), i.e. choose a subset of a 10-element set, and also to split this set into five two-element subsets. The first choice can be done by 2^{10} ways, and the number of splittings is

$$\frac{\binom{10}{2} \cdot \binom{8}{2} \cdot \binom{6}{2} \cdot \binom{4}{2} \cdot \binom{2}{2}}{5!}$$

(we choose a two-element subset, then a two-element subset of the remaining eight elements, etc. since the splitting is non-ordered, we have to divide the whole product by 5!). In total this yields

$$2^{10} \cdot \frac{10!}{2^5 \cdot 5!} = 10 \cdot 9 \cdot 8 \cdot 7 \cdot 6 \cdot 2^5 < 2^{20}$$

distinguishable interpretations.

Exercise 8.4

1. The translations of the English sentences into predicate logic are:

(a) ¬∃x. [man(x) ∧ woman(x)]

(b) ∃x. [woman(x) ∧ beautiful(x)]

(c) ∀x. [friend(x, John) ⇒ ¬beautiful(x)]

(d) beautiful(John) ∧ man(John)

(e) ∀x. [¬friend(x,x) ⇒ ¬∃y.friend(y,x)], or equivalently
    ∀y.∀x.∀x.[¬friend(x, x) ⇒ ¬friend(y, x)]

(f) ∀x. [man(x) ⇒ ∃y.
          [woman(y) ∧ beautiful(y) ∧ friend(x,y)]]
          ∧ ¬∀x.[[woman(x) ∧ beautiful(x)] ⇒
          ∃y. [man(y) ∧ friend(x,y)]]

   The reading of 'but not vice versa' is ambiguous. One can read it as 'but not every beautiful woman is a friend of some man' or another reading is 'but the beautiful woman is not a friend of the man'. A third reading is 'not every friend of some beautiful woman is a man'.

   The third reading can be translated as
   ¬∀x. ∀y. [woman(y) ∧ beautiful(y) ∧ friend(x,y)]
                ⇒ man(x)].

   The moral is that natural language is very, very ambiguous.

(g) ∀x. ∀y. ∀z. [friend(x,y) ∧ friend(y,z) ⇒ friend(x,z)]

(h) ∀x. [[∀y. [friend(y,x) ⇒ beautiful(y)]] ⇒ woman(x)]

(i) ∀x. [man(x) ∨ woman(x)]

2. Possible translations of the predicate logic sentences into English are:

   (a) There is someone who is a woman if women (do indeed) exist.

   (b) Everyone has someone who would reciprocate his friendship.

   (c) If there is someone who befriends himself then all around are men.

3. In the expression

   ```
   ∃x.  [[[ ∃x. friend(x, y)] ⇒ friend(y, y)] ∧
   friend(x,y) ∧ woman(x) ∧ [woman(y) ⇒ woman(x)] ∧
   ∀y. friend(y, y)]
   ```

   x is bound by the outermost ∃x. y is free everywhere except in the last conjunct.

4. The sentences about numbers translate as:

   (a) ∀x.∃y. x<y

   (b) ∀x. (prime(x) ⇒ ∃y. (prime(y) ∧ x<y))

   (c) ∃x.∀y. ¬(y<x)

   (d) prime(y)

   (e) We have no symbols for the predicate *divide* so we cannot express it directly. For this particular example, it can be expressed as $(z < 1) \vee ((1 < z)$ $\wedge$ $(z < 3)) \vee ((3 < z) \wedge (z < 9))$.

   (f) We have no predicate for *love* and so the sentence cannot be expressed.

5. The barber paradox is a true paradox.

   Let $S(x, y)$ stand for 'x shaves y'. Then the barber formula becomes

   $$\exists x.\forall y.(S(x, y) \Leftrightarrow \neg S(y, y))$$

   This formula is inconsistent.

   Let y be x and we get

   $$S(x, x) \Leftrightarrow \neg S(x, x)$$

   which is impossible.

   The reason that it is not immediately obvious to us that the statement is not consistent is because we think of the barber as shaving other people, not himself. (That is, we do not allow $y = x$.)

Exercise 8.5

The outline proofs of the validity of the quantifier equivalences are:[1]

1. $\forall \mathbf{x}.[\varphi(\mathbf{x}) \wedge \psi(\mathbf{x})]$
    $\equiv [\varphi(a_1) \wedge \psi(a_1)] \wedge [\varphi(a_2) \wedge \psi(a_2)] \wedge [\varphi(a_3) \wedge \psi(a_3)] \wedge \ldots$
    $\equiv [\varphi(a_1) \wedge \varphi(a_2) \wedge \varphi(a_3) \wedge \ldots] \wedge [\psi(a_1) \wedge \psi(a_2) \wedge \psi(a_3) \wedge \ldots]$
    $\equiv [\forall \mathbf{x}.\varphi(\mathbf{x})] \wedge [\forall \mathbf{x}.\psi(\mathbf{x})]$

2. $\exists \mathbf{x}.\ [\varphi(\mathbf{x}) \vee \psi(\mathbf{x})]$
    $\equiv [\varphi(a_1) \vee \psi(a_1)] \vee [\varphi(a_2) \vee \psi(a_2)] \vee [\varphi(a_3) \vee \psi(a_3)] \vee \ldots$
    $\equiv [\varphi(a_1) \vee \varphi(a_2) \vee \varphi(a_3) \vee \ldots] \vee [\psi(a_1) \vee \psi(a_2) \vee \psi(a_3) \vee \ldots]$
    $\equiv [\exists \mathbf{x}.\ \varphi(\mathbf{x})] \vee [\exists \mathbf{x}.\ \psi(\mathbf{x})]$

3. $\exists x.\forall y.(\varphi(x) \Rightarrow \varphi(y)) \equiv \exists x.(\varphi(x) \Rightarrow \forall y\ \varphi(y)) \equiv \forall x.\varphi(x) \Rightarrow \forall y.\varphi(y).$

    The latter formula is true because $\forall x.\varphi(x)$ and $\forall y.\varphi(y)$ correspond to the same
    (maybe infinite) conjunction

    $$\varphi(a_1) \wedge \varphi(a_2) \wedge \ldots$$

Exercise 8.7

1. $\exists x.\forall y.p(x, y) \wedge \exists x.\forall y.q(x, y)$ first should be rewritten:

    $$\exists x.\forall y.p(x, y) \wedge \exists z.\forall u.q(z, u)$$

    Then we can apply quantifier equivalences and get

    $$\exists x.(\forall y.p(x, y) \wedge \exists z.\forall u.q(z, u))$$
    $$\equiv \exists x.\forall y.(p(x, y) \wedge \exists z.\forall u.q(z, u))$$
    $$\equiv \exists x.\forall y.\exists z.(p(x, y) \wedge \forall u.q(z, u))$$
    $$\equiv \exists x.\forall y.\exists z.\forall u.(p(x, y) \wedge q(z, u))$$

    Other solutions are:

    $$\exists z.\forall u.\exists x.\forall y.(p(x, y) \wedge q(z, u)),$$
    $$\exists x.\exists z.\forall u.\forall y.(p(x, y) \wedge q(z, u)), \text{ etc.}$$

2. The same method. First we rewrite the formula as

    $$\exists x.\forall y.p(x, y) \Rightarrow \forall z.\exists u.q(z, u)$$

---

[1] If the domain is infinite, we get infinite disjunctions and conjunctions in the proof below, and we should consider the 'proof' as informal and intuitive.

Then we get subsequently

$$\forall z.(\exists x.\forall y.p(x,y) \Rightarrow \exists u.q(z,u))$$
$$\equiv \forall z.\exists u.(\exists x.\forall y.p(x,y) \Rightarrow q(z,u))$$
$$\equiv \forall z.\exists u.\forall x.(\forall y.p(x,y) \Rightarrow q(z,u))$$
$$\equiv \forall z.\exists u.\forall x.\exists y.(p(x,y) \Rightarrow q(z,u))$$

There are also other solutions:

$$\forall x.\forall z.\exists u.\exists y.(p(x,y) \Rightarrow q(z,u)),$$
$$\forall z.\forall x.\exists y.\exists u.(p(x,y) \Rightarrow q(z,u)), \text{ etc.}$$

Exercise 8.10

1. The definitions are:

(a)
$$\langle \mathcal{M}, V \rangle \vDash \neg\varphi$$

iff $\langle \mathcal{M}, V \rangle \vDash \varphi \Rightarrow \bot$

iff $\langle \mathcal{M}, V \rangle \vDash \varphi$ implies $\langle \mathcal{M}, V \rangle \vDash \bot$

iff $\langle \mathcal{M}, V \rangle \vDash \varphi$ implies false

iff $\langle \mathcal{M}, V \rangle \nvDash \varphi$

(b)
$$\langle \mathcal{M}, V \rangle \vDash \varphi\lor\psi$$

iff $\langle \mathcal{M}, V \rangle \vDash (\varphi\Rightarrow\bot)\Rightarrow\psi$

iff $\langle \mathcal{M}, V \rangle \vDash (\varphi\Rightarrow\bot)$ implies $\langle \mathcal{M}, V \rangle \vDash \psi$

iff $\langle \mathcal{M}, V \rangle \nvDash \varphi$ implies $\langle \mathcal{M}, V \rangle \vDash \psi$

iff $\langle \mathcal{M}, V \rangle \vDash \varphi$ or $\langle \mathcal{M}, V \rangle \vDash \psi$

(c)
$$\langle \mathcal{M}, V \rangle \vDash \varphi\land\psi$$

iff $\langle \mathcal{M}, V \rangle \vDash (\varphi\Rightarrow(\psi\Rightarrow\bot))\Rightarrow\bot$

iff $\langle \mathcal{M}, V \rangle \nvDash \varphi\Rightarrow(\psi\Rightarrow\bot)$

iff $\langle \mathcal{M}, V \rangle \vDash \varphi$ and $\langle \mathcal{M}, V \rangle \nvDash \psi\Rightarrow\bot$

iff $\langle \mathcal{M}, V \rangle \vDash \varphi$ and $\langle \mathcal{M}, V \rangle \vDash \psi$ and $\langle \mathcal{M}, V \rangle \nvDash \bot$

iff $\langle \mathcal{M}, V \rangle \vDash \varphi$ and $\langle \mathcal{M}, V \rangle \vDash \psi$

(d)
$$\langle \mathcal{M}, V \rangle \vDash \forall \mathbf{x}. \varphi$$

iff $\langle \mathcal{M}, V \rangle \vDash (\exists \mathbf{x}. (\varphi\Rightarrow\bot))\Rightarrow\bot$

iff $\langle \mathcal{M}, V \rangle \nvDash \exists \mathbf{x}. \varphi\Rightarrow\bot$

iff there does not exist $d \in \mathcal{D}$ such that $\langle \mathcal{M}, V_{[x\mapsto d]} \rangle \vDash \varphi\Rightarrow\bot$

iff there does not exist $d \in \mathcal{D}$ such that $\langle \mathcal{M}, V_{[x\mapsto d]} \rangle \nvDash \varphi$

iff for all $d \in \mathcal{D}$ $\langle \mathcal{M}, V_{[x\mapsto d]} \rangle \vDash \varphi$

2. The truth values of the formulae are:

(a) $\langle M, V \rangle \vDash p(f(a),b)$ iff
$\pi_{pred}(p)(\pi_{term}(f(a)),\pi_{term}(b)) = \top$ iff
$\pi_{pred}(p)(\pi_{func}(f)(\pi_{cons}(a)),\pi_{cons}(b)) = \top$ iff
$\pi_{pred}(p)(\pi_{func}(f)(1),3) = \top$ iff
$\pi_{pred}(p)(2,3) = \top$, which it is.

(b) $\langle M, V \rangle \vDash r(a,f(b),c)$ iff
$\pi_{pred}(r)(\pi_{term}(a),\pi_{term}(f(b)),\pi_{term}(c)) = \top$ iff
$\pi_{pred}(r)(\pi_{cons}(a),\pi_{func}(f)(\pi_{cons}(b)),\pi_{cons}(c)) = \top$ iff
$\pi_{pred}(r)(1,\pi_{func}(f)(3),5) = \top$ iff
$\pi_{pred}(r)(1,5,5) = \top$, which it is not.

(c) $\langle M, V \rangle \vDash \exists x. \quad (\neg q(x) \Rightarrow p(f(a),g(x,2)))$ iff
there exists $d \in \mathcal{D}$ such that
$\langle M, V_{[x \mapsto d]} \rangle \vDash \neg q(x) \Rightarrow p(f(a),g(x,2))$ iff
there exists $d \in \mathcal{D}$ such that $\langle M, V_{[x \mapsto d]} \rangle \vDash \neg q(x)$ implies
$\langle M, V_{[x \mapsto d]} \rangle \vDash p(f(a),g(x,2))$ iff
there exists $d \in \mathcal{D}$ such that $\langle M, V_{[x \mapsto d]} \rangle \nvDash q(x)$ implies
$\langle M, V_{[x \mapsto d]} \rangle \vDash p(f(a),g(x,2))$
Since the premise $\neg q(x)$ is false for $x = 2$, the full expression holds.

(d) In this case the full expression must hold for every choice of x. In particular, for the cases where $\neg q(x)$ holds we must check the consequent $p(f(a), g(x, 2))$. The choice of $x = 3$ makes $\neg q(x)$ true and the consequent false. Hence the sentence does not hold in the model.

Exercise 8.11

(a) $s(x, x, x)$,
because $x + x = x$ holds iff $x = 0$.
Another solution is

$$\forall y. s(x, y, y)$$

(b) $p(x, x, x) \land \neg s(x, x, x)$,
because $x \cdot x = x$ holds iff $x = 0$ or $x = 1$.

Another solution is

$$\forall y. p(x, y, y)$$

(c) $\exists y. (\forall z. p(y, z, z) \land s(y, y, x))$,
because $2 = 1 + 1$.
Another solution is:

$$\exists y. (p(x, x, y) \land s(x, x, y)) \land \neg s(x, x, x)$$

because $x \cdot x = x + x$ iff $(x = 0$ or $x = 2)$.

(d) $\exists y.s(y, y, x)$.

(e) $\forall y.\forall z.(p(y, z, x) \Rightarrow p(y, y, y) \lor p(z, z, z)) \land \neg p(x, x, x)$.

Explanation: the first conjunct says that if $y \cdot z = x$ then one of the numbers y, z is either 0 or 1. If we require also that $x \cdot x \neq z$ (i.e. $x \neq 0, x \neq 1$) then the first conjunct is equivalent to

$$\forall y.\forall z.(y \cdot z = x \Rightarrow y = 1 \lor z = 1)$$

which, taken together with $x \neq 1$, means that x is prime.

(f) One solution is to say that $x \neq 0 \land x \neq 1 \land \cdots \land x \neq 27$.

Another method is to say that

$$\exists y.(27 + y = x \land y \neq 0)$$

or that

$$\exists y.\exists z.(y \neq 0 \land y + z = x \land z = 27)$$

We know how to express the first two conjuncts. $z = 27$ can be expressed, for example, as

$$\exists x.\exists y.(x = 3 \land y = x \cdot x \land z = x \cdot y)$$

Now the problem is to say that $x = 3$. This can be done as follows:

$$\exists y.\exists z.(y + z = x \land y = 1 \land z = y + y)$$

and we can use exercise (c).

Bringing everything together, we obtain the formula

$$\exists y.\exists z.[\neg s(y, y, y) \land s(y, z, x) \land \exists x.\exists y.(p(x, x, y) \land p(x, y, z) \land$$
$$\exists y.\exists z.(s(y, z, x) \land p(y, y, y) \land \neg s(y, y, y) \land s(y, y, z)))]$$

(Note that x has free and bound occurrences here.)

(g) We can express this by saying that $x + 0 = y$, which is equivalent to

$$\exists z.(z = 0 \land x + z = y)$$

i.e. the formula is

$$\exists z.(s(z, z, z) \land s(x, z, y))$$

(h) Similarly, we can say that $\exists z.(z \neq 0 \land x + z = y)$, which is written thus:

$$\exists z.(\neg s(z, z, z) \land s(x, z, y))$$

(i) This is expressed as follows: $\forall x.\exists y.(x < y \land y \text{ is prime})$. The expressions for conjuncts are found in (h) and (e).

Exercise 8.12

(a) No. To show this, we can use quantifier equivalences:

$$\exists x.\forall y.(Q(x, x) \wedge \neg Q(x, y))$$
$$\equiv \exists x.(Q(x, x) \wedge \forall y.\neg Q(x, y))$$
$$\equiv \exists x.Q(x, x) \wedge \forall y.\neg Q(x, y)$$
$$\equiv \exists x.Q(x, x) \wedge \neg \exists y.Q(x, y)$$

If the latter is true, we have for some a in the model:

$$Q(a, a) \wedge \neg \exists y.Q(a, y) = \top$$

But $Q(a, a) = \top$ implies that $\exists y.Q(a, y) = \top$ (namely, one can take $y = a$).

Hence $Q(a, a) \wedge \neg \exists y.Q(a, y) = \top \wedge \bot = \bot$, and this is a contradiction.

(b) Yes. We can take a two-element model

$$D = \{d_1, d_2\}$$
$$\pi_{\mathrm{pred}}(P)(x) = \top \text{ iff } x = d_1$$

Then $P(d_1) \wedge \neg P(d_2) = \top$, implying that $\langle D, \pi_{\mathrm{pred}}, [\ ] \rangle \vDash (b)$.

(c) Obviously, yes. Take any model in which $\pi_{\mathrm{pred}}(Q)$ sends every pair to $\bot$. Then the premise of the implication is false under any assignment of x, y.

(d) Obviously, yes. Take any model in which $\pi_{\mathrm{pred}}(P)$ sends every element to $\bot$.

Exercise 8.13

(a) No. We can make $\exists x.P(x) = \top$ and $\forall x.P(x) = \bot$ in a model where $P(x)$ is sometimes true and sometimes false. For instance, take the model with $D = \{d_1, d_2\}$,
$\pi_{\mathrm{pred}}(d_1) = \top, \pi_{\mathrm{pred}}(d_2) = \bot$.

(b) No, because $\exists x.P(x) \Rightarrow \forall x.P(x)$ has a model. It can be the same as for (d) in the previous exercise.

(c) Yes. Assume that $\langle \mathcal{U}, V \rangle \vDash \exists x.\forall y.Q(x, y)$, and show that $\langle \mathcal{U}, V \rangle \vDash \forall y.\exists x.Q(x, y)$.

By assumption, $\langle \mathcal{U}, V_{[x \mapsto a]} \rangle \vDash \forall y Q(x, y)$ for some a, and thus for any b, $\langle \mathcal{U}, V_{[x \mapsto a, y \mapsto b]} \rangle \vDash Q(x, y)$. Hence for any b, $\langle \mathcal{U}, V_{[y \mapsto b]} \rangle \vDash \exists x.Q(x, y)$, and therefore $\langle \mathcal{U}, V \rangle \vDash \forall y.\exists x.Q(x, y)$.

(d) No. Take a model with $D = \{a, b\}$,

$$\pi_{\mathrm{pred}}(Q) : \{(a, a) \mapsto \top, (b, b) \mapsto \top, (a, b) \mapsto \bot, (b, a) \mapsto \bot\}$$

Then

$$\exists y.Q(z,y) = \top \text{ since } Q(a,a) = \top$$
$$\exists y.Q(b,y) = \top \text{ since } Q(b,b) = \top$$

Thus $\forall x.\exists y.Q(x,y) = \top$.

On the other hand,

$$\forall x.Q(x,a) = \bot \text{ since } Q(b,a) = \bot$$
$$\forall x.Q(x,b) = \bot \text{ since } Q(a,b) = \bot$$

Thus $\exists y.\forall x.Q(x,y) = \bot$.

So we obtain that (d) $= \bot$ in this model.

Exercise 9.5

1. p(a,f(z)) and p(x,f(b)) unify with most general unifier $\theta = \{x/a, z/b\}$.

2. q(f(g(x))) and r(c) do not unify as the predicates differ!

3. r(x,x,f(b)) and r(g(f(b)),g(y),y) unify with most general unifier
$\theta \qquad\qquad\qquad =$
{x/g (f(b)),y/f(b)}.

4. p(a,f(g(x))) and p(y,g(z)) do not unify as the functors of the second arguments differ.

5. q(b,x) and q(y,f(x)) do not unify as x occurs within the term f(x).

6. q(f(a,x)) and q(f(y,f(z))) unify with most general unifier $\theta = \{y/a, x/f(z)\}$.

Exercise 9.6

1. Because the y does not appear in the matrix of the formula, there is no position to place its Skolem function, so it is omitted (if it had appeared, it would have been of the form f(x)), since it is only in the scope of the $\forall x$. The other existentially quantified variable, v, is in the scope of three universal quantifiers, on x, z and u. Thus v's Skolem function g has three arguments:

$$\forall x.\forall z.\forall u. [R(x, z) \Rightarrow \neg Q(u, g(x,y,u))]$$

2. The Skolemized forms are:

(a) $\forall x.\forall y. [A(x, y) \Rightarrow B(x)]$

(b) $\neg A(f) \vee \neg B(g)$

(c) $A(f) \wedge \forall z. B(z, g)$

(d) $\forall x.\forall y. [A(x, y) \Rightarrow B(x, f(x,y)) \wedge C(g(x,y))]$
   (Since u and v do not appear in the matrix, they can be eliminated. The Skolem constants do not depend on them.)

Exercise 9.10

A translation into logic of the argument is

1. ∀x. [interrupt(x) ⇒ ¬desirable(x)]
2. ∃x. [control(x) ∧ interrupt(x)]
    _____
3. ∃x. [control(x) ∧ ¬desirable(x)]

From assumption 2 using ∃ elimination (Skolemization) with the new constant k, we get

4. control(k) ∧ interrupt(k)

Using ∀ instantiation for k in assumption 1 we get

5. interrupt(k) ⇒ ¬desirable(k)

From sentences 4 and 5, using propositional ∧ elimination and *modus ponens*, we get

6. ¬desirable(k)

From sentences 4 and 6, using ∧ elimination and ∧ introduction, we get

7. control(k) ∧ ¬desirable(k)

Finally, ∃ introduction on sentence 7 gives

3. ∃x. [control(x) ∧ ¬desirable(x)]

Exercise 9.16

1. $\forall x.(a(x) \lor b(x)), \neg \exists x.a(x) \vdash \ \vdash \forall x.b(x)$

    | rewrite

    $\forall x.(a(x) \lor b(x)), \forall x.\neg a(x), \exists x.\neg b(x) \vdash \bot \ \vdash$

    | rewrite

    $a(x) \lor b(x), \neg a(x), \exists x.\neg b(x) \vdash \bot \ \vdash$

    | Skolemize

    $a(x) \lor b(x), \neg a(x), \neg b(k) \vdash \bot \ \vdash$

    | rewrite

    $(a(x) \Rightarrow \bot) \Rightarrow b(x), a(x) \Rightarrow \bot, b(k) \Rightarrow \bot \vdash \bot \ \vdash$

    | rule for atoms using $b(k) \Rightarrow \bot$

    $(a(x) \Rightarrow \bot) \Rightarrow b(x), a(x) \Rightarrow \bot, b(k) \Rightarrow \bot \vdash b(k) \ \vdash$

$$\Big| \text{ substitution } \{x/k\}$$

$$(a(k) \Rightarrow \bot) \Rightarrow b(k), a(k) \Rightarrow \bot, b(k) \Rightarrow \bot \vdash b(k) \quad \vdash$$

$$\Big| \text{ rule for atoms}$$

$$(a(k) \Rightarrow \bot) \Rightarrow b(k), a(k) \Rightarrow \bot, b(k) \Rightarrow \bot \vdash a(k) \Rightarrow \bot \quad \vdash$$

$$\Big| \text{ rule for } \Rightarrow$$

$$(a(k) \Rightarrow \bot) \Rightarrow b(k), a(k) \Rightarrow \bot, b(k) \Rightarrow \bot, a(k) \vdash \bot \quad \vdash$$

$$\Big| \text{ rule for atoms using } a(k) \Rightarrow \bot$$

$$(a(k) \Rightarrow \bot) \Rightarrow b(k), a(k) \Rightarrow \bot, b(k) \Rightarrow \bot, a(k) \vdash a(k) \quad \vdash$$

$$\Big|$$

success

2. $\exists x.(a(x) \Rightarrow b(x)) \vdash (\exists x.a(x)) \Rightarrow \exists x.b(x) \quad \vdash$

$$\Big| \text{ rule for } \Rightarrow$$

$$\exists x.(a(x) \Rightarrow b(x)), \exists x.a(x) \vdash \exists x.b(x) \quad \vdash$$

$$\Big| \text{ Skolemize}$$

$$a(k) \Rightarrow b(k), a(l) \vdash \exists x.b(x) \quad \vdash$$

$$\Big| \text{ rewrite}$$

$$a(k) \Rightarrow b(k), a(l) \vdash b(u) \quad \vdash$$

$$\Big| \text{ substitution } \{u/k\}$$

$$a(k) \Rightarrow b(k), a(l) \vdash b(k) \quad \vdash$$

$$\Big| \text{ rule for atoms}$$

$$a(k) \Rightarrow b(k), a(l) \vdash a(k) \quad \vdash$$

The proof fails, because k, l are constants, and we are not allowed to unify $a(l)$ and $a(k)$.

3. $\exists x.\forall y.a(x, y) \vdash \forall y.\exists x.a(x, y) \quad \vdash$

$$\Big| \text{ rewrite}$$

$$\exists x.\forall y.a(x, y), \exists y.\forall x.(a(x, y) \Rightarrow \bot) \vdash \bot \quad \vdash$$

$$\Big| \text{ Skolemize}$$

$\forall y.a(k, y), \forall x.(a(x, l) \Rightarrow \bot) \vdash \bot \quad \vdash$

$\quad\quad\quad\Big|$ rewrite

$a(k, y), a(x, l) \Rightarrow \bot \vdash \bot \quad \vdash$

$\quad\quad\quad\Big|$ rule for atoms

$a(k, y), a(x, l) \Rightarrow \bot \vdash a(u, l) \quad \vdash$

$\quad\quad\quad\Big|$ substitution $\{u/k, y/l\}$

$a(k, l), a(x, l) \Rightarrow \bot \vdash a(k, l) \quad \vdash$

$\quad\quad\quad\Big|$

$\quad\quad$ success

The proof can be made shorter, if we Skolemize at the very beginning:

$\forall y.a(k, y) \vdash \exists x.a(x, l) \quad \vdash$

$\quad\quad\quad\Big|$ rewrite

$a(k, y) \vdash a(u, l) \quad \vdash$

$\quad\quad\quad\Big|$ substitution $\{u/k, y/l\}$

$a(k, l) \vdash a(k, l) \quad \vdash$

$\quad\quad\quad\Big|$

$\quad\quad$ success

4.

$$\begin{array}{c}
\exists x.\exists y.r(x,y), \forall x.\forall y.(r(x,y) \Rightarrow r(y,x)), \\
\forall x.\forall y.\forall z.(r(x,y) \wedge r(y,z) \Rightarrow r(x,z))
\end{array} \qquad \vdash \forall x.r(x,x)$$

$$\Big|\; \text{Skolemize}$$

$$\begin{array}{c}
r(k,l), \forall x.\forall y.(r(x,y) \Rightarrow r(y,x)), \\
\forall x.\forall y.\forall z.(r(x,y) \wedge r(y,z) \Rightarrow r(x,z))
\end{array} \qquad \vdash r(m,m)$$

$$\Big|\; \text{rewrite}$$

$$r(k,l), r(x,y) \Rightarrow r(y,x), r(x,y) \wedge r(y,z) \Rightarrow r(x,z) \vdash r(m,m)$$

$$\Big|\; \text{substitute } \{x/m, z/m\}$$

$$r(k,l), r(m,y) \Rightarrow r(y,m), r(m,y) \wedge r(y,m) \Rightarrow r(m,m) \vdash r(m,m)$$

$$\Big|\; \text{rule for atoms}$$

$$r(k,l), r(m,y) \Rightarrow r(y,m), r(m,y) \wedge r(y,m) \Rightarrow r(m,m) \vdash r(m,y) \wedge r(y,m)$$

$$\Big|\; \text{rule for } \wedge$$

$$\begin{array}{c}
r(k,l), r(m,y) \Rightarrow r(y,m) \\
r(m,y) \wedge r(y,m) \Rightarrow r(m,n)
\end{array} \qquad \vdash r(m,y) \qquad \cdots$$

$$\Big|\; \text{substitute } \{y/m\}$$

$$r(k,l), r(m,m) \Rightarrow r(m,m) \vdash r(m,m)$$

Now the proof fails because $r(k,l)$ and $r(m,m)$ cannot be unified. (We do not show the right branch, because the left one already fails.)

There is no other way to continue a proof, and in fact the goal is not provable from the data, as one can check by doing a countermodel.

5. See 3 above, and Example 8.1.7.

Exercise 10.19

1. We give truth tables for M. Recall that for any B and any world w, $h(w, \Box B) = \top$ iff $h(w', B) = \top$ for all worlds w' such that $R(w, w')$. So clearly in M, $h(s, \Box B) = \top$ for *any* formula B, because there is *no* world w' such that $R(s, w')$.

	p	q	$\neg q$	$p \Rightarrow \neg q$	A	$\neg A$	$\Box \neg A$	$\Box q$	$\neg \Box q$	B_1
0	T	⊥	T	T	⊥	T	⊥	T	⊥	T
s	⊥	T	⊥	T	T	⊥	T	T	⊥	⊥
t	T	T	⊥	⊥	⊥	T	T	⊥	T	T

	$\Box q \vee p$	$\Box(\Box q \vee p)$	$\Box\Box(\Box q \vee p)$	B_2
0	T	T	T	⊥
s	T	T	T	⊥
t	T	T	T	⊥

It helps in the second half of the table if we note:

Fact: if B is any formula and $h(w, B) = \top$ for all worlds w, then $h(w, \Box B) = \top$ for all w.

This holds in all modal structures. Why?

2. In M' the truth tables do not change much. We note that p, q have the same truth values at every world, and thus the first six columns are the same, because $\Box$ is not involved.

Eventually we have

	p	q	$\neg q$	$p \Rightarrow \neg q$	A	$\neg A$	$\Box \neg A$	$\Box q$	$\neg \Box q$	B_1
0	T	⊥	T	T	⊥	T	⊥	⊥	T	T
s	⊥	T	⊥	T	T	⊥	⊥	T	⊥	T
t	T	T	⊥	⊥	⊥	T	T	⊥	T	T

Then we observe that $\Box q \vee p$ is always true, and thus again B_2 is always false.

Exercise 9.4.2

1. From Definition 9.4.1 it follows that

$$\langle M, V \rangle \vDash^t \forall v.\varphi \text{ iff for any } d \in D_t, \langle M, V_{[v \mapsto d]} \rangle \vDash^t \varphi$$

- Now consider the formula φ_1. We have

$$\langle M, V \rangle \vDash^0 \forall x.\forall y.(p(x, y) \Rightarrow \Diamond q(y))$$

iff for any $k \in D_0, \langle M, V_{[x \mapsto k]} \rangle \vDash^0 \forall y.(p(x, y) \Rightarrow \Diamond q(y))$
iff for any $k, l \in D_0, \langle M, V_{[x \mapsto k, y \mapsto l]} \rangle \vDash^0 p(x, y) \Rightarrow \Diamond q(y)$.

But for $k = a, l = b$ we get:

$$\langle \mathcal{M}, V_{[x \mapsto a, y \mapsto b]} \rangle \models^0 p(x, y) \Rightarrow \Diamond q(y)$$

iff $\langle \mathcal{M}, V_{[x \mapsto a, y \mapsto b]} \rangle \models^0 p(x, y)$ implies $\langle \mathcal{M}, V_{[x \mapsto a, y \mapsto b]} \rangle \models^0 \Diamond q(y)$.

Now $\langle \mathcal{M}, V_{[x \mapsto a, y \mapsto b]} \rangle \models^0 p(x, y)$

iff $\pi^0_{\text{pred}}(p)(\pi^0_{\text{term}}(x), \pi^0_{\text{term}}(y)) = \top$

iff $\pi^0_{\text{pred}}(p)(V_{[x \mapsto a, y \mapsto b]}(x), V_{[x \mapsto a, y \mapsto b]}(y)) = \top$

iff $\pi^0_{\text{pred}}(p)(a, b) = \top$, which holds.

On the other hand, $\langle \mathcal{M}, V_{[x \mapsto a, y \mapsto b]} \rangle \models^0 \Diamond q(y)$

iff for some $s \geq 0$, $\langle \mathcal{M}, V_{[x \mapsto a, y \mapsto b]} \rangle \models^s q(y)$

iff $(\langle U, V_{[x \mapsto a, y \mapsto b]} \rangle \models^0 q(y)$ or $\langle \mathcal{M} V_{[x \mapsto a, y \mapsto b]} \rangle \models^1 q(y))$

iff $(\pi^0_{\text{pred}}(q)(b) = \top$ or $\pi^1_{\text{pred}}(q)(b) = \top)$,

which fails.

Thus $\langle \mathcal{M}, V_{[x \mapsto a, y \mapsto b]} \rangle \not\models^0 p(x, y) \Rightarrow \Diamond q(x, y)$, and therefore $\langle \mathcal{M}, V \rangle \not\models^0 \varphi_1$.

Now consider φ_1 at 1. Below we use the abbreviated notation explained in Definition 7.3.2. Similarly to the above we have
$\langle \mathcal{M}, V \rangle \models^1 \varphi_1$
iff for any $k, l \in D_1, \langle \mathcal{M}, V \rangle \models^1 p(k, l) \Rightarrow \Diamond q(l)$,
iff for any $k, l \in D_1, (\langle \mathcal{M}, v \rangle \models^1 p(k, l)$ implies $\langle \mathcal{M}, V \rangle \models^1 \Diamond q(l))$.

Now take $k = c, l = d$. Then

$\langle \mathcal{M}, V \rangle \models^1 p(c, d)$ iff $\pi^1_{\text{pred}}(p)(c, d) = \top$, which holds.

But $\langle \mathcal{M}, V \rangle \models^1 \Diamond q(d)$ iff for some $s \geq 1, \langle \mathcal{M}, V \rangle \models^s q(d)$ iff $\langle \mathcal{M}, V \rangle \models^1 q(d)$
iff $\pi^1_{\text{pred}}(q)(d) = \top$, which fails.

Thus $\langle \mathcal{M}, V \rangle \not\models^1 \varphi_1$.

Next, consider φ_2. $\langle \mathcal{M}, V \rangle \models^t \varphi_2$ iff for any $k, l \in D_t, \langle \mathcal{M}, V \rangle \models^t p(k, l) \Rightarrow \exists z. \Diamond q(z)$.

We notice that the latter holds if $\langle \mathcal{M}, V \rangle \models^t \exists z. \Diamond q(z)$, i.e. if for some $k \in D_t$ we have $\langle \mathcal{M}, V \rangle \models^t \Diamond q(k)$.

If $t = 0$ we can take $k = c$ since $\langle \mathcal{M}, V \rangle \models^0 q(c)$ and $0 \leq 0$.

If $t = 1$ we can also take $k = c$, since $\langle \mathcal{M}, V \rangle \models^1 q(c)$ and $1 \leq 1$.

Thus we obtain that φ_2 is always true in our model.

2. Let us show that φ_3 is always true. $\langle \mathcal{M}, V \rangle \models^t \varphi_3$ iff for some $k \in D_t$, $\langle \mathcal{M}, V \rangle \models^t \Box q(k)$
iff for some $k \in D_t$, for any $s \geq t, \langle \mathcal{M}, V \rangle \models^s q(k)$. ·

Now if $t = 1$, then $s = t$, and we can take $k = c$.

If $t = 0$, we can also take $k = c$ because

$$\pi_{\text{pred}}(q)(c) = \pi_{\text{pred}}^1(q)(c) = \top$$

Let us show that φ_4 is always true too. $\langle M, V \rangle \vDash^t \varphi_4$ iff for all $s \geq t$, $\langle U, V \rangle \vDash^s$
$\exists x.\exists y.(p(x, y) \wedge \neg q(y))$
iff for all $s \geq t$ there exist $k, l \in D_s$ such that
$\langle M, V \rangle \vDash^s p(k, l) \wedge \neg q(l)$.

Now it is sufficient to show that the latter holds for any s, which is true since

$$\langle M, V \rangle \vDash^0 p(a, b) \wedge \neg q(b)$$
$$\langle M, V \rangle \vDash^1 p(c, d) \wedge \neg q(d)$$

Exercise 9.4.3

1. This is a tautology. In fact,

$$\langle M, V \rangle \vDash^t [\Diamond \forall x.\varphi(x)] \Rightarrow \forall x.\Diamond \varphi(x)$$

iff $\langle M, V \rangle \vDash^t \Diamond \forall x.\varphi(x)$ implies $\langle M, V \rangle \vDash^t \forall x.\Diamond \varphi(x)$.

To show this, assume that $\langle M, V \rangle \vDash^t \Diamond \forall x.\varphi(x)$, i.e. that for some $s_0 \geq t$, for
any $k \in D_{s_0}$, $\langle M, V \rangle \vDash^{s_0} \varphi(k)$.

Let us prove that $\langle M, V \rangle \vDash^t \forall x.\Diamond \varphi(x)$, i.e. that for any $l \in D_t$, $\langle M, V \rangle \vDash^t$
$\Diamond \varphi(l)$.

So take any $l \in D_t$. Since $t \leq s_0$, we have that $D_t \subseteq D_{s_0}$, and thus $l \in D_{s_0}$.
Then $\langle M, V \rangle \vDash^s \varphi(l)$ by our assumption.

Thus $\langle M, V \rangle \vDash^t \Diamond \varphi(l)$ holds for an arbitrary l.

2. This is also a tautology.

   In fact, for any formulae α, β, $(\alpha \Rightarrow \beta) \equiv (\neg \beta \Rightarrow \neg \alpha)$ because
   $(\langle M, V \rangle \vDash^t \alpha$ implies $\langle M, V \rangle \vDash^t \beta)$ iff
   $(\langle M, V \rangle \nvDash^t \beta$ implies $\langle M, V \rangle \nvDash^t \alpha)$.

   Furthermore, if $\alpha \equiv \beta$, then $\Diamond \alpha \equiv \Diamond \beta$, and also $\Box \alpha \equiv \Box \beta$, as follows from
   Definition 9.4.1.

   Now we have the following equivalences:

$$[[\exists x.\Box \varphi(x)] \Rightarrow \Box \exists x.\varphi(x)]$$
$$\equiv [(\neg \Box \exists x.\varphi(x)) \Rightarrow \neg \exists x.\Box \varphi(x)]$$
$$\equiv [(\neg \neg \Diamond \neg \exists x.\varphi(x)) \Rightarrow \neg \exists x.\neg \Diamond \neg \varphi(x)]$$
$$\equiv [\Diamond \forall x.\neg \varphi(x) \Rightarrow \forall x.\Diamond \neg \varphi(x)]$$

The latter is a tautology (item 1).

The argument above uses quantifier equivalences

$$\forall x.\neg\varphi(x) \equiv \neg\exists x.\varphi(x)$$

and

$$\exists x.\neg\varphi(x) \equiv \neg\forall x.\varphi(x)$$

which are easily observed in temporal logic as well.

3. This is not a tautology for the case when $\varphi(x)$ is $P(x)$ (P atomic).

Consider a model $\mathcal{M}$ with two moments of time, $0 \le 1$, and $D_0 = D_1 = \{a, b\}$. Let

$$\pi^0_{pred}(P)(a) = \pi^1_{pred}(P)(b) = \top$$

$$\pi^0_{pred}(P)(b) = \pi^1_{pred}(P)(a) = \bot$$

Then $\langle \mathcal{M}, V \rangle \models^0 \forall x.\Diamond P(x)$
iff for all $d \in D$, $\langle \mathcal{M}, V \rangle \models^0 \Diamond P(b)$,
which holds because $\langle \mathcal{M}, V \rangle \models^0 \Diamond\forall x.P(x)$.

On the other hand, $\langle \mathcal{M}, V \rangle \models^0 \Diamond\forall x.P(x)$
iff $\langle \mathcal{M}, V \rangle \models^0 \forall x P(x)$ or $\langle \mathcal{M}, V \rangle \models^1 \forall x P(x)$.

This fails because $\langle \mathcal{M}, V \rangle \not\models^0 P(b)$ and $\langle \mathcal{M}, V \rangle \not\models^1 P(a)$.

Thus $\langle \mathcal{M}, V \rangle \not\models^0 (\forall x.\Diamond P(x)) \Rightarrow \Diamond\forall x.P(x)$.

4. This is also not a tautology for the case of $\varphi(x)$ atomic ($P(x)$). Take the same model as in 3. We have

$\langle \mathcal{M}, V \rangle \models^0 \Box\exists x.P(x)$
iff $\langle \mathcal{M}, V \rangle \models^0 \exists x.P(x)$ and $\langle \mathcal{M}, V \rangle \models^1 \exists x.P(x)$,
which holds because $\langle \mathcal{M}, V \rangle \models^0 P(a), \langle \mathcal{M}, V \rangle \models^1 P(b)$.

On the other hand,

$$\langle \mathcal{M}, V \rangle \models^0 \exists x.\Box P(x)$$

iff $\langle \mathcal{M}, V \rangle \models^0 \Box P(a)$ or $\langle \mathcal{M}, V \rangle \models^0 \Box P(b)$.
But $\langle \mathcal{M}, \rangle \not\models^0 \Box P(a)$ since $\langle \mathcal{M}, V \rangle \not\models^1 P(a)$,
and $\langle \mathcal{M}, V \rangle \not\models^0 \Box P(b)$ since $\langle \mathcal{M}, V \rangle \not\models^0 P(b)$,
Thus $\langle \mathcal{M}, V \rangle \not\models^0 \exists x.\Box P(x)$, and therefore 4 fails.

BIBLIOGRAPHY

[Abramsky *et al.*, 1992– 94] S. Abramsky, D. M. Gabbay and T. Maibaum, eds. *Handbook of Logic in Computer Science*, 4 vols. Oxford University Press, Oxford, 1992–1994.

[Adler, 1967] C. Adler. *Modern Geometry*, 2nd edition. McGraw Hill, 1967.

[Aleksander and Burnett, 1987] I. Aleksander and P. Burnett. *Thinking Machines*. Oxford University Press, Oxford, 1987.

[Aleksander and Morton, 1995] I. Aleksander and H. Morton. *An Introduction to Neural Computing*. 2nd Edition. International Thompson Computer Press, London, 1995.

[Antoniou, 1996] G. Antoniou. *Nonmonotonic Reasoning*. The MIT Press, Cambridge, MA, 1996.

[Apt, 1996] K. R. Apt. *From Logic Programming to Prolog*. Prentice Hall, 1996.

[Avron, 1988] A. Avron. *Foundations and proof theory of three valued logic*, LFCS reports, University of Edinburgh, 1988.

[Barendregt, 1984] H. Barendregt. *The Lambda Calculus*. 2nd Edition. North-Holland, Amsterdam, 1984.

[Barwise, 1977] J. Barwise, ed. *Handbook of Mathematical Logic*. North-Holland, Amsterdam, 1977.

[Ben-Ari, 1993] M. Ben-Ari. *Mathematical Logic for Computer Science*, Prentice Hall, 1993.

[Besnard, 1989] P. Besnard. *Default Logic*. Springer-Verlag, Heidelberg, 1989.

[Bizam and Herczeg, 1978] G. Bizam and J. Herczeg. *Sokszin Logika* (175 logikai feladat). Müszaki könyvkiado, Budapest, 1975 (in Hungarian); Russian translation: Mir, Moscow, 1978.

[Blumenthal, 1980] L. M. Blumenthal. *A Modern View of Geometry*. Dover, New York, 1980.

[Bradley and Swartz, 1979] R. Bradley and P. Swartz. *Possible World: An Introduction to Logic and its Philosophy*. Blackwell, Oxford, 1979.

[Brewka, 1991] G. Brewka. *Nonmonotonic Reasoning: Logical Foundations of Commonsense*. Cambridge University Press, Cambridge, 1991.

[Brewka *et al.*, 1997] G. Brewka, J. Dix and K. Konolige. *Nonmonotonic Reasoning: An Overview*. CSLI, 1997.

[Broda *et al.*, 1994] K. Broda, S. Eisenbach, H. Khoshnevisian and S. Vickers. *Reasoned Programming*. Prentice Hall, 1994.

[Burke and Foxley, 1996] E. Burke and E. Foxley. *Logic and its Applicatons*. Prentice Hall, 1996.

[Chellas, 1980] B. F. Chellas. *Modal Logic, An Introduction*. Cambridge University Press, Cambridge, 1980.

[Chiswell and Hodges, 2007] I. Chiswell and W. Hodges. *Mathematical Logic*, Oxford Texts in Logic, Oxford University Press, 2007, 250pp.

[Clarke and Gabbay, 1987] M. Clarke and D. M. Gabbay. An intuitionistic basis for non-monotonic reasoning. In *Automated Reasoning for Non-standard Logic*, ed. P. Smets, pp. 163–179. Academic Press, London, 1987.

[Copeland, 1993] J. Copeland. *Artificial Intelligence*. Blackwell, Oxford, 1993.

[Copi, 1986] I. M. Copi. *Introduction to Logic*, 7th Edition. Macmillan, London, 1986.

[Fagin *et al.*, 1995] R. Fagin, J. Y. Halpern, Y. Moses and M. Y. Vardi. *Reasoning about Knowledge*. The MIT Press, Cambridge, MA, 1995.

[Faulkner, 1949] T. Faulkner. *Projective Geometry*, Oliver andBoyd, 1949.

[Field and Harrison, 1988] A. J. Field and P. G. Harrison. *Functional Programming*. Addison Wesley, Reading, 1988.

[Fitting, 1996] M. Fitting. *First Order Logic and Automated Theorem Proving*, 2nd Edition. Springer-Verlag, Berlin, Heidelberg, New York, 1996.

[Flach, 1994] P. Flach. *Simply Logical*. Wiley, 1994.

[Gabbay, 1976] D. M. Gabbay. *Investigations in Modal and Tense Logics*. D. Reidel, Dordrecht, 1976.

[Gabbay, 1981] D. M. Gabbay. *Semantical Investigations in Heyting's Intuitionistic Logic*. D. Reidel, Dordrecht, 1981.

[Gabbay, 1982] D. M. Gabbay. Intuitionistic basis for non-monotonic logic. In *Proceedings of CADE-6*, LNCS vol. 138, pp. 260–273. Springer-Verlag, Berlin, Heidelberg, New York, 1982.

[Gabbay, 1985] D. M. Gabbay. Theoretical foundations for non-monotonic reasoning. In *Expert Systems, Logic and Models of Concurrent Systems*, ed. K. Apt, pp. 439–459. Springer-Verlag, Berlin, Heidelberg, New York, 1985.

[Gabbay, 1988] D. M. Gabbay. *The Tübingen Lectures*, Technical report 90-55, pp. 1–127. University of Tübingen, 1988.

[Gabbay et al., 1994] D. M. Gabbay, I. Hodkinson and M. Reynolds. *Temporal Logic: Mathematical Foundations and Computational Aspects, Vol 1: Mathematical Foundations*, Oxford University Press, 1994.

[Gabbay, 1996] D. M. Gabbay. *Labelled Deductive Systems, Vol. 1, Basic Theory*. Oxford University Press, Oxford, 1996.

[Gabbay and Guenthner, 1977–99] D. M. Gabbay and F. Guenthner, eds. *Handbook of Philosophical Logic*, vols 1–4. Kluwer, Dordrecht, 1979–1986; 2nd Edition 10–12 vols. to appear during 1998–1999.

[Gabbay and Hunter, 1991] D. M. Gabbay and A. B. Hunter. Making inconsistency repsectable, part 1. In *Fundamentals of Artificial Intelligence Research (FAIR '91)*, eds. Ph. Jorrand and J. Kelemen, LNAI Vol. 535, pp. 19–32. Springer-Verlag, Berlin, Heidelberg, New York, 1991.

[Gabbay, 1998] D. M. Gabbay. *Fibring Logics*. Oxford University Press, 1998.

[Gabbay and Olivetti, 2000] D. M. Gabbay and N. Olivetti. *Goal Directed Algorithmic Proof Theory*, to appear. Kluwer, Dordrecht, 2000.

[Gabbay and Reyle, 1984] D. M. Gabbay and U. Reyle. *N*-Prolog: An extension of Prolog with hypothetical implications 1. *Journal of Logic Programming*, **1**, 319–355, 1984.

[Gabbay et al., 1993–95] D. M. Gabbay, C. Hogger and J. A. Robinson, eds. *Handbook of Logic in Artificial Intelligence and Logic Programming*, 5 vols., Oxford University Press, Oxford, 1993–1996.

[Gabbay et al., 1994] D. M. Gabbay, I. Hodkinson and M. Reynolds. *Temporal Logic, Vol. 1*. Oxford University Press, Oxford, 1994.

[Gabbay et al., 1995] D. M. Gabbay, L. Giordano, A. Martelli and N. Olivetti. Hypothetical updates, priority and inconsistency in a logic programming langauge. *Logic Programming and Nonmonotonic Reasoning*, eds. V. W. Marek, A. Nerode and M. Truszczynski, LNCS Vol. 928, pp. 203–216. Springer-Verlag, Berlin, Heidelberg, New York, 1995.

[Gabbay et al., 2001] D. M. Gabbay, R. Kempson and W. Meyer-Viol. *Dynamic Syntax: The Flow of Language Understanding*. Blackwells, 2001, 360pp.

[Gabbay et al., 2002] D. M. Gabbay, A. S. D'Avila Garcez and K. Broda. *Neural-symbolic Learning Systems: Foundations and Applications*. Springer-Verlag, 2002, 350pp.

[Gabbay and Woods, 2003] D. M. Gabbay and J. Woods. *Agenda Relevance*. Elsevier, 2003. 521pp

[Gabbay et al, 2003] D. M. Gabbay, A. Kurucz, F. Wolter and M. Zakhryaschev. *Many Dimensional Modal Logics*. Elsevier, 2003.

[Gabbay et al., 2004] D. M. Gabbay, K. Broda, L. Lamb and A. Russo. *Compiled Labelled Deductive Systems for Modal and Conditional Logics*. Research Studies Press, 2004.

[Gabbay and Woods, 2005] D. M. Gabbay and J. Woods. *The Reach of Abduction*. Elsevier, 2005. 476pp

[Gabbay and Maksimova, 2005] D. M. Gabbay and L. Maksimova. *Interpolation and Definability, Volume 1: Modal and Intuitionistic Logic*. Oxford University Press, 2005.

[Gabbay et al., 2007] D. M. Gabbay, W. Carnielli, M. Coniglio, P. Gouveia and C. Sernadas. *Analysis and Synthesis of Logics*, Springer, 2007.

[Gabbay et al., 2007a] D. M. Gabbay, K. Engesser and D. Lehmann. *Quantum Logic*. College Publications, 2007.

[Gabbay et al., 2007b] D. M. Gabbay, R. Schmidt and A. Szalas. *Second-order Quantifier Elimination*. College Publications, 2007.

[Gabbay et al., 2008] D. M. Gabbay, A. S. D'Avila Garcez and L. C. Lamb. *Connectionist Nonclassical Logics: Distributed Reasoning and Learning in Neural Networks*. Springer-verlag, 2008.

[Gabbay et al., to appear] D. M. Gabbay, G. Metcalfe and N. Olivetti. *Proof Theory for Fuzzy Logics*. RSP, Wiley, to appear.

[Gabbay et al., 2008] D. M. Gabbay, V. Shehtman and D. Skvortsov. *Quantification in Non-classical Logics*. To appear with Elsevier, 2008.

[Gabbay et al., in preparation] D. M. Gabbay, O. Rodrigues and A. Russo. *Revision by Translation*. Partial draft available, 300pp.

[Gallier, 1986] J. H. Gallier. *Logic for Computer Science: Foundations of Automatic Theorem Proving*. Harper and Row, New York, 1986.

[Galton, 1990] A. Galton. *Logic for Information Technology*, John Wiley and sons, 1990, 304pp.

[Gibbins, 1988] P. Gibbins. *Logic with Prolog*. Oxford University Press, Oxford, 1988.

[Gillies, 1996] D. Gillies. *Artificial Intelligence and Scientific Method*. Oxford University Press, Oxford, 1996.

[Gottwald, 1993] S. Gottwald. *Fuzzy Sets and Fuzzy Logic*. Vieweg, Braunschweig, 1993.

[Goubault-Larrecq and Mackie, 1997] J. Goubault-Larrecq and I. Mackie. *Proof Theory and Automated Deduction*, Applied Logic Series. Kluwer, Dordrecht, 1997.

[Hájek and Valdes, 1994] P. Hájek and J. Valdes. An analysis of MYCIN like expert systems. *MathwareandSoft Computng*, **1**, 45–68, 1994.

[Hankin, 2004] C. L. Hankin. *An Introduction to Lambda Calculi for Computer Scientists*. College Publications, 2004.

[Hein, 1995] J. L. Hein. *Discrete Structures. Logic and Computability*. Jones and Bartlett, Sudbury, Massachusetts, 1995.

[Hindley and Seldin, 1986] J. R. Hindley and J. P. Seldin. *Introduction to Combinators and λ-calculus*. Cambridge University Press, Cambridge, 1986.

[Hodges, 1977] W. Hodges. *Logic*. Pelican, Harmondsworth, 1977.

[Hodges, 1977a] W. Hodges. *A Shorter Model Theory*. Cambridge University Press, 1977.

[Hogger, 1994] C. J. Hogger. *Essentials of Logic Programming*. Oxford University Press, Oxford, 1994.

[Hughes and Cresswell, 1996] G. E. Hughes and M. J. Cresswell. *A New Introduction to Modal Logic*. Routledge, London, 1996.

[Hunter, 1996] A. Hunter. *Uncertainty in Information Systems*. McGraw Hill, New York, 1996.

[Huth and Ryan, 2004] M. Huth and M. Ryan. *Logic in Computer Science: Modelling and Reasoning about Systems*, Cambridge University Press, 2004, 440pp.

[Kahane, 1990] H. Kahane. *Logic and Philosophy*, 6th Edition. Wadsworth, Belmont, California, 1990.

[Klir and Folger, 1988] G. J. Klir and T. A. Folger. *Fuzzy Sets, Uncertainty and Information*. Prentice Hall, London, 1988.

[Kowalski, 1979] R. A. Kowalski. *Logic for Problem Solving*. North-Holland, Amsterdam, 1979.

[Kowalski and Sergot, 1986] R. A. Kowalski and M. Sergot. A logic based calculus of events. *New Generation Computing*, **4**, 1986.

[Kraus et al., 1990] S. Kraus, D. Lehmann and M. Magidor. Nonmonotonic reasoning, preferential models and cumulative logics. *Artificial Intelligence*, **44**, 167–208, 1990.

[Kuliakowski, 1984] C. Kuliakowski. *A Practical Guide to Designing Expert Systems*. 1984.

[Lalement, 1993] R. Lalement. *Computation as Logic*. Prentice Hall, 1993.

[Lambert and Ulrich, 1980] K. Lambert and W. Ulrich. *The Nature of Argument*. Macmillan, London, 1980.

[Lavrov and Maksimova, 1995] I. A. Lavrov and L. L. Maksimova. *Problems in Set Theory, Mathematical Logic and Theory of Algorithms*, 3rd Edition. Nauka, Moscow, 1995. (in Russian).

[Łukasiewicz, 1990] W. Łukasiewicz. *Non-monotonic Reasoning: Formalisation of Commonsense Reasoning*. Ellis Horwood (now Prentice Hall), Chichester, 1990.

[Malinowski, 1993] G. Malinowski. *Many Valued Logics*. Oxford University Press, Oxford, 1993.

[Marek and Truszczynski, 1993] V. W. Marek and M. Truszczynski. *Nonmonotonic Logic*. Springer-Verlag, Berlin, Heidelberg, New York, 1993.

[Mendelson, 1964] E. Mendelson. *Introduction to Mathematical Logic*. Van Nostrand, 1964; 3rd Edition, Wadsworth, Belmont, California, 1987.

[Müller et al., 1997] J. P. Müller, M. J. Wooldridge and N. R. Jennings, eds. *Intelligent Agents III*, LNAI, vol. 1193, Springer-Verlag, Berlin, Heidelberg, New York, 1997.

[Nidditch, 1962] P. H. Nidditch. *Propositional Calculus*. RKP, London, 1962.

[Novikov, 1964] P. S. Novikov. *Elements of Mathematical Logic*. Oliver and Boyd, Edinburgh, 1964.

[Nwana and Azarmi, 1997] H. S. Nwana and N. Azarmi, eds. *Software Agents and Soft Computing*. LNAI, vol. 1198, Springer-Verlag, Berlin, Heidelberg, New York, 1997.

[Potter *et al.*, 1991] B. Potter, J. Sinclair and D. Till. *An Introduction to Formal Specification and Z*. Prentice Hall, London, 1991.

[Reeves and Clarke, 1990] S. Reeves and M. Clarke. *Logic for Computer Science*. Addison Wesley, Reading, 1990.

[Russell and Norvig, 1995] S. Russell and P. Norvig. *Artificial Intelligence: A Modern Approach*. Prentice Hall, London, 1995.

[Sainsbury, 2000] M. Sainsbury. *Logical Forms: An Introduction to Philosophical Logic*, Blackwell, 2000,432pp.

[Sandewall, 1994] E. Sandewall. *Features and Fluents: Volume 1: A Systematic Approach to the Representation of Knowledge about Dynamical Systems*. Oxford University Press, Oxford, 1994.

[Shoham, 1988] Y. Shoham. *Reasoning about Change*. The MIT Press, Cambridge, MA, 1988.

[Spivak, 1995] A. V. Spivak. *Mathematical festival*. Moscow Centre of Continuous Mathematical Education, Moscow, 1995 (in Russian).

[Truss, 1991] J. K. Truss. *Discrete Mathematics for Computer Scientists*. Addison Wesley, Reading, 1991.

[van Dalen, 1994] D. van Dalen. *Logic and Structure*, 3rd Edition. Springer-Verlag, Berlin, Heidelberg, New York, 1994.

[Walton, 1989] D. Walton. *Informal Logic*. Cambridge University Press, Cambridge, 1989.

[Woods and Walton, 1982] J. Woods and D. Walton. *Argument, The Logic of the Fallacies*. McGraw-Hill, New York, 1982.

INDEX

reasoning with, 340
voting, 114

well-formed formulae, 321
wff, 321
WTA example for $\mathbb{E}$ and $\mathbb{S}$ rules, 422

Lightning Source UK Ltd.
Milton Keynes UK
UKOW05f1001241016

285990UK00007BA/434/P